TRIANGLE CLASSICS

ILLUMINATING THE GAY AND LESBIAN EXPERIENCE

And the Band Played On
by Randy Shilts

The Autobiography of Alice B. Toklas
by Gertrude Stein

The Beebo Brinker Chronicles
by Ann Bannon

Bertram Cope's Year
by Henry Blake Fuller

Borrowed Time/Love Alone/Becoming a Man
by Paul Monette

A Boy's Own Story/
The Beautiful Room Is Empty
by Edmund White

Brideshead Revisited
by Evelyn Waugh

The Celluloid Closet
by Vito Russo

City of Night
by John Rechy

Dancer from the Dance
by Andrew Holleran

Death in Venice
and Seven Other Stories
by Thomas Mann

Family Dancing
by David Leavitt

The Family of Max Desir
by Robert Ferro

Giovanni's Room
by James Baldwin

The Lord Won't Mind/One for the Gods
by Gordon Merrick

The Lure
by Felice Picano

The Naked Civil Servant/How to Become a Virgin/
Resident Alien
by Quentin Crisp

Nightwood/Ladies Almanack
by Djuna Barnes

Olivia
by Olivia

Oranges Are Not the Only Fruit
by Jeanette Winterson

Orlando
by Virginia Woolf

The Picture of Dorian Gray
by Oscar Wilde

The Price of Salt
by Patricia Highsmith

Rubyfruit Jungle
by Rita Mae Brown

Sexual Politics/Sita
by Kate Millett

A Single Man
by Christopher Isherwood

Skinflick/Gravedigger/Nightwork
by Joseph Hansen

The Sophie Horowitz Story/Girls, Visions and Everything/
After Dolores
by Sarah Schulman

Stone Butch Blues
by Leslie Feinberg

Surpassing the Love of Men
by Lillian Faderman

The Well of Loneliness
by Radclyffe Hall

What Is Found There/An Atlas of the Difficult World/
The Fact of a Doorframe
by Adrienne Rich

Zami/Sister Outsider/Undersong
by Audre Lorde

SEXUAL POLITICS

SITA

SEXUAL POLITICS

SITA

KATE MILLETT

QUALITY PAPERBACK BOOK CLUB
NEW YORK

SEXUAL POLITICS

For
FUMIO
YOSHIMURA

CONTENTS

INTRODUCTION TO THE
ILLINOIS PAPERBACK

It is a great pleasure to me to see a new edition of this work, my first book, back in print after an absence of nearly seven years. When a book goes out of print, its author feels an erasure, almost as if it had never been published, as if a beloved offspring has become one of the "disappeared." While going out of print was almost accidental in this title's case, getting it back in print was a big problem. I had regained the copyright from Simon and Schuster to bestow it on my new editor, Mary Cunane, at W. W. Norton. Simon and Schuster had been doing little for this book and my other titles, and Norton was such a sound academic press that I was sure it would keep *Sexual Politics* in print. Then suddenly, after over twenty years with Norton and as a vice president to boot, Mary Cunane simply quit the house. Its other editors were uninterested in my work. In a trice, I was without an editor and a publisher. Recovering from this state of orphanhood was no easy matter then. The field of feminist texts had become dominated by a prodigious number of collections of essays by professors of this new discipline who selected one another other's work and assigned it for university courses: secondary sources. Primary sources such as *Sexual Politics* were now seen as passé.

I had the surreal experience of being informed by Doubleday, the origin publisher of *Sexual Politics*, that it was one of the ten most important books it had published in its hundred years of existence and the honor of seeing an excerpt of the book selected for a self-congratulatory coffee-table volume of these ten stellar texts—this from the trade division. But from the paperback division of Doubleday Anchor, the bad news was that they could not consider doing a reprint of the book itself because *Sexual Politics* was now "not at all right" for the "present market in women's studies." The Feminist Press, which tends to specialize in texts no longer covered by copyright, would venture to reprint *Sexual Politics* but only a few years hence and only after it had gathered a number of "prominent women's studies scholars" to write prefaces and introductions vouching for its importance. One imagined these authorities would be well remunerated for their efforts. On its first offer, I was to be paid only five hundred dollars.

My "feminist classic" had become a radical text, dubious, "far out," a risky proposition. This had an amusing as well as an irritating side as one trade publisher or university press after another considered putting the book back into print and then backed off. Parts of the text were routinely plagiarized for class use without permission; then with the new rules at the copy houses, portions were duly reprinted with permission, but you still couldn't get the whole book. Meanwhile, readers who once couldn't believe that *Sexual Politics* was actually out of print began to realize the book was now unobtainable and grew incensed.

One might account for this quiet type of censorship (I was surely not the only one to feel it) through "backlash" or the false rationale of "the marketplace"—as the vast corporate conglomerates that control American publishing explain it to us as they systematically eliminate thought-provoking materials from public view. But for me, the long blackout was a grievous period. I had recovered all my copyrights and wanted several other titles back in print as well. Everything I had ever written had vanished from the world except for *The Politics of Cruelty*. These were years of a curious spectral experience of having lived beyond my time. Was there any point in writing new books when the earlier ones were already dead? To continue to write was made harder and more uncertain than it need to have been.

Trying to get back into print was tedious, humiliating, and time consuming, sapping the energy for new writing. Life was on hold for months and then years while one or another editor failed to call back. I held out not only for *Sexual Politics*, my doctoral thesis and first book, but also for the handful of titles that were my life's work. Then one day Will Regier, prompted by Kim Grossmann, of the University of Illinois Press called up out of the blue and offered to reprint the four titles in this series: *Sexual Politics, Sita, Flying* and *The Loony Bin Trip*. The heavens opened.

In the thirty years since the composition of *Sexual Politics* and in the seven years it has been out of print, I have had more than enough time to consider what I might say in an introduction to a new edition. Three decades have brought a great many changes, a great second wave of feminist insurgency in this country and throughout the West, but also considerable backlash and reaction despite a steady wave of patriarchal reform through the United Nations responding to international feminism. That would surely be another book—in fact, it has been thousands and must go on being so. But in 1970 my main interest was to restate and reestablish the fact of historical patriarchy in modern terms and for my generation, to see it as a controlling political institution built on status, temperament, and role, a socially conditioned belief system presenting itself as nature or necessity. Thirty years have focused this understanding but could not alter it significantly. Of course there are hindsight perceptions as well. Reading Gerda Lerner's magnificent *Creation of Patriarchy*, published in 1986, I regretted not having had its fine prose and confident scholarship to guide me when I approached the subject. Differing with Lerner, I wish I had placed more emphasis on the discovery of paternity as the critical factor in establishing the groundwork for patriarchy's triumph over earlier fertility culture, as Elizabeth Fischer does. This great early scientific discovery, a hunch I shared with friends in discussion but theorists still do not emphasize, has struck me more and more over the years as the cause of what Engels called "the great historical defeat of woman"—the creation of patriarchy. Engels attributed it to the introduction of monogamy. And of course without monogamy and the ownership and sequestration of women, paternity is hard to ascertain. But in a free sexual culture only maternity is evident: the infant's head in the birth canal is visible proof of parenthood, whereas a chance encounter among how many others nine months earlier can hardly establish fatherhood and all that came with it in the ownership of persons (women, children, and slaves), private property, and the state. In Engels's Victorian imagination, itself a product of exploitative patriarchal sexual practices, sexuality was so odious to women that he reasoned they would prefer ownership by one man rather than "use" by some communal horde. All this implies the existence of an onerous and coercive sexuality instead of a free one: patriarchy, in fact. But before the establishment of patriarchy through the discovery of paternity, sexual intercourse might have had a very different meaning, a pleasure quite removed from consequences.

If paternity was not clear until the example of animal husbandry, with its use of breeding pens and sequestration, made the discovery of human paternity possible through analogy, the economic potential and social control over human birth and issue were not available to human males. Knowledge of paternity is the key; until its discovery, the religious and monetary uses of the phallus and the seed were also not available. The discovery once made, patriarchy could and did invalidate all female participation in the spiritual creation of life, nominate the female as a mere vessel in which the magic seed grew, invent male gods who gave birth alone to Adam or Athena, and begin the long subordination of woman in every avenue of human experience and civilization—even to its symbols. The ovum was not discovered until the nineteenth century, and it appears to have had no such social or political significance.

If the biological discovery of paternity had monumental ramifications for human social organization at the onset of patriarchy, today, when that institution is under attack and perhaps about to be reformed out of existence, other biological discoveries have, perhaps even fortuitously, come into being. In vitro fertilization, cloning, and surrogate motherhood—the products of an essentially masculine science—have made human reproduction subject to human manipulation as it has never been previously. It is in the interpretation of scientific knowledge that power lies, and the social consequence of these discoveries is still unclear, but control over them is in the hands of a male scientific establishment increasingly driven by corporate profit and Western and class interests. Why not wombs rented from the poor for the rich? As amniocentesis has made it possible to chose boy infants over girls, many have done so. The consequences of knowledge as power may be staggering; the discovery of paternity need not have had any social or political effect at all, yet it came to shape the iron form of human society in the entire historical period. What uses may be made of the new biology, by whom, and for what ends?

Another perception that hindsight might have emphasized is the role of force in patriarchy. When I finished *Sexual Politics* in 1970, feminists were still so intent on a reasonable civil rights argument that it seemed almost "shrill" to look very far into domestic violence and rape, which had always been presented as "aberrant" behavior. Only later did we become aware that there was a normative element in patriarchal violence, still later we began to understand the depth of worldwide poverty among women, even the widespread malnourishment of female children. The brutality visited on female adolescents that I studied in *The Basement* was too shocking for me to write about yet; although I already knew the story of Sylvia Likens, it was fourteen years before I could put it on paper. And the explosion of state violence within patriarchy that I studied in *The Politics of Cruelty* took another ten years to understand.

Patriarchy is "in trouble" worldwide; institutions in trouble get tough. Vicious. Patriarchal powers still have the military and financial means. Patriarchy is not only male domination of females but also a militaristic hierarchy among males. Many of its concessions in the modern period—a universal franchise and representative democracy, rules of war or international law, constitutional and civil rights, individual rights, and human rights—have been canceled during this century in the breathtaking creation of concentration camps and gulags, the reintroduction of torture on a wide scale, massacres and genocide, and the use of rape or starvation as policy. The scramble of greed presented to us as Darwinian necessity through the "global market" has undermined world labor and the integrity of trade, manufacture, and even medicine. Human organs are for sale, and the Chinese state can time its executions exactly to provide vital organs freshly air-expressed for Western hospitals.

Fundamentalist Christianity constantly thwarts feminism, and fundamentalist Islam has built its entire political program on a new subjection of women. Dictatorships return again and again to a more virulent patriarchy. The length of patriarchy is its greatest strength, its seeming permanence; its pretensions to a divine or natural base have been repeatedly served by religion, pseudoscience, or state ambition. Its dangers and oppression are not easily done away with. But surely the very future of freedom requires it — not only for women but for humanity itself.

—Kate Millett
New York, 2000

INTRODUCTION TO THE
TOUCHSTONE PAPERBACK

It happened because I got fired. Of course I had a thesis plan, had handed it in even before the Columbia strike in '68. I'd been doing the reading for years; a whole summer for Lawrence. But what I mean is that this became the book it is, even that it became a book at all, taking off with that "to hell with it" first chapter, rather than another Ph.D. thesis, because at the end of 1968 I was fired from a three-hundred-and-eight-dollar-a-month job as a lecturer in English at Barnard College, a job I would have worked at gladly the rest of my life. It was my life, at least a third of it; the rest was Fumio and my existence as a downtown sculptor—a precarious existence ricocheting between the fine arts and scholarship. As a doctoral candidate in literature at Columbia I led a double life; during my preliminary examination the fact that two of my sculptures had recently appeared in *Life* magazine was thrown up to me as proof I was not a serious scholar.

I had been serious at Oxford, won first class honors and had been consecrated to the profession. Then I fell in love with sculpture and threw it all away, as my colleagues put it, when I resigned my first teaching post to come to New York to spend a year in a freezing studio on the Bowery, and headed for two years in Japan, living on nothing, sculpting a lot. When I came home the only employment for which I qualified was file-clerking, which I did, and teaching English, which I could not go on doing without a doctoral degree. By now I was living with the Japanese sculptor Fumio Yoshimura; he was getting a dollar and a half an hour in the sweatshops of display. One of us had to do better: that meant resigning myself to the doctoral program in English and Comparative Literature at Columbia in order to continue devotedly teaching my students at Barnard. I had finished the coursework, passed the language and qualifying examinations, and outlined a thesis. Then came the Columbia strike. I was both a student and a teacher as well as a committed feminist, a protestor against the war in Vietnam, and a pacifist (the strike revolved around secret government research at Columbia), so I took the students' part, asking for amnesty for the strikers in order that they would not be expelled. The strike transformed Columbia, made it wonderful for a time: ideas came alive, faculty debates were high drama, principles were at issue. The academy asserted itself, drew away from government and business, existed for a while on its own terms. Intellectual values became as real as I remembered them at Oxford; more than that, they grew into the movielike scenario of revolutionary change. Everything came together—the radical agenda of the youth movement, the New Left and civil rights, the radical new feminist politics we were inventing downtown— all confronting the university's president and trustees, their compromising connections with big money and military research. Their power finally asserted itself on that terrible night the police were given the run of the campus to beat and bludgeon the university's own young undergraduate students.

I was there that night and saw it, staying on deliberately past the danger point when the big iron gates closed us in with riot police, to witness whatever harm might come to them—our kids. There were very few faculty members who stayed; a handful of them were young and untenured and vulnerable. The strike was in May; Nixon was elected in November; Barnard fired me before Christmas. In the whirlwind I heard that the other instructors, young men from Columbia, were gone too.

Life stopped. I drank martinis in the daytime and wept. We'd starve, we'd die. Fumio grinned and listened to me rave. Columbia's gates were shut now; I was outside the walls of academe forever; I had lost my profession. But I could still write that damn thesis. So I did. The whole world was ahead of me and I didn't know it. But in the desert of time around that holiday season and into the new year I toiled over what became chapter two, the "Theory of Sexual Politics." Tried a little version of it out in a speech at Cornell, wore my best jumper and a silk blouse and even got paid seventy-five dollars. Driving back into the city of New York over the George Washington Bridge, I had a panic attack and confessed to my comrades that I had lost my job.

I was now on my own. Fumio went off to paint Persian miniatures by the hour. I had the whole day ahead of me, so I started to play, to work at writing the way I'd made sculpture, for fun. At the end of a week I had a rough draft of chapter one, exemplary quotations of sexual intercourse with commentary, and read it to our pal Jim Wagenvoord, a young writer who stopped by for a drink that Friday evening. He laughed his head off. So did Fumio. With this encouragement I called up Betty Prashker at Doubleday, who had politely refused to publish the little pamphlet I wrote with the education committee of NOW, but had offered to read whatever I wrote next. She did. She liked the first chapter and offered me an advance of four thousand dollars.

Now it remained to find someone at Columbia who would direct such a thesis. The professor assigned to me declined and moved on to Harvard. I went after Steven Marcus: marshaling my outrageous attack on patriarchy into a semblance of academic respectability, I waited for him in the hall and hoped he'd listen. He did. The book holds water, thanks not only to his intellectual courage but to his dogged insistence upon proof and more proof, exhaustive reading, research, and analysis. He raised the argument above feminist rhetoric into the kind of cultural criticism it aimed for and hoped to help invent. Betty Prashker was an editor who really worked on a text. I was an angry young woman with a message, a graduate student who wanted to be a scholar, a sculptor who wanted to learn to write. They taught me by being tough and patient and exacting; the book owes them both a great debt.

It is dedicated to Fumio, and the nightly martini over which he listened to each day's pages, laughed and crowed, criticized, and egged me on. *Sexual Politics* also owes a great deal to a long-vanished debating society called Downtown Radical Women, where each detail of the theory of patriarchy was hatched, rehearsed, and refined upon again; to friends in New Haven, graduate women at Yale, who would stay up nights speculating on the origins of patriarchy, the discovery of paternity, the population explosion following upon the implementation of that discovery in the rise of slavery, property, and the city-state. Sexual politics, the idea, was an ongoing project among a great many women in the months I was writing it. And I had their support and companionship, their intellectual energy running through me so actively I felt I composed it for all of us, was the scribe of many. Without Lucinda Cisler's amazing bibliography to draw upon, I couldn't have located many of my sources. Other books were emerging at the same time too: Robin Morgan's *Sisterhood Is Powerful*, Shulamith Firestone's *Dialectic of Sex*, all the pamphlets that were collected together into the *Notes from the First Year*. We were all in this together, knew each other, were collaborators in the creation of a different consciousness.

There was Columbia Women's Liberation too, founded with friends in the graduate school and faculty; we devoted hundreds of hours of research to documenting the university's unfair salary schedules, deliberately using the tools of our academic training to attack the system. We were dedicated to scholarship, loved it, believed in it so much that we dreamed about it out loud, lying on someone's rug uptown and outlining a curriculum freed of sexual prejudice, a whole new way to see history, literature, economics, psychology, political events. We were beginning to invent women's studies, we were reinterpreting knowledge, discovering a new learning.

These were the days of the millennium. As the book took shape, so did events. By the time *Sexual Politics* was published, our actions and demonstrations, meetings, issues, were running through this and other countries, mobilizing women. By the summer of 1970, the moment this text was released, there was a great wave of feminism building. It was the fiftieth anniversary of the suffrage, there were marches and strikes of women workers in New York and throughout the United States. It was the right moment. The rest is history.

And the history of the emancipation of women is—like other stories that describe the long, difficult winding down of oppressive systems—circular; a little forward, almost as much backward, then standstill, reaction, repression, then another surge. We have seen the Equal Rights Amendment almost pass and then be defeated again, abortion won and then nearly lost—a woman's right to choose whether to have a child or not, become once again something men quibble over. So we know it's a long haul, the oldest struggle; we know that as feminists now we stand at one still vital ringing moment in a file of years stretching behind us and before us. Failure is impossible: Susan B. Anthony said it for us. If it isn't easy, it's always interesting. And the work of enlarging human freedom is such nice work we're lucky to get it.

—Kate Millett
New York, 1990

PREFACE

Before the reader is shunted through the relatively uncharted, often even hypothetical territory which lies before him, it is perhaps only fair he be equipped with some general notion of the terrain. The first part of this essay is devoted to the proposition that sex has a frequently neglected political aspect. I have attempted to illustrate this first of all by giving attention to the role which concepts of power and domination play in some contemporary literary descriptions of sexual activity itself. These random examples are followed by a chapter analyzing the social relationship between the sexes from a theoretical standpoint. This second chapter, in my opinion the most important in the book and far and away the most difficult to write, attempts to formulate a systematic overview of patriarchy as a political institution. Much here, and throughout the book, is tentative, and in its zeal to present a consistent argument has omitted (although it need not preclude) the more familiar ambiguities and contradictions of our social arrangements.

The second section, chapters three and four, are largely historical, outlining the great transformation in the traditional relationship between the sexes which took place in the nineteenth and early twentieth centuries, and then giving an account of the climate of reaction which later set in, assuring the continuation of a modified patriarchal way of life, and frustrating the possibility of revolutionary social change in this area for some three decades. The later chapters of the book focus specifically upon the work of three figures I take to be representative of this latter period, examining their responses to the prospect of radical changes in sexual politics and their participation in a mood of reaction against such an impulse. The final chapter, devoted to the writings of Jean Genet, is intended to present a contrast, first in approaching sexual hierarchy from the oblique angle of homosexual dominance order as Genet describes and exposes it in his novels, and secondly, through the emphasis given in his plays to the theme of sexual oppression and the necessity, in any radical program, for its eradication.

It has been my conviction that the adventure of literary criticism is not restricted to a dutiful round of adulation, but is capable of seizing upon the larger insights which literature affords into the life it describes, or interprets, or even distorts. This essay, composed of equal parts of literary and cultural criticism, is something of an anomaly, a hybrid, possibly a new mutation altogether. I have operated on the premise that there is room for a criticism which takes into account the larger cultural context in which literature is conceived and produced. Criticism which originates from literary history is too limited in scope to do this; criticism which originates in aesthetic considerations, "New Criticism," never wished to do so.

I have also found it reasonable to take an author's ideas seriously when, like the novelists covered in this study, they wish to be taken seriously or not at all. Where I have substantive quarrels with some of these ideas, I prefer to argue on those very grounds, rather than to take cover under the tricks of the trade and mask disagreement with "sympathetic readings" or the still more dishonest pretense that the artist is "without skill" or a "poor technician." Critics who disagree with Lawrence, for example, about any issue are fond of saying that his prose is awkward—a judgment purely subjective. It strikes me as better to make a radical investigation which can demonstrate why Lawrence's analysis of a situation is inadequate, or biased, or his influence pernicious, without ever needing to imply that he is less than a great and original artist, and in many respects a man of distinguished moral and intellectual integrity.

The ambitious, often rather overwhelming, undertaking this study became as I proceeded, could not have been accomplished without the guidance, the support, and the much-needed criticism of a number of people: I should like to thank George Stade, Theodore Solataroff, Betty Prashker, Annette Baxter, Mary Mothersill, Lila Karp, Suzanne Shad-Somers, Catherine Stimpson, Richard Gustafson, Laurie Stone, Frances Kamm, and Sylvia Alexander for providing all of them. I am particularly grateful to Steven Marcus who gave the manuscript the most careful reading and could always find time and patience to insist rhetoric give way to reason.

—Kate Millett
New York, 1970

I

SEXUAL POLITICS

ONE

Instances of Sexual Politics

I

I would ask her to prepare the bath for me. She would pretend to demur but she would do it just the same. One day, while I was seated in the tub soaping myself, I noticed that she had forgotten the towels. "Ida," I called, "bring me some towels!" She walked into the bathroom and handed me them. She had on a silk bathrobe and a pair of silk hose. As she stooped over the tub to put the towels on the rack her bathrobe slid open. I slid to my knees and buried my head in her muff. It happened so quickly that she didn't have time to rebel or even to pretend to rebel. In a moment I had her in the tub, stockings and all. I slipped the bathrobe off and threw it on the floor. I left the stockings on—it made her more lascivious looking, more the Cranach type. I lay back and pulled her on top of me. She was just like a bitch in heat, biting me all over, panting, gasping, wriggling like a worm on the hook. As we were drying ourselves, she bent over and began nibbling at my prick. I sat on the edge of the tub and she kneeled at my feet gobbling it. After a while I made her stand up, bend over; then I let her have it from the rear. She had a small juicy cunt, which fitted me like a glove. I bit the nape of her neck, the lobes of her ears, the sensitive spot on her shoulder, and as I pulled away I left the mark of my teeth on her beautiful white ass. Not a word spoken.[1]

This colorful descriptive prose is taken from Henry Miller's celebrated *Sexus*, first published in Paris in the forties but outlawed from the sanitary shores

[1] Henry Miller, *Sexus* (New York: Grove Press, 1965), p. 180.

of his native America until the Grove Press edition of 1965. Miller, alias
Val, is recounting his seduction of Ida Verlaine, the wife of his friend Bill
Woodruff. As an account of sexual passage, the excerpt has much in it of note
beyond that merely biological activity which the narrator would call "fucking." Indeed, it is just this other content which gives the representation of
the incident its value and character.

First, one must consider the circumstances and the context of the scene.
Val has just met Bill Woodruff outside a burlesque theater where Ida Verlaine is performing. In the rambling fashion of Miller's narrative, this meeting calls up the memory of the hero's sexual bouts with Ida ten years before,
whereupon follow eleven pages of vivid re-enactment. First, there is Ida herself:

> She was just exactly the way her name sounded—pretty, vain, theatrical, faith-
> less, spoiled, pampered, petted. Beautiful as a Dresden doll, only she had raven
> tresses and a Javanese slant to her soul. If she had a soul at all! Lived entirely
> in the body, in her senses, her desires—and she directed the show, the body
> show, with her tyrannical little will which poor Woodruff translated as some
> monumental force of character. . . . Ida swallowed everything like a pythoness.
> She was heartless and insatiable.[2]

Woodruff himself is given out as a uxorious fool: "The more he did for her
the less she cared for him. She was a monster from head to toe."[3] The narrator claims to be utterly immune to Ida's power but is nonetheless subject
to coldly speculative curiosity:

> I just didn't give a fuck for her, as a person, though I often wondered what
> she might be like as a piece of fuck, so to speak. I wondered about it in a de-
> tached way, but somehow it got across to her, got under her skin.[4]

As a friend of the family, Val is entitled to spend the night at the Woodruff house, followed by breakfast in bed while husband Bill goes off to work.
Val's initial tactic of extracting service from Ida is important to the events
which follow:

> She hated the thought of waiting on me in bed. She didn't do it for her husband
> and she couldn't see why she should do it for me. To take breakfast in bed was
> something I never did except at Woodruff's place. I did it expressly to annoy
> and humiliate her.[5]

In accord with one of the myths at the very heart of a Miller novel, the
protagonist, who is always some version of the author himself, is sexually

[2] *Ibid.*, p. 178.
[3] *Ibid.*
[4] *Ibid.*, p. 179.
[5] *Ibid.*

irresistible and potent to an almost mystical degree. It is therefore no very great surprise to the reader that Ida falls into his hands. To return to the plucking then, and the passage quoted at length above. The whole scene reads very much like a series of strategems, aggressive on the part of the hero and acquiescent on the part of what custom forces us to designate as the heroine of the episode. His first maneuver, for example, is to coerce further service in the form of a demand for towels, which reduces Ida to the appropriate roles of a hostess and a domestic. That Ida has dressed herself in a collapsible bathrobe and silk stockings is not only accommodating but almost romancelike. The female reader may realize that one rarely wears stockings without the assistance of other paraphernalia, girdle or garters, but classic masculine fantasy dictates that nudity's most appropriate exception is some gauzelike material, be it hosiery or underwear.

Val makes the first move: "I slid to my knees and buried my head in her muff." The locution "muff" is significant because it is a clue to the reader that the putative humility of the action and the stance of petition it implies are not to be taken at face value. "Muff" carries the tone, implicit in the whole passage, of one male relating an exploit to another male in the masculine vocabulary and with its point of view. Considerably more revealing as to the actual character of the action is the comment which follows: "It happened so quickly she didn't have time to rebel or even to pretend to rebel." Since the entire scene is a description not so much of sexual intercourse, but rather of intercourse in the service of power, "rebel" is a highly charged word. Val had already informed the reader that "she wanted to bring me under her spell, make me walk the tight-rope, as she had done with Woodruff and her other suitors." The issue, of course, is which of the two is to walk a tight-rope, who shall be master?

Having immediately placed Ida under his domination, Val acts fast to forestall insubordination. This prompts the next remarkable event—Val brings her into his element, as it were, and places her in the distinctly ridiculous position of being in a bathtub with her clothes on. Again the language indicates the underlying issue of power: "I had her in the bathtub." The reader is also advised that credit should be given the narrator for his speed and agility; Ida is swooshed into the tub in a trice. Having assumed all initiative, Val then proceeds to divest his prey of her redundant bathrobe and throw it on the floor.

The display of stockings and nudity is brought forward for aesthetic delectation; it contributes to make Ida "more lascivious looking, more the Cranach type." The frail perfection of a Cranach nude had been mentioned earlier as Ida's comparable body type. Juxtaposing the innocence and rarity of this image with the traditional "girlie" figure in silk stockings is an eminent bit of strategy. The word "lascivious" implies a deliberate sensuality and is dependent upon a relish for the prurient, and particularly for the degrading in sexual activity, which, in its turn, relies on the distinctly puritanical conviction that sexuality is indeed dirty and faintly ridiculous. Webster defines "lascivious" as "wanton; lewd; lustful" or a "tendency to produce lewd emotions." The Cranach in question is most likely to be the delicate and rather morbid Eve of the Genesis Panel, now depreciated to a calendar girl.

Val proceeds—his manner coolly self-assured and redolent of comfort: "I lay back and pulled her on top of me." What follows is purely subjective description. Ceasing to admire himself, the hero is now lost in wonder at his effects. For the fireworks which ensue are Ida's, though produced by a Pavlovian mechanism. Like the famous programed dog, in fact "just like a bitch in heat," Ida responds to the protagonist's skillful manipulation: ". . . biting me all over, panting, gasping, wriggling like a worm on the hook." No evidence is ever offered to the reader of any such animal-like failure of self-restraint in the response of our hero. It is he who is the hook, and she who is the worm: the implication is clearly one of steely self-composure contrasted to loverlike servility and larval vulnerability. Ida has—in the double, but related, meaning of the phrase—been had.

In the conventional order of this genre of sexual narrative, one position of intercourse must rapidly be followed by another less orthodox and therefore of greater interest. Miller obliges the reader with a quick instance of dorsal intercourse, preceded by a flitting interlude of fellatio. But more pertinent to the larger issues under investigation is the information that Ida is now so "hooked" that it is she who makes the first move: ". . . she bent over and began nibbling at my prick." The hero's "prick," now very center stage, is still a hook and Ida metamorphosed into a very gullible fish. (Perhaps all of this aquatic imagery was inspired by the bathtub.)

Furthermore, positions are significantly reversed: "I sat on the edge of the tub and she kneeled at my feet gobbling it." The power nexus is clearly outlined. It remains only for the hero to assert his victory by the arrogance of his final gesture: "After a while I made her stand up, bend over; then I let her have it from the rear."

What the reader is vicariously experiencing at this juncture is a nearly supernatural sense of power—should the reader be a male. For the passage is not only a vivacious and imaginative use of circumstance, detail, and context to evoke the excitations of sexual intercourse, it is also a male assertion of dominance over a weak, compliant, and rather unintelligent female. It is a case of sexual politics at the fundamental level of copulation. Several satisfactions for the hero and reader alike undoubtedly accrue upon this triumph of the male ego, the most tangible one being communicated in the following: "She had a small juicy cunt which fitted me like a glove."

The hero then caters to the reader's appetite in telling how he fed upon his object, biting ". . . the nape of her neck, the lobes of her ears, the sensitive spot on her shoulder, and as I pulled away I left the mark of my teeth on her beautiful white ass." The last bite is almost a mark of patent to denote possession and use, but further still, to indicate attitude. Val had previously informed us that Bill Woodruff was so absurd and doting a groveler that he had demeaned himself to kiss this part of his wife's anatomy. Our hero readjusts the relation of the sexes by what he believes is a more normative gesture.

Without question the most telling statement in the narrative is its last sentence: "Not a word spoken." Like the folk hero who never condescended to take off his hat, Val has accomplished the entire campaign, including its *coup de grace*, without stooping to one word of human communication. The recollection of the affair continues for several more pages of diversified stimulation by which the hero now moves to consolidate his position of power through a series of physical and emotional gestures of contempt. In answer to her question " 'You don't really like me, do you?' " he replies with studied insolence, " 'I like *this*,' said I, giving her a stiff jab."[6] His penis is now an instrument of chastisement, whereas Ida's genitalia are but the means of her humiliation: "I like your cunt, Ida . . . it's the best thing about you."[7]

All further representations conspire to convince the reader of Val's superior intelligence and control, while demonstrating the female's moronic complaisance and helpless carnality; each moment exalts him further and degrades her lower: a dazzling instance of the sexual double standard:

> "You never wear any undies do you? You're a slut, do you know it?"
> I pulled her dress up and made her sit that way while I finished my coffee.
> "Play with it a bit while I finish this."
> "You're filthy," she cried, but she did as I told her.
> "Take your two fingers and open it up. I like the color of it."
> . . . With this I reached for a candle on the dresser at my side and I handed it to her.
> "Let's see if you can get it in all the way . . ."
> "You can make me do anything, you dirty devil."
> "You like it, don't you?"[8]

Val's imperious attitude sets the tone for the dramatic events which follow, and the writing soars off into that species of fantasy which Steven Marcus calls "pornotopic," a shower of orgasms:

> I laid her on a small table and when she was on the verge of exploding I picked her up and walked around the room with her; then I took it out and made her walk on her hands holding her by the thighs, letting it slip out now and then to excite her still more.[9]

In both the foregoing selections the most operative verbal phrases are: "I laid her on a small table" (itself a pun), "made her walk on her hands," "she

[6] *Ibid.*, p. 181.
[7] *Ibid.*
[8] *Ibid.*, pp. 181–82.
[9] *Ibid.*, p. 183.

did as I told her," and "I pulled her dress up and made her sit that way." Ida is putty, even less substantial than common clay, and like a bullied child, is continually taking orders for activity which in the hero's view degrades her while it aggrandizes him.

Meanwhile, the hero's potency is so superb and overwhelming that he is lost in admiration: "It went on like this until I had such an erection that even after I shot a wad into her it stayed up like a hammer. That excited her terribly."[10] And emerging from his efforts covered with so much credit and satisfaction, he takes account of his assets: "My cock looked like a bruised rubber hose; it hung between my legs, extended an inch or two beyond its normal length and swollen beyond recognition."[11]

Ida, who has never demanded much of his attention, nor of ours, is quickly forgotten as the hero goes off to feast in his inimitable fashion: "I went to the drug store and swallowed a couple of malted milks."[12] His final pronouncement on his adventure also redounds to his credit: "A royal bit of fucking, thought I to myself, wondering how I'd act when I met Woodruff again."[13] Royal indeed.

During the course of the episode, Val obliges the reader with intelligence of the Woodruffs' marital incompatibility, a misalliance of a curiously physical character. Mr. Woodruff possesses a genital organ of extraordinary proportions, "a veritable horse cock." "I remember the first time I saw it—I could scarcely believe my eyes"[14] whereas Mrs. Woodruff's dimensions have already been referred to under the rubric "small juicy cunt." But lest this irreconcilable misfortune in any way excuse her in seeking out other satisfaction, it is repeatedly underlined, throughout the section of the novel where she figures that she is an uppity woman. Therefore the hero's exemplary behavior in reducing her to the status of a mere female. Moreover, we are given to understand that she is an insatiable nymphomaniac—thus his wit and prosperity in discovering and exploiting her.

The figure of Ida Verlaine appears to have haunted Miller's imagination. It is not enough that his hero should discover her "whorish" nature and bring her to paroxysms of sensual capitulation while congratulating himself on cuckolding her adulating husband. In an earlier work, *Black Spring*, she appears as a woman discovered at prostitution and properly chastised. Here Miller's didactic nature obtrudes itself and one is made to perceive the validity of his claim that his is a deeply moral imagination.

Bill Woodruff's brilliant reaction when the news is passed along to him

10 *Ibid.*, pp. 182–83.
11 *Ibid.*, p. 183.
12 *Ibid.*
13 *Ibid.*
14 *Ibid.*, p. 184.

by another buddy is narrated at length and with obvious relish. The narrator, again a version of Miller, regards the anecdote as "cute":

This night, however, he waited up for her and when she came sailing in, chipper, perky, a little lit up and cold as usual he pulled up short with a "where were you to-night?" She tried pulling her usual yarn, of course. "Cut that," he said. "I want you to get your things off and tumble into bed." That made her sore. She mentioned in her roundabout way that she didn't want any of that business. "You don't feel in the mood for it, I suppose," says he, and then he adds: "that's fine because now I'm going to warm you up a bit." With that he up and ties her to the bedstead, gags her, and then goes for the razor strop. On the way to the bathroom, he grabs a bottle of mustard from the kitchen. He comes back with the razor strop and he belts the piss out of her. And after that he rubs the mustard into the raw welts. "That ought to keep you warm for to-night," he says. And so saying he makes her bend over and spread her legs apart. "Now," he says, "I'm going to pay you as usual," and taking a bill out of his pocket he crumples it and then shoves it up her quim.[15]

Miller concludes the saga of Ida and Bill with a last joke at the cuckold's expense, for Bill is still a cuckold, and a maxim for the reader in capital letters, is put forward as "the purpose of all this"—merely "To prove that

THE GREAT ARTIST IS HE WHO CONQUERS THE ROMANTIC IN HIMSELF."[16]

Miller's educational intentions in the passage are abundantly clear. Females who are frigid, e.g., not sexually compliant, should be beaten. Females who break the laws of marital fidelity should also be beaten, for the barter system of marriage (sex in return for security) must not be violated by outside commerce. Rather more informative than this sober doctrine of the cave is the insight it provides into Miller's sexual/literary motives and their undeniably sadistic overtones. They are closer to the vicarious politic of the cock-pit than of the boudoir, but the former often casts considerable light on the latter.

II

"I have nothing in me," she said. "Do we go ahead?"
"Who knows," I said, "keep quiet."
And I could feel her beginning to come. The doubt in me had tipped her off, the adjuration to be quiet had thrown the bolt. She was a minute away, but she was on her way, and just as if one of her wily fingers had thrown some switch in me, I was gone like a bat and shaking hands with the Devil once more. Rare greed shone in her eyes, pleasure in her mouth, she was happy. I was ready to chase, I was gorged to throw the first spill, high on a choice, like some

[15] Henry Miller, Black Spring (1938) (New York: Grove Press, 1963), pp. 227–28.
[16] Ibid., p. 228.

cat caught on two wires I was leaping back and forth, in separate runs for separate strokes, bringing spoils and secrets up to the Lord from the red mills,
bearing messages of defeat back from that sad womb, and then I chose—ah,
but there was time to change—I chose her cunt. It was no graveyard now, no
warehouse, no, more like a chapel now, a modest decent place, but its walls
were snug, its odor was green, there was a sweetness in the chapel, a muted
reverential sweetness in those walls of stone. "That is what prison will be like
for you," said a last effort of my inner tongue. "Stay here!" came a command
from inside of me; except that I could feel the Devil's meal beneath, its fires
were lifting through the floor, and I waited for the warmth to reach inside, to
come up from the cellar below, to bring booze and heat up and licking tongues,
I was up above a choice which would take me on one wind or another, and I
had to give myself, I could not hold back, there was an explosion, furious,
treacherous and hot as the gates of an icy slalom with the speed at my heels
overtaking my nose. I had one of those splittings of a second where the senses
fly out and there in that instant the itch reached into me and drew me out and
I jammed up her ass and came as if I'd been flung across the room. She let out
a cry of rage.[17]

The foregoing is a description of heterosexual sodomy from Norman
Mailer's *An American Dream*. The practice is not only one of the book's primary attractions, but so central to the action that one might even say the
plot depended on it. Mailer's hero, Stephen Rojack, has just finished murdering his wife and is now relieving his feelings by buggering his maid.

Mailer transparently identifies with his hero, who has little motive for the
killing beyond the fact that he is unable to "master" his mate by any means
short of murder. The desire for such mastery is perfectly understandable to
Mailer and even engages his sympathy. So does Rojack's surprisingly old-
fashioned stance of the outraged husband. Mrs. Rojack, to whom Mr.
Rojack's many affairs are perfectly well known, has found the temerity to
advise him that since their separation she too has indulged herself. Moreover,
and here is where one must depend on the forceful role of sodomy in the
book, she admits that she has been enjoying this very activity with her new
lovers. Now sodomy is a specialty in which our hero takes personal pride.
Though he boasts to her face that his mistresses far excel her in this activity,
the notion that his wife is committing sodomous adultery is evidently too
severe a trial on his patience. It is the final blow to his vanity, his sense of
property, and most material of all, his fancied masculine birthright of su-
perordination, so he promptly retaliates by strangling the upstart. As Mrs.
Rojack is one of those Celtic sporting women, it is not easy work, and Rojack
is exhausted when he finishes and all the more triumphant: "I was weary
with a most honorable fatigue, and my flesh seemed new. I had not felt so

[17] Norman Mailer, *An American Dream* (New York, Dial, 1964), pp. 45–46.

nice since I was twelve. It seemed inconceivable at this instant that anything in life could fail to please."[18]

To return to the maid. Rojack had entered her room to find her busily masturbating, surely a fortuitous circumstance. The rest is easy. He calmly removes her hand from her genitals and replaces it with his bare foot "drawing up on the instant out of her a wet spicy wisdom of all the arts and crafts of getting along in the world."[19] The comment is indicative of the heavy heuristic value which the hero is to obtain from his sexual exploits. For an instant Rojack toys with the idea of simply murdering the maid—"I was ready to kill her easy as not, there was an agreeable balance in the thought that I was ready to kill anyone at this moment"[20]—but he decides instead to take her on. Three pages of sexual activity then follow before a word is spoken; and, as the hero boasts, "it must have been five minutes before I chose to give her a kiss, but I took her mouth at last."[21] In doing so, he undertakes to absorb her soul, which is that of a German proletarian. It appears that Mr. Rojack's employee smells, and it is chiefly through her odor that Rojack, a Harvard man, a college professor, a United States congressman, a television personality, and the very recent widower of a rich woman, stumbles upon the understanding outlined in the next statement.

> But then, as abruptly as an arrest, a thin high constipated smell (a smell which spoke of rocks and grease and the sewer-damp of wet stones in poor European alleys) came needling its way out of her. She was hungry, like a lean rat she was hungry, and it could have spoiled my pleasure except that there was something intoxicating in the sheer narrow pitch of the smell, so strong, so stubborn, so private, it was a smell which could be mellowed only by the gift of furs and gems.[22]

Although her patron, Rojack is almost too repelled to continue: "it could have spoiled my pleasure." Then he decides that even this unworthy creature can serve him in some way: "I had a desire suddenly to skip the sea and mine the earth, a pure prong of desire to bugger, there was canny hard-packed evil in that butt, that I knew."[23]

It is at this point that the first word is spoken; the servant resists the will of her master. But Ruta's *"verboten"* makes little impression on Rojack. He has convinced himself that her essence lies in her rectum and that it is a quality which might be convenient to him. As a newly arrived homicide, he is in immediate need of a bit of that canny lower-class self-preservation Ruta is presumed to contain. For if nothing else, she has the invaluable "knowledge

[18] *Ibid.*, p. 32.
[19] *Ibid.*, p. 42.
[20] *Ibid.*
[21] *Ibid.*, pp. 42–43.
[22] *Ibid.*, p. 43.
[23] *Ibid.*, p. 44.

of a city rat." Furthermore, Rojack regards himself in the light of a moralist in search of wisdom and Ruta's anus can teach him about evil.

How evil resides in her bowels or why Ruta has a greater share of it than her master may appear difficult to explain, but many uncanny things are possible with our author. In most of Mailer's fiction sexuality has such a mystical and metaphysical import that genitals acquire definite personalities. Ruta's "box," as Rojack refers to it, has very little to offer; nothing resides therein but "cold gasses from the womb and a storehouse of disappointments."[24] In *An American Dream* female sexuality is depersonalized to the point of being a matter of class or a matter of nature. Ruta behaves like a guttersnipe, Deborah, the former Mrs. Rojack, like a cruel duchess. Cherry, the mistress Rojack later wins, has the virtues of nature, unavailable to poor Ruta, and excelling those of the privileged female (Deborah) who is now too dangerously insubordinate to stay alive. As the hero and a male, Rojack, of course, transcends any such typology.

Finding where Ruta's true serviceability lies, the hero disdains her vagina to continue rooting in her nether orifice. (Her name appears to be a cruel English pun on this: in German, *Rute*, pronounced nearly the same as Ruta, refers both to the switch or birch of chastisement as well as to the penis, and perhaps more than mere linguistic coincidence is involved.) As her resistance renders her difficult to penetrate, Rojack hits upon the device of pulling her hair, noting with fastidious justification that, anyway, it is dyed red: "I could feel the pain in her scalp strain like a crowbar the length of her body and push up the trap and I was in, that quarter-inch more was gained, the rest was easy."[25] As further justification for his inquiry into her he resorts again to the odor of her presumably vicious, but now fascinating, character:

> What a subtle smell came from her then, something back of the ambition, the narrow stubbornness, the monomaniacal determination to get along in the world, no, that was replaced by something tender as the flesh but not as clean, something sneaky, full of fear.[26]

Just as homicide produced an honorable fatigue in him, Rojack now hits on the glittering idea that in forcibly buggering his servant he is actually performing an act of patriotism because Ruta is a "Nazi." The reader may have some difficulty in accepting this; twenty-three years old and therefore a child during the war, Ruta is hardly a fit subject for Rojack's instant justice. But the hero continues to take an uncommon satisfaction in his racial revenge: "There was a high private pleasure in plugging a Nazi, there was something clean despite all—I felt as if I were gliding in the clear air above

24 *Ibid.*, p. 44.
25 *Ibid.*
26 *Ibid.*

Luther's jakes."[27] And through this shift, Rojack, a wizard at manipulative ethics, arrives at a position of moral leverage for any further exploits.

Sodomy has a number of possible meanings in Rojack's mind: homosexuality (he confesses to Cherry that he has some doubts about his heterosexual vocation); a forbidden species of sexuality at which he is an expert and over which he holds copyright; or anal rape, which is his way of expressing contemptuous mastery. It is the acting out of this last attitude which is reserved for Ruta.

Throughout the rest of the passage, Rojack entertains the reader with his contrasting impressions of Ruta's rectum, "a bank of pleasures," and her vagina, "a deserted warehouse, that empty tomb." But this virtuosity is accomplished with certain misgivings. As one might expect, these have nothing to do with her pleasure, which is never at issue, but with Rojack's peculiar notion of sexual honor. After all, he muses, her womb might contain "one poor flower growing in a gallery." Because he has deprived her of the opportunity to bear his seed, a substance Rojack regards with reverential awe, he feels obliged to regard himself as a "great thief."[28] Later he will indulge in a number of "might have beens" about the ill fortune of "that empty womb," that "graveyard which gambled a flower and lost."[29] The fact that his precious semen has been discharged in her rectum and not in her cervix is a source of bemusement, not uncomfortably experienced as guilt. Ruta has missed the radiant opportunity to be impregnated by a higher power and he can only pity her: "I had thought then of what had been left in her. It was perishing in the kitchens of the Devil." And then he wonders: "Was its curse on me? . . . Was that the cloud of oppression which had come to me in the dark? That the seed was expiring in the wrong field?"[30] Perhaps it is this monomania about his own sexual discharge that has made Rojack a specialist in existential dread.

As for Ruta, she responds magically, just as the relevant masculine fantasy dictates. Indeed, her gratitude at being sodomized is positively astonishing: "I do not know why you have trouble with your wife. You are absolutely a genius, Mr. Rojack."[31] Accordingly, the final stages in which this man has his will with his maid take place under the most ideal conditions. Ruta now responds quite as masculine egotism would prescribe: ". . . she was becoming mine as no woman ever had, she wanted to be part of my will."[32] It would seem that she could want nothing better for herself, and at once her "feminine," or again "true woman," instincts emerge and she acquires

27 *Ibid.*
28 *Ibid.*, p. 45.
29 *Ibid.*, p. 49.
30 *Ibid.*
31 *Ibid.*, p. 46.
32 *Ibid.*, p. 45.

what her master relays to be ". . . the taste of power in her eyes and her mouth, that woman's look that the world is theirs."[33] This delusion of success is, of course, most advantageous to her lord's purposes.

Sexual congress in a Mailer novel is always a matter of strenuous endeavor, rather like mountain climbing—a straining ever upward after achievement. In this, as in so many ways, Mailer is authentically American. Rojack is presently doing very well at his cliff-face, but Ruta begins to waver. She turns with guilty admission of possible failure, "a little look of woe was on her face, a puckered fearful little nine-year-old afraid of her punishment, wishing to be good."[34] In his vast composure, Rojack orders her to "keep quiet." Not only is he more conscious than she of the state of her orgasm, he enjoys a complacent sadistic awareness of what "punishment" might ensue, if she isn't "good."

What follows is the passage I have quoted at the outset, almost exclusively a description of Rojack's activity—and properly so—as coitus here is simply his accomplishment as enacted upon Ruta, and therefore its value is precisely its value to him. Very much a solo flight, it is by no means inappropriate that the imagery employed is aeronautic, "I was gone like a bat," etc. It is also a summary of Rojack's major interests: sport—"I was ready to chase"; "leaping back and forth in separate runs for separate strokes"; "an icy slalom with the speed at my heels"; alcohol—"to bring booze and heat up and licking tongues"; and religion.

By now it is hardly surprising that his orgasm should take on cosmic and metaphysical implications: "a choice which would take me on one wind or another," "one of those splittings of a second where the senses fly out" and give rise to visions of a "huge city in some desert, was it a place on the moon?" What is more noteworthy are the elaborate configurations in the act of the Lord and the Devil. The Devil is manifestly an anal force. The Lord smiles upon Rojack's high mission to fertilize the humble and bring the "spoils and secrets" of his semen to the "sad womb" of this lowly woman through the favor of his visitation. Indeed, Ruta's "cunt" as Rojack calls it, has prospered through association with him and grown respectable: "It was no graveyard now, no warehouse, no, more like a chapel now." But despite the purloined phrases from William Blake it is still no great shakes, simply ". . . a modest decent place, but its walls were snug," and appropriately, it is aware of its exalted, if only sporadic, honor in housing Rojack himself, who deigns to find in it "a muted reverential sweetness." But having defined the organ in question in terms of several types of public buildings, Rojack finally comes to detect in it a prison with "walls of stone."

The result of this discovery is that, at the last moment, he escapes back to the freewheeling Devil of sodomy. The chief function of this passage is to

[33] *Ibid.*
[34] *Ibid.*

provide a way for Rojack to commit his crime a second time in symbolic circumstances. Given the often emphasized choice between the Devil (sodomy) and the Lord (procreation), or death and life, Rojack once again opts for death. Just as he refuses what we are asked to believe is a portentous existential opportunity to sweeten Ruta's womb with his magical semen (infallible in its power to bring about conception), so too does Rojack refuse the choice of acknowledging his crime, accepting responsibility for it and going to prison. Ruta's vagina has constituted his foretaste of prison. " 'That is what prison will be like for you' said a last effort on my inner tongue. 'Stay here!' came a command from inside of me." But the Devil has more exotic and dynamic attractions. Rojack claims that he is compelled to his decision and he explains it in terms of a generosity which pertains only to himself: "I had to give myself, I could not hold back." Ruta and prison must do without the hallowed presence of the hero so that Rojack may have his ultimate satisfaction: "I jammed up her ass and came as if I'd been flung across the room. She let out a cry of rage." It seems that Mailer is both a romantic manichean and a romantic diabolist.

After receiving his servant's congratulations on his dazzling performance, Rojack proceeds calmly to the next floor and throws his wife's body out of the window. He has elected to remain with the Devil and stay alive. Ruta has been a vessel of considerable utility. Through her, or rather through her "ass," the hero has made his major decision: to pass the murder off as an accident. And as Ruta was compliant to an outlandish degree, so is the rest of the world. All obstacles melt before Rojack, who hereafter is a miracle of tough dispatch. Once almost a "loser," he is rejuvenated and remade through the act of murder: he wins a fight with a black gangster who cowers before him, a fortune at the tables at Las Vegas, and the love of a nightclub singer who wants him to make her a lady (the last detail a fatuity which is better passed over in silence). Even the police look on Rojack with eyes blinded by admiring comradery, and he is permitted to escape to Yucatan. In fact, Mailer's *An American Dream* is an exercise in how to kill your wife and be happy ever after. The reader is given to understand that by murdering one woman and buggering another, Rojack became a "man."

The humanist convictions which underlie *Crime and Punishment* (the original and still the greatest study in what it is like to commit murder), may all go by the board. Both Dostoyevsky and Dreiser, in *An American Tragedy*, gradually created in their murderers an acceptance of responsibility for the violation of life which their actions constituted, and both transcend their crimes through atonement. Rojack has some singularity in being one of the first literary characters to get away with murder; he is surely the first hero as homicide to rejoice in his crime and never really lose his creator's support. In *Native Son*, Richard Wright understood Bigger Thomas' crime while never condoning it and made of it a prototypical fable of the logic of rage in a racist society. Mailer also appears to find in Rojack a symbolic figure whose crime is diagnostic of conditions in American society. But the condition appears to be simply a hostility between the sexes so bitter that it has reached the proportions of a war waged in terms of murder and sodomy. (Rojack knew "all women were killers," who "must kill" unless "we" master them "altogether.")[35] And Mailer is to be on the winning side, to which end he has created in Rojack the last warrior for a curious cause, none other than male supremacy. Rojack is a far cry from Wright's underdog from a Chicago slum acting only through desperation in a novel that is both a plea for racial justice and a threatening vision of what may come to pass should the hope of it fail. Rojack belongs to the oldest ruling class in the world, and like one of Faulkner's ancient retainers of a lost cause, he is making his stand on the preservation of a social hierarchy that sees itself as threatened with extinction. His partial Jewish ancestry and his "liberal" views to the contrary, Rojack is the last surviving white man as conquering hero. Mailer's *An American Dream* is a rallying cry for a sexual politics in which diplomacy has failed and war is the last political resort of a ruling caste that feels its position in deadly peril.

III

A few days later, when I met him near the docks, Armand ordered me to follow him. Almost without speaking, he took me to his room. With the same apparent scorn he subjected me to his pleasure.

Dominated by his strength and age, I gave the work my utmost care. Crushed by that mass of flesh, which was devoid of the slightest spirituality, I experienced the giddiness of finally meeting the perfect brute, indifferent to my happiness. I discovered the sweetness that could be contained in a thick fleece on torso, belly and thighs and what force it could transmit. I finally let myself be buried in that stormy night. Out of gratitude or fear I placed a kiss on Armand's hairy arm.

"What's eating you? Are you nuts or something?"

"I didn't do any harm."

I remained at his side in order to serve his nocturnal pleasure. When we went to bed, Armand whipped his leather belt from the loops of his trousers and made it snap. It was flogging an invisible victim, a shape of transparent flesh. The air bled. If he frightened me then, it was because of his powerlessness to be the Armand I see, who is heavy and mean. The snapping accompanied and supported him. His rage and despair at not being *him* made him tremble like a horse subdued by darkness, made him tremble more and more. He would not, however, have tolerated my living idly. He advised me to prowl around the station or the zoo and pick up customers. Knowing the terror inspired in me by his person, he didn't deign to keep any eye on me. The money I earned I brought back intact.[36]

[35] *Ibid.,* p. 82, p. 100.

[36] Jean Genet, *The Thief's Journal,* translated from the French by Bernard Frechtman (New York: Grove Press, 1964), p. 134.

This quotation, from Jean Genet's autobiographical novel *The Thief's Journal*, is the first passage in which the author's identification is with the "female figure." Jean Genet is both male and female. Young, poor, a criminal and a beggar, he was also initially the despised drag queen, the *maricone* (faggot), contemptible because he was the female partner in homosexual acts. Older, distinguished by fame, wealthy and secure, he became a male; though never ascending to the full elevation of the pimp (or supermale).

Sexual role is not a matter of biological identity but of class or caste in the hierocratic homosexual society projected in Genet's novels. Because of the perfection with which they ape and exaggerate the "masculine" and "feminine" of heterosexual society, his homosexual characters represent the best contemporary insight into its constitution and beliefs. Granted that their caricature is grotesque, and Genet himself is fully aware of the morbidity of this pastiche, his homosexuals nonetheless have unerringly penetrated to the essence of what heterosexual society imagines to be the character of "masculine" and "feminine," and which it mistakes for the nature of male and female, thereby preserving the traditional relation of the sexes. Sartre's brilliant psychoanalytic biography of Genet describes the sexual life of the pimps and queens, male and female figures, in terms that bear out these distinctions of character and prestige:

This is murder: submissive to a corpse, neglected, unnoticed, gazed at unmindfully and manipulated from behind, the girl queen is metamorphosed into a contemptible female object. She does not even have for the pimp the importance that the sadist attributes to his victim. The latter, though tortured and humiliated, at least remains the focal point of her tormentor's concern. It is indeed she whom he wishes to reach, in her particularity, in the depths of her consciousness. But the fairy is only a receptacle, a vase, a spittoon, which one uses and thinks no more of and which one discards by the very use one makes of it. The pimp masturbates in her. At the very instant when an irresistible force knocks her down, turns her over and punctures her, a dizzying word swoops down upon her, a power hammer that strikes her as if she were a medal: "Encule!" [Faggot][37]

This is mainly a description of what it is to be female as reflected in the mirror society of homosexuality. But the passage also implies what it is to be male. It is to be master, hero, brute, and pimp. Which is also to be irremediably stupid and cowardly. In this feudal relationship of male and female, pimp and queen, one might expect exchange of servitude for protection. But the typical pimp never protects his slave, and allows him/her to be beaten, betrayed, or even killed, responding only with ambiguous amuse-

[37] Jean-Paul Sartre, *Saint Genet, Actor and Martyr*, translated from the French by Bernard Frechtman. (New York: Braziller, 1963), p. 125. In a footnote, Frechtman translates "Encule" as one who gets buggered, but as English lacks such an expression, he suggests "cock-sucker" as the best equivalent of the insult.

ment. One is naturally curious to discover just what the queen does receive in return. The answer appears to be an intensity of humiliation which constitutes identity for those who despise themselves. This, in turn, leads us to the reasons for such self-despair.

With Genet they are quite explicit, and Sartre has little difficulty outlining them. A bastard, Genet was repudiated at birth and left at an orphanage; the double rejection of what can only be described as an error from inception. Adopted then by a family of narrow Morvan peasants, he was found stealing and sent to grow up in a children's prison. There he experiences his final ostracism in being subjected to rape by older and stronger males. He has now achieved the lowest status in the world as he saw it; a perfection of opprobrium in being criminal, queer, and female. It remained only to study and refine his role, thus the wallowing in self-hatred which both Sartre and Genet describe as the "femininity" of the passive homosexual. He is feminine because ravished and subjugated by the male; therefore he must study the slavish gestures of "femininity" that he may better exalt his master. As a criminal he is obliged to controvert every decency of the property-owning class not only through a life of larceny (material) but through one of betrayal (moral) as well. And as an outcast, his life's demeanor must be plotted both to imitate and to contradict every notion of the world beyond whose boundaries he lives in exile.

But having gone this far, having plunged this low, Genet studies the values of those who live above him so that he may further desecrate them. In doing so he acquires the pride of the utterly abject, a condition which turns out to be next door to saintliness. As a young beggar and whore in the Barrio Chino of Barcelona, Genet attained this sanctity and the unshakable self-respect of one who has truly nothing more to lose. Out of this sprang a wily urge to live. And for those who continue in downright ignominy, the will to live may very plausibly become the will to triumph. This whole cast of thought is generously supported by the French tradition wherein martyrdom is still the highest boon open to the religious imagination. In Catholic Europe sainthood remains, even among the renegades, the loftiest state of grace. That is why Divine, the hero/heroine of *Our Lady of the Flowers,* who is also Genet, is uncontestably a larger spirit than Darling, Gorgui, Armand, Stilitano, and all the other pimps. Not only has she greater courage, humor, imagination, and sensibility than the male oppressors before whom she prostrates herself; she alone has a soul. She has suffered, while they have not, because the consciousness required for suffering is inaccessible to them. And in Divine's mortification, both in the flesh and in the spirit, lies the victory of the saint.

Thus Genet's two great novels, *Our Lady of the Flowers* and *The Thief's Journal,* are tales of an odium converted to grandeur. But together with the rest of his prose fiction they also constitute a painstaking exegesis of the barbarian vassalage of the sexual orders, the power structure of "masculine" and "feminine" as revealed by a homosexual, criminal world that mimics with brutal frankness the bourgeois heterosexual society.

In this way the explication of the homosexual code becomes a satire on the heterosexual one. By virtue of their earnestness, Genet's community of pimps and fairies call into ridicule the behavior they so fervently imitate:

> As for slang Divine did not use it, any more than did her cronies the other Nellys . . .
> Slang was for men. It was the male tongue. Like the language of men among the Caribees, it became a secondary sexual attribute. It was like the colored plumage of male birds, like the multi-colored silk garments which are the prerogatives of the warriors of the tribe. It was a crest and spurs. Everyone could understand it, but the only ones who could speak it were the men who at birth received as a gift the gestures, the carriage of the hips, legs and arms, the eyes, the chest, with which one can speak it. One day at one of our bars, when Mimosa ventured the following words in the course of a sentence ". . . his screwy stories . . ." the men frowned. Someone said with a threat in his voice: "Broad acting tough."[38]

The virility of the pimp is a transparent egotism posing as strength. His "masculinity" is in fact the most specious of petty self-inflations and is systematically undermined by the true heroes of these adventures, the queens. Though Genet is a great romantic and has created in Divine what is perhaps the last and possibly the most illustrious of those archetypal great-hearted whores so dear to the French tradition, Genet is just as certainly a cold-blooded rationalist whose formidable analytic mind has fastened upon the most fundamental of society's arbitrary follies, its view of sex as a caste structure ratified by nature.

Beginning with the dissection of sexual attitudes in his prose fiction, Genet has gone on in his plays to survey the parent world of the parasitic homosexual community—that larger society where most of us imagine we are at home. Emerging from the little world of homosexual crime which still concerned him in *Deathwatch* and *The Maids*, he brought the truths he had learned there to bear on the complacencies of the "normal" world which for so long had banished and condemned him. His most scathing critique of sexual politics is found in his most recent works for the theater, *The Blacks*, *The Balcony*, and *The Screens*.

What he has to tell this snug and pious enclave will hardly furnish it with the reassuring bromides they have begun to feel the need of and take as a balm from old retainers like Norman Mailer and Henry Miller. Genet submits the entire social code of "masculine" and "feminine" to a disinterested scrutiny and concludes that it is odious.

[38] Jean Genet, *Our Lady of the Flowers*, translated by Bernard Frechtman (New York: Grove Press, 1963), p. 90.

If Armand is but a brute and a fool, there is really, as Genet demonstrates, no cause for surprise. He was schooled to be such through every element of his education and was clearly given to understand that these traits were no less than the fulfillment of his very nature as a male. All he has learned has taught him to identify "masculine" with force, cruelty, indifference, egotism, and property. It is no wonder that he regards his penis as a talisman: both an instrument to oppress and the very symbol, in fact the reality, of his status: "My cock," he once said, "is worth its weight in gold . . ."[39] At other times he boasts that he can lift a heavy man on the end of it. Armand automatically associated sexuality with power, with his solitary pleasure, and with the pain and humiliation of his partner, who is nothing but an object to him in the most literal sense. Intercourse is an assertion of mastery, one that announces his own higher caste and proves it upon a victim who is expected to surrender, serve, and be satisfied.

Armand, for all his turpitude, is at once both more primitive and more logical than a "gentleman," and more honest and direct than the respectable bourgeois whose real convictions he has simply put into practice, and who, by no accident, enjoys reading such passages for the vicarious illusion of mastery which he fancies is offered therein.

The Balcony is Genet's theory of revolution and counterrevolution. The play is set in a brothel and concerns a revolution which ends in failure, as the patrons and proprietors of a whorehouse are persuaded to assume the roles of the former government. Having studied human relationships in the world of pimp and faggot, Genet has come to understand how sexual caste supersedes all other forms of inegalitarianism: racial, political, or economic. *The Balcony* demonstrates the futility of all forms of revolution which preserve intact the basic unit of exploitation and oppression, that between the sexes, male and female, *or* any of the substitutes for them. Taking the fundamental human connection, that of sexuality, to be the nuclear model of all the more elaborate social constructs growing out of it, Genet perceives that it is in itself not only hopelessly tainted but the very prototype of institutionalized inequality. He is convinced that by dividing humanity into two groups and appointing one to rule over the other by virtue of birthright, the social order has already established and ratified a system of oppression which will underlie and corrupt all other human relationships as well as every area of thought and experience.

The first scene, which takes place between a prostitute and a bishop, epitomizes the play much as it does the society it describes. The cleric holds power only through the myth of religion, itself dependent on the fallacy of sin, in turn conditional on the lie that the female is sexuality itself and therefore an evil worthy of the bishop's condign punishment. By such devious routes does power circle round and round the hopeless mess we have made

[39] *The Thief's Journal*, p. 135.

of sexuality. Partly through money: for it is with money that the woman is purchased, and economic dependency is but another sign of her bondage to a system whose coercive agents are actual as well as mythical. Delusions about sex foster delusions of power, and both depend on the reification of woman.

That the Bishop is actually a gasman visiting the bordello's "chambers of illusions" so that he can vicariously share in the power of the church only clarifies the satire on the sexual class system. Those males relegated to reading gas meters may still participate in the joys of mastery through the one human being any male can buy—a female as whore. And the whore, one wonders, what profits her? Nothing. Her "role" in the ritual theater where sexual, political, and social institutions are so felicitously combined is merely to accommodate the ruling passion of each of her rentiers.

In the second scene, the whore is a thief and a criminal (versions of Genet himself) so that a bank clerk may play at justice and morality. Her judge may order her whipped by a muscular executioner or grant her mercy in a transcendent imitation of the powers-that-be, powers reserved to other more fortunate males. The General of Scene III, following his own notions of masculine majesty, converts his whore into his mount and plays at hero while her mouth bleeds from the bit. No matter with which of the three leading roles of sinner, malefactor, or animal the male client may choose to mime his delusions of grandeur, the presence of the woman is utterly essential. To each masquerading male the female is a mirror in which he beholds himself. And the penultimate moment in his illusory but purchasable power fantasy is the moment when whether as Bishop, Judge, or General, he "fucks" her as woman, as subject, as chattel.

The political wisdom implicit in Genet's statement in the play is that unless the ideology of real or fantasized virility is abandoned, unless the clinging to male supremacy as a birthright is finally foregone, all systems of oppression will continue to function simply by virtue of their logical and emotional mandate in the primary human situation.

But what of the madame herself? Irma, *The Balcony*'s able and dedicated administrator, makes money by selling other women, wherein it may be observed how no institution holds sway without collaborators and overseers. Chosen as queen under the counterrevolution, Irma does nothing at all, for queens do not rule. In fact, they do not even exist in themselves; they die as persons once they assume their function, as the Envoy graciously explains. Their function is to serve as figureheads and abstractions to males, just as Chantal, a talented former whore who moves for a moment toward human realization by means of her hope in the revolution, wavers, and then is sold anew and converted into the sexual figurehead for the rising when it becomes corrupt and betrays its radical ideals under the usual excuse of expediency. "In order to win" it adopts the demented consciousness of its opponent and establishes a rotten new version of all it had once stood against. In no time it turns the rebellion into a suicidal carnival, an orgy of blood connected to the old phallic fantasy of "shoot and screw." Its totem is the ritual scapegoat provided by every army's beauty queen since Troy. Once Chantal enters upon the mythical territory of a primitive standard and prize over whom males will tear each other apart, the revolution passes irrevocably into counterrevolution.

Throughout *The Balcony* Genet explores the pathology of virility, the chimera of sexual congress as a paradigm of power over other human beings. He appears to be the only living male writer of first-class literary gifts to have transcended the sexual myths of our era. His critique of the heterosexual politic points the way toward a true sexual revolution, a path which must be explored if any radical social change is to come about. In Genet's analysis, it is fundamentally impossible to change society without changing personality, and sexual personality as it has generally existed must undergo the most drastic overhaul.

If we are to be free at last, Genet proposes in the last scenes of the play, we must first break those chains of our own making through our blind acceptance of common ideas. The three great cages in which we are immured must be dismantled. The first is the potential power of the "Great Figures"—the cleric, the judge and the warrior—elements of myth which have enslaved consciousness in a coil of self-imposed absurdity. The second is the omnipotence of the police state, the only virtual power in a corrupt society, all other forms of coercion being largely psychological. Last, and most insidious of all, is the cage of sex, the cage in which all others are enclosed: for is not the totem of Police Chief George a six-foot rubber phallus, a "prick of great stature"? And the old myth of sin and virtue, the myth of guilt and innocence, the myth of heroism and cowardice on which the Great Figures repose, the old pillars of an old and decadent structure, are also built on the sexual fallacy. (Or as one is tempted to pun, phallacy.) By attempting to replace this corrupt and tottering edifice while preserving its foundations, the revolution's own bid for social transformation inevitably fails and turns into the counterrevolution where the Grand Balcony, a first-class whorehouse, furnishes both costumes and actors for the new pseudo-government.

Genet's play ends as it had begun. Irma turning out the lights informs us we may go home, where all is falser than the theater's rites. The brothel will open again tomorrow for an identical ritual. The sounds of revolution begin again offstage, but unless the Police Chief is permanently imprisoned in his tomb and unless the new rebels have truly forsworn the customary idiocy of the old sexual politics, there will be no revolution. Sex is deep at the heart of our troubles, Genet is urging, and unless we eliminate the most pernicious of our systems of oppression, unless we go to the very center of the sexual politic and its sick delirium of power and violence, all our efforts at liberation will only land us again in the same primordial stews.

TWO

Theory of Sexual Politics

The three instances of sexual description we have examined so far were remarkable for the large part which notions of ascendancy and power played within them. Coitus can scarcely be said to take place in a vacuum; although of itself it appears a biological and physical activity, it is set so deeply within the larger context of human affairs that it serves as a charged microcosm of the variety of attitudes and values to which culture subscribes. Among other things, it may serve as a model of sexual politics on an individual or personal plane.

But of course the transition from such scenes of intimacy to a wider context of political reference is a great step indeed. In introducing the term "sexual politics," one must first answer the inevitable question "Can the relationship between the sexes be viewed in a political light at all?" The answer depends on how one defines politics.[1] This essay does not define the political as that relatively narrow and exclusive world of meetings, chairmen, and parties. The term "politics" shall refer to power-structured relationships, arrangements whereby one group of persons is controlled by another. By way

---

[1] The American Heritage Dictionary's fourth definition is fairly approximate: "methods or tactics involved in managing a state or government." *American Heritage Dictionary* (New York: American Heritage and Houghton Mifflin, 1969). One might expand this to a set of strategems designed to maintain a system. If one understands patriarchy to be an institution perpetuated by such techniques of control, one has a working definition of how politics is conceived in this essay.

of parenthesis one might add that although an ideal politics might simply be conceived of as the arrangement of human life on agreeable and rational principles from whence the entire notion of power *over* others should be banished, one must confess that this is not what constitutes the political as we know it, and it is to this that we must address ourselves.

The following sketch, which might be described as "notes toward a theory of patriarchy," will attempt to prove that sex is a status category with political implications. Something of a pioneering effort, it must perforce be both tentative and imperfect. Because the intention is to provide an overall description, statements must be generalized, exceptions neglected, and subheadings overlapping and, to some degree, arbitrary as well.

The word "politics" is enlisted here when speaking of the sexes primarily because such a word is eminently useful in outlining the real nature of their relative status, historically and at the present. It is opportune, perhaps today even mandatory, that we develop a more relevant psychology and philosophy of power relationships beyond the simple conceptual framework provided by our traditional formal politics. Indeed, it may be imperative that we give some attention to defining a theory of politics which treats of power relationships on grounds less conventional than those to which we are accustomed.[2] I have therefore found it pertinent to define them on grounds of personal contact and interaction between members of well-defined and coherent groups: races, castes, classes, and sexes. For it is precisely because certain groups have no representation in a number of recognized political structures that their position tends to be so stable, their oppression so continuous.

In America, recent events have forced us to acknowledge at last that the relationship between the races is indeed a political one which involves the general control of one collectivity, defined by birth, over another collectivity, also defined by birth. Groups who rule by birthright are fast disappearing, yet there remains one ancient and universal scheme for the domination of one birth group by another—the scheme that prevails in the area of sex. The study of racism has convinced us that a truly political state of affairs operates between the races to perpetuate a series of oppressive circumstances. The subordinated group has inadequate redress through existing political institutions, and is deterred thereby from organizing into conventional political struggle and opposition.

Quite in the same manner, a disinterested examination of our system of sexual relationship must point out that the situation between the sexes now, and throughout history, is a case of that phenomenon Max Weber defined

2 I am indebted here to Ronald V. Samson's *The Psychology of Power* (New York: Random House, 1968) for his intelligent investigation of the connection between formal power structures and the family and for his analysis of how power corrupts basic human relationships.

as *herrschaft,* a relationship of dominance and subordination.[3] What goes largely unexamined, often even unacknowledged (yet is institutionalized nonetheless) in our social order, is the birthright priority whereby males rule females. Through this system a most ingenious form of "interior colonization" has been achieved. It is one which tends moreover to be sturdier than any form of segregation, and more rigorous than class stratification, more uniform, certainly more enduring. However muted its present appearance may be, sexual dominion obtains nevertheless as perhaps the most pervasive ideology of our culture and provides its most fundamental concept of power.

This is so because our society, like all other historical civilizations, is a patriarchy.[4] The fact is evident at once if one recalls that the military, industry, technology, universities, science, political office, and finance—in short, every avenue of power within the society, including the coercive force of the police, is entirely in male hands. As the essence of politics is power, such realization cannot fail to carry impact. What lingers of supernatural authority, the Deity, "His" ministry, together with the ethics and values, the philosophy and art of our culture—its very civilization—as T. S. Eliot once observed, is of male manufacture.

If one takes patriarchal government to be the institution whereby that half of the populace which is female is controlled by that half which is male, the principles of patriarchy appear to be two fold: male shall dominate female, elder male shall dominate younger. However, just as with any human institution, there is frequently a distance between the real and the ideal; contradictions and exceptions do exist within the system. While patriarchy as an institution is a social constant so deeply entrenched as to run through all other political, social, or economic forms, whether of caste or class, feudality or bureaucracy, just as it pervades all major religions, it also exhibits great variety in history and locale. In democracies,[5] for example, females have often held no office or do so (as now) in such minuscule numbers as to

[3] "Domination in the quite general sense of power, i.e. the possibility of imposing one's will upon the behavior of other persons, can emerge in the most diverse forms." In this central passage of *Wirtschaft und Gesellschaft* Weber is particularly interested in two such forms: control through social authority ("patriarchal, magisterial, or princely") and control through economic force. In patriarchy as in other forms of domination "that control over economic goods, i.e. economic power, is a frequent, often purposively willed, consequence of domination as well as one of its most important instruments." Quoted from Max Rheinstein's and Edward Shil's translation of portions of *Wirtschaft und Gesellschaft* entitled *Max Weber on Law in Economy and Society* (New York: Simon and Schuster, 1967), pp. 323–24.

[4] No matriarchal societies are known to exist at present. Matrilineality, which may be, as some anthropologists have held, a residue or a transitional stage of matriarchy, does not constitute an exception to patriarchal rule, it simply channels the power held by males through female descent—, e.g. the Avunculate.

[5] Radical democracy would, of course, preclude patriarchy. One might find evidence of a general satisfaction with a less than perfect democracy in the fact that women have so rarely held power within modern "democracies."

be below even token representation. Aristocracy, on the other hand, with its emphasis upon the magic and dynastic properties of blood, may at times permit women to hold power. The principle of rule by elder males is violated even more frequently. Bearing in mind the variation and degree in patriarchy—as say between Saudi Arabia and Sweden, Indonesia and Red China—we also recognize our own form in the U.S. and Europe to be much altered and attenuated by the reforms described in the next chapter.

I IDEOLOGICAL

Hannah Arendt[6] has observed that government is upheld by power supported either through consent or imposed through violence. Conditioning to an ideology amounts to the former. Sexual politics obtains consent through the "socialization" of both sexes to basic patriarchal polities with regard to temperament, role, and status. As to status, a pervasive assent to the prejudice of male superiority guarantees superior status in the male, inferior in the female. The first item, temperament, involves the formation of human personality along stereotyped lines of sex category ("masculine" and "feminine"), based on the needs and values of the dominant group and dictated by what its members cherish in themselves and find convenient in subordinates: aggression, intelligence, force, and efficacy in the male; passivity, ignorance, docility, "virtue," and ineffectuality in the female. This is complemented by a second factor, sex role, which decrees a consonant and highly elaborate code of conduct, gesture and attitude for each sex. In terms of activity, sex role assigns domestic service and attendance upon infants to the female, the rest of human achievement, interest, and ambition to the male. The limited role allotted the female tends to arrest her at the level of biological experience. Therefore, nearly all that can be described as distinctly human rather than animal activity (in their own way animals also give birth and care for their young) is largely reserved for the male. Of course, status again follows from such an assignment. Were one to analyze the three categories one might designate status as the political component, role as the sociological, and temperament as the psychological—yet their interdependence is unquestionable and they form a chain. Those awarded higher status tend to adopt roles of mastery, largely because they are first encouraged to develop temperaments of dominance. That this is true of caste and class as well is self-evident.

II BIOLOGICAL

Patriarchal religion, popular attitude, and to some degree, science as well[7] assumes these psycho-social distinctions to rest upon biological differ-

[6] Hannah Arendt, "Speculations on Violence," *The New York Review of Books*, Vol. XII No. 4, February 27, 1969, p. 24.
[7] The social, rather than the physical sciences are referred to here. Traditionally, medical science had often subscribed to such beliefs. This is no longer the case today,

ences between the sexes, so that where culture is acknowledged as shaping behavior, it is said to do no more than cooperate with nature. Yet the temperamental distinctions created in patriarchy ("masculine" and "feminine" personality traits) do not appear to originate in human nature, those of role and status still less.

The heavier musculature of the male, a secondary sexual characteristic and common among mammals, is biological in origin but is also culturally encouraged through breeding, diet and exercise. Yet it is hardly an adequate category on which to base political relations *within civilization*.[8] Male supremacy, like other political creeds, does not finally reside in physical strength but in the acceptance of a value system which is not biological. Superior physical strength is not a factor in political relations—vide those of race and class. Civilization has always been able to substitute other methods (technic, weaponry, knowledge) for those of physical strength, and contemporary civilization has no further need of it. At present, as in the past, physical exertion is very generally a class factor, those at the bottom performing the most strenuous tasks, whether they be strong or not.

It is often assumed that patriarchy is endemic in human social life, explicable or even inevitable on the grounds of human physiology. Such a theory grants patriarchy logical as well as historical origin. Yet if as some anthropologists believe, patriarchy is not of primeval origin, but was preceded by some other social form we shall call pre-patriarchal, then the argument of physical strength as a theory of patriarchal *origins* would hardly constitute a sufficient explanation—unless the male's superior physical strength was released in accompaniment with some change in orientation through new values or new knowledge. Conjecture about origins is always frustrated by lack of certain evidence. Speculation about prehistory, which of necessity is what this must be, remains nothing but speculation. Were one to indulge in it, one might argue the likelihood of a hypothetical period preceding pa-

---

when the best medical research points to the conclusion that sexual stereotypes have no bases in biology.

8 "The historians of Roman laws, having very justly remarked that neither birth nor affection was the foundation of the Roman family, have concluded that this foundation must be found in the power of the father or husband. They make a sort of primordial institution of this power; but they do not explain how this power was established, unless it was by the superiority of strength of the husband over the wife, and of the father over the children. Now, we deceive ourselves sadly when we thus place force as the origin of law. We shall see farther on that the authority of the father or husband, far from having been the first cause, was itself an effect; it was derived from religion, and was established by religion. Superior strength, therefore, was not the principle that established the family." Numa Denis Fustel de Coulanges, *The Ancient City* (1864). English translation by Willard Small (1873), Doubleday Anchor Reprint, pp. 41–42. Unfortunately Fustel de Coulanges neglects to mention how religion came to uphold patriarchal authority, since patriarchal religion is also an effect, rather than an original cause.

triarchy.[9] What would be crucial to such a premise would be a state of mind in which the primary principle would be regarded as fertility or vitalist processes. In a primitive condition, before it developed civilization or any but the crudest technic, humanity would perhaps find the most impressive evidence of creative force in the visible birth of children, something of a miraculous event and linked analogically with the growth of the earth's vegetation.

It is possible that the circumstance which might drastically redirect such attitudes would be the discovery of paternity. There is some evidence that fertility cults in ancient society at some point took a turn toward patriarchy, displacing and downgrading female function in procreation and attributing the power of life to the phallus alone. Patriarchal religion could consolidate this position by the creation of a male God or gods, demoting, discrediting, or eliminating goddesses and constructing a theology whose basic postulates are male supremacist, and one of whose central functions is to uphold and validate the patriarchal structure.[10]

So much for the evanescent delights afforded by the game of origins. The question of the historical origins of patriarchy—whether patriarchy originated primordially in the male's superior strength, or upon a later mobilization of such strength under certain circumstances—appears at the moment to be unanswerable. It is also probably irrelevant to contemporary patriarchy, where we are left with the realities of sexual politics, still grounded, we are often assured, on nature. Unfortunately, as the psycho-social distinctions made between the two sex groups which are said to justify their present political relationship are not the clear, specific, measurable and neutral ones of the physical sciences, but are instead of an entirely different character—vague, amorphous, often even quasi-religious in phrasing—it must be admitted that many of the generally understood distinctions between the sexes in the more significant areas of role and temperament, not to mention status, have in fact, essentially cultural, rather than biological, bases. Attempts to prove that temperamental dominance is inherent in the male (which for its advocates, would be tantamount to validating, logically as well as historically, the patriarchal situation regarding role and status) have been notably unsuccessful. Sources in the field are in hopeless disagreement

[9] One might also include the caveat that such a social order need not imply the domination of one sex which the term "matriarchy" would, by its semantic analogue to patriarchy, infer. Given the simpler scale of life and the fact that female-centered fertility religion might be offset by male physical strength, pre-patriarchy might have been fairly equalitarian.

[10] Something like this appears to have taken place as the culture of Neolithic agricultural villages gave way to the culture of civilization and to patriarchy with the rise of cities. See Louis Mumford, *The City in History* (New York: Harcourt, Brace, 1961), Chapter One. A discovery such as paternity, a major acquisition of "scientific" knowledge might, hypothetically, have led to an expansion of population, surplus labor and strong-class stratification. There is good reason to suppose that the transformation of hunting into war also played a part.

about the nature of sexual differences, but the most reasonable among them have despaired of the ambition of any definite equation between temperament and biological nature. It appears that we are not soon to be enlightened as to the existence of any significant inherent differences between male and female beyond the bio-genital ones we already know. Endocrinology and genetics afford no definite evidence of determining mental-emotional differences.[11]

Not only is there insufficient evidence for the thesis that the present social distinctions of patriarchy (status, role, temperament) are physical in origin, but we are hardly in a position to assess the existing differentiations, since distinctions which we know to be culturally induced at present so outweigh them. Whatever the "real" differences between the sexes may be, we are not likely to know them until the sexes are treated differently, that is alike. And this is very far from being the case at present. Important new research not only suggests that the possibilities of innate temperamental differences seem more remote than ever, but even raises questions as to the validity and permanence of psycho-sexual identity. In doing so it gives fairly concrete positive evidence of the overwhelmingly *cultural* character of gender, i.e. personality structure in terms of sexual category.

What Stoller and other experts define as "core gender identity" is now thought to be established in the young by the age of eighteen months. This is how Stoller differentiates between sex and gender:

Dictionaries stress that the major connotation of *sex* is a biological one, as for example, in the phrases *sexual relations* or *the male sex*. In agreement with this, the word *sex*, in this work will refer to the male or female sex and the component biological parts that determine whether one is a male or a female; the word *sexual* will have connotations of anatomy and physiology. This obviously leaves tremendous areas of behavior, feelings, thoughts and fantasies that are related to the sexes and yet do not have primarily biological connotations. It is for some of these psychological phenomena that the term gender will be used: one can speak of the male sex or the female sex, but one can also talk about masculinity and femininity and not necessarily be implying anything about anatomy or physiology. Thus, while *sex* and *gender* seem to common sense inextricably bound together, one purpose of this study will be to confirm the fact that the two realms (sex and gender) are not inevitably bound in anything like a one-to-one relationship, but each may go into quite independent ways.[12]

[11] No convincing evidence has so far been advanced in this area. Experimentation regarding the connection between hormones and animal behavior not only yields highly ambivalent results but brings with it the hazards of reasoning by analogy to human behavior. For a summary of the arguments see David C. Glass (editor), *Biology and Behavior* (New York: Rockefeller University and the Russell Sage Foundation, 1968).

[12] Robert J. Stoller, *Sex and Gender* (New York, Science House, 1968), from the preface, pp. viii-ix.

In cases of genital malformation and consequent erroneous gender assignment at birth, studied at the California Gender Identity Center, the discovery was made that it is easier to change the sex of an adolescent male, whose biological identity turns out to be contrary to his gender assignment and conditioning—through surgery—than to undo the educational consequences of years, which have succeeded in making the subject temperamentally feminine in gesture, sense of self, personality and interests. Studies done in California under Stoller's direction offer proof that gender identity (I am a girl, I am a boy) is the primary identity any human being holds—the first as well as the most permanent and far-reaching. Stoller later makes emphatic the distinction that sex is biological, gender psychological, and therefore cultural: "*Gender* is a term that has psychological or cultural rather than biological connotations. If the proper terms for sex are "male" and "female," the corresponding terms for gender are "masculine" and "feminine"; these latter may be quite independent of (biological) sex."[13] Indeed, so arbitrary is gender, that it may even be contrary to physiology: ". . . although the external genitalia (penis, testes, scrotum) contribute to the sense of maleness, no one of them is essential for it, not even all of them together. In the absence of complete evidence, I agree in general with Money, and the Hampsons who show in their large series of intersexed patients that gender role is determined by postnatal forces, regardless of the anatomy and physiology of the external genitalia."[14]

It is now believed[15] that the human fetus is originally physically female until the operation of androgen at a certain stage of gestation causes those with *y* chromosomes to develop into males. Psychosexually (e.g., in terms of masculine and feminine, and in contradistinction to male and female) there is no differentiation between the sexes at birth. Psychosexual personality is therefore postnatal and learned.

> . . . the condition existing at birth and for several months thereafter is one of psychosexual undifferentiation. Just as in the embryo, morphologic sexual differentiation passes from a plastic stage to one of fixed immutability, so also does psychosexual differentiation become fixed and immutable—so much so, that mankind has traditionally assumed that so strong and fixed a feeling as personal sexual identity must stem from something innate, instinctive, and not subject to postnatal experience and learning. The error of this traditional assumption is that the power and permanence of something learned has been underestimated.

[13] *Ibid.*, p. 9.
[14] *Ibid.*, p. 48.
[15] See Mary Jane Sherfey, "The Evolution and Nature of Female Sexuality in Relation to Psychoanalytic Theory," *Journal of the American Psychoanalytic Association,* vol. 14, January 1966, no. 1 (New York, International Universities Press Inc.), and John Money, "Psychosexual Differentiation," in *Sex Research, New Developments* (New York, Holt, 1965).

The experiments of animal ethologists on imprinting have now corrected this misconception.[16]

John Money who is quoted above, believes that "the acquisition of a native language is a human counterpart to imprinting," and gender first established "with the establishment of a native language."[17] This would place the time of establishment at about eighteen months. Jerome Kagin's[18] studies in how children of pre-speech age are handled and touched, tickled and spoken to in terms of their sexual identity ("Is it a boy or a girl?" "Hello, little fellow," "Isn't she pretty," etc.) put the most considerable emphasis on purely tactile learning which would have much to do with the child's sense of self, even before speech is attained.

Because of our social circumstances, male and female are really two cultures and their life experiences are utterly different—and this is crucial. Implicit in all the gender identity development which takes place through childhood is the sum total of the parents', the peers', and the culture's notions of what is appropriate to each gender by way of temperament, character, interests, status, worth, gesture, and expression. Every moment of the child's life is a clue to how he or she must think and behave to attain or satisfy the demands which gender places upon one. In adolescence, the merciless task of conformity grows to crisis proportions, generally cooling and settling in maturity.

Since patriarchy's biological foundations appear to be so very insecure, one has some cause to admire the strength of a "socialization" which can continue a universal condition "on faith alone," as it were, or through an acquired value system exclusively. What does seem decisive in assuring the maintenance of the temperamental differences between the sexes is the conditioning of early childhood. Conditioning runs in a circle of self-perpetuation and self-fulfilling prophecy. To take a simple example: expectations the culture cherishes about his gender identity encourage the young male to develop aggressive impulses, and the female to thwart her own or turn them inward. The result is that the male tends to have aggression reinforced in his behavior, often with significant anti-social possibilities. Thereupon the culture consents to believe the possession of the male indicator, the testes, penis, and scrotum, in itself characterizes the aggressive impulse, and even vulgarly celebrates it in such encomiums as "that guy has balls." The same process of reinforcement is evident in producing the chief "feminine" virtue of passivity.

In contemporary terminology, the basic division of temperamental trait

---

[16] Money, op cit., p. 12.

[17] Ibid., p. 13.

[18] Jerome Kagin, "The Acquisition and Significance of Sex-Typing," in *Review of Child Development Research*, ed. M. Hoffman (New York, Russell Sage Foundation, 1964).

is marshaled along the line of "aggression is male" and "passivity is female." All other temperamental traits are somehow—often with the most dexterous ingenuity—aligned to correspond. If aggressiveness is the trait of the master class, docility must be the corresponding trait of a subject group. The usual hope of such line of reasoning is that "nature," by some impossible outside chance, might still be depended upon to rationalize the patriarchal system. An important consideration to be remembered here is that in patriarchy, the function of norm is unthinkingly delegated to the male—were it not, one might as plausibly speak of "feminine" behavior as active, and "masculine" behavior as hyperactive or hyperaggressive.

Here it might be added, by way of a coda, that data from physical sciences has recently been enlisted again to support sociological arguments, such as those of Lionel Tiger[19] who seeks a genetic justification of patriarchy by proposing a "bonding instinct" in males which assures their political and social control of human society. One sees the implication of such a theory by applying its premise to any ruling group. Tiger's thesis appears to be a misrepresentation of the work of Lorenz and other students of animal behavior. Since his evidence of inherent trait is patriarchal history and organization, his pretensions to physical evidence are both specious and circular. One can only advance genetic evidence when one has genetic (rather than historical) evidence to advance. As many authorities dismiss the possibility of instincts (complex inherent behavioral patterns) in humans altogether, admitting only reflexes and drives (far simpler neural responses),[20] the prospects of a "bonding instinct" appear particularly forlorn.

Should one regard sex in humans as a drive, it is still necessary to point out that the enormous area of our lives, both in early "socialization" and in adult experience, labeled "sexual behavior," is almost entirely the product of learning. So much is this the case that even the act of coitus itself is the product of a long series of learned responses—responses to the patterns and attitudes, even as to the object of sexual choice, which are set up for us by our social environment.

The arbitrary character of patriarchal ascriptions of temperament and role has little effect upon their power over us. Nor do the mutually exclusive, contradictory, and polar qualities of the categories "masculine" and "feminine" imposed upon human personality give rise to sufficiently serious question among us. Under their aegis each personality becomes little more, and often less than half, of its human potential. Politically, the fact that each group exhibits a circumscribed but complementary personality and range of activity is of secondary importance to the fact that each represents a status or power division. In the matter of conformity patriarchy is a governing

[19] Lionel Tiger, *Men in Groups* (New York, Random House, 1968).

[20] Through instinct subhuman species might undertake the activity of building a complex nest or hive; through reflex or drive a human being might simply blink, feel hunger, etc.

ideology without peer; it is probable that no other system has ever exercised such a complete control over its subjects.

III Sociological

Patriarchy's chief institution is the family. It is both a mirror of and a connection with the larger society; a patriarchal unit within a patriarchal whole. Mediating between the individual and the social structure, the family effects control and conformity where political and other authorities are insufficient.[21] As the fundamental instrument and the foundation unit of patriarchal society the family and its roles are prototypical. Serving as an agent of the larger society, the family not only encourages its own members to adjust and conform, but acts as a unit in the government of the patriarchal state which rules its citizens through its family heads. Even in patriarchal societies where they are granted legal citizenship, women tend to be ruled through the family alone and have little or no formal relation to the state.[22]

As co-operation between the family and the larger society is essential, else both would fall apart, the fate of three patriarchal institutions, the family, society, and the state are interrelated. In most forms of patriarchy this has generally led to the granting of religious support in statements such as the Catholic precept that "the father is head of the family," or Judaism's delegation of quasi-priestly authority to the male parent. Secular governments today also confirm this, as in census practices of designating the male as head of household, taxation, passports etc. Female heads of household tend to be regarded as undesirable; the phenomenon is a trait of poverty or misfortune. The Confucian prescription that the relationship between ruler and subject is parallel to that of father and children points to the essentially feudal character of the patriarchal family (and conversely, the familial character of feudalism) even in modern democracies.[23]

Traditionally, patriarchy granted the father nearly total ownership over wife or wives and children, including the powers of physical abuse and often even those of murder and sale. Classically, as head of the family the father is both begetter and owner in a system in which kinship is property.[24] Yet

[21] In some of my remarks on the family I am indebted to Goode's short and concise analysis. See William J. Goode, *The Family* (Englewood Cliffs, New Jersey, Prentice-Hall, 1964).

[22] Family, society, and state are three separate but connected entities: women have a decreasing importance as one goes from the first to the third category. But as each of the three categories exists within or is influenced by the overall institution of patriarchy, I am concerned here less with differentiation than with pointing out a general similarity.

[23] J. K. Folsom makes a convincing argument as to the anomalous character of patriarchal family systems within democratic society. See Joseph K. Folsom *The Family and Democratic Society* (New York: John Wiley, 1934, 1943).

[24] Marital as well as consanguine relation to the head of the family made one his property.

in strict patriarchy, kinship is acknowledged only through association with the male line. Agnation excludes the descendants of the female line from property right and often even from recognition.[25] The first formulation of the patriarchal family was made by Sir Henry Maine, a nineteenth-century historian of ancient jurisprudence. Maine argues that the patriarchal basis of kinship is put in terms of dominion rather than blood; wives, though outsiders, are assimilated into the line, while sister's sons are excluded. Basing his definition of the family upon the *patria potestes* of Rome, Maine defined it as follows: "The eldest male parent is absolutely supreme in his household. His dominion extends to life and death and is as unqualified over his children and their houses as over his slaves."[26] In the archaic patriarchal family "the group consists of animate and inanimate property, of wife, children, slaves, land and goods, all held together by subjection to the despotic authority of the eldest male."[27]

McLennon's rebuttal[28] to Maine argued that the Roman *patria potestes* was an extreme form of patriarchy and by no means, as Maine had imagined, universal. Evidence of matrilineal societies (preliterate societies in Africa and elsewhere) refute Maine's assumption of the universality of agnation. Certainly Maine's central argument, as to the primeval or state of nature character of patriarchy is but a rather naïf[29] rationalization of an institution Maine tended to exalt. The assumption of patriarchy's primeval character is contradicted by much evidence which points to the conclusion that full patriarchal authority, particularly that of the *patria potestes* is a late development and the total erosion of female status was likely to be gradual as has been its recovery.

In contemporary patriarchies the male's *de jure* priority has recently been modified through the granting of divorce[30] protection, citizenship, and property to women. Their chattel status continues in their loss of name, their obligation to adopt the husband's domicile, and the general legal assumption

[25] Strict patriarchal descent is traced and recognized only through male heirs rather than through sister's sons etc. In a few generations descendants of female branches lose touch. Only those who "bear the name," who descend from male branches, may be recognized for kinship or inheritance.

[26] Sir Henry Maine, *Ancient Law* (London, Murray, 1861), p. 122.

[27] Sir Henry Maine, *The Early History of Institutions* (London), pp. 310–11.

[28] John McLennon, *The Patriarchal Theory* (London, Macmillan, 1885).

[29] Maine took the patriarchal family as the cell from which society evolved as gens, phratry, tribe, and nation grew, rather in the simplistic manner of Israel's twelve tribes descending from Jacob. Since Maine also dated the origin of patriarchy from the discovery of paternity, hardly a primeval condition, this too operates against the eternal character of patriarchal society.

[30] Many patriarchies granted divorce to males only. It has been accessible to women on any scale only during this century. Goode states that divorce rates were as high in Japan during the 1880s as they are in the U.S. today. Goode, *op. cit.*, p. 3.

that marriage involves an exchange of the female's domestic service and (sexual) consortium in return for financial support.[31]

The chief contribution of the family in patriarchy is the socialization of the young (largely through the example and admonition of their parents) into patriarchal ideology's prescribed attitudes toward the categories of role, temperament, and status. Although slight differences of definition depend here upon the parents' grasp of cultural values, the general effect of uniformity is achieved, to be further reinforced through peers, schools, media, and other learning sources, formal and informal. While we may niggle over the balance of authority between the personalities of various households, one must remember that the entire culture supports masculine authority in all areas of life and—outside of the home—permits the female none at all.

To insure that its crucial functions of reproduction and socialization of the young take place only within its confines, the patriarchal family insists upon legitimacy. Bronislaw Malinowski describes this as "the principle of legitimacy" formulating it as an insistence that "no child should be brought into the world without a man—and one man at that—assuming the role of sociological father."[32] By this apparently consistent and universal prohibition (whose penalties vary by class and in accord with the expected operations of the double standard) patriarchy decrees that the status of both child and mother is primarily or ultimately dependent upon the male. And since it is not only his social status, but even his economic power upon which his dependents generally rely, the position of the masculine figure within the family—as without—is materially, as well as ideologically, extremely strong.

Although there is no biological reason why the two central functions of the family (socialization and reproduction) need be inseparable from or even take place within it, revolutionary or utopian efforts to remove these functions from the family have been so frustrated, so beset by difficulties, that most experiments so far have involved a gradual return to tradition. This is strong evidence of how basic a form patriarchy is within all societies, and of how pervasive its effects upon family members. It is perhaps also an admonition that change undertaken without a thorough understanding of the sociopolitical institution to be changed is hardly productive. And yet radical social

[31] Divorce is granted to a male for his wife's failure in domestic service and consortium: it is not granted him for his wife's failure to render him financial support. Divorce is granted to a woman if her husband fails to support her, but not for his failure at domestic service or consortium. But see Karczewski versus Baltimore and Ohio Railroad, 274 F. Supp. 169.175 N.D. Illinois, 1967, where a precedent was set and the common law that decrees a wife might not sue for loss of consortium overturned.

[32] Bronislaw Malinowski, *Sex, Culture and Myth* (New York, Harcourt, 1962), p. 63. An earlier statement is even more sweeping: "In all human societies moral tradition and the law decree that the group consisting of a woman and her offspring is not a sociologically complete unit." *Sex and Repression in Savage Society* (London, Humanities, 1927), p. 213.

change cannot take place without having an effect upon patriarchy. And not simply because it is the political form which subordinates such a large percentage of the population (women and youth) but because it serves as a citadel of property and traditional interests. Marriages are financial alliances, and each household operates as an economic entity much like a corporation. As one student of the family states it, "the family is the keystone of the stratification system, the social mechanism by which it is maintained."[33]

IV CLASS

It is in the area of class that the castelike status of the female within patriarchy is most liable to confusion, for sexual status often operates in a superficially confusing way within the variable of class. In a society where status is dependent upon the economic, social, and educational circumstances of class, it is possible for certain females to appear to stand higher than some males. Yet not when one looks more closely at the subject. This is perhaps easier to see by means of analogy: a black doctor or lawyer has higher social status than a poor white sharecropper. But race, itself a caste system which subsumes class, persuades the latter citizen that he belongs to a higher order of life, just as it oppresses the black professional in spirit, whatever his material success may be. In much the same manner, a truck driver or butcher has always his "manhood" to fall back upon. Should this final vanity be offended, he may contemplate more violent methods. The literature of the past thirty years provides a staggering number of incidents in which the caste of virility triumphs over the social status of wealthy or even educated women. In literary contexts one has to deal here with wish-fulfillment. Incidents from life (bullying, obscene, or hostile remarks) are probably another sort of psychological gesture of ascendancy. Both convey more hope than reality, for class divisions are generally quite impervious to the hostility of individuals. And yet while the existence of class division is not seriously threatened by such expressions of enmity, the existence of sexual hierarchy has been re-affirmed and mobilized to "punish" the female quite effectively.

The function of class or ethnic mores in patriarchy is largely a matter of how overtly displayed or how loudly enunciated the general ethic of masculine supremacy allows itself to become. Here one is confronted by what appears to be a paradox: while in the lower social strata, the male is more likely to claim authority on the strength of his sex rank alone, he is actually obliged more often to share power with the women of his class who are economically productive; whereas in the middle and upper classes, there is less tendency to assert a blunt patriarchal dominance, as men who enjoy such status have more power in any case.[34]

It is generally accepted that Western patriarchy has been much softened by the concepts of courtly and romantic love. While this is certainly true,

[33] Goode, *op. cit.*, p. 80.
[34] Goode, *op. cit.*, p. 74.

such influence has also been vastly overestimated. In comparison with the candor of "machismo" or oriental behavior, one realizes how much of a concession traditional chivalrous behavior represents—a sporting kind of reparation to allow the subordinate female certain means of saving face. While a palliative to the injustice of woman's social position, chivalry is also a technique for disguising it. One must acknowledge that the chivalrous stance is a game the master group plays in elevating its subject to pedestal level. Historians of courtly love stress the fact that the raptures of the poets had no effect upon the legal or economic standing of women, and very little upon their social status.[35] As the sociologist Hugo Beigel has observed, both the courtly and the romantic versions of love are "grants" which the male concedes out of his total powers.[36] Both have had the effect of obscuring the patriarchal character of Western culture and in their general tendency to attribute impossible virtues to women, have ended by confining them in a narrow and often remarkably conscribing sphere of behavior. It was a Victorian habit, for example, to insist the female assume the function of serving as the male's conscience and living the life of goodness he found tedious but felt someone ought to do anyway.

The concept of romantic love affords a means of emotional manipulation which the male is free to exploit, since love is the only circumstance in which the female is (ideologically) pardoned for sexual activity. And convictions of romantic love are convenient to both parties since this is often the only condition in which the female can overcome the far more powerful conditioning she has received toward sexual inhibition. Romantic love also obscures the realities of female status and the burden of economic dependency. As to "chivalry," such gallant gesture as still resides in the middle classes has degenerated to a tired ritualism, which scarcely serves to mask the status situation of the present.

Within patriarchy one must often deal with contradictions which are simply a matter of class style. David Riesman has noted that as the working class has been assimilated into the middle class, so have its sexual mores and attitudes. The fairly blatant male chauvinism which was once a province of the lower class or immigrant male has been absorbed and taken on a certain glamour through a number of contemporary figures, who have made it, and a certain number of other working-class male attitudes, part of a new, and at the moment, fashionable life style. So influential is this working-class ideal of brute virility (or more accurately, a literary and therefore

<hr/>

[35] This is the gist of Valency's summary of the situation before the troubadours, acknowledging that courtly love is an utter anomaly: "With regard to the social background, all that can be stated with confidence is that we know nothing of the objective relationships of men and women in the Middle Ages which might conceivably motivate the strain of love-poetry which the troubadours developed." Maurice Valency, *In Praise of Love* (Macmillan, New York, 1958), p. 5.

[36] Hugo Beigel, "Romantic Love," *The American Sociological Review*, Vol. 16, 1951, p. 331.

middle-class version of it) become in our time that it may replace more discreet and "gentlemanly" attitudes of the past.[37]

One of the chief effects of class within patriarchy is to set one woman against another, in the past creating a lively antagonism between whore and matron, and in the present between career woman and housewife. One envies the other her "security" and prestige, while the envied yearns beyond the confines of respectability for what she takes to be the other's freedom, adventure, and contact with the great world. Through the multiple advantages of the double standard, the male participates in both worlds, empowered by his superior social and economic resources to play the estranged women against each other as rivals. One might also recognize subsidiary status categories among women: not only is virtue class, but beauty and age as well.

Perhaps, in the final analysis, it is possible to argue that women tend to transcend the usual class stratifications in patriarchy, for whatever the class of her birth and education, the female has fewer permanent class associations than does the male. Economic dependency renders her affiliations with any class a tangential, vicarious, and temporary matter. Aristotle observed that the only slave to whom a commoner might lay claim was his woman, and the service of an unpaid domestic still provides working-class males with a "cushion" against the buffets of the class system which incidentally provides them with some of the psychic luxuries of the leisure class. Thrown upon their own resources, few women rise above working class in personal prestige and economic power, and women as a group do not enjoy many of the interests and benefits any class may offer its male members. Women have therefore less of an investment in the class system. But it is important to understand that as with any group whose existence is parasitic to its rulers, women are a dependency class who live on surplus. And their marginal life frequently renders them conservative, for like all persons in their situation (slaves are a classic example here) they identify their own survival with the prosperity of those who feed them. The hope of seeking liberating radical solutions of their own seems too remote for the majority to dare contemplate and remains so until consciousness on the subject is raised.

As race is emerging as one of the final variables in sexual politics, it is pertinent, especially in a discussion of modern literature, to devote a few words to it as well. Traditionally, the white male has been accustomed to concede the female of his own race, in her capacity as "his woman" a higher

[37] Mailer and Miller occur to one in this connection, and Lawrence as well. One might trace Rojack's very existence as a fictional figure to the virility symbol of Jack London's Ernest Everhard or Tennessee Williams' Stanley Kowalski. That Rojack is also literate is nothing more than an elegant finish upon the furniture of his "manhood" solidly based in the hard oaken grain of his mastery over any and every "broad" he can better, bludgeon, or bugger.

status than that ascribed to the black male.[38] Yet as white racist ideology is exposed and begins to erode, racism's older protective attitudes toward (white) women also begin to give way. And the priorities of maintaining male supremacy might outweigh even those of white supremacy; sexism may be more endemic in our own society than racism. For example, one notes in authors whom we would now term overtly racist, such as D. H. Lawrence —whose contempt for what he so often designates as inferior breeds is unabashed—instances where the lower-caste male is brought on to master or humiliate the white man's own insubordinate mate. Needless to say, the female of the non-white races does not figure in such tales save as an exemplum of "true" womanhood's servility, worthy of imitation by other less carefully instructed females. Contemporary white sociology often operates under a similar patriarchal bias when its rhetoric inclines toward the assertion that the "matriarchal" (e.g. matrifocal) aspect of black society and the "castration" of the black male are the most deplorable symptoms of black oppression in white racist society, with the implication that racial inequity is capable of solution by a restoration of masculine authority. Whatever the facts of the matter may be, it can also be suggested that analysis of this kind presupposes patriarchal values without questioning them, and tends to obscure both the true character of and the responsibility for racist injustice toward black humanity of both sexes.

V   ECONOMIC AND EDUCATIONAL

One of the most efficient branches of patriarchal government lies in the agency of its economic hold over its female subjects. In traditional patriarchy, women, as non-persons without legal standing, were permitted no actual economic existence as they could neither own nor earn in their own right. Since women have always worked in patriarchal societies, often at the most routine or strenuous tasks, what is at issue here is not labor but economic reward. In modern reformed patriarchal societies, women have certain economic rights, yet the "woman's work" in which some two thirds of the female population in most developed countries are engaged is work that is

[38] It would appear that the "pure flower of white womanhood" has at least at times been something of a disappointment to her lord as a fellow-racist. The historic connection of the Abolitionist and the Woman's Movement is some evidence of this, as well as the incidence of white female and black male marriages as compared with those of white male and black female. Figures on miscegenation are very difficult to obtain: Goode (op. cit., p. 37) estimates the proportion of white women marrying black men to be between 3 to 10 times the proportion of white men marrying black women. Robert K. Merton "Intermarriage and the Social Structure" Psychiatry, Vol. 4, August 1941, p. 374, states that "most intercaste sex relations—not marriages—are between white men and Negro women." It is hardly necessary to emphasize that the more extensive sexual contacts between white males and black females have not only been extramarital, but (on the part of the white male) crassly exploitative. Under slavery it was simply a case of rape.

not paid for.[39] In a money economy where autonomy and prestige depend upon currency, this is a fact of great importance. In general, the position of women in patriarchy is a continuous function of their economic dependence. Just as their social position is vicarious and achieved (often on a temporary or marginal basis) through males, their relation to the economy is also typically vicarious or tangential.

Of that third of women who are employed, their average wages represent only half of the average income enjoyed by men. These are the U. S. Department of Labor statistics for average year-round income: white male, $6704, non-white male $4277, white female, $3991, and non-white female $2816.[40] The disparity is made somewhat more remarkable because the educational level of women is generally higher than that of men in comparable income brackets.[41] Further, the kinds of employment open to women in modern patriarchies are, with few exceptions, menial, ill paid and without status.[42]

In modern capitalist countries women also function as a reserve labor force, enlisted in times of war and expansion and discharged in times of peace and recession. In this role American women have replaced immigrant labor and now compete with the racial minorities. In socialist countries the female labor force is generally in the lower ranks as well, despite a high incidence of women in certain professions such as medicine. The status and rewards of such professions have declined as women enter them, and they are permitted to enter such areas under a rationale that society or the state (and socialist countries are also patriarchal) rather than woman is served by such activity.

Since woman's independence in economic life is viewed with distrust, prescriptive agencies of all kinds (religion, psychology, advertising, etc.)

[39] Sweden is an exception in considering housework a material service rendered and calculable in divorce suits etc. Thirty-three to forty per cent of the female population have market employment in Western countries: this leaves up to two thirds out of the market labor force. In Sweden and the Soviet Union that figure is lower.

[40] U. S. Department of Labor Statistics for 1966 (latest available figures). The proportion of women earning more than $10,000 a year in 1966 was 7/10 of 1%. See Mary Dublin Keyserling, "Realities of Women's Current Position in the Labor Force" in Sex Discrimination in Employment Practices, a report from the conference (pamphlet) University extension, U.C.L.A. and the Women's Bureau, September 19, 1968.

[41] See The 1965 Handbook on Women Workers, United States Department of Labor, Women's Bureau: "In every major occupational group the median wage or salary income of women was less than that of men. This is true at all levels of educational attainment." A comparison of the income received by women and men with equal amounts of schooling revealed that women who had completed four years of college received incomes which were only 47% of those paid to men with the same educational training; high school graduates earned only 38%, and grade school graduates only 33%.

[42] For the distribution of women in lower income and lower status positions see Background Facts on Working Women (pamphlet) U. S. Department of Labor, Women's Bureau.

continuously admonish or even inveigh against the employment of middle-class women, particularly mothers. The toil of working-class women is more readily accepted as "need," if not always by the working-class itself, at least by the middle-class. And to be sure, it serves the purpose of making available cheap labor in factory and lower-grade service and clerical positions. Its wages and tasks are so unremunerative that, unlike more prestigious employment for women, it fails to threaten patriarchy financially or psychologically. Women who are employed have two jobs since the burden of domestic service and child care is unrelieved either by day care or other social agencies, or by the co-operation of husbands. The invention of labor-saving devices has had no appreciable effect on the duration, even if it has affected the quality of their drudgery.[43] Discrimination in matters of hiring, maternity, wages and hours is very great.[44] In the U. S. a recent law forbidding discrimination in employment, the first and only federal legislative guarantee of rights granted to American women since the vote, is not enforced, has not been enforced since its passage, and was not enacted to be enforced.[45]

In terms of industry and production, the situation of women is in many ways comparable both to colonial and to pre-industrial peoples. Although they achieved their first economic autonomy in the industrial revolution and now constitute a large and underpaid factory population, women do not participate directly in technology or in production. What they customarily produce (domestic and personal service) has no market value and is, as it were, pre-capital. Nor, where they do participate in production of commodities through employment, do they own or control or even comprehend the process in which they participate. An example might make this clearer: the refrigerator is a machine all women use, some assemble it in factories, and a very few with scientific education understand its principles of operation. Yet the heavy industries which roll its steel and produce the dies for its parts are in male hands. The same is true of the typewriter, the auto, etc. Now, while knowledge is fragmented even among the male population, collectively they could reconstruct any technological device. But in the absence of males, women's distance from technology today is sufficiently great that it is doubtful that they could replace or repair such machines on any significant scale. Woman's distance from higher technology is even greater: large-scale

[43] "For a married woman without children the irreducible minimum of work probably takes between fifteen to twenty hours a week, for a woman with small children the minimum is probably 70–80 hours a week." Margaret Benston, "The Political Economy of Women's Liberation," *Monthly Review*, Vol. XXI, September 1969.

[44] See the publications of the Women's Bureau and particularly *Sex Discrimination in Employment Practices* (op. cit.) and Carolyn Bird, *Born Female* (New York: McKay, 1968).

[45] Title VII of the 1964 Civil Rights Act. The inclusion of "sex" in the law upholding the civil right of freedom from discrimination in employment was half a joke and half an attempt on the part of Southern congressmen to force Northern industrial states to abandon passage of the bill.

building construction; the development of computers; the moon shot, occur as further examples. If knowledge is power, power is also knowledge, and a large factor in their subordinate position is the fairly systematic ignorance patriarchy imposes upon women.

Since education and economy are so closely related in the advanced nations, it is significant that the general level and style of higher education for women, particularly in their many remaining segregated institutions, is closer to that of Renaissance humanism than to the skills of mid-twentieth-century scientific and technological society. Traditionally patriarchy permitted occasional minimal literacy to women while higher education was closed to them. While modern patriarchies have, fairly recently, opened all educational levels to women,[46] the kind and quality of education is not the same for each sex. This difference is of course apparent in early socialization, but it persists and enters into higher education as well. Universities, once places of scholarship and the training of a few professionals, now also produce the personnel of a technocracy. This is not the case with regard to women. Their own colleges typically produce neither scholars nor professionals nor technocrats. Nor are they funded by government and corporations as are male colleges and those co-educational colleges and universities whose primary function is the education of males.

As patriarchy enforces a temperamental imbalance of personality traits between the sexes, its educational institutions, segregated or co-educational, accept a cultural programing toward the generally operative division between "masculine" and "feminine" subject matter, assigning the humanities and certain social sciences (at least in their lower or marginal branches) to the female—and science and technology, the professions, business and engineering to the male. Of course the balance of employment, prestige and reward at present lie with the latter. Control of these fields is very eminently a matter of political power. One might also point out how the exclusive dominance of males in the more prestigious fields directly serves the interests of patriarchal power in industry, government, and the military. And since patriarchy encourages an imbalance in human temperament along sex lines, both divisions of learning (science and the humanities) reflect this imbalance. The humanities, because not exclusively male, suffer in prestige:

[46] We often forget how recent an event is higher education for women. In the U.S. it is barely one hundred years old; in many Western countries barely fifty. Oxford did not grant degrees to women on the same terms as to men until 1920. In Japan and a number of other countries universities have been open to women only in the period after World War II. There are still areas where higher education for women scarcely exists. Women do not have the same access to education as do men. The Princeton Report stated that "although at the high school level more girls than boys receive grades of "A," roughly 50% more boys than girls go to college." *The Princeton Report to the Alumni on Co-Education* (pamphlet), Princeton, N.J. 1968, p. 10. Most other authorities give the national ratio of college students as two males to one female. In a great many countries it is far lower.

the sciences, technology, and business, because they are nearly exclusively male reflect the deformation of the "masculine" personality, e.g., a certain predatory or aggressive character.

In keeping with the inferior sphere of culture to which women in patriarchy have always been restricted, the present encouragement of their "artistic" interests through study of the humanities is hardly more than an extension of the "accomplishments" they once cultivated in preparation for the marriage market. Achievement in the arts and humanities is reserved, now, as it has been historically, for males. Token representation, be it Susan Sontag's or Lady Murasaki's, does not vitiate this rule.

VI FORCE

We are not accustomed to associate patriarchy with force. So perfect is its system of socialization, so complete the general assent to its values, so long and so universally has it prevailed in human society, that it scarcely seems to require violent implementation. Customarily, we view its brutalities in the past as exotic or "primitive" custom. Those of the present are regarded as the product of individual deviance, confined to pathological or exceptional behavior, and without general import. And yet, just as under other total ideologies (racism and colonialism are somewhat analogous in this respect) control in patriarchal society would be imperfect, even inoperable, unless it had the rule of force to rely upon, both in emergencies and as an ever-present instrument of intimidation.

Historically, most patriarchies have institutionalized force through their legal systems. For example, strict patriarchies such as that of Islam, have implemented the prohibition against illegitimacy or sexual autonomy with a death sentence. In Afghanistan and Saudi Arabia the adulteress is still stoned to death with a mullah presiding at the execution. Execution by stoning was once common practice through the Near East. It is still condoned in Sicily. Needless to say there was and is no penalty imposed upon the male corespondent. Save in recent times or exceptional cases, adultery was not generally recognized in males except as an offense one male might commit against another's property interest. In Tokugawa Japan, for example, an elaborate set of legal distinctions were made according to class. A samurai was entitled, and in the face of public knowledge, even obliged, to execute an adulterous wife, whereas a chōnin (common citizen) or peasant might respond as he pleased. In cases of cross-class adultery, the lower-class male convicted of sexual intimacy with his employer's wife would, because he had violated taboos of class and property, be beheaded together with her. Upper-strata males had, of course, the same license to seduce lower-class women as we are familiar with in Western societies.

Indirectly, one form of "death penalty" still obtains even in America today. Patriarchal legal systems in depriving women of control over their own bodies drive them to illegal abortions; it is estimated that between two and five thousand women die each year from this cause.[47]

Excepting a social license to physical abuse among certain class and ethnic groups, force is diffuse and generalized in most contemporary patriarchies. Significantly, force itself is restricted to the male who alone is psychologically and technically equipped to perpetrate physical violence.[48] Where differences in physical strength have become immaterial through the use of arms, the female is rendered innocuous by her socialization. Before assault she is almost universally defenseless both by her physical and emotional training. Needless to say, this has the most far-reaching effects on the social and psychological behavior of both sexes.

Patriarchal force also relies on a form of violence particularly sexual in character and realized most completely in the act of rape. The figures of rapes reported represent only a fraction of those which occur,[49] as the "shame" of the event is sufficient to deter women from the notion of civil prosecution under the public circumstances of a trial. Traditionally rape has been viewed as an offense one male commits upon another—a matter of abusing "his woman." Vendetta, such as occurs in the American South, is carried out for masculine satisfaction, the exhilarations of race hatred, and the interests of property and vanity (honor). In rape, the emotions of aggression, hatred, contempt, and the desire to break or violate personality, take a form consummately appropriate to sexual politics. In the passages analyzed at the outset of this study, such emotions were present at a barely sublimated level and were a key factor in explaining the attitude behind the author's use of language and tone.[50]

Patriarchal societies typically link feelings of cruelty with sexuality, the latter often equated both with evil and with power. This is apparent both in the sexual fantasy reported by psychoanalysis and that reported by pornography. The rule here associates sadism with the male ("the masculine role") and victimization with the female ("the feminine role").[51] Emotional response to violence against women in patriarchy is often curiously ambivalent;

[47] Since abortion is extralegal, figures are difficult to obtain. This figure is based on the estimates of abortionists and referral services. Suicides in pregnancy are not officially reported either.

[48] Vivid exceptions come to mind in the wars of liberation conducted by Vietnam, China, etc. But through most of history, women have been unarmed and forbidden to exhibit any defense of their own.

[49] They are still high. The number of rapes reported in the city of New York in 1967 was 2432. Figure supplied by Police Department.

[50] It is interesting that male victims of rape at the hands of other males often feel twice imposed upon, as they have not only been subjected to forcible and painful intercourse, but further abused in being reduced to the status of a female. Much of this is evident in Genet and in the contempt homosexual society reserves for its "passive" or "female" partners.

[51] Masculine masochism is regarded as exceptional and often explained as latently homosexual, or a matter of the subject playing "the female role"—e.g., victim.

references to wife-beating, for example, invariably produce laughter and some embarrassment. Exemplary atrocity, such as the mass murders committed by Richard Speck, greeted at one level with a certain scandalized, possibly hypocritical indignation, is capable of eliciting a mass response of titillation at another level. At such times one even hears from men occasional expressions of envy or amusement. In view of the sadistic character of such public fantasy as caters to male audiences in pornography or semi-pornographic media, one might expect that a certain element of identification is by no means absent from the general response. Probably a similar collective *frisson* sweeps through racist society when its more "logical" members have perpetrated a lynching. Unconsciously, both crimes may serve the larger group as a ritual act, cathartic in effect.

Hostility is expressed in a number of ways. One is laughter. Misogynist literature, the primary vehicle of masculine hostility, is both an hortatory and comic genre. Of all artistic forms in patriarchy it is the most frankly propagandistic. Its aim is to reinforce both sexual factions in their status. Ancient, Medieval, and Renaissance literature in the West has each had a large element of misogyny.[52] Nor is the East without a strong tradition here, notably in the Confucian strain which held sway in Japan as well as China. The Western tradition was indeed moderated somewhat by the introduction of courtly love. But the old diatribes and attacks were coterminous with the new idealization of woman. In the case of Petrarch, Boccaccio, and some others, one can find both attitudes fully expressed, presumably as evidence of different moods, a courtly pose adopted for the ephemeral needs of the vernacular, a grave animosity for sober and eternal Latin.[53] As courtly love was transformed to romantic love, literary misogyny grew somewhat out of fashion. In some places in the eighteenth century it declined into ridicule and exhortative satire. In the nineteenth century its more acrimonious forms almost disappeared in English. Its resurrection in twentieth-century attitudes and literature is the result of a resentment over patriarchal reform, aided by the growing permissiveness in expression which has taken place at an increasing rate in the last fifty years.

Since the abatement of censorship, masculine hostility (psychological or physical) in specifically *sexual* contexts has become far more apparent. Yet as masculine hostility has been fairly continuous, one deals here probably less with a matter of increase than with a new frankness in expressing hostility in specifically sexual contexts. It is a matter of release and freedom to express

[52] The literature of misogyny is so vast that no summary of sensible proportions could do it justice. The best reference on the subject is Katherine M. Rogers, *The Troublesome Helpmate, A History of Misogyny in Literature* (Seattle, University of Washington Press, 1966).

[53] As well as the exquisite sonnets of love, Petrarch composed satires on women as the "De Remediis utriusque Fortunae" and *Epistolae Seniles*. Boccaccio too could balance the chivalry of romances (Filostrato, Ameto, and Fiammetta) with the vituperance of Corbaccio, a splenetic attack on women more than medieval in violence.

what was once forbidden expression outside of pornography or other "underground" productions, such as those of De Sade. As one recalls both the euphemism and the idealism of descriptions of coitus in the Romantic poets (Keats's *Eve of St. Agnes*), or the Victorian novelists (Hardy, for example) and contrasts it with Miller or William Burroughs, one has an idea of how contemporary literature has absorbed not only the truthful explicitness of pornography, but its anti-social character as well. Since this tendency to hurt or insult has been given free expression, it has become far easier to assess sexual antagonism in the male.

The history of patriarchy presents a variety of cruelties and barbarities: the suttee execution in India, the crippling deformity of footbinding in China, the lifelong ignominy of the veil in Islam, or the widespread persecution of sequestration, the gynacium, and purdah. Phenomenon such as clitoroidectomy, clitoral incision, the sale and enslavement of women under one guise or another, involuntary and child marriages, concubinage and prostitution, still take place—the first in Africa, the latter in the Near and Far East, the last generally. The rationale which accompanies that imposition of male authority euphemistically referred to as "the battle of the sexes" bears a certain resemblance to the formulas of nations at war, where any heinousness is justified on the grounds that the enemy is either an inferior species or really not human at all. The patriarchal mentality has concocted a whole series of rationales about women which accomplish this purpose tolerably well. And these traditional beliefs still invade our consciousness and affect our thinking to an extent few of us would be willing to admit.

VII Anthropological: Myth and Religion

Evidence from anthropology, religious and literary myth all attests to the politically expedient character of patriarchal convictions about women. One anthropologist refers to a consistent patriarchal strain of assumption that "woman's biological differences set her apart . . . she is essentially inferior," and since "human institutions grow from deep and primal anxieties and are shaped by irrational psychological mechanisms . . . socially organized attitudes toward women arise from basic tensions expressed by the male."[54] Under patriarchy the female did not herself develop the symbols by which she is described. As both the primitive and the civilized worlds are male worlds, the ideas which shaped culture in regard to the female were also of male design. The image of women as we know it is an image created by men and fashioned to suit their needs. These needs spring from a fear of the "otherness" of woman. Yet this notion itself presupposes that patriarchy has already been established and the male has already set himself as the human norm, the subject and referent to which the female is "other" or alien. What-

[54] H. R. Hays, *The Dangerous Sex, the Myth of Feminine Evil* (New York: Putnam, 1964). Much of my summary in this section is indebted to Hays's useful assessment of cultural notions about the female.

ever its origin, the function of the male's sexual antipathy is to provide a means of control over a subordinate group and a rationale which justifies the inferior station of those in a lower order, "explaining" the oppression of their lives.

The feeling that woman's sexual functions are impure is both world-wide and persistent. One sees evidence of it everywhere in literature, in myth, in primitive and civilized life. It is striking how the notion persists today. The event of menstruation, for example, is a largely clandestine affair, and the psycho-social effect of the stigma attached must have great effect on the female ego. There is a large anthropological literature on menstrual taboo; the practice of isolating offenders in huts at the edge of the village occurs throughout the primitive world. Contemporary slang denominates menstruation as "the curse." There is considerable evidence that such discomfort as women suffer during their period is often likely to be psychosomatic, rather than physiological, cultural rather than biological, in origin. That this may also be true to some extent of labor and delivery is attested to by the recent experiment with "painless childbirth." Patriarchal circumstances and beliefs seem to have the effect of poisoning the female's own sense of physical self until it often truly becomes the burden it is said to be.

Primitive peoples explain the phenomenon of the female's genitals in terms of a wound, sometimes reasoning that she was visited by a bird or snake and mutilated into her present condition. Once she was wounded, now she bleeds. Contemporary slang for the vagina is "gash." The Freudian description of the female genitals is in terms of a "castrated" condition. The uneasiness and disgust female genitals arouse in patriarchal societies is attested to through religious, cultural, and literary proscription. In preliterate groups fear is also a factor, as in the belief in a castrating *vagina dentata*. The penis, badge of the male's superior status in both preliterate and civilized patriarchies, is given the most crucial significance, the subject both of endless boasting and endless anxiety.

Nearly all patriarchies enforce taboos against women touching ritual objects (those of war or religion) or food. In ancient and preliterate societies women are generally not permitted to eat with men. Women eat apart today in a great number of cultures, chiefly those of the Near and Far East. Some of the inspiration of such custom appears to lie in fears of contamination, probably sexual in origin. In their function of domestic servants, females are forced to prepare food, yet at the same time may be liable to spread their contagion through it. A similar situation obtains with blacks in the United States. They are considered filthy and infectious, yet as domestics they are forced to prepare food for their queasy superiors. In both cases the dilemma is generally solved in a deplorably illogical fashion by segregating the act of eating itself, while cooking is carried on out of sight by the very group who would infect the table. With an admirable consistency, some Hindu males do not permit their wives to touch their food at all. In nearly every patriarchal group it is expected that the dominant male will eat first or eat better, and even where the sexes feed together, the male shall be served by the female.[55]

All patriarchies have hedged virginity and defloration in elaborate rites and interdictions. Among preliterates virginity presents an interesting problem in ambivalence. On the one hand, it is, as in every patriarchy, a mysterious good because a sign of property received intact. On the other hand, it represents an unknown evil associated with the mana of blood and terrifyingly "other." So auspicious is the event of defloration that in many tribes the owner-groom is willing to relinquish breaking the seal of his new possession to a stronger or older personality who can neutralize the attendant dangers.[56] Fears of defloration appear to originate in a fear of the alien sexuality of the female. Although any physical suffering endured in defloration must be on the part of the female (and most societies cause her—bodily and mentally—to suffer anguish), the social interest, institutionalized in patriarchal ritual and custom, is exclusively on the side of the male's property interest, prestige, or (among preliterates) hazard.

Patriarchal myth typically posits a golden age before the arrival of women, while its social practices permit males to be relieved of female company. Sexual segregation is so prevalent in patriarchy that one encounters evidence of it everywhere. Nearly every powerful circle in contemporary patriarchy is a men's group. But men form groups of their own on every level. Women's groups are typically auxiliary in character, imitative of male efforts and methods on a generally trivial or ephemeral plane. They rarely operate without recourse to male authority, church or religious groups appealing to the superior authority of a cleric, political groups to male legislators, etc.

In sexually segregated situations the distinctive quality of culturally enforced temperament becomes very vivid. This is particularly true of those exclusively masculine organizations which anthropology generally refers to as men's house institutions. The men's house is a fortress of patriarchal association and emotion. Men's houses in preliterate society strengthen masculine communal experience through dances, gossip, hospitality, recreation, and religious ceremony. They are also the arsenals of male weaponry.

David Riesman has pointed out that sports and some other activities provide males with a supportive solidarity which society does not trouble to provide for females.[57] While hunting, politics, religion, and commerce may play a role, sport and warfare are consistently the chief cement of men's

---

[55] The luxury conditions of the "better" restaurant affords a quaint exception. There not only the cuisine but even the table service is conducted by males, at an expense commensurate with such an occasion.

[56] See Sigmund Freud, *Totem and Taboo,* and Ernest Crawley, *The Mystic Rose* (London, Methuen, 1902, 1927).

[57] David Riesman, "Two Generations," in *The Woman in America,* edited by Robert Lifton (Boston, Beacon, 1967). See also James Coleman, *The Adolescent Society.*

house comradery. Scholars of men's house culture from Hutton Webster and Heinrich Schurtz to Lionel Tiger tend to be sexual patriots whose aim is to justify the apartheid the institution represents.[58] Schurtz believes an innate gregariousness and a drive toward fraternal pleasure among peers urges the male away from the inferior and constricting company of women. Notwithstanding his conviction that a mystical "bonding instinct" exists in males, Tiger exhorts the public, by organized effort, to preserve the men's house tradition from its decline. The institution's less genial function as power center within a state of sexual antagonism is an aspect of the phenomenon which often goes unnoticed.

The men's houses of Melanesia fulfill a variety of purposes and are both armory and the site of masculine ritual initiation ceremony. Their atmosphere is not very remote from that of military institutions in the modern world; they reek of physical exertion, violence, the aura of the kill, and the throb of homosexual sentiment. They are the scenes of scarification, headhunting celebrations, and boasting sessions. Here young men are to be "hardened" into manhood. In the men's houses boys have such low status they are often called the "wives" of their initiators, the term "wife" implying both inferiority and the status of sexual object. Untried youths become the erotic interest of their elders and betters, a relationship also encountered in the Samurai order, in oriental priesthood, and in the Greek gymnasium. Preliterate wisdom decrees that while inculcating the young with the masculine ethos, it is necessary first to intimidate them with the tutelary status of the female. An anthropologist's comment on Melanesian men's houses is applicable equally to Genet's underworld, or Mailer's U. S. Army: "It would seem that the sexual brutalizing of the young boy and the effort to turn him into a woman both enhances the older warrior's desire of power, gratifies his sense of hostility toward the maturing male competitor, and eventually, when he takes him into the male group, strengthens the male solidarity in its symbolic attempt to do without women."[59] The derogation of feminine status in lesser males is a consistent patriarchal trait. Like any hazing procedure, initiation once endured produces devotees who will ever after be ardent initiators, happily inflicting their own former sufferings on the newcomer.

The psychoanalytic term for the generalized adolescent tone of men's house culture is "phallic state." Citadels of virility, they reinforce the most saliently power-oriented characteristics of patriarchy. The Hungarian psychoanalytic anthropologist Géza Róheim stressed the patriarchal character of men's house organization in the preliterate tribes he studied, defining their communal and religious practices in terms of a "group of men united in the cult of an object that is a materialized penis and excluding the women

[58] Heinrich Schurtz, *Altersklassen und Männerbünde* (Berlin, 1902), and Lionel Tiger, *op. cit.*
[59] Hays, *The Dangerous Sex*, p. 56.

from their society."[60] The tone and ethos of men's house culture is sadistic, power-oriented, and latently homosexual, frequently narcissistic in its energy and motives.[61] The men's house inference that the penis is a weapon, endlessly equated with other weapons, is also clear. The practice of castrating prisoners is itself a comment on the cultural confusion of anatomy and status with weaponry. Much of the glamorization of masculine comradery in warfare originates in what one might designate as "the men's house sensibility." Its sadistic and brutalizing aspects are disguised in military glory and a particularly cloying species of masculine sentimentality. A great deal of our culture partakes of this tradition, and one might locate its first statement in Western literature in the heroic intimacy of Patroclus and Achilles. Its development can be traced through the epic and the saga to the *chanson de geste*. The tradition still flourishes in war novel and movie, not to mention the comic book.

Considerable sexual activity does take place in the men's house, all of it, needless to say, homosexual. But the taboo against homosexual behavior (at least among equals) is almost universally of far stronger force than the impulse and tends to effect a rechanneling of the libido into violence. This association of sexuality and violence is a particularly militaristic habit of mind.[62] The negative and militaristic coloring of such men's house homosexuality as does exist, is of course by no means the whole character of homosexual sensibility. Indeed, the warrior caste of mind with its ultravirility, is more *incipiently* homosexual, in its exclusively male orientation, than it is *overtly* homosexual. (The Nazi experience is an extreme case in point here.) And the heterosexual role-playing indulged in, and still more persuasively, the contempt in which the younger, softer, or more "feminine" members are held, is proof that the actual ethos is misogynist, or perversely rather than positively heterosexual. The true inspiration of men's house association therefore comes from the patriarchal situation rather than from any circumstances inherent in the homo-amorous relationship.

If a positive attitude toward heterosexual love is not quite, in Seignebos' famous dictum, the invention of the twelfth century, it can still claim to be a novelty. Most patriarchies go to great length to exclude love as a basis of mate selection. Modern patriarchies tend to do so through class, ethnic, and religious factors. Western classical thought was prone to see in heterosexual love either a fatal stroke of ill luck bound to end in tragedy, or a contempti-

[60] Géza Róheim, "Psychoanalysis of Primitive Cultural Types," *International Journal of Psychoanalysis* Vol. XIII, London, 1932.

[61] All these traits apply in some degree to the bohemian circle which Miller's novels project, the Army which never leaves Mailer's consciousness, and the homosexual subculture on which Genet's observations are based. Since these three subjects of our study are closely associated with the separatist men's house culture, it is useful to give it special attention.

[62] Genet demonstrates this in *The Screens;* Mailer reveals it everywhere.

ble and brutish consorting with inferiors. Medieval opinion was firm in its conviction that love was sinful if sexual, and sex sinful if loving.

Primitive society practices its misogyny in terms of taboo and mana which evolve into explanatory myth. In historical cultures, this is transformed into ethical, then literary, and in the modern period, scientific rationalizations for the sexual politic. Myth is, of course, a felicitous advance in the level of propaganda, since it so often bases its arguments on ethics or theories of origins. The two leading myths of Western culture are the classical tale of Pandora's box and the Biblical story of the Fall. In both cases earlier mana concepts of feminine evil have passed through a final literary phase to become highly influential ethical justifications of things as they are.

Pandora appears to be a discredited version of a Mediterranean fertility goddess, for in Hesiod's *Theogony* she wears a wreath of flowers and a sculptured diadem in which are carved all the creatures of land and sea.[63] Hesiod ascribes to her the introduction of sexuality which puts an end to the golden age when "the races of men had been living on earth free from all evils, free from laborious work, and free from all wearing sickness."[64] Pandora was the origin of "the damnable race of women—a plague which men must live with."[65] The introduction of what are seen to be the evils of the male human condition came through the introduction of the female and what is said to be her unique product, sexuality. In *Works and Days* Hesiod elaborates on Pandora and what she represents—a perilous temptation with "the mind of a bitch and a thievish nature," full of "the cruelty of desire and longings that wear out the body," "lies and cunning words and a deceitful soul," a snare sent by Zeus to be "the ruin of men."[66]

Patriarchy has God on its side. One of its most effective agents of control is the powerfully expeditious character of its doctrines as to the nature and origin of the female and the attribution to her alone of the dangers and evils it imputes to sexuality. The Greek example is interesting here: when it wishes to exalt sexuality it celebrates fertility through the phallus; when it wishes to denigrate sexuality, it cites Pandora. Patriarchal religion and ethics tend to lump the female and sex together as if the whole burden of the onus and stigma it attaches to sex were the fault of the female alone. Thereby sex, which is known to be unclean, sinful, and debilitating, pertains to the fe-

---

[63] Wherever one stands in the long anthropologists' quarrel over patriarchal versus matriarchal theories of social origins, one can trace a demotion of fertility goddesses and their replacement by patriarchal deities at a certain period throughout ancient culture.

[64] Hesiod, *Works and Days*, translated by Richmond Lattimore (University of Michigan, 1959), p. 29.

[65] Hesiod, *Theogony*, translated by Norman O. Brown (Indianapolis, Liberal Arts Press, 1953), p. 70.

[66] Hesiod, *Works and Days*, phrases from lines 53–100. Some of the phrases are from Lattimore's translation, some from A. W. Mair's translation (Oxford, 1908).

male, and the male identity is preserved as a human, rather than a sexual one.

The Pandora myth is one of two important Western archetypes which condemn the female through her sexuality and explain her position as her well-deserved punishment for the primal sin under whose unfortunate consequences the race yet labors. Ethics have entered the scene, replacing the simplicities of ritual, taboo, and mana. The more sophisticated vehicle of myth also provides official explanations of sexual history. In Hesiod's tale, Zeus, a rancorous and arbitrary father figure, in sending Epimetheus evil in the form of female genitalia, is actually chastising him for adult heterosexual knowledge and activity. In opening the vessel she brings (the vulva or hymen, Pandora's "box") the male satisfies his curiosity but sustains the discovery only by punishing himself at the hands of the father god with death and the assorted calamities of postlapsarian life. The patriarchal trait of male rivalry across age or status line, particularly those of powerful father and rival son, is present as well as the ubiquitous maligning of the female.

The myth of the Fall is a highly finished version of the same themes. As the central myth of the Judeo-Christian imagination and therefore of our immediate cultural heritage, it is well that we appraise and acknowledge the enormous power it still holds over us even in a rationalist era which has long ago given up literal belief in it while maintaining its emotional assent intact.[67] This mythic version of the female as the cause of human suffering, knowledge, and sin is still the foundation of sexual attitudes, for it represents the most crucial argument of the patriarchal tradition in the West.

The Israelites lived in a continual state of war with the fertility cults of their neighbors; these latter afforded sufficient attraction to be the source of constant defection, and the figure of Eve, like that of Pandora, has vestigial traces of a fertility goddess overthrown. There is some, probably unconscious, evidence of this in the Biblical account which announces, even before the narration of the fall has begun—"Adam called his wife's name Eve; because she was the mother of all living things." Due to the fact that the tale represents a compilation of different oral traditions, it provides two contradictory schemes for Eve's creation, one in which both sexes are created at the same time, and one in which Eve is fashioned later than Adam, an afterthought born from his rib, peremptory instance of the male's expropriation of the life force through a god who created the world without benefit of female assistance.

[67] It is impossible to assess how deeply embedded in our consciousness is the Eden legend and how utterly its patterns are planted in our habits of thought. One comes across its tone and design in the most unlikely places, such as Antonioni's film *Blow-Up*, to name but one of many striking examples. The action of the film takes place in an idyllic garden, loaded with primal overtones largely sexual, where, prompted by a tempter with a phallic gun, the female again betrays the male to death. The photographer who witnesses the scene reacts as if he were being introduced both to the haggard knowledge of the primal scene and original sin at the same time.

The tale of Adam and Eve is, among many other things, a narrative of how humanity invented sexual intercourse. Many such narratives exist in preliterate myth and folk tale. Most of them strike us now as delightfully funny stories of primal innocents who require a good deal of helpful instruction to figure it out. There are other major themes in the story: the loss of primeval simplicity, the arrival of death, and the first conscious experience of knowledge. All of them revolve about sex. Adam is forbidden to eat of the fruit of life or of the knowledge of good and evil, the warning states explicitly what should happen if he tastes of the latter: "in that day that thou eatest thereof thou shalt surely die." He eats but fails to die (at least in the story), from which one might infer that the serpent told the truth.

But at the moment when the pair eat of the forbidden tree they awake to their nakedness and feel shame. Sexuality is clearly involved, though the fable insists it is only tangential to a higher prohibition against disobeying orders in the matter of another and less controversial appetite—one for food. Róheim points out that the Hebrew verb for "eat" can also mean coitus. Everywhere in the Bible "knowing" is synonymous with sexuality, and clearly a product of contact with the phallus, here in the fable objectified as a snake. To blame the evils and sorrows of life—loss of Eden and the rest—on sexuality, would all too logically implicate the male, and such implication is hardly the purpose of the story, designed as it is expressly in order to blame all this world's discomfort on the female. Therefore it is the female who is tempted first and "beguiled" by the penis, transformed into something else, a snake. Thus Adam has "beaten the rap" of sexual guilt, which appears to be why the sexual motive is so repressed in the Biblical account. Yet the very transparency of the serpent's universal phallic value shows how uneasy the mythic mind can be about its shifts. Accordingly, in her inferiority and vulnerability the woman takes and eats, simple carnal thing that she is, affected by flattery even in a reptile. Only after this does the male fall, and with him, humanity —for the fable has made him the racial type, whereas Eve is a mere sexual type and, according to tradition, either expendable or replaceable. And as the myth records the original sexual adventure, Adam was seduced by woman, who was seduced by a penis. "The woman whom thou gavest to be with me, she gave me of the fruit and I did eat" is the first man's defense. Seduced by the phallic snake, Eve is convicted for Adam's participation in sex.

Adam's curse is to toil in the "sweat of his brow," namely the labor the male associates with civilization. Eden was a fantasy world without either effort or activity, which the entrance of the female, and with her sexuality, has destroyed. Eve's sentence is far more political in nature and a brilliant "explanation" of her inferior status. "In sorrow thou shalt bring forth children. And thy desire shall be to thy husband. And he shall rule over thee." Again, as in the Pandora myth, a proprietary father figure is punishing his subjects for adult heterosexuality. It is easy to agree with Róheim's comment on the negative attitude the myth adopts toward sexuality: "Sexual maturity is regarded as a misfortune, something that has robbed mankind of happiness . . . the explanation of how death came into the world."[68]

What requires further emphasis is the responsibility of the female, a marginal creature, in bringing on this plague, and the justice of her suborned condition as dependent on her primary role in this original sin. The connection of woman, sex, and sin constitutes the fundamental pattern of western patriarchal thought thereafter.

VIII   Psychological

The aspects of patriarchy already described have each an effect upon the psychology of both sexes. Their principal result is the interiorization of patriarchal ideology. Status, temperament, and role are all value systems with endless psychological ramifications for each sex. Patriarchal marriage and the family with its ranks and division of labor play a large part in enforcing them. The male's superior economic position, the female's inferior one have also grave implications. The large quantity of guilt attached to sexuality in patriarchy is overwhelmingly placed upon the female, who is, culturally speaking, held to be the culpable or the more culpable party in nearly any sexual liaison, whatever the extenuating circumstances. A tendency toward the reification of the female makes her more often a sexual object than a person. This is particularly so when she is denied human rights through chattel status. Even where this has been partly amended the cumulative effect of religion and custom is still very powerful and has enormous psychological consequences. Woman is still denied sexual freedom and the biological control over her body through the cult of virginity, the double standard, the proscription against abortion, and in many places because contraception is physically or psychically unavailable to her.

The continual surveillance in which she is held tends to perpetuate the infantilization of women even in situations such as those of higher education. The female is continually obliged to seek survival or advancement through the approval of males as those who hold power. She may do this either through appeasement or through the exchange of her sexuality for support and status. As the history of patriarchal culture and the representations of herself within all levels of its cultural media, past and present, have a devastating effect upon her self image, she is customarily deprived of any but the most trivial sources of dignity or self-respect. In many patriarchies, language, as well as cultural tradition, reserve the human condition for the male. With the Indo-European languages this is a nearly inescapable habit of mind, for despite all the customary pretense that "man" and "humanity" are terms which apply equally to both sexes, the fact is hardly obscured

[68] Géza Róheim, "Eden," *Psychoanalytic Review*, Vol. XXVII, New York, 1940. See also Theodor Reik, *The Creation of Woman*, and the account given in Hays, *op. cit.*

that in practice, general application favors the male far more often than the female as referent, or even sole referent, for such designations.[69]

When in any group of persons, the ego is subjected to such invidious versions of itself through social beliefs, ideology, and tradition, the effect is bound to be pernicious. This coupled with the persistent though frequently subtle denigration women encounter daily through personal contacts, the impressions gathered from the images and media about them, and the discrimination in matters of behavior, employment, and education which they endure, should make it no very special cause for surprise that women develop group characteristics common to those who suffer minority status and a marginal existence. A witty experiment by Philip Goldberg proves what everyone knows, that having internalized the disesteem in which they are held, women despise both themselves and each other.[70] This simple test consisted of asking women undergraduates to respond to the scholarship in an essay signed alternately by one John McKay and one Joan McKay. In making their assessments the students generally agreed that John was a remarkable thinker, Joan an unimpressive mind. Yet the articles were identical: the reaction was dependent on the sex of the supposed author.

As women in patriarchy are for the most part marginal citizens when they are citizens at all, their situation is like that of other minorities, here defined not as dependent upon numerical size of the group, but on its status. "A minority group is any group of people who because of their physical or cultural characteristics, are singled out from others in the society in which they live for differential and unequal treatment."[71] Only a handful of sociologists have ever addressed themselves in any meaningful way to the minority status of women.[72] And psychology has yet to produce relevant studies on the

---

[69] Languages outside the Indo-European group are instructive. Japanese, for example, has one word for man (*otōko*), another for woman (*ōnna*) and a third for human being (*ningen*). It would be as unthinkable to use the first to cover the third as it would be to use the second.

[70] Philip Goldberg, "Are Women Prejudiced Against Women?" *Transaction*, April 1968.

[71] Louis Wirth, "Problems of Minority Groups," in *The Science of Man in the World Crisis*, ed. by Ralph Linton (New York, Appleton, 1945), p. 347. Wirth also stipulates that the group see itself as discriminated against. It is interesting that many women do not recognize themselves as discriminated against; no better proof could be found of the totality of their conditioning.

[72] The productive handful in question include the following:
Helen Mayer Hacker, "Women as a Minority Group," *Social Forces*, Vol. XXX, October 1951.
Gunnar Myrdal, *An American Dilemma*, Appendix 5 is a parallel of black minority status with women's minority status.
Everett C. Hughes, "Social Change and Status Protest: An Essay on the Marginal Man," *Phylon*, Vol. X, First Quarter, 1949.
Joseph K. Folsom, *The Family and Democratic Society*, 1943.
Godwin Watson, "Psychological Aspects of Sex Roles," *Social Psychology, Issues and Insights* (Philadelphia, Lippincott, 1966).

subject of ego damage to the female which might bear comparison to the excellent work done on the effects of racism on the minds of blacks and colonials. The remarkably small amount of modern research devoted to the psychological and social effects of masculine supremacy on the female and on the culture in general attests to the widespread ignorance or unconcern of a conservative social science which takes patriarchy to be both the status quo and the state of nature.

What little literature the social sciences afford us in this context confirms the presence in women of the expected traits of minority status: group self-hatred and self-rejection, a contempt both for herself and for her fellows—the result of that continual, however subtle, reiteration of her inferiority which she eventually accepts as a fact.[73] Another index of minority status is the fierceness with which all minority group members are judged. The double standard is applied not only in cases of sexual conduct but other contexts as well. In the relatively rare instances of female crime too: in many American states a woman convicted of crime is awarded a longer sentence.[74] Generally an accused woman acquires a notoriety out of proportion to her acts and due to sensational publicity she may be tried largely for her "sex life." But so effective is her conditioning toward passivity in patriarchy, woman is rarely extrovert enough in her maladjustment to enter upon criminality. Just as every minority member must either apologize for the excesses of a fellow or condemn him with a strident enthusiasm, women are characteristically harsh, ruthless and frightened in their censure of aberration among their numbers.

The gnawing suspicion which plagues any minority member, that the myths propagated about his inferiority might after all be true often reaches remarkable proportions in the personal insecurities of women. Some find their subordinate position so hard to bear that they repress and deny its existence. But a large number will recognize and admit their circumstances when they are properly phrased. Of two studies which asked women if they would have preferred to be born male, one found that one fourth of the sample admitted as much, and in another sample, one half.[75] When one inquires of children, who have not yet developed as serviceable techniques of evasion, what their choice might be, if they had one, the answers of female children in a large majority of cases clearly favor birth into the elite group,

[73] My remarks on the minority status of women are summarized from all the articles listed, and I am particularly indebted to an accomplished critique of them in an unpublished draft by Professor Marlene Dixon, formerly of the University of Chicago's Department of Sociology and the Committee on Human Development, presently of McGill University.

[74] See The Commonwealth v. Daniels, 37 L.W. 2064, Pennsylvania Supreme Court, 7/1/68 (reversing 36 L.W. 2004).

[75] See Helen Hacker, op. cit., and Carolyn Bird, op. cit.

whereas boys overwhelmingly reject the option of being girls.[76] The phenomenon of parents' prenatal preference for male issue is too common to require much elaboration. In the light of the imminent possibility of parents actually choosing the sex of their child, such a tendency is becoming the cause of some concern in scientific circles.[77]

Comparisons such as Myrdal, Hacker, and Dixon draw between the ascribed attributes of blacks and women reveal that common opinion associates the same traits with both: inferior intelligence, an instinctual or sensual gratification, an emotional nature both primitive and childlike, an imagined prowess in or affinity for sexuality, a contentment with their own lot which is in accord with a proof of its appropriateness, a wily habit of deceit, and concealment of feeling. Both groups are forced to the same accommodational tactics: an ingratiating or supplicatory manner invented to please, a tendency to study those points at which the dominant group are subject to influence or corruption, and an assumed air of helplessness involving fraudulent appeals for direction through a show of ignorance.[78] It is ironic how misogynist literature has for centuries concentrated on just these traits, directing its fiercest enmity at feminine guile and corruption, and particularly that element of it which is sexual, or, as such sources would have it, "wanton."

As with other marginal groups a certain handful of women are accorded higher status that they may perform a species of cultural policing over the rest. Hughes speaks of marginality as a case of status dilemma experienced by women, blacks, or second-generation Americans who have "come up" in the world but are often refused the rewards of their efforts on the grounds of their origins.[79] This is particularly the case with "new" or educated women. Such exceptions are generally obliged to make ritual, and often comic, statements of deference to justify their elevation. These characteristically take the form of pledges of "femininity," namely a delight in docility and a large appetite for masculine dominance. Politically, the most useful persons for such a role are entertainers and public sex objects. It is a common trait of minority status that a small percentage of the fortunate are permitted to entertain their rulers. (That they may entertain their fellow subjects in the process is less to the point.) Women entertain, please, gratify, satisfy and flatter men with their sexuality. In most minority groups athletes or intellectuals are allowed to emerge as "stars," identification with whom should content their less fortunate fellows. In the case of women both such eventualities are discouraged on the reasonable grounds that the most popular

---

[76] "One study of fourth graders showed ten times as many girls wishing they could have been boys, as boys who would have chosen to be girls," Watson, op. cit., p. 477.

[77] Amitai Etzioni, "Sex Control, Science, and Society," Science, September 1968, pp. 1107–12.

[78] Myrdal, op. cit., Hacker, op. cit., Dixon, op. cit.

[79] Hughes, op. cit.

explanations of the female's inferior status ascribe it to her physical weakness or intellectual inferiority. Logically, exhibitions of physical courage or agility are indecorous, just as any display of serious intelligence tends to be out of place.

Perhaps patriarchy's greatest psychological weapon is simply its universality and longevity. A referent scarcely exists with which it might be contrasted or by which it might be confuted. While the same might be said of class, patriarchy has a still more tenacious or powerful hold through its successful habit of passing itself off as nature. Religion is also universal in human society and slavery was once nearly so; advocates of each were fond of arguing in terms of fatality, or irrevocable human "instinct"—even "biological origins." When a system of power is thoroughly in command, it has scarcely need to speak itself aloud; when its workings are exposed and questioned, it becomes not only subject to discussion, but even to change. Such a period is the one next under discussion.

II

HISTORICAL
BACKGROUND

The Sexual Revolution

FIRST PHASE
1830–1930

POLITICAL

DEFINITION

The term "sexual revolution" has such vogue at present it may be invoked to explain even the most trivial of socio-sexual fashions. Such usage is at best naïve. In the context of sexual politics, truly revolutionary change must have bearing on that political relationship between the sexes we have outlined under "theory." Since the state of affairs defined there as patriarchy had obtained for so long and with such universal success, there seemed little reason to imagine it might alter. Yet it did. Or at least it began to—and for nearly a century it must have looked as though the organization of human society were about to undergo a revision possibly more drastic than any it had ever known within the historical period. During this time it must have often appeared as if the most fundamental government of civilization, patriarchy itself, was so disputed and besieged that it stood at the verge of collapse. Of course, nothing of the sort occurred: the first phase ended in reform and was succeeded by reaction. Nonetheless, very substantial change did emerge from its revolutionary ferment.

Just because the period in question did not in fact complete the drastic transformation it seemed to promise, it might be well to speculate for a moment upon what a fully realized sexual revolution might be like. A hypothetical definition may be of service in measuring the shortcomings of the first phase. It might also be of use in the future since there is reason to suppose that the reaction which set in after the first decades of the twentieth century is about to give way before another upsurge of revolutionary spirit.

A sexual revolution would require, perhaps first of all, an end of traditional sexual inhibitions and taboos, particularly those that most threaten patriarchal monogamous marriage: homosexuality, "illegitimacy," adolescent, pre- and extra-marital sexuality. The negative aura with which sexual activity has generally been surrounded would necessarily be eliminated, together with the double standard and prostitution. The goal of revolution would be a permissive single standard of sexual freedom, and one uncorrupted by the crass and exploitative economic bases of traditional sexual alliances.

Primarily, however, a sexual revolution would bring the institution of patriarchy to an end, abolishing both the ideology of male supremacy and the traditional socialization by which it is upheld in matters of status, role, and temperament. This would produce an integration of the separate sexual subcultures, an assimilation by both sides of previously segregated human experience. A related event here would be the re-examination of the traits categorized as "masculine" and "feminine," with a reassessment of their human desirability: the violence encouraged as virile, the excessive passivity defined as "feminine" proving useless in either sex; the efficiency and intellectuality of the "masculine" temperament, the tenderness and consideration associated with the "feminine" recommending themselves as appropriate to both sexes.

It seems unlikely all this could take place without drastic effect upon the patriarchal proprietary family. The abolition of sex role and the complete economic independence of women would undermine both its authority and its financial structure. An important corollary would be the end of the present chattel status and denial of rights to minors. The collective professionalization (and consequent improvement) of the care of the young, also involved, would further undermine family structure while contributing to the freedom of women. Marriage might generally be replaced by voluntary association, if such is desired. Were a sexual revolution completed, the problem of overpopulation might, because vitally linked to the emancipation of women, cease to be the insoluble dilemma it now appears.

Such conjecture leads us a long way from the period under discussion. What are its claims to have made a beginning at sexual revolution? One might object, that since the Victorian period was so notoriously inhibited, the era between 1830 and 1930 could accomplish nothing at all in the area of sexual freedom. Yet it is important to recall that as sexual suppression in the form of "prudery" reached a crisis in this period, only one course out of it was possible—relief. The last three decades of the nineteenth as well as the first three decades of the twentieth century were a time of greatly increasing sexual freedom for both sexes. This in particular meant the attainment of a measure of sexual freedom for women, the group who in general had never been allowed much, if any, such freedom without a devastating loss of social standing, or the dangers of pregnancy in a society with strong sanctions against illegitimate birth. The first phase achieved a good measure of sexual freedom and/or equity by struggling toward a single standard of morality. The Victorians worked rather illogically at this in two ways. While they strove to remove the onus from the "fallen woman," they tried with a frequently naïve optimism to raise boys to be as "pure" as girls. However humorous a spectacle they present in these efforts, theirs was the first period in history that faced and tried to solve the issue of the double standard and the inhumanities of prostitution. A superficial knowledge of the reactionary era which succeeded the first phase might lead one to imagine it to be the more significant era of sexual freedom. Such is not in fact the case, for the liberalization of this period is hardly more than a continuation or diffusion of that begun before it. Often subverted for patriarchal ends it acquired a new exploitative character of its own. Any increase in sexual freedom for women in the period 1930–60 (for at its close the first phase had given them a rich increase) is probably due less to social change than to better technology in the manufacture of contraceptive devices and their proliferation. Wide distribution of what is as yet the most useful of these, "the pill," falls outside the counterrevolutionary period. Save for this handy specific, the "New Woman" of the twenties was as well off, and possibly better provided with sexual freedom, than the woman of the fifties.

During the first phase, the most important problem was to challenge the patriarchal structure and to furnish an initial impetus for the enormous transformations a sexual revolution might effect in the areas of temperament, role, and status. It must be clearly understood that the arena of sexual revolution is within human consciousness even more pre-eminently than it is within human institutions. So deeply embedded is patriarchy that the character structure it creates in both sexes is perhaps even more a habit of mind and a way of life than a political system. Because the first phase challenged both habit of mind and political structures—but had much greater success with the latter than with the former—it was unable to withstand the onset of reaction and failed to fulfill its revolutionary promise. Yet as its goal was a far more radical alteration in the quality of life than that of most political revolutions, it is easy to comprehend how this type of revolution, basic and cultural as it is, has proceeded fitfully and slowly, more on the pattern of the gradual but fundamental metamorphosis which the industrial revolution or the rise of the middle class accomplished, than on the model of spasmodic rebellion (followed by even greater reaction) one observes in the French Revolution. Moreover, as the result of the rapid onset of a period of reaction, the first phase of the sexual revolution, like a moving object arrested mid-course, could not proceed even to the expenditure of its initial momentum. When we recall that this force has been revitalized only as recently as the last five years, and after some four decades of dormancy, we realize how amorphous and contemporary is the phenomenon we seek to describe—how recalcitrant before the precision historians seek to impose on more distant and defined events.

It cannot be emphasized too strongly that many, indeed most, of those first affected by the sexual revolution had neither a systematic understanding of it, nor foresight into its possible implications. Few, even of those who believed they were sympathetic, would have been committed to all its possible consequences. This is even true, to a varying degree, of its theorists: Mill never guessed at the effects it might have upon the family, and Engels seems quite unaware of its enormous psychological ramifications.

Changes as drastic and fundamental as those of a sexual revolution are not easily arrived at. Nor should it be surprising that such change might take place by stages that are capable of interruption and temporary regression. In view of this fact, the shortcomings of the first phase are understandable, and even the arrest and subversion of its progress which one encounters in the next era, while irritating and deplorable, is, to a degree, explicable as a comprehensible pause or plateau within an ongoing process. Although the first phase fell woefully short of accomplishing the aims of its theorists and its most far-seeing exponents, it did nevertheless make some monumental progress and furnish a groundwork on which the present and the future can build. Although failing to penetrate deeply enough into the substructure of patriarchal ideology and socialization, it did attack the most obvious abuses in its political, economic, and legal superstructure, accomplishing very notable reform in the area of legislative and other civil rights, suffrage, education, and employment. For a group excluded—as women were —from minimal civil liberties throughout the historical period, their very attainment was a great deal to achieve in one century.

By an oversight too conspicuous to be accidental, historians have ignored the issue of sexual revolution, dismissed it with frivolous footnotes intended to demonstrate the folly of "votes for women," or mistaken it for a trivial exhibitionist ripple in sexual fashion. Yet the great cultural change which the beginnings of a sexual revolution represent is at least as dramatic as the four or five other social upheavals in the modern period to which historiographical attention is zealously devoted.

Since the Enlightenment, the West has undergone a number of cataclysmic changes: industrial, economic, and political revolution. But each appeared to operate, to a large extent, without much visible or direct reference to one half of humanity. It is rather disturbing how the great changes brought about by the extension of the franchise and by the development of democracy which the eighteenth and nineteenth century accomplished, the redistribution of wealth which was the aim of socialism (and which has even had its effect upon the capitalist countries) and finally, the vast changes wrought by the industrial revolution and the emergence of technology—all, had and to some degree still have, but a tangential and contingent effect upon the lives of that majority of the population who might be female. Knowledge of this is bound to draw our attention to the fact that the primary social and political distinctions are not even those based on wealth or rank but those based on sex. For the most pertinent and fundamental consideration one can bestow upon our culture is to recognize its basis in patriarchy.

And it was against patriarchy that the sexual revolution was directed. Difficult as it is to explain such a radical shift in collective consciousness, it is almost as difficult to date it precisely. One might look back as far as the Renaissance and consider the effect of the liberal education it devised when such learning was finally permitted to women. Or one might reflect on the influence of the Enlightenment: the subversive impact of its agnostic rationalism upon patriarchal religion, the tendency of its humanism to extend dignity to a number of deprived groups, and the invigorating clarity which the science it sponsored exercised upon traditional notions both of the female and of nature. One might also speculate upon the marginal impetus provided by the French Revolution in breaking down other ancient hierarchies of power. Two beliefs which French radicalism had bequeathed to the American Revolution must also have had an effect: the idea that government relies for its legitimacy on the consent of the governed, and the faith in the existence in inalienable human rights. Out of this intellectual milieu came Mary Wollstonecraft's *Vindication*, the first document asserting the full humanity of women and insisting upon its recognition. A friend of Paine and of French revolutionaries, its author was sufficiently in touch with revolutionary thought to urge the application of its basic premises to that majority still excluded from the Rights of Man.

Although it is beyond question that the culture of the eighteenth century in France had much to do with the suggestion that democracy apply in sexual as well as class politics, the purview of the present essay, coming as it does from America, must be confined to the English-speaking cultures, and as even the reforming influence of the French Revolution was throttled in England until the danger of revolution had passed, and consequently did not emerge in any fullness until the 1830s, it seems appropriate to begin this chapter's discussion in the nineteenth century. The date set for its beginnings can be justified to some extent on the grounds that these years saw the emergence of actual political organization on the issues of sexual politics, excited public controversy on the implications of a sexual revolution, and in literature, an obsessive concern with the emotions and experiences of such a revolution. Finally, the period recommends itself for the pioneering, significant reforms in sexual politics which were actually accomplished within it. If the sexual revolution was born in the thirties and forties of the nineteenth century, it enjoyed, nevertheless, a very generous period of gestation in the womb of time; possibly it was conceived in the eighteenth century, perhaps a glint of the desire which begat it may even be observed in the splendid eye of Renaissance. But the decade of the 1830s demands our attention on specific grounds, the coming of age of the reform movement in England, and the first female anti-slavery convention in America in 1837.[1] Both events had profound implications. The British reform movement opened the way to an extension of suffrage to many groups previously excluded. It also inaugurated a series of investigations into the conditions working women endured, followed by measures improving those conditions. In America, the abolition movement offered the first occasion upon which women were able to organize in a political manner. With the 1840s and particularly with 1848, one is on very sure ground indeed, for in that year the meeting in Seneca Falls, New York, marked the beginning of the political organization of women in their own behalf. British women began agitation under Mill's leadership in the sixties, but it was in America and at Seneca Falls that the first challenge was issued in a seventy-year struggle which became the international Woman's Movement.

PARADOXES

Before embarking on a study of any historical period it is instructive to contrast its own divers impressions of itself against each other. When one examines the various types of evidence available from the period 1830–1930, one is struck by a disparity and contradiction between fact and faith nearly breathtaking. It is perhaps most revealing to compare the two prevailing official versions of the culture's sexual politics: polite and legal. The conventional chivalrous attitude (and the nineteenth century carried this affectation very far indeed) asserted authoritatively that woman was superbly well cared for by her "natural protector." Yet the legal system, what must here be called the fact rather than the pious hope of the matter, furnished information far less optimistic. The reformation of the abject legal status of women is one of the major achievements of the Woman's Movement and feminist agitation during the first phase of the sexual revolution. Patriarchal law did not surrender readily or gracefully. In the United States it was amended piecemeal, slowly and laboriously, state by state all through the fifties, sixties, seventies, and eighties. In England the case was much the same; the Married Woman's Property Act, touching upon a whole series of civil rights, was first introduced in 1856, enacted in 1870, amended in 1874, and consolidated in the Act of 1882, then added to and enlarged upon on

---

[1] The Reform Act of 1832, landmark that it is, did not reform very much. In fact it was the first English legislation specifically (de jure rather than de facto) to exclude women from legal privileges such as the franchise. But it did open the way to a whole spate of highly important legislative changes in the decades which followed. In America the year 1837 saw another auspicious event; Mount Holyoke was opened, the first college for women in either country.

various occasions up to 1908. In both countries even an approach to a sensible divorce law was not made until very late.[2]

Under the common law which prevailed in both countries at the opening of the period, a woman underwent "civil death" upon marriage, forfeiting what amounted to every human right, as felons now do upon entering prison. She lacked control over her earnings, was not permitted to choose her domicile, could not manage property legally her own,[3] sign papers, or bear witness. Her husband owned both her person and her services, could—and did—rent her out in any form he pleased and pocket the profits. He was permitted to sue others for wages due her and confiscate them. All that the wife acquired by her labor, service, or act during "coverture" became the legal property of the male. Save for owning property, single women enjoyed nearly as few civil rights under law as did married women. The principle of "coverture" or *femme couverte*, general throughout Western jurisprudence, placed the married woman in the position both of minor and chattel throughout her life. Her husband became something like a legal keeper, as by marrying she succumbed to a mortifying process which placed her in the same class with lunatics or idiots, who were also "dead in the law."

No matter how irresponsible an individual a husband might be, nor how careless of the welfare of his children, he was legally entitled to demand and receive the wife's wages at any moment, even to the peril of his dependents' lives. As head of the proprietary family, the husband was the sole "owner" of wife and children, empowered to deprive the mother of her offspring, who were his legal possessions, should it please him to do so upon divorcing or deserting her. A father, like a slaver, could order the law to reclaim his chattel-property relatives when he liked. Wives might be detained against their will; English wives who refused to return to their homes were subject to imprisonment.

Should the husband die intestate, the state might pick over his property (for all property was legally his) leaving the widow nothing at all, or as little as it chose to bestow upon her. New York law was edifying and punc-

[2] The first divorce law in England to make any reform was passed in 1858. But it was based on double-standard premises and its provisions ensured that divorce remain very difficult and expensive to obtain. Further reform did not come until after the first world war. In America some states initiated progressive change in the later nineteenth century, others not until the twentieth century.

[3] The husband had complete rights over a wife's personal estate and income. Over real estate he also possessed a large number of rights, although wealthy and landed families had worked out elaborate dodges here in the form of "settlements," arranged according to rules of equity, as common law did not recognize ownership in women. But settlement was available only to the comfortable classes (English law stipulated it applied only to property over £200). It was permitted in the interests of class rather than of women, who, whatever their settlement, were prevented from the free use of what might legally be theirs.

tilious here; regardless of the number of her children, it enumerated the following as her due:

> The family Bible, pictures, school books, and all books not exceeding the sum of $50; spinning wheels, weaving looms, and stoves; ten sheep and their fleeces, two swine and their pork . . . All necessary wearing apparel, beds, bedsteads, and bedding; the clothing of the widow and ornaments proper to her station—one table, six chairs, six knives and forks, six tea-cups and saucers, one sugar dish, one milk pot, one tea-pot, and six spoons.[4]

The closest analogue to marriage was feudalism. Lest a woman entertain any doubts over her serf status, the wedding ceremony, with its injunctions to subordinance and obedience, was perfectly clear upon this point. St. Paul abjured the bride to be obedient unto her husband as unto the Lord, a behest more powerful to the pious (and care was taken that women receive large doses of piety) than any mere secular command. Secular law was equally explicit and ruled that when man and woman became "one," that one was the man. It would be difficult to find a more perfect definition of subservience than the one Blackstone's Commentary gives in explaining the wife's position in common law:

> By marriage, the husband and wife are one person in law: that is, the very being or legal existence of the woman is suspended during marriage, or at least is incorporated and consolidated into that of the husband . . . But though our law in general considers man and wife as one person, yet there are some instances in which she is separately considered; as inferior to him, and acting by his compulsion.[5]

When Henry Blackwell married Lucy Stone in 1855, this liberal gentleman and feminist renounced a formidable set of legal prerogatives which came to him with the contract. The text of this abdication has a certain period charm:

> While we acknowledge our mutual affection by publicly assuming the relationship of husband and wife . . . we deem it a duty to declare that this act on our part implies no sanction of, nor promise of voluntary obedience to such of the

---

[4] Susan B. Anthony, Elizabeth Cady Stanton, and Mathilda Gage, *The History of Woman Suffrage* (Rochester, New York, 1881), Vol. I, pp. 175–76. This quotation, like a number of others from *HWS* and the congressional debates, is quoted by Flexner, *op. cit.,* p. 63.

[5] Blackstone's *Commentaries,* Vol. I, "Rights of Persons," 3d Edition, 1768, Chapter 14, p. 442. "And therefore all deeds executed, and acts done by her during coverture are void"—it is ironic how after this flat statement of legal nonentity Blackstone can say this is "for the most part, intended for her benefit," and forgetting his dullness in blandishment proclaim "so great a favorite is the female sex of the laws of England." The last two phrases are from Blackstone's *Laws of England* (1765) Bk. I, Ch. 15, p. 433.

present laws of marriage as refuse to recognize the wife as an independent, rational being, while they confer upon the husband an injurious and unnatural superiority . . . We protest especially against the laws which give the husband:

1. The custody of the wife's person.
2. The exclusive control and guardianship of their children.
3. The sole ownership of her personal and the use of her real estate, unless previously settled upon her, or placed in the hands of trustees, as in the case of minors, lunatics and idiots.
4. The absolute right to the product of her industry.
5. Also against any laws which give to the widower so much larger and more permanent an interest in the property of his deceased wife than they give to the widow in that of the deceased husband.
6. Finally, against the whole system by which "the legal existence of the wife is suspended during marriage" so that, in most States, she neither has a legal part in the choice of her residence, nor can she make a will, nor sue or be sued in her own name, nor inherit property.[6]

It is an interesting exercise to contrast the customary attitudes and protestations of what society judged were its most "responsible" males with certain prosaic examples of their effects in actual life. The muddle of unction and apprehension which passed for chivalry is clear in this legislator's oratory:

Sir, it has been said that "the hand that rocked the cradle ruled the world," and there is truth as well as beauty in that expression. Women in this country by their elevated social position, can exercise more influence upon public affairs, than they could coerce by the use of the ballot. When God married our first parents in the garden according to that ordinance they were made "bone of one bone and flesh of one flesh;" and the whole theory of government and society proceeds upon the assumption that their interests are one, that their relations are so intimate and tender that whatever is for the benefit of the one is for the benefit of the other . . . The woman who undertakes to put her sex in the adversary position to man, who undertakes by the use of some independent political power to contend and fight against man, displays a spirit which would, if able, convert all the now harmonious elements of society into a state of war, and make every home a hell on earth.[7]

In answering the objection of a New York senator that in attaining human and civil rights women might lose their "femininity," the labor organizer Rose Schneiderman describes a different reality altogether:

We have women working in the foundries, stripped to the waist, if you please, because of the heat. Yet the Senator says nothing about these women losing

---

[6] Anthony, Stanton, and Gage, *HWS*, Vol. I, pp. 260–61. Quoted in Flexner, *op. cit.*, p. 64.

[7] The speaker is Senator Williams of Oregon. From the *Congressional Globe*, 39th Congress (1867), 2nd Session, Part I, p. 56. Quoted in Flexner, *op. cit.*, p. 148.

their charm . . . Of course you know the reason they are employed in foundries is that they are cheaper and work longer hours than men. Women in the laundries, for instance, stand for thirteen or fourteen hours in the terrible steam and heat with their hands in hot starch. Surely these women won't lose any more of their beauty and charm by putting a ballot in a ballot box once a year than they are likely to lose standing in foundries or laundries all year round. There is no harder contest than the contest for bread, let me tell you that.[8]

Wanda Neff's scholarly and informative study of Victorian working women has documented the effects of benign masculine protection in England. As in America women generally suffered from longer hours, duller tasks, more noxious working conditions, and lower wages than men in every trade. Parliamentary Blue Books, Kay-Shuttleworth's reports, and Engels' *Conditions of the Working Class in England* all present appalling descriptions of the outrages English women endured in the industrial revolution while the doctrine of manly guardianship was gravely proclaimed. Neff prints the personal testimony of a "drawer" in the coal mines of Little-Bolton—the reader's attention is directed toward the position this woman occupies in relation to her connubial master as well as to the abuses perpetrated on her by her employers:[9]

I have a belt around my waist and a chain passing between my legs, and I go on my hands and feet. The road is very steep, and we have to hold by a rope, and when there is no rope, by anything we can catch hold of . . . The pit is very wet where I work, and the water comes over our clogs always, and I have seen it up to my thighs: it rains in at the roof terribly: my clothes are wet through almost all day long. I never was ill in my life but when I was lying-in. My cousin looks after my children in the daytime. I am very tired when I get home at night; I fall asleep sometimes before I get washed. I am not so strong as I was, and cannot stand my work so well as I used to do. I have drawn till I have had the skin off me; the belt and chain is worse when we are in the family way. My feller [husband] has beaten me many a time for not being ready. I were not used to it at first, and he had little patience. I have known many a man beat his drawer.[10]

[8] From an address, "Senators versus Working Women," given at Cooper Union before the Wage Earners Suffrage League of New York, March 29, 1912, p. 5. Quoted in Flexner, *op. cit.*, pp. 258–59.

[9] Another English historian has this to say about the position of women in labor: "Although eminent historians of the labor and trade union movements have preferred to scuttle hurriedly across this dangerous ground, the women's battle in the unions was with the men rather than with the employers—with the domestic not the economic boss." Roger Fulford, *Votes for Women* (London, Faber, 1957), p. 101.

[10] Wanda Neff, *Victorian Working Women* (Columbia University Press, New York, 1929), p. 72. The speaker was thirty-seven years old and named Betty Harris. Neff describes the task of her occupation: " . . . drawers dragged the wagon behind them in places too low for horses to be used, or carried loads of coal on their backs from half a

Other contradictions intrude upon the student. The Victorians are renowned for their devotion to "purity," and "chastity." Yet in the 1860s Parliament passed a series of measures entitled The Contagious Diseases Acts by which the government legalized and regulated prostitution.[11] The age of consent was set at twelve years of age. The Acts provided that any woman might be taken for a prostitute on the word of the police or their agents and subject to involuntary medical examination, imprisonment should she refuse, and the indignity of being reduced to a species of slave or pariah in either case.

All systems of oppression have invented, and granting poetic license, have even believed, whole libraries of legends as to the beneficent effect their despotism produced upon their subjects, dimly perceived in the mellow light of cherished dependents whose role of servitude enriches the lives of their masters. Here is another statement of the cloistered circumstances of female service:

> It seems to me as if the God of our race has stamped upon [the woman] a milder gentler nature which not only makes them shrink from but disqualifies them from the turmoil and battle of public life. They have a higher and holier mission. It is in retiracy [sic] to make the character of coming men. Their mission is at home, by their blandishments and their love to assuage the passions of men as they come in from the battle of life, and not themselves by joining in the contest to add fuel to the very flames . . . It will be a sorry day for this country when those vestal fires of love and piety are put out.[12]

The famous Triangle Fire is some evidence of how serious the discrepancy between illusion and reality could become. On March 25, 1911, the premises of the Triangle Shirtwaist company burned. The company occupied a loft building where New York University now stands. The firm's 700 employees sat back to back, wedged tightly into rows between their machines. As the fire spread rapidly to the ninth and tenth floors at the top of the factory, workers panicked. Elevators proved inadequate. Iron gates shut off the staircases. The exits leading to the fire escapes were in many cases shuttered and locked. The building had no outside fire escapes and only one inside with a twenty-five foot jump at the bottom. It soon broke with the weight of the hundreds swarming over it. The fire department's tallest ladders reached only

---

hundred weight to a hundred weight and a half, for twelve, fourteen, sixteen hours daily, sometimes, in extreme cases, for thirty-six hours." *Ibid.*

[11] This is truly paradoxical; the contradiction is of course only apparent, not real, for as the historian Halévy observes, "European sex morality rests on the complementary pillars of marriage and prostitution." Elie Halévy, *History of the English People in the Nineteenth Century*, Vol. VI, The Rule of Democracy, 1905–14), p. 498.

[12] The speaker is Senator Frelinghuysen of New Jersey. From the *Congressional Globe*, 39th Congress (1867), 2nd Session, Part I, p. 5. Quoted in Flexner, *op. cit.*, pp. 148–49.

to the sixth floor. Nets were spread but the bodies hurtled down too fast and broke them. As the afternoon drew to a close, one hundred and forty-six operatives, all women, most of them young girls, were dead. Some had been burned to death, some died as their bodies hit the pavement, some were impaled upon an iron fence. The two men who owned the vast sweatshop were tried and then acquitted. One partner was later fined $20.[13]

In their fatuity, those who sounded the dominant note of chivalrous pretense acknowledged almost no restraints whatsoever in the degree of self-indulgence and regressive nostalgia they permitted themselves. Here is a typical anti-suffragist passage dedicated to the favorite theme of motherhood:

> Whether the child's heart pulses beneath her own or throbs against her breast, motherhood demands above all tranquility, freedom from contest, from excitement, from the heart burnings of strife. The welfare, mental and physical, of the human race rests, to a more or less degree, upon that tranquility.[14]

To this stimulating stuff one might oppose the words of the great feminist and abolitionist, Sojourner Truth, a slave in New York until that state finally abolished slavery in 1827, whereupon she was licensed to graduate to domestic service. Speaking at a woman's rights convention in Akron, Ohio in 1851, Sojourner Truth answered a cleric who had argued with courtly aplomb that as women were helpless physical weaklings, they were not entitled to civil rights:

> That man over there says women need to be helped into carriages and lifted over ditches, and to have the best place everywhere. Nobody ever helps me into carriages or over puddles, or gives me the best place—and ain't I a woman?
>
> Look at this arm! I have ploughed and planted and gathered into barns, and no man could head me—and ain't I a woman?
>
> I could work as much and eat as much as a man—when I could get it—and bear the lash as well! And ain't I a woman?
>
> I have borne thirteen children, and seen most of 'em sold off to slavery, and

[13] This account is put together from information in Aileen Kraditor's *The Ideas of the Woman Suffrage Movement* (New York, Columbia University, 1965), p. 155, and Mildred Adams *The Right to Be People* (New York, Lippincott, 1966), pp. 123-24. Flexner (*op. cit.*) records the bizarre fact that at the trial it came out that the stairway exits were locked to prevent theft of merchandise or a sudden walk-out strike. Adams points out that the disaster led to a series of excellent factory laws strongly supported by the suffragist movement. Two years before the fire the great Triangle strike afforded one of the first proofs that women could organize in employment and was a triumph both for the Woman's Movement, which supported it handsomely, and the Union Movement.

[14] The speaker is Senator McCumber of North Dakota, arguing against female suffrage in one of the final Congressional debates. The Nineteenth Amendment was defeated by two votes the next day. From the Congressional Record, 65th Congress, 2nd Session, Vol. 56, Part II, p. 10774 (1919). Quoted in Flexner, *op. cit.*, p. 309.

when I cried out with my mother's grief, none but Jesus heard me. And ain't I a woman?[15]

It is necessary to realize that the most sacrosanct article of sexual politics in the period, the Victorian doctrine of chivalrous protection and its familiar protestations of respect, rests upon the tacit assumption, a cleverly expeditious bit of humbug, that all women were "ladies"—namely members of that fraction of the upper classes and bourgeoisie which treated women to expressions of elaborate concern, while permitting them no legal or personal freedoms. The psycho-political tactic here is a pretense that the indolence and luxury of the upper-class woman's role in what Veblen called "vicarious consumption"[16] was the happy lot of all women. The efficacy of this maneuver depends on dividing women by class and persuading the privileged that they live in an indulgence they scarcely deserve. A use of intimidation in one class and envy in another effectively prevents solidarity. The young middle-class woman could be frightened into social and sexual conformity with the specters of governessing, factory work, or prostitution. And the less favored female is left only to dream of becoming a "lady," the single improvement to her situation she is permitted to conceive of, the hope of acquiring social and economic status through attracting the sexual patronization of the male. Despite the fact that class feeling prevented this from happening very often, it is a recurrent and favorite fantasy in the literature of the period. When the only known "freedom" is a gilded voluptuousness attainable through the largesse of someone who owns and controls everything, there is little incentive to struggle for personal fulfillment or liberation.

To succeed, both the sexual revolution and the Woman's Movement which led it would have to unmask chivalry and expose its courtesies as subtle manipulation. It would also have to cross class lines and join lady to factory hand, the loose and the respectable, in a common cause. To the extent it could be so, it succeeded.

THE WOMAN'S MOVEMENT

Education

As a number of competent historians have already documented this event it is my purpose here simply to recapitulate directing the reader's glance across its general surface so that I may comment upon its effects in a wider cultural context and particularly that of literature.

Curiously enough, the dictionary supplies us with a definition of "fem-

---

[15] Anthony, Stanton, and Gage, *History of Woman Suffrage*, Vol. I, p. 116. The passage is printed in dialect in the original and set in Gage's descriptive prose. I have standardized the spelling and excerpted the words of the speaker.

[16] In *The Theory of the Leisure Class* Thorstein Veblen argues that the bourgeois class displays its wealth through its women whose idleness and expensive vanities are an exhibition of the industry and prestige of their proprietors, their husbands and fathers.

inism" which is, in fact, neither more nor less than a complete and satisfactory characterization of the ends of the sexual revolution itself: ". . . a system of political, economic, and social equality between the sexes." As this is so sweeping a formula, involving the radical transformation of an entire society with which this whole essay attempts to deal—a sexual revolution in fact—this section is confined to the Woman's Movement and the concrete reforms it effected in the specific areas of education, the political organization of women (particularly around the issue of suffrage), and employment. We must acknowledge however, that most other related changes effected within society during the first phase arose from or co-operated with the vanguard which the Woman's Movement represented.

As with the liberation of any group long oppressed, the first priority was education. Since Plato's liberal suggestions in *The Republic* were never followed, it was the Renaissance which furnished the first applied theories of education for women. Alberti's *Della Famiglia* is fairly representative of these. The purpose of such minimal training as it recommends is merely an aesthetic and convenient docility. It bears some resemblance to the plan of mental sedation which inspired the white founders of black colleges in the United States, intent primarily on the creation of less incompetent agriculturalists and a more tractable servant class. With women too, the concession was gradually made that a barely literate service might have more to recommend it than the illiterate variety. Such inferior association as the products of the former might provide are still better company than utter ignorance; while at the same time, they hold none of the terrors posed by equals. The education of women was not thought of as a course of study beyond the threshold level of learning, a genteel polish its major achievement. And in most cases it was deliberately cynical in its emphasis upon "virtue"—a sugared word which meant obedience, servility, and a sexual inhibition perilously near to frigidity.

Coming from a man who contributed so much to the French Revolution, Rousseau's impressions of the proper education for women were as reactionary as they were influential:

> The whole education of women ought to be relative to men. To please them, to be useful to them, to make themselves loved and honored by them, to educate them when young, to care for them when grown, to counsel them, to make life sweet and agreeable to them—these are the duties of women at all times, and what should be taught them from their infancy.[17]

Most education for women in the nineteenth century followed this prescription scrupulously—a great deal of it does so to this day. There are an endless number of statements from the period advocating higher education

---

[17] Jean-Jacques Rousseau, *L'Émile or A Treatise on Education,* edited by W. H. Payne (New York and London, 1906), p. 263.

for women on the grounds that it would make them better housewives and mothers; there are an equal number which argue against the effort, predicting its malevolent influence should the newly educated go beyond the agreed-upon end of subordination.[18]

Even with such perfect co-operative subjection as an ideal, the project of educating depressed groups has always the seeds of its own subversion within it. A little knowledge is indeed a dangerous thing if only because it so often induces a thirst for more. Serious study can grow even from the rudiments of prescribed frivolity; can give rise to analysis, direction, organization—finally the way out of present circumstances. And the nineteenth century saw this thirst grow to Gargantuan proportions, while it produced such phenomena as the crazy pathos of Mary Lyon's green bag and its travels over New England begging contributions of five, three, and one dollar—and even, in its graceful lack of discrimination, accepting an offering of six cents—that a real college might open for women in America.[19]

Mount Holyoke opened its doors in 1837. Oberlin had admitted women to its degree the same year and was the first college to offer women an education unquestionably equal to that of men. Over the following decades a handful of eastern colleges for women sprang up: Vassar in 1865, Smith and Wellesley in 1875, Radcliffe (the Harvard Annex) in 1882, and Bryn Mawr in 1885. In England, Queen's College was founded at London University in 1848, and Bedford in 1849. In England as in America, the decade of the seventies saw great progress: Girton was opened at Cambridge in 1872, Lady Margaret Hall and Somerville opened at Oxford in 1879, and in 1874 a woman's school of medicine was founded in London. As the specific aim of these colleges was the education of women, they were at first more significant than co-education: in 1875 Vassar alone had as many women students enrolled in its collegiate course as the eight state universities combined which admitted women.[20] In America, the land grant institutions were also capitulating to the demand and furnishing women with higher education, but as the public institutions admitted women largely out of their own economic need, the result of a decline in their male enrollment before and during the Civil War, rather than out of any special commitment toward their new students, and as for a long time they confined women to their "normal

---

[18] *The Saturday Review*, for example, flatly referred to the intellectual inferiority of women. But most of the argument was carried out on the gallant line of "concern" lest women lose their health or charm through higher learning. Most disagreement with the "usefulness" of opening higher education to women has a solid financial bottom: patriarchal economic and social arrangements both prevent women from making large endowment contributions, or from putting professional education to use. The best account of the discussion is found in Mabel Newcomer's *A Century of Higher Education for American Women* (New York, Harcourt, 1959).

[19] See Flexner, *op. cit.*, p. 34 and the Mount Holyoke College catalogue.

[20] Mabel Newcomer, *op. cit.*, p. 20.

school" departments, they never came to feel any particular obligation to the education of women.

In both countries the growth of higher education for women was the result of two factors: the opening of teaching to women, and feminist agitation.[21] The spread of universal primary and secondary education was one of the great ideals of the nineteenth century. Since in both England and America, the cheapest system of public education was obtained through hiring women as schoolteachers, women had to be conceded better education if only so that they might teach children. Higher education for women on an equal basis with men was one of the feminists' chief objectives. Yet so fearful were its advocates of compromising their cause, that they were occasionally timid about the more doubtful campaign for suffrage.

One can say with considerable certainty that the sexual revolution would have had little impetus, the Woman's Movement still less, without the growth of higher education for women, one of the major achievements of the period. While the first phase gave women their initial opportunity for higher education, much impetus was lost in the reaction which followed. An equal education is yet to come. But even the taste of knowledge was sufficiently revolutionary to spark an enormous unrest and provide the movement with its leaders, a large number of whom came fresh from the new colleges.

In order to explore the depth and complexity of the issue of education for women, literary sources are particularly illustrative. In England Tennyson's *The Princess* furnished the spectacle of a major poet composing a long work devoted to the problem. The poem tends to fall apart at its joints, leaving a heap of shining lyrics as its relic. In Tennyson's uneasy asides one finds sufficient evidence of his difficulty in deciding on the proper tone to adopt. Indeed, the subject matter, educational polemic, is hardly one that instantly recommends itself as poetic material. Tennyson starts out bravely enough in the vein of smug badinage. But immediately it begins to betray him. First of all, he grows a bit ashamed of his own levity. The opening of university education to women, a topic he was sure could afford nothing but comic material, begins to turn unexpectedly serious when he projects himself into his heroine's position.

In his early poetry, Tennyson was fond of describing his own moods through lilylike maidens, Shalott, Mariana, etc. But in *The Princess* the fable becomes something of a case history of the poet's own problems of sexual

[21] In institutions originally exclusively male it was financial need which again opened doors to women during the Depression and World War II. In ending its long tradition of refusing women admission, Princeton recently named a similar reason, its need to compete in drawing power with co-educational colleges. In integrating, both Princeton and Yale proclaim (as Harvard has long done) a quota system against women applicants. Most co-educational colleges are thought to exercise quotas as well: they are simply more discreet.

identity. The prince who tells the story is not promising material—an epileptic with long golden curls who goes about in drag, and sings falsetto while courting. Tennyson veers between identifying with this paragon and the princess herself, also a poet, whose fierce desire for learning makes her a passionate and fairly commanding spirit. However, his initial "gamesome" tone rather soon begins to tire under the conflicts produced by Tennyson's own male chauvinism. A teasing patronization then gives way to a more urgent insecurity.

Tennyson for a time is almost persuaded by the eloquence of Ida's feminism which comes through despite the heavy-handed burlesque under which he tries to drape it. Princess Ida is exciting .The poet's hero wishes to marry her, but he is not prepared to marry an equal. Siege must be laid to tame her into a docile but slightly above-average housewife whose additional accomplishment is a discarded bit of learning, abdicated to the higher cause of service to ego and his heirs. An unpleasant presentiment has occurred to the poet— what would happen to men if women were their intellectual equals? Would they be rejected, no longer served and soothed? Ida's demand for equality in education is obviously cutting too close. In fact it might wreck Victorian marriage. Years later, Mill twitted anti-feminist resistance by saying that it regarded marriage—as it was—as so uninviting a proposition that all other options had to be closed to women, lest they refuse to marry. This might appear to be mere sarcasm, but in fact chivalry did apprehend that women would cease to enter into marriage on the terms expected of them when education gave them other choices. That is why *The Princess*, in a curious, otherwise inexplicable manner proceeds to "change the subject" from education to marriage. Masculine security appears to depend on Tennyson's ability to turn the rebel's head from learning to love.

Ida's almost humble request to be allowed to enter upon the cultural heritage of civilization must be made to seem outrageous and grotesque. Tennyson insists on turning her woman's college hope of attaining intellectual equality into a separatist Amazon fantasy of his own, part mockery, part titillation. The poem makes use of a "framing" narrative device, and the tale of the princess herself is told by a bunch of undergraduates. There are songs interspersed throughout the text, the bulk of them frank propaganda for hearth and home and these latter morsels of domestic piety are placed in the mouths of the girls who listen—they are not otherwise permitted to intervene in the discussion of their fate. Tennyson's actual premise is that Ida may study *or* love; not both. As the male has no intention of sharing his university, the female can only set up her own artificial alternate culture, a project the poet regards as both futile and silly. He has loaded the question by blowing up the period's own solution of segregated education to the proportions of a totally segregated society. All this is an interesting comment on the Victorian feeling that the female must relinquish sexuality if she is to be in any sense autonomous, a variant on the bondage of "virtue" which demands sexual inhibition in a woman if she is to maintain her social and therefore her economic position.

Having stumbled upon what remained disconcerting questions, Tennyson bundles the whole thing toward an awkward conclusion, for he seems to have an uneasy prescience that the entire system he calls "love" is in some danger. Princess Ida has flatly refused to marry the prince. The poet complicates the plot with side issues of "colorful" antiquarian character such as wars of rapine, property interests as big as kingdoms, forced marriages arranged by contract in childhood, and that species of masculine vanity called honor. The poet's choice of a pseudo-medieval setting in which to "debate" the "problem of woman" and her very present demand for educational opportunity has the effect of diluting a contemporary issue nearly to the point of insipidness. To fend off the troublesome implications he intuits lie in his subject, Tennyson is reduced to the expedient of having his hero wounded in a tournament and require the decorous attentions of a nurse-mother in order to recover. Ida is beaten when he plays dead. By feigning infantile helplessness he can convert his virago into the glowing image of mama, which the poem repeatedly exalts. This (to the Victorian sensibility) is perhaps safely asexual. In any case it fends off the peril of competition.

As fantasy is the only vehicle which Tennyson can use to conduct his discussion, Ida is a shadowy princess abiding in a Cloud-Cuckoo-Land college from which all men are rigidly excluded. Having invaded the sanctuary anyway, the prince has fallen desperately in love with her according to the hyperbole of chivalrous stereotype; her hair is somehow "a stately fretwork in the sun," despite the fact that it is black, and her companions are "a hundred airy does" . . . all step with "tender feet, light as air," and so forth.

But when the bargaining begins, and the prince shifts from courting to the marriage contract, the submission he wants to impose upon Ida is not forthcoming. Yet the conditions of the union are ones our poet and his readers would regard as just. With commendable logic Ida still refuses the swain who would coerce her. Tennyson then grows so nervous he turns Ida into an Amazon caricature. To complicate things and obscure the issue even further, the prince is fitted out with a father who is a male supremicist of the most vulgar and abusive variety:

> Man for the field and woman for the hearth;
> Man for the sword and for the needle she;
> Man with the head, and woman with the heart;
> Man to command, and woman to obey;
> All else confusion.

The irascible old man sees in Ida a likely breeder of warriors, and advises his son to get her:

Man is the hunter; woman is his game.
The sleek and shining creatures of the chase,
We hunt them for the beauty of their skins;
They love us for it and we ride them down.

With transparent falsity and a devious but strenuous attempt to be "fair," the poet urges the reader to side with the prince who is said to advocate moderation. He is really his father's boy, but a diplomat—"Wild natures need wise curbs"—who scorns open warfare. He will conquer through the subtle method of flattery, and when this fails, he can always play invalid until Ida capitulates and abandons her scheme of liberating education and takes up royal housewifery. The prince is too canny to parley over equality; he prefers to render inherent biological differences into pretty phrases which only disguise the old king's rigid categories. He would pretend to side-step the issue of status altogether. He sets up a theory of complementary difference, justifying cultural disparity through genital dissimilarity—"Either sex alone is half itself." Given the social circumstances of conditioning this is even the case with regard to personality; but Tennyson believes temperamental differences reside in nature. The male is thesis, the female antithesis—and marriage is synthesis. Together, the poet promises in a particularly banal figure, they will harmonize into "perfect music." He then insists that the fact of sexual dimorphism shall determine personality and role just as before: "For woman is not undevelopt, man, but diverse." The "diverse" is of course wonderfully familiar—*Vive la différence*. His bromide "Not like to like, but like to difference" simply passes off traditional inequalities as interesting variety. Under this formulation the male will continue as of old to represent force, authority, and status, "the wrestling thews that throw the world," the female will go on at "childward care" as well as supplying the "childlike in the larger mind." Flattery gives way to insult.

Under the force of sickbed sympathy, Ida says yes. Now thoroughly in command, the prince abandons the role of invalid. With great assurance he dismisses the subject of education altogether, by conceding woman only what one guesses to be the usual minimal literary finish—"all that not harms distinctive womanhood." Ida's college is closed; the prince has co-opted all her theories with the unctuous ingenuity of the doctrine of the separate spheres.

The dangers which masculine sensibility believes are inherent in equal educational opportunities could not be better displayed than here—nor the emotional strategies necessary to deal with and subvert them. One begins to understand how tactically vital is the chivalrous posture, its emphasis on heart and home and happy marriage—how desperately it rallied to the defense of the status quo. The Victorian belief in marriage—nearly an article of faith—is an attempt to beautify the traditional confinement of women at any cost. The cloying sweetness, the frenetic sentimentality, all conspire to hide the fact that this is only candy-coated sexual politics.

Political Organization

After education, the next step was organization. It was the Abolitionist Movement which gave American women their first opportunity for political action and organization. In the United States, where the Woman's Movement began and from whence it spread to other Western countries and beyond the Western world, it was the cause of eradicating slavery which provided the impetus for the emancipation of women. It was around this issue American women acquired their first political experience and developed the methods they were to use throughout most of their campaign and until the turn of the century: petition, and agitation carried on to educate the public. There is something logical in the fact that they should first band together for another cause than their own: it fulfills the "service ethic" in which they were indoctrinated. Slavery was probably the only circumstance in American life sufficiently glaring in its injustice and monumental evil to impel women to break that taboo of decorum which stifled and controlled them more efficiently than the coil of their legal, educational, and financial disabilities. Eleanor Flexner's *Century of Struggle,* the major scholarly history of women in the United States, assesses the campaign against slavery in these terms:

> It was in the abolition movement that women first learned to organize, to hold public meetings, to conduct petition campaigns. As abolitionists they first won the right to speak in public and began to evolve a philosophy of their place in society and of their basic rights. For a quarter of a century the two movements, to free the slave and to liberate the woman, nourished and strengthened one another.[22]

The first generation of feminists were active and dedicated abolitionists: the Grimké sisters, Lucy Stone, Elizabeth Cady Stanton, Lucretia Mott, and Susan B. Anthony. This does not, of course, imply that abolitionists were always remarkably sympathetic towards feminism. Frederick Douglass and Henry Blackwell were, Garrison too; but the plight of Lucy Stone is fairly typical—she was encouraged to speak on the rights of blacks during weekends for the larger crowds, but allowed to devote herself to the rights of women only on weekdays, lest her espousal of the latter detract from public support for the former.[23]

The Woman's Movement in America was officially inaugurated with the Seneca Falls convention of July 19 and 20, 1848. This meeting also grew out of abolition, for at the World Anti-Slavery Convention held in London in 1840, Lucretia Mott and Elizabeth Cady Stanton, mere women, were

---

[22] Flexner, *op. cit.,* p. 41. Historians of the Woman's Movement are in agreement upon this. See also Mildred Adams, *The Right to Be People* (New York, Lippincott, 1967) and Andrew Sinclair, *The Emancipation of the American Woman* (New York, Harper and Row, 1965).

[23] See Flexner, *op. cit.*

excluded from the proceedings,[24] a circumstance that threw them together and into the alliance which resulted in the Seneca Falls adventure. Lucretia Mott was a Nantucket Quaker whose house served as a station on the underground railroad and a founder of the first female Anti-Slave Society. She was some twenty years older than Stanton, whom she coached to become the leading intellectual in the American movement. The "Statement of Sentiments" composed at Seneca Falls began with a simple paraphrase of the Declaration of Independence. Seventy-five years after the American Revolution, women were daring to apply this document to themselves, extending its premises—the proposition of inalienable human rights and the legitimacy of government relying upon the consent of the governed—even, and at last to their own case. The reforms they advocated here and in the women's rights conventions which began to spring up everywhere, were control of their earnings and the right to own property, access to education and divorce, the guardianship of their children, and most explosively, the demand for suffrage. Of the 250 women who met at Seneca Falls, only one, a nineteen-year-old seamstress named Charlotte Woodward, lived to vote for president in 1920.[25] The Wesleyan chapel which saw the birth of a great national and international movement is now a gas station, marked only by a sign on the sidewalk. And yet, in the sense of formal politics, the first insurrectionary gathering of the revolution had taken place.

Through a New York *Herald Tribune* account of a Woman's Rights Convention at Worcester, Massachusetts, in 1850, the news of practical political organization reached Harriet Taylor in London, who greeted the event with enthusiasm in the *Westminster Review*. But there were still no feminist societies formed in England until the sixties. Mill presented the first suffrage petition to Parliament in 1866 and published his *Subjection of Women* in 1869. The movement now had strong and growing roots in England. It was given a wider international character when Susan B. Anthony began the international feminist movement during a visit abroad in 1883. Carrie Chapman Catt gave much of her life to the international, and in the years of reaction after suffrage was won in America, an international woman's movement continued to function through various organizations, its latest manifestation the United Nations Committee on the Status of Women. By 1920 the number of nations who had granted some form of civil rights

[24] Their public exclusion and the denial of their "recognition as persons" dramatized the situation of women before delegates from all over the world. Furious, Garrison left the convention and sat with the women. See Abbie Graham, *Ladies in Revolt* (New York, The Woman's Press, 1934).

[25] A farm girl who plied her trade at home, Woodward has left a record of how she felt: "I can say that every fiber of my being rebelled, although silently, all the hours I sat and sewed gloves for a miserable pittance which, after it was earned, could never be mine. I wanted to work, but I wanted to choose my task, and I wanted to collect my wages. That was my form of rebellion against the life into which I was born." Quoted in Sinclair, *op. cit.,* p. 60.

and the franchise to women was 26; by 1964 it was 104. Though it continues to be largely ignored, a profound social change had come about, its seed sown in nineteenth-century England and America.

In the long and tortuous years of campaigning for a whole series of reforms, the final and signal achievement of the woman's movement came to lie in winning the franchise. The best-known, the most specific, and the best-documented aspect of the first phase of the sexual revolution, a historical field in its own right, the story has been told many times, often well.[26] In broad outline, there was a considerable similarity between the movements in England and America, both as regards tactics and the split that developed between the "constitutional" and the "militant" wings. Until well into this century the woman's movement had worked only through the slow, persevering methods of petition, pamphleteering, speechmaking and a careful canvas and appeal for male votes in local elections and in the debates of Congress and Parliament. But the task of "educating" the public was long, seemingly endless. The apparent futility of their quiet patience provoked the need for more spectacular methods: mass demonstrations, parades, pickets. An increasing frustration with disingenuous governmental delay led the Pankhursts' English "suffragette" group to adopt the tactics of disruption and arrest, finally the theatrics of arson and window breaking. In America, members of Alice Paul's rather less desperate militant group, the Congressional Union, suffered arrest and abuse for quietly picketing the White House in wartime. There is much disagreement about the value of the militants' contribution. It is probable militant methods were necessary to keep the issue alive over so long and discouraging a campaign; they were unquestionably important for the public sympathy they enlisted when government replied to them with police brutality, harsh prison terms, and forced feeding for hunger strikers. Even in their angriest moods, Engilsh and American suffragettes were violent toward property rather than persons, and in its more general use of nonviolent methods the Woman's Movement had hit upon tactics which went beyond the methods of earlier reform movements, and may even possibly have provided later political leaders and causes with an example: Gandhi, the Union Movement, and Civil Rights.

The friends of the suffrage movement in America were a mixed lot: in the West, populism and the frontier spirit; in the Middle West, temperance; in the East, reform. In England, the Liberal party seemed a friend until it had the power of office; Labour was sympathetic. Nowhere would a party commit itself. The enemies of the suffrage movement were also an interesting

---

[26] As well as Flexner, Adams, and Sinclair, *op. cit.* (American), see Roger Fulford, *Votes for Women* (London, Faber, 1957) and Ray Strachey, *The Cause* (London, 1928) for short histories of the Woman's Movement in England. Further analysis of the American Movement can be found in William J. O'Neill's *Everyone Was Brave* (Chicago, Quadrangle, 1968), and Aileen Kraditor's *The Ideas of the Woman's Suffrage Movement* (New York, Columbia University Press, 1965).

group: Southern racists fearful of the votes of black women, middle-western liquor interests, eastern capitalism, and machine politics. In the last two there was considerable, finally largely unjustified anxiety, that women might play a strong role in unionization and political reform. Corporations opposed the vote for women, and like the liquor trust stood willing to finance anti-suffrage campaigns; both were rash enough to leave the evidence behind.[27]

The moderate wing of the American suffrage movement became the League of Women Voters. Looking back on the objectives of the League in its early years, there is some evidence women were effective at first in gaining a measure of the sort of legislative reform for which they needed the vote: the protection of women in industry, child welfare, child labor laws, social hygiene, collective bargaining, minimum wage laws, pure food laws, honest election practices, municipal reform, compulsory education, and a unification of the laws concerning the civil status of women.[28] In the twentieth century tide of welfare and reform legislation, the enfranchisement of women probably did play some role and had some actual effect: what is disturbing is that it has not had more. When their constitutional amendment for a strong child-labor law failed to attain state ratification in 1934, the League had already entered its decline. As a deliberately non-partisan group it did not or could not make use of the ballot for direct purposes of women's self-interest as other interest groups traditionally have done. Since public feeling, together with party practices (and women's growing new reticence in the face of both), combined to prevent candidacy or election to office for women, the vote grew more and more meaningless as reaction set in. Prejudice against the employment of women (a group of workers still generally outside the union movement) mounted during the Depression and was repeated again after the Second World War. In the fifties anti-feminism culminated in a fairly solid feeling against women's participation in public life. The groundswell of the Woman's Movement was utterly spent by then. "Feminist" became a derogatory term.

The cause of suffrage was the focal point of the formal politics of the first phase of the sexual revolution; around it were marshaled other issues such as education, equality before the law, and equal pay. One must recognize the central significance of the franchise in that it aroused the greatest opposition and mobilized the greatest consciousness and effort. Yet in many ways it was the red herring of the revolution—a wasteful drain on the energy of seventy years. Because the opposition was so monolithic and unrelenting, the struggle so long and bitter, the vote took on a disproportionate importance. And when the ballot was won, the feminist movement collapsed in what can

[27] See Alan P. Grimes, *The Puritan Ethic and Woman Suffrage* (New York, Oxford, 1967) and Flexner, *op. cit.* Both authors substantiate the charge.

[28] Adams, *op. cit.*, p. 191.

only be described as exhaustion.[29] The suffrage campaign reminds one of nothing so much as a flat tire encountered early on a long journey—a flat which takes so much time, labor, and expense to repair that the journey is dejectedly abandoned. Aileen Kraditor has documented the type of co-option and collusion to which the American suffragists were driven in their desperation to achieve that imperative "next step" which took so long to take that it engulfed the whole movement. The second generation of suffragists were pioneers like the first, but a newer, more conventional breed. Suffrage became respectable, "smart," even possible, if one were willing to play politics and make the requisite compromises. The compromises were decidedly unpalatable: unsavory understandings with southern racism to win congressional votes from the southern states, a grating irony in a movement whose origins were in abolition. And as the machine-held districts where new immigrant populations were centered voted time and time again against the option of granting suffrage to them, native American women became bitter for a time against the foreign-born.[30]

If suffrage's ability to limit a whole social revolution to one issue was a great fault, the bourgeois character of the movement was another. Never, even at the last, was it sufficiently involved with working women, the most exploited group among its numbers. Although the women's suffrage movement did have moments of solidarity which cut across class lines in a way quite new to American politics, probably never recaptured again until Civil Rights, the hopelessly exploited character of female employment today is proof of its shortcoming in labor organization. Certain nearly inevitable factors contributed to its too frequently middle-class character; generally only women of this class enjoyed the leisure and education necessary for the endless effort the suffrage battle demanded.[31]

The chief weakness of the movement's concentration on suffrage, the factor which helped it to fade, disappear, and even lose ground when the

[29] The same phenomenon may be observed in abolition and black emancipation; agitation here produced only literal manumission after sixty years of effort. The gains of 1868 were withdrawn or ended in the next hundred years. It took some sixteen years of Civil Rights work to restore to black Americans those rights that had been conceded them a century before. In Carrie Chapman Catt's triumphant speech dismissing the crowd of American suffragists, one can also detect overconfidence and short-sightedness: "Now we will all go our separate ways . . . I have lived to see the great dream of my life—the enfranchisement of women. We are no longer petitioners, we are not wards of the nation, but free and equal citizens." Quoted in Adams *op. cit.*, p. 170.

[30] Aileen Kraditor, *The Ideas of the Woman Suffrage Movement, 1890–1920* (New York, Columbia University, 1965).

[31] Catt estimated that there were 56 campaigns to referendum, 480 campaigns to get legislatures to submit suffrage to voters, 47 campaigns to get state constitutional conventions to include woman's suffrage, 277 campaigns to get state party conventions to add a suffrage plank, and 19 campaigns to 19 successive Congresses. See Carrie Chapman Catt and Nettie Rogers Shuler *Woman Suffrage and Politics* (New York, Scribner's, 1923), p. 107.

vote was gained, lay in its failure to challenge patriarchal ideology at a sufficiently deep and radical level to break the conditioning processes of status, temperament and role. A reform movement, and especially one which has fixed its attention on so minimal an end as the ballot, the sort of superficial change which legislative reform represents, and which, when it has attained this, becomes incapable even to putting it to use, is hardly likely to propose the sweeping radical changes in society necessary to bring about the completion of a sexual revolution—changes in social attitudes and social structure, in personality and institutions. Marriage was preserved nearly intact despite women's new legal rights within it, and divorce. The "home" was still creditable enough to be refurbished in gleaming colors in the ensuing period of reaction. Although they felt they had escaped economic dependence as far as "the right to work," women were not yet able to pursue the question all the way to equal rights in work; nor did they continue to view work as responsibility or a fundamental social contribution. In affluence or before social pressure, they returned to idleness or dependency. The next generation found it easy to exploit women as a "reserve labor force," bringing them out to the job when it suited a wartime economy, and sending them back to the "home" when it didn't. Most crucial of all, the whole elaborate processes of sexual "socialization" were left in such good repair that they could be reorganized into newer and more subtle patterns of control. Despite the reform of its legal system and the (finally minor) humiliation to its political pride, the patriarchal mentality reasserted itself with great strength at the end of the first phase. Patriarchy, reformed or unreformed, is patriarchy still: its worst abuses purged or foresworn, it might be actually more stable and secure than before.

Employment

The issue of women's entrance into the professions is a spectacular case of the contradictions in the chivalrous mentality with which the sexual revolution had to contend. Women have always worked. They have generally worked longer hours for smaller rewards and at less agreeable tasks than have men. The issue of employment during the period of the first phase was simply their demand that they be paid for their efforts, have an opportunity to enter the most prestigious fields of work, and when paid be allowed to retain and control their earnings. Even before the industrial revolution brought them to the factory, women had always done menial labor, most of it physically exhausting and tedious, much of it agricultural. Yet chivalry's accessory police ethic, "decorum" found it outrageous for a "lady" to use her mind rather than her hands and back. Such powerful feeling against such infraction of taboo affords a glimpse of how economically and politically useful taboo can be. In embarking upon the intellectually and socially responsible employment which the professions constituted, pioneers in each field met with ruthless and nearly overwhelming opposition in law, medicine, science, scholarship, and architecture.

If among the middle classes the obsessive fetish of decorum could be damaging to women's own interests, among the working class the passivity it implied took another form—despair. When the settlement houses began to reach the poor, they found, much as they would find today, that the women were at the bottom of the heap among slum dwellers; no one was paid less or needed unions more desperately than the women, more often unskilled and held back by the more severely inhibiting traditions of European patriarchy. Inured to servitude, they were listless and afraid to pursue their own interests, no matter how great their suffering. One of the pioneers in labor organization reported the situation in these depressing terms:

> . . . the habit of submission and acceptance without question of any terms offered them, with the pessimistic view of life in which they see no ray of hope. Such people cannot be said to live, as living means the enjoyment of nature's gifts, but they simply vegetate like partially petrified creatures . . . many women are deterred from joining labor organizations by foolish pride, prudish modesty, and religious scruples; and a prevailing cause, which applies to all who are in the flush of womanhood, is the hope and expectancy that in the near future marriage will lift them out of the industrial life to the quiet and comfort of a home, foolishly imagining that with marriage their connection with and interest in labor matters end; often finding, however, that their struggle has only begun when they have to go back to the shop for two instead of one. All this is the result or effect of the environments and conditions surrounding women in the past and present, and can be removed only by constant agitation and education.[32]

Both in England and America investigations of the conditions of women and child labor had all along brought an appalled public response. This was particularly true in Britain where Parliament conducted hearings and published blue books of its findings for decades. The result was the beginning of modern protective legislation, curbing the greed of capitalist laissez faire policy, and finally assuring minimum standards of decent working conditions for all workers, men as well as women. While men, women and children benefited hugely from reform, men benefited still more from the labor movement, whereas women did not. Working women needed unions even more than they needed votes, but the labor movement showed (and still shows) remarkably little interest in organizing them. As unorganized and notoriously cheap labor, cheap enough to be used to undersell male labor, women, when they were permitted to work, could also be more easily exploited in labor or more easily fired, laid off, or pushed out when it was convenient not to permit them to work.[33]

---

[32] *Proceedings of the Knights of Labor,* "Report of General Investigator of Women's Work and Wages," 1886, pp. 155–56. Leonara Barry is the reporter. Quoted in Flexner, *op. cit.,* pp. 190–200.

[33] Things have not changed very much. In America, among the occupations in which women are employed, there is either no union to protect them, as with domestics, typists,

One of the first major labor reforms was legislation limiting the hours of work.[34] But in both England and America, most agitation for the improvement of the barbarous circumstances under which women worked was carried out with essential disregard of their human rights as workers, and instead, typically preferred to put its emphasis either on the indecorum of their shocking and disorganized lives, or on the subversive effects their working conditions must have on their breeding ability, their service to infants, their "morals" or "virtue." In many places there was real sympathy for the sufferings of women in industry, but a great deal of the motivation behind reform was little more than protection of patriarchal culture and institutions: family structure was becoming disrupted (including the authority of the father as provider and head of household); women in industry had access to sexual freedom; they were worked too hard in one circumstance (the factory) to serve properly in another (the home).[35] The prevailing male attitude in both countries seemed to find the perfect remedy in getting women out of the factory altogether and back into the safety of the "home."

It is important to understand that economic independence was consciously as well as unconsciously perceived to be a direct threat to male authority. The freedom of sexual choice, the competence and self-sufficiency of a skilled woman worker, single and receiving top wages, was possibly as frightening to certain onlookers as the ghastly poverty of the majority of women factory workers, harassed by family duties, and ridden with disease or malnutrition. The second might be handy exempla of the follies of earning your own living; the first could only entice one to freedom. A number of observers have pointed out that the elite women of the working class fared rather better than those women of the middle class who were driven to the humiliations of governessing with its low pay, servant status and eternal spying supervision.[36]

In few cases, or none, was it ever an affair of moment to those in power

---

and stenographers, or one too weak or corrupt to give them real assistance, as with retail clerks and waitresses. Nowhere else in American employment is pay differential so great as it is between unionized male employment and the unprotected female occupations; by comparison, even the professions treat women with a semblance of fairness, some actually feel their discrimination is better concealed.

[34] Both men and women benefited here from child labor law for as the number of hours permitted to the young in factory labor decreased, it became necessary to limit those of adults doing tasks which depended upon the child labor force as well.

[35] See Neal J. Smelser, *Social Structure and the Industrial Revolution* (University of Chicago, 1959, see particularly Chapters IX–XI). Neff, *op. cit.* and the Blue Books bear this out. One must remember too that woman's domestic "work" was (and is) never seen as work, with the dignity that term implies in a market or money economy—and that it was always there to be done, no matter how many hours she might spend employed outside her home. Hired domestics, who made up a large part of the female labor force during this period, lived under conditions very near to serfdom.

[36] This is attested to in the more perceptive and sympathetic social literature of the period and borne out in Neff, *op. cit.*

enacting measures for their protection, that women have beneficial conditions so that they might enjoy or profit from meaningful work; still less were they concerned with equality between the sexes, least of all in the matter of wages. About all the chivalrous reform which was finally accomplished there was a frequently patronizing air of concessions made to the physically inferior. Women and children are generally lumped together in Parliamentary blue books: both had the status of minors. Louis Brandeis' famous "Oregon Brief" which won a decisive victory for protective legislation in America is based on the smug assumption that "women are fundamentally weaker than men in all that makes for endurance, in muscular strength, in nervous energy, in the power of persistent application and attention.[37] . . . History discloses the fact that woman has always been dependent on man . . . Differentiated by these matters from the other sex, she is properly placed in a class by herself, and sustained even when like legislation is not necessary for men and could not be sustained. It is impossible to close one's eyes to the fact that she still looks to her brother and depends on him."[38]

English and American studies of the period cannot help but persuade one that women workers were habitually rescued for what amounted to the wrong reasons. Yet the fact remains that the sexual revolution began to accomplish a great deal for women economically. Despite the dreadful hardships of exploitative and discriminatory employment, they attained through it a measure of that economic, social, and psychological independence which is the *sine qua non* of freedom.

POLEMICAL

MILL VERSUS RUSKIN

Had the older, cynical expressions of male supremacy continued to carry much weight, a first phase of sexual revolution might never have taken place. Instead, the struggle was carried out between two opposing camps, rational and chivalrous, each of them claiming to have at heart the best interests of both sexes and the larger benefit of society. Just as it was enlightening to contrast the chivalrous attitude with the reality of women's economic and

[37] Decision of the United States Supreme Court in Curt Muller vs. the State of Oregon, U.S. 412, 421, 422 (1908) and Brief for the State of Oregon by Louis D. Brandeis.

[38] *Ibid.* The doctrine that "sex is a valid basis for classification" enunciated in the Muller case has always been one open to abuse. Protective legislation enacted for their benefit has often been used to discriminate against women: regulations on the hours of work or limitations on weights they can lift can become "reasons" why they may not work overtime, be promoted, etc.

legal situation—the result of such paternalism—it should be quite as revealing to compare two of the central documents of sexual politics in the Victorian period—Mill's *Subjection of Women,* and Ruskin's "Of Queen's Gardens."[39] Compressed within these two statements is nearly the whole range and possibility of Victorian thought on the subject.

In Mill one encounters the realism of sexual politics, in Ruskin its romance and the benign aspect of its myth. Much of the other portion of Victorian sexual myth is included in Ruskin by implication, for his virtuous matron relies for her very existence on that spectral figure of the temptress, her complement in the period's dichotomous literary fantasy—just as in life, the two classes of women, wife and whore, account for the socio-sexual division under the double standard. If Mill's essay recommends itself for its lucid statement of an actual situation, Ruskin's lecture recommends itself as one of the most complete insights obtainable into that compulsive masculine fantasy one might call the official Victorian attitude. Its other side, the darker side of male attitude, can be found in fiction, and especially in poetry. The dark woman, the period avatar of feminine evil, lurks there in subterranean menace, stationed at intervals all the way from Tennyson's verse to the more scabrous pornography of the age. But the daytime lady in "Of Queen's Gardens" is an expression of the more normative beliefs of the Victorian middle class at the moment of their most optimistic and public profession.

It must always be understood that the sexual revolution made headway slowly and against enormous odds of cultural resistance. While the Victorian period is the first in history to face the issue of patriarchy and the condition of women under its rule, it did so in a bewildering variety of ways: courageously and intelligently as in Mill and Engels; half-heartedly as in the tepid criticism of the novelists who describe it, with bland disingenuousness as in Ruskin; or with turbulent ambivalence as in the poets Tennyson, Rossetti, Swinburne, and Wilde. Intermittent degrees and variations on all these patterns are to be found everywhere, and the subject is a vexed and difficult one. Dickens, for example, achieved a nearly perfect indictment of both patriarchy and capitalism in *Dombey and Son,* a novel virtually inspired by the phenomenon of prenatal preference, and a superb illustration of Engels' state-

[39] John Stuart Mill, *The Subjection of Women* (1869), reprinted in *Three Essays by J. S. Mill,* World's Classics Series (London, Oxford University Press, 1966). John Ruskin's "Of Queen's Gardens" in *Sesame and Lilies,* first published in 1865, reprinted in an American edition (Homewood Publishing Company, 1902). After having found in "Of Queen's Gardens" a representative, and perhaps even a definitive expression of the chivalrous position, it is pleasant to discover that so distinguished a Victorian scholar as Walter Houghton is in agreement as to its significance in the period: "This lecture of Ruskin's is the most important single document I know for the characteristic idealization of love, women, and the home in Victorian thought." Walter Houghton, *The Victorian Frame of Mind* (Yale, 1957), p. 343. In view of the present neglect of this work (Victorian scholars tend to look embarrassed when it is mentioned), it is material to recall that *Sesame and Lilies* was also Ruskin's most popular volume.

ments on the subordination of women within the system of property. Yet
Dickens did this without ever relinquishing the sentimental version of women
which is the whole spirit of Ruskin's "Of Queen's Gardens." It is one of the
more disheartening flaws in the master's work that nearly all the "serious"
women in Dickens' fiction, with the exception of Nancy and a handful of her
criminal sisters, are insipid goodies carved from the same soap as Ruskin's
Queens. Indeed, an acquaintance with Ruskin's "Of Queen's Gardens" is a
great aid in the study of Victorian fiction.

One is tempted to see in Victorian chivalry a transition phase between the
open male supremacy of earlier ages, such as the bullying license of the
Regency, and the revolutionary climate of the early twentieth century
when feminism was at its height. While one might object that it is to this latter period which Mill and Engels belong in spirit, they wrote in 1869 and
1884 respectively, and their very modern books were also products of the
Victorian era, however advanced or before their time they may appear. The
realities they deal in were ones that impinged on Victorian sensibility very
acutely, either directly through the growing feminist agitation for reform, or
indirectly in the strictures on women's social and legal disabilities which began to appear in the novel. Among the poets the effects of change are mir-
rored in the unconscious fantasies of a masculine sensibility often guilty, resentful, or at bay, and driven to compensatory myths of feminine evil, while
among women writers one sees the new ideas producing a growing restlessness and rebellion at their condition.

Ruskin presented his lecture at the Town Hall of Manchester in 1864 before a mixed audience of middle-class men and women. It appeared in book
form with the publication of *Sesame and Lilies* in 1865, and was reissued in
1871 with an additional preface perfumed with Ruskin's middle-aged infatu-
tion over Rose La Touche, with whom he had fallen in love back in 1858,
when she was nine and he thirty-nine years of age. That the beaming gallantry in "Of Queen's Gardens" has often the aspect of senile eroticism addressing itself to beautiful ignorance should perhaps call for little astonishment in
an age when every woman was legally a minor.

Despite the lavish flattery with which Ruskin approaches the women in his
audience, a group of bourgeoises whom he addresses with grating regularity
as "Queens," he had in fact felt and probably smarted under the pressure of
feminist insurgence. "There never was a time when wilder words were
spoken or more vain imagination permitted respecting this question" he be-
moans—the "question" is of course "the 'rights' of women," Ruskin fussily
putting rights in quotation marks.[40]

<hr>

[40] Ruskin *op. cit.*, p. 128. The preface (1871) refers to further "questions" which
have arisen since the lecture "respecting the education and claims of women." These
have "greatly troubled simple minds and excited restless ones." Disdaining to pursue such
nonsense, Ruskin proceeds to harangue the female reader on virtue, his tone growing
didactic ("Take out your Latin dictionary and look out "sollenis" and fix the word well

Assuring us at the outset that he is no crude chauvinist, Ruskin asserts that he is steering a middle course. He seems to direct his efforts against the "left" of feminism and the effect of his lecture should be to refute it with the courtly platitude that women are loved and honored, have nothing to complain of and are even royalty, so long as they stay at home. His strategy appears to be an attempt to subvert the new heresy through the doctrine of the "separate spheres," the period's most ingenious mechanism for restraining insurgent women.

Mill did not speak for queens, nor was he arrested at the nubile level of Rose La Touche. The Subjection of Women was written in 1861, three years before "Of Queen's Gardens," but as Mill took great care in the timing of his books, it was not published until 1869, two years before Ruskin reprinted his own statement. Mill composed his essay in collaboration with his stepdaughter, Helen Taylor, and claimed that his own part in it was largely inspired by his wife, Harriet Taylor. There is no reason to doubt that the knowledge of female psychology which infuses the book required a woman's assistance, but the style and the logic are Mill's own. The Subjection of Women is a reasoned and eloquent statement of the actual position of women through history as well as an attack on the conditions of legal bondage, debilitating education, and the stifling ethic of "wifely subjection" within the Victorian period. It is argued as powerfully as the essay On Liberty and is as full of Mill's splendidly controlled humanist outrage as any of his statements on slavery or serfdom, to which he draws frequent parallels.

A political realist, Mill was quite aware of the revolutionary character of his thesis:

That the principle which regulates the existing social relations between the two sexes—the legal subordination of one sex to the other—is wrong in itself, and now one of the chief hindrances to human improvement; and that it ought to be replaced by a principle of perfect equality, admitting no power or privilege on the one side, nor disability on the other.[41]

This was a drastic recommendation to make then, just as it is now, and Mill was fully awake to the resistance he would meet, the appalled uproar, the irrationality of the old school, chauvinist or chivalrous, neither of whom would have dreamed of producing real evidence for their assertion that things were quite as they should be between man and woman. Mill even predicts the uncritical bigotry of the opposition: "In every respect the burden is hard on those who attack an almost universal opinion. They must be very fortunate as well as unusually capable if they obtain a hearing at all."[42] For

in your mind") and even punitive ("Of all the insolent, all the foolish persuasions that by any chance could enter and hold your empty little heart"), etc. Preface, pp. 9, 10, 13.
[41] Mill, op. cit., p. 427.
[42] Mill, op. cit., p. 428.

all his extraordinary capability, Mill was scarcely fortunate before a male audience: the reaction in the reviews was disastrous; he was denounced as mad or immoral, often as both.[43]

I The Problem of Nature

Reason has always been an intruder in the area of sexual prejudice. Ruskin, who was by no means a stupid man, has recourse to less intellectual energy in "Of Queen's Gardens" than anywhere else in his work. In turning his mind toward *Lilies* it was enough for him to rely on sentiment, a vague nostalgia about the heroic middle ages, and saccharine assertions about The Home. Mill remarks that one of the most tedious and characteristic mental habits of the nineteenth century is its reaction against eighteenth-century rationalism, and its quirk of trusting instead to "the unreasoning elements in human nature."[44] Ruskin's lecture is a demonstration of this observation.

If Ruskin may be said to have a thesis, it is altogether a simpler affair than Mill's, calculated to stroke rather than ruffle his listeners. Beginning with the rather complacent assumption that the educated middle classes exercise a "kingship" over the "illguided and illiterate," Ruskin's task is simply to divide a little section of the realm off for Queens, or as he is pleased to put it, determine "what special portion of this royal authority, arising out of noble education, may be rightly possessed by women."[45] If there was just an element of pandering to social pretension in the industrialists he had addressed as "kings," Ruskin is unrestrained in the unction he directs toward his female hearers, who "if they rightly understood and exercised this royal or gracious influence, the order and beauty induced by such benignant power would justify us in speaking of the territories over which each of them reigned as 'Queen's Gardens.' "[46]

In professing that one cannot conclude what the "queenly power of women should be until we are agreed what their ordinary power should be,"[47] Ruskin is only saying that the role of upper- and middle-class female is dependent on the nature and abilities of the female herself. Were these equal

---

[43] A reviewer rebuked Mill for his interest in "the strangest" and the "most ignoble and mischievous of all the popular feelings of the age," another was incredulous that Mill could imagine the relations of men and women might ever "work on a purely voluntary principle," while others found the book indecent. Thirty years later it could still be anathematized as "rank moral and social anarchy." See Michael St. John Packe, *The Life of John Stuart Mill* (New York, Macmillan, 1954), p. 495. Mill's biographer comments: "Of anything Mill ever wrote, *The Subjection of Women* aroused the most antagonism." *Ibid.* Women received the book rather differently than did men; the Woman's Movement welcomed it as a handmade text.

[44] Mill, *op. cit.*, p. 430.

[45] Ruskin, *op. cit.*, pp. 125, 126, 127. (The preceding lecture, "Of King's Treasuries," dealing with education and poverty and addressed largely to men, is excellent and by no means complacent: nothing could afford a greater contrast than the two pieces.)

[46] *Ibid.*, p. 127.

[47] *Ibid.*

to the male's, she could be a full member of the elite, not just the auxiliary he proposes. It was precisely to avoid the danger of sexual equality within this or any other class, that he and his fellows invented the doctrine of the separate spheres and proclaimed it "Nature." The two great poles of influence in the Victorian period are Mill and Carlyle. Frequently at odds with the rational tradition which Mill represents, Ruskin, following Carlyle, tends to rely more upon emotionalism than reason. And to those under Carlyle's influence Nature is not only an emotional term, but all too often an eminently convenient gadget which can be directed at random to justify class, absolutism, feudalism, or any other system they choose to endorse. Ruskin was never a democrat like Mill.[48] Instead, he combined moral outrage against the plight of the poor with an excited longing for the heroism and grace he found in aristocratic and medieval revivalism. Yet at his best moments he transcends this snobbery altogether in a splendid compassion for the poor, Biblical in the energy of its denunciation of Philistine avarice.

As he is far too canny to speak openly of sexual status, Ruskin arrives at it inevitably through adhering to traditional sexual stereotype in role and temperament. However silly and old-fashioned his phraseology may appear, his tactic is perennially popular; it re-emerged in more sophisticated terms in the period of reaction which set in with the 1930s. He immediately renounces all claims to speak of the "superiority" of one sex to another, as if they could be compared in similar things. "Each has what the other has not; each completes the other. They are in nothing alike, and the happiness and perfection of both depends on each asking and receiving from the other what the other only can give."[49] This sounds nice enough until one remembers it is the threadbare tactic of justifying social and temperamental differences by biological ones. For the sexes are inherently in everything alike, save reproductive systems, secondary sexual characteristics, orgasmic capacity, and genetic and morphological structure. Perhaps the only things they can uniquely exchange are semen and transudate. One would like to be sure it was not upon this method of barter that Ruskin intended to construct his social economy.

Having through mere assertion "proven" that the sexes are complementary opposites, Ruskin then proceeds to map out their worlds, reserving the entire scope of human endeavor for the one, and a little hothouse for the other:

> Now their separate characters are briefly these. The man's power is active progressive, defensive. He is eminently the doer, the creator, the discoverer, the defender. His intellect is for speculation and invention; his energy for adventure,

48 "I am, and my father was before me, a violent Tory of the old school—Walter Scott's school, that is to say, and Homer's." John Ruskin, *Praeterita*, reprinted in part in *The Genius of John Ruskin*, Selections from his writings edited by John D. Rosenberg (Houghton Mifflin, Boston, 1963), p. 461.

49 Ruskin, "Of Queen's Gardens," p. 143.

for war and for conquest . . . But the woman's power is for rule, not for battle
and her intellect is not for invention or recreation, but sweet ordering, arrangement, and decision . . . By her office and place, she is protected from all danger
and temptation. The man, in his rough work in the open world, must encounter all peril and trial—to him therefore must be the failure, the offence,
the inevitable error; often he must be wounded or subdued, often misled, and
always hardened.[50]

Of course Ruskin has not only glossed over the fact of ruler and ruled in
pretentious and inflated language. He has also deliberately confused the customary with the natural, the convenient with the inevitable. Mill is aware
that the culturally created distinctions of temperament and role underlie
and support the invidious distinctions of sexual status, and are indeed the
latter's method of inculcation and perpetuation. He also believes that the
practice of splitting male and female humanity into two neat little divisions
and calling the distinctions in their social and intellectual situation "Nature"
is pre-eminently a political gesture.

To those who might object to his comparisons with other "forms of unjust
power" Mill answers that the master class have always regarded their privileges as natural; Aristotle could see no harm in slavery—nor could the American planter class. Both justified their injustices on the grounds of nature and
insisted the subordinate group were born to their position and reserved for it
by God. Monarchy was often defended on the same grounds as springing
from a still more ancient patriarchal authority still more "natural": "So true is
this that the unnatural generally means only uncustomary, and that everything which is usual appears natural. The subjection of women to men being
a universal custom, any departure from it quite naturally appears unnatural."[51]

Ruskin's whole structure of complementary and separate spheres based on
natural proclivity is undermined by Mill's logical objection that nothing can
be known of the inherent nature of a personality so subject to—as to be virtually created by—circumstantial conditioning:

Standing on the ground of common sense and the constitution of the human
mind, I deny that anyone knows, or can know, the nature of the two sexes,
so long as they have only been seen in their present relation to one another . . .
What is now called the nature of woman is an eminently artificial thing—the

---

[50] *Ibid.,* pp. 143–44. It is hardly necessary to comment on the wonderful license such
a system grants to the male to exploit other human beings. At home his "better half"
remains virtuous and ready to replenish his vanishing humanity. It is a perfect ethic for
a harsh business society. Home and the little wife enclosed there represent—then as now—
the last idyll, the final pastoral. Today the suburbs serve this function and there the
harried commercial man keeps his mate and flock of kids at pasture.

[51] Mill, *op. cit.,* p. 441.

result of forced repression in some directions, unnatural stimulation in others. It may be asserted without scruple, that no other class of dependents have had their character so entirely distorted from its natural proportions by their relation with their masters.[52]

Mill realized that what is commonly regarded as feminine character is but the predictable outcome of a highly artificial system of cultivation, or to adopt his own metaphor, society's female is a plant grown half in a steam bath and half in the snow. He foretells that the idolatrous attitude toward the myth of nature is bound to disintegrate before a "sound psychology." Deplorably, such assistance has yet to appease, but in the meantime one may rely on Mill's own. For its psychological contribution is the book's great achievement: Mill's psychology is grounded in a more lucid distinction between prescription and description than one encounters in Freud,[53] and a far more intelligent grasp of the effects of environment and circumstance. Mill is also sensitive to the mechanisms by which conservative thought construes the status quo into the inevitable, a fine trait in a social psychologist. Until we undertake "an analytic study of the most important departments of psychology, the laws of the influence of circumstances on character"—we are, Mill observes, unlikely to be able to know anything about the natural differences of sexual personality, for "the most elementary knowledge of the circumstances in which they have been placed clearly points out the causes that have made them what they are."[54] Meanwhile, since nothing is known it is presumption in man to "lay down the law to women as to what is, or is not, their vocation."[55]

[52] *Ibid.*, p. 451.

[53] Freud knew and disliked Mill's essay. He had even translated it. He probably did not know Ruskin's lecture, but it is easy to see how much more he would have approved of it. Freud responded to Mill by arguing that the sexes are inherently different in temperament, and then, despite the logical contradiction, by deploring changes in upbringing which might erode these differences. He pays chivalrous compliment to "the most delightful thing the world can offer us—our ideal of womanhood." He is also convinced that "nature has determined woman's destiny through beauty, charm, and sweetness." Yet he jumps from ridiculing Mill and his book ("one simply cannot find him human") ("he lacked in many matters, the sense of the absurd, for example in that of female emancipation and the woman's question altogether") to a stance of personal defensiveness about his fiancée: "If for instance, I imagined my gentle sweet girl as a competitor it would only end by my telling her, as I did seventeen months ago, that I am fond of her and that I implore her to withdraw from the struggle into the calm uncompetitive activity of my home." Ernest Jones, *The Life and Work of Sigmund Freud,* Vol. I (New York, Basic Books, 1953), pp. 175–76. In his letters, Freud was in the habit of addressing his fiancée with paternal condescension as "my precious little woman," "my sweet child," etc. See Ernst Freud, *Letters of Sigmund Freud* (New York, 1960), letter 76, p. 161.

[54] Mill, *op. cit.,* pp. 452–53.

[55] *Ibid.*, p. 457.

II The Problem of Education

Because he understands how conditioning produces a sexual temperament appropriate to sexual role, Mill is in an excellent position to understand how woman is the product of the system which oppresses her: how all her education, formal and informal, is dedicated to perpetuating it. He also believes "the mental differences supposed to exist between women and men are but the natural effects of the differences in their education and circumstances, and indicate no radical differences, far less radical inferiority of nature."[56] Mill's description of the education assigned to women tallies exactly with Ruskin's. Yet there is one alarming difference: Ruskin finds it a very good thing, whereas Mill despises it as a minimal literary acquaintance with decorative Culture deliberately designed to be superficial—in Mill's derogatory phrase, "an education of the sentiments rather than of the understanding,"[57] calculated to render women fit for submission, vicarious experience, and a service ethic of largely ineffective philanthropy.

Since he has delineated their sphere, it remains for Ruskin to "fit" women to it. Whereas Mill is eager to train women in every branch of arts and science, to open professional learning to them, that the world's available talent might be doubled—Ruskin would not be so precipitate: "We cannot consider how education may fit them for any widely extending duty until we are agreed what is their true constant duty."[58] Translated (it is continually necessary to translate chivalrous sentiment) this only means that women should not be educated in any real sense at all, least of all for the sake of education itself. Instead they should be indoctrinated to contribute their "modest service" to the male. Ruskin's formula is an education deliberately inferior by any standard, and Ruskin's standards are high in the case of young men. In an earlier lecture, he had derided short-sighted parents who aspired no further than adjusting their heirs to "their station in life."[59] He can rail at the pragmatic middle class for its unimaginative vocational interest, a low instinct for which he expresses an unqualified contempt, yet he feels it imperative that the education of women be no more ambitious than merely habituating them to "their place."

Ruskin believes in the "subjection" of wives and says so. In general the task of the woman is to serve man and the family through "womanly guidance," exercise some vague and remote good influence on everyone, and dispense a bit of charity from time to time. It is to this end that education should prepare her. As a theory of education it is nearly an exact parallel of Rousseau's, save for its greater emphasis upon good works. But Ruskin also furnishes definitive propositions about female education; it is to be directed toward

---

[56] *Ibid.*, p. 489.
[57] *Ibid.*, p. 532.
[58] Ruskin, *op. cit.*, p. 128.
[59] Ruskin, "Of King's Treasuries," *Sesame and Lilies*, p. 46.

making women wise, "not for self-development, but for self-renunciation."[60] This is surely graphic enough. It is sufficient that a woman be well-intentioned and a model listener: "A man ought to know any language or science he learns, thoroughly; while a woman ought to know the same language or science only so far as may enable her to sympathize in her husband's pleasures, and in those of his best friends."[61]

Ruskin is solicitous to warn women away from accomplishment. They may get a smattering of information, but they are given orders to halt at the point of difficulty: "understand the meaning, the inevitableness of natural laws; and follow at least one of them as far as to the threshold of that bitter valley of humiliation, into which only the wisest and bravest of men can descend."[62] Theology is explicitly forbidden them, Ruskin apprehending that serious female interference would be fatal to patriarchal religion. Here a certain personal hostility lurking behind the chivalrous posture obtrudes itself. Ruskin irritably complains that while they generally admit they have no aptitude for the hard sciences, women plunge right into divinity, "that science in which the greatest men have trembled and the wisest erred."[63] A passage of invective follows, castigating those impious females who, as Ruskin puts it, crawl up the steps of God and attempt to divide His throne with Him.[64]

Much of Ruskin's educational program is eked out of the Lucy poems of William Wordsworth, from whence he appears to have procured a recipe for the "delicate strength" and the "perfect loveliness of a woman's countenance" which are the end products of a salutary acquaintance with sun and shower. Joan of Arc, he informs us blandly, was entirely educated by Nature. The obsession with Nature is very strong in conjunction with statements on women: boys must be "chiseled" into shape, but as females are "Nature," Ruskin is assured they grow effortlessly like flowers. Even classical libraries have no effect on them as blossoms do not give themselves to the contaminations of learning. Together with the graceful studies of music, art, and literature, Nature itself constitutes the fourth branch of female education in Ruskin's pedagogy. Through Nature she will grow in piety, which is well; piety is less dangerous than theology. Under the influence of such thoughts, the glowing texture of Ruskin's prose begins to melt and flow like the unctuous sludge of Chapel preaching. Metaphysics and astronomy should be taught to a female on the following plan: "She is to be taught somewhat to understand

---

[60] Ruskin, "Of Queen's Gardens," *Sesame and Lilies*, p. 145.

[61] *Ibid.*, p. 153.

[62] *Ibid.*, pp. 149–50. The rhetorical stress on "wisest and bravest," and the "valley of humiliation" is directly at odds with the earlier statement that "a man ought to learn any language or science he learns thoroughly." This is *any* man, not the "wisest and bravest."

[63] *Ibid.*, pp. 151–52.

[64] Ruskin's own unfortunate experiences with religious women, his mother and Rose La Touche, create strongly extenuating circumstances for the animosity here.

the nothingness of the proportion which that little world in which she lives and loves, bears to the world in which God lives and loves."[65] As it is "not the object of education to turn the woman into a dictionary," he is persuaded she need not trouble much over geography and history.[66] As regards the latter study, Ruskin advises she confine herself simply to an appreciation of the romantic drama and the demonstrations of religious law afforded by the past.

In Mill's opinion, the precious educational conditioning Ruskin has just outlined with gallant protestations of his affection, is nothing less than the most ingenious system of mental enslavement in history:

> All causes, social and natural, combine to make it unlikely that women should be collectively rebellious to the power of men. They are so far in a position different from all other subject classes that their masters require something far more from them than actual service. Men do not want solely the obedience of women, they want their sentiments. All men, except the most brutish, desire to have, in the woman most nearly connected with them, not a forced slave but a willing one; not a slave merely, but a favorite. They have therefore put everything in practice to enslave their minds. The masters of all other slaves rely, for maintaining of obedience, on fear; either fear of themselves, or religious fears. The masters of women wanted more than simple obedience, and they turned the whole force of education to effect their purpose.[67]

It is hard to believe that Mill and Ruskin are discussing the same subject— or, since each claims he has the best interests of women at heart—that one of the two does not prevaricate. Both are sincere, yet Ruskin, whose educational scheme is patently not the favor he proclaims it to be, is much like a paternal racist of the more genial variety, fairly unconscious of the real drift of his statements. Only occasionally does his hostility peek forth, carefully disguised as a moralist's wrath against frivolous "queens" who forsake their heaven of good works to gad about in petty snobbery or vanity. Moreover, Ruskin's purpose is to ennoble a system of subordination through hopeful rhetoric, whereas Mill's purpose is to expose it.

III THE DOMESTIC THEME

This antithesis grows to greater proportion when the two come to discuss two favorite Victorian themes—The Home and the Goodness of Women. Ruskin's passage on the domestic scene, which he presents in the strongest language as the "woman's true place," is a classic of its kind.

> This is the true nature of home—it is the place of peace; the shelter, not only from all injury, but from all terror, doubt, and division. In so far as it is not

[65] "Of Queen's Gardens," p. 151.
[66] *Ibid.*, p. 150.
[67] Mill, *op. cit.*, pp. 443–44.

this, it is not home; so far as the anxieties of the outer life penetrate into it, and the inconsistently-minded, unknown, unloved, or hostile society of the outer world is allowed by either husband or wife to cross the threshold it ceases to be a home; it is then only a part of the outer world which you have roofed over and lighted fire in. But so far as it is a sacred place, a vestal temple, a temple of the hearth watched over by household gods, before whose faces none may come but those whom they can receive with love—so far as it is this, and the roof and the fire are types only of a nobler shade and light, shade as of the rock in a weary land, and the light as of Pharos in the stormy sea—so far it vindicates the name and fulfills the praise of home.

And wherever a true wife comes, this home is always round her. The stars only may be over her head, the glow-worm in the night-cold grass may be the only fire at her foot, but home is wherever she is; and for a noble woman it stretches far round her, better than ceiled with cedar or painted with vermillion, shedding its quiet light far for those who else were homeless.[68]

Mill sees it differently. The home is the center of a system he defines as "domestic slavery." Since she lives under the first as well as the last, or longest, rule of force in the history of tyranny, Mill calmly declares that woman is no more than a bondservant within marriage. He then summarizes the history of this institution as based on sale or enforcement; the husband holding the power of life or death over his wife. He has some impressive legal-historical evidence: although a husband might divorce his wife, she could not escape him; English law defined the murder of a husband as petty treason (as distinguished from high treason) because a husband stood to a wife in the relation of a sovereign; the penalty was death by burning.[69] Most slaves, Mill argues, had greater rights than wives under the law: the Romans reserved their *pecuniam* to them and some leisure was always permitted them. Even female slaves were sometimes spared coercion into sexual intimacy with their masters. Yet no wife is exempt from sexual assault, however much both partners might despise each other.[70] Under the law, as Mill points out, a man owns wife and child entirely. Should his wife leave him, she is entitled to take nothing with her, and her husband may, if he wishes to exercise his legal rights, compel her to return. Divorce, Mill urges with ironic force, would seem the least concession in a system where "a woman is denied any lot in life but that of being the personal body-servant of a despot."[71]

While admitting that he has "described the wife's legal position, not her actual treatment,"[72] Mill argues that law is not custom, but permission. No

[68] Ruskin, "Of Queen's Gardens," pp. 144–45.

[69] Mill, *op. cit.*, p. 461.

[70] The theme of enforced sexual relations within marriage figures rather prominently in Victorian literature, notably in Browning's *The Ring and The Book*.

[71] Mill, *op. cit.*, p. 464.

[72] *Ibid.*, p. 465.

tyranny exerts its possibilities without mitigation: "Every absolute king does not sit at his window to enjoy the groans of his tortured subjects."[73] But they are within his reach in every legal sense, should he crave them. "Whatever gratifications of pride there is in the possession of power, and whatever personal interest in its exercise, is in this case not confined to a limited class, but common to the whole male sex."[74] As Mill remonstrates, one deals here with absolute power, for the law allows it, and while probably not resorted to as frequently as once, it is still there for the wise and the foolish, the loving and the hating. Fortunately marriages, and the people who make them, are far better than the law, but every danger yet remains inherent in such law, and one of the main objects of Mill's essay is to argue in the strongest terms for changes in the legal status of women.

In both Roman and American slavery, Mill reminds one, affection was by no means uncommon. But it is as perniciously naïve to judge "domestic slavery" by its best instances, the loving rule and loving submission which Ruskin dwells on, as it is foolish to neglect its worst occasions. And of those worst occasions, Mill is too acute a student of nineteenth-century life to be ignorant.[75] Even Ruskin shows he has heard of them in a reference of tasteless levity to "Bill and Nancy," whom he deliberately misrepresents as sparring partners, "down in that back street . . . knocking each other's teeth out."[76] The allusion is of course to Bill Sykes and the woman he clubbed to death in Dickens' *Oliver Twist*.[77] Such instances of brutality, ranging from blows to murder, were very common occurrences in the period, and though Ruskin tosses them off with a loutish attempt at class humor, Mill is far too humane either to try to find them funny, or, as in Ruskin's Punch-and-Judy show version, to misrepresent the facts.

Mill is perfectly aware that among the poor the female is subject to greater indignities than anywhere else, as she is the only creature in the world over whom an exploited man can claim superiority and "prove" it by crude force.

And how many thousands are there among the lowest classes in every country, who, without being in a legal sense malefactors in every other respect, because in every other quarter their aggressions meet with resistance, indulge the utmost habitual excesses of bodily violence toward the unhappy wife, who

[73] *Ibid.*, p. 466.

[74] *Ibid.*, p. 438.

[75] The Criminal Procedures Act of 1853 attempted, with disastrous effect, to abridge somewhat an Englishman's "right" to beat his wife. Resentment at such a suggestion appears to have but increased the practice. See W. L. Burns, *The Age of Equipose* (London, 1964).

[76] Ruskin, "Of King's Treasuries," *Sesame and Lilies*, p. 46.

[77] The description of Nancy's hideous death is one of the most dynamic in Dickens' work and likely to be the most appalling in the period. Dickens had a sick fascination for the episode, hastening his own death by dramatizing hers at public readings, counting the evening a success only if a great many women fainted. See Edmund Wilson's historic essay, "Dickens, The Two Scrooges," in *The Wound and The Bow* (Oxford, 1965).

alone, at least of grown persons, can neither repel nor escape from their brutality; and toward whom the excess of dependence inspires their mean and savage natures, not with generous forbearance and a point of honor to behave well to one whose lot in life is trusted entirely to their kindness, but on the contrary with a notion that the law has delivered her to them as their thing, to be used at their pleasure, and that they are not expected to practice the consideration towards her which is required from them towards everybody else.[78]

In the nineteenth century, as today, unreported, even unremarked upon, assault among women too servile or too intimidated to risk further attacks was a customary event among the lower classes. Mill urges that as "there can be little check to brutality consistent with leaving the victim still in the power of the executioner," divorce should be permitted upon conviction of assault, lest convictions become unobtainable "for want of a prosecutor, or for want of a witness."[79] Further down the rungs of connubial sensibility: "the vilest malefactor has some wretched woman tied to him, against whom he can commit any atrocity except killing her, and if tolerably cautious, can do that without much danger of the legal penalty."[80] Such occasions were a favorite Victorian theme, particularly in the melodrama. The treatment afforded such subject matter, then as now, is often a curiously hypocritical mixture of prurient delight and moral compunction.

Since the conditions of any institution are so liable to abuse and Mill's contentions are grounded in legal reality, Ruskin's domestic idyll is somewhat more difficult to infer from the facts than Mill's description. Ruskin will trust to chivalry. Mill regards it as an evolutionary stage, only a slight improvement over the barbarities which preceded it and hardly a reliable deterrent, depending as it does upon the gratuitous good will of an elite. Mill had consulted social history and law; Ruskin trusted to poetry, and his history of women is based on the gossamer of literary idealization. Out of the political wisdom afforded by the portraits of Shakespearian heroines, "perfect women," "steadfast in grave hope and errorless purpose," "strong always to sanctify, infallibly faithful"—together with the tender beauties of Walter Scott's romances—"patient," full of "untiring self-sacrifice" and "deeply restrained affection," Ruskin attempts to re-create the sexual history of the Western peoples.[81] As further evidence, he introduces the posture of the courtly lover encountered in Dante and the troubadours, sworn to serve and obey a mistress. Then, with impressive bravura, Ruskin declares that ancient Greek "knights" also practiced courtly love, boasting he could quote antique originals to this effect, were it not that his audience might have difficulty in following him. In any case, he will not be so mean with his hearers as to deny them some descriptions of the "simple mother and wife's heart of Andromache," the

[78] Mill, _op. cit._, pp. 467–68.
[79] _Ibid._, p. 468.
[80] _Ibid._, p. 467.
[81] Ruskin, "Of Queen's Gardens," pp. 133, 134, 135.

housewifely calm of Penelope, the "bowing down of Iphegenia, lamb-like and silent," and Alcestis' self-immolation to save her husband's life.[82] Ruskin rejoices in this piece of "self-sacrifice" presenting it as evidence that the Greek mind had a premonition of the Christian doctrine of Resurrection. The entire "historical" passage in the lecture, lengthy and presumably central to its argument, is hard to account for. Ruskin was not an ignorant man.

It seems at times that historical misrepresentation can never appear too egregious when its subject is woman. Certain of his contentions, Ruskin calls upon his stout middle-class audience to doubt the validity of his assertions. He appears convinced, and is sure they will be as well, that the poetry to which he has alluded is no less than a true and accurate picture of the condition of women in the societies in which these literary productions originated, since it is inconceivable that great authors "in the main works of their lives, are amusing themselves with a fictitious and ideal view of the relation between man and woman." Nor can this be mere empty abstraction, but must be fact, for Ruskin declares it is "worse than fictitious or idle—for a thing to be imaginary, yet desirable, if it were possible."[83]

While insisting that "in all Christian ages which have been remarkable for their purity of progress, there has been absolute yielding of obedient devotion, by the lover to his mistress,"[84] Ruskin neatly reassures the nervous suspicion mounting among the burghers who hear him that while this may be all very well for courtship, it is not appropriate for marriage where he agrees that the proper thing is a "true wifely subjection."[85] What follows is that tidy duplicity in social policy which Ruskin codified in the dogma of separate spheres: the wife shall be subject but will "guide," even "rule" her lord by serving as his conscience. This pretends to forfeit status through semantics. Yet no forfeiture is involved. Maintaining the most traditional roles, Ruskin prudently reserves the world for the male, leaving the female an ancillary circle of housewifely and philanthropic activity. Moreover, the capricious gallantry of his enunciations about the "respect" due to "virtuous women" would suggest that status—dignity and equality in human affairs— were not the issue at all. And at its most fulsome it would even insinuate that because of the gratitude of her "lord" (as Ruskin refers to that personage) the female actually enjoys a higher status than the male. By transposing political position to moral rectitude, we are given to imagine that women are "better" than men. Unless, of course, they are worse—then God help them.

What Mill has to say on the subject is directly at odds with all this. While in the lower classes the ethic of male supremacy may take the form of brutality, in the middle classes it tends toward the rankest hypocrisy; among the educated "the inequality is kept as much as possible out of sight; above all out

82 *Ibid.*, pp. 137, 138.
83 *Ibid.*, p. 139.
84 *Ibid.*, p. 140.
85 *Ibid.*, p. 142.

of sight of the children," with "the compensations of the chivalrous feeling being made prominent, while the servitude which requires them is kept in the background."[86] But the facts of the situation intrude themselves quickly enough on the minds of young men, however they are raised. If their education is chivalrous they are only being preserved from an actuality they soon enough discover. Mill was raised by a domestic tyrant who encouraged his children to despise their mother. Ruskin's childhood was very different and he undoubtedly acquired a becoming politeness of attitude. Mill was spared the pretension of chivalry; Ruskin appears to have known it so long he became unable to recognize it for what it was until he no longer wished to do so. Mill's observations are an interesting glimpse into boyhood:

> . . . people are little aware . . . how early the notion of his inherent superiority to a girl arises in his mind; how it grows with his growth and strengthens with his strength; how it is inoculated by one schoolboy upon another; how early the youth thinks himself superior to his mother, owing her perhaps forbearance, but no real respect; and how sublime and sultan-like a sense of superiority he feels, above all, over the woman whom he honours by admitting her to a partnership of his life. Is it imagined that all this does not pervert the whole manner of existence of the man, both as an individual and as a social being . . . Above all, when the feeling of being raised above the whole of the other sex is combined with personal authority over one individual among them; the situation, if a school of conscientious and affectionate forbearance to those whose strongest points of character are conscience and affection, is to men of another quality, a regularly constituted Academy or Gymnasium for training them in arrogance and overbearingness . . .[87]

The effect of male ascendency upon human society in general and the masculine character (which governs society) in particular is such that it fosters notions of superiority and satisfaction over differential or prejudicial treatment from earliest youth. In Mill's analysis, the system of sexual dominance is the very prototype of other abuses of power and other forms of egotism. Just as Engels came to see in sexual super- and subordination the model for later hierarchies of rank, class, and wealth, Mill had discovered in it the psychological foundations of other species of oppression. "All the selfish propensities, the self-worship, the unjust self-preference, which exist among mankind, have their source and root in, and derive their principal nourishment from, the present constitution of the relation of men and women."[88]

Chivalry and all—marriage is really feudal, and Mill hates feudalism. At present little more than a "school of despotism in which the virtues of des-

---

[86] Mill, *op. cit.*, p. 523.

[87] *Ibid.*, pp. 523-24. One is reminded of Jefferson's eloquent demonstration of how slavery corrupted white youth even from their childhood.

[88] *Ibid.*, p. 522.

potism, but also its vices, are largely nourished"[89] the family can afford no real love to its members until it is based on a situation of total equality among them. His position of authority is less likely to inspire the husband to affection than to "an intense feeling of the dignity and importance of his own personality; making him disdain a yoke for himself . . . he is abundantly ready to impose on others for his own interest and glorification."[90] With an admirable touch of candor, Mill admits that no man would wish for himself the conditions of life he chivalrously consigns to women: the pastoral coign of a Queen's Garden would appall any man confined to it—perhaps Ruskin most of all.

The single concession Ruskin's sphere theory makes to its rule that male "duties," meaning privileges, are "public" (war, money, politics, and learning) whereas female "duties," meaning responsibilities, are "private," e.g., domestic —is in the realm of philanthropy.[91] In pursuit of its kind offices, Ruskin is inclined to permit woman a narrow latitude to step beyond her sphere, never into the great world of nineteenth-century reform, but into the little world of the homes of what were then known as the "honest poor." There, while sewing garments and exchanging recipes, the respectable wife might make some minuscule restitution for the ravages her masculine class-counterpart had been busy accomplishing all day through his worldly prerogatives of politics, money, and technology.

Ruskin, who had thought of a scheme whereby English boys might be "knighted" and English girls "invested" with the official title of "lady" under the auspices of a national chivalry movement something like the boy scouts, has a kindred inspiration for the adult middle class.[92] The word "Lady," he tells them, means "bread-giver"; or "loaf-giver"; "Lord" means "maintainer of laws."[93] Role should be determined accordingly: under the euphemism of "maintainer of laws" the male appropriates all power, and the female dispenses charity. In its ersatz-medieval character, the whole thing is not only depressingly fantastical, it is singularly inappropriate to the conditions of nineteenth-century industrialism whose nearly infinite economic injustices Ruskin felt so keenly. These could scarcely be ameliorated by the trifling charities of a middle-class housewife posing as some outlandish medieval almsgiver.

Ruskin's typically Victorian insistence that social responsibility is a female province is somewhat ridiculous in the light of two considerations: first, as dispossessed persons themselves, both legally and economically, women were quite unable to give any really material help to other dispossessed groups; secondly, the device enabled men, and especially men of the ruling class, to

---

[89] *Ibid.*, p. 479.
[90] *Ibid.*, pp. 479–80.
[91] Ruskin, "Of Queen's Gardens," p. 164.
[92] *Ibid.*, p. 166.
[93] *Ibid.*, pp. 166–67.

ignore or deputize their own enormous responsibilities to the poor whom they oppressed—since, rather than terminate such oppression they preferred to alleviate it with charitable solace.[94] Like most Victorians Ruskin believed women to have finer instincts, for men are "feeble in sympathy," and can even "bear the sight of misery" and "tread it down" "in their own struggle."[95] Mill answers this cherished sentimentality with a certain ironic logic:

> They are declared to be better than men; an empty compliment which must provoke a bitter smile from every woman of spirit, since there is no other situation in life in which it is the established order, and considered quite natural and suitable, that the better should obey the worse. If this piece of talk is good for anything, it is only as an admission by men, of the corrupting influence of power . . . it is true that servitude, except when it actually brutalizes, though corrupting to both, is less so to the slaves than to the slave-masters.[96]

The philanthropy which Ruskin advocates for women as their sole opportunity outside the Home, is to Mill's better understanding of social economy merely an "unenlightened and short-sighted benevolence" which is pernicious to those it pretends to serve by sapping "the foundations of the self respect" which is the only pride left the independent poor and their only route of escape.[97] The paternalism of the charity and gratitude system is humiliating to the poor—far more so than Ruskin would permit his queens to realize.[98] Mill would remind them:

> A woman born to the present lot of women, and content with it, how should she appreciate the value of self-dependence? She is not self-dependent; her destiny is to receive everything from others, and why should what is good enough for her be bad for the poor? Her familiar notions of good are of blessings descending from a superior. She forgets that she is not free, and that the poor are . . .[99]

[94] Ruskin seems to toady to the genteel pretensions of his audience, urging them to pointless and impractical feudal largesse in statements like this: "Your fancy is pleased with the thought of being noble ladies, with a train of vassals. Be it so; you cannot be too noble and your train too great; but see to it that your train is of vassals whom you serve and feed." *Ibid.*, pp. 167–68.

[95] *Ibid.*, p. 169.

[96] Mill, *op. cit.*, p. 518.

[97] *Ibid.*, p. 532.

[98] Welfare is a contemporary example of the system as it corrodes generation after generation of the poor, presupposing a benevolent master and grateful serf mentality, leaving its victims on the short rations of charity and cultivating an enervating dependence which only further dependence can satisfy. This is, of course, not really welfare, but neo-feudalism.

[99] Mill, *op. cit.*, p. 533.

Considerably beyond chivalrous compliment, Mill is perfectly aware of how adverse an effect feminine influence can have: "He who has a wife has given hostages to Mrs. Grundy."[100] Herself the victim of a narrow and superficial education, woman is often just as likely to exert an influence that is petty, family-centered, and selfish.

As to the feminine self-sacrifice which so inspires Ruskin, it is in Mill's eyes only a despicable self-immolation, both wasteful and tasteless. Because it is not reciprocal, the "exaggerated self-abnegation which is the present artificial ideal of feminine character,"[101] produces only a false altruism. Looking beneath the surface of chivalrous blandishment, Mill has detected expediency, even duplicity:

> . . . we are perpetually told that women are better than men by those who are totally opposed to treating them as if they were as good; so that the saying has passed into a piece of tiresome cant, intended to put a complimentary face upon an injury, and resembling those celebrations of royal clemency which, according to Gulliver, the King of Lilliput always prefixed to his most sanguinary decrees.[102]

On the other hand, if we accept the report of Ruskin's vision, the grief of the world is on the heads of women, so powerful are they in their secluded bowers, those shadowy corners of "higher mystery" at whose behests masculine power "bows itself and will forever bow, before the myrtle crown and the stainless sceptre of womanhood."[103] Carried aloft by his chimera of woman's power, he insists, "there is not a war in the world, no, nor an injustice, but you women are answerable for it; not in that you have provoked, but in that you have not hindered."[104] There is a certain humor in Ruskin's proclamation that woman, confined through history to a vicarious and indirect existence, without a deciding voice in any event, with so much of the burden of military, economic and technological events visited upon her, and so little of their glories, is nevertheless solely accountable for morality on the planet.

Ruskin then launches into a peroration on flowers, whose subject, though he can never bring himself to say so in English, is prostitution, the cancer in chivalry's rose. He begins prosaically enough: "the path of a good woman is indeed strewn with flowers, but they rise behind her steps, not before them."[105] He then takes off in ecstasy, and orders the good women of England, presumably the matrons snugly seated before him in Manchester's Town Hall to go out into the "darkness of the terrible streets" on a mission

100 *Ibid.*, p. 535.
101 *Ibid.*, p. 476.
102 *Ibid.*
103 Ruskin, "Of Queen's Gardens," p. 168.
104 *Ibid.*, p. 169.
105 *Ibid.*, p. 172.

to rescue certain persons there whom he refers to in cipher as "feeble florets," full period euphuism for whore.[106] Ruskin's plan is that the matrons will plant and establish the harlots in "little fragrant beds." Perhaps more in line with his general intentions, is the injunction to "fence them, in their trembling from the fierce wind."[107]

However buried in flowers, the overtones of sexuality in the last passage provoke still others: Ruskin quotes from Tennyson's vaguely erotic lyric "Come into the garden Maude" and transforms the unbalanced young man who is actually the speaker in the poem into a slightly eroticized Christ, and one with whom the lecturer appears to identify in the most curious, oblique, and oddly personal manner. Having now run off into a rather self-indulgent type of piety Ruskin concludes the lecture in a paroxysm of Dissenting fervor:

> Oh you queens, you queens! among the hills and happy greenwood of this land of yours, shall the foxes have holes, and the birds of the air have nests; and in your cities shall the stones cry out against you, that they are the only pillows where the Son of Man can lay his head?[108]

It would almost seem that Ruskin's mind has grown confused and that he is addressing his cold and obdurate child mistress in the language of Bethel chapel. That salvation of the world he is assured should come from its subject women is a concoction of nostalgic mirage, regressive, infantile, or narcissistic sexuality, religious ambition, and simplistic social panacea. It is the very stuff of the age's pet sentimental vapors, enshrined in notions such as "the angel in the house," "the good woman who rescues the fallen," etc. It is the fabric of dreams. But the dreams of an age are part of its life, although perhaps as often a foretaste of its death.

By comparison, Mill's conclusion seems not only more rational but full of a new and promising vigor. He urges the complete emancipation of women not only for the sake of the "unspeakable gain in happiness to the liberated half of the species, the difference to them between a life of subjection to the will of others and a life of rational freedom,"[109] but also for the enormous benefit this would confer on both sexes, on humanity: "We have had the morality of submission and the morality of chivalry and generosity; the time is now come"[110] for "the most fundamental of the social relations" to be

[106] *Ibid.*, p. 173.

[107] *Ibid.* An alliance between whores and ladies, however unlikely, might be the end of chivalry which relies, as Mill is careful to point out, on the double standard for its chief value, "virtuous womanhood." Though undoubtedly sincere, Ruskin can scarcely be taken literally here, so little does he appear to apprehend the consequences of his suggestion.

[108] *Ibid.*, p. 175.

[109] Mill, *op. cit.*, p. 522.

[110] *Ibid.*, p. 478.

"placed under the rule of equal justice."[111] In Mill's tones one hears the precursor of revolution; in Ruskin's only reaction tactfully phrased. In the 1860s Ruskin's muddled gallantry was in every mouth, but by 1920 Mill's clear voice had prevailed.

Engels and Revolutionary Theory

I THE HISTORICAL PARADIGM

Nearly as important as the political breakthrough, that actual change in the quality of their lives which a gradual, painful, and finally partial or conditional emancipation realized for women in the sexual revolution, was the work of the revolutionary theorists who passed beyond agitation to provide an analysis of the past and a new model for the future. Such theorists could give coherence and ideological support to the disputes of the day, otherwise the product of resentment or prejudice. Capable of seeing the events of the present in a historical perspective, they could provide direction for change otherwise the product of unconscious forces. The major theorists were Chernyshevsky, Mill, Engels, Bebel, and Veblen. Much of what they said is still relevant to a sexual revolution and therefore still speaks to us today.[112]

Of all these theoretical writings, Engels' *The Origin of the Family, Private Property, and the State*[113] provided the most comprehensive account of patriarchal history and economy—and the most radical, for Engels alone among the theorists attacked the problem of patriarchal family organization. But in tracing it back to its original roots he was baffled by one of history's conundrums.

Here one must pause to consider a curious quarrel that has absorbed anthropology for some hundred years.[114] One school, which for simplicity shall be called the school of patriarchal origins, takes the patriarchal family to be the primordial form of human social organization, tribe, nation, etc., evolving from it or patterned upon it.[115] Generally, the effect of this argument is to see in patriarchy the primeval, original, hence the "natural" form of society, biologically based in the physical strength of the male, and the

---

[111] *Ibid.*, p. 541.

[112] See N. G. Chernyshevsky's *What Is to Be Done?*, August Bebel's *Women and Socialism*, and Thorstein Veblen, *The Theory of the Leisure Class*. Charlotte Perkins Gilman and Elizabeth Cady Stanton provided the Woman's Movement with argument and ideology as well.

[113] Friedrich Engels, *The Origin of the Family, Private Property, and the State* (1884) (Chicago, Charles Kerr, 1902). Translated from the German by Ernest Untermann.

[114] The battle rages elsewhere than in America, where the social sciences appear serenely adjusted to a settled patriarchal view.

[115] The chief contributions were made by Sir Henry Maine (*Ancient Law*, 1861) and Edward Westermarck (*The History of Human Marriage*, 1891). The first is an account of patriarchal origins through patriarchal law, the second is based on the premise that patriarchal monogamy is a primeval human institution.

"debilitating" effects of pregnancy in the female, working in conjunction with the environmental needs of a hunting culture,[116] to explain the subordination of women as the reasonable, even the necessary outcome of circumstances. There are several weaknesses in this theory making its hypotheses insufficient to constitute *necessary* cause: social and political institutions are rarely based on physical strength, but are generally upheld by value systems in co-operation with other forms of social and technical force; hunting culture was generally succeeded by agricultural society which brought different environmental circumstances and needs; pregnancy and childbirth may be socially construed or socially arranged so that they are very far from debilitating events or the cause of physical inferiority, particularly where child care is communal and fertility reverenced or desired. And finally, since patriarchy is a social and political form, it is well here, as with other human institutions, to look outside nature for its origins.

Probably one ought to be content with questioning the primordial character of patriarchal origins, relying upon the argument that since what we are dealing with is an institution, patriarchy must, like other human institutions, have had an origin and arisen out of circumstances which can be inferred or reconstructed, and since, if this is so, some other social condition must have obtained previous to patriarchy. Members of the matriarchal school, however, were not content with this. Working at a disadvantage because trying to counteract an established theory and strong social prejudices, they found it necessary to posit prepatriarchal conditions in the positive sense of "matriarchy."[117] While only two members of this school went so far as to imagine matriarchy a complete or exact analogue of patriarchy (e.g., a social form where the female was as dominant, the male as oppressed, as the male had been dominant and the female oppressed in patriarchy),[118] nearly every member has argued that patriarchal rule was preceded by some form of matriarchal rule, where mother-right, the "female principle," or fertility dominated social and religious life. They found considerable evidence for the last two items in myth and the early history of religions, as well as in the tendency of agricultural peoples to worship the fertility principle. The discovery of the existence of matrilineality among certain non-Western peoples was construed as a vestige of matriarchy persisting within groups who were in transition between matriarchy and patriarchy.

Despite the possible fascination of the dispute, and its logical attraction

[116] War is frequently urged as another factor. As organized armed conflict, war is too evidently an institution itself to qualify as primeval.

[117] Here the chief contributions were made by Bachofen (*Das Mutterrecht*, 1861), Louis Henry Morgan (*Ancient Society*, 1877), Robert Briffault (*The Mothers*, 1927), McLennon (*Primitive Marriage*, 1875) and Giraud-Teulon (*Les Origines de la Famille*, 1874). See also the works of Sir James Frazer and Joseph Campbell, Robert Graves (*The White Goddess*), and Jane Harrison (*Prolegomena to the Study of Greek Religion*, 1903).

[118] See Mathias and Mathilde Vaertung, *The Dominant Sex* (London, 1923).

as an etiological problem in sexual politics, it appears to be incapable of resolution since the information from prehistory which might settle it is inaccessible.[119] Given that each school works only upon hypothesis, it is more interesting, and perhaps even more pertinent, to understand the sexual-political predilections of each faction. Of course, both sides agree that the present and historical form is patriarchy—what they disagree about is not only prehistory, but also, by implication (as we shall see) the future as well. In general, the most vociferous members of the patriarchal school of origins tend toward conservatism and are often led by the effect of their argument to ratify patriarchy as in some sense the "natural" and original form of human society, from which departure (whether or not it may be recommended) is variation—and deliberate variation. There is a fairly strong implication that any such modification is a concession to modern civilization or "changed social values," possibly dangerous if radical (e.g., affecting the patriarchal family structure or drastically altering its role system) and probably revocable in any case should need arise, or "nature" reassert itself.[120] Members of the matriarchal school are somewhat less complacent as they neither serve a status quo nor contemplate a return to earlier forms. The main force of their argument is to challenge patriarchy's claims to eternal authority, primeval or primordial origins, and biological or environmental necessity. They see patriarchy as but one era of human history and therefore, theoretically, as capable of dissolution as it was of institution.

A liberal, Mill saw no further back in time than a universal rule of force and took the subjection of women to be an eternal feature of human life which "progress" and moral suasion might alleviate as he felt they had tyranny and slavery. A communist, Engels was temperamentally disinclined to accept the optimism of this view of a continuously progressive history; he believed he saw in the institution of slavery, for example, a backward step from a more genial primitive communal life. A revolutionary, he was necessarily at odds with fatalistic or "biological" versions of the origins of human institutions (such as those of the patriarchal school), preferring instead to regard institutions as man-made and hence capable of radical, sudden, even violent alteration, should a conscious revolutionary humanity so desire. Having seen the connection between the patriarchal family and property, Engels believed he had found the origins of property in the subjection and ownership of women upon which patriarchy was founded. Engels was understandably attracted to the work of Bachofen, whose *Das Mutterrecht* was the first formulation of the matriarchal theory of origins. For the matriarchate ap-

[119] As the historical period opens patriarchy has already appeared. Of the social organization in prehistory there is simply insufficient evidence to judge, and the social organization of contemporary preliterate peoples does not provide a reliable guide to the social conditions of prehistorical peoples.

[120] Hence their satisfaction over the failure or relinquishment of experimental arrangements in the kibbutzim, Communist China and Russia, etc.

peared to Engels to be a primordial communism, without property in persons, without familial property interests, that very simplicity which socialism has often sought in the past, partly out of its need for an example of a world without a complex inequitable political order based on wealth, and partly out of its own nostalgia for a golden age.[121] Whatever the character of "matriarchy" (and here Engels' entire anthropological basis is more than problematic by now)[122] it could be demonstrated that patriarchy was accompanied by all the ills Engels deplored, the ownership of persons, beginning with women and progressing to other forms of slavery, the institutions of class, caste, rank, ruling and propertied classes, the steady development of an unequally distributed wealth—and finally the state.

Combining Bachofen with Louis Morgan's pioneering work in anthropology and his own socialist theory, Engels could construct a universal history; one which took account of the family and conditions of human reproduction and social organization as gens, phratry and tribe evolved into city and nation, as well as one which recorded the means of material production as humanity evolved into toolmaker, herdsman, farmer, artisan, merchant, and finally manufacturer and industrialist. Engels constructed a series of stages in social or family history, passing by degrees from matriarchy (mother-right) through a succession of sexual associations: promiscuity, group marriage, the consanguineous family, the Punalua, and ending in patriarchy through pairing and finally monogamous marriage.

II A DIGRESSION ON THE EVIDENCE OF MYTH

Despite the comprehensive and neatly explicit character of this scheme there is one crucial event which Engels and his sources fail to account for adequately—the patriarchal takeover. Whatever form of social organization preceded it, the genesis of patriarchy is still a moot and perhaps even a crucial question in human history. Both Engels and Bachofen presumed patriarchy to have arisen in conjunction with a change from a more communal sexual life to the adoption of certain forms of sexual association, first through pairing and finally through monogamy, both of which established the male's exclusive sexual possession of the female.[123] The existence of pairing marriages has considerable support, strict monogamy being by no means a common form and probably late in developing. The existence of the other forms mentioned: promiscuity, group marriage, etc., has been heatedly debated and appears dubious. According to the very unsatisfactory evidence available, Bachofen and Engels' supposition that patriarchy originated solely or largely

[121] Perhaps there was a need to counteract the idyll of "patriarchal simplicity" as well.

[122] For the most recent discussion of Morgan and Bachofen see Marvin Harris, *The Origins of Anthropological Theory* (New York, Columbia, 1969).

[123] Within pairing marriage (as Engels defines it) the male is free for other attachments; the female is not. It could be absolved by divorce.

through the adoption of certain forms of sexual associations, is probably untenable, other changes—social, ideological, technological, and economic—presenting themselves as more likely. Engels' contention that women constituted
the first property is probably true. However, his belief that women are made
chattels through the establishment of the male's exclusive sexual possession
over woman in marriage (a possession not reciprocal for women) already
presupposes patriarchal circumstances.

Realizing the importance of the cause for this shift or change in the
character of sexual association, realizing too the important role of early
religion in connection with sexuality, Bachofen looked to myth and literature
for evidence of how early society construed biological event in terms one
might call sexual-political. One factor undeniably inherent in the situation,
but certainly difficult to place in historical order, is the discovery of paternity.[124] Bachofen, who heard in ancient myth a thousand echoes both of
the ancient matriarchate and of a patriarchal dispossession of its deities and
values, had pointed out the usefulness of fables, such as the one Aeschylus
employed in the *Oresteia,* for pinpointing a moment when knowledge of
paternity (an undoubtedly much earlier discovery) came to be used to support
patriarchal rule. Conservative factors such as religious myth and kinship ties
are, in the absence of more concrete evidence, the most lasting vestiges of
that vast historical shift whereby patriarchy, probably by slow degrees and
stages, and most likely at different moments in each locale, replaced whatever
order preceded it and instituted that long government of male over female.

The eldest and most religiously conservative of the Greek tragedians,
Aeschylus, made use of the last play in his Oresteian trilogy, *The Furies*
(*Eumenides*) to present a confrontation drama between patriarchal or paternal authority and what appear to be the defeated claims of an earlier order,
one which had placed emphasis upon maternal claims and was in Bachofen's
view matriarchal. Working on the material of much earlier myth, the playwright has sharpened the Olympian decision between the claims of Clytemnestra and the Furies as against those of Agamemnon and Orestes to become
something of an ideological conflict.[125]

One must go back before the scene of the play and recall the chain of
events out of which its action arises. Clytemnestra had killed Agamemnon
upon his return from Troy. A victorious general, coming home in triumph
with a booty of captive women, among them the Trojan princess Cassandra,
now maddened by rape and enslavement—Agamemnon's assassination is a
blow against all patriarchal authority; Clytemnestra's act constitutes the most
outrageous rebellion against the masculine authority of husband and king.

[124] Even Maine took account of this, realizing that certainty of paternity was highly
important to the patriarchal family and patriarchal authority. Somehow it did not occur
to him that his insight was very much at odds with his insistence on the primordial character of patriarchy itself.

[125] One wonders at the linguistic accident of her name.

In further treason to marital and political lordship, she has taken a lover during Agamemnon's ten-year absence, and now aspires to share the throne with him. Above all, Clytemnestra seems to be defending the claims of mother-right in seeking to avenge her daughter Iphigenia, whom Agamemnon had enticed from her by promising that she was to marry Achilles, the pride of his army. Upon the girl's arrival in his camp at Aulis, her father slaughtered the "bride," a human sacrifice to propitiate the winds that carried him to Troy and glory.

Deeply offended at his mother's offense against primogeniture and masculine prerogative, Orestes then revenged his father's death. But in committing matricide, he has provoked the rage of the Furies, who pursue him from city to city. In *The Flies*, Sartre passed off these dark avengers as guilt, remorse, or the force of public opinion. But in Aeschylus they appear as the deposed powers of a matriarchate, reduced already to the level of harridans. And their cry that Orestes' crime must be punished (Clytemnestra already having paid for hers with her life) has something of the sound of matriarchy's last stand in the ancient world.

When the Furies accuse him of matricide, Orestes dodges responsibility; he acted under orders from the Oracle of Apollo. The Furies refuse to believe "a god of prophecy" would recommend such a crime, so they put the prince on trial, assured that justice will be on their side. They have failed to reckon with patriarchal justice. When Orestes observes that they should have hounded Clytemnestra too for the murder she committed, they reply in all the confidence of the mother-right: "The man she killed was not of her own blood."[126] "But am I of my mother's?" Orestes sneers. The Furies are appalled: "Vile wretch, she nourished you in her own womb. Do you disown your mother's blood?" . . . "Do you deny you were born of woman?"[127] This might appear a difficult allegation to deny, but Greek patriarchy had already formulated a rather surprisingly politicized version of biology which Apollo expounds:

> The mother is not the parent of the child
> Which is called hers. She is the nurse who tends the growth
> Of young seed planted by its true parent, the male.
> So, if Fate spares the child, she keeps it, as one might
> Keep for some friend a growing plant . . .
> Father without mother may beget . . .

This last statement would seem to be carrying the discovery of paternity, the knowledge of the seed, rather too far. In finding out his own part in the

126 With the one stated exception, all quotations from the *Eumenides* are from Philip Vellacott's translation for the Penguin edition of the Oresteian trilogy.

127 Here John Lewin's "Do you deny you were born of woman" strikes me as closer in spirit to the original. *The Oresteia,* rendered into English by John Lewin, University of Minnesota, 1966 (New York, Bantam, 1969).

creation of human life, the male, who doubtless once believed that there could be motherhood without a father, has retaliated for his years of ignorance with overstatement. Since the mother's role is observed, conspicuous, the child emerging from her very body, and the father's role only inferred, one cannot but feel a certain awkwardness in this total expropriation of fertility. In the event his genetics fail to persuade, Apollo, sounding something like a mountebank, digs out the other card he holds in his sleeve:

> . . . We have
> Present, as proof, the daughter of Olympian Zeus:
> One never nursed in the dark cradle of the womb;

This is the well-known device of hitting upon a quisling to deal the death blow. Athena, born full-grown from the head of her father Zeus, marches on, spoiling to betray her kind:

> No mother gave me birth. Therefore the father's claim
> And male supremacy in all things, save to give
> Myself in marriage, wins my whole heart's loyalty
> Therefore a woman's death, who killed her husband, is,
> I judge, outweighted in grievousness by his.

This sort of corroboration can be fatal. The Chorus of Furies may cry in vain "O Mother, O Darkness, look on us!" Zeus and the patriarchy have put out the eyes of the Great Mother while this "new" generation of gods "ride rough-shod over Elder Powers," casting out the old fertility goddesses who preceded the Titans. Apollo even baits them: "You have as little honor amongst elder gods as amongst us, the younger. I shall win." The trial is rigged; the Furies haven't a chance.

Through Athena's deciding vote, Orestes is not only acquitted but reinvested with his patrimony. Having entirely appropriated the creative force of fertility for the male, patriarchal dogma shall not stop short of devaluating female existence as well. And such is the force of the decision: "Zeus so ordained and Zeus was right . . . their two deaths are in no way to be compared" Apollo legislates, finding Clytemnestra, in taking the life of Agamemnon, husband, king and father, guilty of a very grave crime indeed, but exonerating Orestes in taking a woman's life, though it be his own mother's.

The Furies, whose wrath Aeschylus had designed to give off the pathos of foregone defeat, are never permitted to pose any real threat, and lament helplessly:

> The old is trampled by the new!
> Curse on you younger gods who overrule
> The ancient laws . . .

The Furies, who are of course fertility goddesses, had considered wreaking their revenge in a murrain all over Greece, "a sterile blight" on "plant and child." But Athena stands by to cajole them out of their rage and into an ancillary role within the new order. By dint of fair talk and the threat that since their day is over they would be wise to co-operate, she coaxes the Furies into a bargain which appears to afford them no benefits beyond survival—yet is an absolute necessity to the new order. For all his boasting that he is the sole source of life, patriarchal man, by tacit concession, appears to acknowledge that he cannot prosper without the assistance of the female principle. So Athena wheedles the Furies to provide.

> Blessings from earth and sea and sky; blessing that breathes
> In wind and sunlight through the land; that beast and field
> Enrich my people with unwearied fruitfulness,
> And armies of brave sons be born . . .

Ignominious in their defeat, The Furies jump at the offer of a home in Athens and launch into five pages of local chamber of commerce rhapsody. In Aeschylus' dramatization of the myth one is permitted to see patriarchy confront matriarchy, confound it through the knowledge of paternity, and come off triumphant. Until Ibsen's Nora slammed the door announcing the sexual revolution, this triumph went nearly uncontested.

III   DIGRESSION ON THE EVIDENCE OF SEXUALITY

Bachofen had felt the importance of the knowledge of paternity and was therefore attracted to mythic and religious statements such as the *Eumenides* furnishes. But, understandably, he refused to rely too heavily on such sources as evidence either as to the discovery of paternity or as to its part in the origins of patriarchy. He sought other reasons. For his part, Engels was not only suspicious of what he called the "mysticism" of Bachofen's thought when it touched on myth or religion, but was disinclined to accept such evidence in any case.[128] So he chose instead to follow Bachofen on a second and much less reliable hypothesis. Asking themselves how women allowed their subjection to overtake them, they responded with a naïveté characteristic of their era, claiming that women submitted willingly to the sexual and social subjection of pairing and then monogamous marriage because in fact women find sexuality burdensome.[129] "They constantly longed for relief by the right

---

[128] In imagining Bachofen was so naïve as to represent "religion as the main lever of the world's history" Engels missed Bachofen's point altogether. Changes in the relation of the sexes are not *made by* but only *reflected in* religion. What was reflected was the discovery of paternity, and it is this which Engels failed to appreciate.

[129] Members of the patriarchal school outlawed the possibility of promiscuity or group marriage altogether. Maine was convinced that sexual jealousy was an inherent instinct in the male and would never have permitted it. Both factions were, to some degree at least, repelled or made uneasy by the prospect of unregulated sexual activity.

of chastity,"[130] Engels informs us and therefore accepted the exclusive sexual possession with which patriarchy originated as a not unwelcome "penalty" for "becoming exempt from the ancient community of men and acquiring the right of surrendering to one man only."[131]

One is tempted to see an absurdity in such confident assumption that women dislike sex. Moreover, there is something unconsciously patriarchal in the assumption that sexual association involves "surrender" as well as in the inference that sexual intercourse is in fact (for women) a political act of submission. One cannot help but be unfavorably impressed at the extent to which Engels' attitudes are affected by the presuppositions of his culture. But in fact, he is only being Victorian. The point of his remark was the widespread appreciation in his own period that, however much sexual resistance militated against the woman's own sensual desires (and the possibility of their existing in any intensity was largely disregarded) it was nevertheless an act of self assertion. The notion of sexual resistance, the defense of integrity with frigidity, or the preservation of independence through chastity, are common themes in Victorian literature. Under the demands of a socially coercive or exploitative sexuality such as patriarchy had instituted, where sexual activity implied submitting to male will, "chastity," frigidity, or some form of resistance to sexuality took on something of the character of a "political" response to the conditions of sexual politics. While chastity, or even the negative attitudes toward coitus which accompany frigidity, operated as patriarchal social and psychological "stratagems" to limit or prohibit woman's pleasure in sexuality, they could also be transformed into protective feminine "stratagems" in a refusal to capitulate to patriarchal force: physical, economic, or social.

While trying to explain conditions prior to patriarchy, Engels reasoned according to assumptions becoming only to patriarchal conditions. And, since it has until very recently been a scientific football or a swamp of superstitious misinformation, he was also ignorant of the nature of female sexuality. In view of recent research in this subject there is little reason to imagine woman would have welcomed in pairing or monogamous marriage a form of sexual association which, in limiting the demands upon her sexually, also involved the subjection of her sensuality, and by extension, of her self, to the will of another. All the best scientific evidence today unmistakably tends toward the conclusion that the female possesses, biologically and inherently, a far greater capacity for sexuality than the male, both as to frequency of coitus, and as to frequency of orgasm in coition.

Even without the aid of science, common sense would persuade anyone who chose to ponder the fact that prostitution requires the female to engage in intercourse with a frequency impossible for males. Yet such sexual experience is only quantitative and physiologically passive, as it does not imply

---

[130] Engels, *op. cit.*, p. 65.
[131] *Ibid.*, p. 62.

orgasm.[132] Prostitutes have little need and usually little opportunity to accompany their availability with either orgasm or pleasure. Their sexual experience is in some manner forced (through economic or through devious psychological needs) and is hard to construe as freely chosen.

Yet the studies of Masters and Johnson prove that the female sexual cycle is capable of multiple orgasms in quick succession, each of which is analogous to the detumescence, ejaculation, and loss of erection in the male. With proper stimulation, a woman is capable of multiple orgasms in quick succession.

> If a female who is capable of having regular orgasms is properly stimulated within a short period after her first climax, she will, in most instances, be capable of having a second, third, fourth, and even a fifth and sixth orgasm before she is fully satiated. As contrasted with the male's usual inability to have more than one orgasm in a short period, many females, especially when clitorally stimulated, can regularly have five or six full orgasms within a matter of minutes.[133]

In view of the long-standing belief in the existence of a "vaginal orgasm" it might be emphasized that the clitoris is the organ specific to sexuality in the human female, the vagina being an organ of reproduction as well as of sexuality, and possessing no erogenous tissue save in the lower third of the vaginal tract, the nerve endings in these cells all deriving from and centering in the clitoris. While there is no "vaginal orgasm" per se, there is of course orgasm in vaginal coitus (and probably one of a different experiential character than that produced by exclusively clitoral stimulation) just as on any occasion when the clitoris is properly stimulated. In heterosexual intercourse, female orgasm is due to the friction of the penis upon the clitoral head or glans and the labia minora of the clitoral area. A distinction must be made between the locus of arousal and the locus of response. The seat of response is in the clitoris, which triggers other responses (the enlargement of the labia majora, the flow of transudate, vaginal spasms, etc.). Sexual arousal may have its source in the stimulation of body tissues, erogenous or otherwise, or in purely psychological excitation (thoughts, emotions, words, pictures, etc.). The clitoris, one might point out, is the only human organ which is specific to sexuality and to sexual pleasure: the penis has other functions both in elimination and in reproduction.

While the male's sexual potential is limited, the female's appears to be

---

[132] So little does the sexual activity of a prostitute give itself to orgasm that prostitutes tend to develop a condition known as Taylor's syndrome, a painful chronic congestion in the pelvic area, the result of experiencing sexual arousal unaccompanied by that release of vascular congestion and tension which is experienced in the orgasm.

[133] W. H. Masters and Virginia Johnson, "Orgasm, Anatomy of the Female," in *Encyclopedia of Sexual Behavior,* ed. by A. Ellis and A. Abarbanel (New York, Hawthorn Books, 1961), Vol. 2, p. 792.

biologically nearly inexhaustible, and apart from psychological considerations, may continue until physical exhaustion interposes.

> The average female with optimal arousal will usually be satisfied with three to five manually-induced orgasms; whereas mechanical stimulation, as with the electric vibrator, is less tiring and induces her to go on to long stimulative sessions of an hour or more during which she may have twenty to fifty consecutive orgasms. She will stop only when totally exhausted.[134]

In an important article on the implications of such research, Dr. Sherfey makes the following observation upon these findings:

> No doubt the most far reaching hypothesis extrapolated from these biological data is the existence of a universal and physically normal condition of woman's inability ever to reach complete sexual satiation in the presence of the most intense, repetitive orgasmic experiences, no matter how produced. Theoretically, a woman could go on having orgasms indefinitely if physical exhaustion did not intervene.[135]

In view of Sherfey's overemphasis upon insatiability, it is perhaps necessary to stress that despite an enormous biological orgasmic capacity, exhaustion can and does intervene in strict accordance with the amount of tension and energy expended; greater in the case of the penis's friction in coitus; lesser in the case of manual or mechanical stimulation. In that sense, female, like male, sexuality is limited. Moreover, biological capacity is hardly psychological need, nor does it always correspond to psychic satisfaction. It is perhaps unnecessary to point out that whatever her biological capacities for sexuality, as a human being, the female is just as able to sublimate them as is the male. And as a member of society, her sexuality is very subject to social forces. So much is this the case that the conditions of patriarchal society have had such profound effects upon female sexuality that its function has been drastically affected, its true character long distorted and long unknown.[136] This is remarkable evidence of culture's ability to affect physiology.

That the nature of female sexuality has been so long uninvestigated says much for the direction knowledge takes from social circumstances. Given woman's extraordinary biological potentiality for sexual arousal and pleasure, no form of sexual association would have satisfied it less than monogamy or

[134] W. H. Masters as quoted by Dr. Mary Jane Sherfey. M. J. Sherfey, "The Evolution and Nature of Female Sexuality in Relation to Psychoanalytic Theory," *The Journal of the American Psychoanalytic Association,* Vol. 14, January 1966, no. 1 (New York, International Universities Press, Inc.), p. 792.

[135] Sherfey, *op. cit.,* p. 117.

[136] The experience of woman herself has not been consulted often in history, but so strong is her conditioning, that such evidence is itself unreliable: generations of women have comforted Freudian analysts as to the reality of the vaginal orgasms they were expected and even enjoined to experience.

polygyny; none more than group marriage. Yet Engels' conviction that women should have preferred the limited sexuality imposed on them by paired marriage is an interesting comment both upon the sexual "climate" of his period and upon the implications which sexuality takes on within social contexts such as patriarchy. Patriarchal myth and belief had always assumed greater sexual capacity in the male and argued from it a greater need which lent sanction to the double standard and perhaps even to polygyny.[137] This is an expedient assumption even if in direct contradiction to biological fact. It is doubtless behind Engels' fancy as to the burdensome claims of the "community of men" which women so longed to escape they accepted every other form of subordination.

The effect of patriarchal social conditions upon women with regard to their sexual lives has had enormous and even anomalous results. One marvels at the proof of socialization's powers found in the fact that the vast inherent potential of female sexuality had come, by Engels' time, to be nearly totally obscured through cultural restraints.[138] One also observes the paradoxical situation that while patriarchy tends to convert woman to a sexual object, she has not been encouraged to enjoy the sexuality which is agreed to be her fate. Instead, she is made to suffer for and be ashamed of her sexuality, while in general not permitted to rise above the level of a nearly exclusively sexual existence. For the great mass of women throughout history have been confined to the cultural level of animal life in providing the male with sexual outlet and exercising the animal functions of reproduction and care of the young. Thus the female has had sexuality visited upon her as a punishment in a way of life which, with few exceptions,[139] and apart from maternity, did not encourage her to derive pleasure in sexuality and limited her to an existence otherwise comprised mainly of menial labor and domestic service.

Only with the relaxation of sexual mores and the lifting of the major prohibitions against woman's pleasure in sexuality, together with the changes which the first phase of the sexual revolution had brought about in social attitudes and in her social position—changes so deep and pervasive that even

---

[137] Under polygyny of the representative Islamic sort which licenses one male to have sole access and total possession of four women, the ratio of sexual opportunity is one to sixteen; each woman has one fourth of a male's sexual potential, whereas the male has that of four women. Under the double standard, the ratio regarding wife and mistress is one to four in favor of the male's opportunity for satisfaction. These are ironic circumstances when one considers the relative sexual capacity of each sex.

[138] That the conditions of the Victorian period still obtain among us today is confirmed by a study of sexual attitudes done among the white working class, Rainwater's *And the Poor Get Children*. One third of the women in this sample were totally negative toward sexuality, and another third largely so. Among both men and women in the study it was agreed that "sex is for the man"—undertaken for his need and pleasure.

[139] Prostitutes are less exceptional here than they might appear. The purpose of their sexual activity is not their own pleasure: a fact which has been recognized since the earliest definitions of their function.

the ensuing period of reaction could not erase their effect—only then could the potential capacity of the female's sexuality reassert itself in any general way. Yet while placing the greatest emphasis on social changes which afforded women education, divorce, economic independence, and greater social freedom, one need not underestimate the influence of increased physiological understanding and improved sexual technique. What was the beginning, in the West at least, of a less oppressively masculine-oriented sexual technique (another legacy of the first phase of sexual revolution) has also contributed to the diminution of that enormous cultural inhibition and distortion which patriarchal conditions had imposed upon woman's bio-sexual organic base.

IV   The Revolutionary Substance

The great value of Engels' contribution to the sexual revolution lay in his analysis of patriarchal marriage and family. Whatever his difficulties in accounting for the genesis of these institutions, the very fact of his attempt to demonstrate that they were not an eternal feature of life was in itself a radical departure. The scholars upon whose work his own is built had of course done so as well, but never with Engels' intentions. Bachofen's interest was myth; Morgan's ethnology. That Engels could subsume their theories into one of his own directed toward revolutionary social reorganization is proof of a pragmatic motivation in his study of prehistory.

If patriarchal marriage and the family, though prehistoric, have their origins in the human past, they cease to be immutable, and become subject to alteration. In treating them as historical institutions, subject to the same processes of evolution as other social phenomena, Engels had laid the sacred open to serious criticism, analysis, even to possible drastic reorganization. Whatever the validity of his thesis that the institution of marriage (pairing and then monogamous) is the factor which ushered in the period of patriarchal rule, Engels' declaration that marriage and the family were built upon the ownership of women was a most damaging charge indeed. All the historical evidence of patriarchal law now supported Mill's charge of "domestic slavery" with a new vehemence. What Mill had thought to be a primordial evil, the inevitable consequence of man's original savagery, Engels' historical account transformed into an oppressive innovation, an innovation which brought with it innumerable other forms of oppression, each dependent upon it. Far from being the last injustice, sexual dominance became the keystone to the total structure of human injustice.

The first course of social change as Engels had charted it[140] was from consanguine group marriage, to the Punaluan consanguine group, then to maternal gens, and finally to paternal gens. And when the gens converts from maternal to paternal lineage, inherited property (and primogeniture) have

---

[140] Engels' main source here was Morgan's *Ancient Society,* an account of social organization as consanguine or gentile association, based both on the Amerindian peoples and those of the ancient Western world.

already intruded as large factors in social and political life. Out of the gens or consanguine tribe who practiced democracy and held their land in common, and finally at the expense and decay of the gens, there arose with the gradual evolution of patriarchy the following institutions: slavery (the model for all later class systems and itself modeled on the ownership of persons first established over women), chiefdom, aristocracy, the social-political differentiation of economic groups into rich and poor. Finally, through the increasing importance of private property, with war serving as its catalyst, grew the state, the organ which solidified and maintained all social and economic disparities. Thus all the mechanisms of human inequality arose out of the foundations of male supremacy and the subjection of women, sexual politics serving historically as the foundation of all other social, political, and economic structures. Pairing marriages incorporated human barter, the buying and selling of women, in itself an instructive precedent for the indiscriminate human slavery which arose thereafter. Under patriarchy, the concept of property advanced from its simple origins in chattel womanhood, to private ownership of goods, land, and capital. In the subjection of female to male, Engels (and Marx as well) saw the historical and conceptual prototype of all subsequent power systems, all invidious economic relations, and the fact of oppression itself.

The subjection of women is of course far more than an economic or even political event, but a total social and psychological phenomenon, a way of life, which Engels (whose psychology is less subtle and individualized than Mill's, and based upon collective states) frames in terms of class emotion:

> The first class antagonism appearing in history coincides with the development of the antagonism of man and wife in monogamy, and the first class oppression with that of the female by the male sex. Monogamy was a great historical progress. But by the side of slavery and private property it marks at the same time that epoch which, reaching down to our days, takes with all progress also a step backwards, relatively speaking, and develops the welfare and advancement of one by the woe and submission of the other. It is the cellular form of civilized society which enables us to study the nature of its now fully developed contrasts and contradictions.[141]

Engels distinguishes between the economic classes of his own time by pointing out that the unpropertied classes make practical use of women, while the propertied, having others to serve them, convert her into a decorative or aesthetic object with only limited uses. In asserting that "sexual love in man's relation to woman becomes and can become the rule among the oppressed classes alone, among the proletarians,"[142] Engels, in the time-honored manner of socialists, appears to romanticize the poor. His other arguments are

[141] Engels, op. cit., pp. 79–80.
[142] Ibid., p. 86.

more convincing. Patriarchy is less strongly entrenched economically among
the dispossessed, for inherited property is germane to the foundation of patriarchal monogamy, and the poor are without property. The sequestration
of women in the home had seriously decayed among the working class by
his time through the employment of women in factories and eventually in
their achieving, for the first time, a right to the profit of their labors. Then
too, the legal enforcement of patriarchal law is more difficult for the poor to
obtain, since law is an expensive commodity. But Engels also ignores the fact
that woman is viewed, emotionally and psychologically, as chattel property
by the poor as well as, and often even more than, the rich. Lacking other
claims to status a working class male is still more prone to seek them in his
sexual rank, often brutally asserted.

Were it not sufficient to account for so much social iniquity through the
two most revered forms in his culture, marriage and the family, Engels proceeded to point out that the monogamy it so publicly admired scarcely existed
in fact, and that the term "monogamous marriage" was itself something of a
misnomer. Primarily, it is only the female who was obliged to be monogamous,
since males have traditionally reserved for themselves certain polygynous
privileges through the double standard "for the simple reason that they
[males], never, even to this day, had the least intention of renouncing the
pleasures of group marriage."[143]

Engels is refreshingly frank about prostitution, a subject as obscured in
his own time, through chivalrous tergiversation as, in ours, it is confused
through a thoughtless equation of sexual freedom with sexual exploitation.[144] Prostitution is, as Engels demonstrates, the natural product of traditional monogamous marriage. This assertion is capable of proof on a
number of grounds, the simplest being numerical. When chastity is prescribed and adultery severely punished in women, marriage becomes monogamous for women rather than men, yet there should not be sufficient females
to satisfy masculine demand unless a sector of women, usually from among the
poor, are bred or reserved for sexual exploitation. This group, who among us,
are largely enlisted from the socially and economically exploited racial minorities, were in Engels' industrial England that group of poor below the working
class. Smaller numbers are often set apart for additional services, such as
conversation or entertainment: hetaera, geisha, courtesan, and call girl. What-

[143] *Ibid.*, p. 65.

[144] Reform here should mean that society should cease to punish the promiscuity in
women it does not think to punish in men. This does not, and should not, mean governmental institution and regulation, which under the deceptive rationale of greater safety
for the client, creates an approved and convenient captivity for the prostitute victim. As
those causes of prostitution which are not economic are psychological, it is pointless for
the state to intervene either to prohibit or to regulate. Only changes in economic opportunity and social and psychological attitude can work effectively toward eliminating
prostitution.

ever society's official attitude may be, the demand for prostitution continues within male-supremacist culture,[145] and as Engels describes it, prostitution

> is as much a social institution as all others. It continues the old sexual free-dom—for the benefit of the men. In reality not only permitted, but also assidu-ously practiced by the ruling class, it is denounced only nominally. Still in practice, this denunciation strikes by no means the men who indulge in it, but only the women. These are ostracised and cast out of society, in order to pro-claim once more the fundamental law of unconditional male supremacy over the female sex.[146]

In this last statement one might find some explanation for the persistence of prostitution even after the reforms of the first phase of the sexual revolution had helped to undermine woman's economic vulnerability and relaxed sexual mores had facilitated the practice of extramarital sexuality for both sexes. Men who might be sexually accommodated by casual pickups without expense still provide a demand for prostitution, supplied at times even by women who are not under economic compulsion. In the case of each partner to such prostitution, some need to "proclaim" or at least affirm male supremacy through the humiliation of woman seems to play a leading role. Prostitution, when unmotivated by economic need, might well be defined as a species of psychological addiction, built on self-hatred through repetitions of the act of sale by which a whore is defined. While such self-denigration is extreme, it is not inexplicable within patriarchal society which tends to hold women in contempt, a contempt which is particularly intense in association with female sexuality. There is also a sense in which the prostitute's role is an exaggeration of patriarchal economic conditions where the majority of females are driven to live through some exchange of sexuality for support. The degradation in which the prostitute is held and holds herself, the punitive attitude society adopts toward her, are but reflections of a culture whose general attitudes toward sexuality are negative and which attaches great penalties to a promis-cuity in women it does not think to punish in men.

Having examined marriage, Engels turns his attention to the patriarchal family, as precious to the Victorians as it later became to conservative sociol-ogy in the period of reaction. In Engels' tart phrase, the family's "essential points are the assimilation of the unfree element and the paternal author-ity."[147] "It is founded on male supremacy for the pronounced purpose of breeding children of indisputable paternal lineage. The latter is required because these children shall later on inherit the fortune of their father."[148]

[145] Communist China is said to be the only country in the world which has no prostitution.

[146] Engels, *op. cit.*, p. 81.

[147] *Ibid.*, p. 70.

[148] *Ibid.*, p. 79.

Despite the decline of inherited wealth, this is still so; legitimacy is quite as important now, and thought to justify the cost and education of rearing the young in the nuclear family.

The ideal type of the patriarchal family and the ancestor of our own is the Roman family, whence come both the term and the legal forms and precedents used in the West. Originally, the word *familia* did not, Engels cheerfully informs us

> . . . signify the composite ideal of sentimentality and domestic strife in the present day philistine mind. Among the Romans it did not even apply in the beginning to the leading couple and its children, but to the slaves alone. Famulus means domestic slave, and familia is the aggregate number of slaves belonging to one man . . . The expression [familia] was invented by the Romans in order to designate a new social organism the head of which had a wife, children and a number of slaves under his paternal authority and according to Roman law, the right of life and death over all of them.[149]

To this, Engels adds Marx's observation that

> the word is, therefore, not older than the ironclad family system of the Latin tribes, which arose after the introduction of agriculture and of lawful slavery . . . The modern family contains the germ not only of slavery (servitus) but also of serfdom . . . It comprises in miniature all those contrasts that later on develop more broadly in society and the state.[150]

In noting its economic character Engels is calling attention to the fact that the family is actually a financial unit, something which his contemporaries, like our own, prefer to ignore. Due to the nature of its origins, the family is committed to the idea of property in persons and in goods. "Monogamy was the first form of the family not founded on natural but on economic conditions, viz. the victory of private property over primitive and natural collectivism."[151]

Whatever the value of Engels' insistence on the priority of a "primitive and natural collectivism," the cohesion of the patriarchal family and the authority of its head have consistently relied (and continue to do so) on the economic dependence of its members.[152] Its stability and its efficiency also rely upon its ability to divide its members by hierarchical roles and maintain them in such through innumerable forms of coercion—social, religious, legal, ideological, etc. As Engels makes clear, such a collection of persons cannot be

[149] *Ibid.*, pp. 70–71.

[150] *Ibid.*, p. 71.

[151] *Ibid.*, p. 79.

[152] Can it be that the first group of persons owned (even if only temporarily) is that of children? Could it be that they should also be the last?

said to be free agents. Historically, nearly the entire basis of their association is not affection but constraint: much of it remains so.

Engels' analysis is not simply negative. It does in fact provide a model for change. His proposals are both equitable and feasible recommendations for the general conduct of sexuality in a revolutionary society. He has a certain reasonable appreciation of fidelity and advocates temporary associations, freed of the economic considerations of the older forms and based on "individual sexlove," his own precise if rather colorless phrase for a phenomenon whose development he traces to fairly recent times, and evolving from courtly and romantic love. In insisting that the economic element be utterly purged from all sexual associations Engels went beyond other nineteenth-century theorists by arguing that marriage would continue to be a variety of prostitution (e.g., sex in return for money or commodities) until it ceases to be in any sense an involuntary contract essentially economic in character. The analogy he adopts here is interesting: a woman who enters upon or perseveres in a marriage for economic motives is in the position of a worker who contracts himself to an employment disadvantageous to his interests or inclinations, merely in order to eat. Other theorists—Mill, for example—urged woman's right to work, to enter the professions etc., but imagined many women and most married women would remain in the home tending children and continuing in economic dependency. But Engels is both more logical and more radical: only with the end of male economic dominion and the entrance of women into the economic world on perfectly equal and independent terms will sexual love cease to be barter in some manner based on financial coercion.

Quite as one would expect, Engels' foresight is strongest in the area of economy. Mill had thought legal change would be sufficient and was content that if women obtained suffrage and a just property law, most might well continue in their traditional roles. Engels realized very well that woman's legal disabilities were not the cause but merely the effect of patriarchy. The removal of such invidious law would not give women equal status unless it were accompanied with total social and economic equality and every opportunity of personal fulfillment in productive work. Engels' argument that one cannot be a dependent and still an equal is very compelling. There is no free contract, such as marriage might ideally become, Engels insists, unless both members are free in every respect, including the economic. Here his argument is based on the observation that the concentration of all economic resources into male hands has made the relation of the sexes much like that of one economic class to another:

> The modern monogamous family is founded on the open or disguised domestic slavery of women, and modern society is composed of molecules in the form of monogamous families. In the great majority of cases the man has to earn a

living and to support his family, at least among the possessing classes. He thereby obtains a superior position that has no need of any legal special privilege. In the family he is the bourgeois, the woman represents the proletariat.[153]

One can judge the depth of Engels' radicalism by realizing that in this argument he has not only exceeded the analysis or the reforms urged by his contemporaries, he has pointed out the very stumbling block to further revolution. For the family did not give way. Comment upon the success of that reaction which in the 1920s followed the first phase of sexual revolution and whose energy centered about the family, the preservation of its roles and the necessity of their maintenance through the corollaries of "masculine" and "feminine" is all furnished by the fact that Engels' objections to marriage and the family are as valid today as they were in his own times.

Again, using the analogy of the proletariat whose invidious economic and social position was never made completely clear until democracy had granted them legal equality, Engels insists that a sexual revolution, begun in the first phase with women's achievement of legal and minimal political equality, shall not be completed until it is economic and social as well: "the emancipation of women is *primarily* dependent on the reintroduction of the whole female sex into the public industries. To accomplish this, the monogamous family must cease to be the industrial unit of society."[154]

Engels was fully aware of how drastic, far-reaching, and significant a social change this might represent, but confident of the success both of socialist and sexual revolution, he prophesied with an optimism which has a somewhat melancholy effect today: "We are now approaching a social revolution in which the old economic foundations of monogamy will disappear just as surely as those of its complement prostitution."[155] The revolution was then still to come—but soon. Nearly one hundred years later we yet await it.

There is one more cardinal point in Engels' theory of sexual revolution, bound to provoke more controversy than all the others: "With the transformation of the means of production into collective property, the monogamous family will cease to be the economic unit of society. *The care and education of children becomes a public matter.*"[156] This last point is perhaps the most crucial of Engels' propositions, though it meets with the greatest resistance. There is something logical and even inevitable in this recommendation, for so long as every female, simply by virtue of her anatomy, is obliged, even forced, to be the sole or primary caretaker of childhood, she is prevented from being a free human being. The care of children, even from the period

---

[153] Engels, *op. cit.*, p. 89.
[154] *Ibid.*, p. 90. Italics added.
[155] *Ibid.*, pp. 91–92. Italics added.
[156] *Ibid.*, pp. 191–92.

when their cognitive powers first emerge, is infinitely better left to the best trained practitioners of both sexes who have chosen it as a vocation, rather than to harried and all too frequently unhappy persons with little time nor taste for the work of educating minds, however young or beloved. The radical outcome of Engels' analysis is that the family, as that term is presently understood, must go. In view of the institution's history, this is a kind fate. Engels was heresy in his age. These many decades after, he is heresy still. But revolution is always heresy, perhaps sexual revolution most of all.

LITERARY

One can locate three different responses to the sexual revolution in the literature of the period. The first is the realistic or revolutionary. It took in a wide spectrum of radical analysis from Engels to Mill, to the critics and reformers such as Ibsen and Shaw, to the moderates such as Dickens and Meredith. If a critical attitude toward the sexual politics of patriarchy precedes reform, reform itself precedes revolution. The first school expressed themselves either deliberately in theory or polemic, or indirectly in the fictive situations of the theatre or the novel.

The second response belongs to the sentimental and chivalrous school of which Ruskin's "Of Queen's Gardens" is the best and most complete example. It operates through an appeal to propriety and protestation of its good intentions, rather than through any specific recommendations for change. In fact, its general intention is to forestall change of any kind by proclaiming the status quo both good and natural. It presupposes an ideal state of awed reverence toward virtuous womanhood while it temporizes hypocritically on the issue of status, idly pretending an eagerness to award a superior position to a group to whom in fact it begrudges egalitarian place, for it is designed specifically to meet the challenge of "levelers." Loath to make any economic concessions, it sentimentalizes the monogamous family, which it refuses to see as an economic unit and would defend to the death. At its most generous moments it might regretfully permit a few legal reforms; but on the whole it finds even these unnecessary, for since all good men cherish their good wives, the fact that they legally own them is not sufficiently important to deserve mention. Even education is a disagreeable subject with the chivalrous because a decorative and slender instruction is not only feminine and aesthetic, it also complements masculine higher learning. Serious education for women is perceived, consciously or unconsciously, as a threat to patriarchal marriage, domestic sentiment, and ultimately to male supremacy—economic, social, and psychological. The phenomena of prostitution or of poverty, the plight of many women at the time, can, under this benign sentimentality, only be deplored. Poverty may be glossed over as a problem to be dealt with through the trivial offices of charity assigned to the female sphere. As to prostitution, it is better ignored as unfit for discussion, especially in polite or literary contexts, or in circles where it might cause a "blush" to arise. Most Victorian poetry is deliberately escapist, resolutely shunning the contemporary world as the verse of probably no other period before had dared to do. Poetry itself has nearly always been identified with the ruling class, its views, values, and interests. Only in the novel did the real world openly intrude. And for all the decorous disguises it assumed in the Victorian novel, the actual contemporary world did intrude very often; the ugly facts of sexual politics and the upsetting facts of the sexual revolution along with it. Yet here too the chivalrous mentality exerted itself and infested candid discussion.

The third school, which we shall call the school of fantasy, involves itself with a point of view nearly exclusively masculine. It often expresses the unconscious emotions of male response to what it perceives as feminine evil, namely, sexuality. However much this may resemble the old myth of feminine evil, there is something new about it—it is painfully self-conscious. Finding that there was much in its culture it could no longer take for granted, the Victorian period tends to exaggerate and be ill at ease in traditional gestures. In its fantasies of feminine evil there is something so uneasily self-aware that a number of tensions and overtones appear which one had not usually met with before in this convention. The disparity between the good and the evil, chaste and sensuous woman, figures older than Christianity, becomes far more overt than it had ever been previously, partly because the cover of religious sanction afforded by the figures of Eve and Mary had pretty well collapsed. Earlier periods had also cherished two separate and contradictory versions of woman—one vicious, one adulatory. But in no period of Western literature had the question of the sexual politics or of woman's experience within it grown so vexing and insistent as it did in this. The myth of feminine evil appears more in the poetry of the age than in other literary forms. In the novel feminine evil is too likely to wear the recognizable social and economic garments of prostitution or penury; in prose fiction the sexuality projected upon the female demands the more honest explanation of the whore, the "fallen woman," the servant seduced: Nancy, Tess, Esther Waters. The more accommodating vehicle of myth which is proper to poetry, deals actually—and rather transparently—with a sexuality the male has perceived in himself, and despising it, casts upon the woman. In the poetry of Tennyson, the myth combines with the other period legend of chivalry, and masculine sensibility weighs the virtuous woman against the vicious woman. We are told that it is the first of whom the poet approves, even if he fails to demonstrate it. Later on in Victorian poetry, there is less and less resort to chivalrous palliation. And with Rossetti and Swinburne, even the eternal need to vent disapproval on the malefic woman begins to disappear.

It does so with a curious and highly significant novelty; what was once simply evil and terrifying remains all this, perhaps even more so, but it is now wonderfully attractive as well. The bitch goddess whom Mailer's Rojack righteously strangles is transformed by *fin de siècle* into a dazzling apparition before whom a poet like Swinburne is willing to prostrate himself in paroxysms of masochistic ecstasy, and a playwright like Wilde is even willing to go so far as to identify *himself* with.

The fantastic is the most ambivalent of the three schools of attitude. Each of the first two had a definite stand to take for or against the sexual revolution, but the third is confused in its response. Despite fantasy's elusive and escapist manner (for it usually refused to face social realities even more resolutely than chivalry, which had at least troubled to prepare a formula), it had a considerable contribution to make to the sexual revolution. Through its tactics of refuge in the unconscious and in fantasy, it released more sexual energy and expressed more tenuous and deeply buried sexual attitudes than did its rivals. As a result it was in the vanguard of the sexual revolution in the area of *sexuality* itself; suggesting, however unsystematically, greater measures for relief in the areas of sexual mores and sexual "deviance," than any other. It was the center also of homosexual sentiment, and of certain other practices, which, unlike homosexuality, deserve to be labeled as sexually perverse.

Although its means were irrational and often circuitous, occasionally even perverse, it was able to explore sexual politics at an inchoate primary level. The chivalrous school, deeply anti-revolutionary and conservative, was, by comparison, utterly unproductive save for its empty proclamations. It was the realists and the fantasists who brought about the revolution. However, the first group were far more practical and to the point, the fantasists often so incoherent as to be liable to subversion, and sometimes so ambivalent that they could hardly be relied upon for more than that cultural information which all representative fantasy affords.

It should be remembered that only at the extreme of each class were unmixed attitudes to be found; needless to say, all three were coterminous. Reformers were often afraid of the effects of any relaxation of sexual mores; members of the fantasy school were afraid, delighted, and guilty all at once. Reforming novels were also full of chivalrous sentiment, even given to optimistic assurances that the unpleasantness they described was unique or exceptional and could be solved by love alone.

It is impossible, even in a chapter so embarrassingly lengthy, to do any real justice to the literature of the first phase, a subject which merits a treatment of its own in one or several volumes. It is imperative therefore that we limit ourselves to these few generalizations and to an examination of a small number of lesser-known but representative works. The most famous products of revolutionary agitation, the plays of Shaw and Ibsen, the work of Virginia Woolf, are, whatever their present fortunes, perhaps too familiar. It seemed more interesting to hit upon a few texts which are not much read, or not read in this context, to furnish us with key examples—three novels by Hardy, Meredith, and Charlotte Brontë, and a prose poem by Oscar Wilde.

Thomas Hardy's *Jude the Obscure* gives an account of the trials of two rebels: Jude is battling the class system in trying to obtain the Oxford education reserved for the elite; Sue Bridehead has set herself against a number of patriarchal institutions, principally marriage and the church. Both are beaten. Jude dies solitary and desolate with the merry echoes of Oxford's Eights Week boat races mocking his agony. Sue returns to the "fanatic prostitution" of living with her first husband, Richard Phillotson, a man she despised.

Hardy's Jude is a complete human being composed of both sense and spirit, mind and body. In a classic instance of the Victorian triangle he is torn between two women who are incomplete beings. Arabella is at one pole, utter carnality, "a complete and substantial female animal—no more, no less."[157] In Hardy's grotesque parody of Cupid's shaft, they first meet when Arabella pitches the scrotum of a butchered barrow-pig at Jude's head. At the other pole stands Sue—pure spirit. They are the familiar Lily and Rose, but Sue is a lily with a difference—she has a brain. Yet she is repelled by sense, for Sue is not only the New Woman, but by a complex set of frequently unsympathetic defenses, at times convincing, and at times only a rather labored ambivalence of Hardy's own—she is the Frigid Woman as well. Hardy is disgusted by Arabella, appalled, if intrigued, by her crude and terrible vitality. He champions Sue through a series of uningratiating maneuvers, but he is always slightly nervous about her. In a defensive postscript written seventeen years after his first preface, he appears to have been rather embarrassed and even annoyed at what the public took her to be:

After the issue of Jude the Obscure as a serial story in Germany, an experienced reviewer of that country informed the writer that Sue Bridehead, the heroine, was the first delineation in fiction of the woman who was coming into notice in her thousands every year—the woman of the feminist movement —that slight, pale, "bachelor" girl—the intellectualized, emancipated bundle of nerves, that modern conditions were producing, mainly in cities as yet; who does not recognize the necessity for most of her sex to follow marriage as a profession, and boast themselves as superior people because they are licensed to be loved on the premises. The regret of this critic was that the portrait of the newcomer had been left to be drawn by a man, and was not done by one of her own sex, who would never have allowed her to break down at the end.[158]

---

[157] Thomas Hardy, *Jude the Obscure*, first published in book form in 1895. (London: Macmillan Library Edition, 1951), p. 42.

[158] *Ibid.*, p. x, 1912 postscript to the Preface to the first edition.

The passage is wonderfully noncommittal: for all the sarcasm Hardy scatters at bachelor girls, colorless bags of emaciated nerves who are indistinguishable from prostitutes since they are "licensed to be loved on the premises" and reject marriage as a "profession"—with the implication that there are but two professions for women—Hardy still never goes on to contradict his German critic. For it is still true that Sue is his heroine and that she had the temerity to be altogether down on marriage. There is a certain irony about the critic's last statement berating Hardy for allowing her to "break down at the end." Even though Hardy was far too astute, or far too timid, to permit himself to be identified with the notorious feminists, quite the finest thing in the book is his sensitive, perceptive account of Sue's capitulation.

This is not to say that the portrait is without flaws. Sue is broken by the arbitrary death of her children; Hardy's murder—their own suicide. Even in her revolt against convention she is uncertain, confused, imperfectly convincing. Jude is inconsistent as well, but his dilemma is a simpler matter of being strung between what Hardy gives us to understand is the deterministic reflex action of his flesh, and the aspirations of his soul toward the Fathers and the Classics. His motivations are always made clear for us; Sue's are not. Like the Continental Naturalists, Hardy fancies he is following scientific law in awarding his characters instincts. Yet it is curious how sexual impulse is an instinct only in males; some females have it, others do not.[159] And when Sue is delivering her diatribes against marriage, Hardy is surely present but to a degree difficult to determine. He never commits himself to Sue as he did to Jude, and insists on seeing her obliquely or at a distance. As the center of consciousness in the novel is Jude's rather than Sue's, we never really understand what thought processes have brought her to the point of chanting Swinburne's atheism in the Oxford moonlight before her clandestine pagan sculptures under the very nose of the High Anglican orthodoxy she so thoroughly detests and so audaciously ridicules.

It is Sue's defeat that persuades us, not her insurrection. Jude's ambitions were noble and of a kind the reader is made liable to identify with at once and without reservations. His defeat is tragic but never humiliating, for he had never betrayed his intentions nor ever surrendered to the system—it simply overran and killed him. Through a series of back-slidings he has fallen into the clutches of Arabella for the third and final time, but these are mere physical weaknesses and Hardy would not have us concern ourselves with them overmuch. Class and poverty have conquered Jude. With Sue it is far otherwise. She collapses from within. Jude indulges in sexuality as his right and in a blundering fashion which is often at odds with his own career ambitions. But from the very beginning, from her first admirer, the Oxford

---

[159] One of the more awkward strands of "science" in the novel is the attribution of hereditary traits to its characters; Sue and Jude's failure in marriage is partly due to the fact that a number of their ancestors had also made a botch of it.

undergraduate whom she drove to suicide, Sue has held sexuality in terror, seen it as evil—her own evil.

The clue to both Sue and Arabella is in their self-hatred and self-contempt. They despise womanhood. Arabella, a conqueror of men, a vaginal trap, a creature utterly devoid of any kind of compunction, helpfully explains her entire sex to Phillotson, squaring the plot's two triangles to a rectangle, while providing the mechanism for Sue's recapture and final internment:

> That's the only way with these fanciful women that chew high—innocent or guilty. She'd have come round in time. We all do! Custom does it! it's all the same in the end! . . . I shouldn't have let her go! I should have kept her chained on—her spirit for kicking would have been broke soon enough! There's nothing like bondage and a stone deaf taskmaster for taming us women. Besides, you've got the laws on your side. Moses knew. Don't you call to mind what he says? . . . I used to think o't when they read it in church, and I was carrying on a bit. "Then shall the man be guiltless; but the woman shall bear her iniquity." Damn rough on us women; but we must grin and put up wi' it!—Haw haw!—Well; she's got her deserts now.[160]

The moment her children are dead Sue breaks like a straw, finding in the atrocity of Father Time's population control—or Hardy's reaching for effect— ample evidence of divine retribution. All her shaky but hard-earned faith in her own intelligence and the critical analysis it had accomplished on the society she inhabited and was assailed by collapses before what she confesses is her "awe or terror of conventions I don't believe in. It comes over me at times like a sort of creeping paralysis."[161] It is sexual guilt that undoes Sue, guilt for ever having known freedom, joy, sexuality, Jude's love, or her cherished illegitimate children.

When they are found hanged, Jude comforts himself with reciting the *Agamemnon* in Greek, but Sue's very soul despairs and dies. The mind that Jude had so admired and which is Hardy's most original note in the novel, that splendid intellect which had "scintillated like a star"[162] and seen the world as the mere error of a somnambulant First Cause, staggers and turns the full force of her affliction into a malign Destiny's punishment for Sin. She falls to the level of lecturing her lover to the tune of "We must conform . . . There is no choice . . . It is no use fighting against God."[163] From here on in she is to grovel at the foot of the cross.

What lies at the root of her capitulation is patriarchy's ancient masochistic system: sex is female and evil. "I cannot humiliate myself too much. I should like to prick myself all over with pins and bleed out the badness that's in

160 *Ibid.*, pp. 383–84.
161 *Ibid.*
162 *Ibid.*, p. 396.
163 *Ibid.*, p. 413.

me."[164] Jude, who, like Hardy, has never been very sure whether "the women are to blame" and all the evils of life are inherent in their natures, or whether the problem is in "the artificial system of things, under which the normal sex impulses are turned into devilish domestic gins and springes to noose and hold back those who want to progress"[165] frantically exhorts Sue to remain true to her former insights: "Is a woman a thinking unit at all, or a fraction always wanting its integer?"[166]

Jude is mistaken. Sue is only too logical. She has understood the world, absorbed its propositions, and finally implemented that guilt which precipitated her self-hatred. Nothing remains to her but to destroy herself. She renounces all hope of bucking the system and in giving up she becomes a collaborator who can out Victorian the Victorian slave-wife. In presenting herself at Richard's bedroom door she is demonstrating the full hideous iniquity of conventional marriage which is Hardy's target in the novel. Her pronouncements now take on the semantic coloration of religious treacle; she mouths pious cliché about "the error of my views:"

> We ought to be continually sacrificing ourselves on the altar of duty! But I have always striven to do what has pleased me. I well deserved the scourging I have got! I wish something would take the evil right out of me, and all my monstrous errors, and all my sinful ways![167]

Her final psychotic self-mutilation in offering herself to Richard is the result not only of an abdication to period opinion but is also inspired by her sexual disappointment when she discovers Jude has betrayed her in returning to Arabella. Sue never had all of Jude and she knew it. Hardy, by inventing in Sue Bridehead a woman so "ethereal," has made it impossible for Jude's more complete humanity to be faithful to her.

It is difficult to understand whether Sue is the victim of circumstances, principally those of her own social indoctrination and stronger than any truth that she might acquire on her own, or the victim of a cultural literary convention (Lily and Rose) that in granting her a mind insists on withholding a body from her, or finally, whether she is simply the victim of Hardy's irascible pessimism and the heavy-handed tragic device which poleaxes her hopes by hanging her children.

Hardy himself seems unsure and the product of this uncertainty is that Sue is by turns an enigma, a pathetic creature, a nut, and an iceberg. The book is a significant contribution to the literature of the sexual revolution in a number of ways—first, for its savage criticism of institutions—marriage and sexual ownership—its impassioned plea for easy divorce. Most of Hardy's

[164] *Ibid.*, p. 417.
[165] *Ibid.*, p. 261.
[166] *Ibid.*, p. 424.
[167] *Ibid.*, p. 416.

novels are this. *Jude* is the first of them where people manage to obtain divorce but even this cannot help them in a world where marriage is corrupt. Secondly, Hardy is to be commended for creating in Sue an intelligent rebel against sexual politics and in understanding the forces which defeat such a rebel. Finally, the novel's greatest fascination resides in its demonstration of how very difficult a struggle such a revolution can be—not only for its participants but even for the author who would describe it. *Jude the Obscure* is on very solid ground when attacking the class system, but when it turns to the sexual revolution, Hardy himself is troubled and confused.

Nothing could be further removed from the air of grim futility Hardy breathed upon *Jude the Obscure* than Meredith's gay and civilized urbanity in *The Egoist*. Yet both novels attack the conventions surrounding patriarchal marriage. Meredith's plot is as slight and agreeable as any of Austen's. To say that the novel is nearly that good is high praise indeed. It too is a comedy of manners over the trifling question of "who she'll marry," but Meredith has made it the vehicle of much satire as well. The complexities of poverty within which Hardy had obscured the issues of sexual politics in *Jude* are not to be found in *The Egoist,* for Meredith deliberately chose to play out his scenes among the upper class, where one is most likely to find the extreme cases of social convention and artifice. He sensed that in this setting sex is most distorted by ritual etiquette, conventionalized language and emotion. Here the sex-as-barter system should be most unnecessary. Yet the economic factor does not cease to be operative.

Meredith's heroine, Clara Middleton, has no money of her own and is prevented from earning any. She is therefore to be sold into security. It is Meredith's conviction that many of the evils of society are due to an unconscious and conditioned falseness, a sickness so thoroughly "socialized" that it lies below the level of even political remedy. In other words, he has discovered that sexual politics is a mental habit buried deep in our culture which transcends the politics of class, however deeply intertwined the two may be.

Perhaps Meredith's most important contribution is his indictment of chivalry as a selfish custom of complacency which property and power have engendered in the male. The entire novel might have been based upon Mill's observations on the vicious effects that the superior status awarded to men must necessarily have upon their characters. For the book's real subject is its painstaking investigation of the egoist of its title; it is a veritable anatomy of masculine vanity in the person of Sir Willoughby Patterne. Here, for example, one is privileged to see the man in love:

> Clara was young, healthy, handsome; she was therefore fitted to be his wife, the mother of his children, his companion picture. Certainly they looked well side by side. In walking with her, in drooping to her, the whole man was made conscious of the female image of himself by her exquisite unlikeness. She

completed him, added the softer lines wanting to his portrait before the world. He had wooed her ragingly; he courted her becomingly; with the manly self-possession enlivened by watchful tact which is pleasing to girls. He never seemed to undervalue himself in valuing her.[168]

Meredith knows his subject. One might call it the case of a man who looked into his heart—and those of his fellows—and wrote. This is the manner in which Robert Louis Stevenson responded:

Here is a book to send the blood into men's faces . . . It is yourself that is hunted down; these are your faults that are dragged into the day and numbered, with lingering relish, with cruel cunning and precision. A young friend of Mr. Meredith's (as I have the story) came to him in an agony. "This is too bad of you," he cried, "Willoughby is me!" "No, my dear fellow," said the author, "he is all of us." . . . I am like the young friend of the anecdote—I think Willoughby an unmanly but a very serviceable exposure of myself.[169]

The surprising parallels to Meredith's own life are unmistakable. Clara Middleton is his own first wife, Mary Nicolls. Her irresponsible epicurean parent is Thomas Love Peacock, Meredith's former father-in-law. Willoughby jilted is Meredith deserted after some seven years of bitter cohabitation, when Mary left him for Henry Wallis the painter. What is astonishing is that the book is not the revenge one would inevitably expect, but is instead a careful analysis of incompatibility. Willoughby's conceit is something Meredith recognizes in himself and everyman, part of his training and expectation; an unconscious tendency to overbear, yet a manner for which Meredith is willing to take responsibility. What is brilliant about the achievement is how much Meredith can reveal without unnecessary rancor. The entire satire is rendered in the most delightful comic spirit.

Better even than such description is Meredith's explanation of how circumstances are so arranged that there can be little peace between the sexes; Meredith not only knows how things are ordered in sexual politics, he knows why. His virtues lie in his sympathetic understanding of all his characters (even to the rare wonder of his comprehension of the women in the book—a feat of astounding empathy) and in his superb background information on the powers of environment and conditioning that have made these people what they are.

It is impossible to hate Willoughby, so thoroughly do we come to know that conspiracy of worship which has labored to construct his vanity, fond product of a lifetime association with obsequious female dependents who have convinced him he is god. Raised by a doting mother and two demented

---

[168] George Meredith, *The Egoist*, first published in 1879. (Cambridge, Massachusetts; Riverside Press, 1958), p. 36.

[169] Quoted in Lionel Stevenson's Introduction to the Riverside Edition. The source is R. L. Stevenson's essay, "Books Which Have Influenced Me."

aunts, he has already discovered his divinity in childhood and standing on a
chair proclaimed himself Louis the Sun King, an event recalled in anecdote
by his miniature court with rapturous nods and smiles.

Once Meredith has described the conditions of her education, it is just as
difficult to blame Clara Middleton for allowing herself to become engaged
to Willoughby, rather than send him packing the moment he appeared.
Clara is hemmed in by the circumstances of her meager education, her innocence, her economic impotence, and her conditioning to docility and respectability. The last item, a tribal policing technique, held the most terror
for a marriageable young woman and was the dragon which the sexual
revolution had first to slay. If Clara breaks her engagement it will be a
major scandal; if she fails to do so it will be—as she finally comes to realize—
a catastrophe. Meredith's great interest is in psychological conflict, bind and
double bind, the war of motive within the individual, the welter of destructive urges, the fears and frustrations due to artificial codes and the acceptance of false standards of values.

He is an avowed feminist who sees in women an oppressed class dominated
through male self-interest, prevented from developing as human beings
by a system which prostitutes them in and out of marriage and deliberately
miseducates them. Clara Middleton, the product of such a learning process,
cannot at first comprehend what it is in her rich and handsome fiancé that
she finds so utterly repellent. Her senses revolt at his peremptory embraces,
but she cannot immediately fathom why. The discussion of volition and sexuality which Hardy bungles so in frigid Sue is far better done in *The Egoist*.
Meredith is sensitive not only to what one might call "timing," but also to
the fact that sexual freedom is freedom of choice and occasion, and he recognizes that Clara feels her own will coerced in Willoughby's clumsy assertive
advances. Sexuality is an affair of possession with this young lord and Clara
has learned in an instant that she is to be "claimed" as "his apparent
right."[170] She reacts like any creature who senses captivity and springs
back, but this never ruffles Willoughby's confidence, for he regards it as only
proper his wife be cold; it is a sign she is appropriately "pure." Virginity is
also part of the bargain. When Clara loses her purse, Meredith plays on the
double entendre in Willoughby's satisfaction that his former servant Flitch
has returned it "intact"; on the same occasion the master refers to one of his
cast off women as "an ancient purse."

Clara is to be sold to this connoisseur by a bookish father who is humbled
at the princely price Willoughby has condescended to pay. At a moment
when things are not going smoothly and it seems the prize might escape
him, Willoughby sits up over an exquisite port with her parent. "Ladies are
creation's glory but they are an anti-climax, following a wine of a century
old."[171] The suitor then presents his bribe—there are fifty dozen bottles of

[170] *Ibid.*, p. 49.
[171] *Ibid.*, p. 161.

the same port for Middleton when he becomes father-in-law to this magnificent cellar. "I have but a girl to give," blushes the old gourmand.[172] The bargain is struck. "Note the superiority of wine over Venus," the old scholar chuckles while trolling the more rakish passages of Catullus and exclaiming over the manner in which Willoughby's bottles are corked, a series of sexual pens which Meredith brings off with remarkable flair.

Willoughby is Clara's education. Having come to perceive Willoughby's irremediable fatuity, Clara can serve as a tutor to Laetitia Dale, curing this sentimentalist of her doglike devotion to a man who had trifled with her for ten years, holding her always as a sort of reserve love-force on days when it seemed nothing better might turn up. Of Willoughby's treatment of Laetitia, Meredith comments in mock-sententiousness: "In the hundred and fourth chapter of the thirteenth volume of the Book of Egotism, it is written: Possession without obligation to the object possessed approaches felicity."[173] One of the most delicious moments in the book occurs upon Willoughby's return from a trip abroad:

> Willoughby returned to his England after an absence of three years. On a fair April morning, the last of the month, he drove along his park palings, and by the luck of things, Laetitia was the first of his friends whom he met. She was crossing from field to field with a bank of school-children, gathering wild flowers for the morrow May-day. He sprang to the ground and seized her hand. "Laetitia Dale!" he said. He panted. "Your name is sweet English music! And you are well?" The anxious question permitted him to read deeply in her eyes. He found the man he sought there, squeezed him passionately, and let him go, saying, "I could not have prayed for a lovelier home-scene to welcome me . . ."[174]

Meredith is an expert at satirizing the enormous bulk of egotism that masculine chivalrous sentiment had injected into love, Romantic or Courtly. Willoughby, who finds society a "weltering human mass"[175] without feminine "virtue" intends by that chivalric desideratum an eternal fidelity to a masculine proprietor:

> Clara! to dedicate your life to our love! Never one touch! one thought, not a dream! Could you?—it agonizes me to imagine . . . be inviolate? mine above? —mine before all men, though I am gone—true to my dust. Tell me. Give me that assurance. True to my name!—Oh! I hear them "His relict." Buzzing about Lady Patterne. "The widow." If you knew their talk of widows! Shut your ears my angel! Consent; gratify me; swear it. Say, "Beyond death." Whisper it. I ask for nothing more. Women think the husband's grave breaks the bond,

[172] *Ibid.*, p. 159.
[173] *Ibid.*, p. 108.
[174] *Ibid.*, pp. 23–24.
[175] *Ibid.*, p. 44.

cuts the tie, sets them loose. They wed the flesh—pah! What I call on is nobility; the transcendent nobility of faithfulness beyond death. "His widow!" let them say; a saint in widowhood.[176]

Willoughby's gallant professions of protection are in fact nothing but an odious form of patronization: "Whenever the little brain is in doubt, perplexed, undecided, which course to adopt, she will come to me, will she not."[177]

So imperturbable is Willoughby that when Clara warns him, "I fear we do not often agree, Willoughby," he replies with irritating assurance, "When you are a little older!"[178]

The great wellspring of their quarrel concerns what the couple both refer to as "the world." For his part, Willoughby "wanted her simply to be material in his hands for him to mold her, he had no other thought."[179] There is a hitch in the scheme: "he had made the discovery that their minds differed on one or two points and a difference of view in his bride was obnoxious to his repose."[180] Willoughby, who intends to go into Parliament and in the days of the British Empire at its zenith proposes to rule that entity he calls the world, insists that for true lovers there should be an absolute exclusion of the world from their blisses. Translated, this means that the dyadic withdrawal he pretends to recommend for both parties should apply exclusively to his bride; he intends Clara to spend the rest of her days in his home catering to his comfort. It is Ruskin's irrepressible formula of separate spheres once again. Clara begins to view the prospect as tantamount to undergoing interment alive.

Willoughby is a lord. To marry him is to enter into the hierarchal obligations of feudalism. From his birth he has been taught and encouraged to command and he expects to continue when Clara is added to his retinue. When she finally gathers courage to reject him, he refuses to release her from an engagement she informs him in the most lucid terms is unpalatable. How dare she wish to be free of him: "Volatile, unworthy, liberty—my dearest! . . . you are at liberty within the law, like all good women; I shall control and direct your volatility; and your sense of worthiness must be re-established when we are more intimate; it is timidity. The sense of unworthiness is a guarantee of worthiness ensuing."[181]

So obtuse is Willoughby that it takes Clara four hundred more pages to persuade him that she truly means not to marry him. The situation of a vain man who refuses to be refused in marriage by a spirited young woman, is a

---

[176] *Ibid.*, pp. 42–43.
[177] *Ibid.*, p. 88.
[178] *Ibid.*, p. 83.
[179] *Ibid.*, p. 39.
[180] *Ibid.*, pp. 38–39.
[181] *Ibid.*, p. 89.

fine subject for comedy, and Meredith milks it for all it is worth. The result is very entertaining. Yet the conclusion of the book, a falling into the slender stuff of drawing-room comedy, overheard conversations, mistaken identity and so forth, is—for all its hilarity—somehow disappointing. Clara is married off to Vernon Whitford, a nice enough fellow, and the reader is expected to feel that her fate is happily settled. This hardly seems satisfactory. It would be a splendid thing if the bitter generality of sexual politics were all to be solved in marrying the right person, and the sexual revolution confined to and completed by a honeymoon in Switzerland. The "world" is a bit more complex than this and one cannot help wishing, like Clara, that there were a bit more of it in the book. Comedies are always concluded in marriage, but there is something poignant in the realization that Clara's marriage is rather like a death. Throughout the novel she was a person in the process of *becoming*, but by the last page she has not succeeded in becoming anyone but Mrs. Vernon Whitford, which is to say, no one at all. Meredith knows how to save her from the egoist, but he can think of nothing else to do for her. A life more occupied and interesting than mere mating—for good or ill—never seems to have occurred to him in connection with an intelligent young woman. This is a notably deficient and a rather tritely masculine attitude; for all his good intentions regarding the crippling character of feminine education, the feudal character of patriarchal marriage, and the egotism of male assumptions, Meredith appears incapable of transcending them and consequently mistakes the liberating turmoil of the sexual revolution for the mundane activities of a matchmaking bureau.

So far we have observed the sexual revolution as it was reflected in the minds of male writers responding to it with gallant enthusiasm or dubious ambiguity. But the period did provide something more informative than this; it permitted the first expression of a feminine point of view. Mill had remarked that most of what women produced when they began to write was but sycophancy to male attitude and ego: the caveat is profoundly true both then and now. Yet, inasmuch as the first phase made possible the emergence of a truly feminine sensibility, one can find in the Brontës the real thing. "Living in sin," George Eliot lived the revolution as well perhaps, but she did not write of it. She is stuck with the Ruskinian service ethic and the pervasive Victorian fantasy of the good woman who goes down into Samaria and rescues the fallen man—nurse, guide, mother, adjunct of the race. Dorothea's predicament in *Middlemarch* is an eloquent plea that a fine mind be allowed an occupation; but it goes no farther than petition. She marries Will Ladislaw and can expect no more of life than the discovery of a good companion whom she can serve as secretary. Virginia Woolf glorified two housewives, Mrs. Dalloway and Mrs. Ramsay, recorded the suicidal misery of Rhoda in *The Waves* without ever explaining its causes, and was argumentative yet somehow unsuccessful, perhaps because unconvinced, in conveying the frustrations of the woman artist in Lily Briscoe. Only in *A Room of One's Own*, essay rather than fiction, could she describe what she knew.

Lucy Snowe, the heroine of Charlotte Brontë's *Villette*,[182] a book too subversive to be popular, is another matter. In Lucy one may perceive what effects her life in a male-supremacist society has upon the psyche of a woman. She is bitter and she is honest; a neurotic revolutionary full of conflict, backsliding, anger, terrible self-doubt, and an unconquerable determination to win through. She is a pair of eyes watching society; weighing, ridiculing, judging. A piece of furniture whom no one notices, Lucy sees everything and reports, cynically, compassionately, truthfully, analytically. She is no one, because she lacks any trait that might render her visible: beauty, money, conformity. Only a superb mind imperfectly developed and a soul so omnivorously large it casts every other character into the shadows, she is the great exception, the rest only the great mediocre rule.

Lucy is a woman who has watched men and can tell you what they are as seen by the woman they fail to notice. Some are like John Graham Bretton, charming egoists. Their beauty, for Brontë is perhaps the first woman who ever admitted in print that women find men beautiful, amazes and hurts her. Bretton is two people: one is Graham the treasured and privileged man-child seen through the eyes of a slighted sister, whether the distant idolator be Lucy or Missy Home. Brontë keeps breaking people into two parts so we can see their divided and conflicting emotions; Missy is the worshipful sister, Lucy the envious one. Together they represent the situation of the girl in the family. Bretton is both the spoiled son Graham, and the successful doctor John, and in both roles Lucy envies, loves and hates him. Never does the situation permit her to love him in peace, nor him to take notice of her in any but the most tepid and patronizing good humor: sterile, indifferent. His beauty and goodness make him lovable; his privilege and egotism make him hateful. The enormous deprivation of her existence causes Lucy to resemble a ghetto child peering up at a Harvard man—envy, admiration, resentment and dislike; yet with a tremendous urge to love—if it were possible to love one so removed, so diffident, so oppressive, so rich, disdainful and unjustly superior in place.

If the male is not the delightful and infuriating egoist whom maturity means learning to relinquish one's "crush" on, he is the male one encounters a bit later in life when one tries to make one's way. He is Paul Emanuel, the voice of piety, conventionality, male supremacy, callow chauvinism terrified of female "competition." John is unconquerable; he will never acknowledge any woman who is not beautiful or rich, his only qualifications; he loved Fanshawe's stupidity just as readily as Paulina Mary's virtue. Women

---

[182] Charlotte Brontë, *Villette*, first published in 1853 under the pseudonym Currer Bell. Reprinted by the Gresham Publishing Company, London, undated. Page numbers refer to this edition. Throughout my remarks I am indebted to an unpublished essay on Charlotte Brontë's *Shirley* written by Laurie Stone.

are decorative objects to him. Paul is easier to cope with; in his sexual antagonism there is something more tractable. John Graham never saw Lucy; Paul sees her and hates her. Here it is possible to establish contact and, as the story is all a fantasy of success (a type of success utterly impossible to achieve in Brontë's period, and so necessarily fantastic) Paul is met and persuaded. To his sneer that she is ignorant and women are dolts, Lucy replies with phenomenal intellectual effort. Despite the impossible atmosphere he gives off as a pedagogue, the bullying, the captivity in overheated rooms, the endless spying, the bowdlerizing of her texts—she learns. It is his ridicule that forces her to achieve, pokes her into development, deprives her of the somnolence of ladyhood, its small ambitions, timidity, and self-doubt.

Lucy watches women—again from a double and even more complicated point of vantage. She studies Ginevra Fanshawe the flirt, an idiot beauty callously using men to acquire what she has been carefully taught to want: admiration, money, the petty power of dominating a puppy. Fanshawe is beautiful too, and Lucy, in every respect the product of her society as well as its enemy and rebel, has been schooled to love this beauty. It stirs her. The book is full of references to the desire such beauty arouses in her. To express it, Brontë invents the device of an afternoon of amateur theatrics. Lucy is dragged into them at the last moment to play Fanshawe's lover. It is another of Paul's bullying schemes (he locks her in an attic in the July heat to be sure she learns her lines) to coerce her into courage and achievement. Lucy succeeds miraculously, and she makes love to Fanshawe on stage in one of the most indecorous scenes one may come upon in the entire Victorian novel. (Brontë is too much an insurrectionary to acknowledge any convention beyond the literary and the most astonishing things occur continuously in her fiction.) Just as maturity and success lie in outgrowing an infatuation with Graham's masculine egotism, or Paul's bullying but productive chauvinism, they are also a matter of renouncing a masculine lust for Fanshawe. She is too dumb to love, too silly to want or to permit oneself to be wounded by. The dialogue between the two young women is brutal; Fanshawe parades her beauty with the double purpose of making Lucy capitulate before it, acknowledge herself an ugly woman and therefore inferior; or propose herself a suitor to it and therefore a captive through desire. For Ginevra knows critical Lucy would be the best catch of all, the biggest conquest. Lucy holds her own in these cruel sessions and won't be had either way. Ultimately, she transcends them and Fanshawe altogether, who fades into the mere butterfly she is and disappears from the book.

The other women Lucy watches are Madame Beck and Mrs. Bretton. Both are older women, one a mother, one a businesswoman and head of a school. They are two of the most efficient women one can meet anywhere in fiction. Lucy, who, like Charlotte Brontë, lacked a mother, regards older women as the embodiment of competence, and what she loves in them is their brilliant ability to manage. While Victorian masculine fantasy saw only tender, quivering incapacity in such women, Lucy perceives them as big, capable ships and herself only a little boat. But the big ships are afloat because they knew how to compromise; Lucy does not plan to. The big ships are convention. For all the playful banter of her relationship with her son, Mrs. Bretton stands for a stale and selfless maternity, bent on living vicariously through her adored boy's success. Pleasant matron that she is, she would sacrifice any daughter in the world for the comfort of his lordly breakfast, and Lucy knows it. Mrs. Bretton's conventional motherhood is only the warm perfection of chauvinist sentiment. Then there is Madame Beck, a tower of convention, the tireless functionary of European sexual inhibition, watching every move of the young women under her Jehovah-like and unsleeping surveillance; getting up at night to examine Lucy's underwear, reading her letters to sniff out traces of sex in them, watching for missives thrown from windows to her pupils. Both these women are still young and ripe for sexuality. Mrs. Bretton fulfills her own in flirtation with her son:

> "Mamma, I'm in a dangerous way."
> "As if that interested me," said Mrs. Bretton.
> "Alas! the cruelty of my lot!" responded her son. "Never man had a more unsentimental mother than mine; she never seems to think that such a calamity can befall her as a daughter-in-law."
> "If I don't, it is not for want of having that same calamity held over my head; you have threatened me with it for the last ten years. 'Mamma, I am going to be married soon!' was the cry before you were well out of jackets."
> "But mother, one of these days it will be realized. All of a sudden, when you think you are most secure, I shall go forth like Jacob or Esau, or any other patriarch, and take me a wife, perhaps of these which are of the daughters of the land."
> "At your peril, John Graham! that is all."[183]

Beck is more sensually alive and would be delighted to take on John Graham, but of course she is not sufficiently young, beautiful, or socially prominent for his tastes. Real as her own sexuality is, she will gracefully acknowledge his rejection, and serenely carry on the business, while cheerfully stamping out the intrusion of the least hint of sex in any corner of her establishment. As the educator of young females, Madame Beck is a perpetual policewoman, a virtual forewoman of patriarchal society. No system of subjection could operate for two seconds without its collaborators, and Beck is a splendid example of the breed.

Finally, there is Paulina Mary, the golden one, the perfect woman, John Graham's pretty Polly, the apple of her daddy's eye. Lucy had no father to dote upon her, nor any John to court her, and she is painfully aware that

Paulina is lucky. Yet there is one flaw in this female paragon—she is a child of eight—delightful when she appears as Missy Home at the beginning of the book; clever, affectionate, precocious—but nauseating when she reappears as a woman of nineteen and still a mental infant. Paulina is well-meaning and well loved. Even Lucy is fond of her from time to time, but she is also appalled that society's perfect woman must be a cute preadolescent. Having surveyed the lot, Lucy prefers to be like none of them. Looking over all the "role models" her world presents, the adoring mother, the efficient prison matron, the merciless flirt, the baby-goddess, Lucy, whose most genuine trial is that she has been born into a world where there are no adequate figures to imitate so that she is forced to grope her way alone, a pioneer without precedents, turns her back on the bunch of them. Better to go back to something solidly her own—deal with mathematics, Paul Emanuel, and the job.

Lucy has watched men look at women, has studied the image of woman in her culture. There is probably nothing so subversive in the book as that afternoon in the Brussels museum when she scrutinizes the two faces of woman whom the male has fashioned, one for his entertainment, one for her instruction: Rubens' Cleopatra and the Academician's four pictures of the virtuous female. Lucy's deliberately philistine account of Cleopatra is very entertaining:

> It represented a woman, considerably larger, I thought, than the life. I calculated that this lady, put into a scale of magnitude suitable for the reception of a commodity of bulk, would infallibly turn from fourteen to sixteen stones. She was indeed extremely well fed. Very much butchers' meat, to say nothing of bread, vegetables, and liquids, must she have consumed to attain that breadth and height, that wealth of muscle, that affluence of flesh. She lay half-reclined on a couch, why, it would be difficult to say; broad daylight blazed round her; she appeared in hearty health, strong enough to do the work of two plain cooks; she could not plead a weak spine; she ought to have been standing, or at least sitting bolt upright. She had no business to lounge away the noon on a sofa . . . Then, for the wretched untidiness surrounding her, there could be no excuse. Pots and pans, perhaps I ought to say vases and goblets, were rolled here and there on the foreground; a perfect rubbish of flowers was mixed amongst them, and an absurd and disorderly mass of certain upholstery smothered the couch, and cumbered the floor.[184]

This "coarse and preposterous canvas," this "enormous piece of claptrap," as Lucy nominates the masturbatory fantasy she perceives in it, is the male dream of an open and panting odalisque, the sheer carnality floating always in the back of his mind, and can be matched only by its obverse—the image of woman he would foist on the woman herself. Cleopatra is for masculine delectation only, and when Paul catches Lucy contemplating the painting he is deeply shocked: "How dare you, a young person, sit coolly down, with

[184] *Ibid.*, p. 183.

the self-possession of a garçon, and look at *that* picture?"[185] A despot, as Lucy describes him so often, he is deeply offended, even affronted, that a young woman should see what he immediately settles down to gaze at. Paul forbids Lucy to look upon Cleopatra, and forces her to sit in a dull corner and study several mawkish daubs the conventional mind has designed for her:

> . . . a set of four, denominated in the catalogue, "La vie d' une femme." They were painted in a remarkable style, flat, dead, pale and formal. The first represented a "Jeune Fille," coming out of a church door, a missal in her hand, her dress very prim, her eyes cast down, her mouth pursed up—the image of a most villainous, little, precocious she-hypocrite. The second, a "Mariée" with a long white veil, kneeling at a prie-dieu in her chamber, holding her hands plastered together, finger to finger, and showing the whites of her eyes in the most exasperating manner. The third, a "Jeune Mère" hanging disconsolate over a clayey and puffy baby with a face like an unwholesome full moon. The fourth, a "Veuve," being a black woman, holding by the hand a black little girl [black because in mourning] and the twain studiously surveying an elegant French monument . . . All these four "Anges" were grim and grey as burglars, and cold and vapid as ghosts. What women to live with! insecure, ill-humored, bloodless, brainless nonentities! As bad in their way as the indolent gipsy giantess, the Cleopatra, in hers.[186]

In this comic instance of sight taboo, the social schizophrenia within masculine culture, not only the hypocrisy of the double standard, but its purpose and intentions are exposed. It has converted one woman into sex symbol, flesh devoid of mentality or personality, "cunt"—this for itself to gaze upon. And unto woman herself is reserved the wearisome piety of academic icons with their frank propaganda of serviceable humility.

The disparity in the contradiction of images represented by the two pictures explains the techniques of *Villette* better than any other moment in the novel. It is a division in the culture which Brontë is retorting to by splitting her people in half and dividing Lucy's own responses into a fluctuating negative and positive. The other dichotomy is between her newness, her revolutionary spirit, and the residue of the old ways which infects her soul. This inner conflict is complemented by an exterior one between her ambitions and desires and the near impossibility of their fulfillment. There are obstacles everywhere, social and financial. The hard realities of the sexual caste system frustrate her as well as its mentality. Curiously enough, the obstacles drive her on. Lucy represents not only Brontë's, but what must have been, and probably still remains, the ambition of every conscious young woman in the world. She wants to be free; she is mad to escape, to learn, to work, to go places. She envies every man his occupation, John his medicine,

[185] *Ibid.*, p. 184.
[186] *Ibid.*, p. 185.

Paul his scholarship, just as she envied them their education. Both had the finest obtainable and it was given to them as a preparation for life. Lucy was given nothing so substantial:

> . . . picture me for the next eight years, as a bark slumbering through halcyon weather, in a harbour as still as glass—the steersman stretched on the little deck, his face up to heaven, his eyes closed . . . A great many women and girls are supposed to pass their lives something in that fashion; why not I with the rest? . . . However, it cannot be concealed that in that case, I must somehow have fallen overboard, or there must have been a wreck at last.[187]

She is traumatically cast out of the middle class quite unprepared to live, for all the world had expected her to exist parasitically. She now lacks the prerequisites: a face, respectable social connections, and parents to place her. She is a serf without a proprietor who must become a wage slave, namely a governess or teacher. The only way out, and it's a desperate track, is to learn the world and books. *Villette* chronicles her formal and informal education in the acquisition of her own competence through both.

But what work can Lucy do; what occupations are open to her? Paid companion, infant nurse, governess, schoolteacher. As they are arranged, each is but another name for servant. Each involves starvation wages which only a lifetime of saving could ever convert to ransom. There is another humiliation in the fact of servant status which rested with particular severity on middle-class women who in taking employment are falling a step below the class of their birth. (While a paid companion, Lucy encounters a schoolmate now the mistress of a household—Lucy had been visiting another servant in the kitchen.) Furthermore, these occupations involve "living-in" and a twenty-four-hour surveillance tantamount to imprisonment. The only circumstances under which Lucy is permitted an occupation are such that they make financial independence and personal fulfillment impossible. It is not very hard to understand her envy at the gratification and status which Paul and John are given automatically in their professions. One might well ask, as Lucy does unceasingly, is it worth it then, under these conditions, to work? Is it not easier to keep falling into daydreams about prince charmings who will elevate one to royalty, or so they claim? At any rate, they could provide easy security and a social position cheaply attained. They will provide, if nothing else, the sexual gratification which women occupied like Lucy are utterly forbidden to enjoy.

Villette reads, at times, like another debate between the opposed mentalities of Ruskin and Mill. Lucy is forever alternating between hankering after the sugared hopes of chivalric rescue, and the strenuous realism of Mill's analysis. Brontë demonstrates thereby that she knows what she is about. In her circumstances, Lucy would not be creditable if she were not continuously

<hr>

[187] *Ibid.*, p. 32.

about to surrender to convention; if she were not by turns silly as well as sensible. So there are many moments when she wishes she were as pretty as Fanshawe, as rich as Polly, occasions when she would happily forgo life itself at a sign that Graham recognizes she was alive. Born to a situation where she is subject to life-and-death judgments based on artificial standards of beauty, Lucy is subject to a compulsive mirror obsession, whereby each time she looks in the glass she denies her existence—she does not appear in the mirror. One of the most interesting cases of inferiority feelings in literature, Lucy despises her exterior self, and can build an inner being only through self-hatred. Yet living in a culture which takes masochism to be a normal phenomenon in females, and even conditions them to enjoy it, Lucy faces and conquers the attractions Paul's sadism might have held.

Charlotte Brontë has her public censor as well as her private one to deal with. This accounts for the deviousness of her fictional devices, her continual flirtation with the bogs of sentimentality which period feeling mandates she sink in though she be damned if she will. Every Victorian novel is expected to end in a happy marriage; those written by women are required to. Brontë pretends to compromise; convention is appeased by the pasteboard wedding of Paulina Mary and Prince John; cheated in Lucy's escape.

Escape is all over the book; *Villette* reads like one long meditation on a prison break. Lucy will not marry Paul even after the tyrant has softened. He has been her jailer all through the novel, but the sly and crafty captive in Lucy is bent on evading him anyway. She plays tame, learns all he has to teach her of the secrets of the establishment—its mathematics and Latin and self-confidence. She plays pupil to a man who hates and fears intelligent women and boasts of having caused the only woman teacher whose learning ever challenged his own to lose her job. Lucy endures the baiting about the "natural inferiority of females" with which Paul tortures her all through the lesson, and understands that only the outer surface of his bigotry melts when she proves a good student and thereby flatters his pedagogic vanity. Yet in his simplicity he has been hoodwinked into giving her the keys. The moment they are in her hand, and she has beguiled him into lending her money, renting her a school of her own, and facilitated her daring in slipping from the claws of Madame Beck—she's gone. The keeper turned kind must be eluded anyway; Paul turned lover is drowned.

Lucy is free. Free is alone; given a choice between "love" in its most agreeable contemporary manifestation, and freedom, Lucy chose to retain the individualist humanity she had shored up, even at the expense of sexuality. The sentimental reader is also free to call Lucy "warped," but Charlotte Brontë is hard-minded enough to know that there was no man in Lucy's society with whom she could have lived and still been free. On those occasions when Brontë did marry off her heroines, the happy end is so fraudulent, the marriages so hollow, they read like satire, or cynical tracts against love itself.

There was, in Lucy's position, just as in the Brontës' own, no other solution available.

As there is no remedy to sexual politics in marriage, Lucy very logically doesn't marry. But it is also impossible for a Victorian novel to recommend a woman not marry. So Paul suffers a quiet sea burial. Had Brontë's heroine "adjusted" herself to society, compromised, and gone under, we should never have heard from her. Had Brontë herself not grown up in a house of half-mad sisters with a domestic tyrant for father, no "prospects," as marital security was referred to, and with only the confines of governessing and celibacy staring at her from the future, her chief release the group fantasy of "Angria," that collective dream these strange siblings played all their lives, composing stories about a never-never land where women could rule, exercise power, govern the state, declare night and day, death and life—then we would never have heard from Charlotte either.[188] Had that been the case, we might never have known what a resurrected soul wished to tell upon emerging from several millennia of subordination. Literary criticism of the Brontës has been a long game of masculine prejudice wherein the player either proves they can't write and are hopeless primitives, whereupon the critic sets himself up like a schoolmaster to edit their stuff and point out where they went wrong, or converts them into case histories from the wilds, occasionally prefacing his moves with a few pseudo-sympathetic remarks about the windy house on the moors, or old maidhood, following with an attack on every truth the novels contain, waged by anxious pedants who fear Charlotte might "castrate" them or Emily "unman" them with her passion. There is bitterness and anger in *Villette*—and rightly so. One finds a good deal of it in Richard Wright's *Black Boy*, too. To label it neurotic is to mistake symptom for cause in the hope of protecting oneself from what could be upsetting.

What should surprise us is not Lucy's wry annoyance, but her affection and compassion—even her wit. *Villette* is one of the wittier novels in English and one of the rare witty books in an age which specialized in sentimental comedy. What is most satisfying of all is the astonishing degree of consciousness one finds in the work, the justice of its analysis, the fairness of its observations, the generous degree of self-criticism. Although occasionally flawed with mawkish nonsense (there is a creditable amount of Victorian syrup in *Villette*), it is nevertheless one of the most interesting books of the period and, as an expression of revolutionary sensibility, a work of some importance.

Mill and Engels dealt with the sexual revolution on a theoretical and rational level; Hardy, Meredith, and Brontë described it in fiction with less objectivity but with the informative addition of the conflicts it involved and the emotions it awakened; the poets respond on still another, often uncon-

[188] See Fannie Ratchford, *The Brontës' Web of Childhood* (New York: Columbia University Press, 1941).

scious level. What one finds in the poetry of the Victorian period is often a disguised arrangement of what is the most inhibited and negative material in the age—its ambivalence, its uncertainty, its guilt. It is reacting less to practical sexual politics than to the promise—and threat—of sexual freedom. Victorian poetry is in general the vehicle of the period's grave misgivings on three subjects: the death, disappearance or erosion of God through the progress of the sciences, both social (history, anthropology, economics) and natural (biology, geology, archaeology); democracy and the possibility of class warfare; and that affront to the ancient pieties and hated restraints which the sexual revolution represented. The poetry of the period responded to these contemporary tempests by being not of the period at all, but of a different age. Only under the disguise of medieval or ancient situations did the poets feel safe enough to cope. Arnold revived the pastoral to describe the grief of a shaken religious disposition; Tennyson the romance, in order to inhabit a feudal asylum where he could deal with the failure of marriage and the wearying perils of sexuality.

Medievalism and the securely remote flavor of courtly love seemed the best setting for this sort of discussion. Actually, it was Keats who started it all with that fatal woman in *La Belle Dame Sans Merci* who kept her knight hanging about disconsolate and "palely loitering."[189] Such a posture of lassitude was attractive to Tennyson, and he adopted it becomingly in *Tithonus* and *The Lotus Eaters*. It is probably more natural to him than the bootstrap determination of *Ulysses*. Throughout his poetic career, Tennyson appears to be torn between a vivid appreciation of the good woman of chivalrous sentiment (the buxom matron or virginal adolescent), and the fatal woman. They are neatly categorized under the era's elaborate conventional floral imagery of Lily and Rose. Tennyson's early lyrics describe the fortunes of Shalott and Mariana, imprisoned high-born maidens full of sensibility and melting with sexual frustration—Lilies. Though it has a lily maid upon the scene as well, his major poem, *The Idylls of the King,* introduced the Rose element in two different manifestations of that temptation: Guinevere and Vivian. The subversive sexuality of the first brings down the entire Utopian dream of the Round Table. Tennyson's ideal kingdom based on ideal marriage, the union of soul and sense, male and female, a Victorian synthesis of opposites, is a resounding failure. Arthur is all soul, a pure disembodied spirit, a Christ figure. Guinevere appears to be irredeemably human and is therefore classed as pure sensuality. Yet for all that, she has some dignity and is probably Tennyson's best female character. Vivian, who renders Merlin helpless and so hastens the ruin of Arthur's kingdom and Tennyson's ideal state, is another matter. She is carnality unrelieved by a single sympathetic trait; a vaginal trap, a *vagina dentata,* a snakelike presence whose every cell is another bit of guile. In Tennyson's adherence to the separate spheres' dogma,

---

[189] Any discussion of the fatal woman must, of necessity, owe a debt to Mario Praz's, *The Romantic Agony* (Oxford, 1933).

the male is given over to intellect, rule, warfare and other altruistic projects calculated to serve mankind and promote civilization, but the female, as Vivian obligingly confesses, knows only the animal level of sexuality:

> "Man dreams of fame while woman wakes to love."
> Yea! love, tho' love were of the grossest, carves
> A portion from the solid present, eats
> And uses, careless of the rest; but fame
> The fame that follows death is nothing to us;[190]

At times this insatiable female appetite may be decorated with motherhood and called the "rose of womanhood" as in *The Two Voices,* a very early poem, but in the *Idylls,* his most mature production, Tennyson has occasion to see below this into the chasm of chaotic, uninhibited copulation which Vivian the Abstract Female presages; a world where if such as she takes any equal part can only roll "back into the beast."

All this rabid lechery may appear particularly unlikely as one remembers the inhibited sexuality of the actual Victorian woman. The poets, however, did not deal in practicalities but in fantasy, and their fantasies were their own, and therefore masculine.[191] Recognizing her for the polluted creature Tennyson knows her to be, Merlin mutters "harlot." Like any witch, Vivian responds to the magic of a name with her hideous true colors:

> Leapt from her session on his lap, and stood as
> Stiff as a viper frozen; loathesome sight,
> How from the rosy lips of life and love
> Flash'd the bare-grinning skeleton of death![192]

Tennyson had very mixed emotions about Lilies and Roses; was tempted and repulsed alternately. Lilies are creatures forced into dull, vicarious existence like Shalott, or hopelessly fed upon shadows like the Lily Maid of Astolat, or they suffer endless hallucinatory attendance upon sexual affirmation like Mariana. Delicate and poetic sensibilities as they are, they have a poor time of it until they starve and die. Their virginity is their only life, their curse and mortality as well. Roses, their sensual opposites (outside of the Brontës no woman is a complete human being in the period, surely the most damning thing one can say about its sexual culture) also pose a terrible threat, particularly depressing to a poet as diffident and tepid toward the prospect of active sexuality as Tennyson. The problem is never resolved in his work, which is a virtue, for it creates tension and interest. Despite his moral objections to them, it is clear that Tennyson is not just negative but un-

---

190 Tennyson, *The Idylls of the King,* "Merlin and Vivian," ll. 458–62.
191 For some glimpses of female sexual fantasy in the Victorian period, the reader is recommended to Christina Rossetti's *Goblin Market.*
192 *The Idylls of the King,* "Merlin and Vivian," ll. 843–46.

decided about the Rose type. Yet there is something discouraging about both floral patterns: to be a Lily is to be condemned to die; to be a Rose is to be fatal to others; it would be difficult to find a more uncongenial way to sum up sexuality or the other sex.

The conflict continued with Rossetti who made a valiant effort to heal the disparity between sexuality and sensibility in the synthesis of *The House of Life,* a brave but not very successful attempt to unite masculine idealism (Courtly and Platonic) with a rich sensuality, more admirable for its intention than its achievement. Elsewhere Rossetti also indulges in fantasies of feminine sexuality, but with fewer reservations, less inhibiting restraint. *The Blessèd Damozel* is a bid to eroticize Christian Platonism, not only via the warm, naked breast the damozel generously exposes to the bar of heaven, but in the even more ambitious notion that when the lovers of the poem are reunited in Dante Gabriel's worldly paradise, they will be encouraged to practice their ardor, naked and unashamed before the eyes of the Blessed Virgin. Contemporary critics find the impropriety of all this more in their own hearts than in Rossetti's; but it is undeniable that he has embarked on an impossible mission. *Jenny,* his finest poem, is the dramatic monologue of a prostitute's client seeing, or trying to see, through the double standard and sexual politics to justice and the social and economic circumstances of Jenny's fate. The poem is so subtle and sophisticated in technique, so ironic in the hermetic perfection of its only speaker, that one never knows, or perhaps Rossetti never has to divulge, whether it is the inherent evil in the world, "a toad within a stone," or simply the way things have been arranged by fellows like our monologist, that is finally accountable for Jenny's degradation. Unaffected by the usual Victorian melodrama and mawkishness when dealing with such a subject, *Jenny* is in the best analytical and rational vein of the novelists. The majority of Rossetti's lyrics are not, and their chief contribution is to convert the fatal woman into a symbol such as The Card Dealer, or the bosomy Helen of *Troy Town,* abstract icons of death and fate. This distancing device will be useful for later poets like Swinburne and Wilde, as it makes Tennysonian moral scruples irrelevant and permits the poet to enjoy the fatal woman undisturbed.

Tennyson preserved propriety by castigating the wanton Rose with vice and always pronouncing loudly for the Lily; Rossetti kept a shred of decorum by clinging to the notion of the Virgin, or Beatrice, or some other Lily, however secularized. Swinburne went all the way and pronounced loudly for the evil itself. In the course of his devotions to Dolores, "Our Lady of Pain," he begs this pagan princess to "Forgive us our virtues," "We" would change "the lilies and languors of virtue/For the raptures and roses of Vice." It is at moments like this that Swinburne most reminds one of a prurient schoolboy jerking off.

The earlier Victorian poets had dealt with the onsurge of doubt and agnosticism by turning sadly to the Christian middle ages; Swinburne, with a logical and forthright courage one cannot help but admire, went right across the line into atheism. Since this was far too risky even for him to do in modern dress, he generally hunted about for some vaguely plausible classical setting. Among the ancients it might just be conceivable for dramatic characters to refer to the deity as "The supreme evil, God," even if the speakers are the chorus of Athenian maidens in *Atalanta*. Since its introduction in the Renaissance, classicism has always represented a certain competitive or seductive danger to Christianity, but in Swinburne its use is a deliberate piece of sabotage. A self-conscious immoralist, he initiated a classical revival flagrantly based on a reversion to primitivism, and a certain calculated savagery, rich in overtones of the Marquis de Sade.

In fact, all the pagan terror Tennyson built into Albion and set up the reign of Arthur to restrain, Swinburne released in the flood of uninhibited sexuality which Tennyson had set himself to withstand. The lid, as it were, began to loosen in Tennyson; Swinburne gaily, irresponsibly, encouraged it to pop. The latter poet's unfortunate sexual peculiarities are well known: his impotence, his algolagnia—that incorrigible craving to be whipped—the cultural masochism he had imbibed at England's finest school over the birching block of Eton. All the enormity of these sad diversions are well documented in Swinburne's unpublished or happily forgotten verses.[193] Edmund Wilson informed us that Swinburne's fixation is one of the clues to the age and its sexual culture, a culture that forced its elite to identify pain and unsatisfied homosexuality with its earliest sexual experiences.[194] It is somehow logical after a long period of sexual repression, when sexual energy finally finds means of release and its pent-up dynamism discovers an avenue of egress, it may take rather devious routes into neurosis, perversity, and other antisocial forms of sexuality. Swinburne is such a case and the era of *fin de siècle*, which he opened with the publication of his *Poems and Ballads* in 1866, represents something analogous for a whole society. Swinburne's case is instructive; a failed rebel, he was not content to renounce established religion but had to become a militant atheist and finally indulge in a counterreligion of paganism and masochistic ritual; an exponent of sexual freedom, he was compelled to carry it to license and childish frenzy; a patrician republican, he was not satisfied until he had gone full circle and become an Imperial Tory babbling jingoism in his old age.

There is something impractical, irrational, sudden, incoherent about the sexual liberation of *fin de siècle*, as if the surge of long-damned sexual energy became a flood that somehow overwhelmed its initiators so that they were incapable of distinguishing any values save those of untrammeled expression

[193] See Georges LaFourcade, *Swinburne: A Literary Biography* (London: Bell, 1932) and *La Jeunesse de Swinburne* (Paris: Les Belles Lettres, 1928). Also *Chastelard, The Queen Mother, Whippingham Papers*, etc.

[194] Edmund Wilson, "Swinburne of Capheaton and Eton," a critical introduction to the *Novels of A. C. Swinburne* (New York: Noonday Press, 1963).

—at whatever cost to themselves. And the deliberately outrageous professions of its participants, Swinburne in particular, had something of panic in them, and a great deal of unresolved guilt. The source of this guilt lies unmistakably in his formative years, and the unhealthy conditions of a restrictive culture. The reprisals which surprised convention took upon Wilde must also command our sympathy. Yet the very disorganized character of *fin de siècle* sexuality has about it a fairly certain hazard to the sexual revolution and carries within it the inevitable threat of reaction. The very abruptness of the release predicts a faltering later; the uncertainty of its unpremeditated rush forbodes its arrest.

Wilde's *Salomé* was published in French in 1893. Ibsen's *A Doll's House* was written in Norwegian in 1879, but not performed in English until 1889. There is an irony in the fact that Wilde's play followed Ibsen's on the English scene by only four years. To the new theatre and its revolutionary naturalist manifesto in that real and contemporary slam of Nora's door, contrast Wilde's perfumed fantasy based on a Near Eastern myth. *A Doll's House* represented the actuality of the sexual revolution. *Fin de siècle* replied with the weary irrelevance of an unconscious dream, based on self-induced fright and titillation. Interesting and neglected work that it is, and key to so much that came after it, *Salomé* always seems remarkably contingent in the very midst of the sexual revolution, somehow oblique and aside from the point.

It is a dialogue between sensuality and asceticism: Salomé and Jokanaan—an awesome but extremely unpleasant version of John the Baptist. Both antagonists are artists; Salomé does pagan aestheticism, Jokanaan prophetic fervor; her style is the lyric and the dance, his is rhetoric, denunciation, and rhapsody. But the style of the play itself is Salomé's, and it is Salomé who wins the duel, though it be a Pyrrhic victory. Following Swinburne's lead, Wilde casts his vote for the fatal woman Tennyson earnestly resisted, even commending in Salomé that "castrating" female whom masculine fantasy invented and by now had grown to approve; the Bitch of Mailer's hostile imagination turned into a goddess. Salomé is presented as a blinding manifestation of sexuality itself, more an idea than a personality, the success of the play depending on the actress who plays her. For all the languorous and powerful sensuality of the character and the speeches, it is an imperious *sexual will* which Salomé represents, rather than sexuality. Nothing so passive as a vaginal trap, she is an irresistible force and is supposed to betoken an insatiable clitoral demand that has never encountered resistance to its whims before. Every man in Herod's court palpably desires her, from the king to the lowest guard. Only Jokanaan disdains her, declining with the fixed convictions of an immovable object. No mere vampire or seductress, like Vivian and earlier fatal ladies, Salomé is a despot, something of a rapist. And it is not poor old impotent Merlin whom she makes her demands upon, but patently virile and hairy young Jokanaan, the holy prophet of God. Rossetti held on to the hope of gently eroticizing Christianity; Swinburne wrote tracts against it; it is Wilde's shameless intention to titillate it with the dance of the seven veils and Salomé's wonderfully explicit come-on—a series of statements so forthright one had not heard their like since the Wife of Bath:

> I am amorous of thy body Jokanaan. Thy body is white as the lilies of a field that the mower hath mowed. . . . Suffer me to touch thy body.[195]

Jokanaan responds with an enviable awareness of his sanctitude:

> Back daughter of Sodom! Touch me not. Profane not the temple of the Lord God.[196]

While a young Syrian, infatuated with desire for her, looks on and then stabs himself out of jealousy and frustration, Salomé croons to the Baptist:

> It is thy mouth that I desire, Jokanaan. Thy mouth is like a band of scarlet on a tower of ivory. It is like a pomegranate cut in twain by a knife of ivory . . . There is nothing in the world so red as thy mouth . . . Suffer me to kiss thy mouth.
> Jokanaan: Never! Daughter of Babylon! Daughter of Sodom! Never.
> Salomé: I will kiss thy mouth, Jokanaan. I will kiss thy mouth.[197]

Jokanaan, who sounds more like Doc Hines (the sex fanatic and evangelical puritan in Faulkner's *Light in August*) than anything one might encounter in the New Testament, answers this with the repelled horror of an Orthodox Jew tempted by the "stranger woman":

> Back! Daughter of Babylon! By woman came evil into the world. Speak not to me. I will not listen to thee. I listen but to the voice of the Lord God.[198]

He is also supposed to represent the asceticism of the early Christian era, the fascinated denunciatory antisexuality of the Dissenter mentality, while serving as a mouthpiece for appalled respectability when confronted with the nudity of Beardsley's bare-breasted dancer.

For all her exhibitionism and imperious clitoral command, Salomé is not exclusively or even fundamentally female; she is Oscar Wilde too. The play is a drama of homosexual guilt and rejection followed by a double revenge. Salomé repays the prophet's rebuttal by demanding his head, and then, in Wilde's uneasy vision of retribution, Salomé is slain by Herod's guards.

[195] Oscar Wilde, *Salomé*, translated into English by Wilde and Alfred Douglas, reprinted in *The Portable Oscar Wilde*, edited by Richard Aldington (New York: Viking Press, 1946), p. 403.

[196] *Ibid.*, p. 404.

[197] *Ibid.*

[198] *Ibid.*, p. 403.

The brazen sexuality Salomé represents, is, in the play's last moment, punished with terrible force as the despicable tyrant Herod turns on the stairs, beholds Salomé in an ecstasy kissing the dismembered head of Jokanaan, and calls out the climactic last line: "Kill that woman!"[199]

Despite the stunning virtuosity of this ultimate *volte face*, it appears to have something arbitrary about it unless we comprehend the play's disguised and therefore elusive homosexual imagery. It is Herod's command that slays Salomé, but Herod is a corrupt authority in a corrupt state. Were Wilde to suffer such condemnation, he might assuage his own guilt, but he would, like Salomé, still emerge as the heroine of the play. Yet the order was issued before and came from the mouth of the desirable prophet:

> The Voice of Jokanaan: Let the captains of the host pierce her with their swords, let them crush her beneath their shields.[200]

In vain will Salomé appeal to the bloody head she is now free to kiss:

> Well, thou hast seen thy God, Jokanaan, but me, me, thou didst never see. If thou hadst seen me thou hadst loved me. I saw thee, and I loved thee. Oh, how I loved thee! I love thee yet, Jokanaan, I love only thee . . . I am athirst for thy beauty; I am hungry for thy body; and neither wine nor apples can appease my desire. What shall I do now, Jokanaan? Neither the floods nor the great waters can quench my passion. I was a princess, and thou didst scorn me. I was a virgin, and thou didst take my virginity from me. I was chaste, and thou didst fill my veins with fire. . . . Ah! Ah! wherefore didst thou not look at me? If thou hadst looked at me thou hadst loved me. Well I know that thou wouldst have loved me, and the mystery of love is greater than the mystery of death.[201]

Jokanaan will never forgive her, never desire her. The kiss she courted, the ivory knife cutting the pomegranate, the scarlet band on a tower of ivory—all are images of anal penetration or fellatio. And to the stern voice of Judaeo-Christian interdiction to ask this kiss is to castrate or murder the beloved. Should he comply, convention calls him effeminate; should he refuse, the hurt pride of desire takes its vengeance in psychic murder, here rendered in the convenient rubric of the myth as decapitation, followed with imaginary suicide or execution. In the stern court of Herod's corrupt justice the whole scenario when completed is punishable by swift and arbitrary death. Yet even here there is satisfaction—the death comes by Jokanaan's order, and it is a death of crushing and penetration under an army of males: one thinks of Genet. As with Swinburne, so here, guilt will find ways of satisfying itself in pain, punishment, and condemnation. And *Salomé* is a secret

[199] *Ibid.*, p. 429.
[200] *Ibid.*, p. 414.
[201] *Ibid.*, p. 428.

dream of guilt rather than an open act of rebellion in the clear daylight of action.

In creating a fatal woman who castrates the male with what seems to be the full favor of the author's approval (for whatever the *deus ex* ending may mean, Salomé carries the play, every word of its ornate Near Eastern exoticism, its jewels and peacocks, a tribute to the sensuality she stands for), Wilde would appear to be reacting to the sexual revolution with the enthusiasm of overkill. The feminists merely wanted equality and the vote—need one respond with a heroine who goes about cutting off heads? Indeed, Salomé resembles nothing so little as the actual Victorian woman of her time. But then she is not a woman anyway, but the product of Wilde's homosexual guilt and desire. This consideration, together with the practical obstacle that he could not contemplate even a closet drama where one male made love to another, necessitated subterfuge. Victorian pornography and other underground or unpublished works went a good deal further. But Wilde wanted to publish and to shine. *Dorian Gray* is also disguised homosexuality and just misses being the first important homosexual novel because it is too timid to tell us what Dorian's "crime" really was and so must lean upon the frummery of "vice"—those plastic whorehouses and opium dens we are asked to believe were his downfall. The substitution spoils the book, whose flirtatious first chapter is very good indeed.

And so, unable to say what he liked, because of historical and personal reasons of fear and guilt, Wilde had to resort to myth, the oriental mime of an imitation Noh play, the picturesque inspiration of Doré's and Gustav Moreau's paintings, presenting us with a fatal woman who is not even a female. The revolutionary energy of Wilde's assertion of homosexuality, which sheer circumstance years later forced him to enact in the martyrdom of his trial and imprisonment, is, in his writing itself, diverted into reactionary fantasy[202] which still parades the fatal woman of misogynous myth, the feminine evil. Ibsen's Nora Helmer is the true insurrectionary of the sexual revolution; Salomé a retreat into archaic slanderous accusation, that symbolic emptiness which predicts the counterrevolution. It was personal necessity which led Wilde to traffic in symbols and to refuse to deal with the actual woman responding to her circumstances, a product of history and conditioning struggling to free herself from both. In writers who followed him the resort of depicting woman as an idea, an abstraction, had other motivations. Yet a whole series of symbolic and unreal feminine avatars succeeded Salomé: Yeats' notion of genteel elegance, Eliot's fear of life, everyone's Eternal Feminine, Earth Mother, Castrator, or whatever.

Both *A Doll's House* and *Salomé* are confrontation drama, where action is unnecessary and plot an impertinence because all interest is hypnotized into awaiting the explosion. Nora confronted every convention and the chiv-

[202] In the writing published in Wilde's lifetime, rather than the unexpurgated *De Profundis*, finally released in 1959.

alrous masculine prejudice that caged her within a child's toy structure, hoping to insure she would remain a house pet and infant there forever. Salomé, standing in for Wilde, confronted the frowning British public which penalized "unnatural acts" with years in prison and still kept a Scots law on the books which made sodomy punishable by hanging. He also confronted the rejection of the men he would court. And by this one does not impugn the powers of Wilde's sexual attractiveness. The two most debilitating homosexual fears—both the direct product of society's hostility—are fear of public exposure, and fear of rejection. The first fear produced the spectacle of Salomé's "drag"—those naked breasts her alter ego hides behind. The second produced Jokanaan's refusal, which accounts for the play's only motivation. Whatever the sex of the "heroine," *Salomé* is a breathtaking evocation of desire on the stage; all of its ringing tension a function of its public display. Whatever the enormity of Salomé's revenge, there is actual pathos in her pain at being scorned. Wilde managed this so well we react not just to her carnality, nor even to her attempts to coerce. And Jokanaan's adamantine rebuff has something of arrogance and much of twisted puritanism in it.

Perhaps what was hardest of all for Wilde to confront was not even this rejection but the appalling and dizzying accusation of the direst kind of Sin, the sin of all others against which both convention and "manliness" had set their faces, the sin against which the entire Judaeo-Christian ages cried out "Sodom!" Nora was battling the sexual politic openly and rationally. Wilde was not able to. He could dare only a brief demonstration; then came condign sentence and silence. When Wilde fell in 1895, Nora and her band of revolutionaries had a few more years of insurrection left; Shaw and Woolf and the vote were yet to come. Wilde had broken even stronger patriarchal taboo, and the punishment was swift and terrible. It took somewhat longer for patriarchy to respond to the greater threat which Nora represented and to which it could at first reply with the concession of mild reforms. But here, too, reaction came; slowly, powerfully, the great impetus of the sexual revolution was brought to a halt.

FOUR

The Counterrevolution
1930–60

REACTIONARY POLICY
The Models of Nazi Germany and the Soviet Union

The first phase ended in reform rather than revolution. For a sexual revolution to proceed further it would have required a truly radical social transformation—the alteration of marriage and the family as they had been known throughout history. Without such radical change it remained impossible to eradicate those evils attendant upon these institutions which reformers found most offensive: the economic disabilities of women, the double standard, prostitution, venereal disease, coercive marital unions, and involuntary parenthood. A completed sexual revolution would have entailed, even necessitated, the end of the patriarchal order through the abolition of its ideology as it functions through a differential socialization of the sexes in the areas of status, temperament, and role. While patriarchal ideology was eroded and patriarchy reformed, the essential patriarchal social order remained. As most people could conceive of no other form of social organization, the only alternative to its perpetuation appeared to be chaos. In the words of one recent analysis, it was not so much that "social order required the subordination of women: rather, to the conservatives it required a *family structure* that involved the subordination of women."[1]

It seemed, finally, that patriarchy was necessary for the family system. In conservative economies with an ethos of aggressive competition, the "home" seemed to offer the last vestiges of humane feeling, the only haven of communal emotion. For a society unwilling to extend such activity beyond the nuclear family (open to criticism both on the grounds of its self-centered character and as a wasteful and inefficient body)[2] there was nothing left but to salvage the private hearth. As an educational arm of the state, the patriarchal family has much to recommend it. Heads of families may be subjects, perhaps even something like vassals, to the state, while members of such families are subject or vassal to their head. Authoritarian governments appear to favor patriarchy especially; the atmosphere of fascist states and of dictatorships depends heavily upon their patriarchal character.[3] Another form of totalitarianism, such as that which occurred in the Soviet Union, began to flourish about the same time as the sexual revolution, inaugurated there on a large scale, began to be abandoned.[4] As the patriarchal family depends

[1] Aileen Kraditor, *Up From the Pedestal, Selected Writings in the History of American Feminism* (Chicago, Quadrangle Books, 1968) p. 13. In our analysis emphasis has been put upon the persistence of the family as a force frustrating revolutionary change. Other factors less basic undoubtedly contributed: the collapse of organized feminism in 1920, the Depression, and the death of radicalism in the thirties, postwar reaction after 1945—and the labor situation which accompanied it, and finally, the general conservatism of the fifties. The hypothesis that the counterrevolution began to show signs of abatement after 1960 is attested to by the recent revival of feminism.

[2] Not only is woman's contribution to the larger society generally precluded by the nuclear family, her full-time employment in menial domestic tasks is wasteful both to herself and to society, and the traditional method of child care (from which her attention is continuously diverted by household tasks) carried on in an unsystematic and individualistic manner, is also inefficient.

[3] Marcuse, Horkheimer, and other thinkers have pointed this out. Reich puts it well: "The authoritarian state has a representative in every family, the father, in this way he becomes the state's most valuable tool." "Since authoritarian society reproduces itself in the structure of the mass individual by means of the authoritarian family, it follows that political reaction must defend the authoritarian family as the basis of the state, of culture and of civilization." Wilhelm Reich, *The Mass Psychology of Fascism* (1933) translated by Theodore Wolfe (New York: Orgone Institute, 1946), pp. 44 and 88.

[4] The problem of the relation of the family to state control is a difficult one. The Müller-Lyer theory, which Bertrand Russell recapitulates as supposing that "where the state is strong the family is weak and the position of women is good, whereas where the state is weak the family is strong and the position of women is bad" does not appear to operate with strong states such as Fascist Germany, Spain, and Italy or even militarist Japan, where a strong state operated either by exploiting, fostering, or even reestablishing an extreme patriarchal family structure. In this case the co-operation of males with the state may be obtained by the confirmation or even reintroduction of their authority over females. See Bertrand Russell, "Style in Ethics," *The Nation* 118:197–99 (1924).

for its cohesiveness primarily on the economic dependence of women and children, financial equality is almost impossible within it, and its unity is rooted in its economic and legal entity rather than upon its exclusively emotional ties. Finally, and what is most germane, is that even the modern nuclear family, with its unchanged and traditional division of roles, necessitates male supremacy by preserving specifically human endeavor for the male alone, while confining the female to menial labor and compulsory child care. Differences in status according to sex follow inevitably.

In two very different societies, Nazi Germany and Soviet Russia, official governmental experimentation with the family furnishes something like a model that might clarify the problems other societies faced in the sexual revolution. The National Socialist Party in Germany drew its first and most consistent support from a group of disgruntled war veterans. Its mood was the national, sexual, and racial chauvinism one would expect from such a political base. Historians and sociologists have described the Nazi state as a return to tribal solidarity, playing stipulated in-groups against out-groups.[5] Beyond this, it was also probably the most deliberate attempt ever made to revive and solidify extreme patriarchal conditions. Led by their Führer, tribal members themselves would play master to members of the tribal cells, the women, and children.

From the first, National Socialism saw the sexual revolution and feminism as forces to be dealt with seriously. The Woman's Movement had begun late in Germany. Not until the first decade of the twentieth century had it made any inroads there. But five years before the Nazi party came to power feminism had organized some millions of German women into a huge federation of women's organizations in four great divisions. By 1928, when the great women's federation was formed, feminism was in fact a fortress.[6] Nazism

---

[5] Joseph K. Folsom, *The Family and Democratic Society* (New York, John Wiley, 1934, 1943). Folsom describes the Nazi state as showing "strong trends backward toward a caste society and authoritarianism." (p. 193). Clifford Kirkpatrick, *Nazi Germany, Its Women and Family Life* (Indianapolis: Bobbs Merrill, 1938). Kirkpatrick speaks of a ". . . general readiness for primitive thinking, reliance on force and authority and a regression, if possible, to a narrow intimacy in living, thrusting roots into a native soil, stress on blood ties, unanimity of opinion, love of friend and hatred of foe." P. 28.

[6] Feminism began with Helene Lange's pioneering efforts for the school reforms of 1908. Other early German feminists were Alice Salomon, Marie Baum and Marie Elizabeth Lüders. Women were enfranchised under the Weimar Constitution and won seats in the Reichstag. Gertrud Bäumer, the leader of German feminism was a member of the Reichstag and a high official in the Ministry of the Interior; she was purged from public life when the Nazis came to power. Yet the Weimar reforms had not really altered, or at least not struck hard enough, even at the legal surface of German patriarchy. One finds ample proof of the very tenuous character of woman's new freedom in the fact that the Bürgerliches Gesetzbuch or civil code continued to authorize male authority in the husband in the matter of residence, power of decision and control in most economic areas and over the children. (This was not repealed until 1957.)

set about storming it in a very methodical way: by factionalizing, by infiltrating, by forcing elections, commandeering leadership positions, purging feminist leaders both from the movement and from public life, and then pre-empting the feminist organizations into the Nazi folds under the orders of the Party in organs such as the *Frauenorden,* the *Frauenschaft,* and later the *Frauenfront* (renamed the *Frauenwerk* a few years later), ostensibly headed by a *Führerin* and anti-feminist women collaborators, but controlled by men close to the party such as Krummacher and Hilgenfeldt. Although only 3 per cent of party members were women, the takeover of women's groups had proceeded so skillfully that in 1933 National Socialist women's organizations were now the in-group and feminists the out-group.[7]

When the process of "bringing into line" (*Gleichshaltung*) was accomplished and the older women's organizations, often not only feminist, but pacificist, internationalist, and socialist, were co-opted, often at enormous cost, what the Nazis inherited in the case of the two most powerful of the four groups, the Federation of German Women's Clubs and the League of University Women, was merely a name. The first group and the teachers' branch of the second had voted themselves into dissolution during 1933 rather than be absorbed. Nevertheless, some six to eight million women were mobilized for Party ends in the *Frauenwerk,* ready to be put at the service of the Nazi state.

[7] Party instructions for taking over the feminist organizations stipulate: "The bringing-in-line" [Gleichshaltung] of the women's organizations does not mean a deviation from the clear line of National Socialism . . . Fill the other women's organizations with the National Socialism spirit . . . In social work the most important places in the country as well as the city must be occupied . . . The executive bodies of the other women's associations are to be slowly penetrated . . . The religious groups are to be handled with caution. They cannot be brought into line in the same way as the other women's clubs. Detailed instructions will appear shortly." Later orders were specific as to tactics: "In every province a woman commissioner who must be a National Socialist will be appointed by the province leader . . . The commissioner . . . shall cause the women's organizations themselves to accept a newly chosen leadership. Only when the organization refuses to accept the new staff does the commissioner take over this office. Severity in this connection is to be avoided if possible." Discipline within the new order was strict; "The leaders of the National Socialist Frauenschaft warn that no unsocial behavior may take place in other associations. In case such should take place the woman commissioner of the German Frauenschaft is to be given the facts. The commissioner for the province shall act in association with the German Frauenfront to restrain forbidden activity." Amtswalterinnenblatt der N. S. Frauenschaft (Deutscher Frauenorden) München, Gässler Nos. 14, p. 43 (May 21, 1933), 15, p. 51 (June 7, 1933) and 23, pp. 181–82 (Oct. 1, 1933). Here, as in all of the quotations from Nazi sources (save those from Hitler's *Mein Kampf,* readily available in translation) appearing in this section, I am indebted to Clifford Kirkpatrick's invaluable study which supplied translations on pp. 60, 61, 64, 50, 246, 52, 109, 110, 111–12, 112–13, 114, 116–17, 118. My remarks on Germany are further indebted to Reich's *Mass Psychology of Fascism,* Folsom's comparison of Germany, Russia, and Sweden in *The Family in Democratic Society,* and Walter Laquer's *Young Germany,* Robert Brady's *The Spirit and Structure of German Fascism,* and Max Seydewitz's *Civil Life in Wartime Germany.*

The part women were assigned to play in Hitler's Germany was to be one strictly confined to utter dedication to motherhood and the family,[8] and yet (here there is perhaps less inherent contradiction than one might suppose) women were to make up the factory population which serviced and produced the German war machine, at least at the outset, and until their numbers were augmented with slave labor from Eastern Europe. By 1935 the National Labor Service Law of July 26 obliged members of both sexes to participate in state labor, which by 1940, few women could escape. For all the thundering propaganda about marriage, holy motherhood and home, the number of employed women, even working mothers, increased under Nazi rule from 1933 onward.[9] This in itself is hardly surprising, for the population of women employees all over the world increased during this period, and one would expect such an increase following upon the opening of higher education to women. But in Nazi Germany, a government decree[10] stipulated that women be held to a quota of one in ten university students; women constituted only one third of high school students. This is

[8] The emphasis on loyal motherhood was based on the sound assumption that nationalist emotion is largely imbibed in early childhood through parental influence. Motherhood was used as a lever with which to organize women into the Nazi controlled women's clubs. A Party worker looking over prospective members categorizes them: "A part are Marxist, today still tense, inflamed, embittered [e.g., militant feminists]. But it is false to go ahead from the standpoint of classification . . . According to my experience there is only one way, to speak as woman to woman, as mother to mother. We come to our point of view by the way of Christianity. God be praised! . . . National Socialism is more difficult to make comprehensible since every woman has a bit of pacifism in her. The national will indeed grows in women through the men. One thing we can do. Teach women to rear their children to love the homeland. So if we cultivate the will to sacrifice in every German woman, they will be ready, albeit with heavy hearts, to give that which is most dear for the Fatherland." Amtswalterinnenblatt der N. S. Frauenschaft (Deutscher Frauenorden) München, Gässler, No. 15, p. 62 (June 7, 1933).

[9] When Hitler came to power (January 1933) women were 37.3% of all workers employed in industry. By 1936 their share was reduced to 31.8%. But in 1940 it was back up to 37.1%. And in absolute numbers, the female labor force rose from 4,700,000 in 1933 to 6,300,000 in 1938 and 8,420,000 in January 1941. The total estimated number of women fit for work was then set at 10–12 million and there was continual discussion of how to mobilize those women still unemployed: figures from Franz Neuman, *Behemoth, The Structure and Practice of National Socialism 1933–44* (New York: Oxford, 1942, 44). By the end of 1943 as many as 13.5 to 14 million women had been conscripted into work. Helge Press points out that the number of women in *paid* positions during World War I was greater than that during World War II in Germany. Helge Press "West Germany" in Patai, Woman in the Modern World (New York, Free Press, 1967) p. 259. Folsom, *op. cit.*, reports that while the percentage of women employed in 1933–36 declined (more men became employed after the depression) in actual numbers, women employed increased by 1,200,000 even during this period, the three years the Nazis were trying hardest to get women out of the labor market that their jobs might be given to men.

[10] The decree was put in effect in 1933, rescinded in 1935. But it seems to have had its effect, for the quota of university women was still just 10% in 1938.

a far lower ratio than one would have expected in view of the rapid strides of feminism in Germany; it is far lower than in England and America. What does make Germany unique among Western states at this period was its reversal of the feminist thrust into the professions and the higher economic and social positions. The actual purpose of Nazi ideology was not, as stated, to return women to the home, but to "take women out of professions and put them into low-paid occupations."[11] Speaking at a meeting of the Nazi medical panel in December 1934, Dr. Wagner, the appointed leader of the medical profession, cried out before a mixed audience, "We will strangle higher education for women."[12] The dissenting feminist voices still heard within the new order were silenced one by one, Dr. Thimm, Anna Pappritz, and Sophie Rogge-Börner. When the new regime had taken over, German women were forbidden to sit as judges; in 1936 they were forbidden to hold office in the courts. There were thirty women in the Reichstag when the Nazis came to power; they were apparently not "the right kind," for by 1938 there were none. One gathers some insight into Nazi emotions below the chivalrous eulogies of motherhood in the jeer which a National Socialist member called out to a Social Democrat who regretted the death of her son in World War I: "For that you she-goats were made."[13]

As in the case of the Jews (why persecute your finest talents?) the Nazi method with women was hardly practical. It would have been far more expedient for a nation about to embark on years of military exploit, empire and colonization, to have declared sexual equality and provided day care centers for the rise in birth rate it demanded to fill the colonies and perpetuate its glorious race. Then, even if it were not sufficiently pragmatic to enroll the female population in the mighty army of the thousand-year Reich (Hitler had made it clear from the start that the Nazis desired "no women to throw grenades") it would still be sure of having a replica society at home to run the state in the absence of its warriors. A nation which plans to mobilize nearly all of its male population into the army is surely in need of a corps of women doctors, lawyers, judges, and other functionaries.

One may find economic reasons for the exclusion of women from participation in higher level work in the hypothesis that the Nazis may have felt the need for that cheap labor force which all other twentieth-century states have enjoyed from women's employment; and as long as it reserved military service for males alone it could hardly staff the munitions plants with men. Yet this would not account for the plethora of propaganda for motherhood and the home, which must be explained as an effort to purge women from the upper levels of the labor force (which in fact was done on a large scale, through legislation against "double income families," and the flat

[11] Folsom, *op. cit.*, p. 195.

[12] Dr. L. Thimm, "Leistungsprinzip oder 'Neider mit den Frauen,'" *Die Ärztin* Vol. 10, No. 1, pp. 3-4 and 28 (January 1934).

[13] Gehrke, Martha Marie, "Fraenwahl," *Vossische Zeitung*, July 26, 1932.

firing of married and unmarried women alike) so that when they were called back into the labor market, women would accept the humble status of server and helper which had been decreed for them as auxiliary to the great masculine project of the state. For all the pontification on "feminine" and "womanly work" (social work, nursing, teaching) the arduous labor required of German women was in the factories and the fields of the Nazi state.

The policy of Dr. Wilhelm Frick,[14] Minister of the Interior, was very concise, both as to ideology and economics:

> The mother should be able to devote herself entirely to her children and her family, the wife to the husband. The unmarried girl should be dependent only upon such occupations as correspond to the feminine type of being. As for the rest, employment should remain given over to the man.

While the German male could be kept loyal and content by receiving those positions from which women were dismissed in large numbers during the first Nazi years, he would also be willing to enter the army when the "war effort" expanded, while the female, properly cowed as to her worth and place, was made to do the growing labor of the Reich.

Yet the most basic motivations behind the Nazi manipulation of its female subjects were neither economic (related to male unemployment) nor dictated by population policy (related to imperialist expansion). The final reasons for the male supremacist temperament of the Nazi state are psychological and emotional, a policy line clarified by the pronouncements of the Party authorities themselves. Gottfried Feder, one of the Party's founding "thinkers" defined feminism for the masses:

> The Jew has stolen woman from us through the forms of sex democracy. We, the youth, must march out to kill the dragon so that we may again attain the most holy thing in the world, the woman as maid and servant.[15]

In a coy, inadvertent tribute to Ruskin, a Nazi woman leader, Guida Diehl, suggested "queen" be added to the list.[16] In his Nuremberg speech of September 8, 1934, Hitler himself corroborated the theory that Jewish Communism, an alien and Semitic outrage, was the source of the detested sexual revolution:

> The message of woman's emancipation is a message discovered solely by the Jewish intellect and its content is stamped with the same spirit.[17]

[14] Wilhelm Frick, "Die Deutsche Frau im nationalsozialistischen Staate," *Volkischer Beobachter*, June 12, 1934.

[15] Gottfried Feder, quoted in "Die Deutsche Frau im Dritten Reich," *Reichstagskorrespondenz der Bayrischen Volkspartei*, April 4, 1932.

[16] Guida Diehl, *Die Deutsche Frau und der Nationalsozialismus*, 2nd. rev. ed., Eisenach, Neuland, 1933, pp. 114–20.

[17] Adolf Hitler, quoted in N. S. *Frauenbuch*, München, J. F. Lehmann, 1934, pp. 10–11.

The views of this remarkable personality on woman's place are very explicit. The conventional separation of male and female spheres occurs as naturally to a Hitler as to other reactionaries:

> For her world is her husband, her family, her children and her home. But where would the greater world be if no one cared to tend the smaller world? . . . We do not find it right when the woman presses into the world of the man. Rather we find it natural when these two worlds remain separate . . . To one belongs the power of feeling, the power of the soul . . . to the other belongs the strength of vision, the strength of hardness . . . The man upholds the nation as the woman upholds the family. The equal rights of women consist in the fact that in the realm of life determined for her by nature she experience the high esteem that is her due. Woman and man represent two quite different types of being. Reason is dominant in man. He searches, analyses and often opens new immeasurable realms. But all things that he approaches merely by reason are subject to change. Feeling in contrast is much more stable than reason and woman is the feeling and therefore the stable element.[18]

In *Mein Kampf* Hitler had stated that "the German girl is a State Subject and only becomes a State Citizen when she marries."[19] The original Nazi program called for abolition of women's suffrage and when the regime came to power the franchise, granted by Weimar as early as 1918, was limited, for the exclusion of women from public life and office was Nazi policy. There is a brood-mare theory of women implicit in all Nazi pronouncements and Hitler's statement in *Mein Kampf* that the "aim of feminine education is invariably to be the future mother"[20] has a special irony when one remembers how closely linked is population growth with the ambitions of a military state; more children must be born to die for country. And as Reich points out in *The Mass Psychology of Fascism*, and *Mein Kampf* illustrates again and again, the mystical idealization of chaste motherhood is a particularly efficient means not only of utterly equating sexuality with procreation (facilitated by the Nazi ban on contraception and abortion) but also of suppressing and inhibiting female sexuality altogether and converting it into a state-directed process of human reproduction for what were often lethal state ends.

As Germany had come under attack both by the international feminist movement and the liberal West for its treatment of women, Hitler defended the new state against the charge that "we have instituted a tyrannical regimentation of women":

> The outside world says, "Yes, the men! But the women they cannot be optimistic with you. They are oppressed, downtrodden and enslaved. You do not

[18] *Ibid.*

[19] Adolf Hitler, *Mein Kampf*, translated by Chamberlain et al. (New York, Reynal and Hitchcock, 1940), p. 659.

[20] *Ibid.*, p. 621.

want to give them any freedom, any equality of rights." But we reply, what you regard as a yoke others experience as a blessing. What for one appears as heaven, for another is hell . . . I am often told, "you want to force women out of professions." No, I only want to create to the greatest extent the possibility of founding a family and having children because our folk needs them above all things.[21]

The Führerin Frau Scholtz-Klink concurred with a docile definition that the only work of the German woman is to serve the German male—"to minister in the home" attending to "the care of man, soul, body and mind" continuously "from the first to the last moment of man's existence."[22] There was never any question among Party notables that the Nazi idea was a purely masculine affair, which women might serve but never partake of. As Minister of Propaganda, Goebbels made this clear:

The National Socialist movement is in its nature a masculine movement . . . The realms of directing and shaping are not hard to find in public life. To such realms belong for one thing the tremendously great sphere of politics. This sphere without qualification must be claimed by man . . . When we eliminate women from public life, it is not because we want to dispense with them but because we want to give them back their essential honor . . . The outstanding and highest calling of woman is always that of wife and mother, and it would be unthinkable misfortune if we allowed ourselves to be turned from this point of view.[23]

The Nazi "experiment" is particularly noteworthy in that, unlike other Western governments, it legislated the female sphere, rather than merely presenting it in the form of a biological edict, or simply propagandizing through a suasion often gallant in tone. For the Nazi state took a number of actual measures to insure the family, so often elsewhere merely the subject of propaganda, doubt, or wailing prophecy. The Nazi regime taxed bachelors and spinsters, and on June 1, 1933, it enacted its infamous Marriage Loans, under which one third of all German marriages were contracted thereafter, with tax and interest rebates for each child born in the marriage. In the early years of the regime the purpose of this was to remove women from the labor force (at the higher levels anyway) but still more deliberately to offset the declining birth rate which had accompanied German defeat in a First World War followed by the Depression, as well as to fight the tendency toward divorce, free union, contraception, and abortion, which had grown up under both the liberal Weimar climate and feminist

---

[21] Adolf Hitler, quoted in *Die Frau*, Vol. 44, p. 48 ff. (October 1936).

[22] Gertrud Scholtz-Klink, *The German Woman* (Mimeographed leaflet prepared by the Reichsfrauenführung).

[23] Josef Goebbels, quoted in *Der Nationalsozialistische Staat* (Walter Gehl, ed. *op. cit.*).

influence. Women took out the loan, but it was paid to the men. The wives created by the loan were not allowed to work unless the husband could show cause for welfare qualification and extreme need. The law took 800,000 women out of the labor market in 1933–35, but by 1936 there were already 1,200,000 more women employed than when Hitler came to power in January 1933 and their numbers kept rising with the armament efforts until the number of employed women was double what it had been at the start of the regime.

The campaign to raise the birth rate succeeded far better; the number of live births arose from 971,174 in 1933 to 1,261,273 in 1935.[24] The Nazi program was operated on coercion and bribery as well as propaganda: Folsom contrasts this with the more democratic method Sweden pursued by improving housing, guaranteeing maternity leaves, etc. Governments who manipulate population growth have two choices: making maternity pleasant, or making it inescapable. Moreover, when the Nazis came to power in 1933 there were two million women in excess of the male population, who, despite the force of a state inspired prescription to marry, clearly could not, and so continued to be victims of the endless cant about home and motherhood.

To provide contraceptive information in Nazi Germany was dangerous and punishable even in physicians. All the Weimar marriage clinics which had distributed contraceptives were closed after 1933. Contraceptive devices could no longer be advertised or sold save by specially licensed permit. Yet condoms were sold openly in vending machines in Berlin. This may appear utterly inconsistent. In fact it is not, for condoms were advocated, not as contraception, but as health measures to protect the populace and particularly the soldiery against infection by venereal disease.[25] After 1934 the Nazi state performed its own very different birth control in the notorious eugenic clinics through countless, largely indefensible, sterilizations. Sex education in Nazi Germany was quite simply racism, a course in Aryan eugenics. Abortion became a very risky affair, penalized by extreme measures, the criminal law of May 1933 making even the act of assistance in obtaining an abortion a penal offense. Unless there were suspicion of congenital defect, generally understood as non-Aryan parentage, all pregnancies must be brought to term. The liberal sexual reformers of the Weimar period were purged; Wilhelm Reich's books were banned. The Nazis found communism and Jewry responsible for the "sexual license" they claimed had preceded their regime and instituted an ethos of their own, generally neo-puritan as it applied to women, often neo-pagan as it applied to men.

[24] Figures for the Marriage Loans from Kirkpatrick, *op. cit.,* p. 149–73 and Folsom, *op. cit.,* p. 195.
[25] Syphilis was something of a private obsession with Hitler and innumerable references are made to it in *Mein Kampf* where it is repeatedly equated with sexual freedom or, in Hitler's view, bolshevik license.

Homosexuality was vigorously denounced, and there were frequent homosexual purges in the military, despite the continued presence of Captain Roehm, a well-known homosexual, as leader of the storm troopers. The virility cult of Nazi male culture, its emphasis upon "leaders" and male community, lent the entire Nazi era a curious tone of repressed homosexuality, neurotically anti-social and sadistic in character. The men's house culture of the Nazi *Männerbünde* constituted something very like an instance of state-instituted deviance. Prostitution and pornography were both proscribed ineffectively and for puritanical reasons quite removed from economic or humanitarian considerations; both became the privileges of the S.S. and other favored Nazi functionaries. In certain areas the police busily prohibited women from smoking; Dr. Krummacher issued edicts against cosmetics. Meanwhile the double standard flourished and prostitution, regulated and protected by the police, was looked upon as an indispensable convenience in a military state, so long as the "street picture" were not too offensive to innocent German youth. Fertility was considered so valuable that when a husband's vagary resulted in illegitimate birth, he was not held to have committed adultery in the legal sense. Unmarried women were thought to have transgressed but little in presenting the state with new children, but illegitimacy was not acceptable as a forgivable addition to the population in married women. Every aspect of Nazi sexual regulations, including its masculine tinge of neo-paganism, was of a character which might well be described as a state-sponsored and legally enforced sexual counterrevolution.

In reviewing the Nazi state, one can only conclude that economic motives superseded those not only of "sacred motherhood" (its favorite shibboleth) but even those of bolstering the family and the home.[26] Not only were German women deprived of professional or political participation that they might be exploited in the most exhausting labor the state needed done, its factory and agricultural work, but the home as a tribal unit was in continual competition with the state, which created time-consuming and compulsory organizations for each family member.

Yet the overriding reason for the flagrantly patriarchal and male-suprema-

[26] Folsom describes its effect on the family unit as deleterious: "The Nazis have wanted to strengthen the family as an instrument of the State. State interest is always paramount. Germany does not hesitate to turn a husband against a wife or children against parents when political disloyalty is involved. Much of the time of children and youth, as well as adults, is taken from the family for the use of group activities. Courts may take custody of children if parents refuse to teach them the Nazi ideology." Folsom, *op. cit.*, p. 196. Kirkpatrick sums up the Nazi attempt to solve what it fancied to be the "woman's problem" this way: ". . . the Nazis were not willing to pay the price. Theirs was a halfway program. They harried a few women out of their jobs, paid out a little money to encourage births, distributed a vast amount of propaganda and went right ahead with military preparations. An opportunistic demand for women's energies and capacities in the service of war preparations was hostile to defining woman's role in marriage." Kirkpatrick, *op. cit.*, p. 284.

cist character of the Nazi state seems to be temperamental rather than political or economic. In its regressive tribal mood a structure built on the suppression of women represented the perfect vehicle of authoritarian, jingoist, and militarist sentiment.[27] Again, one is forced to conclude that sexual politics, while connected to economics and other tangibles of social organization, is, like racism, or certain aspects of caste, primarily an ideology, a way of life, with influence over every other psychological and emotional facet of existence. It has created, therefore, a psychic structure, deeply embedded in our past, capable of intensification or attenuation, but one which, as yet, no people have succeeded in eliminating.

The Soviet Union did make a conscious effort to terminate patriarchy and restructure its most basic institution—the family. After the revolution every possible law was passed to free individuals from the claims of the family: free marriage and divorce, contraception, and abortion on demand. Most material of all, the women and children were to be liberated from the controlling economic power of the husband. Under the collective system, the family began to disintegrate along the very lines upon which it had been built. Patriarchy began, as it were, to reverse its own processes, while society returned to the democratic work community which socialist authorities describe as matriarchy.

On December 19, 1917, and October 17, 1918, Lenin issued two decrees which invalidated the prerogatives of males over their dependents and affirmed the complete right to economic, social, and sexual self-determination in women, declaring it a matter of course that they freely choose their own domicile, name, and citizenship.[28] Every legal provision was made for political and economic equality. One cannot legislate a sexual revolution by fiat, however, as Lenin was aware, and efforts were made to make the financial independence of both women and children a reality: nurseries were to be established, housekeeping was to be collectivized to spare women its

---

[27] Abrahamsen (probably relying upon Reich's rather superior account in *The Mass Psychology of Fascism*) argues that much of the Nazis' success was due to the consistently high level of "patriarchalism" present in German culture. In a more recent book, Robert Lowie argues against this thesis. But Abrahamsen, and Reich still more, comprehend the formalization of authoritarian patriarchy in the Nazi state as intimately connected with the national mass psychology and Lowie's depreciation of Germanic patriarchalism, on the grounds that motherhood was respected or that individual housewives were strong characters, is somewhat naïve. See David Abrahamsen, *Men, Mind, and Power* (New York, Columbia University Press, 1945) and Robert Lowie, *Toward Understanding Germany* (Chicago, University of Chicago Press, 1954).

[28] See Rudolph Schlesinger, *The Family in the U.S.S.R. Documents and readings* (London, Routledge & Kegan Paul, 1949). Illegitimacy was no longer recognized. Incest, adultery and homosexuality were dropped from the criminal code. On November 20, 1920, abortion under hospital conditions was legalized. The new code of January 1, 1927 recognized common-law marriages.

drudgery, maternity leave would be granted, and women welcomed on an equal footing into the labor force, which together with education and the household, were to be made collective.

With all this, the Soviet experiment failed and was abandoned. Through the thirties and forties Soviet society came to resemble the modified patriarchy of other Western countries; at times the zeal of its propaganda for the traditional family was indistinguishable from that of other Western nations, including Nazi Germany. The reasons for the counterrevolution are many and complex, yet a good number of conservative observers have rejoiced so in the event that they are willing to attribute it to nature, the "biological tragedy of women," the eternal life and validity of the patriarchal family and so forth.[29]

The chief causes appear to be the difficulty of establishing a complete social revolution when one is overwhelmed, as the Russians were, with both political (the White Russian wars against the revolution) and economic problems (women were declared economically independent, but this scarcely made them so, particularly in the New Economic Policy years of unemployment). A still deeper cause is the fact that beyond declaring that the compulsive family must go, Marxist theory had failed to supply a sufficient ideological base for a sexual revolution, and was remarkably naïve as to the historical and psychological strength of patriarchy. Engels had supplied nothing but a history and economy of the patriarchal family, neglecting to investigate the mental habits it inculcates. Lenin admitted that the sexual revolution, like the social and sexual processes in general, were not adequately understood; he also stated on a number of occasions that he did not find them important

---

[29] Scholars freely admit this widespread bias: "A good deal has been written on the subject and many writers have concluded that the Soviet experience proves that the family cannot be dispensed with." H. Kent Geiger, *The Family in Soviet Russia* (Cambridge, Harvard University Press, 1968), p. 96. An article on "The Changing Soviet Family," by Urie Bronfenbrenner in *The Role and Status of Women in the Soviet Union,* ed. by Donald R. Brown (New York, Teachers College, Columbia University Press, 1968) speaks of "a number of Western Scholars" who have interpreted the "dramatic shift in Soviet policy on the family" as "a return to and vindication of" traditional Western family patterns (pp. 102–3) and traces this attitude to its most authoritative enunciator, Alex Inkeles, who in 1949 took satisfaction in the Soviet abandonment of revolutionary policies as "striking affirmation of the importance" of the family in "Western civilization." Alex Inkeles, "Family and Church in Postwar USSR," *Annals of the American Academy of Political and Social Sciences,* CCLXIII (May 1949), pp. 33–44. Timasheff, whose material on the Soviet family was incorporated into Bell and Vogel, the most authoritative American text on the subject of the family, makes it clear that the radical sexual policy had to be abandoned as its effects "were found to endanger the very stability of the new society and its capacity to stand the test of war." (This last phrase has a certain unintentional irony.) Nicholas Timasheff, *The Great Retreat* (New York, Dutton, 1946). In popular American opinion during the forties and fifties (cold war years) it was frankly believed that "since the Russians had tried and failed to change the family it couldn't be done."

enough to speak on.[30] Trotsky, who did not deign to treat of sex in his supposedly practical book *Everyday Questions*, is vehement about the ideological vacuum, Soviet failure, and Stalinist regression in *The Revolution Betrayed*,[31] but this is the hindsight of 1936. Indeed, it seems as though Reich's charge that sex itself were somehow beneath the notice of the great social thinkers is correct.[32] Therefore, with the collapse of the old patriarchal order, there was no positive and coherent theory to greet the inevitable confusion.

In addition to this, there was no realization that while every practical effort should be made to implement a sexual revolution, the real test would be in changing attitudes. For Soviet leadership had declared the family defunct in a society composed entirely of family members, whose entire psychic processes were formed in the patriarchal family of Tsarist Russia. Women in such a society were loath to relinquish the dependency and security of the family and the domination over children which it accorded them; men were just as reluctant to waive their traditional prerogatives and privileges; everyone talked endlessly about sexual equality, but none, or few, were capable of practicing it. Nearly all were afraid of sexual autonomy and freedom. Moreover, the collective was difficult, if not impossible, to establish in direct proportion to the strength of family feeling and organization. There were, moreover, several ancient errors embedded in the revolutionary mentality: a belief that sexuality is incompatible with social effort and dedication, an assumption that sexuality is antithetical to collective or to cultural achievement (one finds this in Freud too),[33] an attitude in which pregnancy and childbirth were continually referred to as "biological infirmities," and a questionable, even dangerously superficial, presumption that family and marriage are merely economic or material phenomena, capable of solution by economic and institutional methods alone.

Even here the Soviets failed miserably. As Trotsky comments icily, "You cannot 'abolish' the family, you have to replace it."[34] The communal housekeeping and crèches simply did not materialize. Geiger, who feels the failure to provide these two services was the "fatal flaw" in the revolution's effort to emancipate women reports that in 1925 only three out of every one hundred

---

[30] Klara Zetkin, *Reminiscences of Lenin*, London, 1929. Lenin to Klara Zetkin: "Perhaps one day I shall speak or write on these questions—but not now. Now all our time must be dedicated to other matters." P. 61.

[31] Leon Trotsky, *The Revolution Betrayed* (1936), translated by Max Eastman (New York, Merit, 1965).

[32] Wilhelm Reich, *The Sexual Revolution* (1945) (New York, Noonday, 1967).

[33] A. A. Soltz, a party official, had stressed this as early as 1926, and Zalkind, the party officer who first mapped out the ideological line for a retreat from sexual freedom in developing a theory of "revolutionary sublimation" admitted to his debt to Freud. As leader of the conservative movement between 1923 and 1936, Zalkind developed a theory of "conservation of energy" very like Freud's theory of libido; energy taken from the socialist effort through sexuality is energy stolen from the revolution and the proletariat.

[34] Trotsky, *op. cit.*, p. 145.

children were accommodated outside the home.[35] The entire burden of child care and housework was left upon women, frequently alone, as paternal responsibility was so often neglected. Urged into employment such women were in fact only being awarded the responsibility of three occupations to shoulder simultaneously. In the absence of crèches and communal housekeeping, children were often homeless and neglected; juvenile delinquency became a considerable threat.

Much of the problem was economic. The government, just recovering from the terrible poverty of the early Soviet years gave its priority to heavy industry and armaments.[36] Allowing reaction to replace revolution is simply easier in troubled situations, and by 1936 party official Svetlov could announce that since the state is "temporarily unable to take upon itself family functions" it is forced to "conserve the family."[37]

Approaching such great social change with misconceptions and an outright failure to supply the promised provisions, the inevitable confusion following upon such radical social transformation unaccompanied by sufficient institutional replacement was interpreted by party functionaries as chaos. A population so recently freed did not know how to use its freedom, and (especially under the conditions of poverty following the civil wars of 1918–22) sexuality was brutalized. There appears to have been a good deal of exploitative or irresponsible sexuality as well, arising partly out of ignorance or guilt (a failure or inability on the part of the people to avail themselves of contraception)[38] and partly from the callousness of inherited attitudes, particularly male-supremacist ones. The Bischoff and Harvard Project studies documenting individual cases illustrate how, no longer entitled to the tyrannical position tsarist patriarchy had awarded him, Soviet man still satisfied his impression of sexual superiority in objectified promiscuity and domestic irresponsibility.[39] In practice the new sexual freedom applied largely as a freedom for men. There is considerable evidence that in many ways the conditions of women worsened in the first decades of the revolution and that they were sexually exploited on a large scale. The great mass of women, illiterate, submissive after centuries of subordination, with little realization of their rights, could scarcely take advantage of the new free-

[35] Geiger quoted in discussion in Brown, *The Role and Status of Women in the Soviet Union, op. cit.,* p. 51; and Geiger, *The Family in Soviet Russia, op. cit.,* p. 58.

[36] Where crèches were built on some scale after 1936 and 1944 their function was to raise population and release women for Stalin's factories. By this time the ideal of sexual freedom and the emancipation of women with which the revolution had begun and still gave lip service had ceased to matter.

[37] Schlesinger, *op. cit.,* p. 346.

[38] Accounts of the use of contraception in the twenties and thirties vary. In *Soviet Journey* (1935) Louis Fischer reported a widespread use, but Geiger denies this and stresses the government's fear of sponsoring a rigorous drive for contraception. In view of the misery the lack of it caused this appears little short of criminal.

[39] Examined in Geiger, *op. cit.,* and elsewhere.

doms to the degree which men could. Trotsky's observation of how the male party member forged ahead (only 10 percent of party members were women in the twenties) and finding his overworked wife "regressive" simply discarded her, has become a commonplace in the literature of the period.

The abuses which arose from the government's own failures and omissions opened the way for the experts and the moralists, the party pundits, and the gradual erosion of the new liberties under the banner of humanistic justification of traditional strictures. The revisionists had arrived on the scene and the radical views of the feminists and revolutionaries Kollontai and Wolffson were publicly censured as unsound.

At the Congress of Kiev in 1932 abortion was decried for innumerable reasons, all of which came down to authoritarian state interest in forcing women to bear children, explained as population policy (the birth rate had boomed after the revolution and now a slight decline was interpreted as catastrophic). There was much cant about "preserving the race," "humanity dying out," "morality collapsing," and so forth. The other prevailing rationale was based on an equally authoritarian distaste over the fact women now enjoyed the control of their bodies; functionaries fussed that women were no longer ashamed of abortion and now "considered it their legal right."[40] Dr. Koroliov urged his colleagues that "criminal abortion is a sign of immorality which finds support in the legalization of abortion . . . It prevents motherhood . . . Its intention is not that of helping the mother or society; it has nothing to do with the protection of maternal health."[41] The effect here is to force motherhood on the unwilling as a social obligation, to deny that sexuality may be removed from procreation, and to create a negative attitude toward sexuality itself under the guise of pious concern over women and babies. The last was hardly necessary, so great was the shame and distaste for sexuality in Soviet women, a legacy from prerevolutionary attitudes, that the same congress could affirm that 60–70 per cent of women were incapable of experiencing sexual pleasure. Despite legalization it had taken ten years to stamp out the underground trade in abortions and the excessive or abusive resort to abortion was the result of so negative an attitude toward sexuality that women felt guilty in using contraception.[42] Despite strong public objection, Stalin's Second Five Year Plan in 1936 outlawed abortion in first pregnancies. This is often said to be the last occasion on which Stalin consulted public opinion. In 1944 all legal abortion was abolished, with two-year prison terms for persons who aided a woman in securing it. Acute observers perceived that the rationalization for the repeal of the right to legal abortion as a desire to protect

[40] Quoted in Reich, *The Sexual Revolution, op. cit.,* p. 206. The speaker is Stroganov.
[41] Quoted in Reich, *op. cit.,* p. 199.
[42] This phenomenon may also be observed today in America where students and other young women neglect contraception, unconsciously willing pregnancy to occur, the "punishment" courted for repressed "guilt."

the health of the mother was a hypocrisy which "obviously camouflaged"[43] the desire for a rise in the birth rate as the result of war preparations. "We have need of people" Soltz proclaimed, oblivious to the number of homeless children, the housing shortage and harried involuntary mothers. Just as in Nazi Germany, the mood had changed to one which dictated large population growth in an increasingly militarized society.

Abortion was the first wedge, but other reactionary attitudes which had persisted soon began to reassert themselves. Revolutionary legislation had thrown out the old Tsarist paragraph penalizing homosexuality; and in March 1934, after fifteen years, it was reintroduced, with penalties of from three to eight years. It is an interesting insight into reawakened patriarchal sentiment to observe that in Russia, as elsewhere, homosexuality is recognized and punished only between males; homosexuality between females is presumed to be unthinkable or nonexistent.[44] There were mass arrests of homosexuals and widespread persecution, together with propaganda campaigns to the effect that homosexuality was "decadent," "oriental," "bourgeois," and even "fascist" (guilt through association with the Nazi Männerbünde).

One very real problem facing the Soviet Union was whether it could, through a revolutionary education, set up a new psychic structure in its members to replace that of patriarchy. And here it failed signally. After a period of experimentation, it gradually instituted its own moralistic, inhibiting ideology, a new authoritarian structure, stressing its own kind of attitudes toward the sexes and sexuality, and its own standard of the masculine as the ideal and the norm, by continual adulation of militaristic achievements and the exploits of revolutionaries. Education was again antisexual; every effort was made to hamper, divert, and thwart the sexuality of the young. Asceticism began to reassert itself as the ideal in schools and among the Pioneers (youth groups). Progressive schools such as Vera Schmidt's kindergarten, an experiment in raising children without sexual guilt or inhibition, was closed at the behest of "the authorities" in educational theory. The youth communes (Komsomol) floundered for economic and psychological reasons, turned authoritarian,[45] and finally failed and were discontinued

[43] Geiger's phrase, *op. cit.*, p. 100.

[44] Only in Sweden have the laws been equalized. Homosexual acts between consenting adults, men or women, are not illegal. Homosexual assault and the seduction of minors are legal offenses in both sexes.

[45] It is interesting that Makarenko, author of the chief codification of the new state-oriented authoritarian family first distinguished himself as leader of a particularly ascetic and militaristic Komsomol established under the auspices of the Soviet Secret Political Police for delinquent boys. Makarenko had great contempt for libertarian child-centered theories of the twenties; with his rise to eminence progressives had been defeated and the new party line supported traditional educational methods and discipline. At times it is hard to know if sexual counterrevolution betrayed the women or the youth more bitterly in Russia. See Makarenko, *A Book for Parents* (1937, published in 1940).

after 1932. Their efforts to establish a model communal life are studies in the psychic incapacity of family-produced youth to establish a collective life style; they lacked housing conducive to privacy or order, and vacillated dizzily between the sexual climate of the harem and that of the convent. The powers of an oppressive sexual ethic triumphantly reasserted themselves in this statement of the Commissar for Public Health to students:

> Comrades, you have come to the universities and technical institutes for your studies. That is the main goal of your life. And as all your impulses and attitudes are subordinated to this goal, as you must deny yourself many enjoyments because they might interfere with your main goal, that of studying and becoming collaborators in the reconstruction of the state, so you must subordinate all other aspects of your existence to this goal. The state is as yet too poor to take over the support of you and the education of the children. Therefore, our advice to you is: *Abstinence!*[46]

Despite the obvious alternative of contraception, this admonition became standard official advice in the Soviet Union as it was elsewhere during the era of reaction.

The Russian retreat from a sexual revolution began with the worried discussions of the twenties, but did not get under way until the mid-thirties, and was not completed until 1944.[47] Everything was done to re-enforce the family. In the new law of 1935 parents were again held responsible for their children's education and behavior. Soviet ideology now announced that sexual union was to be "in principle a life-long union with children." Sex and the family, sex and procreation, were welded together again. Having declined to fulfill its promise of crèches and collective housekeeping, and in view of its experience without them, as well as in view of the priority it put upon industrial projects, particularly armaments, Stalin's Russia preferred to bolster the family so that it might perform the functions the state had promised but did not choose to afford. At the same time it now felt secure that the "new Soviet family" (the old, consisting of an earlier generation, had posed a threat) which Makarenko promulgated, with Stalin's support, would be an admirable vehicle of state-directed socialization. Paternal authority was to be upheld again, which is not surprising when one understands that the state saw itself as *delegating* its authority to parents and in turn *demanding* them to rear the young in the *correct* manner.[48]

[46] Quoted in Reich, *The Sexual Revolution,* pp. 189–90.
[47] With the "Thaw" the situation began to improve; in 1954–55 the right of abortion was restored and in 1964–65 bastardy ceased to be registered. In 1964 the distinguished social philosopher Strumilin raised new discussion by the suggestion of a kibbutzlike collective education very reminiscent of early Soviet hopes. A return to Marxist principles in this area might possibly be in the offing.
[48] "In delegating to you a certain measure of societal authority the Soviet State demands from you the correct upbringing of its future citizens." Anton S. Makarenko,

The new divorce law of 1936 punished the error of "mistaking infatuation with love" in fines levied for divorce of 30–50 roubles. In 1944 a harsher law raised the fine to 500–2000 roubles and required petition to a lower and higher court, both of which specialized in reconciliations. Free divorce had once been "the gift of the revolution"; now great financial, judicial, and ideological barriers were raised against it. Common law marriage, recognized since 1927 was revoked. The ZAG (civil registry) offices were smartened up and marriage and divorce no longer transacted at the same counter; encouragement was given so that weddings might become ritualistic again. Illegitimacy was reinstituted as a concept, severely penalized and stigmatized both in mother and child. The father was in such cases no longer held responsible. This of course permitted sexuality to become more exploitative than it had been in the 1920s. It is ironic that the reaction, put through in the name of protecting women and children ("the weak") actually made their situation far worse. Women now had very little relief or escape from the total housekeeping and child-care burden as the old ideal of sexual equality became increasingly irrelevant to a nation preparing for war through the imposition of a militarist and authoritarian atmosphere often scarcely indistinguishable from traditional patriarchy. The archetypal figures of the mother and the soldier replaced the revolutionary comrades and lovers. Svetlov exulted that "motherhood has become a joy." Vast campaigns were launched to honor mothers of large families, the law of 1936 awarded bonuses to women with six or more children; the law of 1944 rewarded mothers of seven or more with honorary titles and decorations.

A new type of propaganda had appeared in the mid-thirties through domestic melodrama, sentimental films, and editorials in *Pravda,* which in a more and more official tone assured the world that the Soviets regarded the "family as a big and serious thing," asserted that "only a good family man could be a good Soviet citizen" and that "marriage is the most serious affair of life." Stalin paid a much-publicized visit to his aged mother in the Caucasus. Engels' belief in individual sex love and the rights of sexual life to be beyond the province of the state were now called "bourgeois" and "irresponsible" while un-Marxist pronouncements poured forth: "The state cannot exist without the family." Marxism was stood on its head: "There are people who dare to assert that the Revolution destroys the family; this is entirely wrong: the family is an especially important phase of social relations in the socialist society . . . One of the basic rules of Communist morals is that of strengthening the family."[49]

A *Book for Parents,* translated by Robert Daglish as *The Collective Family, A Handbook for Russian Parents* (New York, Doubleday & Company, Inc., 1967), pp. 27–28.

[49] These very un-Marxist slogans are reprinted in Timasheff, *op. cit.,* pp. 197–98.

International Communism followed suit, and France's *Humanité* gave out the alarming cry:

> Save the family! Help us in our great inquiry in the interest of the right to love . . . The Communists are confronted by a very grave situation. The country which they are to revolutionize, the French world, runs the danger of being crippled and depopulated. The maliciousness of a dying capitalism, its immorality, the egotism it creates, the misery, the clandestine abortion which it provokes, *destroy the family*. The Communists want to fight in the defense of the French family . . . They want to take over a strong country and a fertile race. The USSR points the way. But it is necessary to take active measures to save the race.[50]

Of course this is not only in direct contradiction to Marxist principles, but in essence much the same sort of thing one reads in Nazi pronouncements. Even the *Ladies' Home Journal,* by no means in disagreement as to the family point of view, compares creditably with it as to style of persuasion. It is a remarkable fact that, as John Stuart Mill pointed out long before, the authoritarian and patriarchal mind cannot separate the liberation of women from racial extinction and the death of love, an equation of human affection and reproduction with slavish subordination, excessive or accidental progeny, and servile affection which never fails to convict the speaker.

Twenty-seven years after the revolution, the Soviet position had completely reversed itself. The initial radical freedoms in marriage, divorce, abortion, child care, and the family were largely abridged and the reaction gained so that, by 1943, even coeducation was abolished in the Soviet Union. The sexual revolution was over, the counterrevolution triumphant. In the following decades conservative opinion elsewhere rejoiced in pointing to the Soviet as an object lesson in the folly of change.

THE REACTION IN IDEOLOGY

Freud and the Influence of Psychoanalytic Thought

The pressures of official suppression cannot account for the counterrevolution. For in most places the sexual revolution collapsed from within and was undermined more through its own imperfections than from hostile forces which combined to crush it. The real causes of the counterrevolution appear to lie in the fact that the sexual revolution had, perhaps necessarily, even inevitably, concentrated on the superstructure of patriarchal policy, changing its legal forms, its more flagrant abuses, altering its formal educa-

---

[50] P. Vaillant-Courturier, *Humanité*, October 31, 1935.

tional patterns, but leaving the socialization processes of temperament and role differentiation intact. Basic attitudes, values, emotions—all that constituted the psychic structure several millennia of patriarchal society had built up—remained insufficiently affected, if not completely untouched. Moreover, the major institutions of the old tradition, patriarchal marriage and the family, were never or rarely challenged. Only the outer surface of society had been changed; underneath the essential system was preserved undisturbed. Should it receive new sources of support, new ratification, new ideological justifications, it could be mobilized anew. Patriarchy could, as indeed it did, remain in force as a thoroughly efficient political system, a method of social governance, without any visible superstructure beyond the family, simply because it lived on in the mind and heart where it had first rooted itself in the conditioning of its subjects, and from which a few reforms were hardly likely to evict it.

Recently, a number of studies have begun to explore the conservative trends that operated between 1930–60, causing a deterioration in the economic and educational status of American women.[51] They attribute it to postwar reaction, conservative or anti-Communist animus toward the Soviet or other Socialist experimentation, an economic situation where women are exploited as a reserve labor force, periodically and widely purged from employment, and when reintroduced, confined to its lower reaches, and finally, to the ideology of the "higher domesticity."[52] As such phenomena have, to some degree, already been documented, what shall concern us here are the more diffuse currents of opinion in literature and in scholarship, the intellectual origins and the atmosphere of the counterrevolutionary era.

If new ideological support were to come to the patriarchal social order, its sex roles and its differentiated temperaments of masculine and feminine, it could not come from religion, although the decades in question did see a religious revival, particularly in the prestigious and influential quarters of literature and the university. T. S. Eliot's piety and the sanctity of the fashionable neo-orthodoxy at Oxford and in the New Criticism could scarcely serve as a lifeboat for an entire society any more than could the wholesale defection of literary and critical minds from rationality into the caverns of myth. The new formulation of old attitudes had to come from science and particularly from the emerging social sciences of psychology, sociology, and anthro-

---

[51] See The President's Report on the Status of Women, William L. O'Neill's *Everyone Was Brave, The Rise and Fall of Feminism in America* (Chicago, Quadrangle, 1969), Betty Friedan's *The Feminine Mystique* (New York, Norton, 1963), and Marlene Dixon's "Why Women's Liberation?" *Ramparts*, November 1969. The gap between male and female earnings has been growing since the thirties. In 1940 women still held 45 per cent of all professional and technical occupations, by 1967 they held only 37 per cent. In the 1930s women received two out of five of the B.A. and M.A. degrees and one in seven of the Ph.Ds. Yet in 1962 only one in three persons who received a B.A. or M.A. was a woman, one in ten of those who received Ph.Ds. (figures from Dixon).

[52] The term is O'Neill's.

pology—the most useful and authoritative branches of social control and manipulation. To be unassailable, there should be some connection, however dubious, with the more readily validated sciences of biology, mathematics, and medicine. To fill the needs of conservative societies and a population too reluctant or too perplexed to carry out revolutionary changes in social life, even to the drastic modification of basic units such as the family, a number of new prophets arrived upon the scene to clothe the old doctrine of the separate spheres in the fashionable language of science.

The most influential of these was Sigmund Freud, beyond question the strongest individual counterrevolutionary force in the ideology of sexual politics during the period. Although popular in England and on the continent in Lawrence's time, the prestige of Freud's sexual theories did not arrive at, still less maintain, such complete ascendancy there as they achieved in the United States. In America, the influence of Freud is almost incalculable, and America, in many ways the first center of the sexual revolution, appears to have need of him. Although generally accepted as a prototype of the liberal urge toward sexual freedom, and a signal contributor toward softening traditional puritanical inhibitions upon sexuality, the effect of Freud's work, that of his followers, and still more that of his popularizers, was to rationalize the invidious relationship between the sexes, to ratify traditional roles, and to validate temperamental differences.

By an irony nearly tragic, the discoveries of a great pioneer, whose theories of the unconscious and of infant sexuality were major contributions to human understanding, were in time invoked to sponsor a point of view essentially conservative. And as regards the sexual revolution's goal of liberating female humanity from its traditional subordination, the Freudian position came to be pressed into the service of a strongly counterrevolutionary attitude. Although the most unfortunate effects of vulgar Freudianism far exceeded the intentions of Freud himself, its anti-feminism was not without foundation in Freud's own work.

In a moment of humble confusion Freud once confessed to his students: "If you want to know more about femininity, you must interrogate your own experience, or turn to the poets, or else wait until science can give you more coherent information."[53] On another occasion he admitted to Marie Bonaparte "the great question that has never been answered and which I have not been able to answer, despite my thirty years of research into the feminine soul, is 'What does a woman want?' "[54] In the face of such basic uncertainty it is most unfortunate that Freud insisted on proceeding so far in constructing a psychology of women.

Probably the real tragedy of Freudian psychology is that its fallacious in-

[53] Freud, "Femininity," New Introductory Lectures on Psychoanalysis (1933), translated by James Strachey (New York, Norton, 1964), p. 135.

[54] Freud in a letter to Bonaparte quoted in Ernest Jones, The Life and Work of Sigmund Freud (New York, Basic Books, 1953), Vol. II, p. 421.

terpretations of feminine character were based upon clinical observations of great validity. For the women who sought out psychoanalysis were (and in many cases still are) the "unadjusted women" of their time, all those who in Viola Klein's eloquent description, were symptomatic of a "widespread, in fact, a general dissatisfaction with their sexual role":

> It was expressed in inferiority feelings, in contempt for their own sex, in revolt against their passive role, in envy of man's greater freedom, in the ambition to equal man in intellectual or artistic achievements, in strivings for independence . . . and in all sorts of devices to make up for the social disadvantages of not being a man.[55]

Through his clinical work Freud was able to observe women suffering from two causes: sexual inhibition (sometimes sufficiently great as to bring on severe symptoms, even hysteria),[56] and a great discontentment with their social circumstances. In general, his tendency was to believe the second over-dependent upon the first, and to recommend in female sexual fulfillment a panacea for what were substantial symptoms of social unrest within an oppressive culture.

I

In reconsidering Freud's theories on women we must ask ourselves not only what conclusions he drew from the evidence at hand but also upon what assumptions he drew them. Freud did not accept his patient's symptoms as evidence of a justified dissatisfaction with the limiting circumstances imposed on them by society, but as symptomatic of an independent and universal feminine tendency.[57] He named this tendency "penis envy," traced its origin to childhood experience and based his theory of the psychology of women upon it, aligning what he took to be the three corollaries of feminine psychology, passivity, masochism, and narcissism, so that each was dependent upon, or related to, penis envy.

As the Freudian understanding of female personality is based upon the idea of penis envy, it requires an elaborate, and often repetitious, exposition.[58] Beginning with the theory of penis envy, the definition of the female

[55] Viola Klein, *The Feminine Character, History of an Ideology* (London, Kegan Paul, 1946), pp. 72–73.

[56] Freud's first cases were hysterics; see Vol. I of his *Collected Papers* (1893–1905) pp. 9–272, and *Dora. An Analysis of a Case of Hysteria* (1905–9) edited by Philip Rieff (New York, Collier, 1966).

[57] Here Freud's procedure was very different from the liberal and humane attitude he adopted toward patients suffering from sexual inhibition.

[58] See especially "Femininity." After making use of such patently invidious terms as "the boy's far superior equipment" (p. 126), "her inferior clitoris" (p. 127), "genital deficiency" (p. 132), and "original sexual inferiority" (p. 132), Freud proposes to his audience that penis envy is the foundation of his whole theory of female psychology, warning them that should they demur before his hypothesis, they would sabotage the

is negative—what she is is the result of the fact that she is not a male and "lacks" a penis. Freud assumed that the female's discovery of her sex is, in and of itself, a catastrophe of such vast proportions that it haunts a woman all through life and accounts for most aspects of her temperament. His entire psychology of women, from which all modern psychology and psychoanalysis derives heavily, is built upon an original tragic experience—born female. Purportedly, Freud is here only relaying the information supplied by women themselves, the patients who furnished his clinical data, the basis of his later generalities about all women. It was in this way, Freud believed, he had been permitted to see how women accepted the idea that to be born female is to be born "castrated":

> As we learn from psycho-analytic work, women regard themselves as wronged from infancy, as undeservedly cut short and set back; and the embitterment of so many daughters against their mothers derives, in the last analysis, from the reproach against her of having brought them into the world as women instead of as men.[59]

Assuming that this were true, the crucial question, manifestly, is to ask why this might be so. Either maleness is indeed an *inherently* superior phenomenon, and in which case its "betterness" could be empirically proved and demonstrated, or the female misapprehends and reasons erroneously that she is inferior. And again, one must ask why. What forces in her experience, her society and socialization have led her to see herself as an inferior being? The answer would seem to lie in the conditions of patriarchal society and the inferior position of women within this society. But Freud did not choose to pursue such a line of reasoning, preferring instead an etiology of childhood experience based upon the biological fact of anatomical differences.

While it is supremely unfortunate that Freud should prefer to bypass the more likely social hypothesis to concentrate upon the distortions of infantile subjectivity, his analysis might yet have made considerable sense were he sufficiently objective to acknowledge that woman is born female in a masculine-dominated culture which is bent upon extending its values even to anatomy and is therefore capable of investing biological phenomena with symbolic force. In much the same manner we perceive that the traumatizing circumstance of being born black in a white racist society invests skin color with symbolic value while telling us nothing about racial traits as such.

In dismissing the wider cultural context of feminine dissatisfaction and

---

entire construct: "If you reject the idea as fantastic and regard my belief in the influence of lack of a penis on the configuration of femininity as an idée fixe, I am of course defenceless." (P. 132.) My critique of Freud's notions of women is indebted to an unpublished summary by Frances Kamm.

[59] Freud, "Some Character Types Met With in Psycho-Analysis Work" (1915) *Collected Papers of Sigmund Freud*, edited by Joan Riviere (New York, Basic Books, 1959), Vol. IV, p. 323.

isolating it in early childhood experience, Freud again ignored the social context of childhood by locating a literal feminine "castration" complex in the child's discovery of the anatomical differentiation between the sexes. Freud believed he had found the key to feminine experience—in that moment when girls discover they are "castrated"—a "momentous discovery which little girls are destined to make":

> They notice the penis of a brother or playmate, strikingly visible and of large proportions, at once recognize it as the superior counterpart of their own small and inconspicuous organ, and from that time forward fall a victim to envy for the penis.[60]

There are several unexplained assumptions here: why is the girl instantly struck by the proposition that bigger is better? Might she just as easily, reasoning from the naïveté of childish narcissism imagine the penis is an excrescence and take her own body as norm? Boys clearly do, as Freud makes clear, and in doing so respond to sexual enlightenment not with the reflection that their own bodies are peculiar, but, far otherwise, with a "horror of the mutilated creature or triumphant contempt for her."[61] Secondly, the superiority of this "superior counterpart," which the girl is said to "recognize at once" in the penis, is assumed to relate to the autoerotic satisfactions of childhood; but here again the child's experience provides no support for such an assumption.

Much of Freudian theory rests upon this moment of discovery and one is struck how, in the case of the female, to recapitulate the peculiar drama of penis envy is to rehearse again the fable of the Fall, a Fall that is Eve's alone.[62] As children, male and female first inhabit a paradisiacal playground where roles are interchangeable, active and passive, masculine and feminine. Until the awesome lapsarian moment when the female discovers her inferiority, her castration, we are asked to believe that she had assumed her clitoris a penis. One wonders why. Freud believes it is because she masturbated with it, and he assumes that she will conclude that what is best for such purposes must be a penis.[63] Freud insists upon calling the period of clitoral autoeroticism "phallic" in girls.

[60] Freud, "Some Psychological Consequences of the Anatomical Distinctions Between the Sexes" (1925) *Collected Papers*, Vol. V, p. 190.

[61] *Ibid.*, p. 191.

[62] Not only has Adam grace within his loins to assure him he belongs to a superior species, but even his later fears of castration which come to him after a glimpse of the "mutilated creature" causes him to repress his Oedipal desires (out of fear of a castrating father's revenge) and in the process develop the strong super-ego which Freud believes accounts for what he took to be the male's inevitable and transcendent moral and cultural superiority.

[63] Because she feels free, equal, and active then, Freud says "the little girl is a little man." "Femininity," p. 118. So strong is Freud's masculine bias here that it has obliterated linguistic integrity: the autoerotic state might as well, in both cases, be

Moreover, the revelation which Freud imagined would poison female life is probably, in most cases, a glimpse of a male playmate urinating or having a bath. It is never explained how the girl child makes the logical jump from the sight of bathing or urination to knowledge that the boy masturbates with this novel article. Even should her first sight of the penis occur in masturbatory games, Freud's supposition that she could judge this foreign item to be more conducive to autoerotic pleasure than her own clitoris (she having no possible experience of penile autoeroticism as males have none of clitoral) such as assumption is groundless. Yet Freud believed that female autoeroticism declines as a result of enlightenment, finding in this "yet another surprising effect of penis-envy, or of the discovery of the inferiority of the clitoris."[64] Here, as is so often the case, one cannot separate Freud's account of how a child reasons from how Freud himself reasons, and his own language, invariably pejorative, tends to confuse the issue irremediably. Indeed, since he has no objective proof of any consequence to offer in support of his notion of penis envy or of a female castration complex,[65] one is struck by how thoroughly the subjectivity in which all these events are cast tends to be Freud's own, or that of a strong masculine bias, even of a rather gross male-supremacist bias.[66]

This habitual masculine bias of Freud's own terms and diction, and the attitude it implies, is increased and further emphasized by his followers: Deutsch refers to the clitoris as an "inadequate substitute" for the penis; Karl Abraham refers to a "poverty in external genitals" in the female, and all conclude that even bearing children can be but a poor substitute for a

---

called "clitoral" for all the light shed by these terms. Freud's usage is predicated on the belief that masturbation is the active pursuit of pleasure, and activity masculine *per se*. "We are entitled to keep to our view that in the phallic phase of girls the clitoris is the leading erotogenic zone." *Ibid.*

[64] "Some Psychological Consequences of the Anatomical Distinctions Between the Sexes," p. 193.

[65] The entirety of Freud's clinical data always consists of his analysis of patients and his own self-analysis. In the case of penis envy he has remarkably little evidence from patients and his description of masculine contempt and feminine grief upon the discovery of sexual differences are extraordinarily autobiographical. Little Hans (Freud's own grandson) a five-year-old boy with an obsessive concern for his "widdler" furnishes the rest of the masculine data. Though an admirable topic of precise clinical research, it was and is, remarkably difficult for Freud, or anyone else, to make generalizations about how children first come to sexual knowledge, family and cultural patterns being so diverse, further complicated by the host of variable factors within individual experience, such as the number, age, and sex of siblings, the strength and consistency of the nakedness taboo, etc.

[66] Ernest Jones aptly described Freud's attitude here as "phallocentric." There is something behind Freud's assumptions reminiscent of the ancient misogynist postulate that females are but incomplete or imperfect males—e.g., deformed humans, the male being accepted as the norm—a view shared by Augustine, Aquinas etc.

constitutional inadequacy.[67] As Klein observes in her critique of Freud, it is a curious hypothesis that "one half of humanity should have biological reasons to feel at a disadvantage for not having what the other half possess (but not vice versa)."[68] It is especially curious to imagine that half the race should attribute their clear and obvious social-status inferiority to the crudest biological reasons when so many more promising social factors are involved.

It would seem that Freud has managed by this highly unlikely hypothesis to assume that young females negate the validity, and even, to some extent, the existence, of female sexual characteristics altogether. Surely the first thing all children must notice is that mother has breasts, while father has none. What is possibly the rather impressive effect of childbirth on young minds is here overlooked, together with the girl's knowledge not only of her clitoris, but her vagina as well.

In formulating the theory of penis envy, Freud not only neglected the possibility of a social explanation for feminine dissatisfaction but precluded it by postulating a literal jealousy of the organ whereby the male is distinguished. As it would appear absurd to charge adult women with these values, the child, and a drastic experience situated far back in childhood, are invoked. Nearly the entirety of feminine development, adjusted or maladjusted, is now to be seen in terms of the cataclysmic moment of discovered castration.

So far, Freud has merely pursued a line of reasoning he attributes, rightly or wrongly, to the subjectivity of female youth. Right or wrong, his account purports to be little more than description of what girls erroneously believe. But there is prescription as well in the Freudian account. For while the discovery of her castration is purported to be a universal experience in the female, her response to this fate is the criterion by which her health, her maturity and her future are determined through a rather elaborate series of stages: "After a woman has become aware of the wound to her narcissism, she develops, like a scar, a sense of inferiority. When she has passed beyond her first attempt at explaining her lack of a penis as being a punishment personal to herself and has realized that that sexual character is a universal one, she begins to share the contempt felt by men for a sex which is the lesser in so important a respect."[69] The female first blames her mother, "who sent her into the world so insufficiently equipped" and who is "almost always held responsible for her lack of a penis."[70] Again, Freud's own language makes no distinction here between fact and feminine fantasy. It is not enough the girl

[67] Karl Abraham, "Manifestations of the Female Castration Complex," *International Journal of Psychoanalysis*, Vol. 3, March 1922.

[68] Klein, *op. cit.*, pp. 83–84.

[69] "Some Psychological Consequences of the Anatomical Distinction Between the Sexes," p. 192.

[70] *Ibid.*, p. 193.

reject her own sex however; if she is to mature, she must redirect her self positively toward a masculine object. This is designated as the beginning of the Oedipal stage in the female. We are told that the girl now gives up the hope of impregnating her mother, an ambition Freud attributes to her. (One wonders how youth has discovered conception, an elaborate and subtle process which children do not discover by themselves, and not all primitive adults can fathom.) The girl is said to assume her female parent has mutilated her as a judgment on her general unworthiness, or possibly for the crime of masturbation, and now turns her anxious attention to her father.[71]

At this stage of her childhood the little girl at first expects her father to prove magnanimous and award her a penis. Later, disappointed in this hope, she learns to content herself with the aspiration of bearing his baby. The baby is given out as a curious item; it is actually a penis, not a baby at all: "the girl's libido slips into position by means—there is really no other way to put it—of the equation 'penis-child.'"[72] Although she will never relinquish some hope of acquiring a penis ("we ought to recognize this wish for a penis as being *par excellence* a feminine one")[73] a baby is as close to a penis as the girl shall get. The new penis wish is metamorphosed into a baby, a quaint feminine-coated penis, which has the added merit of being a respectable ambition. (It is interesting that Freud should imagine the young female's fears center about castration rather than rape—a phenomenon which girls are in fact, and with reason, in dread of, since it happens to them and castration does not.) Girls, he informs us, now relinquish some of their anxiety over their castration, but never cease to envy and resent penises[74] and so while "impotent" they remain in the world a constant hazard to the well-provided male. There are overtones here of a faintly capitalist antagonism between the haves and the have nots. This seems to account for the considerable fear of women inherent in Freudian ideology and the force of an accusation of penis envy when leveled at mature women.

The Freudian "family romance," domestic psychodrama more horrific than a soap opera, continues. The archetypal girl is now flung into the Oedipal stage of desire for her father, having been persuaded of the total inadequacy of her clitoris, and therefore of her sex and her self. The boy, meanwhile is so aghast by the implications of sexual enlightenment that he at first represses the information. Later, he can absorb it only by accompanying the discovery of sexual differentiation with an overpowering contempt for the female. It is difficult to understand how, setting aside the social context, as

[71] The description of female psychological development is from Freud's *Three Contributions to the Theory of Sex,* "Femininity," "Some Psychological Consequences of the Anatomical Distinction Between the Sexes," and "Female Sexuality."

[72] "Some Psychological Consequences of the Anatomical Distinctions Between the Sexes," p. 195.

[73] "Femininity," p. 128.

[74] See "Female Sexuality" (1931), *Collected Works,* Vol. V, pp. 252–72.

Freud's theory does so firmly, a boy could ever become this convinced of the superiority of the penis. Yet Freud assures us that "as a result of the discovery of women's lack of a penis they [females] are debased in value for girls just as they are for boys and later perhaps for men."[75]

Conflict with the father warns the boy that the castration catastrophe might occur to him as well. He grows wary for his own emblem and surrenders his sexual desires for his mother out of fear.[76] Freud's exegesis of the neurotic excitements of nuclear family life might constitute, in itself, considerable evidence of the damaging effects of this institution, since through the parents, it presents to the very young a set of primary sexual objects who are a pair of adults, with whom intercourse would be incestuous were it even physically possible.

While Freud strongly prescribes that all lingering hopes of acquiring a penis be abandoned and sublimated in maternity, what he recommends is merely a displacement, since even maternal desires rest upon the last vestige of penile aspiration. For, as she continues to mature, we are told, the female never gives up the hope of a penis, now always properly equated with a baby. Thus men grow to love women, or better yet, their idea of women, whereas women grow to love babies.[77] It is said that the female doggedly continues her sad phallic quest in childbirth, never outgrowing her Oedipal circumstance of wanting a penis by having a baby. "Her happiness is great if later on this wish for a baby finds fulfilment in reality, and quite especially so if the baby is a little boy who brings the longed-for penis with him."[78] Freudian logic has succeeded in converting childbirth, an impressive female accomplishment, and the only function its rationale permits her, into nothing more than a hunt for a male organ. It somehow becomes the male prerogative even to give birth, as babies are but surrogate penises. The female is bested at the only function Freudian theory recommends for her, reproduction. Furthermore, her libido is actually said to be too small to qualify her as a constructive agent here, since Freud repeatedly states she has less sexual drive than the male. Woman is thus granted very little validity even within her limited existence and second-rate biological equipment: were she to deliver an entire orphanage of progeny, they would only be so many dildoes.

Until active "phallic" autoeroticism ceases, with the acceptance of clitoral inferiority, correct maturation cannot proceed. Here Freud is particularly prescriptive: "masturbation, at all events of the clitoris, is a masculine activity and the elimination of the clitoral sexuality is a necessary pre-

[75] "Femininity," p. 127.
[76] "Some Psychological Consequences of the Anatomical Distinction Between the Sexes" and elsewhere in connection with the Oedipus complex in males.
[77] "Femininity," p. 134.
[78] Ibid., p. 128.

condition for the development of femininity."[79] (Femininity is prescribed as both normal and healthy. Later we shall investigate what it consists of more thoroughly.) Adolescent autoeroticism is outlawed; abstinence is essential to correct female development. In a girl whose development is fortunate so far, there are still obstacles: "she acknowledges the fact of her castration, the consequent superiority of the male and her own inferiority, but she also rebels against these unpleasant facts."[80] Freud finds it typical of nature that "the constitution will not adapt itself to its function without a struggle."[81] And so it is that while the regenerate female seeks fulfillment in a life devoted to reproduction, others persist in the error of aspiring to an existence beyond the biological level of confinement to maternity and reproduction—falling into the error Freud calls "the masculinity complex."[82] This is how one is to account for the many deviant women, both those who renounce sexuality or divert it to members of their own sex, as well as those who pursue "masculine aims." The latter group do not seek the penis openly and honestly in maternity, but instead desire to enter universities, pursue an autonomous or independent course in life, take up with feminism, or grow restless and require treatment as "neurotics." Freud's method was to castigate such "immature" women as "regressive" or incomplete persons, clinical cases of "arrested development."[83]

How penis envy, repressed but never overcome, becomes the primary source of health or pathology; good or evil in female life is left to a mysterious deciding force called the "constitutional factor."[84] Consequently, if a woman takes her fate gracefully, though still a member of an obviously inferior species, she may at least acknowledge her plight and confine herself to maternity. But should she grow insubordinate, she will invade the larger world which Freud is unthinkingly convinced is, of itself, male "territory" and seek to "compete," thereby threatening men. She may then be convicted of "masculinity complex" or "masculine protest."

In such cases Freud and his school after him will do all in their power to convince her of the error of her ways: by gentle persuasion, harsh ridicule, and when vulgar Freudianism has come to power, by the actual mental policing of "pop psych." The renegade must adjust or succumb. One is never enlightened as to what proof exists that all human (as distinct from

---

[79] "Some Psychological Consequences of the Anatomical Distinctions Between the Sexes," p. 194.

[80] "Female Sexuality," p. 257.

[81] "Femininity," p. 117.

[82] "And if the defence against femininity is so vigorous, from what other source can it derive its strength than from that striving for masculinity which found its earlier expression in the child's penis-envy and might well take its name from this." "Female Sexuality," p. 272.

[83] See "Femininity," p. 130, and elsewhere, also "Analysis Terminable and Interminable," Collected Works, Vol. V.

[84] "Femininity," p. 130.

biological or reproductive) pursuits, interesting or uninteresting, designated male "territory," are in fact intrinsically so, or on what biological grounds it can be proven that literacy, the university, or the professions are really inherently male. It would be easy to say that Freud mistakes custom for inherency, the male's domination of cultural modes for nature, but his hypothesis is so weighted with expedient interest that to do this would be to call him naïve.

A philosophy which assumes that "the demand for justice is a modification of envy,"[85] and informs the dispossessed that the circumstances of their deprivation are organic, therefore unalterable, is capable of condoning a great deal of injustice. One can predict the advice such a philosophy would have in store for other disadvantaged groups displeased with the status quo, and as the social and political effects of such lines of reasoning are fairly clear, it is not difficult to see why Freud finally became so popular a thinker in conservative societies.

Freud had spurned an excellent opportunity to open the door to hundreds of enlightening studies on the effect of male-supremacist culture on the ego development of the young female, preferring instead to sanctify her oppression in terms of the inevitable law of "biology." The theory of penis envy has so effectively obfuscated understanding that all psychology has done since has not yet unraveled this matter of social causation. If, as seems unlikely, penis envy can mean anything at all, it is productive only within the total cultural context of sex. And here it would seem that girls are fully cognizant of male supremacy long before they see their brother's penis. It is so much a part of their culture, so entirely present in the favoritism of school and family, in the image of each sex presented to them by all media, religion, and in every model of the adult world they perceive, that to associate it with a boy's distinguishing genital would, since they have learned a thousand other distinguishing sexual marks by now, be either redundant or irrelevant. Confronted with so much concrete evidence of the male's superior status, sensing on all sides the depreciation in which they are held, girls envy not the penis, but only what the penis gives one social pretensions to. Freud appears to have made a major and rather foolish confusion between biology and culture, anatomy and status. It is still more apparent that his audience found such a confusion serviceable.

However complacent he may appear, the feminist movement appears to have posed a considerable threat to Freud. His statements on women are often punctuated with barbs against the feminist point of view. The charge of penis envy against all rebels is reiterated again and again, an incantation to disarm the specter of emancipated or intellectual women, oddities who are putting themselves to unnecessary trouble in a futile effort to compensate for their organic inferiority by stabs at cultural achievement, for which Freud assumes

[85] *Ibid.*, p. 134.

the possession of a penis is a *sine qua non*. He even complains that the women who consult him in psychoanalysis do so to obtain a penis.[86] Since this is obscure, it is necessary to translate: female patients consulted him in the hope of becoming more productive in their work; in return for their fees Freud did what he could to cause them to abandon their vocations as unnatural aberrations.[87] Convinced that the connection between the penis and intellectual ability is unquestionably organic, Freud protests with a genial shrug "in the psychic field the biological factor is really the rock bottom."[88] The intellectual superiority of the male, constitutionally linked with the penis, is close to an ascertainable fact for Freud, a rock bottom of remarkable comfort.

Freud believed that two aspects of woman's character are directly related to penis envy: modesty and jealousy. It is her self-despair over the "defect" of her "castration," we are told, which gives rise to the well-known shame of women. One is struck at how much kinder Victorian chivalry could be with its rigamarole about "purity." Freud designated shame as a feminine characteristic *"par excellence."*[89] Its purpose, in his view, is simply the concealment of her hapless defect. As among the primitives, so today, the woman hides her parts to hide her wound. When Freud suggests that modesty in women was originally designed "for concealment of genital deficiency" he is even willing to describe pubic hair as the response of "nature herself" to cover the female fault.[90]

Although it is one of Freud's favorite notions that women have not, and for constitutional reasons cannot, contribute to civilization (Otto Weininger, a misogynist thinker to whom Freud was often indebted, thought genius itself masculine and a female genius a contradiction in terms) Freud does allow that women might have invented weaving and plaiting—discoveries

---

[86] "The wish to get the longed-for penis eventually, in spite of everything, may contribute to the motives that drive a mature woman to analysis . . . a capacity, for instance, to carry on an intellectual profession—may often be recognized as a sublimated modification of this repressed wish." ("Femininity," p. 125.) What should happen however, is this: "the unsatisfied wish for a penis should be converted into a wish for a child and for a man who possesses a penis." ("Analysis Terminable and Interminable," p. 355.) Intellectual striving or an urge for human fulfillment beyond this confining recipe is castigated as unrepressed bisexuality or "masculine striving" where "the wish for masculinity persists in the unconscious, and . . . exercises a disturbing influence." (*Ibid.*)

[87] It is difficult work, and Freud confesses that "at no point in one's analytic work does one suffer more from the oppressive feeling that one is 'talking to the winds' than when one is trying to persuade a female patient to abandon her wish for a penis on the ground of its being unrealizable." "Analysis Terminable and Interminable," p. 356.

[88] "We often feel that when we have reached the penis wish and the masculine protest we have penetrated all the psychological strata and reached 'bedrock' and that our task is accomplished. And this is probably correct, for in the psychic field the biological factor is really the rock bottom. The repudiation of femininity must surely be biological fact, part of the great riddle of sex." *Ibid.*, p. 356-57.

[89] "Femininity," p. 132.

[90] *Ibid.*

that spring from an identical impulse—the need to hide their deformity.[91]

A folk-like accusation of female jealousy is also part of Freud's program and he assures us this vice springs from penis envy as well.[92] He is of the opinion that males are less prone to sexual jealousy (on many occasions Freud puts in a good word for the double standard which makes men's lives richer in sexual opportunity) and he sees in the vigilance of husbands, fathers and brothers, only the watchful care of property owners. Monogamous marriage is an institution with which he found much fault, but mainly on the grounds that it hampers masculine freedom. The attribution of moral jealousy and a low moral sense to women inspires Freud to remarks of this kind—"the fact that women must be regarded as having little sense of justice, is no doubt related to the predominance of envy in their mental life."[93] In view of the social position of women this is a remarkably damaging accusation, for to accuse a deprived group of spitefulness and no sense of fairness, is to discredit or deprive its members of the moral position which is their only claim for just treatment.

Coming as it did, at the peak of the sexual revolution, Freud's doctrine of penis envy is in fact a superbly timed accusation, enabling masculine sentiment to take the offensive again as it had not since the disappearance of overt misogyny when the pose of chivalry became fashionable. The whole weight of responsibility, and even of guilt, is now placed upon any woman unwilling to "stay in her place." The theory of penis envy shifts the blame of her suffering to the female for daring to aspire to a biologically impossible state. Any hankering for a less humiliating and circumscribed existence is immediately ascribed to unnatural and unrealistic deviation from her genetic identity and therefore her fate. A woman who resists "femininity," e.g., feminine temperament, status, and role, is thought to court neurosis, for femininity is her fate as "anatomy is destiny." In so evading the only destiny nature has granted her, she courts nothingness.

Freud's circular method in formulating penis envy begins by reporting children's distorted impressions, gradually comes to accept them as the correct reaction, goes on to present its own irresponsible version of the socio-sexual context, and then, through a nearly imperceptible series of transitions, slides from description to a form of prescription which insures the continuance of the patriarchal status quo, under the guise of health and normality. Apart from ridicule, the counterrevolutionary period never employed a more withering or destructive weapon against feminist insurgence than the Freudian accusation of penis envy.

[91] *Ibid.*
[92] *Ibid.*, p. 134. The charge is made in "Female Sexuality" and a number of other places as well.
[93] *Ibid.*

II

Since Freud's conception of female character depends as much upon his understanding of biology as it does upon the psychological motive of penis envy, it is necessary to outline the former before proceeding. For the gravest distortion in Freud's theory of female psychology stems from his incapacity, unconscious or deliberate, to separate two radically different phenomena, female biology and feminine status. By inferring the latter is as much, or nearly as much, the product of nature as the former, and somehow inevitable, rather than the product of a social situation, he seems eager to convince us that what a man's world has made of woman is only what nature had made of her first.

In general, Freud defines and identifies the masculine with activity, the feminine with passivity.[94] He rationalizes this on two grounds: the sexual behavior of his contemporaries, both in its social and in its coital manifestations, and the attributes of biosexual materials and processes: sperm and penetration are said to be active, vaginal reception and the ova are said to be passive.[95] The biological data are themselves overstated; not only does the ova journey through the Fallopian tubes and so partake of activity, the sperm are caught, held, and lifted by the plungerlike movement of the cervix and so partake of passivity. Yet it is scarcely rational to attempt to formulate the workings of an entire society upon minor distinctions in the properties of microscopic human cells. Nor does Freud ever go so far. He does, however, appear to use sexual cells as sources of analogy both of temperament and role and in the psychological aspects of masculine and feminine.

Failing to pause and to consider fully how "masculine" and "feminine" are elaborate behavioral constructs for each sex within society, obviously cul-

---

[94] On a number of occasions Freud reminds the reader that the rule associating masculine with activity, feminine with passivity is not always borne out by observation of the animal world, and that in human maternity the female is to some extent active (giving suck, etc.). His reservation about the generalization, however, is only that it is somewhat too sweeping and imprecise. Of its essential validity he appears to have no real doubt, since on its premise he has built a large number of his contentions: the label "phallic" for the autoerotic stage in females, the constitutional passivity of women, the masculine character of the libido, etc. See "Femininity," pp. 114–15, Chapter 4 of *Civilization and Its Discontents* (1930) and "The Transformation of Puberty." The following statement is a good description of Freud's practice in working with these definitions: ". . . psychoanalysis cannot elucidate the intrinsic nature of what in conventional or in biological phraseology is termed 'masculine' and 'feminine': it simply takes over the two concepts and makes them the foundation of its work." "The Psychogenesis of a Case of Homosexuality in a Woman" *Collected Papers of Sigmund Freud* (London; Hogarth, 1920), pp. 202–3.

[95] "The male sex-cell is actively mobile and searches out the female one, and the latter, the ovum, is immobile and waits passively. The behavior of the elementary sexual organisms is indeed a model for the conduct of sexual individuals during intercourse." "Femininity," p. 114.

tural and subject to endless cross-cultural variation, Freud somewhat precipi-
tously equates such behavior with inherency, with the biologically inevitable,
and finally arrives at prescriptive conformity to a social norm built upon what
he believes to be an anatomical base.

To accommodate the many disturbing exceptions to sexual temperamental
norms Freud made use of a sliding scale of gradation and variation of masculine and feminine, with Platonic ideals at either end, probably borrowed
from Weininger. To this he added the theory of bisexuality. Bisexuality could
be invoked, as Freud explained, when dealing with "ladies" who "whenever
some comparison turned out to be unfavorable to their sex were able to utter
a suspicion that we, the male analysts, had been unable to overcome certain deeply-rooted prejudices against what was feminine and this was being
paid for in the partiality of our researches." Freud then informs the reader
how he responded: "Standing on the ground of bisexuality, we had no difficulty in avoiding impoliteness. We had only to say: 'This does not apply to
you. You're the exception; on this point you are more masculine than feminine.'"[96] Women who dispute logic are called men for their pains. And since
the sexual-temperamental differentiation is, although supported by behavioral
differences which constitute social norms, still thought by Freudians to be
physiological in origin, to say that a female is not feminine is merely confusing. Nor does the theory of bisexuality provide much relief to the individual since femininity is forcefully prescribed and praised as the mature
resolution of the child's bisexual dilemma.

On a number of occasions Freud allowed that masculine and feminine in
their pure form are theoretical constructs of uncertain character.[97] He further allows, as most social science has done since—to insidious effect—for over-
lap and graduated patterns. Yet the general effect of Freudian thought was,
despite the theory of bisexuality, to equate, even to prescribe, what it defines as masculine with the biological male, feminine with the biological
female. By 1933, when he came to write his definitive work on the subject,
"Femininity" Freud had come to define the feminine as a "preference" for
passive aims, or to put it in his own somewhat paradoxical phrase "the active pursuit of a passive function."[98] Freud had gradually rejected his earlier
hypothesis that feminine temperament might be largely formed by the effect
of learning processes and social pressure and, though still sometimes acknowledging in passing a social component, went further and further in identifying "feminine" attributes with "constitutional" "instinctive" or genetic
tendencies.[99]

[96] "Femininity," pp. 116–17.
[97] "Female Sexuality," p. 197 and elsewhere.
[98] "Femininity," p. 115.
[99] Even as late as 1933: "The suppression of women's aggressiveness which is prescribed for them constitutionally and imposed on them socially, favors the development
of powerful masochistic impulses." "Femininity," p. 116. The sentence is by no means

In the work of Freud, and still more in that of his disciples, it is generally assumed that masculine and feminine are analogous to male and female, and deviance from either norm is regarded as symptomatic of mental malady according to degree. Yet if the first assumption were in fact true, there should have been less need to make masculine and feminine also prescriptive, as they came to be with such overpowering force in the counterrevolutionary period, when divergence was considered not only unhealthy but even vicious. One might even argue that if masculine and feminine are, or are related to, natural or constitutional products, all behavior on the part of a male is masculine, on the part of a female feminine. Removed from their contexts of social behavior, where they function to maintain an order not only of differentiation but of dominance and subordinance, the words "masculine" and "feminine" mean nothing at all and might well be replaced with what is biologically or naturally verifiable—male and female.

Very early, in 1905, Freud defined the libido (a term which denotes far more than sexual drive and for practical purposes is roughly equivalent to the life force or to every variety of human energy) as masculine "regularly and lawfully of a masculine nature whether in the man or in the woman."[100] This not only seems to invalidate the theory of bisexuality, but gives one some insight into the Victorian character of Freud's own sexual attitudes, through its assumption that sexual activity is "for men." In 1923 he shifted ground a bit and conceded that the libido had no sex.[101] Yet he appears to go right on seeing it as a masculine function with enormous cultural and creative possibilities, a species of life force and male property nearly exclusively. Complementing this was Freud's feeling that culture was in general inimical to sexuality; if one were to devote oneself to "higher" pursuits, one must renounce, or at any rate, sublimate sexuality. Since, by his definition, women have very low libido ("woman is endowed with a weaker sexual instinct")[102] and so cannot pursue civilization, sublimation means, practically speaking, that the male, whose higher libido equips him for it, must shun the temptations afforded by the female and go on to loftier goals.[103]

---

clear as to how each force operates—social or constitutional—and to what proportional extent. But it does support the general Freudian assumption that, in regard to the female, social imposition only supports or reinforces organic conditions.

[100] Freud, *Three Contributions to the Theory of Sex* (1908), *Basic Writings of Sigmund Freud,* edited by A. A. Brill (New York, Random House, Modern Library, 1938), pp. 612–13.

[101] Freud, "The Infantile Genital Organization of the Libido" (1923), *Collected Papers,* Vol. II.

[102] " 'Civilized' Sexual Morality and Modern Nervousness" (1908), *Collected Papers,* Vol. II, p. 87.

[103] The belief in a stronger sexual drive in males has traditionally been put forward to justify the double standard. To the Victorians this was proof of the female's "higher" nature; in Freud it becomes proof of her lower nature, as the amount of sublimated libido

At a time when "instinctual" forces were highly regarded, Freud entrusted not only human culture but the preservation of the human race to the male:

Nature has paid less careful attention to the demands of the female function than to those of masculinity . . . the achievement of the biological aim is entrusted to the aggressiveness of the male, and is to some extent independent of the cooperation of the female.[104]

A later translator is more explicit and expresses the last phrase as "independent of the woman's consent." The very male libido is now to be respected as a power in the service of life and must be permitted to wreak its will on the female whether she has the wit to co-operate or not. The frigid woman (and Freud studied a great many of them) is brought on as an example of the male's superior regard for posterity. Nature, Freud concludes, has simply neglected to provide the female with a forceful libido; what happens then is her fault. The whole balance of male sexual aggression toward the female is hereby subsumed under a huge abstract force only concerned with the continuation of the species. This attitude gave rise to a whole battery of military diction which psychology has ever since employed to describe sexuality: surrender, dominance, mastery.

The male pursues the female for the purposes of sexual union, seizes hold of her and penetrates into her . . . by this you have precisely reduced the characteristic of masculinity to the factor of aggressiveness.[105]

It is not very difficult once this type of language has gained respectability for writers affected by the Freudian point of view to deprecate a less bellicose mating as tepid, epicene, or prissy.

The emphasis on procreational instinct is curiously at odds with Freud's pronouncements on other occasions when he makes it clear that procreation is far from the only or even the nearest reason for sexual desire: ". . . the sexual instinct in man does not originally serve the purposes of procreation, but has as its aim the gain of a particular kind of pleasure."[106] Living in an age when female frigidity or hyposexuality was widespread Freud did not fully understand its social implications, not merely those of guilt or a

predicts the amount of cultural potentiality. He has combined the privileges of a freer sexual expression always accorded to males with traditional assertion of the male's superiority in the intellectual and cultural sphere.

[104] This is from the first English translation of "Femininity," entitled "The Psychology of Women," in W. J. H. Sprott's translation (1933), the second phrase is from Strachey's "Femininity" translation (p. 131) used, with this exception throughout.

[105] "Femininity," pp. 114–15. After sketching this caricature, Freud himself admits that one does not "gain any advantage" from using the terms masculinity and femininity thus—for the same reasons alleged in footnote 94. His followers were rarely or never this forbearing.

[106] " 'Civilized' Sexual Morality and Modern Nervousness," p. 83.

negative attitude toward sexuality, but those of female resistance as well. He appears to have accepted frigidity as further evidence in some degree at least, of a lesser libidinous energy, finding its incidence in many cases "constitutional."[107] He concluded with the simple formula that the female does not "hunger" for sex to the extent that the male does and her lower sexual drive then must be "organic." The recent research of Masters and Johnson has done a great deal to rule out this prim conclusion, but the supposition falls in line with other "Victorian" notions Freud never relinquished.

III

The three most distinguishing traits of female personality, were, in Freud's view, passivity, masochism, and narcissism. Even here, one can see a certain merit in the Freudian paradigm taken as pure *description*. The position of women in patriarchy is such that they are expected to be passive, to suffer, and to be sexual objects; it is unquestionable that they are, with varying degrees of success, socialized into such roles. This is not however what Freud had in mind. Nor had he any intention of describing social circumstances. Instead, he believed that the elaborate cultural construction we call "femininity" was largely organic, e.g., identical with, or clearly related to, femaleness.[108] He therefore proceeded to define femininity as constitutional passivity, masochism, and narcissism. He also prescribed it as the norm not only of general development, but of healthy development. The leading feminine characteristic, passivity, is achieved for example "with the abandonment of clitoridal masturbation" and the onset of maternal craving in the Oedipal stage, and this upsurge of femininity is "accompanied *principally with the help of passive instinctual impulses.*"[109]

Masochism and passivity, Freud would have us understand, are not only both feminine but dynamically interrelated: masochism comprises all passive attitudes to sexual life and object.[110] It is therefore normal in females, abnormal in males. He also provides another general description by saying that in masochism "the subject is placed in a situation characteristic of womanhood, i.e., they mean that he is being castrated, is playing the passive role in coitus, or is giving birth."[111] Masochism is female; femininity is masochistic. It is ingenious to describe masochism and suffering as inherently feminine. Not only does it express masculine attitudes toward female functions (they are painful, degrading, etc.), it justifies any conceivable domination or humiliation forced upon the female as mere food for her nature. To

[107] "Sometimes it [frigidity] is psychogenic and in that case accessible to influence; but in other cases it suggests the hypothesis of its being constitutionally determined and even of there being a contributing anatomical factor." "Femininity," p. 132.

[108] See also preceding footnote where even frigidity is thought to be constitutional.

[109] "Femininity," p. 128 (italics mine).

[110] Freud, "The Economic Problems of Masochism" (1924), *Collected Papers*, Vol. II.

[111] *Ibid.*, p. 258.

carry such a notion to its logical conclusion, abuse is not only good for woman but the very thing she craved; *The Story of O* is an extreme statement made upon such assumptions. No better rationalization could be found for continuing to punish the victim. As an added attraction cruelty is erotic since it fulfills both partners' natures. Nearly any atrocity committed against woman may eventually be extenuated on the theory of her innate masochism. Freud might have been appalled had he dwelt on the full possibilities of such an attribution to this or any other disadvantaged group.

Of the three varieties of masochism Freud outlined—"erotogenic," "moral," and "feminine," he merged two, the feminine with the erotogenic's "lust for pain," which he admitted is in itself difficult to explain, even in women. Hinting at the inscrutable, the inexplicable—a favorite technique when discussing woman—Freud hovers provocatively over such ideas as "some secret relationship with masochism" and titillates us with reports of an appetite for pain which "remains incomprehensible unless one can bring oneself to make certain assumptions about matters that are veiled in obscurity."[112]

Freud is sure, however that pain is enjoyable to the masochist, and he appears to be equally sure that coitus must be painful to the female; this seems to be his only evidence that females enjoy heterosexual intercourse.[113] For the rest, Freud is not far from agreement with Acton, a nineteenth-century physician whose famous dictum is often quoted in evidence of the Victorian attitude that any attribution of sexual pleasure to women was a "vile aspersion." Freud even hoped to cast this in scientific terms by positing "a general female tendency to ward off sexuality."[114] The notion that woman's role in coitus is passive and therefore masochistic, its only delight in enduring pain, while a very revealing projection of masculine attitude toward the female situation in intercourse, is unlikely to be the source of further wisdom.

Freud appears to believe not only that masochism is "feminine" but that it accords with a woman's position in marriage which he denominated as "thralldom," an adjective not without some ironic justification in view of the legal position of women. Yet, notwithstanding his moving description of defloration customs which place the vulnerable virgin bride in the position of "sexual thralldom," "dependent and helpless," he appears to see nothing to object to in the system or in its proceedings. In this situation the female responds, as Freud expects, with "thralldom and gratitude," although disap-

---

[112] *Ibid.*, p. 257.

[113] Freud describes the "lust for pain" as an expression of femininity, a concept which "can be supported on biological and constitutional grounds." (*Ibid.*) Further, that this pain is the nature of female sexual experience: "sexual excitation arises as an accessory effect of a large series of internal processes as soon as the intensity of these processes has exceeded certain quantitative limits . . . an excitation of physical pain and feelings would surely have this effect." Even when masochism occurs in males it is a "form of masochism *a potiori* feminine." *Ibid.*, p. 259 and p. 258.

[114] Freud, "The Taboo of Virginity" (1918), *Collected Papers*, Vol. IV, p. 218.

pointed and in pain, suffering a second wound in addition to the sorrows of her first castration, and knowing too that she is diminished in value because no more a virgin.[115] All this is customary and well enough, unless she so forgets her position as to respond with hostility, or attempts to transcend her role, a response Freud interprets as a desire to "castrate" the male in revenge. Just as with women who show signs of "masculinity complex" or "masculine protest" Freudian theory mobilizes itself against the threat of insubordinate women, specifically stipulated as "emancipated" or intellectual, whose penis envy has gone beyond the knowledge of unworthiness and whose new educational privileges have alienated them from their "instinctual" nature. All the forces of psychoanalysis came to be gathered to force woman to "adjust" to her position, that is to accept it and submit, for the security of society and the strength of traditional marriage depend upon her accepting her fate.

Having satisfied himself that masochism is genetically female, founded both on constitutional affinity and unchangeable psychological nature, Freud advises his students, "if as happens so often you meet with masochism in man, what is left to you but to say that these men exhibit very plainly feminine traits."[116] As such, they are neurotic in some measure. Despite the hypothesis that we are all, to some degree, bisexual, one is made to grow anxious when males display feminine traits, just as masculine traits are unbecoming to females, evidence of penis envy. It is remarkable how Freudian prescription tends to ignore its own notion of bisexuality or to find symptoms of it as backsliding.

Having established passivity and masochism, Freud proceeds to the third of his "feminine" triad—narcissism. Like the categories of medieval scholasticism, it is divided into two headings. The first is the feminine form, which although natural to women, is nevertheless denominated a "perversion."[117] It involves the female's investment of her love in her own body or her self, treating it in the same way as the male would respond to it. Male narcissism, called anaclitic, is of a higher type and sounds more like admiration of others than vanity over self. Narcissism in the male is only the process of overestimating an idealized woman by projecting unto her the male's own finest traits. Narcissistic men improve upon their love object, narcissistic women persist in an inferior form of affection, not rising to the altruism of "object-love."[118] A good deal of this is a reworking of Weininger's remarks on love

115 *Ibid.* The entire description is summarized from the article, esp. pp. 227–28.

116 "Femininity," p. 132.

117 Freud, "On Narcissism, An Introduction" (1914), *Collected Papers,* Vol. IV. p. 30 and p. 46. Freud remarks that the same tendency is observed to occur in homosexuals and megalomaniacs; but in women one expects it.

118 ". . . the anaclitic type is, properly speaking, characteristic of the man. It displays the marked sexual over-estimation which is derived from the original narcissism of the child, now transferred to the sexual object" (e.g., the beloved woman who replaces the maternal figure). *Ibid.,* p. 45. "A different course if followed in the type most frequently

and the idealization of women in literature, notably Dante's Beatrice. Despite woman's intrinsic lesser worth, a man who can create fine poetry by turning her into an idea leaves us all so much better off. As for that vast majority of women who do not live on pedestals, Freud realizes it is psychologically necessary for men to debase them in prostitution and brutalized sexuality, and thus we arrive at "The Most Prevalent Form of Degradation in Erotic Life."

Narcissism is not only constitutionally female, it is also produced by penis envy: "The effect of penis-envy has a share, further, in the physical vanity of women, since they are bound to value their charms more highly as a late compensation for their original sexual inferiority."[119] Even woman's beauty is but another symptom of the need to be born with a penis. One grows to pity Freud's condition. If carried far, the female might grow too engrossed in her narcissism and exclude males altogether from her affection. Freud's attitude on the subject is both resigned (it's her nature) and prescriptive (women must control their vanity).

In convincing himself that the three traits of femininity were in fact constitutional and biologically destined, Freud had made it possible to prescribe them and for his followers to attempt to enforce them, perpetuating a condition which originates in oppressive social circumstances. To observe a group rendered passive, stolid in their suffering, forced into trivial vanity to please their superordinates, and, after summarizing these effects of long subordination, choose to conclude they were inevitable, and then commence to prescribe them as health, realism, and maturity, is actually a fairly blatant kind of Social Darwinism. As a manner of dealing with deprived groups, it is hardly new, but it has rarely been so successful as Freudianism has been in dealing with women.

IV

It is difficult to continue to describe the female as an incomplete male without eventually concerning oneself with the quality of intellect in a creature so curtailed. Freud's early interpretation of what he regarded as the undeveloped feminine intellect was that it was due to social inhibitions on her sexuality which in turn inhibited all other mental effort.[120] As the female's greatest interest was sex, he reasoned—feeling no contradiction with

---

met with in women, which is the purest and truest feminine type . . . this is unfavorable to the development of a true object love . . . there arises in the woman a certain self-sufficiency (especially when there is a ripening of beauty) . . . strictly speaking such women love only themselves with an intensity comparable to that of the man's love for them. Nor does their need lie in the direction of loving, but of being loved." *Ibid.*, p. 46. Women relinquish this sort of narcissism by creating love-objects in children. It is particularly interesting how this whole formulation has avoided the issue of personal vanity or egotism in men.

[119] "Femininity," p. 132.

[120] " 'Civilized' Sexual Morality and Modern Nervousness," p. 94.

his repeated stress that she had little sex drive or pleasure—and since this was the one subject she is forbidden to study, terrorized on all sides that her "greatest thirst for knowledge" might end in the "pronouncement that such curiosity is inwardly a sign of immoral tendency," she can only inhibit and repress, rarely sublimate and transcend. Intimidated from pursuing the strongest interest she is capable of entertaining, the young woman is soon directed away from any study and soon "all mental effort and knowledge in general is depreciated in their eyes."[121] And so the mere fact of sexual repression at first seemed sufficient cause for what Freud took to be the manifestly inferior mentality of the female: ". . . the undoubted fact of the intellectual inferiority of so many women can be traced to that inhibition of thought necessitated by sexual suppression."[122] One is edified not only by the safety-valve phrase "so many women," but by the confused fatalism of "necessitated."

These remarks were made in 1908 when, still a young man, Freud was willing to contradict Moebius' contention that the female was inherently inferior in mental ability, and was still willing to attribute a certain amount of female resistance to her situation, however euphemized as "conflict," etc., to social and educational factors—cultural rather than inherent biological or psychological elements. As the years went by Freud underwent a considerable change of attitude in respect to this question and grew to have a greater and greater need of stronger formulations to convince us that the female character is a static thing ordained by Nature and the unalterable laws of her anatomy. Inferior, vice-ridden, half savage; she comes to be seen as all this simply by virtue of her deformed, castrated physiology.

Since the possibility of social factors in regard to woman's relation to human culture and intellectual achievement did not satisfy him very long, Freud desired surer evidence that woman fails to contribute to civilization not because she is prevented but because she is constitutionally incapable of doing so. Proof of such came to be supplied by Freud's description of female psycho-organic development through the stages of infancy and adolescence.

Freud may take large credit for the lucrative either/or controversy between the clitoris and the vagina which has provided careers and put bread on the table for an army of disciples in the past three decades.[123] Freud himself thought the basic female organ was the clitoris, not the vagina. But he is just as confident that the female could only achieve "normal" and "mature" sex-

121 *Ibid.*

122 *Ibid.*

123 See the history of the "vaginal orgasm" by Daniel Brown, "Female Orgasm and Sexual Inadequacy," reprinted in Edward and Ruth Brecher's *Human Sexual Response* (New York: New American Library, 1966), pp. 125-75.

uality through the vagina, renouncing the clitoris.[124] Herein lies the dilemma. Clearly the woman's task is to transfer her sexuality from clitoris to vagina—a difficult passage in which Freud foresaw that many women might go astray. Even among the successful the project has consumed so much of their productive youth that their minds stagnate. And so the intellectual inferiority of women of which Freud was so comfortably convinced is explained on what are, finally, biological grounds. In between the child's early clitoroidal masturbation, which Freud would have us believe ceases at the discovery of her castration and the onset of penis envy, cowing her so that she henceforth inhibits all sexual activity until the defloration and penetration of her first experience of coitus, the major part of normal female youth was, as Freud would suggest it be, spent in a sexual limbo. The result is what a prurient patriarchy has always found so desirable, the virginal maiden utterly unsexual to herself. While he occasionally catalogued the ill effects of official morality, Freud did not seriously question the basis of patriarchal family life nor the necessity, occasionally unfortunate (but always attractive), for a chaste and sexually inactive young womanhood to be preserved.[125] Champion of the correctly passive type of feminine sexual fulfillment, Freud is also capable of lapsing into accounts of the charms of a relatively frigid or narcissistic womanhood in a vaguely archaic vein. The male appetite and attitude is clearly his chief referent and consideration. One recalls Reich's anecdote of the nineteenth-century gentleman's disgusted reprimand to his enthusiastic bride: "Ladies don't move."

In Freudian terms, there are three hurdles to female development—transference from one zone to another (clitoroidal to vaginal), replacement of the first sex object (mother) with the second (father), and the tediously inescapable factor of penis envy. Should the female lapse into "pathological regression" (an affinity for clitoral stimulation)[126] it is hardly to be wondered at with so many pitfalls all about her. The male program of transferring his love from mother to another woman is seen as a happy and uncomplicated continuum. Freud has a relatively complete system of answers for all female "maladjustment" to the masculine society she inhabits; somewhere

---

[124] Freud, "Three Contributions to the Theory of Sex, The Transformations of Puberty" *Basic Writings of Sigmund Freud*, pp. 613–14 and elsewhere. ". . . the sexual function of many women is crippled by their obstinately clinging to this clitoris excitability." "On the Sexual Theories of Children" (1908), *Collected Papers*, Vol. II, p. 67. Freud's theory that the clitoris is a vestigial stunted penis is not only inaccurate but even, it now seems, directly contrary to fact. Recent embryological research leads to the conclusion that the female is the race type—e.g., that all embryos begin as girls until a number, through the operation of androgen in their chromosomal structure, differentiate themselves into males and commence to grow the penis.

[125] " 'Civilized' Sexual Morality" and elsewhere. In this article Freud states expressly that *excessive* inhibition (i.e., presumably beyond that needed to keep them chaste) may cause frigidity or vaginal anesthesia in brides. His recommendation is not premarital intercourse for women, but second marriages.

[126] "Female Sexuality," pp. 255–57.

the offender has missed a hurdle. All protest is a futile struggle against her own nature and her identity, a masculinity complex, a masculine protest, corroding penis envy, or immaturity. Since activity in women which is not sexual (or rather, reproductive and maternal) is some evidence of penis envy or masculine protest, it is already suspect. And as "feminine nature" is only fulfilled through the renunciation of "masculine" or intellectual pursuits, it is unbecoming, even some sign of neurotic maladjustment, for women to attempt them.

Yet Freud's intent is not only to limit female life to the sexual-reproductive, but also to persuade us that women live at a low cultural level because this is the only one of which they are capable. There must, therefore, be better assurance of woman's cultural incapacity than mere scolding over "masculine protest." Might it be, Freud pondered, that because women have such a big responsibility to the race that they have no surplus energy left for "higher" things? This is happily conservative, in that it appears to salute motherhood, while tying the woman to a mere biological existence.[127]

This position has much to recommend in it, but perhaps it is not quite invidious enough. Freud finally concluded with evident gratification that here again the answer should lie in the facile and well worn but seemingly irrefutable business of organic constitution. Women have contributed little to civilization; it follows that they are incapable of contributing at all. For civilization is made through sublimation, and "women, as the true guardians of the race, are endowed with the power of sublimation only in a limited degree."[128] Moreover, as Freud emphasized, the female since she is not required, as is the male, to conceal and transcend her Oedipal complex for fear of castration (she has been through this surgery once and nothing worse can befall her) fails to develop sufficient super ego.[129] Man makes his contribution to civilization through sublimation and the development of a strong super ego goaded on by fear of castration—as a result of possessing a penis— and the fear of losing it. Never having had a penis and so, unafraid to lose it, the female has far less super ego than the male. This is why, Freud explains, she is largely without moral sense, inclined to be less ethically rigorous, has little perception of justice, submits easily to the necessities of life, is more subject to emotional bias in judgment, and contributes nothing to

[127] See Freud's *Civilization and Its Discontents* (London, Hogarth Press, 1930).

[128] " 'Civilized' Sexual Morality," p. 78. The flummery about "guardians of the race" being incapable of sublimating sexual instinct is odd in the light of Freud's belief that women have so little sexual instinct to sublimate anyway. The method he recommends for their minimal needs is, predictably, that of maternity.

[129] "Femininity." See pages 119, 125, and 129—also "Female Sexuality." "The formation of the super ego must suffer; it cannot attain the strength and independence which give it its cultural significance, and feminists are not pleased when we point out to the effects of this factor on the average feminine character." "Femininity," p. 129. "Character-traits which critics of every epoch have brought against women" are due to the failure of the super ego, despite the "denials of the feminists." "Female Sexuality," p. 197.

high culture. Again her inferiority—real now and not childishly imagined—is the result of her lack of a penis. With a penis, one might have acquired moral understanding and contribute to human progress, art, and civilization. In fact, it appears that girls who believe in the superiority of the penis, are—by all Freud's "proof," entirely correct.

Civilization, we are informed, is created through sublimation, or, in a more recondite Freudian phrase "instinctual renunciation," and again, this is the result of development which, due to her psychological history and physiological constitution the female is, for want of a penis, incapable of achieving. One of Freud's happiest thoughts along this line is an entertaining specimen of his logical processes, and a particularly quaint instance of his unflagging enthusiasm for glorifying the inestimable male organ. Speculating on how man discovered fire, Freud concludes that it was the result of "instinctual renunciation" of the impulse to extinguish the fire by urinating on it. It must be perfectly clear to all that the female could not discover fire because she could not renounce the impulse to urinate on it, lacking as she does the only adequate organ of long-distance urination. Here one has an extreme and pristine case of how, anatomically, woman is disqualified from contributing to the advancement of knowledge.[130]

While he continued to toy with the notion that her biological responsibility to the race impeded the female intellect, Freud progressed to an even more negative position; together with her inherent and psychological incapacities, the female's "sexual role," the function that defines her in life and in the family (Freud regarded the patriarchal family's emergence out of the primal horde as one of civilization's achievements) has made her not only incompetent, but necessarily hostile to intellect and high culture, a type of natural philistine:

> Women represent the interests of the family and the sexual life; the work of civilization has become more and more men's business; it confronts them with ever harder tasks, compels them to sublimations of instinct which women are not easily able to achieve. Since man has not an unlimited amount of mental energy at his disposal, he must accomplish his tasks by distributing his libido to the best advantage. What he employs for cultural purposes he withdraws to a great extent from women and his sexual life; his constant association with men and his dependence on his relations with them even estrange him from his duties as husband and father. Woman finds herself thus forced into the background by the claims of culture and she adopts an inimical attitude towards it.[131]

Through the sober wisdom of *Civilization and Its Discontents* Freud warns against the regressive effect of the female, inferior to the male in social in-

[130] *Civilization and Its Discontents*, pp. 50–51, footnote one. See also "The Acquisition of Power over Fire" (1932). *Collected Papers*, Vol. V.
[131] *Ibid.*, p. 73.

stinct, imbued with the selfishness of her all-sufficient relationship with lover and family around which she is compelled (in order to fulfill her nature) to build her life. The male invests his time and libido in civilized pursuits; the female comes increasingly to view civilization as her rival. Despite the fact that she has little sexual instinct to suppress, her ability to sublimate and renounce is minimal or negligible, and as civilization requires more and more that one do so, the woman may be said to be constitutionally unfitted for civilized life and therefore finds it hard to progress, or presumably, even to keep up with and stay in human society. This view of woman as a species unalterably primitive is remarkably popular in our century; a staple in modern literary attempts to invent romantic fantasies of primeval verities. But one may also, with Freud, see her as a surly savage, a drag on any social amelioration, an unassimilated tribeswoman.

On another occasion, when speaking of the success of psychotherapy in the case of a man over thirty who became "creative" through treatment, Freud regretted that women of the same age are rigid and incapable of growth, their characters having long before responded to their limited natural patterns. Although "an individual woman may be a human being in other respects as well" one must remember Freud warns that "their nature is determined by their sexual function" and that "that influence extends very far."[132] In woman's case it extends far enough to place her in a category one might, in general, term infra-human. Such is the effect of the "anatomy is destiny" formula; it has the incontestable force of primate limitations.

In another age, it might have been easy to excuse Freud on the grounds of a particularly severe patriarchal upbringing, but his most influential work was done in the first three decades of the twentieth century, much of it in the very midst of the sexual revolution. There was, therefore, plenty of historical information, and a whole climate of opinion at hand to assist him in recovering from a male-supremacist bias. In reply to feminist critics (and he was continually beset by them during these years) Freud conceded nothing, or responded with irrelevant banter, amused to acknowledge that not all men are paragons of masculinity, and that some women can nearly attain the characteristic virtues of masculinity, unseemly and misguided though they be to do so.[133] Somewhat analogously, other forms of prejudice are eager to concede an exceptional peasant or Negro or native; this confirms the rule. Refusing to debate the matter seriously, Freud took refuge in a circular tautology: when attacked for masculine prejudice, he responded by accusing his detractors of defensiveness, claiming they were male-oriented in aspiring to objectivity. He himself seemed incapable of imagining objectivity as a non-masculine related quality. Freud is not only confident his opponents were

[132] "Femininity," p. 135.
[133] "Some Psychological Consequences of the Anatomical Distinctions Between the Sexes," p. 197.

wrong in believing otherwise, but that his own theoretical model of the debilitated female super-ego *proved* them wrong.[134]

The lines of influence which psychoanalysis will exercise over sexual politics are set; generations of practitioners will follow, reputable or ridiculous. Yet more effective even than penis envy is the school's tendency toward a pseudoscientific unification of the cultural definition of masculinity and femininity with the genetic reality of male and female. Dressing the thing up in jargon—"passivity," "low libido," "masochism," "narcissism," "undeveloped super ego"—one gives the old myth of feminine "nature" a new respectability. Now it can be said scientifically that women are inherently subservient, and males dominant, more strongly sexed and therefore entitled to sexually subjugate the female, who enjoys her oppression and deserves it, for she is by her very nature, vain, stupid, and hardly better than barbarian, if she is human at all. Once this bigotry has acquired the cachet of science, the counterrevolution may proceed pretty smoothly. Sex, like race, is something one cannot really change. It is a sign of a rather superior female to wish herself out of such a case, seeing and aspiring to the virtues of the ruling group. But it is futile to hope to escape one's birth caste. Aspiration on the part of the truly incapacitated only forbodes frustration. And, after all, psychoanalysis promised fulfillment in passivity and masochism, and greater fulfillment, indeed, the very meaning of woman's life lay in reproduction, and there alone. Then too, in venal hands, psychoanalysis could not only discredit the revolution and turn it back, but give work, make money, sell itself and consumerism as well.[135]

Some Post-Freudians

In general, Freudian psychology would posit an irreducible human nature, an essential and universal human psychology; the Oedipus complex should develop in matriarchal or communal society as well as in patriarchal; penis envy in a sexually egalitarian as well as in a male-supremacist culture. Its tendency is to view each personality as the result not of individual choices or social conditions, nor as the interaction of the two, but as the product of a childhood biography imposed upon inherent constitution by parental behavior. Finally, having misapprehended the physiological data it claims to be based on, it imagines sexual temperament to be the function of biology (masculine is active, feminine is passive) and genetics (the activity and passivity

---

134 See "Some Psychological Consequences of the Anatomical Distinctions Between the Sexes" (p. 197) and "Female Sexuality" (pp. 281–82).

135 Betty Friedan's *The Feminine Mystique* furnishes a good deal of convincing evidence that psychoanalytic thought was exploited by the greedy manipulations of "market research" for the most cynical economic ends. See Chapter Nine, "The Sexual Sell."

of the sperm and ova). Having done all this, it concludes that sexual status, role, and temperament are fixed entities—that culture is based upon anatomy, and must, therefore, be destiny.

As this point of view not only pervaded later psychoanalysis but insinuated itself into the other social sciences, many of Freud's own followers began to take some note of social factors; some, like Karen Horney and Clara Thompson, attempted to revise Freudian theory in recognition of the social conditions of the sexes. But the essential line of theoretical orientation had been set. While some might demur or take exception to Freud's psychology of women, others embraced it and carried it still further. In either case a definite trend of influence had been set in motion which was reactionary in effect, for even gainsayers could not go beyond adjustive revision.

Two early and prominent enunciators of Freudian theory were Marie Bonaparte and Helene Deutsch. In a chapter entitled "Essential Feminine Masochism," Bonaparte carries the potentially malevolent aspect of a Freudian view of sexual intercourse to its logical conclusion:

> Throughout the whole range of living creatures, animal or vegetal, passivity is characteristic of the female cell, the ovum whose mission is to *await* the male cell, the active mobile spermatazoan to come and *penetrate* it. Such penetration, however, implies infraction of its tissue, but infraction of a living creature's tissue may entail destruction: death as much as life. Thus, the fecundation of the female cell is initiated by a kind of wound; in its way, the female cell is primordially "masochistic."[136]

In keeping with this fancy of sexuality as lethal assault, the infant male is presented with histrionic brutality:

> What the small boy apparently yearns to accomplish is an anal, cloacal, intestinal penetration of the mother; a bloody disembowelling even. The child of two, three, or four, despite, or rather because of, its infancy, is truly then a potential Jack the Ripper.[137]

While the young male is given over to such violent self-expression, we are told that the girl can only lay claim to a self-assertion as truncated as the clitoris, her phallus, whose very size "dooms her aggression":[138]

> Constitutionally, no doubt, female aggression, like her libido, is generally weaker than the male's . . . Boys' constitutionally stronger aggression . . . partly determines the male's superiority.[139]

[136] Marie Bonaparte, *Female Sexuality* (New York, Grove Press, 1965), pp. 79–80. First published by International Universities Press, 1953.
[137] *Ibid.*, p. 80.
[138] *Ibid.*, p. 82.
[139] *Ibid.*, p. 81.

While the male *"must* protest" against the "passive attitude," since it is not "biologically imposed on him," both passivity and masochism *"must* be accepted by the female" upon whom they are biologically imposed,[140] and whose life is necessarily unpleasant:

> All forms of masochism are related, and in essence, more or less female, from the wish to be eaten by the father in the cannibalistic oral phase, through that of being whipped or beaten by him in the sadistic-anal stage, and of being castrated in the phallic stage, to the wish, in the adult feminine stage, to be pierced.[141]

Miss Bonaparte, whose own predilections one has little trouble in deducing from her work, takes a strongly prescriptive line with regard to female masochism. Taking off from Freud's essay "A Child Is Being Beaten," she adds— "or a woman"—and reveals that flagellation is but healthy intercourse:

> Vaginal sensitivity in coitus for the adult female, in my opinion, is thus largely based on the existence, and more or less unconscious, acceptation of the child's immense masochistic beating fantasies. In coitus, the woman, in effect, is subjected to a sort of beating by the man's penis. She receives its blows and often, even, loves their violence. This sensitivity must be a deep and truly vaginal sensitivity to the blows of the penis.[142]

Against women who might raise objection against this transformation of "adult" sexuality into a punitive activity, the analyst is armed with invincible arguments: "Women who show . . . an aversion to men's brutal games may be suspect of masculine protest and excessive bisexuality. Such women may very well be clitoroidal."[143]

> When a woman protests so energetically against her masochism, her passivity, and her femininity, it is because the makeup against which she protests is already overdetermined, owing to constitutionally preponderant bisexuality. But for that, she would perfectly and without any great conflict have accepted the feminine masochism essential to her sex.[144]

It is carefully stipulated that the penis should not touch the clitoris during proper coitus,[145] as such an event would only encourage immaturity and an unbecoming disregard for the selfless surrender prescribed as true feminine response to a grave and somewhat pompous ritual of pain. In texts of this

140 *Ibid.*, p. 82.
141 *Ibid.*, p. 83.
142 *Ibid.*, p. 87.
143 *Ibid.*
144 *Ibid.*, p. 88.
145 *Ibid.*, p. 105.

nature the Freudian triad of passivity, narcissism, and masochism are given elaborate explication and application. There is a surprising resemblance between this view of sexuality and that prescribed for the Victorian wife—each knows she must submit and endure, but the woman who has benefited from psychoanalysis has been taught that she must do so without withholding her will:

> As we know in sexual intercourse, as in life, man is the actor, woman the passive one, the receiver, the acted upon. There is a tremendous surging physical ecstasy in the yielding itself, in the feeling of being the passive instrument of another person, of being stretched out supinely beneath him, taken up will-lessly by his passion as leaves are swept before a wind.[146]

Helene Deutsch established her reputation in the psychoanalytic world through studies of masochism and has written a two-volume work on female sexuality generally accepted as the definitive statement of "true femininity":

> In the light of psychoanalysis, the sexual act assumes an immense, dramatic, and profoundly cathartic significance for the woman—but only this under the condition that it is experienced in a feminine, dynamic way and is not transformed into an act of erotic play or sexual "equality."[147]

Carefully avoiding the twin hazards of egalitarianism and delight, sexual politics during the era of counterrevolution began in bed; having established its doctrine of female subjection there, it confidently applied it to the rest of life.

In 1947 an extremely influential popularization of Freudian theory was brought out by a New York psychiatrist named Farnham and a sociologist named Lundberg, dramatically titled *Modern Woman, The Lost Sex*.[148] As this book is so definitive a statement of counterrevolutionary attitude and had enormous influence both on the general public and as a textbook in the academic curriculum under the title of "marriage and the family," "life adjustment" and other didactic innovations, it is necessary to devote somewhat more attention to it than it perhaps deserves. It offered a "psychoanalytic" version of history, advertised the Middle Ages as a golden period of sanity and blamed all the ills of the world on the industrial revolution and Copernicus. Lumping feminism with nihilism, anarchism, anti-Semitism, Com-

---

[146] Marie N. Robinson, *The Power of Sexual Surrender* (New York, Doubleday & Company, Inc., 1959), p. 158.

[147] Helene Deutsch, *Female Sexuality, The Psychology of Women*, 2 vols. (New York, 1945), Vol. II, p. 103.

[148] Ferdinand Lundberg and Marynia F. Farnham, *Modern Woman, The Lost Sex* (New York: Universal Library, 1947).

munism, and racism, by claiming they all preach hatred and violence, it made a broadside attack on revolutionary movements, which it bundled together with Nazism and the Ku Klux Klan. Its particular grudge was the sexual revolution, which had made woman a "lost sex" around whom "much of the unhappiness of our day revolves, like a captive planet."[149]

While lamenting that women too have taken up with these "movements of the unhappy and the damned,"[150] it especially deplores their adherence to the Woman's Movement which "stood on a bedrock foundation of hatred"[151] somehow analogous to Nazism. There is a free indulgence in the game of biographical neurosis: Marx is accounted for by an "unconscious hatred of political authority"; Mill, dismissed with the derogatory label "passive-feminine man," is described as a sissy driven by hatred of his father. The real enemy is Mary Wollstonecraft, who began the madness the authors designate the sexual revolution. Wollstonecraft is suspect not only as a psychiatric case history,[152] and one guilty through association with the "fires of the French Revolution,"[153] but because she and the folly the authors designate as feminism had so corrupted youth as to bring about a state of "sexual indulgence" indistinguishable from a "monkey house,"[154] caused a sad decline in the birth rate, and a rise in abortion and divorce.

Yet it is not enough to find feminism evil—it must be diagnosed as an illness, a pathology, a "complex," a mass delusion and an enemy of the hearth: "The cohesive integrated home has been destroyed and women are adrift."[155] The authors gently deplore the status of women in the previous century, blaming it on the industrial revolution and even expressing a tempered approval of feminist goals which they see as "an attempt to restore earlier rights and privileges."[156] Yet whatever slender validity their objectives might have had, both feminism and the feminists were "an expresson of emotional sickness, of neurosis . . . at its core, a deep illness."[157] Taking off from the thesis that if the sexes were equal they should be identical (a biological impossibility) the authors label equality a "fetish," and go on to inform us that the feminists wanted to be males, and suffered from penis envy. Lundberg and Farnham unhesitatingly equate status and social position with male genitals in curious equations such as "male power—maleness,"[158] and "this is what equality means: identity."[159] Wollstonecraft and the rest were "making a

---

[149] *Ibid.*, p. 24.
[150] *Ibid.*, p. 33.
[151] *Ibid.*
[152] *Ibid.*, p. 149.
[153] *Ibid.*, p. 33.
[154] *Ibid.*, p. 35.
[155] *Ibid.*, p. 142.
[156] *Ibid.*, p. 143.
[157] *Ibid.*
[158] *Ibid.*, p. 150.
[159] *Ibid.*, p. 147.

plea for the admission of women to the company of men on the factually erroneous premise that they were identical to men."[160] "It should be apparent that, far from being a movement for the greater self-realization of women . . . feminism was the very negation of femaleness . . . It bade women commit suicide as women, and attempt to live as men."[161] In demanding equal rights the feminists were asking to be men, a psychic derangement as lamentable as that of a man trying to achieve femininity. When one perceives that any ambition beyond motherhood is an ambition after the "impossible"—an ambition to be a man—then "everything falls into place."[162] It does indeed.

The Lost Sex is explicit about what it takes to be the real feminist threat, an end to home, family and motherhood. Following the bromide that "marriage is an institution evolved . . . to protect women"[163] comes the admission that feminism had not attacked marriage and the family per se, and then the charge that in "simply denying they were women . . . asserting they needed no male protection," "clamoring" for economic independence, the revolutionaries were removing the beneficial "economic drives pushing women into marriage."[164] It is this which is most bitterly resented, this could make it possible to "avoid being women,"[165] which the authors unappetizingly define as the process of forming a "sentimental bond" with an "economic overlord."[166]

Through divorce, through abortion, through contraception, the sexual revolution had undermined marriage. Feminists had even attacked the double standard, with one clear motive—"their own deep desire to engage in lecherous and sensual activities."[167] This tragic error was, like all the rest, motivated by a futile desire to "emulate the male."[168] In advocating a single non-ascetic standard, feminists were actually scheming for a "condition of sexual promiscuity." Our authors endorse premarital chastity, but only for females as they find the double standard "not only inevitable but desirable" and a single standard "inwardly psychopathological" and "outwardly farcical."[169]

Having attacked sexual reform and put their opposition on the defensive with the charge of penis envy and an ingenious interpretation of history, Lundberg and Farnham bring on their more insidious "soft line." This is a glorification of "femininity," the family, female submission, and above all, motherhood. To do so requires nothing more elaborate than the forensic equipment which served Ruskin, but at times there is a curious tone of "fe-

---

[160] *Ibid.*, p. 150.
[161] *Ibid.*, p. 166.
[162] *Ibid.*, p. 162.
[163] *Ibid.*, p. 191.
[164] *Ibid.*, p. 192.
[165] *Ibid.*
[166] *Ibid.*, p. 163.
[167] *Ibid.*, p. 196.
[168] *Ibid.*
[169] *Ibid.*, pp. 274–75.

male chauvinism" about many of their pronouncements. At its positive moments, however *The Lost Sex* only rewrites a "Queen's Gardens" doctrine of separate spheres. One grows appalled at how monotonous polemic in this area can be.

Employing a tactic that was to become a reactionary classic, the authors insist that the sexual revolution must have been error for so many women are still imperfectly happy; witness how they suffer from "conflicts," from "problems." Under the guise of solicitude, such comforters end by punishing the sufferer of these vague and convenient symptoms still further. If woman is "maladjusted" the fault lies in herself rather than in the social situation to which she is exhorted to adjust by assuming her unchangeable constitutional passivity.[170] Accusation poses as diagnosis, prescription as description. Much of the book might also pass for a parody of D. H. Lawrence (were it not so abominably written) for the whole is so steeped in Lawrentian attitudes that it has the air of pastiche. It continuously advises us to turn our backs on the machine and the "brave new facade of modernity"[171] and return to the old instinctual ways, never actually defined, yet always asserted to be better.

About midway through this enormous and empty book, one realizes that the authors have begun to exude confidence that the danger is passing, the revolution has been thwarted, and the "bringing in line" may proceed in less venomous tones. There are still recurrent attacks and condemnations of "castrators" who fail to comply or object to the notion of obedience to male authority,[172] but, on the whole, the authors come to prefer the method of positive injunction; feminine subordination is phrased as "supporting" "manliness" in its "wishes for domination."[173] At times one even detects a note of petition. All male activity, maleness, perhaps patriarchy itself, depend upon penile erection: "Here it is that mastery and domination, the central capacity of the man's sexual nature must meet acceptance or fail."[174] To achieve erection, the male must be master. More recently, advocates of this notion of physiology have termed this the "cichlid effect," a theory of human sexuality modeled on the reactions of a prehistoric fish whom Konrad Lorenz examined to conclude that male cichlids failed to find the courage to mate unless the female of their species responded with "awe." How one measures "awe" in a fish is a question perhaps better left unanswered, but the implications of this notion that the female's awe of the male is physically nec-

---

[170] Marie Robinson's *The Power of Sexual Surrender* took over Lundberg and Farnham's thesis intact and in ascribing frigidity to feminism advertises a treatment of learning to accept and enjoy male dominance.

[171] Lundberg and Farnham, *op. cit.*, p. 201.

[172] *Ibid.*, p. 236.

[173] *Ibid.*, p. 241.

[174] *Ibid.*

essary to sexual intercourse are surely transparent enough if applied to men
and women.[175]

Perhaps what is most distressing about *The Lost Sex* is its pervasive odor
of commercialization. Psychoanalysis is presented here as a business enterprise built on the grave of feminism and professing to be the only cure for
the recalcitrant and "unhappy" woman the authors see everywhere about
them, undergoing conflict between a new life style and traditional or constitutional needs.

"Inner Space"

Recently, two new statements on sexual differences have appeared. Both
argue from "nature" by presupposing congenital temperaments for the two
sexes. Lionel Tiger has defined patriarchy and male dominance as the function of a "bonding" instinct inherent in the male. This is patently a case
of endorsement through rationalization, the "instinct" a method of converting history to biology. Erik Erikson's formulation that a relation to inner
and outer space differentiates the sexes is more benign and probably more influential. Retaining a Freudian or psychoanalytic theory of female personality
and the notion that this is innate, Erikson adds something new in suggesting
"femininity" is socially and politically useful.

Erikson begins his famous essay "Womanhood and the Inner Space"[176]
by deprecating that part of male achievement which has brought the race
to the brink of destruction, appealing to women to save it:

> Maybe if women could only gain the determination to represent publicly what
> they have always stood for privately in evolution and in history (realism of
> upbringing, resourcefulness in peace-keeping and devotion to healing), they
> might well add an ethically restraining, because truly supranational, power
> to politics in the widest sense.[177]

One cannot but note in passing that the force of this recommendation is to
urge that women participate in political power not because such is their human right, but because an extension of their proper feminine sphere into
the public domain would be a social good. This is to argue from expediency
rather than justice. However, let us meet Erikson on his own chosen ground.
One finds it hard not to agree that the conduct of human affairs under male

[175] See Jesse Bernard's *The Sex Game* (Englewood Cliffs, N.J., Prentice-Hall, 1968).
Lorenz's comment on the cichlid is as follows "A male can only pair with an awe-inspiring
and therefore dominant male." Konrad Lorenz, *On Aggression*, New York: Harcourt,
1966), p. 99. Needless to say, Lorenz himself did not apply this instance of subhuman
behavior (offset by different or even opposite behavior in other species) to human beings.
[176] Erik Erikson "Womanhood and the Inner Space" (1964), *Identity, Youth and
Crisis* (New York, W. W. Norton, 1968). First printed in *Daedalus*, The Journal of
the American Academy of Arts and Sciences, Spring 1964.
[177] *Ibid.*, p. 262.

dominance has produced our present predicament (the essay was written un-der the shadow of the Bomb) and that the temperamental traits Erikson as-signs to women would be eminently useful in the conduct of society. What Erikson does not recognize is that the traits of each group are culturally con-ditioned and depend upon their political relationship, which has been rela-tively constant throughout history regardless of contemporary crises. Instead, the entire emphasis of his essay, and the whole force of the experiment on which his theory is based, is to convince us that complementary masculine and feminine traits are inherently male and female. Erikson has perceived that much of what we know as masculine in our culture is and must be recog-nized as progressively antisocial and dangerous even to the preservation of the species, while much of what we know as feminine is directly related to its well-being. The logical recommendation to be made from this does seem to be a synthesis of the two sexual temperaments. Even acknowledging that, under the present circumstances of two sharply divided sexual cultures, we could achieve a human balance only through co-operation of the two groups with their fragmented collective personalities, one must really go further and urge a dissemination to members of each sex of those socially desirable traits previously confined to one or the other while eliminating the bellicosity or excessive passivity useless in either. But to do this is considerably beyond Erikson's scope, since he believes in the existence of innate sexual tempera-ment and imagines the experiment he relates is proof of it.

Erikson is dedicated to the hope of maintaining sexual polarity, its "vital tension," which might be lost in "too much sameness, equality, and equiva-lence,"[178] yet at the same time he wishes to humanize society:

> A new balance of Male and Female, of Paternal and Maternal is obviously presaged not only in contemporary changes in the relation of the sexes to each other, but also in the wider awareness which spreads wherever science, tech-nology and genuine self-scrutiny advance.[179]

Although one is not usually aware that masculine civilization advances through paternal impulse, there is no question in Erikson's mind that the contribution he would encourage in women should be offered on the au-thority of motherhood: "The question arises whether such a potential for annihilation as now exists in the world should continue to exist without the representation of the mothers of the species in the councils of image-making and decision."[180]

Erikson professes he is deeply impressed by "that everyday miracle, preg-nancy and childbirth" (maternity is something of a preoccupation with him) and the experiment he is about to relate is put forward as proof that the

[178] *Ibid.*, p. 264.
[179] *Ibid.*
[180] *Ibid.*, p. 265.

maternal instinct exists through some inherent "somatic" awareness in the female and constitutes her "identity." Here Erikson, who imposes no such limiting perspective in his studies of identity in males, appears to limit individual identity in women to a nearly exclusively sexual basis, believing "much of a young woman's identity is already defined in her kind of attractiveness" and its function is largely confined to selecting a mate in "her search for the man (or men) by whom she wishes to be sought."[181] The period of formal education when she is permitted to extend her interest to activities "removed from the future function of childbearing" is, in Erikson's view, simply a "moratorium."[182] But "a true moratorium must have a term and a conclusion: womanhood arrives when attractiveness and experience have succeeded in selecting what is to be admitted to the welcome of the inner space 'for keeps.' "[183] The stages of female growth are all dedicated to the moment when she will "commit herself to the love of a stranger and to the care to be given to his and her offspring:"[184]

> Here, whatever sexual differences and dispositions have developed in earlier life become polarized with finality because they must become part of the whole process of production and procreation which marks adulthood. But how does the identity formation of women differ by dint of the fact that their somatic design harbors an "inner space" destined to bear the offspring of chosen men, and with it, a biological, psychological, and ethical commitment to take care of human infancy?[185]

Much of the uneasy, even contradictory, tone of the essay is due to the fact that Erikson vacillates between two versions of woman, Freud's chauvinism and a chivalry of his own. He wishes to insist both that female anatomy is destiny (and personality as well) yet at the same time pleads that the preordained historical subordination of women be abridged by a gallant concession to maternal interests. He compliments "the richly convex parts of the female anatomy which suggest fullness, warmth, and generosity"[186]—yet maintains the hallowed Freudian definition of the female as a creature with a "woundlike aperture," "missing" a penis.[187] He is by no means willing to relinquish the Freudian concept of female masochism, and even expands it

181 *Ibid.*, p. 283.
182 *Ibid.*
183 *Ibid.*
184 *Ibid.*, p. 265.
185 *Ibid.*, pp. 265–66.
186 *Ibid.*, p. 267.
187 *Ibid. In Childhood and Society* (1950), Erikson compared female penis envy with Negro fantasies of whiteness and gave the impression he perfectly understood it to have cultural origins. Yet in that context, as well as in this, he is still free with such phrases as "loss from the genital region," "genital scar," and "absent penis." See pp. 244, 231, and 228.

to include the menses, "inner periodicities in addition to the pain of child-birth, which is explained in the Bible as the eternal penalty for Eve's de-linquent behavior," all of which prompts Erikson to employ the poetic epithet "dolorosa."[188] Beneath the sympathetic surface of the essay there is a rather disturbing complacency. Erikson is content, until we invent a "new kind of biocultural history," to interpret the long oppression of woman as due to her innate masochism, which explains how she has come to

> lend herself to a variety of roles conducive to an exploitation of masochistic po-tentials; she has let herself be confined and immobilized, enslaved and infanti-lized, prostituted and exploited, deriving from it at best what in psychology we call "secondary gains" of devious dominance.[189]

Erikson would, to some degree, balance the Freudian theory of penis envy with one of his own that girls derive satisfaction and personality structure from an intuitive knowledge of "the existence of a productive inner bodily space safely set in the center of female form and carriage," claiming this "makes any sense of inadequacy impossible."[190] Freud's penis-envy formula-tion has the effect of an edict that women shall stay out of male "territory" because they are anatomically incapable of participating in it; Erikson's uterine glorification is a gentler form of persuasion purportedly based on the findings of a great laboratory experiment.

> Over a span of two years, I saw 150 boys and 150 girls three times and presented them, one at a time, with the task of constructing a "scene" with toys on a table. The toys were rather ordinary—a family, some uniformed figures (policemen, aviator, Indian, monk, etc.), wild and domestic animals, furniture, automo-biles—but I also provided a large number of blocks. The children were asked to imagine that the table was a moving-picture studio; the toys, actors and props; and they themselves, moving-picture directors. They were to arrange on the table "an exciting scene from an imaginary moving picture," and then tell the plot. This was recorded, the scene photographed, and the child complimented. It may be necessary to add that no "interpretation" was given . . . Sex differ-ences thus were not the initial focus of my interest. I concentrated my attention on how the construction in progress moved forward to the edge of the table or back to the wall behind it; how they rose to shaky heights or remained close to the table surface . . . That all of this "says" something about the constructor is the open secret of all "projective techniques." This too cannot be discussed here. But I soon realized that in evaluating a child's play construction, I had to take into consideration the fact that girls and boys used space differently, and that certain configurations occurred strikingly often in the construction of one sex and rarely in those of the other. The differences themselves were so simple that at first they seemed a matter of course. History in the meantime has offered

[188] "Womanhood and The Inner Space," p. 284.
[189] Ibid.
[190] Ibid., p. 267.

a slogan for it: the girls emphasized *inner* and the boys *outer* space . . . This, then, is typical: the girl's scene is a house *interior* represented either as a configuration of furniture without any surrounding walls or by a simple *enclosure* built with blocks. In the girl's scene, people and animals are mostly *within* such an interior or enclose, and they are primarily people or animals in a static (sitting or standing) position. Girls' enclosures consist of low walls, i.e. only one block high, except for an occasional *elaborate doorway*. These interiors of houses with or without walls were, for the most part, expressly *peaceful*. Often, a little girl was playing the piano. In a number of cases the interior was *intruded* by animals or dangerous men . . . Boys' scenes are either houses with elaborate walls or facades with *protrusions* such as cones or cylinders representing ornaments or cannons. There are *high towers,* and there are entirely *exterior* scenes. In boys' constructions more people and animals are *outside* enclosures or buildings, and there are more *automotive* objects and animals moving along streets and animals *moving* along streets and intersections. There are elaborate automotive *accidents*. . . . While high structures are prevalent in the configurations of the boys, there is also much play with the danger of *collapse* or downfall; *ruins* were exclusively boys' constructions.

The male and female spaces, then, were dominated, respectively, by height and downfall and by strong motion and its channeling or arrest; and by static interiors which were open or simply enclosed, and peaceful or intruded upon. It may come as a surprise to some and seem a matter of course to others that here sexual differences in the organization of a play scene paralleled the morphology of genital differentiation itself; in the male, an external organ, erectable and intrusive in character, serving the channelization of mobile sperm cells; in the female, internal organs, with vestibular access, leading to statically expectant ova. The question is: what is really surprising about this, what only too obvious, and in either case, what does it tell us about the two sexes?[191]

What indeed? Since Erikson admits, without further reference to age and education, that these were young people in their "teens," it is likely to prove they have absorbed the socialization imposed upon them by their culture—policemen, Indians, story-book animals and all. He admits that youth of this age found his experiment banal and tiresome, and performed to be obliging. Erikson invites us to co-operate in his vision of piano playing as "static" and "peaceful" rather than boring,[192] and a moving automobile as equivalent to "mobile sperm cells." We are further asked to accept these distinctions as based on "somatic design," an elaborate term for body parts, and to find in the paraphernalia of Erikson's playroom, nature's explanation for the sexual polarity our culture has created between the roles, temperament, and status of the sexes.

---

[191] *Ibid.,* pp. 268–72.

[192] In view of the assignment—"an exciting scene from an imaginary moving-picture" —Erikson's satisfaction over the static quality of the girls' scene is rather surprising. It must have been difficult for American girls to "imagine" themselves "motion-picture directors" in any case since their society totally deprives them of such role models.

What the experiment does seem to illustrate, and with remarkable clarity, is that each group responded with extreme sensitivity to its conditioning; one to passive domesticity, the other to egoistic achievement, partly constructive (towers, machines, ornament) and partly destructive (cannons, accidents, ruins). Yet for all the efficiency of the socialization (perhaps somewhat facilitated by Erikson's standardized Hollywood movie equipment) not every youth responded as planned. Some unaccounted for number failed to conform: a girl who did outside scenes is dismissed as a "tomboy," a boy who was insufficiently aggressive would also register as a deviate (effeminate), popularly regarded as a graver danger. One must also recall the normative attitude in which sexual identity is viewed. In 1964, when this study was first publicized, sexual reaction had created a climate where failure to conform to sexual category was seen as unhealthy or disturbing.

In analyzing the behavior of each sex, Erikson has solicitously italicized all the clue words in his somewhat overdeliberate verbal interpretation of the events he beheld into a sort of anatomical predestination. The description, which for the sake of fairness, has been reprinted almost in its entirety, has its amusing moments. The vulva, less the author's interest than the womb, is to be derived from the phrase "elaborate doorways"; one wonders if the clitoris may be construed from some element of entrance decor. The time-honored device of equating "femininity" with the passive ("static") so that one may prescribe and enforce it is balanced by the equation of the penis with grandiose towers, speeding and colliding autos, cannons and ruins. "Do we have wars because of detumescence?" one is expected to ask. Feminine "passivity" is always reasoned from anatomy, but masculine activity is generally reasoned from history and technology; a logical inconsistency which leaves the parallel with an asymmetry that is aesthetically unsatisfying.[193]

As an experiment, there is so much in Erikson's report and in the implications he derives from it, which will not bear scrutiny, that its claim to be accepted as scientific evidence is negligible indeed. It does however, tell us a good deal about Erikson, a man genuinely interested in peace and the "feminine" virtues, although apparently quite unable to conceive that since they are humanly valuable they should, logically, be equally valuable for both sexes. Within the experiment no variable was employed, no attempt to reverse proceedings, both of which are essential when one is trying to prove inherency, since what is not arbitrary, imposed, irrelevant, acquired, or learned, will continue to be manifest despite other instructions or modifications in the situation. Erikson's whole theory is built on psychoanalysis' persistent error of mistaking learned behavior for biology. The elaborate phraseology of "somatic design" is calculated to appeal to the common reader and to convince social scientists, often remarkably gullible in respect to physi-

---

[193] The very notion of active spermatozoa on which the Freudian theory of male activity ultimately relies depends upon the microscope's evidence. Do male children "intuit" it?

ological evidence. When describing behavior by hypotheses which are so often intuitive, even literary, they are all too prone to make vague appeals to the natural sciences for the support of ascertainable evidence, enlisted to confirm the mythic with incontrovertible data.

Erikson believes he has answered objections by the disclosure that photos of his subjects' constructions were sex-identifiable to his colleagues. This is not very conclusive, since his teen-agers themselves proved so adept at taking such conspicuous cultural clues. The behavior of the subjects themselves is insisted on: "If the boys thought primarily of their present or anticipated roles, why, for example, is the policeman their favorite toy?"[194] Why indeed? One is often mystified by the incongruity of giving middle-class children police and fireman toys with which to identify, functionaries whom it would mortify their parents to see them grow up to be. Yet possibly the motive is revealed in Erikson's question—a policeman is an authority figure operating by physical force, and it is just this idea of himself that official educators such as public schools and the producers of textbooks wish to inculcate in the little male. Why boys choose policemen to align themselves with and girls do not is hardly a question; apart from the fact that they are taught to make sex-category identifications and policemen are not women, every child, or rather most of those in Erikson's test, is fully aware that boys are supposed to play with policemen and girls are not. What might be more productive to study is the child who has broken the magic circle of programmed learning so that one could isolate elements which helped in transcending the cultural mold. How, for example, does a tomboy arrive at the positive "aggression" of an outdoor scene, or a boy arrive at a peaceful scene; the one escaping the doll house which has been successfully inflicted on her peers, the other the malevolence inflicted on his.

Eleanor Maccoby's informative article on female intelligence[195] offers some clues to this sort of question by pointing out that the independence and ego-strength necessary for first-rate achievement in certain analytical fields is completely absent from the cultural experience of nearly every girl child. Other experiments[196] have proven that the field orientation and dependency, the reliance upon approval and destructive attention which is the general course of female upbringing, produces in boys, a condition of passivity and infantilism considered extremely detrimental to achievement and even to maturity. The double standard of formal, and even informal, education decrees that what is harmful to one group is beneficial to another. And so it

[194] Erikson, "Womanhood and the Inner Space" *op. cit.,* p. 272.

[195] Eleanor Maccoby, "Woman's Intellect," *The Potential of Woman* (New York, McGraw-Hill, 1963), edited by Farber and Wilson.

[196] Maccoby mentions the following studies: D. M. Levy, *Maternal Overprotection* (New York, Columbia University Press, 1943); H. A. Witkin, Helen B. Lewis, M. Herzman, Karen Machover, Pearl Meissener and S. Wepner, *Personality Through Perception* (New York, Harper and Row, 1954); H. A. Witkin, R. B. Dyk, H. E. Faterson, D. R. Goodnough, S. A. Karp, *Psychological Differentiation* (New York, Wiley, 1962).

is if one approves an arrested development for half the race at the level of "playing house." While it is indisputable that the games of both sexes were, as the result of Erikson's choice of materials, notably banal, those for the girls were, for all the sedate feminine virtue the investigator found in them, but the prediction of stereotypical domestic lives; those of the boys had the seeds of something that might become real achievement, architectural, technological and exploratory, as well as moronic violence and war.

The pacific, rather than merely passive character which Erikson ascribes to the girl's play is of course most depressing in view of the fact it lacks all possibility of social implementation until the female "sphere" becomes not the doll's house inner space Erikson endorses, but the world. What is perhaps most discouraging of all is not even the masculine fixation on violence but the futility of the girls' sedentary dream, even its barrenness, for they sit awaiting the "intrusion of men and animals" (a remarkable combination) and doing nothing at all—not even the "nurturance" expected of them.

> Could the role of playing the piano in the bosom of their families really be considered representative of what these girls (some of them passionate horseback riders and all future automobile drivers) wanted to do most or, indeed thought they should pretend they wanted to do?[197]

Unless we assume, as Erikson does, that the pianos in some obscure manner do pertain to inherent female nature as "natural reasons which must claim our interest," the very "spatial order" of their sex, one can only conclude that the female is more completely and more negatively conditioned than the male. And it seems she has to be in order to fulfill the far more limited existence or, in jargon, "role" which Erikson and his confreres would continue to prescribe for her. Erikson himself takes satisfaction from the more "limited circle of activities" which girls are permitted in society, and the "less resistance to control" they exhibit than do males. The latter phrase may be rendered in one word—docility.[198]

Yet Erikson's entire project in the article was to make this more palatable, to shift

> theoretical emphasis from the loss of an external organ to a sense of vital inner potential; from a hateful contempt for the mother to a solidarity with her and other women; from a "passive" renunciation of male activity to the purposeful competent pursuit of activities consonant with the possession of ovaries, a uterus, and a vagina; and from a masochistic pleasure in pain to an ability to stand (and to understand) pain as a meaningful aspect of human experience in general and of the feminine role in particular. And so it is in the

[197] Erikson, *op. cit.*, p. 272.
[198] *Ibid.*, p. 287.

"fully feminine" woman, as such outstanding writers as Helene Deutsch have recognized.[199]

There is a certain awkwardness in the fact that no matter how he tries to brighten the picture, Erikson is incapable of stopping at the right moment, but must always go on to exhibit his own distaste or misgiving for the situation he is trying to reinterpret in such positive terms. Even the possession of a womb becomes a detriment, leaving the female "unfulfilled" every moment she is not pregnant:

No doubt also, the very existence of the inner productive space exposes women early to a specific sense of loneliness, to a fear of being left empty or deprived of treasures, of remaining unfulfilled and of drying up . . . For, as pointed out, clinical observation suggests that in female experience an "inner space" is at the center of despair even as it is the very center of potential fulfillment. Emptiness is the female form of perdition—known at times to men of the inner life . . . but standard experience for all women. To be left, for her, means to be left empty . . . Such hurt can be re-experienced in each menstruation; it is a crying to heaven in the mourning over a child; and it becomes a permanent scar in the menopause.[200]

To attempt to equate pregnancy with artistic creation (referred to as a male monopoly of the "inner life") attracts attention at once, but this is soon lost in the rich prose picture of menstruation as bereavement. One cannot help but find the latter an interesting poetic conceit, but essentially absurd as a description of woman's emotions. It might be amusing to pursue Erikson's fancy: by rough computation, a woman menstruates some 450 times in her life. One begins to grasp the multiple sorrow of this many bereavements, that many children she didn't bear, as a demographer's nightmare.[201]

Sensitive to the contemporary interest in animal societies, Erikson introduces the baboon. Like our author himself, the baboons Washburn and de Vere photographed in their famous study appeared to be chivalrous, "the greatest warriors display a chivalry" which protects the weak female with her "lesser fighting equipment."[202] Here Erikson invokes Freud's phrase

[199] *Ibid.*, p. 275.

[200] *Ibid.*, pp. 277–78.

[201] An archetypal bearer relying upon Erikson's picture of opportunities would aim at some 40–50 children were she exceptionally, flawlessly fertile, and strong enough to survive the ordeal. Fortunately, there is no evidence that the good man wishes to make this fertility emphasis bilateral, in which case it would be necessary to preserve all semen (whether the product of masturbation, wet dreams or homosexual activities). At moments, however, this would appear to be the attitude of the Catholic church.

[202] *Ibid.*, p. 290.

about the "rock bottom of sexual differentiation"[203] inferring that evidence of infrahuman species confirms traditional notions of sexually differentiated roles. The author proceeds to generalize from primate evidence and the length of mammalian gestation to justify the seclusion of women ("limited circle of activities") and their subordinate position ("less resistance to control").[204] But as a pacifist, Erikson has just committed a fatal error: baboon society is built on war, he believes, and human society is said to hold certain traits constant in its evolutionary descent from primate life. It is just as likely then that war is as inherent and inevitable as the psycho-sexual behavior he insists upon and therefore, that female co-operation in the hope of peace can affect it no more than can the efforts of female baboons. This scheme of secluded motherhood guarded by aggressive and predatory male "chivalry" is very close to Ruskin's. In urging woman's participation in the larger social and political life, yet insisting she stay within her traditional domestic sphere and passive temperament (or insisting that such is innate) Erikson has defeated his own purpose. The female continues to be socially ineffective because confined by a menial, domestic or bioreproductive role, while the male who *does* control every avenue of public efficacy, continues (and is authorized to continue) to exercise the aggression defined as his nature. If human sexual temperament is inherent, there is really very little hope for us.

Erikson disclaims any intention to "doom" woman to perpetual motherhood or "deny her the equivalence of individuality and the equality of citizenship;" he is simply eager that she not "compete" or participate in the "active male proclivities" of civilization. Since "woman is never not-a-woman," as he states with assumed profundity, it is clear that once she has proven herself equal to "men's performance and competence in most spheres of achievement"—and it is said that she has—Erikson is content to assume that the potential equality of the sexes is proven, without requiring that their actual inequality be modified. He implies woman would do well to rely upon her "right to be uniquely creative" through maternity and think little further. Like Ruskin, Erikson appears to believe women are "better" and therefore should offer a vicarious and remote moral assistance to the male. Yet in both men there is a fairly clear understanding that civilization is a male department. And since both masculine vanity and masculine uneasiness lest "femininity" be lost (and with it, the only kindness either men profess to see in human beings) prevents the male from acquiring the humanity attributed to woman, or woman from transcending her politically and socially powerless role, Erikson is as unlikely to realize his hopes as Ruskin's queens were powerless to abridge the evils of industrialism. Others, less sincere than Erikson, may find in his theory a splendid rationale to insure that the "outer space" of the technological future and every means of social and political control remain ex-

[203] *Ibid.*, p. 281.
[204] *Ibid.*

clusively male prerogative. And to such an end fables about "inner space" are very expedient myth.

The Influence of Functionalism

During the period of the reaction, the social sciences tended to turn from political or historical considerations to focus their attention upon social structures, providing careful descriptions of how theoretic models operated. Hence the leading school of thought named itself "functionalism." At first glance, its method is one of purely objective description; on the surface it would present itself as value-free. Utility alone detains its clear and disinterested glance; if a pattern works, it may be said to function. Yet all systems which perpetuate themselves may be called functional in this minimal sense: peonage, racism, feudalism. Despite their stability, many oppressive forms do not function efficiently. The debilitated patriarchy which functionalists describe when they turn their attention to sociosexual matters operates with enormous waste and friction. But when functionalists recognize the latter as "conflict," they tend to put the burden of responsibility for it upon the individual who experiences it.

Were such a thing as a value-free social science even possible, it would very likely be monstrous; one which disguises its values is insidious. Since functionalism does not go beyond the status quo for its enunciated frame of reference, it produces a description of the present arrived at by means of the measurements it has devised. These might in themselves be somewhat suspect, for, like all methodologies, they are end-oriented. But without quarreling over methods, the description itself is sufficient evidence of bias. For taking the situation at hand, measuring, stating, and generalizing from it, functionalism, notwithstanding its fetish for the mathematical sciences, operates at odds with the scientific method in neglecting causality: one scarcely needs pages of tables to know that the poor are poor. And so in its measurement of sex difference, every form of passivity and aggression in sex-linked behavior is tested continuously, yet little thought is given as to the causality of such phenomena, either as learned behavior, or as behavior specifically appropriate to patriarchal society. When the differentiation of roles is regarded as functional, no serious explanation of the political character of such function is given: any set of complementary roles may be called functional to the extent they promote stable operation within a system.

Moreover, functionalist description inevitably becomes prescriptive. The discovery that a mode is functional tends to grant it prescriptive authority. In an atmosphere where "normality" and even worth are made to depend upon conformity (in this case to sexual category based on statistical average) such conformity is strongly urged. While early studies were content to measure and generalize, later rationalizations of a sexual differentiation in temperament (and by extension, role) grew altogether bolder. Having found traditional behavior functional, functionalists could now prescribe it: having found the status quo operable, they could proceed to find it "natural" hence biologically "necessary." This was effected either by taking refuge in psychoanalysis' erroneous biological explanations, or through hazy generalizations of their own. The main service of functionalism appears to reside in its justification of the system it perceives and covertly identifies with, followed by prescriptive recommendations on how to "adjust" groups or individuals to this system. When it filters down to practical application in schools, industry, and popular media, it may simply become a form of cultural policing.

Functionalism finds it agreeable to operate in an endless present. Against the dynamism of growth and change it proposes an ideal of stability. In ignoring values, it ignores history, either through an appeal to historical naïveté or by an elimination of historical evidence altogether. History is information, and as such it might well provide sociology with a perspective on institutions such as patriarchy. Such historical perspective might permit it to interpret sex role in terms of a system which is no longer even utilitarian, was always unjust, and is becoming increasingly wasteful. Functionalism either fails to mention patriarchy (it is hard to find the word in functionalist texts save in the sense of an adjective with some vague Biblical coloring), or gives no recognition to patriarchy as a form of social government, or simply assumes that patriarchy is the first form of human grouping, the origin of all society, and therefore too fundamental to merit discussion. The great social transformation which the sexual revolution had accomplished in the partial emancipation of women is deliberately overlooked or semantically obliterated in such phrases as "change in role"—accompanied by the assumption that change has brought much social maladjustment. Where stability is the measure of success, change is not viewed favorably.

One of the most unfortunate aspects of civilization is the extent to which learning and scientific interest are so deeply affected by the culture in which such study is done. A Nazi state invents its own Nazi social investigation; a racist state can formulate a racist science to sanction its most passionate hatreds.[205] While the social sciences in America are just now being purged of a racist bias indulged with considerable freedom over many decades, a strong "sexist" bias, the product of several decades of reaction, still pervades such areas of study.

As the major trend of the sexual revolution had been to de-emphasize traditional distinctions between the sexes both as to role and to temperament, while exposing the discrepancy in status, the most formidable task of reactionary opinion was to blur or disguise distinctions in status while reemphasizing sexual differences in personality by implying that they are innate rather than cultural. A differentiation of roles followed upon that of tempera-

205 See Peter Rose, *The Subject Was Race*, Traditional Ideologies and the Teaching of Race Relations, Oxford, 1968.

ment, and it too was regarded as eminently useful, even necessary. As this return to a conservative prerevolutionary system required validation, the whole weight of public authority which the social sciences had gradually amassed was now exerted in favor of patriarchal ideology, attitudes, and institutions. The preservation of conservative notions of marriage and the family, of sex role, of temperamental trait and identity through conformity to sexual norms, took on something of the nature of defense of holy ground. Socialist experiment or change generally came to be viewed with pity or derision.

Since the model on which such attitudes are formed comes from the past, functionalism has a nostalgic flavor under its impersonal exterior. Perhaps this is nowhere more quaintly evident than in Talcott Parsons' functionalist evocation of "youth culture" as student life in some golden past when all was varsity prom and varsity football.[206] One can often discern some faintly glamorized version of the social scientist's own childhood in the comfortable middle class. The orientation is small town and Middle West, a world of some twenty years back, before the dangers and innovations of the present ever occurred to the investigator. One sees it echoed in the media's bland portraits of comfort, in the children's texts illustrated with blond and bourgeois parents, prosperously equipped with an automobile and a house of their own, neatly divided into breadwinner in business suit and housewife beaming behind her apron.

Each of the social disciplines contributed to re-establishing and then maintaining a reactionary status quo in sexual politics, each through its own method of reasoning: anthropologists might study cross-cultural divisions of labor and ascribe them to a fundamental biological source, while sociologists, in announcing they merely recorded social phenomena, gradually came to ratify them by noting that nonconformist behavior is in fact deviant and produces "problems." The psychologist, in deploring individual maladjustment to social and sexual role, finally came to justify both as inherent psychological nature, fundamental to the species and biological in essence. Later this point of view acquired sufficient confidence to go on the offensive. The habit of discovering and deploring instances of feminine dominance grew obsessive. It became eminently fashionable to regard sexual identity, especially for the male, as so crucial to ego development that any frustration of the demands of masculine prerogative would result in considerable psychic damage, described either as neurosis or homosexuality. In its extreme forms, this attitude insists it is therapeutic necessity, somehow an issue of social health, that male supremacy continue unchallenged.

I have chosen two examples of the type of thinking representative of these attitudes. One is a study entitled "A Cross-cultural Survey of Some

[206] Talcott Parsons, "Age and Sex in the Social Structure of the United States," 1942, in *Essays in Sociological Theory* (New York: Macmillan, 1949).

Sex Differences in Socialization," by Berry, Bacon, and Child, whose orientation is comparative cultural anthropology, and another called "Family Structure and Sex Role Learning by Children," by Orville G. Brim Jr., whose point of view derives from social psychology.[207] Both shall be analyzed at length so that their logic may be fully explored; their representative character will be established by short quotations affirming their position from comparable sources.[208] Both articles were published in reputable professional journals (the first in the *Journal of Abnormal and Social Psychology* and *The American Anthropologist*; the second in *Sociometry*) before their inclusion in a popular and influential college textbook, *Selected Studies in Marriage and the Family*, edited by Winch, McGinnis and Barringer, regarded as reputable and widely used in many kinds of social science courses.

The method of establishing representative opinion from the common denominator of college texts is the one used in C. Wright Mills's valuable study, "The Professional Ideology of Social Pathologists,"[209] and can be defended on evident and logical grounds. This is how Mills describes the method:

> By virtue of the mechanism of sales and distribution, textbooks tend to embody a content agreed upon by the academic groups using them. In some cases texts have been written only after an informal poll was taken of professional opinion as to what should be included and other texts are consulted in the writing of a new one. Since one test of their success is wide adoption, the very spread of the public for which they are written tends to insure textbook tolerance of the commonplace. Only elements admitted into the more stable textbook formulations have come within my view: the aim is to grasp typical perspectives and key concepts.[210]

The first of our articles[211] agrees to the general liberal sociological recognition that "masculine" and "feminine" behavior is the result of long and careful years of "socialization," the conditioned product of reinforcement by punishment and reward. Yet it maintains that culture here only imitates or carries out the inevitable demands of nature. It is prone to the widespread

[207] Herbert Barry, III, Margaret K. Bacon, and Irwin L. Child, "A Cross-cultural Survey of Some Sex Differences in Socialization," and Orville G. Brim, Jr., "Family Structure and Sex Role Learning by Children: A Further Analysis of Helen Koch's Data," in *Selected Studies in Marriage and the Family*, edited by Robert Winch, Robert McGinnis and Herbert Barringer (New York: Holt, Rinehart and Winston, 2nd ed., 1962). Three of the four authors hold academic positions, one at the University of Connecticut, two at Yale University; the fourth is connected with the Russell Sage Foundation.

[208] See Appendix for further quotations.

[209] C. Wright Mills, "The Professional Ideology of Social Pathologists," (1943), *Power, Politics and People* (Oxford University Press, 1963).

[210] *Ibid.*, p. 525.

[211] Barry, Bacon and Child, *op. cit.*

tactic of falling back on a biological mystique and maintaining that the order of things which it describes (often mistakenly) is in fact the very order of necessity. The article also conforms to the common habit of obscuring and romanticizing through the giving of names: female subservience is called "obedience, nurturance and responsibility." Male dominance is phrased as "self-reliance and achievement."[212] Anthropology is then invoked to justify this in terms of the activities of tribal life: "Participation in warfare, as a male prerogative, calls for self-reliance and a high order of skill where survival or death is the immediate issue. The childbearing which is biologically assigned to women, and the child care which is socially assigned primarily to them, lead to nurturant behavior and often call for a more continuous responsibility than do tasks carried out by men.[213] There is really very little difference between this and Ruskin even as to the meaning of terms; only period style intervenes. The change is aesthetic rather than substantive. The first feminine trait mentioned, "obedience," is left without further explanation; perhaps it is better so.

On the strength of such a model of the world, the male at war, the female in her hut responsible for the child, our social science team is satisfied to conclude that "most of these distinctions in adult role are not inevitable, but the biological differences between the sexes strongly predispose the distinction of role."[214] So far the language is still a bit tentative.

To the layman it may appear abstruse that warfare is the inevitable biological destiny of the male, just as it is difficult or obscure how "nurturance" is the lifelong biological destiny of all females if one has already conceded that while childbirth and breast-feeding are biological, child care itself is only culturally assigned to women. Furthermore, classic studies in cultural anthropology used to prove that there was a nearly infinite variety in the division of roles and of labor. It is also highly relevant to examine the *status* line along which division of labor is established. In a culture where men weave and women fish, just as in a culture where men fish and women weave, it is axiomatic that whichever activity is assigned to the male is the activity with the greater prestige, power, status, and rewards.[215]

Having established the validity of their archetypal sex roles satisfactorily, it only remains to these authorities to insist that the conditioning be pervasive and efficient; prescription swiftly follows on description:

If each generation were left entirely to its own devices, therefore, without even

[212] *Ibid.*, p. 274.
[213] *Ibid.*, p. 270. Note that war is "achievement"; child rearing is not.
[214] *Ibid.*
[215] Margaret Mead, "Prehistory and the Woman," *Barnard College Bulletin*, April 30, 1969, Supplement p. 7: "One aspect of the social valuation of different types of labor is the differential prestige of men's activities and women's activities. Whatever men do—even if it is dressing dolls for religious ceremonies—is more prestigious than what women do and is treated as a higher achievement."

an older generation to copy, sex differences in role would presumably be almost absent in childhood and would have to be developed after puberty at the expense of considerable relearning on the part of one or both sexes.[216]

Hence, the advocacy of every means of enforcing orthodoxy to the sex role stereotype, as such educated opinion is now convinced of its "useful function"[217] and even more determined that deviance or lack of pressure may produce that state of misfortune they refer to as "discontinuities in cultural conditioning."[218] Our authors are pleased to end their investigation of this branch of the subject on a complacent note: "The differences in socialization between the sexes in our society, then, are no arbitrary custom of our society, but a very widespread adaptation of culture to the biological substratum of human life."[219] As warfare is cultural and so is the question of who cares for children, it is still very unclear what the biological substratum might be. But biology is a word to conjure by, particularly in the social sciences; a vague reference to the male's larger musculature is expected to silence criticism. It is also to be expected that, even though it is intellectually understood that (beyond breast-feeding) the assignment of child care is cultural rather than biological, middle-class Americans will let that slip by and infer that childbirth must mean child care, the two together again constituting "biology." It is one of conservatism's favorite myths that every woman is a mother.

Somehow the writers of this article are still insecure: the dubious dovetailing of archetypal culture with the inevitability of biology does not explain the present softening of sexual stereotype brought about by the industrial revolution and the emancipation and education of women. They are faced now with a "nuclear" family in place of the virtues of the extended family and polygyny, two forms of social organization which they see in benign terms as cases of clearer and more sensible sex-role differentiation. Yet to admit to inutility in any aspect of a conservative and therefore desirable version of the present would be to admit defeat. Therefore the nuclear family is granted pragmatic sanction on the humorously specious grounds that in emergencies father and mother can "fill in" for each other.[220]

While vaguely aware that "our mechanized economy is perhaps less dependent than any previous economy upon the superior average strength of the male,"[221] the authors are unable to admit that although a technological and capitalist culture puts a very low salary value on the muscle it attributes to the male, it never for a moment relinquishes male control. In fact, muscle is class—lower class. The difference between a stevedore and a scrub-

[216] Barry, Bacon and Child, *op. cit.*, p. 270.
[217] *Ibid.*
[218] *Ibid.*
[219] *Ibid.*
[220] *Ibid.*, p. 273.
[221] *Ibid.*

woman, on the one hand, and an executive or physicist on the other, is a difference measured in the one's confinement and the other's escape from physical labor; other factors at issue being education, economic power, and prestige.

In the same fashion the article acknowledges that "the conditions favoring low sex differentiation appear to be more characteristic of the upper segments of our society, in socioeconomic and educational status, than of lower segments."[222] What is actually meant is that some degree of privilege and education may be shared by both sexes in certain favored classes. The authors appear to be quite blind to the fact that the "biological mission" of full-time child rearing which they ascribe to the female is actually a modern and middle-class luxury. However much the working class is devoted to sexual status, it does nevertheless produce vast numbers of women engaged in menial work in and out of the home and a very large number of households headed by women employed in physically exhausting labor. But it does not appear to be this class of women, mere "lower segments," to whom the authors address themselves. To their middle-class bias such women are not competitors but cheap and useful labor. It is against the middle-class woman, at this moment a college student, that their wisdom is leveled, and its message is that she will limit her auxiliary role to "homemaker."

It is curious how reactionary thinking clings to "biology" as a desperate hope. Only in the area of sex is the position of an oppressed group still ascribed to their physical nature, only here is biological difference still brought forward to explain and rationalize inferior status.[223] Having begun their discussion with a fraudulent "open question"—"In the differential rearing of the sexes does our society make an arbitrary imposition on an infinitely plastic biological base, or is this cultural imposition found uniformly in all societies as an adjustment to the real biological differences between the sexes?"[224] —the study comes out soundly in favor of the latter alternative. Although it puts up no actual evidence for its biological assumptions, it is determined that they form the real base of any division of labor role or temperament without reference to the far more crucial and probable elements of status, political, and economic power—factors far easier and more germane for social research to investigate than nebulous biological assumptions intended to elevate common wisdom to natural necessity.

The article ends on a caveat, which is also something of an omen. Were its implicit suggestion put into effect, it would be a desperate recommendation indeed. Sensing further insubordination within the society they would freeze and immobilize, and a continuing erosion of the old way, they have prepared themselves: "The increase in our society of conditions favoring small

---

[222] *Ibid.*
[223] Jensen should probably be seen as an atavism, rather than an exception.
[224] Barry, Bacon and Child, *op. cit.*, p. 267.

sex difference has led some people to advocate a virtual elimination of sex differences in socialization. This course seems dysfunctional even in our society."[225] As objective pragmatism is their announced philosophy, it is hard to believe that favorable conditions could also be dysfunctional; or that when the supposed need for a thing is palpably no longer present, it could still be functional to keep it about. One senses the writers' insecurity. It is not surprising that they now feel it necessary for the voice of authority to emerge at this point in somewhat axiomatic terms. Therefore a slightly dogmatic tone is adopted in adjudicating the following formula: "a differentiation of role similar to the universal pattern of sex differences is an important and perhaps inevitable development in any social group."[226] (One cannot help noting how handy a rule this might be in advocating class and caste divisions as well.) And now the clincher—biology: ". . . biological differences between the sexes make most appropriate the usual division of those roles between the sexes."[227] Before this juggernaut all argument is expected to confess defeat; the division of labor by sexual status as well as the division of human personality by biological category may be permanently sanctioned. As a final admonition, the kibbutz is hauled on to convince one that failure to enforce sex role differentiation ends in failure altogether. Such radical change is both suspicious and drastic activity; nature is bound to assert itself and bring back the old methods.

The authors cannot rest here. Like others of their kind, they perceive all about them threats to the stereotypes they are committed to defend and reinforce: every species of formal education, even the public school, is undermining their efforts:

> In our training of children, there may now be less differentiation in sex role than characterizes adult life—so little indeed, as to provide inadequate preparation for adulthood. This state of affairs is likely to be especially true of formal education, which is more subject to conscious influence by an ideology than is informal socialization at home. With childrearing being more oriented toward the male than the female role in adulthood, many of the adjustment problems of women in our society today may be partly traced to conflicts growing out of inadequate childhood preparations for their adult role.[228]

This of course requires translation out of the bland abstract jargon of the trade. The subversive ideology referred to as corrupting formal education is, in fact, the egalitarianism still implicit in public schooling and even more

---

[225] *Ibid.*, p. 274.

[226] *Ibid.* (The authors are of course paraphrasing Talcott Parsons, the foremost authority of their school.) See Talcott Parsons and R. F. Bales, *Family, Socialization and Interaction Process* (New York, Free Press). (The remark appears to apply not only to the family, but to groups in general.)

[227] *Ibid.*

[228] *Ibid.*

rampant at the universities—the heritage of the sexual revolution. The recommendation is clearly to eliminate this destructive attitude of intellectual parity from institutions of learning, which, our authors insist, are, by their very nature "oriented toward the male role." Here it is necessary to pause and consider that the male role has undergone a drastic change without notice being served to the reader. Suddenly and inexplicably, it is that of intellect where we had naïvely expected it to continue for all time as "biological" muscle. Unconsciously, our authors have slipped from tribal warfare and hunting, once so prestigious as to be male monopolies, whizzed past the industrial and technological revolutions, and landed squarely in the twentieth century, where learning is understood to be a newer male prerogative. They have foreseen the necessity of withdrawing woman from any education beyond the fairly stultifying sequestration they describe as "the informal socialization of the home," lest she fail to be perfectly conditioned and thereby end up in that deplorable state labeled "inadequately prepared for adulthood." The implication forced upon the reader is that a university education is quite appropriate for the male yet damaging to the female since it is likely to produce "adjustment problems" or cases of arrested development (inadequate preparation for adulthood). Under the guise of objective description, our authors would undo the work of the previous generation. The logical outcome of their suggestion is an end to higher education for women.

To a dispassionate judge of reactionary tactic, functionalist formulation must appear a rather more admirable technique than the earlier and rather tarnished charge of penis envy. Like the latter, it points an accusatory finger of maladjustment at any woman who fails to conform to its arrogant program, but it avoids the openly invidious character of Freud's formula, and appears, through the very turgid cipher of its language, disinterested and beyond opinion. It also avoids pitfall references to sexual status without resorting to Ruskin's or Erikson's chivalrous fatuity. The spheres are separate still, isolated by "science" while this attack mumbles on, clinical and efficient, the arm of a blind justice, its prosaic jargon nearly negating meaning itself, yet remarkably successful at camouflaging even the most ambitiously regressive strictures in its deadening verbiage.

If the orthodoxy of sex role as social benefit as well as biological necessity is inculcated successfully, it is not very difficult for this type of expedient "science" to survey the present population, assign traits to each group, gloss them in a blurred and neutral-seeming terminology, and imply that, while subject to variation and gradation, they are in some way inherently sex-linked. As "biology" determined sex role in the previous study, it will hover helpfully in the background of the next study[229] to assure that what are, in fact, the assigned characteristics of two political classes must also, even if

[229] Brim, *op. cit.*

acquired, be nature as well. In Brim's "Survey of Some Sex Differences in Socialization," the author has hardly any need for prescription. Although he is anxious that sex role be properly absorbed, his main interest is simply to define it. The normal will not neglect to learn.

For if one accepts masculine as male, feminine as female, and if one allows sociology to define masculine and feminine one is caught in the biological trap again. It might be too clearly invidious if "workers" in the area stated outright that the male was "tenacious," "aggressive," "ambitious," "a good planner," "responsible," "original," and "self-confident," and the female, who should be all "obedience," "cheerfulness," and "friendliness," is in fact all too often given to "quarrelsomeness," is "revengeful," "exhibitionist," "uncooperative," "negative," and a "tattler."[230] Therefore authorities in the field have hit upon the expedient of a mediating terminology. We are indebted to Talcott Parsons,[231] the leading functionalist and chief source of inspiration behind our studies for the insight that the male is "instrumental," and the traits of aggressiveness, originality, etc., are only instrumental traits which do and should happen also to be male in that they "pertain to the male role." The female is designated by the euphemism "expressive," and it is the expressive which is obedient, cheerful, friendly, etc. While "instrumental" translates easily to the older, more obviously prejudicial category of intellectual capacity and mastery, "expressive" is but a new name for emotional. Parsons is perhaps not an original thinker here. Yet there is much to commend in this device, for without some such polite intervening semantics, the list of female traits might read like misogyny; devoid of some linguistic cushion it might give rise to ridicule.

The table itself is sufficiently quaint to merit reproduction. It appears to be the work of Orville G. Brim, Jr., himself, but based on data and ideas provided by Koch, Parsons, Terman, and Tyler.

This catalogue provides the unhurried reader with ample material for speculation. It is in fact a perfect paradigm of class. While to the male is assigned every virtue of human rationality, the preponderance of traits valued by the very society in which he predominates, there is yet sufficient candor and self-criticism to admit that he is capable of the faintheartedness of "dawdling and procrastinating" as well as the venial offense of "wavering in decision." Here is honest admission of the ardors of persevering in the role of a superior caste. Under the beguiling rubric of "expressive" is ascribed to the female nearly every conceivable vice of character. One recalls not only the misogynous tradition but the seven deadly sins.

Perhaps nothing is so depressing an index of the inhumanity of the male-

[230] See the table which follows.

[231] Talcott Parsons and R. F. Bales, *op. cit.* The "traits" themselves were arrived at with the help of Parsons' theory, "professional persons" acting as judges, and then checked with the criteria of Terman and Tyler's "Psychological Sex Differences," *Manual of Child Psychology* (2nd. ed.) (New York: Wiley, 1954).

TABLE 1[232]

TRAITS ASSIGNABLE TO MALE (INSTRUMENTAL)
OR FEMALE (EXPRESSIVE) ROLES

Trait	Pertains primarily to instrumental (I) or Expressive (E) role	Trait is congruent (+) or incongruent (−) characteristic of role
1 Tenacity	I	+
2 Aggressiveness	I	+
3 Curiosity	I	+
4 Ambition	I	+
5 Planfulness	I	+
6 Dawdling and procrastinating	I	−
7 Responsibleness	I	+
8 Originality	I	+
9 Competitiveness	I	+
10 Wavering in decision	I	−
11 Self-confidence	I	+
12 Anger	E	−
13 Quarrelsomeness	E	−
14 Revengefulness	E	−
15 Teasing	E	−
16 Extrapunitiveness	E	−
17 Insistence on rights	E	−
18 Exhibitionism	E	−
19 Uncooperativeness with group	E	−
20 Affectionateness	E	+
21 Obedience	E	+
22 Upset by defeat	E	−
23 Responds to sympathy and approval from adults	E	+
24 Jealousy	E	−
25 Speedy recovery from emotional disturbance	E	+
26 Cheerfulness	E	+
27 Kindness	E	+
28 Friendliness to adults	E	+
29 Friendliness to children	E	+
30 Negativism	E	−
31 Tattling	E	−

[232] Brim, *op. cit.*, p. 282.

supremacist mentality as the fact that the more genial human traits are assigned to the underclass: affection, response to sympathy, kindness, cheerfulness. There are a host of what would be termed "nutritive" feminine functions implicit here which it appears the male has ascribed to the female because he disregards their value and utility in himself, preferring they exist in his opposite only that they may cater to his needs. Such a table is a fairly startling revelation of the approved relationship between the sexes and a more accurate index of cultural values than one is generally able to come at. If the Chicago school children who were tested for its efficacy were to live up to the demands of its opprobrious "roles," one could find no more convincing proof of the powers of negative behavioral engineering on childhood. But somehow the machinery has failed to get very creditable results.[233] The expected docility is sometimes present—girls are, as they are expected to be, "obedient"—such indeed is the "congruent characteristic" of their "role," obligingly stated in the right-hand column. But they are also given to anger, jealousy, a desire to revenge themselves, a refusal to co-operate, and perhaps most distressing of all, an "insistence on their rights."

To arrive at the political implications of the table, one has only to exchange its categories with other political classes. Were one to substitute black and white for male and female, one would have a perfect picture of both the expectation and the assumed conditions of a racist society. The obedience and good nature white expects from black would be accounted for, as well as white's dismay to find it accompanied with vengefulness, anger, and a refusal to co-operate. The same holds true of aristocrat and peasant; the former typically fancying himself an intellectual governor and seeing in the latter a warm and jovial servant, but one, alas, given to surliness, petty dodges, "tattling," and frequent insubordination. The table just as adequately reflects the good and evil of capitalist ethics; superiority and intellect on the side of the winning team and greedy spite on the other.

It would be irrelevant to dilate upon the arbitrary character of this division of human nature, just as it would be unprofitable to wonder how such things as tenacity are measured and by what standards they are judged.[234] Yet all unconscious of the insights it affords, the table is a superb analysis

[233] Brim apologizes that at five years of age they are too young to be proficient; the males are as yet impracticed and debilitated by maternal attachment, elder sisters, and other handicaps to echo their fathers as they should and will. He deplores certain cases: "for the boy with the older sister the acquisition of feminine traits would seem to have displaced rather than simply diluted his masculinity" (p. 286). Yet he appears to regard any widespread, long-lasting nonconformity as an "implausibility" (p. 287).

[234] Brim gives it all away by revealing that the whole assessment of the child's possession of a trait was made by kindergarten teachers, sitting in private and subjective judgment on their charges. When one comprehends that the table is the collective achievement of the prejudices of these persons in conjunction with the unconscious sexual-political impressions of the social scientists who invented and assigned the traits, one has understood much. The study is a study of itself.

of master class values, those it invents for itself and those it assigns to the under class it shapes and controls. The governing virtues of a sovereign caste are clearly outlined, with the usual admission that the ruling group is often not sufficiently sure and certain in its dominance. The vices of the oppressed and all their serviceable virtues are acknowledged, with the usual implication that the under class could be much more ingratiating in its place and is expected to bear its ignoble status with a better fortitude and a more accommodating mien than it does. Needless to say, in view of the pressure and concern over children who fail to "adopt" to their role, the table registers prescription as well as expectation.[235] While the scheme is of no use in determining either human or sexual nature, it is a frank, albeit unwitting statement of the actual status of male and female in patriarchy.

Thus sociology examines the status quo, calls it phenomena, and pretends to take no stand on it, thereby avoiding the necessity to comment on the invidious character of the relationship between the sex groups it studies. Yet by slow degrees of converting statistic to fact, function to prescription, bias to biology (or some other indeterminate), it comes to ratify and rationalize what has been socially enjoined or imposed into what is and ought to be. And through its pose of objectivity, it gains a special efficacy in reinforcing stereotypes. Seeing that failure to conform leads to "problems" and "conflicts" as well as other situations it regards as highly undesirable deviant behavior, it counsels a continuous and vigilant surveillance of conditioning that it may proceed on lines of greater proficiency and perfection.

Finally, it has the devastating question of identity with which to threaten its subjects. Young boys whose virtually only permitted self is their maleness are continuously harassed by the danger or the accusation of losing their "masculinity." And the same psycho-social coercion is applied to girls as well. A painful identity crisis is thereby imposed upon every member of either group—to fail to be adequately masculine or feminine is to fail to be true to one's nature. And as we are born undoubtedly male or female, we imagine that should we lose the certainty of gender identity we may fail to exist; gender identity being the primary identity allowed to children as to adults. Girls who are seen as already imperfect in conformity, "maladjusted," etc. (in Brim's study the minus signs for girls are six times the number awarded to boys) evidently through public schooling and the residual lip service occasionally still paid to the sexual revolution's ideal of equality in opportunity and education, are in imminent danger of emerging from their stereotype.

[235] It is interesting to note that Brim's actual purpose in the article was to demonstrate how the number and age of siblings in a family reinforce or fail to reinforce the proper traits of masculinity. Curiously, "responsibleness" is in this study a masculine trait, whereas the other study found it one of the prime characteristics of the female; consistency is perhaps too much to ask where there is otherwise so much agreement.

That this possibility have the full force of catastrophe about it, it is continuously equated with a refusal to perform the biological function of childbearing, endlessly confused and equated with the whole burden of child rearing. Girls are imprisoned in the familiar triad of passivity, masochism, and narcissism by which their whole personality is defined. Boys are also confined by the stereotypical dominance prescribed for them lest they wander into henpeckery or homosexuality. Functionalists, like other reactionaries, are out to save the family.

As the whole subject of sex is covered with shame, ridicule and silence, any failure to conform to stereotype reduces the individual, especially if a child, to an abysmal feeling of guilt, unworthiness, and confusion. In the period of the counterrevolution, adherence to sexual stereotype became, in all fields of activity, including literature and literary criticism, a new morality; good and evil, virtue, sympathy, judgment, disapprobation, were a matter of one's sexual conformity according to category. Scarcely any ideology can lay claim to such merciless, total, and seemingly irrefutable control over its victims. Despite the assumption of inevitable membership by birth (the starting point of ideology) the burden of proof shifts, in fact, to each individual. Unalterably born into one group or another, every subject is forced, moment to moment, to *prove* he or she is, in fact, male or female by deference to the ascribed characteristics of masculine and feminine.

There is no way out of such a dilemma but to rebel and be broken, stigmatized, and cured. Until the radical spirit revives to free us, we remain imprisoned in the vast gray stockades of the sexual reaction. Our subject is now some of those who helped to build these structures—writers, who, after the usual manner of cultural agents, both reflected and actually shaped attitudes. So we proceed to the counterrevolutionary sexual politicians themselves—Lawrence, Miller, and Mailer.

III

THE LITERARY REFLECTION

FIVE

D. H. Lawrence

I DEVOTIONAL

"Let me see you!"

He dropped the shirt and stood still, looking towards her. The sun through the low window sent a beam that lit up his thighs and slim belly, and the erect phallus rising darkish and hot-looking from the little cloud of vivid gold-red hair. She was startled and afraid.

"How strange!" she said slowly. "How strange he stands there! So big! and so dark and cocksure! Is he like that?"

The man looked down the front of his slender white body, and laughed. Between the slim breasts the hair was dark, almost black. But at the root of the belly, where the phallus rose thick and arching, it was gold-red, vivid in a little cloud.

"So proud!" she murmured, uneasy. "And so lordly! Now I know why men are so overbearing. But he's lovely, *really*. Like another being! A bit terrifying! But lovely really! And he comes to *me!*—" She caught her lower lip between her teeth, in fear and excitement.

The man looked down in silence at his tense phallus, that did not change. . . . "Cunt, that's what tha'rt after. Tell lady Jane tha' wants cunt. John Thomas, an' th' cunt o' lady Jane!—"

"Oh, don't tease him," said Connie, crawling on her knees on the bed towards him and putting her arms round his white slender loins, and drawing him to her so that her hanging swinging breasts touched the top of the stirring, erect phallus, and caught the drop of moisture. She held the man fast.

"Lie down!" he said. "Lie down! Let me come!"
He was in a hurry now.[1]

Lady Chatterley's Lover is a quasi-religious tract recounting the salvation of one modern woman (the rest are irredeemably "plastic" and "celluloid") through the offices of the author's personal cult, "the mystery of the phallus."[2] This passage, a revelation of the sacrament itself, is properly the novel's very holy of holies—a transfiguration scene with atmospheric clouds and lighting, and a pentecostal sunbeam (the sun is phallic to Lawrence's apprehension) illuminating the ascension of the deity "thick and arching" before the reverent eyes of the faithful.

Lawrence's working title for the book was "Tenderness," and although Oliver Mellors, the final apotheosis of Lawrentian man, is capable of some pretty drastic sexual animosities (he'd rather like to "liquidate" all lesbians, and what Freudians would call "clitoroidal" women, en masse, together with his own former wife), one still finds in this novel little of the sexual violence and ruthless exploitation so obtrusive in Mailer and Miller, nor, for that matter, the honest recognition of sexual caste one encounters in Genet. With *Lady Chatterley*, Lawrence seems to be making his peace with the female, and in one last burst of passion proposing a reconciliation for the hostilities embarked upon with the composition of *Aaron's Rod* in 1918, nearly ten years before. Compared with the novels and short stories which preceded it, this last work appears almost an act of atonement. And so Constance Chatterley is granted sight of the godhead,[3] which turns out to be a portrait of the creator himself, nude, and in his most impressive state. Whereas the mood of *Kangaroo, Aaron's Rod,* and *The Plumed Serpent* is homoerotic, here it is narcissistic.

In *Lady Chatterley*, as throughout his final period, Lawrence uses the words "sexual" and "phallic" interchangeably, so that the celebration of sexual passion for which the book is so renowned is largely a celebration of the penis of Oliver Mellors, gamekeeper and social prophet. While insisting his mission is the noble and necessary task of freeing sexual behavior of perverse inhibition, purging the fiction which describes it of prurient or prudish euphemism, Lawrence is really the evangelist of quite another cause—"phallic consciousness." This is far less a matter of "the resurrection of the body," "natural love," or other slogans under which it has been advertised, than the transformation of masculine ascendancy into a mystical religion, international, possibly institutionalized. This is sexual politics in its most overpowering form,

[1] D. H. Lawrence, *Lady Chatterley's Lover* (1928). (New York: Random House, 1957), pp. 237–38.

[2] *Ibid.*, p. 238.

[3] It had been Lawrence's consistent practice to veil the sanctities of sex in vague phrases about cosmic flight, movement into space, and so forth, while the trademark adjective droned its tedious "deep, deep, deep" refrain at the reader. Lady Chatterley contains the only wholly explicit sexual descriptions in his work.

but Lawrence is the most talented and fervid of sexual politicians. He is the most subtle as well, for it is through a feminine consciousness that his masculine message is conveyed. It is a woman, who, as she gazes, informs us that the erect phallus, rising phoenixlike from its aureole of golden pubic hair is indeed "proud" and "lordly"—and above all, "lovely." "Dark and cocksure" it is also "terrifying" and "strange," liable to give rise in women to "fear" as well as "excitement"—even to uneasy murmurs. At the next erection, Connie and the author-narrator together inform us the penis is "overweening," "towering" and "terrible."[4] Most material of all, an erection provides the female with irrefutable evidence that male supremacy is founded upon the most real and uncontrovertible grounds. A diligent pupil, Connie supplies the catechist's dutiful response, "Now I know why men are so overbearing." With the ecstasy of the devout, a parody of a loving woman's rapture and delight, she finds the godhead both frightening and sublime. Lawrence's own rather sadistic insistence on her intimidation before biological event is presumably another proof of inherent female masochism. One cannot help admiring the technique: "But he's lovely, *really* . . . A bit terrifying! But lovely really! And he comes to *me!*"—out of the mouth of the inamorata the most abject piety. It is no wonder Simone de Beauvoir shrewdly observed that Lawrence spent his life writing guidebooks for women.[5] Constance Chatterley is as good a personification of counterrevolutionary wisdom as Marie Bonaparte.

Even Mellors is impressed, pleased to refer to his penis in the third person, coyly addressing it in dialect:

> Ay ma lad! Tha'rt theer right enough. Yi, tha mun rear they head! Theer on thy own ey? an ta'es no count o' nob'dy . . . Dost want *her?* Dost want my lady Jane? . . . Say: Lift up your heads, . . . that the king of glory may come in.[6]

John Thomas, this active miracle, is hardly matched by lady Jane, mere passive "cunt." Praise for this commodity is Mellors' highest compliment to his mistress: "Th'art good cunt, though, aren't ter? Best bit o' cunt left on earth . . . Cunt! It's thee down theer; an' what I get when I'm i'side thee . . . Cunt! Eh, that's the beauty o' thee, lass."[7] The sexual mystery to which the novel is dedicated is scarcely a reciprocal or co-operative event—it is simply phallic. Mellors' penis, even when deflated, is still "that which had been the power:" Connie moaning with "a sort of bliss" is its "sacrifice" and a "newborn thing."[8] Although the male is displayed and admired so often, there is, apart from the word cunt, no reference to or description of the female geni-

[4] D. H. Lawrence, *Lady Chatterley's Lover*, p. 238.
[5] Simone de Beauvoir, *The Second Sex* (New York: Knopf, 1953), p. 209.
[6] Lawrence, *op. cit.*, p. 237.
[7] *Ibid.*, p. 201.
[8] *Ibid.*, p. 197.

tals: they are hidden, shameful and subject.[9] Male genitals are not only the aesthetic standard, ". . . the balls between his legs! What a mystery! What a strange heavy weight of mystery . . . The roots, root of all that is lovely, the primeval root of all full beauty,"[10] they become a species of moral standard as well: "The root of all sanity is in the balls."[11] Yet all that is disreputable, even whole classes of society, are anathematized by the words "female" or "feminine."

The scenes of sexual intercourse in the novel are written according to the "female is passive, male is active" directions laid down by Sigmund Freud. The phallus is all; Connie is "cunt," the thing acted upon, gratefully accepting each manifestation of the will of her master. Mellors does not even condescend to indulge his lady in foreplay. She enjoys an orgasm when she can, while Mellors is managing his own. If she can't, then too bad. Passive as she is, Connie fares better than the heroine of *The Plumed Serpent*, from whom Lawrentian man, Don Cipriano, deliberately withdraws as she nears orgasm, in a calculated and sadistic denial of her pleasure:

> By a swift dark instinct, Cipriano drew away from this in her. When, in their love, it came back on her, the seething electric female ecstasy, which knows such spasms of delirium, he recoiled from her. . . . By a dark and powerful instinct he drew away from her as soon as this desire rose again in her, for the white ecstasy of frictional satisfaction, the throes of Aphrodite of the foam. She could see that to him, it was repulsive. He just removed himself, dark and unchangeable, away from her.[12]

Lawrentian sexuality seems to be guided by somewhat the same principle one finds expressed in Rainwater's study of the working class (also the doctrine of the nineteenth-century middle classes)—"sex is for the man."[13] Lawrence's knowledge of Freud was sketchy and secondhand, but he appears to be well acquainted with the theories of female passivity and male activity and doubtless found them very convenient. Ladies—even when they are "cunt"—don't move. In both novels there are a number of severe reprimands delivered against subversive female "friction."

The sexual revolution had done a great deal to free female sexuality. An admirably astute politician, Lawrence saw in this two possibilities: it could

---

[9] This is true despite the great insight Lawrence displays about the nature of sexual inhibition and prurience, brutality and shame in *A Propos Lady Chatterley's Lover* and in his other critical essays on sex and censorship. Here, too, he is busy affirming that the phallus is not only the bridge to the future, but the very essence of marriage and life itself. His silence as regards to female genitals is most remarkable, and evidence, I believe, of considerable inhibition and very probably of strongly negative feelings. In Henry Miller one encounters the same phenomenon in a more severe form.

[10] *Ibid.*, p. 197.

[11] *Ibid.*, p. 246.

[12] D. H. Lawrence, *The Plumed Serpent* (1923). (New York: Knopf, 1951), p. 463.

[13] Lee Rainwater, *And the Poor Get Children* (Chicago: Quadrangle, 1960).

grant women an autonomy and independence he feared and hated, or it could be manipulated to create a new order of dependence and subordination, another form of compliance to masculine direction and prerogative. The frigid woman of the Victorian period was withholding assent, the "new woman," could, if correctly dominated, be mastered in bed as everywhere else. The Freudian school had promulgated a doctrine of "feminine fulfill-ment," "receptive" passivity, the imaginary "adult" vaginal orgasm which some disciples even interpreted as forbidding any penile contact with the clitoris. Notions of this kind could become, in Lawrence's hands, superb instru-ments for the perfect subjection of women.

In thanksgiving for her lover's sexual prowess, Lady Chatterley goes out into the rain before their hut to dance what the reader recognizes to be a mime of King David's naked gyrations before the Lord. Watching her, Mel-lors understands her to be performing a "kind of homage toward him," while "repeating a wild obeisance."[14] Such satisfaction as she is granted by the lordly gamekeeper has converted her to a "wonderful cowering female" whose flashing haunches Mellors perceives in terms of prey. Accordingly, he stirs himself to the chase. Having pursued and caught her, "he tipped her up and fell with her on the path, in the roaring silence of the rain, short and sharp, he took her, short and sharp and finished, like an animal."[15]

Lawrence is a passionate believer in the myth of nature which has ordained that female personality is congenital, even her shame not the product of con-ditioning, but innate. Only the "sensual fire" of the "phallic hunt" can rout this "old, old physical fear which crouches in the bodily roots." On the oc-casion when Lady Chatterley submits to Mellors' anal penetration, we are told that "She would have thought a woman would have died of shame. In-stead of which the shame died . . . she had needed this phallic hunting out, she had secretly wanted it, and she had believed that she would never get it." The "phallus alone" is competent to explore the "core of the physical jungle, the last and deepest recess of organic shame."[16] Having reached the "bedrock of her nature," the heroine breaks off momentarily to preach to the reader that the poets were "liars": "They made one think one wanted senti-ment. When one supremely wanted this piercing, consuming, rather awful sensuality . . . The supreme pleasure of the mind! And what is that to a woman?"[17] Lawrence has killed three birds here, the bluestocking, the courtly pose, and, it would seem, his own sodomous urges.[18] Although Con-

[14] Lawrence, *Lady Chatterley's Lover*, p. 250.

[15] *Ibid.*, pp. 250–51.

[16] *Ibid.*, pp. 280–81.

[17] *Ibid.*, p. 281.

[18] One remembers that Mellors' first love was his colonel. With the exception of *Sons and Lovers* and *The Rainbow*, every Lawrence novel includes some symbolically surrogate scene of pederasty: the rubdowns in *The White Peacock* and *Aaron's Rod*, the consecra-tion scene in *The Plumed Serpent*, the kiss denied in *Kangaroo* and the wrestling scene in *Women in Love*.

stance Chatterley is more credibly a woman than most Lawrentian heroines (there are even casual references to her breasts and she becomes pregnant with the hero's child), the erotic focus of the novel is constantly the magnificent Mellors, "remote," "wild animal," with some superior and "fluid male knowledge," the very personification of phallic divinity, described in caressing phrases which indicate Lawrence himself not only wishes to possess and partake of this power, but be possessed by it as well.

Lady Chatterley's Lover is a program for social as well as sexual redemption, yet the two are inextricable. Early in the novel, Tommy Dukes, one of the author's humbler mouthpieces, has deplored the fact that there are no "real" men and women left in the world, predicting the fall of civilization on this account. We are all doomed unless the one hope of redemption is understood immediately: "It's going down the bottomless pit, down the chasm. And believe me, the only bridge across the chasm will be the phallus!"[19] The metaphor is an unhappy one; in respect of penile length, the future hardly seems promising. Yet the program the novel offers against the industrial horrors it describes with such verve and compassion, is a simple matter: men should adopt a costume of tight red trousers and short white jackets and the working class should cease to desire money. In a single elaboration, Mellors suggests they busy themselves with folk art and country dances. This would be cruel, if it were not ridiculous. While a sexual revolution, in terms of a change in attitudes, and even in psychic structure, is undoubtedly essential to any radical social change, this is very far from being what Lawrence has in mind. His recipe is a mixture of Morris and Freud, which would do away with machinery and return industrial England to something like the middle ages. Primarily the thing is to be accomplished by a reversion to older sexual roles. Modern man is ineffectual, modern woman a lost creature (cause and effect are interchangeable in these two tragedies), and the world will only be put right when the male reassumes his mastery over the female in that total psychological and sensual domination which alone can offer her the "fulfillment" of her nature.

This is why the novel concentrates on rehabilitating Constance Chatterley through the phallic ministrations of the god Pan, incarnated in Mellors. In the novel's early chapters we are instructed that her only meaningful existence is sexual and has been distorted by education and the indecent liberties of the modern woman. Married to an impotent husband, Connie mopes through some hundred and thirty pages of unfulfilled femininity. Neither a wife nor a mother, yearning for a child, her "womb" contracting at certain stated intervals, she seeks her fleeting youth in unsatisfactory trips to the mirror, and endless visits to some hen pheasants, whose "pondering female blood" rebukes "the agony of her own female forlornness"[20] while affording her some solace by being "the only things in the world that warmed her

[19] Lawrence, Lady Chatterley's Lover, p. 82.
[20] Ibid., p. 127.

heart."[21] In the presence of these formidable creatures she "feels herself on the brink of fainting all the time,"[22] and the sight of a pheasant chick breaking its shell reduces her to hysterical weeping. In the best tradition of sentimental narrative we first see "a tear fall on her wrist," followed by the information that "she was crying blindly in all the anguish of her generation's forlornness . . . her heart was broken and nothing mattered any more."[23] Thereupon Mellors intervenes out of pity ("compassion flamed in his bowels for her") and he invites her into the hut for a bit of what she needs.

He is characteristically peremptory in administering it: "You lie there," he orders. She accedes with a "queer obedience"[24]—Lawrence never uses the word female in the novel without prefacing it with the adjectives "weird" or "queer:" this is presumably done to persuade the reader that woman is a dim prehistoric creature operating out of primeval impulse. Mellors concedes one kiss on the navel and then gets to business:

And he had to come into her at once, to enter the peace on earth of that soft, quiescent body. It was the moment of pure peace for him, the entry into the body of a woman. She lay still, in a kind of sleep, always in a kind of sleep. The activity, the orgasm was all his, all his; she could strive for herself no more.[25]

Of course Mellors is irreproachably competent and sexuality comes naturally to him. But the female, though she is pure nature to whom civilized thought or activity were a travesty, must somehow be taught. Constance has had the purpose of her existence ably demonstrated for her, but her conversion must take a bit longer:

Her tormented modern-woman's brain still had no rest. Was it real? And she knew, if she gave herself to the man, it was real. But if she kept herself for herself, it was nothing. She was old; millions of years old, she felt. And at last, she could bear the burden of herself no more. She was to be had for the taking. To be had for the taking.[26]

What she is to relinquish is self, ego, will, individuality—things woman had but recently developed—to Lawrence's profoundly shocked distaste. He conceived his mission to be their eradication. Critics are often misled to fancy that he recommends both sexes cease to be hard struggling little wills and egoists. Such is by no means the case. Mellors and other Lawrentian heroes incessantly exert their wills over women and the lesser men it is their mission

---

[21] *Ibid.*, p. 126.
[22] *Ibid.*, p. 127.
[23] *Ibid.*, p. 129.
[24] *Ibid.*, p. 130.
[25] *Ibid.*, p. 130.
[26] *Ibid.*, pp. 130–31.

to rule. It is unthinkable to Lawrence that males should ever cease to be domineering individualists. Only women must desist to be selves. Constance Chatterley was her husband's typist and assistant: she only ceases to serve this unworthy master when she becomes Mellors' disciple and farm wife. At no point is she given the personal autonomy of an occupation, and Lawrence would probably find the suggestion obscene. Even in the guise of a servant, Mellors has infinite assurance and a solid identity; Lady Chatterley appears an embarrassed impostor beside him.

Under the conventions of the eighteenth- and nineteenth-century novel, gentlemen entered into exploitative sexual liaisons with serving maids. Lawrence appears to have reversed this class relation by coupling the lady with her manservant, and his book is said to display an eloquent democracy by asserting that the class system is an "anachronism." Yet Mellors, a natural gentleman and therefore Lord Chatterley's superior, is just as great a snob as Connie, whose sermons mouth Lawrence's own disgust with the proletariat from whence he was saved by virtue of exceptional merit. Mellors also despises his own class. The lovers have not so much bridged class as transcended it into an aristocracy based presumably on sexual dynamism rather than on wealth or position. The very obnoxious Lord Chatterley represents the insufferable white male of the master caste, pretending to be worthy of the term "ruling class." Mellors and Lawrence are born outsiders to the privileged white man's general sway of empire, mine ownership, and the many other prerogatives of a male elite. But this has not persuaded them to overthrow so much as to envy, imitate, and covet. Rather in the manner of a black who is so corroded with white values that his grandest aspiration is sexual acceptance by the white woman, Lawrence's dark outsiders, whether Mexican Indian or Derbyshire collier, focus their ambition on the "white man's woman"—the Lady. Women of his own class and kind are beneath his contempt; the cruelest caricatures in the novel are Bertha Coutts and Mrs. Bolton, from whom Mellors withholds himself in rigid distaste—they are unbearably "common." Dissatisfaction with Clifford Chatterley's impersonation of the "ruling class" has by no means cured Lawrence of his allegiance to such a notion; to a large extent, his wish is only to install himself in this position. His plan is to begin by suborning the lady-class female, a feat which should give him courage to subordinate other males. Then he may enter upon his inheritance as natural aristocrat. Immersed in the ancient fantasy that he had the wrong father, he has converted his own father into a god; for in addition to being Lawrence himself and a desirable homosexual lover, Mellors is also supposed to be the surly and unpleasant miner of *Sons and Lovers,* Lawrence senior, rehabilitated and transformed into Pan. As it is improbable Mellors can acquire the artistic prestige or political power of other Lawrentian heroes, who are famous writers or generals, he is to be exalted by purely religious means. And although he is a social prophet, even this form of bettering his position is given little emphasis. Instead, he bases his entire claim upon John Thomas. The possession of a penis is itself an accomplishment of such high order (with the unimportant exception of a Venetian laborer who appears on only one page, no other male in the book gives any evidence of potency) that Mellors' divine nature is revealed and established through this organ alone.

When he began to compose his last novel, Lawrence was suffering in the final stages of tuberculosis. After *The Plumed Serpent* he admitted to being weary of the "leader cum follower" bit and had despaired of political success.[27] All other avenues of grandeur appeared to be closed. Public power was a delusion, only sexual power remained. If the last Lawrentian hero is to have but one apostle to glorify him, let it be a woman. Sexual politics is a surer thing than the public variety between males. For all the excursions into conventional political fascism that occupy the middle and late period of his work, it was the politics of sex which had always commanded Lawrence's attention most, both as the foundation and as a stairway to other types of self-aggrandizement. *Lady Chatterley's Lover* is as close as Lawrence could get to a love story. It is also something of a cry of defeat, perhaps even of remorse, in a man who had aspired rather higher, but had to settle for what he could get. As a handbook of sexual technique to accompany a mood of reaction in sexual politics, it was not altogether a failure.

II OEDIPAL

In a letter to Edward Garnett written in 1912, Lawrence provided his own description of *Sons and Lovers:*

A woman of character and refinement goes into the lower class, and has no satisfactions in her own life. She has had a passion for her husband, so the children are born of passion, and have heaps of vitality. But as her sons grow up, she selects them as lovers—first the eldest, then the second. These sons are *urged* into life by their reciprocal love of their mother—urged on and on. But when they come to manhood, they can't love, because their mother is the strongest power in their lives, and holds them . . . As soon as the young men come into contact with women there is a split. William gives his sex to a fribble, and his mother holds his soul. But the split kills him, because he doesn't know where he is. The next son gets a woman who fights for his soul—fights his mother. The son loves the mother—all the sons hate and are jealous of the

[27] D. H. Lawrence, *The Letters of D. H. Lawrence,* edited by Aldous Huxley (New York: Viking, 1932), p. 719. To Witter Bynner, March 13, 1928:

"I sniffed the red herring in your last letter a long time: then at last decided it's a live sprat. I mean about *The Plumed Serpent* and "the hero." On the whole, I think you're right. The hero is obsolete, and the leader of men is a back number . . . the leader-cum-follower relationship is a bore. And the new relationship will be some sort of tenderness, sensitive, between men and men and men and women, and not the one up, one down, lead on I follow, *ich dien* sort of business. . . . But still, in a way, one has to fight . . . I feel one still has to fight for the phallic reality . . ."

father. The battle goes on between the mother and the girl, with the son as object. The mother gradually proves the stronger, because of the tie of blood. The son decides to leave his soul in his mother's hands, and like his elder brother, go for passion. He gets passion. Then the split begins to tell again. But, almost unconsciously, the mother realizes what is the matter and begins to die. The son casts off his mistress, attends to his mother dying. He is left in the end naked of everything, with the drift toward death.[28]

In the same letter Lawrence assured Garnett this would be a great book. Both the précis and the boast have truth, but the latter has more of it. *Sons and Lovers* is a great novel because it has the ring of something written from deeply felt experience. The past remembered, it conveys more of Lawrence's own knowledge of life than anything else he wrote. His other novels appear somehow artificial beside it.

Paul Morel is of course Lawrence himself, treated with a self-regarding irony which is often adulation: "He was solitary and strong and his eyes had a beautiful light"[29]; "She saw him, slender and firm, as if the setting sun had given him to her. A deep pain took hold of her, and she knew she must love him"—and so forth.[30] In the précis, Lawrence (and his critics after him) have placed all the emphasis in this tale of the artist as an ambitious young man, upon the spectral role his mother plays in rendering him incapable of complete relations with women his own age—his sexual or emotional frigidity. That the book is a great tribute to his mother and a moving record of the strongest and most formative love of the author's life, is, of course, indisputable. For all their potential morbidity, the idyllic scenes of the son and mother's walking in the fields, their excited purchases of a flower or a plate and their visit to Lincoln cathedral, are splendid and moving, as only *Sons and Lovers,* among the whole of Lawrence's work, has the power to move a reader. But critics have also come to see Mrs. Morel as a devouring maternal vampire as well, smothering her son with affection past the years of his need of it, and Lawrence himself has encouraged this with the self-pitying defeatism of phrases such as "naked of everything," "with the drift toward death," and the final chapter heading "Derelict."[31]

The précis itself is so determinedly Freudian, after the fact as it were,[32] that it neglects the two other levels at which the novel operates—both the

[28] Lawrence, *The Letters of D. H. Lawrence,* pp. 78–79.

[29] Lawrence, *Sons and Lovers* (1913). (New York: Viking, 1958), p. 356.

[30] *Ibid.,* p. 166.

[31] One of the most influential essays on *Sons and Lovers* is Van Ghent's article, which describes Paul as the victim of scheming and possessive women. Dorothy Van Ghent, *The English Novel: Form and Function* (New York, Rinehart and Company, 1953).

[32] Lawrence rewrote the book at least twice. The final version, like the précis, was done after Frieda had "explained" Freudian theory to Lawrence.

superb naturalism of its descriptive power,[33] which make it probably still the greatest novel of proletarian life in English, but also the vitalist level beneath the Freudian diagram. And at this level Paul is never in any danger whatsoever. He is the perfection of self-sustaining ego. The women in the book exist in Paul's orbit and to cater to his needs: Clara to awaken him sexually, Miriam to worship his talent in the role of disciple and Mrs. Morel to provide always that enormous and expansive support, that dynamic motivation which can inspire the son of a coal miner to rise above the circumstances of his birth and become a great artist. The curious shift in sympathy between the presentation of Mrs. Morel from the early sections of the novel where she is a woman tied by poverty to a man she despises, "done out of her rights"[34] as a human being, compelled, despite her education and earlier aspirations, to accept the tedium of poverty and childbearing in cohabitation with a man for whom she no longer feels any sympathy and whose alcoholic brutality repells and enslaves her, to the possessive matron guarding her beloved son from maturity—is but the shift of Paul's self-centered understanding. While a boy, Paul hates his father and identifies with his mother; both are emotionally crushed and physically afraid before the paternal tyrant. The identification is real enough. When Walter Morel locks his pregnant wife out of the house in a boozy rage, it is Paul with whom she is pregnant, and the scene derives its conviction from the outraged prose of the precious burden himself. When Morel beats her and draws blood, it is Paul's snowy baby clothes that are stained with the sacrifice. As Mrs. Morel cowers, sheltering the infant, a bond is sealed that will last past other attachments.

The book even provides us with glimpses of the Oedipal situation at its most erotic: "I've never had a husband—not really . . . His mother gave him a long fervent kiss."[35] At this critical juncture Walter Morel walks in, justifiably annoyed, to mutter "at your mischief again." Thereupon the two rivals square off and nearly fight it out. But Walter is beaten anyway, and one foresees that Paul is a son who will have much to atone for: "The elderly man began to unlace his boots. He stumbled off to bed. His last fight was fought in that home."[36]

But the Oedipus complex is rather less a matter of the son's passion for the mother than his passion for attaining the level of power to which adult male

[33] The narrative of William's funeral, especially the moment when the coffin is brought into the house, the class honesty of the Christmas parties, and the daily life of Mrs. Morel, are, in my opinion, the most convincing and poignant prose Lawrence ever wrote.

[34] Lawrence, *Sons and Lovers*, p. 66.

[35] *Ibid.*, p. 213. "I was born hating my father: as ever I can remember, I shivered with horror when he touched me . . . This has been a kind of bond between me and my mother. We have loved each other, almost with a husband and wife love . . . We knew each other by instinct." From a letter to Rachel Annand Taylor, Dec. 3, 1910. From the *Collected Letters of D. H. Lawrence*, Ed. by Harry T. Moore (New York, Viking, 1962) Vol. I, pp. 69–70.

[36] *Ibid.*, p. 214.

status is supposed to entitle him. Sexual possession of adult woman may be the first, but is hardly the most impressive manifestation of that rank. Mrs. Morel (in only one short passage of the novel is she ever referred to by her own name—Gertrude Coppard) has had no independent existence and is utterly deprived of any avenue of achievement. Her method of continuing to seek some existence through a vicarious role in the success she urges on her sons, is, however regrettable, fairly understandable. The son, because of his class and its poverty, has perceived that the means to the power he seeks is not in following his father down to the pits, but in following his mother's behest and going to school, then to an office, and finally into art. The way out of his dilemma lies then in becoming, at first, like his mother rather than his father.

We are frequently told that Lawrence made restitution to his father and the men of his father's condition in creating Mellors and others like him. Such, alas, is not the case. Mellors is as one critic observes, "really a sort of gentleman in disguise,"[37] and if the portrait of the broken drunkard in *Sons and Lovers* is cruel, and it is undeniably, it is less cruel than converting this victim of industrial brutality into a blasé sexual superman who is too much of a snob to belong to either the working or the middle classes. The late Lawrentian hero is clearly Lawrence's own fantasy of the father he might have preferred. In the same way, Lady Chatterley is a smartened-up version of his mother herself. Like his own wife Frieda von Richthofen, she is a real lady, not that disappointed little woman of the mining village with chapped red hands who fears her clothes are too shabby to be seen in Lincoln cathedral. Yet Mrs. Morel is a brave, even a great woman, though waitresses in teahouses snub her when she can only order custard, too poor to pay for a full meal. *Sons and Lovers* gives us Lawrence's parents without the glamour with which his snobbishness later invested them. All the romances of his later fiction are a reworking of his parents' marriage, and of his own too, modeled on theirs, but a notable advance in social mobility. For Lawrence saw his course, saw it with a Calvinistic sense of election, as a vocation to rise and surpass his origins.

When Paul's ambition inspires his escape from identical circumstances it will be upon the necks of the women whom he has used, who have constituted his steppingstones up into the middle class. For Paul kills or discards the women who have been of use to him. Freud, another Oedipal son, and a specialist in such affairs, predicted that "he who is a favorite of the mother becomes a 'conqueror.'"[38] Paul is to be just that. By adolescence, he has grown pompous enough under the influence of maternal encouragement to

[37] Graham Hough, *The Dark Sun*, A Study of D. H. Lawrence (New York: Capricorn, 1956), p. 31.

[38] See Alfred Kazin, "Sons, Lovers and Mothers," in the *Viking Critical Edition of Sons and Lovers*, edited by Julian Moynahan (New York: Viking, 1968), p. 599.

proclaim himself full of a "divine discontent"[39] superior to any experience Mrs. Morel might understand. And when his mother has ceased to be of service, he quietly murders her. When she takes an unseasonably long time to die of cancer, he dilutes the milk she has been prescribed to drink: " 'I don't want her to eat . . . I wish she'd die' . . . And he would put some water with it so that it would not nourish her."[40] By a nice irony the son is murdering her who gave him life, so that he may have a bit more for himself: he who once was fed upon her milk now waters what he gives her to be rid of her. Motherhood, of the all-absorbing variety, is a dangerous vocation. When his first plan doesn't work, he tries morphine poisoning: "That evening he got all the morphia pills there were, and took them downstairs. Carefully, he crushed them to powder."[41] This too goes into the milk, and when it doesn't take hold at once, he considers stifling her with the bedclothes.

A young man who takes such liberties must be sustained by a powerful faith. Paul is upheld by several—the Nietzschean creed that the artist is beyond morality; another which he shares with his mother that he is an anointed child (at his birth she has the dream of Joseph and all the sheaves in the field bow to her paragon); and a faith in male supremacy which he has imbibed from his father and enlarged upon himself. Grown to man's estate, Paul is fervid in this piety, but Paul the child is very ambivalent. Despite the ritual observances of this cult which Paul witnessed on pay night[42] and in his father's feckless irresponsibility toward family obligations, he was as yet too young to see much in them beyond the injustices of those who hold rank over him as they did over his mother. Seeing that his father's drinking takes bread from his young mouth, he identifies with women and children and is at first unenthusiastic about masculine prerogative. When a crony comes to call for his father, Paul's vision makes us aware of the man's insolence: "Jerry entered unasked, and stood by the kitchen doorway . . . stood there coolly asserting the rights of men and husbands."[43]

Lawrence later became convinced that the miner's life and the curse of industrialism had reduced this sacred male authority to the oafishness of drinking and wife- and child-beating. Young Paul has been on the unpleasant end of this sort of power, and is acute enough to see that the real control lies in the bosses, the moneyed men at the top. Under industrialism, the male supremacy he yearns after is, in his eyes, vitiated by poverty and brutality, and it grants a noisy power over all too little. This is part of the unfortunately more ignoble side of Lawrence's lifelong hatred for industrial-

---

[39] Lawrence, *Sons and Lovers*, p. 388.

[40] *Ibid.*, p. 388, 393.

[41] *Ibid.*, p. 394.

[42] The miners divide their money out of the presence of women, who are thereby prevented from interfering on the behalf of household and child-rearing expenses. See pages 6, 17, 196, 200.

[43] Lawrence, *Sons and Lovers*, p. 20.

ism. In his middle period he was to concentrate his envy upon the capitalist middle classes, and in his last years he championed primitive societies, where he was reassured male supremacy was not merely a social phenomenon all too often attenuated by class differences, but a religious and total way of life.

The place of the female in such schemes is fairly clear, but in Lawrence's own time it was already becoming a great deal less so. As in *The Rainbow*, this novel's real contrasts are between the older women like his mother, who know their place, and the newer breed, like his mistresses, who fail to discern it. Mrs. Morel has her traditional vicarious joys: "Now she had two sons in the world. She could think of two places, great centers of industry, and feel she had put a man into each of them, that these men would work out what she wanted; they were derived from her, they were of her, and their works would also be hers."[44] When Paul wins a prize for a painting at Nottingham castle, she crows "Hurrah, my boy! I knew we should do it!"[45] For the rest, she is an eager devotee: "He was going to alter the face of the earth in some way which mattered. Wherever he went she felt her soul went with him. Whatever he felt her soul stood by him, ready, as it were, to hand him his tools."[46] She irons his collars with the rapture of a saint: "It was a joy to her to have him proud of his collars. There was no laundry. So she used to rub away at them with her little convex iron, to polish them till they shone from the sheer pressure of her arm."[47] Miriam's mother, Mrs. Leivers, also goes a way toward making a god of the young egoist: "She did him that great kindness of treating him almost with reverence."[48] Lawrence describes with aplomb how Miriam idolizes Paul; even stealing a thrush's nest, he is so superior that she catches her breath: "He was concentrated on the act. Seeing him so, she loved him; he seemed so simple and sufficient to himself. And she could not get to him."[49] Here we are treated not only to idealized self-portraiture but to a preview of the later godlike and indifferent Lawrentian male.

Paul is indeed enviable in his rocklike self-sufficiency, basking in the reverence of the bevy of women who surround him, all eager to serve and stroke—all disposable when their time comes. Meredith's *Egoist* is comic exposure; Lawrence's is heroic romance. When Paul first ventures forth into the larger male world, it is again the women who prepare the way for his victories. In a few days he is a favorite of all the "girls" at Jordan's Surgical Appliances. "The girls all liked to hear him talk. They often gathered in a little circle while he sat on a bench and held forth to them, laughing."[50] We

[44] *Ibid.*, p. 101.
[45] *Ibid.*, p. 253.
[46] *Ibid.*, p. 222.
[47] *Ibid.*, p. 55. (*Portnoy's Complaint* is a healthy antidote to this sort of thing.)
[48] *Ibid.*, p. 223.
[49] *Ibid.*, p. 223.
[50] *Ibid.*, p. 110.

are told that "they all liked him and he adored them."[51] But as Paul makes his way at the factory the adoration is plainly all on their side. They give him inordinately expensive oil colors for his birthday and he comes more and more to represent the boss, ordering silence, insisting on speed and, although in the time-honored manner of sexual capitalism, he is sleeping with one of his underlings, he insists on a rigid division between sex and business.[52]

The novel's center of conflict is said to lie in Paul's divided loyalty to mother and mistresses. In *Fantasia of the Unconscious,* one of two amateur essays in psychoanalysis in which Lawrence disputes with Freud, he is very explicit about the effect of doting motherhood:

> The son gets on swimmingly . . . He gleefully inherits his adolescence and the world at large, mother-supported, mother-loved. Everything comes to him in glamour, he feels he sees wondrous much, understands a whole heaven, mother-stimulated. Think of the power which a mature woman thus infuses into her boy. He flares up like a flame in oxygen.

"No wonder they say geniuses mostly have great mothers."[53] "They mostly have sad fates," he immediately adds with the same sort of self-pity one detects in the précis.[54] About its negative effects on sons, he is equally explicit, for there comes a time when the mother becomes an obstacle: "when faced with the actual fact of sex-necessity," the young man meets with his first difficulty:

> What is he actually to do with his sensual, sexual self? Bury it? Or make an effort with a stranger? For he is taught, even by his mother, that his manhood must not forego sex. Yet he is linked up in ideal love already, the best he will ever know . . . You will not easily get a man to believe that his carnal love for the woman he has made his wife is as high a love as that he felt for his mother or sister.[55]

51 *Ibid.* In Lawrence's day, as in ours, it is customary in business to refer to all low-status female employees, e.g., the vast majority of women workers, as "girls," whatever their age, and some of Paul's co-workers were twice or thrice his age. The custom bears a curious resemblance to that one whereby black men are addressed as "boy" right through senility.

52 Julian Moynahan, "Sons and Lovers; the Search for Form," in the Viking critical edition of *Sons and Lovers,* p. 569. Like much else in the novel, Paul's phenomenal success with the factory women appears to be an instance of wish fulfillment. Lawrence quit a similar factory job "after a few weeks because the factory girls jeered at him and one day removed his trousers in a dark corner of the storerooms."

53 D. H. Lawrence, *Fantasia of the Unconscious* (1922). (New York: Viking, 1960), p. 159.

54 *Ibid.*

55 *Ibid.,* pp. 169–70.

What such a skeptic will do instead is outlined fairly succinctly in Freud's, "The Most Prevalent Form of Degradation in Erotic Life," he will make a rigid separation of sex from sensibility, body from soul; he will also develop a rationale to help him through this trying schizophrenic experience. The Victorians employed the lily-rose dichotomy; Lawrence appeared to have invented something new in blaming it on his mother. But the lily/rose division, which Lawrence is so harsh in excoriating in Hardy,[56] is also a prominent feature of *Sons and Lovers*. Miriam is Paul's spiritual mistress, Clara his sexual one—the whole arrangement is carefully planned so that neither is strong enough to offset his mother's ultimate control. Yet the mother too is finally dispensable, not so that Paul may be free to find a complete relationship with either young woman, but simply because he wishes to be rid of the whole pack of his female supporters so that he may venture forth and inherit the great masculine world which awaits him. Therefore the last words of the book are directed, not at the self-sorrowing of Paul's "nuit blanche," his "dereliction" and "drift towards death," but at the lights of the city, the brave new world which awaits the conqueror.

When Paul wonders incoherently aloud—"I think there's something the matter with me that I can't . . . to give myself to them in marriage, I couldn't, . . . something in me shrinks from her like hell"—just as when Miriam reproaches him, "It has always been you fighting me off," the reader is expected to follow the précis and the critics and understand that this is all part of the young man's unfortunate Oedipal plight. Lawrence himself attempts to provide a better clue to Paul's type of fixation:

> . . . the nicest men he knew . . . were so sensitive to their women that they would go without them forever rather than do them a hurt. Being the sons of women whose husbands had blundered rather brutally through their feminine sanctities, they themselves were too diffident and shy. They could easier deny themselves than incur any reproach from a woman; for a woman was like their mother, and they were full of the sense of their mother . . .[57]

Yet all this well-intentioned puritanism dissolves before the reader's observation of the callowness with which Paul treats both Miriam and Clara. The first girl is, like Paul himself, a bright youngster restless within the narrow limitations of her class and anxious to escape it through the learning which has freed Paul. Less privileged than he, enjoying no support in a home where she is bullied by her brothers and taught the most lethal variety of Christian resignation by her mother, she retains some rebellious hope despite her far

---

[56] D. H. Lawrence, "A Study of Thomas Hardy," reprinted in *Phoenix*, the Posthumous Papers of D. H. Lawrence (New York: Viking, 1936).

[57] Lawrence, *Sons and Lovers*, p. 279.

more discouraging circumstances. Having no one else to turn to, she asks
Paul, whom she has worshiped as her senior and superior, to help her eke out
an education. The scenes of his condescension are some of the most remarkable instances of sexual sadism disguised as masculine pedagogy which
literature affords until Ionesco's memorable *Lesson*.

Paul has grandly offered to teach her French and mathematics. We are
told that Miriam's "eyes dilated. She mistrusted him as a teacher."[58] Well she
might, in view of what follows. Paul is explaining simple equations to her:

> "Do you see?" she looked up at him, her eyes wide with the half-laugh that
> comes of fear. "Don't you?" he cried . . . It made his blood boil to see her
> there, as it were, at his mercy, her mouth open, her eyes dilated with laughter
> that was afraid, apologetic, ashamed. Then Edgar came along with two buckets
> of milk.
> "Hello!" he said. "What are you doing?"
> "Algebra," replied Paul.
> "Algebra!" repeated Edgar curiously. Then he passed on with a laugh.[59]

Paul is roused by the mixture of tears and beauty; Miriam is beautiful to him
when she suffers and cringes: "She was ruddy and beautiful. Yet her soul
seemed to be intensely supplicating. The algebra-book she closed, shrinking,
knowing he was angered."[60]

As she is self-conscious and without confidence (Miriam's sense of inferiority is the key to her character), she cannot learn well: "Things came slowly
to her. And she held herself in a grip, seemed so utterly humble before the
lesson, it made his blood rouse."[61] Blood roused is, of course, the Lawrentian
formula for sexual excitement and an erection; the algebra lesson is something of a symbol for the couple's entire relationship. The sight of Miriam
suffering or humiliated (she later gives Paul her virginity in a delirium of
both emotions) is the very essence of her attractiveness to him, but his response is never without an element of hostility and sadism. His reaction here
is typical: "In spite of himself, his blood began to boil with her. It was
strange that no one else made him in such a fury. He flared against her.
Once he threw the pencil in her face. There was a silence. She turned her
face slightly aside."[62] Of course, Miriam is not angry, for one does not get
angry at God. "When he saw her eager, silent, as it were, blind face, he felt
he wanted to throw the pencil in it . . . and because of the intensity with
which she roused him, he sought her."[63] The reader is made uncomfortably
aware that "pencil" is etymologically, and perhaps even in the author's con-

[58] *Ibid.*, p. 155.
[59] *Ibid.*, p. 156.
[60] *Ibid.*
[61] *Ibid.*
[62] *Ibid.*, p. 157.
[63] *Ibid.*

scious mind as well, related to "penis" and both are instruments which have here become equated with literacy and punishment.

Miriam's aspirations are not respected; her failures are understood to be due to inferiority of talent. There are also a great many explanations provided the reader that she is frigid, and everything in her situation would seem to confirm this. Her mother's literal Victorian repugnance toward sexuality is the most plausible explanation, even without our knowledge of Miriam's debilitating insecurity. When she thinks of giving herself to Paul, she foresees beforehand that "he would be disappointed, he would find no satisfaction, and then he would go away." The chapter where Paul finally brings her to bed is entitled, "The Test on Miriam." Needless to say, she does not measure up, cannot pass his demanding examination. So her prediction comes true and Paul throws her away and takes up Clara. Yet the situation is somehow not this simple; even within the muddled explanations of Lawrence's text, it is several times made clear that Paul withholds himself quite as much as does Miriam.[64] Her famous frigidity appears to be his excuse. In the classic dilemma of the lily/rose choice Paul has been provided with an alibi which passes responsibility on to his mother.

While the first half of Sons and Lovers is perfectly realized, the second part is deeply flawed by Lawrence's overparticipation in Paul's endless scheming to disentangle himself from the persons who have helped him most. Lawrence is so ambivalent here that he is far from being clear, or perhaps even honest, and he offers us two contrary reasons for Paul's rejection of Miriam. One is that she will "put him in her pocket." And the other, totally contradictory, is the puzzling excuse that in their last interview, she failed him by not seizing upon him and claiming him as her mate and property.

It would seem that for reasons of his own, Lawrence has chosen to confuse the sensitive and intelligent young woman who was Jessie Chambers[65] with the tired old lily of another age's literary convention. The same discrepancy is noticeable in his portrait of Clara,[66] who is really two people, the rebellious feminist and political activist whom Paul accuses of penis envy and even man-hating, and who tempts him the more for being a harder conquest, and, at a later stage, the sensuous rose, who by the end of the novel is changed once again—now beyond recognition—into a "loose woman" whom Paul nonchalantly disposes of when he has exhausted her sexual utility. Returning her to her husband, Paul even finds it convenient to enter into one of Lawrence's Blutbruderschaft bonds with Baxter Dawes, arranging an assignation in the country where Clara, meek as a sheep, is delivered over to the man she hated

---

[64] Ibid., p. 284.

[65] See Jessie Chambers, D. H. Lawrence, A Personal Record, by "E.T." 2nd revised edition (New York: Barnes and Noble, 1965).

[66] Actually, Clara is nobody at all. Tradition has it that Lawrence's initiatrix was a Mrs. Dax who simply took pity on the lad: "She took him upstairs one afternoon because she thought he needed it." Julian Moynahan, op. cit., p. 569.

and left years before. The text makes it clear that Dawes had beat and deceived his wife. Yet, with a consummate emotional manipulation, Paul manages to impose his own version of her marriage on Clara, finally bringing her to say that its failure was her fault. Paul, formerly her pupil in sexuality, now imagines he has relieved Clara of what he smugly describes as the "femme incomprise" quality which had driven her to the errors of feminism. We are given to understand that through the sexual instruction of this novice, Clara was granted feminine "fulfillment." Paul is now pleased to make a gift of Clara to her former owner fancying, that as the latter has degenerated through illness and poverty (Paul has had Dawes fired) he ought to be glad of salvaging such a brotherly castoff.

Even before it provides Paul with sexual gratification, the affair offers considerable opportunities for the pleasure of bullying:

> "Here, I say, you seem to forget I'm your boss. It just occurs to me."
> "And what does that mean?" she asked coolly.
> "It means I've got a right to boss you."
> "Is there anything you want to complain about?"
> "Oh, I say, you needn't be nasty," he said angrily.
> "I don't know what you want," she said, continuing her task.
> "I want you to treat me nicely and respectfully."
> "Call you 'sir,' perhaps?" she asked quietly.
> "Yes, call me 'sir.' I should love it."[67]

The sexual therapy Clara affords to Paul is meant to be a balm to his virulent Oedipal syndrome, but is even more obviously a salve to his ego. Only in the fleeting moments of the orgasm can the egoist escape his egotism, but Lawrence's account fails to confirm this:

> She knew how stark and alone he was, and she felt it was great that he came to her, and she took him simply because his need was bigger than either her or him, and her soul was still within her. She did this for him in his need, even if he left her, for she loved him.[68]

This is a dazzling example of how men think women ought to think, but the book is full of them. By relieving his "needs" with a woman he rigidly confines to a "stranger in the dark" category, Paul has touched the great Lawrentian sexual mystery and discovered "the cry of the peewit" and the "wheel of the stars."[69]

Having achieved this transcendence through Clara's offices, he finds it convenient to dismiss her. While watching her swim far out at sea during a holiday they have taken together, Paul converts himself into a species of god

[67] Lawrence, *Sons and Lovers*, p. 266.
[68] *Ibid.*, p. 353.
[69] *Ibid.*

in the universe before whom Clara dwindles to the proportions of microscopic life:

> "Look how little she is!" he said to himself. "She's lost like a grain of sand in the
> beach—just a concentrated speck blown along, a tiny white foam-bubble, almost
> nothing among the morning . . . She represents something, like a bubble of
> foam represents the sea. But what is *she*. It's not her I care for."[70]

This is an impressive demonstration of how subject diminishes object and
having, through his sexual magnetism, reduced this once formidable, independent woman to the level of quivering passion, Paul cannot help but find
her a nuisance. What if their affair were discovered at work? We are told
that "She invariably waited for him at dinner-time for him to embrace her
before she went."[71] Paul reacts to such attentions like the bumptious young
clerk he has become:

> "Surely there's a time for everything. . . . I don't want anything to do with
> love when I'm at work. Work's work—"
> "And what is love?" she asked. "Has it to have special hours?"
> "Yes, out of work hours." . . .
> "Is it only to exist in spare time?"
> "That's all, and not always then."[72]

It is Paul's habit to lecture his mistresses that, as women, they are incapable
of the sort of wholehearted attention to task or achievement that is the
province of the male and the cause of his superiority.

> "I suppose work can be everything to a man . . . But a woman only works
> with a part of herself. The real and vital part is covered up."[73]

The idea seems to be that the female's lower nature, here gently phrased
as her "true nature," is incapable of objective activity and finds its only
satisfactions in human relationship where she may be of service to men and
to children. Men in later Lawrence novels, men such as Aaron, constantly
ridicule trivial female efforts at art or ideas.

Given such views, it is not very surprising that Paul should make such
excellent use of women, Clara included, and when they have outlived their
usefulness to him, discard them. As Clara is a creature of the double standard
of morality, the woman as rose or sensuality, he invokes the double standard
to get rid of her, declaring sententiously that "after all, she was a married

[70] *Ibid.*, pp. 357–58.
[71] *Ibid.*, p. 355.
[72] *Ibid.*
[73] *Ibid.*, p. 416.

woman, and she had no right even to what he gave her.
takes himself to a fustian view of the indissolubility of m.
that she is completely Dawes's property, and with a sense of ι
returns her, no worse, indeed much the better, for wear.

Having rid himself of the two young women, time-consuming se\
who may have posed some other threat as well, possibly one of inteι
competition, Paul is free to make moan over his mother's corpse, give Mι
a final brushoff, and turn his face to the city. The elaborate descriptions \
his suicidal state, however much they may spring from a deep, though much
earlier, sorrow over the loss of his mother, appear rather tacked on in the
book itself, as do certain of the Freudian explanations of his coldness as
being due to his mother's baneful influence. Paul is actually in brilliant condition when the novel ends, having extracted every conceivable service from
his women, now neatly disposed of, so that he may go on to grander adventures. Even here, the force of his mother, the endless spring of Lawrence's
sacred font, will support him: "She was the only thing that held him up,
himself amid all this. And she was gone, intermingled herself."[75] But Paul
has managed to devour all of mother that he needs; the meal will last a
lifetime. And the great adventure of his success will henceforward be his
own. "Turning sharply, he walked toward the city's gold phosphorescence.
His fists were shut, his mouth set fast."[76] Paul may now dismiss his
mother's shade with confidence; all she had to offer is with him still.

III TRANSITIONAL

The Rainbow and *Women in Love* mark a transition in Lawrence's sexual
affinity from mother to mistress, a shift that, when accomplished, finally produces powerful feelings of hostility and a negative attitude toward women
of his own generation, who come more and more to threaten him. Lawrence's
peculiar solution seems to marry and smother them (curiously related gestures
here) and then to fare "beyond women" to homosexual attachments, forming
sexual-political alliances with other males.

The Rainbow is the first of Lawrence's important *fictions*. The most beautiful and lyric of his novels, it is somehow also the most atypical. The novel
is not only a new departure from the naturalism of *Sons and Lovers* into an
original species of psychic narrative which is Lawrence's major technical
achievement; it also contains the key to his later sexual attitudes; here is the
explanation, and perhaps even the root of his final absorption in "phallic consciousness" and his conversion to a doctrinaire male-supremacist ethic. A classic in its genre, the book is the story of three generations. It celebrates the
pastoral life in terms of fertility—never the phallic fertility of the later period,
but the power of the womb. Every event, whether it be falling in love or

[74] *Ibid.,* p. 352.
[75] *Ibid.,* p. 420.
[76] *Ibid.*

ining maturity, is described in terms of fertility, gestation, parturition, and th. In *The Rainbow,* women appear to give birth by parthenogenesis. he power of the womb seems to loom in Lawrence's consciousness, as so ,verwhelming a force, so really terrifying in its self-sufficiency, that it is not hard to see how he found it necessary to reject it in his later novels where there is a complete *volte face* and the male alone is the life force. The idea of "womb envy" might strike one as pure invention, Karen Horney's malicious answer to Freud's doctrine of penis envy. But in Lawrence, we seem to have hit upon an authentic case of this disorder. Accordingly, the early sections of *The Rainbow* show a curious absorption in the myth of the eternal feminine, the earth mother, and constitute a veritable hymn to the feminine mystique.

The heroines of the first two sections of the book, Lydia and Anna Brangwen, mother and daughter, appear to be grand and towering matriarchs. The heroine of the third section, Ursula Brangwen is not, like her predecessors, rooted in the past and the traditional life of the farm wife and mother, but is instead Lawrence's own contemporary, probably of his own age and generation. He has no trouble portraying the traditional women, Lydia and Anna, and is willing to concede them enormous power. Like one of Ruskin's "Queens," the wife of the past was the arbiter of ethical norms: "The man placed in her hands their own conscience, they said to her, 'Be my conscience-keeper, be the angel at the doorway guarding my outgoing and my incoming.' And the woman fulfilled her trust."[77] In these period portraits the women are, in Lawrence's opinion, "dominant," a state of affairs he acquiesces in and even seems to approve; Lydia conquers Tom Brangwen with her inscrutable distant inattention, Anna spoils Will Brangwen's life and her own by becoming a breeder extraordinaire, tying him to the burden of nine children until both his hope and his talent have withered. Yet Lawrence seems to applaud because these earlier persons still lived in a simple primitive "blood knowledge" which contrasts very favorably to the present; the three generations are a devolution from the golden age to the leaden industrial morass of today.

Oddly enough, neither of these two Victorian or late Victorian women are in any way sexually inhibited. Lydia instructs her husband in the art of love, and both Anna and Lydia initiate sexual activity on their own terms and timing—a thing the later Lawrence deplored. In *The Rainbow,* the sexuality of the past is idealized into a healthy freedom it quite certainly was not, while women are given an altogether superior authority they did not possess and it were better they did not exercise in any case.

So entirely does the womb dominate the book that it becomes a symbol, in the arch of Lincoln cathedral, or in the moon, of the spiritual and the supernatural. The womb is so portentous and enviable an organ that the men

[77] D. H. Lawrence, *The Rainbow* (1915). (New York: Viking, 1967), p. 13.

in the book make some effort to participate in the marvel. When Ursula offends Anton Skrebensky, the reader is informed that the youth felt a "dead weight in his womb."[78] When Lydia gives birth, her husband endures the agony of the couvade. During her delivery, Tom is "with his wife in labor, the child was being brought forth out of their one flesh . . . the rent was not in his body, but it was of his body . . . the quiver ran through to him."[79] So entirely do women predominate in the book that all Oedipal relationships of parent and child are a series of father-daughter romances. All masculine attempts to play lord and master and fall back upon patriarchal prerogative, the very stuff of Lawrence's later work, are subjected to ridicule in The Rainbow. Lawrence says it is "shameful and petty" of Will Brangwen to try to recapture "the old position of master of the house." Anna simply calls him a fool. Will himself knows better, is made aware of "what a fool he was," and is "flayed by the knowledge." Lawrence is still capable of separating masculine authority from masculinity, and makes Will himself recognize that his father-in-law "had been a man without arrogating any authority."[80] Patriarchal prejudices are overturned again when young Ursula takes a look at the iconography of religious art and finds the concept of God the Father a nauseating presumption: "The figure of the Most High bored her and roused her resentment. Was this the culmination and the meaning of it all, this draped null figure . . . such a banality for God."[81]

In The Rainbow, Lawrence dealt with the new woman head on in the character of Ursula. Ursula Brangwen is to fulfill the ambitions of her ancestors—for from the first Brangwens, the men had looked back to the fields, the fertile earth, and the women looked out toward learning and the cities. Ursula's mother Anna had been "straining her eyes to something beyond" and "from her Pisgah mount" she could glimpse "a faint gleaming horizon, a long way off,"[82] a promised land she never arrived in, falling into a mindless slattern instead. But Ursula does reach the promised land of the Brangwen women; transcending their confining traditional world she goes out to work and then to the university.

For all his overawed reverence before mother figures—in fact because of it—Lawrence finds the new woman in Ursula fairly hard to bear. It is only when he gets to Ursula that Lawrence begins to lose rapport with his characters and distort the glowing sympathy which so distinguishes the first half of the novel. Ursula is too close to him; she is a rival. Finally, one understands she is a threat and the author's ambivalence toward her is a fascinated combination of sympathy and dislike—even fear. There is a lavish, almost infantile, desire on Lawrence's part to forgo everything before the matriarchal

[78] Ibid., p. 325.
[79] Ibid., p. 70.
[80] Ibid., p. 170.
[81] Ibid., p. 277.
[82] Ibid., p. 192.

figures of the past. He appears overpowered by their fecundity, serenity, their magical correspondence with the earth and the moon. But when a creature equipped with all this redoubtable mana enters into what he prefers here to imagine is the male's own lesser sphere of intellect and social action, he seems caught in a rush of terror. If Ursula has all the same mysterious powers of the female which gave Lydia and Anna such stature, the control of life and the ability to give birth which he finds so impressive, as well as the capacity to live in "the man's world" (as Lawrence calls the chapter in which she earns her living) to succeed and achieve in it, then, Lawrence seems to feel, there is very little left anywhere for the male. He is bettered in his own field and beaten in hers. Most of Lawrence's sexual politics appears to spring from this version of the emancipation of women; many of the preoccupations of his later work are a response to it.

It is important to know that he began in the midst of the feminist movement, and that he began on the defensive. There is a current of bitter animosity which runs throughout Lawrence's description of Ursula's invasion of the "mysteriously man's world," the "world of daily work and duty and existence as a working member of the community" for, really, he keeps reminding the reader, it is neither natural nor necessary that she so transgress. After all, she is, in the vulgar expression, sitting on a fortune and is never without the "price of her ransom—her femaleness." There is a cynical envy in Lawrence's attitude that this is unfair competition—"what she could not get because she was a human being, fellow to the rest of mankind, she would get because she was a female."[83] As she can always sell herself, earning her own living is merely an indulgence, an indulgence made at his expense. Lawrence had made the same difficult climb through the horrors of slum school teaching to the university, and his narrative of Ursula's suffering along the way is an odd mixture of sympathy—when he lapses into autobiography and identification with the character—mingled with acrid resentment, at the thought of one of her sex achieving this much. The splendid maternal old women posed no threat, no competition or rivalry. Ursula as the new woman clearly does. When she rebels at staying on as an upper servant to her parents and fights for a life of her own, Lawrence is torn between trying to respect her position and siding with her elders. He goes to every length to make the lot of the independent woman repellent: Ursula's painful struggle is almost an object lesson. Finally he sides with the opposition: "Let her find out what it's like. She'll soon have enough."[84]

Arrived at her teaching post, a penitentiary which deserves to rank with any of the children's hells which Dickens portrays, Ursula is immediately made aware that working women are sad figures, somewhat like charladies. Even worse, they cease to be attractive to men, who hold their sex as a point

[83] *Ibid.*, p. 333.
[84] *Ibid.*, p. 359.

against them. Oddly enough, they are by nature, as it were, unfitted even for schoolteaching. Lawrence's own theory of education is in general agreement with that of Mr. Harby, Ursula's principal, a martinet who stultifies his pupils while ruling them through sheer will power, brutalizing them so in the process that they exhibit the same fine contempt as he for teachers who employ any more gentle or humane method of instruction.

We are told that much of Harby's nastiness derives from doing work beneath him, mere woman's work, yet we are also assured that the imposition of will which Lawrence assures us is necessary to run classes is above a mere woman's ability. It is demonstrated over and over, that should Ursula succeed, she will lose her "femininity," as did poor Violet Harby, a cadaverous spinster, or destroy the finer part of herself, as she does when she strikes a pupil. Men, it seems, are crude enough to survive and sustain no such damage. Lawrence can only sympathize provisionally, stipulating that the moment Ursula "proves herself" (he will allow her to survive but not to succeed), she must consent to withdraw from his territory on the instant she has satisfied her perverse little desire to try the water.

The driving force behind Ursula's efforts, is, of course, the feminist movement, at its height during the years of *The Rainbow,* and a great force in Lawrence's time, one which he was compelled to deal with. His method here is half· derogatory, half vaporous:

> For her, as for Maggie, the liberty of women, meant something real and deep. She felt that somewhere, in something, she was not free. And she wanted to be. She was in revolt. For once she was free she could get somewhere. Ah, the wonderful real somewhere . . . that she felt deep deep inside her. In coming out and earning her own living she had made a strong, cruel move towards freeing herself. But having more freedom, she only became more profoundly aware of the big want . . . there remained always the want she could put no name to.[85]

Attentive readers will of course know that the big want is a husband, provided in the sequel in the form of Birkin, who is no less a personage than Lawrence himself. But lest we fail to apprehend, we are instructed that "Her fundamental organic knowledge had as yet to take form and rise in utterance," which means that Ursula is unfulfilled femininity. To make matters worse, she had enjoyed a brief homosexual affair with a fellow spirit, Winifred Inger, which illustrates even more clearly the dangers of feminism. Lawrence has recourse here to adjectives such as "corruption" and entitles the chapter where it occurs as "Shame."[86] Ursula earns her freedom and

---

[85] *Ibid.,* pp. 406–7.
[86] *Ibid.,* p. 412. To make his contempt perfectly clear, Lawrence marries Winifred off to an industrialist, declaring that both are mere idolators of machinery; the match is so unlikely it can serve only as punishment. Another feminist friend is left teaching school "in a heavy brooding sadness."

goes on to the university, but Lawrence ridicules her ambitions: "she would take her degree, and she would-ah, she would perhaps be a big woman and lead a movement."[87] Big women are dangerous items unless they be the maternal figures of the past, and so the fate reserved for Ursula is a very different one—Lawrence causes her to fail her examinations, go down in defeat without her coveted B.A. and end her life a contented housewife.

She has one last task, however, and that is to "murder" (jilt, actually, but Lawrence always speaks of the event in terms of homicide to manly pride) Anton Skrebensky, her first lover, whom Lawrence is anxious to execute on several grounds: a class enemy—an aristocrat, colonialist, and snob, Anton is suspect on even more hateful grounds for his robotlike conventionality and even for his blundering faith in democracy and progress, two ideas Lawrence particularly despises. And furthermore, Anton must be sacrificed as an object lesson in how monstrous the new woman can be. Ursula furnishes graphic proof of this first in treating Anton as an instrument or sex object rather in the manner in which men are accustomed to treat women, then in refusing to be his marital appendage, and finally, in "castrating" him by a series of extremely tenuous and hazy bouts of magic. Her vehicle of destruction is moonlight, for Lawrence is addicted to the notion of the moon as a female symbol, once beneficent, but lately malefic and a considerable public danger. Having polished off the unfortunate young man, Ursula beholds the vision of the rainbow and the promise of a new world, for the old is drowned in the flood. She alone survives, the new woman awaiting the new man. Ursula has lived in erotic expectation of a mating between the "Sons of God and the daughters of men."[88] Anton was no son of God, only an empty shell in the midst of the deluge.

Women in Love presents us with the new man arrived in time to give Ursula her comeuppance and demote her back to wifely subjection. It is important to understand how pressing a mission Lawrence conceived this to be, for he came himself upon the errand. The novel, as stated in the preface, is autobiographical;[89] its hero, Rupert Birkin, is Lawrence himself. Much of the description of Birkin is rendered through the eyes of Ursula who is in love with him, so that expressions of admiration abound: his brows have a "curious hidden richness . . . rich fine exquisite curves, the powerful beauty of life itself, a sense of richness and liberty,"[90] we are also asked to see in him "the rare quality of an utterly desirable man"[91] which is rather a lot to say of oneself. Birkin is a prophet, the Son of God at last.

[87] *Ibid.,* p. 407.

[88] *Ibid.,* p. 493 and elsewhere.

[89] "The novel pretends only to be a record of the writer's own desires, aspirations, struggles, in a word, a record of the profoundest experiences in the self," Lawrence, *Women in Love* (1920). (New York: Viking, 1960), Preface, p. viii.

[90] *Ibid.,* p. 37.

[91] *Ibid.,* p. 122.

Women in Love is the first of Lawrence's books addressed directly to sexual politics. It resumes the campaign against the modern woman, represented here by Hermione and Gudrun. Ursula shall be saved by becoming Birkin's wife and echo. The other two women are not only damned but the enemy. The portrait of Hermione is probably the most savage personal attack Lawrence ever wrote. She is the new woman as intellectual, a creature to whom both Birkin and the narrator react with almost hysterical hatred, bombarding her with this sort of description: "macabre, something repulsive," "a terrible void, a lack, a deficiency of being within."[92]

Ursula is to join Birkin, and the two will be the new couple which according to the official pronouncements and rules which Birkin lays down shall be a perfect equilibrium between polarities, "a pure balance of two single beings:—as the stars balance each other."[93] This type of surface assertion is betrayed over and over by the obvious contradictions between preachment and practice. One of the book's most dynamic scenes is Gerald Critch's abuse of a fine Arab mare whom he forces to a railroad crossing, asserting his will in a fashion he fancies is masculine and Birkin finds agreeable, cutting the animal badly in the process. The incident takes on symbolic force as Birkin sermonizes on it, comparing the mare mastered to the woman mastered: "It's the last, perhaps highest love-impulse to resign your will to the higher being . . . And woman is the same as horses: two wills act in opposition inside her. With one will, she wants to subject herself utterly. With the other she wants to bolt, and pitch her rider to perdition."[94] Gerald is an unimaginative fellow who tries to control women with the tired old nostrums of money and physical force. Birkin is a far more sophisticated type who employs psychological warfare.

On the day when Ursula comes to take tea with him and he proposes an alliance with her on the stellar plan, his trump card, and the symbolic explanation of his intentions, turns out to be the object lesson put forward by his cat. Having begun by informing Ursula he will not love her, as he is interested in going beyond love to "something much more impersonal and harder,"[95] he goes on to state his terms: "I've seen plenty of women, I'm sick of seeing them. I want a woman I don't see[96] . . . I don't want your good looks, and I don't want your womanly feelings, and I don't want your

---

[92] *Ibid.,* pp. 10–11. The model of this caricature is Lady Ottoline Morrell, a good friend and Lawrence's mistress for a time. There is a merciless quality in his picture of the affair; the lady is made to grovel at his feet. Although there is certainly an element of class revenge here, the final motivation for the waspishness with which the portrait is done remains always elusive. Lawrence corresponded with Lady Ottoline while writing the book to tell her how well it was going and how good it was.

[93] *Ibid.,* p. 139.

[94] *Ibid.,* pp. 132–33.

[95] *Ibid.,* p. 136.

[96] *Ibid.,* p. 138.

thoughts nor opinions nor your ideas."[97] The "new" relationship, while posing as an affirmation of the primal unconscious sexual being, to adopt Lawrence's jargon, is in effect a denial of personality in the woman. Birkin is full of opinions and ideas and holds forth all through the book while Ursula puts docile leading questions to him. Though she requires some effort to tame, she comes to follow him in apostolic faith. The separate spheres live on in a smart new verbiage, but the real "terms of the contract," a far harsher matter, are supplied by Mino the cat, in his exercise of authority over his inferior mate:

> He, going stately on his slim legs, walked after her, then suddenly, for pure excess, he gave her a light cuff with his paw on the side of her face. She ran off a few steps, like a blown leaf along the ground, then crouched unobtrusively, in submissive, wild patience. The Mino pretended to take no notice of her. He blinked his eyes superbly at the landscape. In a moment she drew herself together and moved softly, a fleecy brown-grey shadow, a few paces forward. She began to quicken her pace, in a moment she would be gone like a dream, when the young grey lord sprang before her and gave her a light handsome cuff. She subsisted at once submissively . . . In a lovely springing leap, like a wind, the Mino was upon her, and had boxed her twice, very definitely, with a white, delicate fist. She sank and slid back, unquestioningly. He walked after her and cuffed her once or twice leisurely.[98]

Ursula draws the parallel, in case we missed it: "It's just like Gerald Critch with his horse—a lust for bullying—a real Wille zur Macht."[99] Birkin defends such conduct and brings home the moral: "With the Mino it is a desire to bring this female cat into pure stable equilibrium . . . It's the old Adam . . . Adam kept Eve in the indestructible paradise when he kept her single with himself, like a star in its orbit."[100] And of course a star in Birkin's orbit is exactly what Ursula's position is to be; Birkin will play at the Son of God, Ursula revolving quietly at his side.

According to a formula which Lawrence was to favor increasingly, Ursula is presented as an incomplete creature, half-asleep in the tedium of her spinster schoolmistress life. Birkin will awake her according to a Lawrentian convention whereby the male gives birth to the female. What is particularly surprising about all this is how very much Lawrentian marriage resembles a plunge into another sleep, even a death. Ursula resigns her position, allowing Birkin to dictate her letter of resignation. We are told over and over that the marriage is to bring her a new life, yet nothing materializes, and she becomes more and more her husband's creature, accepting his instruction even in her own field of botany, which he entered at their first meeting by taking over

[97] *Ibid.*, p. 139.
[98] *Ibid.*, p. 140.
[99] *Ibid.*, p. 142.
[100] *Ibid.*

her classroom, and goes on to master so that he may correct her on the species of a daisy. Lawrence tells us Ursula "was not herself—she was not anything. She was something that is going to be soon-soon-very soon . . . It was all like a sleep."[101] What she does "become" is only a nonentity, utterly incorporated into Birkin, his single follower, proselytizing and sloganeering "if only the world were he! If only he could call a world into being."[102]

Sexually, she comes to be the epitome of passivity: "she wanted to submit, she wanted to know. What would he do to her? . . . She could not be herself . . . she abandoned herself to him."[103] Hereafter, marriage represents not only the taming of the woman, but her extinction.

In Lawrence's short story, "The Fox," this process of anaesthetizing the bride is even more clearly outlined. Henry, the masculine spirit and fox of the title, eliminates his lesbian competition, Jill Banford, murdering her with will power, materially assisted by a tree he fells on her head. He then sits down to await the rigor mortis effect he intends to have on his bride, whose drugged loss of self shall give him that total control over her he requires so that he may transcend her into the male world of achievement.

> No, he wouldn't let her exert her love toward him. No, she had to be passive, to acquiesce, and to be submerged under the surface of love. She had to be like the seaweeds she saw as she peered down from the boat, swaying forever delicately under-water . . . never, never rising and looking forth above the water while they lived. Never. Never looking forth above the water while they lived. Never looking forth above the water until they died, only then washing, corpses, upon the surface . . . it was always under-water, always under-water. And she, being a woman, must be like that. . . . He did not want her to watch any more, to see any more, to understand any more. He wanted to veil her woman's spirit, as Orientals veil the woman's face. He wanted her to commit herself to him, and to put her independent spirit to sleep . . . He wanted to make her submit, yield, blindly pass away out of all her strenuous consciousness. He wanted to take away her consciousness, and make her just his woman. Just his woman. . . . And then he would have her, and he would have his own life at last . . . Then he would have all his own life as a young man and a male.[104]

Women in Love is commonly accepted as the book of Birkin-Lawrence's marriage, but it is actually the story of Birkin's unrequited love for Gerald, the real erotic center in the novel. Ursula (or Frieda) is worn past interest by now—hence the need for another couple, Gerald and Gudrun, to liven things up.[105] The plot is triangular. And since triangles are actually diagrams

101 *Ibid.*, pp. 377–78.
102 *Ibid.*, p. 382.
103 *Ibid.*, pp. 402 and 426.
104 D. H. Lawrence, "The Fox" (1923), *Four Short Novels of D. H. Lawrence* (New York: Viking, 1965), pp. 175–76, 178, and 179.
105 Gudrun and Gerald are Katherine Mansfield and John Middleton Murry. Murry's letters to Frieda after Lawrence's death shed some light on the friendship: it appears

of power in sexual politics, it might be worthwhile to recall what classic triangle situations involved before we embark on the innovation which Lawrence introduced. The courtly triangle featured a lady at its apex, the prize between two rivals, her husband and legal owner, her lover and true possessor. Despite the dangers she endured from the former, she was still given the choice of accepting the latter. The Continental triangle, which is the staple of French and Italian bourgeois literature, has a male at its apex, who represents the ego or center of interest in such fiction as the wife or lady never did.[106] At the bases, vying for his favors, are wife and mistress. His position is one of very considerable power, both social and economic, and is the perfect expression of the double standard.

Lawrence invented a new triangular situation, again with ego, or the masculine consciousness, generally Lawrence himself, at the center or apex. At one corner stands the woman, hereafter generally the wife, soliciting his rather patronizing attention; at the other is a male whom ego courts. This triangle affords even greater power leverage than earlier ones, for the ego at the apex has the choice not of two women, but of a man or a woman, the former often a glamorous or important public personage. The female who is granted ego's favors must now struggle with a male for what is left of the hero's time and interest. There is a strong new double standard built into this, for the wife is allowed no other distractions, either hetero- or homosexual, while the male ego is permitted to enjoy himself in both these directions. While deploring marital infidelity, Lawrence did not consider love between males adulterous.

The old rivalry of wife and mistress might have been transformed under feminist pressures into an entente, and Lawrence has a bitter dread of female alliances of any kind. The most feasible explanation of his hatred for female homosexuality or even friendship seems to be political distrust. Again this is a double standard, for male homosexuality and friendship are one of the great interests of Lawrence's life. Females are pitted against each other, but outside the triangle, where their energies are spent in fighting each other over the hero. Hermione, Birkin's former mistress, and Ursula, his new one, are prevented from forming any dangerous female alliance by what Lawrence rather hopefully assures us is the natural repugnance of women toward each other.

Males, however, are encouraged to build alliances, and Lawrence's introduction seems to direct itself at this: "Every man who is acutely alive must

Murry was in love with Frieda, Lawrence with Murry, and D. H. possibly willing to "make a deal" as it were with his wife's lover, so that he might enjoy Murry too. See Frieda Lawrence, *The Memoirs and Correspondence,* edited by E. W. Tedlock (New York: Knopf, 1964), pp. 340, 360.

[106] The center of consciousness, when there was one, as in the lyric, was nearly always the lover.

wrestle with his own soul . . . Men must speak to one another."[107] As an aid to such communication Lawrence relied upon the cult of Blutbruderschaft. Throughout the book, Birkin courts Gerald, the ineffably beautiful white male of the master class, the epitome of all Birkin and Lawrence are said to hate—the industrialist, the mine owner. Gerald declines the proposition consistently and resists all overtures. This rejection is conveyed to the reader as the death wish, an icy inability to love. Appropriately, Gerald is frozen to death in the Alps and the book is given a Spenglerian ideological superstructure to justify this rather spiteful revenge. Gudrun is made the villain of the piece and Gerald's death is blamed on her, despite Lawrence's equally strong desire to have Gerald execute her as the hateful New Woman and his rival for the love of the blond beast. The fair master-class type of manhood is by no means repellent to Lawrence; it is even highly seductive, and some of his denunciation of it appears to stem really from the rancor of unrequited love. One line rings out in the whole book—Birkin's frantic cry at Gerald's coffin, after a chilly necrophiliac scene with the frozen corpse—"He should have loved me . . . I offered him."[108]

Birkin had in fact wanted Gerald's virginity, if one may refer to such a quality in a rich Lothario to whom sex had been an exploitative hunt carried out against lower-class women, Minnette for example, with whom his rank and money assure him an easy dominance over a slavish prey. We are given to understand that Gerald's death is really the fault of his refusal to enter into a mystical relationship with Birkin before trafficking with dangerous Gudrun. But Gerald isn't having any: "I know you believe something like that. Only I can't feel it, you see."[109]

In revenge for this refusal, the narrator heaps insult upon insult upon Gerald. The odd thing is that Birkin, who is a projection of Lawrence himself, should have desired one who represented so completely everything the narrator, who is also Lawrence, despises. Gerald is really just a better-looking version of Anton, the mechanical man of the system, that embodiment of industrial mentality who is executed in *The Rainbow* with the author's wholehearted approval.

The chapter entitled "Gladiatorial," a wrestling match between Birkin and Gerald, carried out in the luxurious Critch family library, both contestants being naked, is as close as Lawrence cared to come to sodomy. Held back by his own puritan reluctance in such matters he feels safer in flirting, since to his discretion, there is a strong danger of being branded effeminate. As a result, there is always something prurient about the homosexual strain in Lawrence. Though his prose can be as loving a caress to the male body as any of Genet's, it is never as honest. Moreover, the projected masculine alliance, the Blutbruderschaft, is so plainly motivated by the rather sordid political pur-

[107] Lawrence, *Women in Love*, Preface, p. viii.
[108] *Ibid.*, p. 471.
[109] *Ibid.*, p. 345.

pose of clubbing together against women, that this too gives it a perverse rather than a healthy and disinterested character, either as sexuality or as friendship.

If Hermione is the female enemy as intellectual rival, Gudrun is the enemy as rival in love. She is a sculptor, Lawrence's only portrait of the woman as artist. Birkin, a school inspector whom we are to accept as an oracle in such matters, predicts she will fail, and her work is dismissed as "little carvings," "little things," hateful subtleties, which are a "sign of weakness."[110] When Gudrun sees Gerald swimming in his ancestral lake and envies his wealth, freedom, mobility, and masculine privilege, we are given to believe that she is a case of penis envy with whom Ursula compares very favorably by accepting their poverty, pointless employment, and close supervision within their father's home. Ursula escapes all this by accepting Birkin as her husband and leader. For while she is merely an underpaid schoolteacher, Birkin is a superintendent, owns three houses, has a private income, servants, and an automobile. Gudrun, unmarried, continues to practice her art, a free lance and "Glücksritter." Much is done to persuade the reader that she has made the wrong decision.

As a rebuke to the dangerous personal and artistic aspirations Gudrun represents as the new woman, Lawrence introduces a portentous symbol—the African statuette of a woman in labor, reduced to the level of a suffering animal, her face "transfixed and rudimentary." She is said to represent the "extreme of physical sensation, beyond the limits of mental consciousness" and Birkin lectures on her meaning, proving that in the "savage woman" one sees the perfection of female function. Having evaded her primeval female fate, Gudrun is, of course, an instance of contemporary disease. Although she loyally defends Birkin when he is ridiculed for playing Christ, one knows she will never become a disciple. She is therefore to be regarded as the destructive female force, the evil face of the moon. Birkin protects himself from such magic by stoning the image of the moon in a pond and thereby breaking Ursula's sinister female mana. Gerald, who had never made adequate preparations, dies in the snow, the moon just rising as he freezes, the moon which represents Gudrun's malevolence. The Birkin-Ursula couple is the new pair of the new world, Gerald and Gudrun are said to be the old and corrupt, although it is very obvious that Gudrun is the New Woman.

At the end of the book, Birkin is a faintly ridiculous figure, complaining to his wife of how his lover has slighted him. "You've got me," she naïvely reminds him. "Aren't I enough for you?" his model wife asks him, declaring that he is surely enough for her. "No," he said, "you are enough for me as far as a woman is concerned. But I wanted a man friend . . . I wanted eternal union with a man too: another kind of love."[111] In fact, Birkin had harbored ambitions for a ménage à trois. The next novels will explore this theme

---

[110] Ibid., pp. 32–33.
[111] Ibid., pp. 472–73.

of masculine alliance, which grows increasingly political in character, excluding women and revenging itself upon them for the difficulty the Lawrentian male has in subordinating them, turning against their demands for recognition, their claims to personality, and launching out further and further into the jealously guarded masculine prerogatives of formal politics, art, and social action. Lawrence has turned his back on love. Henceforward, it is power he craves: power first over women and then over lesser men.

IV FRATERNAL

Aaron's Rod is a watershed, the book where Lawrence formally renounced love for power, a decision he held to until *Lady Chatterley's Lover*. Yet, as Lawrence sees the two, they are not very different things—a point of view much in line with our premise that in patriarchal culture the relationship between the sexes is essentially political in nature. In Lawrence's mind, love had become the knack of dominating another person—power means much the same thing. Lawrence first defined power as the ability to dominate a woman; later he applied the idea to other political situations, extending the notion of *Herrschaft* to inferior males mastered by a superior male. Thralls to such an elite, lesser men must be as females—subjects. Of course this is the political structure of patriarchy itself, and Lawrence's fine new talk of dark gods, his jargon about spontaneous subordination, is simply a very old form of bullying, which in other contexts we are accustomed to call fascistic. This domination of lesser male by greater has homosexual overtones of a particularly unpleasant kind. For when a man with Lawrence's notion of the sexes starts off in search of more impressive arenas of power, arenas such as those afforded by formal politics, he must necessarily begin to see the men he seeks to dominate in erotic terms, since for him the very nature of *Herrschaft* is erotic.

This novel is a long, hesitating romance between two versions of Lawrence himself: Aaron Sisson, the artist as escaped proletarian, turning his back on his class, and Rawdon Lilly, also a refugee among the middle classes, but now a successful writer and social prophet. One is struck by the narcissistic character of homosexuality in Lawrence. Descriptions of the two heroes are supplied by admiring women who see them as demigods—Aaron, powerful, handsome, even "glamorous," Lilly slight and nervous as was Lawrence himself, yet wise and dark as an Eastern idol.

Aaron's life is a bad dream of what Lawrence's might have been, had he failed to escape in time. Tied to a working-class wife and three hated children (significantly girls), Aaron calmly abandons them on Christmas Eve. In striking contrast to Hardy, England's first major working-class novelist, who was deeply concerned with the salvation of the class in the salvation of the individual, Lawrence is firmly rooted in what we like to think of as a nineteenth-century idea—the notion of individual salvation. The exceptional man will escape and rise above his class, the class itself may remain just exactly where it was. Lawrence insists on having the best of both worlds: he wished to be better than the working class, educated beyond their level, freed of their intimacy, yet at the same time he insisted on being better than the middle and upper class. This is why so much is made of the animal energy and warmth, the earthiness of the working class, making Lawrence and his surrogates so much the superior of those bourgeoise with whom they associate. And it is because Lawrence believes in the rise of the talented individual above his class that he so hates democracy, since it seeks to raise the entire class together; his own preference, the promotion of the isolated case is feudal, or Calvinistic.

Aaron's acceptance by the novel's flimsy smart people of the middle classes is instantaneous and utterly fantastic. On his first night of freedom, he gets drunk and stumbles into a party in the house of his employer. Although very recognizably a miner, he is immediately asked to share a bed with his proprietor's son. Noblewomen fall in love with him; however sullenly and insolently he behaves; however tedious he may be with his put-on dialect, everyone recognizes the natural aristocrat in him, and in his tuxedo he can pass for a gent as well as the rest.

Aaron is the victim of a peculiar malady which one has encountered earlier in Lawrence's work, but is hereafter to become a prominent motif—male frigidity. Just as in the female, this can be a tactical weapon in sexual politics; in her case to resist domination, in his, to acquire it.[112] Aaron turns cold to punish women for a subservience he regards as insufficient. This strategy really began with Paul Morel, Birkin had bouts of it; with Aaron it is a way of life.

While a married man, Aaron's symptoms are an exhausting "withholding of himself," "something in him that would not give in."[113] His wife confirms the diagnosis: "He kept himself back, always kept himself back, couldn't give himself."[114] Coolly assuming that sexuality is not only the most important, but even the only significant experience of which woman is capable, Aaron takes great pleasure in depriving her of it: "All his mad loving was only an effort. Afterwards, he was as devilishly unyielded as ever."[115] Of course all

---

[112] While masculine frigidity is a purely political affair in Lawrence, the general incidence of this misfortune in women is only occasionally political in the strict sense. The repudiation of sexuality, and with it, their own sexual pleasure, which one encounters in women, living then or now, under "Victorian" conditions, is probably partially explicable on the grounds that it is the only resistance permitted them in a culture where they are economic and social dependents. Frigidity (which still continues today in high incidence) is likely to be due to an entire complex of causes: the rigid conditioning of women to fear and abhor sexuality, the frequently humiliating and exploitative character in which it is presented to them, and often perhaps, an unconscious rage asserting itself at their position in patriarchal culture.

[113] D. H. Lawrence, *Aaron's Rod* (1922). (New York: Viking, 1961), p. 18.

[114] *Ibid.*, p. 39.

[115] *Ibid.*, p. 155.

this is "agony and horror"[116] for a woman to endure ". . . in those supreme and sacred times which for her were the whole culmination of life and being, the ecstasy of unspeakable passional conjunction, he was not really hers. He was withheld."[117] We are told that this deliberate difficultness only makes him more precious to woman since "her sacred sex passion" is "the most sacred of all things for a woman."[118] Aaron has become the male analogue of what folk culture calls a "cock-teaser."

He has dinner in London with a young woman. The conversation goes like this:

Josephine: "Won't you kiss me?" . . .
Aaron: "Nay," he said.
Josephine: "Why not?"
Aaron: "I don't want to."[119]

Aaron later arrives at Lilly's bachelor flat, drunk again and infected with influenza, brought on, we are told, because he has permitted himself to be seduced by the same lonely young woman: "I should have been all right if I hadn't given in to her," "I felt it go, inside of me, the minute I gave into her. It's perhaps killed me," he whines.[120] Aaron has reached the point of utter frustration in his relations with women: they continue to refuse him the abject subordination he imagines is his desert as a male. After his latest humiliating experience, which has brought him to the edge of the grave, he resolves to be accessible only to relations with other males. Aaron and Lilly then commence to live in a peculiar domestic bliss, such as Simone de Beauvoir describes in another context as one of the "comedies of love," a wish-fulfilling scene whose scenario dictates that Aaron act as a surly adolescent in need of mothering reassurance.

It is characteristic that when Lawrence can portray a male in bed, with another male in attendance, one of the two must be respectably ill, and nursed by the other. Accordingly, Aaron wastes away with a crudely symbolic stoppage of the bowels which only Lilly can cure. He does so in a remarkable manner, and by means of a rubdown, which is the novel's surrogate for sodomy. It follows another Lawrentian pattern in being a couvade as well:

"I'm going to rub you with oil" . . . "I'm going to rub you as mothers do their babies whose bowels don't work" . . . Quickly he uncovered the blond lower body of his patient, and began to rub the abdomen with oil, using a slow, rhythmic, circulating motion, a sort of massage. For a long time he rubbed finely and steadily, then went over the whole of the lower body, mindless, as if in a

116 *Ibid.*, p. 156.
117 *Ibid.*
118 *Ibid.*
119 *Ibid.*, p. 66.
120 *Ibid.*, p. 84.

sort of incantation. He rubbed every speck of the man's lower body—the abdomen, the buttocks, the thighs and knees, down to his feet, rubbed it all warm and glowing, with camphorated oil, every bit of it, chaffing the toes swiftly, till he was almost exhausted. Then Aaron was covered up again, and Lilly sat down in fatigue to look at his patient. He saw a change. The spark had come back into the sick eyes, and the faint trace of a smile, faintly luminous, into the face. Aaron was regaining himself.[121]

Newborn, the patient and the man who gave him life take up residence. Lilly washes and darns Aaron's socks: "He preferred that no outsider should see him doing these things. Yet he preferred to do them himself."[122] Lilly also cooks, while Aaron sits lordly and idle: "It was not in his nature to concern himself with domestic matters—and Lilly did it best alone."[123] What they have most in common is a fervid hatred of women, and it is around this that all their conversation revolves. Temporarily separated from his own wife, Lilly bewails her intractability:

> She does nothing really but resist me: my authority, or my influence, or just *me*. At the bottom of her heart, she just blindly and persistently opposes me . . . She thinks I want her to submit to me. So I do, in a measure natural to our two selves. Somewhere, she ought to submit to me. But they all prefer to kick against the pricks . . .[124]

Lilly has an obsessive power urge and laments that women, and male disciples too, balk him: "Why can't they submit to a bit of healthy individual authority."[125] Together, Aaron and Lilly indulge in long misogynistic diatribes: they regard children as rivals or burdens who have given women an unnatural power and importance: "The whole world wags for the sake of the children—and their sacred mothers." "Sacred children, and sacred motherhood, I'm absolutely fed stiff by it," Lilly complains.[126] "When a woman's got her children, by God, she's a bitch in the manger," Aaron chimes in. "They look on a man as if he was nothing but an instrument to get and rear children. If I have anything to do with a woman, she thinks it's because you want to get children by her. And I'm damned if it is. I want my pleasure or nothing." "Be damned and be blasted to women and all their importance," cries Aaron, in a paroxysm of chauvinist sentiment, giving the war cry.[127]

Both deplore the terrible ascendancy of modern woman—their version of the sexual revolution. Male solidarity has crumbled before it. In both men's

121 *Ibid.*, pp. 90–91.
122 *Ibid.*, p. 93.
123 *Ibid.*, p. 100.
124 *Ibid.*, p. 91.
125 *Ibid.*
126 *Ibid.*, p. 94.
127 *Ibid.*, p. 95.

devotion to the cause their greatest grief is that males fail to support them—
"the rotten whiners, they're all grovelling before a baby's napkin and a
woman's petticoat."[128] Since the problem of the age is that male status (manhood) is slipping and the masculine side of life neglected—"Men can't move
an inch unless they grovel humbly at the end of the journey"; "The man's
spirit has gone out of the world"; they see the reassertion of male prerogative
as a sacred trust.[129]

The project to reduce woman from her new quasi-equality is discussed
further in a conference the two hold with other males high up in a Florentine tower. Lawrence titles the chapter "Nel Paradiso." From the moment of
his entrance into the city, Aaron rejoices that it is still a masculine stronghold,
built to celebrate male beauty: "It was a town of men," whose piazzas were
packed with men, but all, all men."[130] "Here men had been at their in-
tensest, most naked pitch."[131] He admires the David and even the hideous
Bandinelli as expressions of masculinity, but acting from prejudice rather
than taste, despises the superb Perseus, because he felt the figure looked "female . . . female and rather insignificant; graceful and rather vulgar."[132]
During the council in the tower, the problem of counterrevolutionary strategy
is handled by an overt homosexual named Argyle, together with Lilly, Aaron,
and an Italian major of the mandarin variety. The last warrior leads the discussion by asserting that the real problem lies in the increase in sexual freedom granted to women:

> "It used to be that desire started in the man, and the woman answered. It used
> to be so for a long time in Italy. For this reason the women were kept away
> from the men. For this reason our Catholic religion tried to keep the young
> girls in convents and innocent before marriage. So that with their minds they
> should not know, and should not start this terrible thing, this woman's desire
> over a man, beforehand."[133]

All agree that the relation between the sexes is a matter of rule or be ruled;
all agree that the recent liberation of sexual desire in women, and particularly
the new right of sexual initiative, place women in a position to rule. Like all
who support an ancien régime, the acquisition of any right on the part of the
oppressed is interpreted as a mortal infringement of their own natural
priorities. Argyle speaks for the rest:

> "My dear boy, the balance lies in that, that when one goes up, the other goes
> down. One acts, the other takes. It is the only way in love. And the women

[128] *Ibid.*
[129] *Ibid.*
[130] *Ibid.*, p. 208.
[131] *Ibid.*
[132] *Ibid.*
[133] *Ibid.*, p. 236.

are nowadays the active party. Oh yes, not a shadow of a doubt about it. They take the initiative, and the man plays up. Nice manly proceedings what!"[134]

So far none of them has found a solution to this pressing need to subjugate the female, and all admit that in the interim they find a *pis aller* in homosexuality, frigidity, etc. The Italian's *pis aller* is little girls and prostitutes. But he admits that even this is no adequate alternative; prostitutes submit out of greed, which is not submission at all, and even girl children are "modern women." "Terrible thing, the modern woman,"[135] Argyle sums up. Lilly had been playing the devil's advocate throughout by recommending his official doctrine of "two fighting eagles" and the stellar polarity which was Birkin's formula, but at the end, he "admits" that the others are right, and one realizes his disagreement might well have been no more than an ingenious tactic to spur on his comrades.

There is really only one modern woman in the book—the Marchesa. But the real villain is said to be Lottie, Aaron's wife. She is anything but a feminist or new woman; she is simply poor, without hope, abandoned with three children. While Aaron's fantastic adventures bring him the admiration of ladies whom he is pleased to reject, his real enemy is the working-class wife. Lawrence's picture of her has that surprising disdain and malice that is typical of his treatment of women from the class he escaped. When Aaron decides that to stay in the cramped and sordid world of the poor would only mean to drown, he cheerfully leaves Lottie and his little girls to sink or swim, embarking on the more exciting career of following patronage and wandering about Europe. He explains that deserting them was merely "a natural event,"[136] which needn't even be excused with a reason. "So far man had yielded the mastery to women. Now he was fighting for it back again. And too late, for the woman would never yield."[137] Aaron is never ashamed to admit that he first beat his wife, then experimented with being systematically unfaithful, and finally resorted to utterly ignoring her presence. Lottie is said to deserve all this because of her detestable "female will"—a terrible magical force which is "flat and inflexible as a sheet of iron," yet "cunning as a snake that could sing treacherous songs."[138] Among its other crimes it has enabled Lottie to retain enough dignity to oppose her inhuman treatment and even insist Aaron admit he has treated her unfairly.

Aaron is characteristically arbitrary in that he regards it as perfectly natural she should be stuck with the children—that is woman's fate—but at the same time he hates her for being a mother. In his conversations with Lilly, the book is turned into a tract against Momism. The female is damned either way.

---

[134] *Ibid.*, p. 237.
[135] *Ibid.*, p. 239.
[136] *Ibid.*, p. 141.
[137] *Ibid.*, p. 123.
[138] *Ibid.*, p. 154.

Since all refuse her autonomy or a personal destiny, Lottie can pursue no hope of her own and is even unequipped to earn a living when left to provide the support of three small children. By a wonderful piece of luck, Aaron has a small annuity inherited from his mother. It will last Lottie for a short time; after that she is on her own. It is ironic that the Oedipal mother has come to this in Lawrence's work, and the book's savage rejection of motherhood is surprising; Lottie's maternity is the only existence permitted her, yet by a perfection of injustice it is also her offense. Here, as everywhere else in the novel, Lawrence has shot past the counterrevolutionary mark of renovating and romanticizing masculine dominance and feminine "fulfillment" in subservience, into a male "backlash" of rather alarming animus.

Lawrence has also begun to arrogate the life-giving force entirely to the male: there is Lilly's feat of giving birth to Aaron, and in the symbolism of Aaron's "rod," or penis, his flute (Aaron is a flautist), a curious attempt is made to attribute to this instrument the unique power of self-generating life. On its better days Aaron's flute is said to put forth blossoms, a sort of flowering penis of art, which has rivaled and surpassed the creative function Lawrence first revered in the womb, and has now come to hate and ridicule in women, that he may expropriate it for men.

Despite all its promise, the dedicated alliance between Aaron and Lilly is of short duration. Or rather, their first attempt soon causes them to flounder in an air of charged animosity. Despite their noble mission, cohabitation has brought out between them the same bone of contention they had sought to escape by swearing off women—the dispute over mastery. Just as it is inconceivable that either should debase his manhood before the other, it is just as difficult for two such power-hungry individuals to live without one attempting to subordinate the other. As a result, they squabble in a manner that cannot help but remind us how inescapably they are bound to the heterosexual caste system. When Aaron contradicts him, Lilly's rebuke is "You talk to me like a woman, Aaron."[139] Aaron is naturally outraged at such an egregious insult and protests: a quarrel follows. Perhaps what appalls him most of all is that Lilly, who does the housework, is playing the master: "most irritating of all was the little man's unconscious assumption of priority."[140] They vacillate between homosexual attraction and the antagonism of suppressed sexual desire. "I very much wish there might be something that held us together,"[141] Lilly proposes ruefully, but after a fortnight, the time they have spent together weighs on both of them as a "small eternity."[142]

Strangely enough, it is the very cause which brought them together which drives them apart—male supremacy. For in their bond of masculine solidarity there is also a clause which demands, via the ineluctable logic of Lawrence's

[139] Ibid., p. 100.
[140] Ibid.
[141] Ibid., p. 103.
[142] Ibid., p. 101.

psychology of power, that should their relations assume an erotic character, one must be subjected to the other. As they are both males, both upper caste, this seems impossible. "Have you any right to despise another man?" Aaron protests. "When did it go by rights? . . . You answer me like a woman, Aaron,"[143] Lilly coolly replies, sketching out what will be Aaron's final role and implying that Aaron behaves like a born inferior querulous for attention, fairness, and recognition. All Lilly's efforts to put him in his place are met with Aaron's outraged protest that as a male he can't and won't have it. Only later, when he admits Lilly's superiority, does the stalemate admit a solution. But as the first try is not a success, it leaves Aaron free to bump about the Continent, and be picked up and patronized by two posh homosexuals who like his looks. Aaron likes their money and doesn't mind the admiration.

While off on his own, Aaron's sexual frigidity toward women grows apace until it takes over his whole character and becomes a form of paranoia. Robbed in the street by some Italian soldiers, he blames his misfortune on the woman he has just left. Her conversation, and the party where he met her, have put him in a rare good mood which he claims has made him vulnerable:

". . . if I hadn't got worked up with the Marchesa, and then rushed all kindled through the streets without reserve, it would never have happened. I gave myself away, and there was someone ready to snatch what I gave . . . I should have been on my guard . . . always, always, with God and the devil both, I should be on my guard."[144]

The same rigidity of response poisons his affair with the Marchesa, first with frightened repulsion—"He knew he was sinking towards her"[145]—and later by burgeoning into the crassest egoism—"suddenly and newly flushed with his own male super-power, he was going to have his reward. The woman was his reward."[146] This knowledge is followed by a man's-magazine fantasy wherein he recovers from what appears to be impotence as well as frigidity, boasting he has

something to glory in, something overweening, the powerful male passion, arrogant, royal, Jove's thunderbolt. Aaron's black rod of power, blossoming again with red Florentine lilies and fierce thorns. He moved about in the splendour of his own male lightening, invested in the thunder of the male passion-power. He had got it back, the male godliness, the male godhead.[147]

He hardly lives up to the event itself, for the lady insists on "withstanding him" and his "male super-power" and seems to be "throwing cold water over

143 *Ibid.*, pp. 103–4.
144 *Ibid.*, p. 226.
145 *Ibid.*, p. 243.
146 *Ibid.*, p. 250.
147 *Ibid.*

his phoenix newly risen from the ashes of its nest in flames."[148] Again, Aaron has failed to meet with the servile surrender he demands, and decides henceforth to devote himself to Lilly. He goes back to his hotel delighted the affair has ended, rejoicing to be "alone in his own cold bed, alone, thank God."[149] Lilly finds him there in the last chapter, and the novel's resolution lies in Aaron's acceptance both of Lilly's superior masculinity and his "prophetic message."

This doctrine itself is a combination of political fascism and male supremacy whose emotional correspondence the book establishes with a clarity that excels any other analysis we have come across. Argyle begins by ridiculing a socialist demonstration as "a lot of young louts," and goes on to preach that "the only hope of salvation for the world lies in the reinstitution of slavery,"[150] something everyone will soon realize "when they've had a bit more of this democratic washer-woman business,"[151] he predicts, bringing down the bird of class with the stone of sexual caste. The attack on democracy, like the attack on Christianity—"I think Love and your Christ detestable"—and socialism, derive from the same need in Lawrence—a need to debunk any system with egalitarian potentialities, sexual or social. He realizes these are interrelated ideas: "Because after all, all human society through the course of ages only enacts spasmodically, but still inevitably, the logical development of a given idea."[152] It follows naturally then, Lilly argues, that socialism sprang from the same impulse as Christianity, and Christ, like Marx, or the feminists, was an ugly leveler.

> "The idea and the ideal has for me gone dead—dead as carrion . . . The ideal of love, the ideal that it is better to give than to receive, the ideal of liberty, the ideal of the brotherhood of man, the ideal of the sanctity of human life . . . has all got the modern bee-disease and gone putrid, stinking."[153]

Then Lilly unburdens himself of the novel's concept of government:

> "You've got to have a sort of slavery again. People are not *men*: they are insects and instruments and their destiny is slavery . . . ultimately they will be brought to agree—after sufficient extermination—and then they elect for themselves a proper and healthy and energetic slavery . . . I mean a real committal of the life-issue of inferior beings to the responsibility of a superior being."[154]

---

[148] *Ibid.*, p. 252.
[149] *Ibid.*, p. 256. It is true, however, that he has one last crack at the Marchesa a few days later, but as he explains, he does this only out of "compliance."
[150] *Ibid.*, p. 269.
[151] *Ibid.*, p. 270.
[152] *Ibid.*, p. 271.
[153] *Ibid.*
[154] *Ibid.*, p. 272.

Lilly's racism and anti-Semitism[155] glow in a glandular rhetoric reminiscent
of Carlyle at his worst. His baroque plan is that having achieved democratic
recognition, the poor will elect themselves back into slavery, an idea no more
fatuous than his hope that women will do the same. The euphemism employed here refers to a "voluntary self gift of the inferiors."[156]

Seeing the sage one more time, Aaron is sufficiently impressed that as the
lesson continues, he decides that

> If he had to give into something: if he really had to give in, and it seemed he
> had; then he would rather give in to the devilish little Lilly than to the beastly
> people of the world. If he had to give in, then it should be to no woman, and to
> no social institution. No!—if he had to yield his willful independence, and give
> himself, then he would rather give himself to the little, individual *man* than to
> any of the rest. For to tell the truth, in the man was something incompre-
> hensible, which had dominion over him, if he chose to allow it.[157]

The master begins his final pitch: "There are only two great dynamic
urges in life: love and power."[158] After he has persuaded Aaron to admit
that women and love are "all my eye," "lost illusions," and given a little cap-
sule history of the modern period and the early work of D. H. Lawrence,
Lilly explains that in regard to the "two great life-urges," love and power, we
have erred in "trying to work ourselves . . . from the love urge . . . hating
the power urge and repressing it. And now I find we've got to accept the
very thing we've hated."[159] Lawrence is hereby repudiating his early work's
concern with love and personal relationships, dedicating himself to the power
urge that dominates his late fiction.

Fortunately, for everyone consumed with the will to power, Lilly explains,
there is another who wishes to be overpowered—"willing and urged to be
overpowered." These number at least half the populace:

> Now in the urge of power . . . the woman must submit, but deeply, deeply
> submit. Not to any foolish fixed authority, not to any foolish and arbitrary will.
> But to something deep, deeper. To the soul in its dark motion of power and

[155] Here is a sample of Lilly's racial attitudes:

"I can't do with folk who teem by the billion, like the Chinese and Japs and Orientals
altogether. Only vermin teem by the billion. Higher types breed slower . . . Not like
the flea-bitten Asiatic. Even niggers are better than Asiatics, though they are wallow-
ers." (p. 92) He disposes of Jews in short order: "A jealous God! Could any race be
anything but despicable with such an antecedent?" (p. 105).
[156] *Aaron's Rod*, p. 272.
[157] *Ibid.*, p. 280.
[158] *Ibid.*, p. 284.
[159] *Ibid.*, p. 288.

pride. We must reverse the poles. The woman must submit—but deeply, deeply and richly . . . A deep unfathomable free submission.[160]

This last term would be still more absurd if Lilly had not made it clear that the older patriarchy used the now faintly embarrassing methods of open slavery and thereby failed to coerce a sufficiently resigned subservience in women: one who is forced is not really abject, only compelled. It is Lawrence's mission not only to revoke the minimal freedom women had so far achieved under the sexual revolution, but to reinstate a more complete patriarchy. He is even ambitious enough to seek to improve upon the old oppression, especially its psychological techniques, formerly far from perfect.

Aaron has been such a failure in his own branch of the campaign that he is skeptical. And as the scene is also full of erotic overtones, he is also being coy. "You'll never get it," he demurs. "Yes you will, if you abandon the love idea and the love motive,"[161] Lilly insists, predicting how, from now until *Lady Chatterley's Lover*, Lawrence's fiction will do just this, replacing romantic interest with sexual bullying and a quietly sadistic coercion. And, Lilly continues, when half of humanity is overpowered—"women won't be able to resist"—it will be no very difficult problem to extend this force to lesser males as well:

> Women and men too. Yield to the deep power soul in the individual man and obey him implicitly . . . And men must submit to the greater soul in a man, for their guidance; and women must submit to the positive power-soul in man for their being.[162]

In the subtle difference in phrasing, we have a quick draft of the brave new world—every female abject before every male; most males abject before the super-males.

Then, in the novel's big moment, Lilly turns to Aaron with a proposal, not even of love, for Lilly disdains to love, but of mastery, a curious evasion of physical homosexuality, but in Lawrence's terms, no less erotic:

> You, Aaron, you too have the need to submit. You too have the need livingly to yield to a more heroic soul, to give yourself . . . It's a life-submission. And you know it. But you kick against the pricks. And perhaps you'd rather die than yield . . .
> There was a long pause. Then Aaron looked up into Lilly's face. It was dark and remote-seeming. It was like a Byzantine eikon at the moment.[163]

"And whom shall I submit to?" Aaron asks with pretended naïveté. "Your

[160] *Ibid.*, pp. 288–89.
[161] *Ibid.*, p. 289.
[162] *Ibid.*
[163] *Ibid.*, pp. 289–90.

soul will tell you,"[164] replies the heroic soul right before him, bathos which Lawrence appears to see as darkly mysterious, and critics frequently excuse as inconclusive.

Kangaroo pursues the same theme somewhat further, but its hero, Richard Lovat Somers, is so transparently David Herbert Lawrence, the famous writer, visiting Australia with his wife, that a measure of circumspection is necessary, and thankfully, a bit of humor, to prevent the novel's still more pretentious fantasies from being utterly ridiculous. They follow the same patterns as those of *Aaron's Rod*—a rejection of woman and the pursuit of power in erotic relations with other men which might lead to larger-scale power relations over masses of men and the glory of being proclaimed a great leader and hero, a dictator in fact—a patriarch in the patriarchy.

Here it is perhaps not out of place to review Lawrence's progress, via his well-documented Oedipus complex, to this eminence. In *Women in Love* he graduated from being a son to a lover, while switching his allegiance from heterosexual to homosexual alliance, having already eluded the matronly eternal feminine Freud claimed to be the lifetime object of men who loved their mothers. Lawrence had achieved adult male status in patriarchal society in becoming a husband, if not a father. He had in fact, inherited the social privileges which are one facet of Oedipal concern. It may even be that the sexual content of the Oedipus complex has been exaggerated, the sexual-political ignored, and it is the latter certainly which commands our attention with regard to Lawrence's later work. By the time of *Aaron's Rod*, the Lawrentian protagonist has tired of being a husband, ceased to be a lover of women altogether, and has elected instead to follow power and those who possess it—males. In *Kangaroo*, Lawrence plods on as a bored husband, still childless, still yearning after the power of patriarchal kingship which both Laius and Oedipus enjoyed. Both mother and wife are tedious to him now; he desires what he takes to be his by right—a man's power in a man's world. An artist, a bohemian and a wanderer, Lawrence found it hard to come by these things. Married to a stubborn woman, who though she did devote her life to his service, steadily refused to relinquish her dignity to him, he must have found the tasks of mastery exhausting. While none of the events outlined above are unusual—they are the ordinary progress of masculine experience in our culture—Lawrence is remarkable in having felt them so keenly and recorded them so memorably. He has stressed what concerned him, but in recording his rejection of the father figure in *Sons and Lovers*, and in his passionate early identification with the mother, he appears to have left many readers unprepared for his later rejection of the mother figure, followed by a greedy arrogance for masculine privilege, which at last grew so overweening that it veered toward extremity and invented a religion whose totem was the penis—his own penis at that.

[164] *Ibid.*, p. 290.

Aaron's Rod, Kangaroo, and *The Plumed Serpent* are rather neglected novels, and perhaps justly so. They are unquestionably strident, and unpleasant for a number of reasons, principally a rasping protofascist tone, an increasing fondness of force, a personal arrogance, and innumerable racial, class, and religious bigotries. In these novels one sees how terribly Lawrence strained after triumph in the "man's world" of formal politics, war, priestcraft, art and finance. Thinking of *Lady Chatterley* or the early novels, readers often equate Lawrence with the personal life which generally concerns the novelist, the relations of men and women—for whether he played a woman's man or a man's man, Lawrence was generally doing so before an audience of women, who found it difficult to associate him with the public life of male authority. After *Women in Love,* having solved, or failed to solve, the problem of mastering the female, Lawrence became more ambitious. Yet he never failed to take his sexual politics with him, and with an astonishing consistency of motive, made it the foundation of all his other social and political beliefs.

Lovat Somers went to Australia, by his own account, simply to work and be alone, but in no time every man he meets is begging him to take charge of the country. The "Diggers," a fascist group of disgruntled war veterans, want him to be the brains of their coup d'état. What heightens Somers' excitement at the thought of participating in the "masculine sphere" of government is not only the matey company of other males, but the deliberate exclusion of women, especially his bemused and serviceable wife Harriet. Written only a few years after suffrage, *Kangaroo* makes a great point of excluding women even from discussions of politics. In the bright new order, they will be disenfranchised again and below citizen class. Yet in a man who worships the "dark gods" of phallic supremacy, the blemish of not having established seigniory in his own house is some cause for embarrassment. Lawrence even makes it cause for amusement in the long marital rows that relieve the tedium of his wordy Australian landscapes. And the more the struggle goes on in Lawrence, the more it seems to take out of him, and so the more absolutist and totalitarian he becomes in his male-supremacist beliefs, finally resorting to the magic of phallic religion. Late Lawrence novels have a tendency toward wish-fulfillment, compensatory dream to offset the author's failures at home. Years after his death Frieda Lawrence recorded without bitterness that in the midst of a terrible quarrel Lawrence backed her up against the wall, throttling her while he ground out, "I am the master. I am the master." She replied that he might be if he liked—and what of it. Lawrence let his hands drop in astonishment; Frieda's ready and purely verbal assent—"Is that all? You can be master as much as you like. I don't care"—had quite outwitted him.[165]

With *Kangaroo's* heavy emphasis on masculine privilege, politics, and the public life, from which females, citizens or not, are jealously excluded, come

---

[165] Frieda Lawrence, *op. cit.,* p. 341.

a whole series of other attitudes which we have come to know in this century as particularly dangerous and unpleasant: racism, a lust for violence and for totalitarian authority and control, a hatred for democracy, and a contempt for Christian humanism as a despicably "Jewish" weakness. And with these, *Kangaroo* has also—for all Lawrence's hatred of democracy—a raffish tone, a vulgarity and cheapness of effect which make it the Lawrence novel that commands least critical respect. There is a veteran and buddy atmosphere one associates with the fascist phalanxes of Italy and Hitler's early political cadres. It is the tone of the Patrolmen's Benevolent Association, the Veterans of Foreign Wars and the American Legion; boastfully masculine, jealous of prerogative, stupidly patriotic, and spoiling for a war, the white man's flag and the right to worship a consecrated leader. There is a "male only" exclusiveness, an enormous interest in deep, close, and cloyingly sentimental relationships with other men—on the Australian side, a sticky, palsy mate approach to Somers, mixed with deference, but perhaps not quite enough to suit him. He turns such occasions to rich advantage, posturing as the proletarian boy made good, born of their own kind but a gentleman really.

Lovat patronizes his colonial cousins, but he loves to be courted and is hoping very hard to be won. Unlike Birkin, Somers is being courted rather than being rejected—in fact he is desired on all sides, every man he meets wishes to proclaim him. And this time he can turn them down. With a quaint egotism Lovat permits himself to dream that the leader of a major party would beg, on his deathbed, that the writer grant him a caress and an "I love you." Lovat manages his suitors nicely—he is manly and straight, patronizingly true to his long-suffering wife, yet enjoys the adoration of two males, Jack Callcott and Ben Cooley, both of whom he finds impressive and attractive. Their infatuation is a wonderful tribute to his vanity, and so is his final reluctant refusal of their advances so that he may remain a just man saddled with a fractious wife who has no one or nothing else in the world to live for. This time the Lawrence hero sees himself rejecting the other male as Gerald rejected Birkin. His attitude is more "passive" and "feminine," even coy toward his suitors; at the same time he is more grotesquely authoritarian and "masculine"—as the word is generally understood, toward the females.

A queen bee to desirable males, he is "man enough" to bully his faded and faithful wife. *Kangaroo* is a bizarre account of D. H. Lawrence's extramarital fantasies, fantasies which are never to be charged against him, because they fall just short of consummation, while yet satisfying the whole pack of vanities such dreams spring from. The fantasy love object is male and therefore, by Lawrence's lights, clearly superior to the uninteresting wifely bird in the hand. Yet for all the toying and flirtation, Lawrence is finally too puritanical or too timid to risk the accusation of "unnaturalness"—or more crushing—"unmanliness." He has his code, and Kangaroo's kiss is probably the sweeter for being foregone. By an ingenious fantasy solution, he has assimilated his cake, yet cannot be convicted of eating it.

But the imaginary and surrogate quality of these relationships convinces us their character is predominantly sexual-political, rather than strong or active homosexual impulse. Nor can love between men ever really be the issue, for Lawrence generally meant only power by the word love, and, during his later period, was actually candid enough to adopt the correct term.

V RITUAL

The Plumed Serpent records that moment when Lawrence was led to the ultimate ingenuity of inventing a religion, even a liturgy, of male supremacy. Theological underpinnings for political systems are an old and ever-present need, and so in a sense, Lawrence is only being practical. One of the pillars of the old patriarchy was its religion, and as Lawrence was bored with Christianity, suspicious of its egalitarian potential, and quite uninterested in other established creeds, it was inevitable that he should invent one of his own. Yet as he requires only one service of the supernatural, he is content that it assume the blunt form of phallic worship: his totemic penis is alpha and omega, the word improved into flesh.

That there is a great deal of narcissism in all this was fairly obvious from the inception of the impulse, and a factor in many of the Blutbruderschaft relations described in earlier novels. His phallic cult enables Lawrence to achieve another goal: by investing the penis with magical powers (which might be slightly harder to substantiate without a religious aura) he has been able to rearrange biological fact. For in the new system, life arises by a species of almost spontaneous generation from the penis, bypassing the womb. Now the penis alone is responsible for generating all the vital forces in the world. When one remembers the powers the womb held for Lawrence in *The Rainbow*, it is perhaps not so surprising that he should have wished to effect such drastic alterations in the "facts of life."

The Plumed Serpent is the story of a religious conversion. A rather sensible Irish woman arrives in Mexico, falls in with two ambitious intriguers who wish to set themselves up as incarnations of the ancient Mexican gods in order to take over the country and establish a reactionary government, unmistakably fascist in character, and awkwardly neo-primitivist in program. Mrs. Leslie is torn between her realization that this is all "high-flown bunkem," and the hypnotic masculinity of Don Ramon and Don Cipriano. At last she capitulates to the latter and stays on, married to one man and tempted by both to join the pantheon in the secondary capacity of a goddess.

The novel's point of view is the woman's; its point of interest is the two attractive males. The prose celebrates phallic supremacy continuously. Falling under Cipriano's spell, Kate Leslie is there to observe the "living male power," the "ancient phallic mystery," and the "ancient god-devil of the male Pan," "unyielding forever," "shadowy, intangible, looming suddenly tall, and covering the sky, making a darkness that was himself and nothing but himself."[166] The heroes, Ramon and Cipriano, are Lawrentian men and mouth-pieces, intellectual and earthy respectively. Together with the heroine, they form a characteristic Lawrentian triangle. Cipriano and Kate Leslie appear to be in love with Ramon, who appears to be in love with himself. A very superior being, chief of the deities, the "living Quetzalcoatl," brother anc successor to Jesus Christ, Ramon is understandably self-sufficient. But in more relaxed moments, he enjoys some peculiarly erotic communions with Cipriano, as well as the pleasure of withholding himself from Kate, who is too imperfect to deserve him.

Leavis, and other critics, have remarked upon the impropriety of a heroine as the center of consciousness in this novel.[167] There is some truth in the objection, for Kate Leslie is a female impersonator, yet one cannot neglect her utility as an exemplary case of submission, and the model femininity she represents is surely part of her value. When presented with "the old, supreme phallic mystery," her behavior is unexceptional: after "submitting," and "suc-cumbing," she abdicates self utterly and is "swooned, prone beneath, perfect in her proneness."[168]

> Ah! and what a mystery of prone submission, on her part, this huge erection would imply! Submission absolute, like the earth under the sky. Beneath an over-arching absolute. Ah! what a marriage! How terrible! and how complete! With a finality of death, and yet more than death. The arms of the twilit Pan. And the awful, half-intelligible voice from the cloud. She could conceive now her marriage with Cipriano; the supreme passivity, like the earth below the twilight, consummate in living lifelessness, the sheer solid mystery of passivity. Ah, what an abandon, what an abandon, what an abandon!—"[169]

Overcome by the prospect of this supine future, the lady exclaims "My de-mon lover!" this last epithet a sad instance of Coleridge fallen to the excited cliché of magazine prose.[170]

Kate Leslie is an exemplum, an object lesson placed so as to lead other women "back to the twilight of the ancient Pan world, where the soul of woman was dumb, to be forever unspoken."[171] Her vertiginous passivity is not only an admonition to her sex, but something the author appears to enjoy playing at himself. Through the device of the heroine, Lawrence has found a vehicle to fantasize what seems to be his own surrender to the dark and imperious male in Cipriano.

Throughout the novel, Kate Leslie is schooled in the author's notions of

[166] D. H. Lawrence, *The Plumed Serpent* (1926). (New York: Viking, 1951), p. 342.

[167] See F. R. Leavis, *D. H. Lawrence, Novelist* (New York: Knopf, 1956), p. 70.

[168] Lawrence, *The Plumed Serpent*, p. 341.

[169] *Ibid.*, p. 342.

[170] *Ibid.*

[171] *Ibid.*

primeval truth. Learning that the salvation of the world lies in a reassertion of virility which will also make it possible for women to fulfill their true nature as passive objects and perfect subjects to masculine rule, she undergoes marriage in the new religion, devoutly kissing the feet of her new lord as the service commands her. She studies laboriously to relinquish her will and her individual selfhood, as Lawrence is very punctilious in assuring us female will is an evil and male will a blessing. Yet for all this, one can be fairly sure she won't last very long. Even within the novel it is predicted that she will end as some sort of human sacrifice, a repellent ritual to which the new order is given, described in shocking detail and with a complicity in its barbarism that makes the reader anxious for Lawrence's sanity. Ramon warns her, "if you lived here alone . . . and queened it for a time, you would get yourself murdered—or worse—by the people who had worshipped you."[172] Even as a member of the new regime, her status is so tenuous that her anxious premonitions carry great force: "After all, she was a gringita, and she felt it. A sacrifice? Was she a sacrifice? . . . Now she was condemned to go through these strange ordeals, like a victim."[173]

Lawrence wrote "The Woman Who Rode Away" during the same period as *The Plumed Serpent*, and it is something of a sequel to it. The short story does accomplish the human sacrifice of the female to Lawrence's phallic sect and it is therefore a somewhat franker version of events than the novel. It is the story of a woman in an unhappy marriage, one Lawrence himself describes as an "invincible slavery," which has left her "conscious development . . . completely arrested."[174] On an adventurous gamble, the woman, who significantly is never individualized by a name, rides away into the desert to join the Mexican Indians. She is clearly a woman who needs to run away— to something. What is curious is what Lawrence finds for her to run away to —a death which is astounding in the sadism and malice with which it is conceived.

The cult of primitivism, which provided Lawrence with so much aesthetic gratification, has its political side as well. Having seen in the feminist movement a surge toward the civilized condition which the male had enjoyed so long, Lawrence identified the female (at least his target, the New Woman) as a rather sophisticated enemy. This is quite the opposite tack from that taken by his contemporaries, Faulkner and Joyce, to name two examples, who were fond of presenting woman as "nature" "unspoiled primeval understanding," and the "eternal feminine." Even Freud, with whom Lawrence agrees so well on female character in the matters of passivity and masochism, imagined the female to be a fairly harmless savage. While Lawrence is determined to keep that part of civilization he approves in male hands, he is also

---

[172] *Ibid.*, p. 478.
[173] *Ibid.*, p. 369.
[174] D. H. Lawrence, *The Woman Who Rode Away* (1928). (New York: Knopf, 1928), Berkeley Medallion Edition, p. 8.

realistic enough to acknowledge that since the new breed have arrived, the female has actually escaped the primitive condition others assume to be her nature. Drastic steps must be taken if she is going to be coerced back into it: her will must be broken, her newly found ego destroyed. That is why the heroines of Lawrence's novels spend each book learning their part as females. Indeed, so little can one trust to nature in these matters, that very severe measures must occasionally be taken. "The Woman Who Rode Away" is just this sort of measure. Critics fudge the meaning of this story by mumbling vaguely that it is all allegorical, symbolic.[175] Of course it is—symbolic in the same sense as a head exposed on London Bridge.

The idea of leaving the emancipated woman to the "savage" to kill, delegating the butchery as it were, is really an inspiration; sexism can appear thereby to be liberal and anti-colonialist. Lawrence is able to relish the beauty of dark-skinned males, while congratulating them on what, despite his usual fastidious distaste for non-Aryans, he regards as their stellar virtue—they "keep their women in their place." This is a common fantasy of the white world, the favorite commodity of western movies and the Asian-African spectaculars. Such epics follow a well-paved story line which satisfies a host of white male expectations: the white woman is captured by "savages"—and "we all know how they treat their women"; she is forced to live in a state of utter humiliation and abjection, raped, beaten, tortured, finally stripped and murdered.[176] Such little comedies serve to titillate the white male, intimidate "his woman," and slander the persons upon whom the white male has shifted the burden of his own prurient sadism.

Lawrence has improved upon the rape fantasy by sterilizing the story—removing all traces of overt sexual activity and replacing them with his home-made mythology—the woman is sacrificed to the sun. But there is a sincere "religious impulse" in the tale, apart from the inanities of the pseudo-Indian legend, for the story is Lawrence's most impassioned statement of the doctrine of male supremacy and the penis as deity. The fraudulent myth also prevents

[175] Both Leavis and Tindall take this line. See Leavis' *D. H. Lawrence, Novelist*, and William York Tindall, *The Later D. H. Lawrence* (New York: Knopf, 1952).

[176] Lawrence has a number of stories like this: "None of That" is a grim little piece of hate about an American woman who is gang-raped by a group of shoddy toreadors in gratitude for the fortune she wills to one of them; "The Princess" gives an account of a Mexican guide who rapes and imprisons an American in the mountains—a story done with infinite malice and sexual enmity. There is a premonition of the Lawrence who wrote "The Woman Who Rode Away" as early as *Sons and Lovers*, when little Paul Morel performs strange rites upon his sister Annie's doll. Having broken her "accidentally," he suggests "Let's make a sacrifice of Arabella . . . Let's burn her." Having found her face "stupid" he stands by, watching with satisfaction while the figure melts, then takes the charred remains and smashes them with stones. Annie, whose only toy this had been, stands by helpless and understandably disturbed while Paul shouts, "that's the sacrifice of Misses Arabella . . . And I'm glad there's nothing left of her." *Sons and Lovers*, pp. 57–58.

the story from appearing as the pandering to pornographic dream that it is. On one level of intention, "The Woman Who Rode Away" would reward a careful comparative reading with *The Story of O;* in a number of ways it resembles commercial hard core.

The office of sexual avenger is of course left in the hands of the dark male. Non-Aryan females, like proletarian women, held no interest whatsoever for Lawrence, and never appear in the story. Psychologically, the very pattern of the tale cleverly provides satisfactions for the white male's guilt feelings over the dark peoples and "primitives" whom he exploits. He will atone by throwing them his woman to butcher, advancing his dominion over her in the process, and substituting his own rival as the scapegoat for imperialist excesses. And the liberal, the humanistic, and the well meaning among his numbers are satisfied with the fable at its surface level, while the aggressive, the malign, and the sadistic are provided with greater sustenance below the surface.

It has been fashionable for some time to visit the white man's sins on "his woman." Even LeRoi Jones adopts this line of attack in *The Dutchman,* punishing all whites in the caricature of Lulu, thereby avoiding the more explosive run in with "the man." Genet, whose perceptions are more acute, realizes that the ravishment of the white woman is in reality but an endless, self-seeking white fantasy. This maniacal myth has been both cause and excuse for the white master's reaction to the alleged death or despoilment of "his woman" which has brought on so many atrocities in our national past. So in Genet's play, *The Blacks,* the black "actors" replay "the murder of a white woman" before their white audience, because they know that it is the best entertainment they could offer to interest such a crowd, who are, incidentally, their court of judgment. When the "murder" is revealed as a sham—there is nothing beneath the "catafalque"—it was empty air, an idea, Whiteness itself which the blacks assassinated—the white court are incensed beyond all reason. "You kill us without killing us," they clamor.[177] What Genet had been investigating was not the fact of racial or sexual violence, but the psychic bases of racial-sexual beliefs, exposing them as the myths of a political system.

Lawrence's cautionary tale for white women has odd assumptions common to the white mind: that the dark peoples of the world are fascinated and arrested by yellow hair, an axiomatic assumption of those white fairy tales like *Lord Jim.* It is a common white fancy that when one of the blond folk go to the dark peoples the latter are so overawed, they make him god or king, an event highly satisfactory to his vanity. Lawrence makes this old chestnut do service again while punishing the white woman in the process. The following

---

[177] Jean Genet, *The Blacks, A Clown Show* (1958), translated from the French by Bernard Frechtman (New York: Grove Press, 1960), p. 98.

passage works on both assumptions, and while it humiliates the woman, flatters white egocentricity at the same time:

> There was now absolute silence. She was given a little to drink, then two priests took off her mantle and her tunic, and in her strange pallor she stood there, between the lurid robes of the priests, beyond the pillar of ice, beyond and above the dark-faced people. The throng below gave the low, wild cry. Then the priest turned her round, so she stood with her back to the open world, her long blond hair to the people below. And they cried again.[178]

The scene is shot in MGM technicolor, the whole story reeks of Hollywood, but it also satisfies voyeurism, a sadistic sort of buggery, and the white dream of being uplifted and proclaimed.

One is always struck by the sexual ambiguity in Lawrence. The woman of the fable is bent on going toward death like a bird hypnotized by the eye of a snake. But her fatalism is never explained, save in Lawrence's obsessive wish to murder her. There is a strange quality about this fatalism: while it is supposed to represent the decline of the West or some other abstraction, the narrative derives its power from a participation on the part of the author himself which appears to derive from perverse needs deep in Lawrence's own nature. There is as much attention lavished upon the masochistic as upon the sadistic, and one perceives a peculiar relish for the former in the author, a wallowing in the power of the Indian male, his beauty and indifference and cruelty, exerted not only on the silly woman, his victim, but on Lawrence too. It is the author himself standing fascinated before this silent and darkly beautiful killer, enthralled, aroused, awaiting the sacrificial rape.

Yet the real interest in the story is in the crushing of the woman's will, of which the murder is merely a consummation. As with the *Story of O*, or much of "exotic" pornography (e.g. that set in Near and Far Eastern or in primitive cultures, where a real or assumed contempt for women rationalizes the large dose of sexual sadism which caused the author to choose such a locale to begin with), the interest is not in the physical pain inflicted but in the damage done to will and spirit, the humiliation of the human claim or dignity of the victim. Progress is measured in hundreds of phrases like this: ". . . she was very tired. She lay down on a couch of skins . . . and she slept, giving up everything"[179] . . . "she was utterly strange and beyond herself, as if her body were not her own."[180] Imprisoned in a little hut, drugged day after day as the torture drags on, vomiting continuously, she is reduced to a phenomenal despair and passivity "as if she had no control over herself."[181] Lawrence lingers over her gradual relinquishment of

[178] Lawrence, *The Woman Who Rode Away*, p. 39.
[179] *Ibid.*, p. 24.
[180] *Ibid.*, p. 24.
[181] *Ibid.*, p. 25.

selfhood: "She was not in her own power, she was under the spell of some other control. And at times she had moments of terror and horror . . . the Indians would come and sit with her, casting their insidious spell over her by their very silent presence . . . As they sat they seemed to take her will away, leaving her will-less and victim to her own indifference."[182]

The message—for this story has a message—is revealed at last in a central passage, when the author delivers a formal lecture to the modern woman:

> In the strange towering symbols on the heads of the changeless, absorbed women, she seemed to read once more the Mene Mene Tekel Upharsin. Her kind of womanhood, intensely personal and individual, was to be obliterated again, and the great primeval symbols were to tower once more over the fallen individual independence of women. The sharpness and the quivering nervous consciousness of the highly-bred white woman was to be destroyed again, womanhood was to be cast once more into the great stream of impersonal sex and impersonal passion. Strangely, as if clairvoyant, she saw the immense sacrifice prepared, and she went back to her little house in a trance of agony.[183]

Well she might. With bemused pity one contemplates those women of Africa, Asia, and South America, lobbying in the United Nations for civil rights. Sadly misled, they have failed to grasp Lawrence's wise understanding of the impropriety in their hope of sexual revolution—and their own importance as models to the rest of their sex.

Now that the sermon has been delivered, the proceedings may continue: "She felt always in the same relaxed, confused, victimized state . . . This at length became the only state of consciousness she really recognized, this exquisite sense of bleeding out into the higher beauty and harmony of things."[184] The last phrase is pure gas, but there is no mistaking its intention. Of course, much is made of the masochistic nature of the female, called on to justify any ghastliness perpetrated upon her: "She knew she was a victim, that all this elaborate work upon her was the work of victimizing her. But she did not mind. She wanted it."[185] Of all masculine fantasies, this is perhaps the most revered; not only does it rationalize any atrocity, but even more to the point, it puts such action beyond the moral pale—all these enormities only satisfy her inherent nature." Freud had provided the scientific justification for sadism; Lawrence was not slow to buy the product.

Every effort is made to humiliate her. Since Lawrence's notion of *hubris* is a woman who exhibits any self-assurance, she is rewarded for speaking to the Indians who capture her with cuts at the horse she rides, throwing

[182] *Ibid.,* p. 27.
[183] *Ibid.,* p. 29. Needless to say, the "symbol" which will tower over the fallen freedom of women is none other than the phallus.
[184] *Ibid.,* p. 31.
[185] *Ibid.,* p. 36.

her painfully in the saddle at every step. Later Lawrence has her dismount and crawl. Other details savored are the gratuitous insult of the animal she shares her prison with, "a little female dog," and her rabbitlike terror as she is carried to her death; "she sat looking out of her litter with her big transfixed blue eyes . . . the wan markings of her drugged weariness."[186]

Her captors, who are the embodiment of an idea, and bear no resemblance to living beings of any race whatsoever, are supernatural males, who are "beyond sex" in a pious fervor of male supremacy that disdains any genital contact with women preferring instead to deal with her by means of a knife. These are the final priests of Lawrence's phallicism: "There was nothing sensual or sexual in [their] look. It had a terrible glittering purity"[187] . . . "there was not even derision in the eyes. Only that intense, yet remote, inhuman glitter which was terrible to her. They were inaccessible. They could not see her as a woman at all."[188] We are informed incessantly that they are "darkly and powerfully male,"[189] yet paradoxically, we are told of their "silent, *sexless*, powerful, physical presence."[190] There is no real contradiction here for in this apotheosis of puritanical pornography, Lawrence has separated sexuality from sex. The ersatz Indians are ultimate maleness and therefore can have no relationship with the female, as they are entirely beyond trucking with her. By "male," Lawrence simply means oppressive force, a charisma of mastery, "something primevally male and cruel,"[191] "the ancient fierce human male."[192] Naturally, this is incompatible with any sexual activity, for such might introduce the danger of communicating with or even gratifying a woman. Their relations with their female victim are of an antiseptic antisexual quality which is remarkably obscene, both in its arrogance and in its deliberately inhuman quality:

> "You must take off your clothes, and put these on."
> "If all you men will go out," she said.
> "No one will hurt you," he said quietly.
> "Not while you men are here," she said.
> He looked at the two men by the door. They came quickly forward and suddenly gripped her arms as she stood, without hurting her, but with great power. Then two of the old men came, and with curious skill slit her boots down with keen knives, and drew them off, and slit her clothing so that it came away from her. In a few moments she stood there white and uncovered. The old man on the bed spoke, and they turned her round for him to see. He spoke again,

186 *Ibid.*, pp. 37–38.
187 *Ibid.*, p. 20.
188 *Ibid.*, p. 18.
189 *Ibid.*, p. 27.
190 *Ibid.*, italics added.
191 *Ibid.*, p. 35.
192 *Ibid.*, p. 29.

and the young Indian deftly took the pins and comb from her fair hair, so that it fell over her shoulders in a bunchy tangle.

Then the old man spoke again. The Indians led her to the bedside. The white-haired, glassy-dark old man moistened his finger-tips at his mouth, and most delicately touched her on the breasts and on the body, then on the back. And she winced strangely, each time, as the finger-tips drew along her skin, as if Death itself were touching her.[193]

It is by no means incongruous that the victim feels the touch of death—this is how Lawrence's male supremacy manifests itself at last—lethal, an utter denial of sexuality, of life, and of fertility. One cannot become more sterile than this. The final rites take place before a phallic totem of ice, and there is wonderful propriety in the detail that this penis is an icicle:

Facing, was a great wall of hollow rock, down the front of which hung a great dripping fang-like spoke of ice. The ice came pouring over the rock from the precipice above, and then stood arrested, dripping out of high heaven, almost down to the hollow stones where the stream-pool should be below. But the pool was dry . . . They stood her facing the iridescent column of ice, which fell down marvellously arrested.[194]

In the images of genital topography the reader may perceive the supernatural origin of the penis (dropping out of high heaven), the miracle of an erection (marvellously arrested), and the negation of the womb (a dry pond). The ice-pick is Lawrence's god, an idol, his image of the holy. This is what phallic consciousness can accomplish.

Before the penetration of death, the victim is to be purified, "fumigated," mauled, rubbed, and the reader stimulated through a method possibly the most frankly auto- or perhaps antierotic in pornographic literature. These bits are generally quoted on the flyleaf of cheap paper editions as sex bait—the attraction is obvious.

In the darkness and in the silence she was accurately aware of everything that happened to her: how they took off her clothes, and standing her before a great, weird device on the wall, colored blue and white and black, washed her all over with water . . . Then they laid her on a couch under another great indecipherable image of red and black and yellow, and now rubbed all her body with sweet-scented oil, and massaged all her limbs, and her back, and her sides, with a long, strange, hypnotic massage. Their dark hands were incredibly powerful, yet soft with a water softness she could not understand. And the dark faces, leaning near her white body, she saw were darkened with red pigment, with lines of yellow round the cheeks. And the dark eyes glittered absorbed, as the hands worked upon the soft white body of the woman.

[193] *Ibid.*, pp. 23–24.
[194] *Ibid.*, pp. 38–39.

When she was fumigated, they laid her on a large flat stone, the four powerful men, holding her by the outstretched arms and legs. Behind her stood the aged man, like a skeleton covered with dark glass, holding the knife and transfixedly watching the sun and behind him was another naked priest with a knife.[195]

All sadistic pornography tends to find its perfection in murder. Lawrence's movie priests themselves seem to understand the purpose of the rites and are "naked and in a state of barbaric ecstasy,"[196] as they await the moment when the sun, phallic itself, strikes the phallic icicle, and signals the phallic priest to plunge the phallic knife—penetrating the female victim and cutting out her heart—the death fuck.[197]

With elaborate care, Lawrence has plotted the sexualized landscape to coincide with the sexual scenario—as his victim lies poised and waiting, he works up suspense:

> Turning to the sky she looked at the yellow sun. It was sinking. The shaft of ice was like a shadow between her and it. And she realized that the yellow rays were filling half the cave though they had not reached the altar where the fire was, at the far end of the funnel shaped cavity. Yes, the rays were creeping round slowly. As they grew ruddier, they penetrated farther. When the red sun was about to sink, he would shine full through the shaft of ice deep into the hollow of the cave to the innermost. She understood now that this was what the men were waiting for . . . And their ferocity was ready to leap out into a mystic exultance, of triumph . . . Then the old man would strike, and strike home, accomplish the sacrifice and achieve the power.[198]

This is a formula for sexual cannibalism: substitute the knife for the penis and penetration, the cave for a womb, and for a bed, a place of execution—and you provide a murder whereby one acquires one's victim's power. Lawrence's demented fantasy has arranged for the male to penetrate the female with the instrument of death so as to steal her mana. As he supposes the dark races envy the white, who in his little legend, have "stolen their sun," Lawrence himself seems envious, afraid—murderous.

The act here at the center of the Lawrentian sexual religion is coitus as killing, its central vignette a picture of human sacrifice performed upon the woman to the greater glory and potency of the male. But because sexual potency could accomplish little upon a corpse, it is painfully obvious that

[195] *Ibid.*, pp. 36 and 39.

[196] *Ibid.*

[197] Curiously enough, Lawrence has created a realization of the popular equation of sexuality and violence one finds, for example, in street language, where our obsessive cultural habit of sexual loathing causes "fuck" to become synonymous with kill, hurt, or destroy.

[198] *Ibid.*, pp. 39–40.

the intention of the fable is purely political. The conversion of human genitals into weapons has led him from sex to war. Probably it is the perversion of sexuality into slaughter, indeed, the story's very travesty and denial of sexuality, which accounts for its monstrous, even demented air.

SIX

Henry Miller

Certain writers are persistently misunderstood. Henry Miller is surely one of the major figures of American literature living today, yet academic pedantry still dismisses him as beneath scholarly attention. He is likely to be one of the most important influences on our contemporary writing, but official criticism perseveres in its scandalous and systematic neglect of his work.[1] To exacerbate matters, Miller has come to represent the much acclaimed "sexual freedom" of the last few decades. One finds eloquent expression of this point of view in a glowing essay by Karl Shapiro: "Miller's achievement is miraculous: he is screamingly funny without making fun of sex . . . accurate and poetic in the highest degree; there is not a smirk anywhere in his writings.[2] Shapiro is confident that Miller can do more to expunge the "obscenities" of the national scene than a "full-scale social revolution."[3] Lawrence Durrell exclaims over "how nice it is for once to dispense with the puritans and with pagans," since Miller's books, unlike those of his con-

[1] It may be that his own eccentricity in granting permission is also a factor: Miller regards permission to quote as a personal endorsement of the critic's views. Unfortunately space does not permit me to pay tribute to Henry Miller's considerable achievement as an essayist, autobiographer and surrealist; my remarks are restricted to an examination of Miller's sexual ethos.

[2] Karl Shapiro, "The Greatest Living Author," reprinted as an introduction to the Grove Press edition of *Tropic of Cancer* (New York: Grove Press, 1961), p. xvi.

[3] *Ibid.,* p. xviii.

temporaries, are "not due to puritanical shock."[4] Shapiro assures us that Miller is "the first writer outside the Orient who has succeeded in writing as naturally about sex on a large scale as novelists ordinarily write about the dinner table or the battlefield."[5] Significant analogies. Comparing the *Tropic of Cancer* with Joyce's *Ulysses,* Shapiro gives Miller the advantage, for while Joyce, warped by the constraints of his religious background, is prurient or "aphrodisiac," Miller is "no aphrodisiac at all, because religious or so-called moral tension does not exist for him."[6] Shapiro is convinced that "Joyce actually prevents himself from experiencing the beauty of sex or lust, while Miller is freed at the outset to deal with the overpowering mysteries and glories of love and copulation."[7]

However attractive our current popular image of Henry Miller the liberated man may appear, it is very far from being the truth. Actually, Miller is a compendium of American sexual neuroses, and his value lies not in freeing us from such afflictions, but in having had the honesty to express and dramatize them. There *is* a kind of culturally cathartic release in Miller's writing, but it is really a result of the fact that he first gave voice to the unutterable. This is no easy matter of four-letter words; they had been printed already in a variety of places. What Miller did articulate was the disgust, the contempt, the hostility, the violence, and the sense of filth with which our culture, or more specifically, its masculine sensibility, surrounds sexuality. And women too; for somehow it is women upon whom this onerous burden of sexuality falls. There is plenty of evidence that Miller himself is fleetingly conscious of these things, and his "naive, sexual heroics" would be far better if, as one critic suggests, they had been carried all the way to "self-parody."[8] But the major flaw in his oeuvre—too close an identification with the persona, "Henry Miller"—always operates insidiously against the likelihood of persuading us that Miller the man is any wiser than Miller the character.[9]

And with *this* Miller; though one has every reason to doubt the strict veracity of those sexual exploits he so laboriously chronicles in the first person, though one has every reason to suspect that much of this "fucking" is sheer fantasy—there is never reason to question the sincerity of the emotion which infuses such accounts; their exploitative character; their air of juvenile egotism. Miller's genuine originality consists in revealing and recording a group of related sexual attitudes which, despite their enormous prevalence and power, had never (or never so explicitly) been given literary expres-

[4] Bern Porter, *The Happy Rock* (Berkeley, Packard Press, 1945), pp. 2–4.

[5] Shapiro, *op. cit.,* pp. xvi–xvii.

[6] *Ibid.,* p. xvii.

[7] *Ibid.,* pp. xvii–xviii.

[8] Ihab Hassan, *The Literature of Silence,* Henry Miller and Samuel Beckett (New York: Knopf, 1967), p. 10.

[9] I am pleased to find that Hassan agrees with me here.

sion before. Of course, these attitudes are no more the whole truth than chivalry, or courtly, or romantic love were—but Miller's attitudes do constitute a kind of cultural data heretofore carefully concealed beneath our traditional sanctities. Nor is it irrelevant that the sociological type Miller's impressions represent is that of a brutalized adolescence. The sympathy they elicit is hardly confined to that group but strikes a chord of identification in men of all ages and classes, and constituting an unofficial masculine version of both sexuality and the female which—however it appears to be at variance with them—is still vitally dependent on the official pieties of love: mother, wife, virgin, and matron. The anxiety and contempt which Miller registers toward the female sex is at least as important and generally felt as the more diplomatic or "respectful" version presented to us in conventional writing.[10] In fact, to hear Miller bragging of having "broken down" a "piece of tail" is as bracing as the sound of honest bigotry in a redneck after hours of Senator Eastland's unctuous paternalism.

Miller regards himself as a disciple of Lawrence, a suggestion certain to have outraged the master had he lived to be so affronted. The liturgical pomp with which Lawrence surrounded sexuality bears no resemblance to Miller's determined profanity. The Lawrentian hero sets about his mission with notorious gravity and "makes love" by an elaborate political protocol. In the process, by dint of careful diplomacy and expert psychological manipulation, he effects the subjection of the woman in question. But Miller and his confederates—for Miller is a gang—just "fuck" women and discard them, much as one might avail oneself of sanitary facilities—Kleenex or toilet paper, for example. Just "fucking," the Miller hero is merely a huckster and a con man, unimpeded by pretension, with no priestly role to uphold. Lawrence did much to kill off the traditional attitudes of romantic love. At first glance, Miller seems to have started up blissfully ignorant of their existence altogether. Actually, his cold-blooded procedure is intended as sacrilege to the tenderness of romantic love, a tenderness Lawrence was never willing to forgo. In his brusque way, Miller demonstrates the "love fraud" (a species of power play disguised as eroticism) to be a process no more complex than a mugging. The formula is rather simple: you meet her, cheat her into letting you have "a piece of ass," and then take off. Miller's hunt is a primitive find, fuck, and forget.

Among other things, it was a shared dislike for the sexual revolution that sparked Miller's admiration and drove him to undertake a long essay on Lawrence:

It seems significant that, with all the power that was in him, Lawrence strove to put woman back in her rightful place . . . The masculine world . . . deeply

[10] I have in mind not only traditional courtly, romantic, and Victorian sentiment, but even that of other moderns. Conrad, Joyce, even Faulkner, never approach the sexual hostility one finds in Miller.

and shamefully feminized, is . . . inclined to distrust and despise Lawrence's ideas . . . what he railed against and fought tooth and nail . . . the sickly ideal love world of depolarized sex! The world based on a fusion of the sexes instead of an antagonism . . . [for] the eternal battle with woman sharpens our resistance, develops our strength, enlarges the scope of our cultural achievements: through her . . . we build . . . our religions, philosophies and sciences.[11]

There is a similarity of purpose here, but what Miller fails to recognize, or at least to comment upon, is the total disparity of their methods. Lawrence had turned back the feminist claims to human recognition and a fuller social participation by distorting them into a vegetative passivity calling itself fulfillment. His success prepared the way for Miller's escalation to open contempt. Lawrence had still to deal with persons; Miller already feels free to speak of objects. Miller simply converts woman to "cunt"—thing, commodity, matter. There is no personality to recognize or encounter, so there is none to tame or break by the psychological subtleties of Lawrence's Freudian wisdom.

While both writers enlist the fantastic into the service of sexual politics, Lawrence's use seems pragmatically political, its end is to compel the emotional surrender of an actual woman, generally a person of considerable strength and intelligence. Miller confronts nothing more challenging than the undifferentiated genital that exists in masturbatory revery. In the case of the two actual women, Maude and Mara, who appear in Miller's world amidst its thousand floozie caricatures, personality and sexual behavior is so completely unrelated that, in the sexual episodes where they appear, any other names might have been conveniently substituted. For the purpose of every bout is the same: a demonstration of the hero's self-conscious detachment before the manifestations of a lower order of life. During an epic encounter with Mara, the only woman he ever loved, Miller is as clinical as he was toward Ida; Mara just as grotesque:

And on this bright and slippery gadget Mara twisted like an eel. She wasn't any longer a woman in heat, she wasn't even a woman; she was just a mass of indefinable contours wriggling and squirming like a piece of fresh bait seen upside down through a convex mirror in a rough sea.

I had long ceased to be interested in her contortions; except for the part of me that was in her I was cool as a cucumber and remote as the Dog Star . . .

Towards dawn, Eastern Standard Time, I saw by that frozen condensed-milk expression about the jaw that it was happening. Her face went through all the metamorphoses of early uterine life, only in reverse. With the last dying spark it

[11] Henry Miller, "Shadowy Monomania," *Sunday After the War* (New Directions, New York, 1944), pp. 259–61.

collapsed like a punctured bag, the eyes and nostrils smoking like toasted acorns in a slightly wrinkled lake of pale skin.[12]

The Victorians, or some of them, revealed themselves in their slang expression for the orgasm—"to spend"—a term freighted with economic insecurity and limited resources, perhaps a reflection of capitalist thrift implying that if semen is money (or time or energy) it should be preciously hoarded.[13] Miller is no such cheapskate, but in his mind, too, sex is linked in a curious way with money. By the ethos of American financial morality, Miller was a downright "failure" until the age of forty; a writer unable to produce, living a seedy outcast existence, jobless and dependent on handouts. Before exile in Paris granted him reprieve, Miller felt himself the captive of circumstances in a philistine milieu where artistic or intellectual work was despised, and the only approved avenues of masculine achievement were confined to money or sex. Of course, Miller is a maverick and a rebel, but much as he hates the money mentality, it is so ingrained in him that he is capable only of replacing it with sex—a transference of acquisitive impulse. By converting the female to commodity, he too can enjoy the esteem of "success." If he can't make money, he can make women—if need be on borrowed cash, pulling the biggest coup of all by getting something for nothing. And while his better "adjusted" contemporaries swindle in commerce, Miller preserves his "masculinity" by swindling in cunt. By shining in a parallel system of pointless avarice whose real rewards are also tangential to actual needs and likewise surpassed by the greater gains run up for powerful egotism, his manly reputation is still assured with his friends.

When reporting on the civilized superiority of French sex, his best proof is its better business method. The whore's client is "permitted to examine and handle merchandise before buying," a practice he congratulates as "fair and square."[14] Not only is the patron spared any argument from the "owner of the commodity," overseas trade is so benevolent that there is nothing "to hinder you should you decide to take a half-dozen women with you to a hotel room, provided you made no fuss about the extra charge for soap and towels."[15] As long as you can pay, he explains, full of the complacency of dollar culture, no other human considerations exist. "At the hotel I rang for women like you would ring for whiskey and soda,"[16] he boasts once in a pipe-dream of riches, inebriated with the omnipotence of money and the yanqui Playboy's conviction that the foreigners do these things better.

During his tenure as personnel manager for Western Union, Miller was happily placed to exercise a perfect combination of sexual and economic

[12] Henry Miller, *Sexus* (New York: Grove Press, 1965), p. 143.

[13] See Steven Marcus, *The Other Victorians* (New York: Basic Books, 1966).

[14] Henry Miller, *The World of Sex* (New York: Grove Press, 1965), p. 101.

[15] *Ibid.*, pp. 101–2.

[16] Henry Miller, *Tropic of Capricorn* (New York: Grove Press, 1961), p. 202.

power over the women applying to him for jobs: "The game was to keep them on the string, to promise them a job but to get a free fuck first. Usually it was only necessary to throw a feed into them, in order to bring them back to the office at night and lay them out on the zinc-covered table in the dressing room."[17] As all Americans know, the commercial world is a battle-field. When executives are "fucked" by the company, they can retaliate by "fucking" their secretaries. Miller's is "part-nigger" and "so damned pleased to have someone fuck her without blushing,"[18] that she can be shared out to the boss's pal Curley. She commits suicide eventually, but in business, "it's fuck or be fucked,"[19] Miller observes, providing some splendid insight into the many meanings we attach to the word.

One memorable example of sex as a war of attrition waged upon economic grounds is the fifteen-franc whore whom Miller and his friend Van Norden hire in the Paris night and from whom, despite their own utter lack of appetite and her exhaustion from hunger, it is still necessary to extort the price.[20] As sex, or rather "cunt," is not only merchandise but a monetary specie, Miller's adventures read like so many victories for sharp practice, carry the excitement of a full ledger, and operate on the flat premise that quantity is quality. As with any merchant whose sole concern is profit, the "goods" themselves grow dull and contemptible, and even the amassing of capital pales beside the power it becomes. So enervating is the addiction to sex that Miller and his friends frequently renounce it: "Just cunt Hen . . . just cunt," MacGregor sighs.[21] Van Norden is ashamed of his own obsessive weakness, glad to make do from time to time with an apple, cutting out the core and adding cold cream.[22] Sensually or emotionally, such a surrogate involves no special hardship, since one has so little sense of actual women in Miller's accounts of intercourse. Apples, however, offer no resistance, and the enterprise of conquest, the fun of "breaking her down," is lost thereby.[23]

In the surfeit of Miller's perfervid "fucking," it is surprising how much of sexuality is actually omitted: intimacy, for example, or the aesthetic pleasures of nudity. A very occasional pair of "huge teats" or "haunches" are poor and infrequent spare parts for the missing erotic form of woman. Save for the genitals—the star performers cock and balls—not a word is wasted on the male body. It is not even bodies who copulate here, let alone persons. Miller's fantasy drama is sternly restricted to the dissociated adventures of cunt and prick: "The body is hers, but the cunt's yours. The cunt and the

17 *Ibid.*, p. 29.

18 *Ibid.*, p. 57, p. 180.

19 *Ibid.*, p. 30. This is the sense of the passage.

20 Henry Miller, *Tropic of Cancer* (New York: Grove Press, 1961), p. 141 ff.

21 Henry Miller, *Plexus* (New York: Grove Press, 1965), p. 475.

22 Miller, *Tropic of Cancer*, pp. 291–92.

23 Henry Miller, *Nexus* (New York: Grove Press, 1965), p. 275 and passim. The expression is used often in this book and elsewhere.

prick, they're married," he lectures, after having demonstrated how life has so divorced the couple that "the bodies are going different ways."[24] In so stipulating on a contingent and momentary union, Miller has succeeded in isolating sexuality from the rest of life to an appalling degree. Its participants take on the idiot kinetics of machinery—piston and valve.

The perfect Miller "fuck" is a biological event between organs, its hallmark—its utter impersonality. Of course perfect strangers are best, chance passengers on subways molested without the exchange of word or signal. Paradoxically, this attempt to so isolate sex only loads the act with the most negative connotations. Miller has gone beyond even the empty situations one frequently encounters in professional pornography, blue movies, etc., to freight his incidents with cruelty and contempt. While seeming to remove sexuality from any social or personal context into the gray abstraction of "organ grinding."[25] he carefully includes just enough information on the victim to make her activity humiliating and degrading, and his own an assertion of sadistic will.

Miller boasts, perhaps one should say confesses, that the "best fuck" he "ever had" was with a creature nearly devoid of sense, the "simpleton" who lived upstairs.[26] "Everything was anonymous and unformulated . . . Above the belt, as I say, she was batty. Yes, absolutely cuckoo, though still aboard and afloat. Perhaps that was what made her cunt so marvelously impersonal. It was one cunt out of a million . . . Meeting her in the daytime, watching her slowly going daft, it was like trapping a weasel when night came on. All I had to do was to lie down in the dark with my fly open and wait."[27] Throughout the description one not only observes a vulgar opportunistic use of Lawrence's hocus pocus about blanking out in the mind in order to attain "blood consciousness," but one also intuits how both versions of the idea are haunted by a pathological fear of having to deal with another and complete human personality. Happily, Miller's "pecker" is sufficient to "mesmerize" his prey in the dark: "Come here, you bitch," I kept saying to myself, "come in here and spread that cunt over me . . . I didn't say a word, I didn't make a move, I just kept my mind riveted on her cunt moving quietly in the dark like a crab."[28] One is made very aware here that in the author's scheme the male is represented not only by his telepathic instrument, but by mind, whereas the perfect female is a floating metonymy, pure cunt, completely unsullied by human mentality.

Things are not always this good. To achieve a properly "impersonal fuck" with his despised wife Maude (she persists in the folly of "carnal love"

[24] *Sexus*, p. 83.
[25] Steven Marcus attributes this happy expression to Philip Rahv.
[26] Henry Miller, *Tropic of Capricorn*, pp. 181–82.
[27] *Ibid.*, p. 183.
[28] *Ibid.*, p. 182.

in opposition to her husband's wiser taste for "cold fuck") Miller is put to the trouble of waiting until she sleeps: "Get her half asleep, her blinders off[29] . . . sneak up on her, slip it to her while she's dreaming."[30] The method recommended here is "back-scuttling," preferable for eliminating all superfluous contact and never obliging him to look at her face. Not until his betrayal and imminent departure madden her with grief and fear will she drop her annoying habit (the cause of their incompatibility) of desiring he recognize her as a person, and settle for being a "blind fuck." Earlier she had the gall to protest, "You never had any respect for me—as a human being,"[31] but finally, in a repetitious series of scenes, Miller can play upon her hysteria, put her on the "fucking block" and go at it "with cold-blooded fury."[32] After that it's all "fast, clean work . . . no tears, no love business" until the "ax" falls—a quaint trope which presumably represents his orgasm and her execution.

During a really busy day (Maude, Valeska, Valeska's cousin), Miller awakens from a nap on a West Side pier to discover he has an erection. One must not let such providence go to waste so he hurries to the apartment of a young woman to whom he had been introduced that day at lunch. She opens the door half-asleep and Miller seizes his opportunity: "I unbuttoned my fly and got my pecker out and into position. She was so drugged with sleep that it was almost like working on an automaton."[33] So much the better. More attractive still is the exotic detail, an infringement of several taboos, that she is Jewish passing for Egyptian: "I kept saying to myself—'an Egyptian fuck . . . an Egyptian fuck' . . . It was one of the most wonderful fucks I ever had in my life."[34] Best of all, he manages to escape from her apartment fast enough to avoid the expense of any communication. This is really something for nothing, a free fuck: "I hadn't a word to say to her; the only thought in my head to get out . . . without wasting any words."[35] To complete his satisfaction, Miller's old friend Kronsky has arrived at the door of the apartment, and standing silently outside, is overhearing the entire scene, a crestfallen witness to the conquest.

Miller's ideal woman is a whore. Lawrence regarded prostitution as a profanation of the temple, but with Miller the commercialization of sexuality is not only a gratifying convenience for the male (since it is easier to pay than persuade) but the perfection of feminine existence, efficiently confining it to the function of absolute cunt. To illustrate this he calls upon Germaine,

[29] *Sexus*, p. 83.
[30] *Ibid.*
[31] *Ibid.*, p. 97.
[32] *Ibid.*, p. 100.
[33] *Tropic of Capricorn*, p. 82.
[34] *Ibid.*, p. 83.
[35] *Ibid.*, pp. 83–84.

the archetypal French prostitute of American tourism: "a whore from the cradle; she was thoroughly satisfied with her role, enjoyed it in fact."[36] Launching into a thorough exposition of the subject, Miller explains that Germaine's "twat" is her "glory," her "sense of connection," her "sense of life" because "that was the only place where she experienced any life . . . down there between her legs where women ought to."[37] "Germaine had the right idea: she was ignorant and lusty, she put her heart and soul into her work. She was a whore all the way through—and that was her virtue."[38] Miller states categorically, "I could no more think of loving Germaine than I could think of loving a spider," but he does wish to impress upon us her superiority to another prostitute, Claude, whom he castigates as "delicate" and blames her for "refinement," claiming she offends in having "a soul and a conscience."[39] Most unedifying of all, Claude's evident but unspoken grief is proof she fails to relish her life and even dislikes its active hustle after custom. Such an attitude is inappropriate, morally and aesthetically outrageous: "a whore, it seemed to me, had no right to be sitting there like a lady, waiting . . . for someone to approach."[40]

Since "whores are whores," Miller is also capable of reviling them as "vultures," "buzzards," "rapacious devils," and "bitches"—his righteous scorn as trite as his sentimentality. He is anxious, however, to elevate their function to an "idea"—the Life Force. As with electrical conductors, to plug into them gives a fellow "that circuit which makes one feel the earth under his legs again."[41] Prostitutes themselves speak of their work as "servicing," and Miller's gratified egotism would not only seek to surround the recharge with mystification, but convert the whore into a curious vessel of intermasculine communication—rhapsodizing: "All the men she's been with and now you . . . the whole damned current of life flowing through you, through her, through all the guys behind you and after you."[42] What is striking here is not only the total abstraction Miller makes of sexuality (what could be less solid, less plastic than electricity?) but also the peculiar (yet hardly uncommon) thought of hunting other men's semen in the vagina of a whore, the random conduit of this brotherly vitality.

There is a men's-house atmosphere in Miller's work. His boyhood chums remain the friends of his youth, his maturity, even his old age. Johnny Paul and the street-gang heroes of adolescence continue as the idols of adulthood, strange companions for Miller's literary gods: Spengler, Nietzsche, Dostoiev-

[36] *Tropic of Cancer*, p. 45.
[37] *Ibid.*, pp. 45 and 47.
[38] *Ibid.*, p. 47.
[39] *Ibid.*, pp. 44 and 46.
[40] *Ibid.*, p. 46.
[41] *Ibid.*, p. 47.
[42] *Ibid.*, p. 46.

ski. The six volumes of autobiography, and even the essays, are one endless, frequently self-pitying threnody for the lost paradise of his youth.

As a result, the sexual attitudes of the "undisputed monarch" of the "Land of Fuck,"[43] as Miller chooses to call himself, are those of an arrested adolescence where sex is clandestine, difficult to come by,[44] each experience constituting a victory of masculine diligence and wit over females either stupidly compliant or sagely unco-operative. There's one girl on the block who will take on the whole boy's club, but most are mean numbers who require working over; "good girls" whom parents and religion have corrupted into tough lays. The first afford the easy exultation of superiority, a feeling of utter and absolute contempt, the second, harder to make, provoke the animosity always reserved for the intransigent. The more difficult the assault the greater the glory, but any victory is pointless if it cannot be boasted of and sniggered over. Just as Kronsky is said to hover behind the door, the reader is given the impression that sex is no good unless duly observed and applauded by an ubiquitous peer-group jury. And so Miller's prose has always the flavor of speech, the inflection of telling the boys: "And then I had to get over her again and shove it in, up to the hilt. She squirmed around like an eel, so help me God."[45] His strenuous heterosexuality depends, to a considerable degree, on a homosexual sharing. Not without reason, his love story, *The Rosy Crucifixion,* is one long exegesis of the simple admission "I had lost the power to love."[46] All the sentiment of his being, meanly withheld from "cunt," is lavished on the unattractive souls who make up the gang Miller never outgrew or deserted. What we observe in his work is a compulsive heterosexual activity in sharp distinction (but not opposed to) the kind of cultural homosexuality which has ruled that love, friendship, affection—all forms of companionship, emotional or intellectual—are restricted exclusively to males.

Miller's sexual humor is the humor of the men's house, more specifically, the men's room. Like the humor of any in-group, it depends on a whole series of shared assumptions, attitudes and responses, which constitute bonds in themselves. Here sex is a game whose pleasures lie in a demanding strategic deception and manipulation of a dupe. Its object is less the satisfaction of libido than ego, for the joys of sense are largely forgotten in the fun of making a fool of the victim. But unless sex is hard to get, comic, secretive, and "cunt" transparently stupid and contemptible, the joke disappears in air. As with racist humor or bigot fun in general, failure to agree upon the

[43] *The World of Sex,* p. 114.

[44] It is important to bear in mind that Miller was fifty-eight when *Sexus* was published. The scarcity ethic of callow youth—"Did you get to first base?" "Did you get her to go all the way?"—probably accounts for the sheer quantity, the cloying plenty of Miller's escapades.

[45] *Tropic of Capricorn,* p. 214.

[46] *Nexus,* p. 37.

presumed fundamentals turns the comedy into puerile tedium. The point of Miller's game is to get as much as you can while giving nothing. The "much" in question is not sexual experience, for that might imply depth of feeling: the answer appears to be as much "cunt" or as many "cunts" as possible. In standard English the approximate phrase is probably Kinsey's uninviting "number of sexual outlets."

To love is to lose. In his one honest book, *Nexus*, Miller reveals that he lost very badly. His beloved Mara turned out to be a lesbian who inflicted her mistress upon him in a nightmarish ménage à trois, a female variant of the rigged triangle Lawrence aspired to but never achieved. It would be fascinating to speculate on how much of Miller's arrogance toward "cunt" in general is the product of this one lacerating experience.

For those convinced of the merits of the game, nearly any occasion can be exploited. Here is the redoubtable Henry paying a visit of condolence to a widow he once foolishly reverenced and admired, stammering and blushing before her, fatuously imagining she couldn't be "had." Scrupulously, he first sets the scene, welcoming his comrades to the setting of his triumph: "a low sofa," "soft lights"; the drink is catalogued and then the dress—"a beautiful low-cut morning gown."[47] Halfway through a eulogy of her late husband, Miller is suddenly inspired: "Without saying a word I raised her dress and slipped it into her."[48] The moment of truth is at hand; will the widow balk? As in a dream, this surprise attack meets with instantaneous success: "As I got it into her and began to work it around she took to moaning like . . . sort of delirious . . . with gasps and little shrieks of joy and anguish."[49] Finally the moral: "I thought to myself what a sap you've been to wait so long. She was so wet and juicy down there . . . why, anybody could have come along and had what's what. She was a pushover."[50] So are they all, and the joke is that such opportunities are missed only for lack of enterprise or through adherence to false ideals.

They are not only pushovers, they are puppets. Speaking boy to boy about another "fuck," Miller remarks, "I moved her around like one of those legless toys which illustrate the principle of gravity."[51] Total victory is gratuitous insult; the pleasure of humiliating the sexual object appears to be far more intoxicating than sex itself. Miller's protégé, Curley, is an expert at inflicting this sort of punishment, in this instance, on a woman whom both men regard as criminally overambitious, disgracefully unaware she is only cunt:

> He took pleasure in degrading her. I could scarcely blame him for it, she was such a prim, priggish bitch in her street clothes. You'd swear she didn't own a

[47] Henry Miller, *Black Spring* (New York: Grove Press, 1963), p. 96.
[48] *Ibid.*
[49] *Ibid.*
[50] *Ibid.*
[51] *Sexus*, p. 94. The legless toy in question is Mara.

cunt the way she carried herself in the street. Naturally, when he got her alone, he made her pay for her highfallutin' ways. He went at it cold-bloodedly. "Fish it out!" he'd say, opening his fly a little. "Fish it out with your tongue!" . . . once she got the taste of it in her mouth you could do anything with her. Sometimes he'd stand her on her hands and push her around the room that way, like a wheelbarrow. Or else he'd do it dog fashion, and while she groaned and squirmed he'd nonchalantly light a cigarette and blow the smoke between her legs. Once he played her a dirty trick doing it that way. He had worked her up to such a state that she was beside herself. Anyway, after he had almost polished the ass off her with his back-scuttling he pulled out for a second, as though to cool his cock off . . . and shoved a big long carrot up her twat.[52]

One recalls Shapiro's enthusiasm for the "overpowering mysteries of love and copulation."

Even the orgies which Miller presents to us as lessons in a free and happy sensuality, far removed from the constraints of American puritanism, are really only authoritarian arrangements where male will is given absolute license. One of these events takes place at Ulric's studio. But the brilliant surface of the occasion is marred by the hero's cupidity in wishing to enjoy both women, though insanely anxious that Ulric stay away from his own Mara. Here, just as in legendary suburbia, the women take no active part in the arrangements whereby they are swapped. Usually Miller and his friends are magnanimous; they offer each other some "cunt" whenever they can, an offer casually made in front of the property herself. Several unforeseen occurrences trouble the moment's serenity. Ulric's "blind date," because mulatto, is "rather difficult to handle, at least in the preliminary stages."[53] Moreover, she begins to menstruate: "What's a little blood between bouts?" Ulric giggles, alarmed enough to rush to the bathroom and scrub himself "assiduously," unable to cover a primitive fright which infects the whole gang— Miller himself takes twenty pages to fret over the possibility that contact with menstrual discharge has given him "the syph." In their omnipotence, Miller and his cohorts can do anything to women whose only revenge is venereal disease—a major reason for the continual masculine anxiety on this score.

Another group event takes place between Miller, his estranged wife Maude, and a visitor who stopped in for a drink. On this occasion things begin amiably enough, Miller providing an ecstatic running commentary on the ideal freedom from jealousy, ill will, and guilt, and each of the two

[52] *Tropic of Capricorn*, pp. 1180–81.
[53] *Sexus*, p. 91. Miller has a certain faltering sympathy for blacks which does not extend itself to black women about whom he makes remarks so outrageously racist that (as expressions of the author's own sentiment) they are difficult to match in serious writing. "Try a piece of dark meat now and then. It's tastier, and it costs less," etc. (*Nexus*, p. 261).

female robots behaving splendidly. Finally the hero, tried by the exertion of some five consecutive orgasms, summons his last ounce of strength for neighbor Elsie, who has been most enthusiastic till now: " 'Go on, fuck, fuck,' she cried," etc.[54] Suddenly the evening's pleasant ambiance is shattered and Elsie is in pain. Miller's powerful prose renders this " 'Oh, oh! Don't. Please don't. It hurts!' she yelled."[55] The hero is outraged. He appears to reason that, in consenting, the woman had waived all rights and must be kept to the bargain regardless:

"Shut up, you bitch you!" I said. "It hurts does it? You wanted it, didn't you?" I held her tightly, raised myself a little higher to get it into the hilt, and pushed until I thought her womb would give way. Then I came—right into that snail-like mouth which was wide open. She went into a convulsion, delirious with joy and pain. Then her legs slid off my shoulders and fell to the floor with a thud. She lay there like a dead one, completely fucked out."[56]

The spirit of this sort of evening is incomprehensible, both in its frenzy and in its violence, unless one takes into account the full power of the conventional morality it is written against and depends upon so parasitically—every fear, shame, and thou shalt not. Were there not so much to deny, resist, overcome, and befoul, the operator and his feminine machines would hardly require their belabored promiscuity, nor the hero his righteous brutality.

Miller is very far from having escaped his Puritan origin: it is in the smut of his pals; in the frenzy of his partners; in the violence and contempt of his "fucking." We are never allowed to forget that this is forbidden and the sweeter for being so; that lust has greater excitements than love; that women degrade themselves by participation in sexuality, and that all but a few "pure" ones are no more than cunt and outrageous if they forget it. "The dirty bitches—they like it," he apprises us; clinical, fastidious, horrified and amused to record how one responded "squealing like a pig"; another "like a crazed animal"; one "gibbered"; another "crouched on all fours like a she-animal, quivering and whinnying"; while still another specimen was "so deep in heat" she was like "a bright voracious animal . . . an elephant walking the ball."[57]

The very brutality with which he handles the language of sex; the iconographic four-letter words, soiled by centuries of prurience and shame, is an indication of Miller's certainty of how really filthy all this is. His defense against censorship is incontrovertible—"there was no other idiom possible" to express the "obscenity" he wished to convey.[58] His diction is,

[54] Ibid., p. 384.

[55] Ibid.

[56] Ibid.

[57] Chosen at random: see Sexus, p. 227, Capricorn, p. 213, and Sexus, p. 101, and 377 and 378.

[58] Henry Miller, Remember to Remember (New York: New Directions, 1947), p. 280.

quite as he claims, a "technical device"[59] depending on the associations of dirt, violence, and scorn, in which a sexually distressed culture has steeped the words which also denominate the sexual organs and the sexual act. Miller is completely opposed to dissipating the extrasexual connotations of such diction, but wishes to preserve its force as "magical terms"[60] whose power is immanent in their quality of mana and taboo. Under this sacramental cloak a truly obscene ruthlessness toward other human beings is passed over unnoticed, or even defended. "Obscenity" is analogous to the "uses of the miraculous in the Masters," Miller announces pretentiously.[61] He and the censor have linguistic and sexual attitudes in common: ritual use of the "obscene" is, of course, pointless, unless agreement exists that the sexual is, in fact, obscene.[62] Furthermore, as Miller reminds us again and again, obscenity is a form of violence, a manner of conveying male hostility, both toward the female (who is sex) and toward sexuality itself (which is her fault). Yet, for all his disgust, indeed because of it, Miller must return over and over to the ordure; steel himself again and again by confronting what his own imagination (powerfully assisted by his cultural heritage and experience) has made horrible. The egotism called manhood requires such proof of courage. This is reality, Miller would persuade us: cunt stinks, as Curley says, and cunt is sex.

With regard to the male anatomy, things are very different, since "prick" is power. While urinating in a pissoir or even emptying the garbage, Miller may be smitten with a painful awareness of his own noble destiny. In the "Land of Fuck" the "spermatozoon reigns supreme." God is the "summation of all the spermatozoa." Miller himself is divine: "My name? Why just call me God."[63] Actually, he's even a bit more than this—"something beyond God Almighty. . . . *I am a man.* That seems to me sufficient."[64] Probably, but just in case, it is safer to develop a theology and know one's catechism: "Before me always the image of the body, our triune god of penis and testicles. On the right, God the Father; on the left and hanging a little lower, God the Son! and between them and above them, the Holy Ghost. I can never forget that this holy trinity is man-made."[65]

Cunt is scarcely this inspiring: a "crack"; a "gash"; a "wound"; a "slimy

[59] *Ibid.,* p. 287.

[60] *Ibid.,* p. 288.

[61] *Ibid.,* p. 287.

[62] Unfortunately for the religiously inclined of every persuasion, from Miller to the censors to the Church, fuck is losing its aura of the nefarious and in time may, while meaning all things to all people, mean just what it does mean and cease to function as a synonym for hurt, humble, or exploit. In *Eros Denied* Wayland Young has already demonstrated that it is surely the best English word to convey "sexual intercourse," "coitus," and other pretentious locutions to which expository prose is still confined.

[63] *Tropic of Capricorn,* pp. 203–4.

[64] *Black Spring,* p. 24. Italics Miller's.

[65] *Ibid.,* pp. 24–25.

hole";—but really only emptiness, nothingness, zero. This is no less true of Mara than of the run-of-the-mill female, the taxi-dancer Miller dismisses as a "minus sign" of "absolute vacuity."[66] Gazing at his love, the egoist reports he "finds nothing, nothing except my own image wavering in a bottomless well," admitting at last he is "unable to form the slightest image of her being."[67] In the *Tropic of Cancer* both Miller and Van Norden explore the frightening enigma of "cunt." Sickened, even before he begins, by the very sight of this "dead clam," Van Norden fortifies himself with technology: "I made her hold it open and I trained the flashlight on it . . . I never in my life looked at cunt so seriously . . . And the more I looked at it the less interesting it became. It only goes to show you there's nothing to it after all."[68] Still shaken at the sight, he cannot help exclaiming over the bitter cheat:

> When you look at them with their clothes on you imagine all sorts of things; you give them an individuality like, which they haven't got, of course. There's just a crack there between the legs . . . It's an illusion! . . . It's so absolutely meaningless . . . All that mystery about sex and then you discover that it's nothing—just a blank . . . there's nothing there . . . nothing at all. It's disgusting.[69]

Later on in the book Miller hires a whore himself to have a try at dredging some meaning out of the unfathomable vacuum of the female. Like his fellow investigator, he finds only a "great gulf of nothingness," an "ugly gash" and "the wound that never heals."[70] But he is determined to do better than his buddy. He is also extremely self-conscious about the artist's lofty role in the areas of myth and vision. It is not very far from this to "mystery;" so, doing the best he can, Miller converts the "fucked out cunt of a whore" into a grand "riddle," hoping to convince himself that the planet earth is "but a great sprawling female . . . in the violet light of the stars." After all, he reasons, "out of that dark unstitched wound, that sink of abomination," man is born; part clown; part angel, a thought which leaves him "face to face with the Absolute." And out of this unworthy "zero" derive the "endless mathematical worlds" of masculine civilization, even the holy writ of Dostoievski. There must, therefore, be something to this "festering obscene horror" after all.[71] A false Xavier touching leprosy on a dare, Miller finds it impossible to smother his disgust. There is perhaps a certain unintended irony too, in the fact that Mara, his apotheosis of the eternal and mysterious "female principle," is also a pathological liar.

[66] *Tropic of Capricorn*, pp. 120–21.
[67] *Ibid.*, p. 343.
[68] *Tropic of Cancer*, pp. 139–40.
[69] *Ibid.*, p. 140.
[70] *Ibid.*, p. 249.
[71] *Ibid.*, pp. 248, 9, 50.

Miller has a rather morbid fear of excreta. The only woman whom he actually fails to "fuck" lived in an apartment with a faulty toilet and, in some two-thousand pages, his "most embarrassing moment" (to adopt his own interesting phrase) occurred when it overflowed, a generous amount of his feces along with it. Miller abandons the siege and ducks out, leaving her in charge of his remains. In general, he has irreversibly associated sexuality with the process of waste and elimination, and since his responses to the latter are extraordinarily negative, it is significant that, when he intends to be particularly insulting, he carries on his amours in the "shithouse" as, on one occasion, when he happens upon "an American cunt" in a French rest-room. Standing her "slap up against the wall, he finds he can't "get it into her." With his never-failing ingenuity, he next tries sitting on the toilet seat. This won't do either, so, in a burst of hostility posing as passion, he reports: "I come all over her beautiful gown and she's sore as hell about it."[72] In the *Tropic of Capricorn* he repeats the stunt; in Sexus too. It is a performance which nicely combines defecation with orgasm and clarifies the sense of defilement in sexuality which is the puritan bedrock of Miller's response to women. The unconscious logic appears to be that, since sex defiles the female, females who consent to sexuality deserve to be defiled as completely as possible.[73] What he really wants to do is shit on her.

The men's room has schooled Miller in the belief that sex is inescapably dirty. Meditating there upon some graffiti, "the walls crowded with sketches and epithets, all of them jocosely obscene," he speculates on "what an impression it would make on those swell dames . . . I wondered if they would carry their tails so high if they could see what was thought of an ass here."[74] Since his mission is to inform "cunt" just how it's ridiculed and despised in the men's house, women perhaps owe Miller some gratitude for letting them know.

In a great many respects Miller is avant-garde and a highly inventive artist, but his most original contribution to sexual attitudes is confined to giving the first full expression to an ancient sentiment of contempt. The remainder of his sexual ethos is remarkably conventional. Reading, again in the toilet, he converts his own syndrome into a "great tradition" and fancies himself one of the illustrious company of Rabelais, Boccaccio, and Petronius, "the fine lusty genuine spirits who recognized dung for dung and angels for angels," observing with them the ancient distinctions between good and evil, whore and lady, adamant about the virtues of a "world where the vagina is repre-

[72] *Ibid.*, p. 18.

[73] E.g. Women are dirty because they are sex; "pure" women are those who **deny** this. Some few of these are admirable (mothers, childhood sweethearts, etc.); most, however, are only hypocrites to be punished and exposed.

[74] *Tropic of Cancer*, pp. 174–75.

sented by a crude, honest slit."⁷⁵ Under the brash American novelty is the old story: guilt, fear, a reverence for "purity" in the female; and a deep moral outrage whenever the "lascivious bitch" in woman is exposed. Despite the fact that Don Juan's success lies in proving "they all like it—the dirty bitches," Miller seems each time disappointed that they should, shocked and unsettled by the discovery. Somehow he wishes they wouldn't, is sure they shouldn't. Yet, most do and it appears that it is just to unmask this very hypocrisy that he carries on so many campaigns. Disillusion sets in early. Giving piano lessons, the stripling discovered that his pupil's mother is "a slut, a tramp and a trollop if ever there was one." Worse still, she lives "with a nigger . . . seems she couldn't get a prick big enough to satisfy her." Now the first rule of his code is that no opportunity should be wasted—anyway, "what the hell are you going to do when a hot bitch like that plasters her cunt up against you"—yet Miller seems shocked nevertheless.⁷⁶ He has a hygienic preference for the daughter, who is "fresh cunt," clean as "new-mown hay." When she is "knocked up" he finds a "Jewboy," coughs up a very modest contribution toward the cost of an abortion and lights out for the Adirondacks. Off on a jaunt to the Catskills he meets a pair of girls who, in the manner of medieval "types," represent Dishonesty and Integrity. Agnes is a "dumb Irish Catholic" and consequently, a prude; she "likes it," but is afraid to admit as much. In splendid contrast stands Francie—"one of those girls who are born to fuck. She had no aims, no great desires . . . held no grievances, was constantly cheerful."⁷⁷ She is so exemplary she even relishes a beating: "it makes me feel good inside . . . maybe a woman ought to get beaten up once in a while," she volunteers, and Miller marvels that "It isn't often you get a cunt who'll admit such things—I mean a regular cunt and not a moron."⁷⁸

In the experience of the American manchild sex and violence, exploitation and sentimentality, are strangely, even wonderfully, intermingled. Miller relates how, on one climactic day of his childhood, he murdered a boy in a gang fight, then slicked his hair and returned to the welcoming arms of unsuspecting Aunt Caroline, to bask in the maternal solicitude of her home-made bread—"Mothers had time in those days to make good bread with their own hands, and still do the thousand and one things which motherhood demands of a woman."⁷⁹ The same afternoon brings sexual initiation: "Joey was so happy that he took us down to his cellar later and made his sister pull up her dress and show what was underneath . . .Whereas the other

⁷⁵ Black Spring, pp. 48, 50.
⁷⁶ Tropic of Capricorn, pp. 255–56.
⁷⁷ Ibid., p. 261.
⁷⁸ Ibid., p. 263.
⁷⁹ Remember to Remember (New York: New Directions, 1947), p. 40. The homily, delivered with absolute gravity, echoed by (and echoing) popular magazines, soap opera, etc., is an object lesson in how interrelated the various levels of American media can be.

urchins used to pay to make Weesie lift her dress up, for us it was done with love. After a while we persuaded her not to do it anymore for the other boys —we were in love with her and we wanted her to go straight."[80] The model of the adult world already shines through the boy's excitement: violence, a male prerogative; sexuality, a secret and shameful province of the female, regulated by the cash nexus. And the pieties are neatly arranged: Weesie shall be saved and isolated into "decency" through "love" will mellow in time into Aunt Caroline's handy ignorant nurturance.

Through all his exhausting experiences with enthusiastic "bitches," Miller never abandons the icons of his "pure," early loves, immaculate creatures about whom, he is pleased to announce, he "never had an impure thought." Four decades later his chivalrous ardor toward Una Gifford can still gush forth at the remembered echo of a pop tune: ". . . a thousand times beyond any reach of mine. Kiss me, kiss me *again!*" How the words pierced me! And not a soul in that boisterous, merrymaking group was aware of my agony . . . Sounds of revelry filled the empty street . . . It was for me they were giving the party. And she was there, my beloved, snow-blonde, starry-eyed, forever unattainable Queen of the Arctic."[81] Miller, in love, reverts to all the sentimental tokens of "respect" appropriate to a Victorian suitor. Floundering in a sentimentality largely narcissistic, full of a sludgy "idealism" that complements his cynicism, he sends flowers and writes long letters full of regressive daydreams. Rich in pathos as it is, Miller's long, frustrating attachment to Mara is less a love story than the case history of a neurotic dependence.

Part of Miller's conventionality is to insist on a rigid split between body and mind, sense and soul. Van Norden puts it on the line: "You can get something out of a book, even a bad book . . but a cunt, it's just sheer loss of time."[82] Miller has plenty of time to waste but is just as careful to preserve an obstinate separation between sex and the "higher" life of books and ideas, which can only be experienced alone or in masculine company. His interpretation of the separate spheres is that woman is no more than "cunt," though she is occasionally said to redeem herself by having babies while men write books. Even this uterine mystique is no good unless an abstraction; he has no interest in parenthood, and his compliments to maternity are scanty and without feeling.

Ambivalent about money, Miller is unmoved by the claims of extreme virility, war, and militarism. Yet this hardly makes him any less determined to maintain male hegemony throughout every phase of life. As Lawrence and other prophets have tried to teach us, this can only be done by preserving traditional sexual polarity, the one way to offset the decline of the West and

---

80 *Tropic of Capricorn*, p. 125.
81 *Nexus*, p. 303.
82 *Tropic of Cancer*, p. 140.

redeem the horrors of the twentieth century. In what must be, beyond question, the most novel analysis of World War I, Miller traces the catastrophe to the loss of sexual polarity, e.g., the feminist movement: "The loss of sex polarity is part and parcel of the larger disintegration, the reflex of the soul's death, and coincident with the disappearance of great men, great causes, great wars."[83]

Miller's scheme of sexual polarity relegates the female to "cunt," an exclusively sexual being, crudely biological. Though he shares this lower nature, the male is also capable of culture and intellect. The sexes are two warring camps between whom understanding is impossible since one is human and animal (according to Miller's perception, intellectual and sexual)—the other, simply animal. Together, as mind and matter, male and female, they encompass the breadth of possible experience. The male, part angel, part animal, enjoys yet suffers too from his divided nature. His appetite for "cunt," recurrent and shameful as it is, is, nevertheless, his way of staying in touch with his animal origins. It keeps him "real." Miller staves off the threat of an actual sexual revolution—woman's transcendence of the mindless material capacity he would assign her—through the fiat of declaring her cunt and trafficking with her only in the utopian fantasies of his "fucks." That this is but whistling in the dark is demonstrated by his own defeating experience with Mara, and, even more persuasively by the paralyzing fear which drives him to pretend—so that he may deal with them at all—that women are things.[84]

In *The World of Sex* Miller explains that most of his writing on sex was simply an attempt at "self-liberation."[85] What he has furnished us is an excellent guide to his dungeon but it provides no clue to the world into which he was emancipated. Delivered from the Brahmin eminence of his old age, the following pronunciamento is woefully shaky: "Perhaps a cunt, smelly though it may be, is one of the prime symbols for the connection between all things"[86]—the possibility might exist, but the stench you may be sure of. There are times when Miller seems to catch a glimpse of what chaos is made of human life through the brutality of the sexual ethic he represents: and at one point, profoundly unconscious of patronization, he serves up this staggering naïveté: "No matter how attached I became to a 'cunt,' I was more interested in the person who owned it. A cunt doesn't live a separate independent existence."[87]

The impulse to see even women as human beings may occur momentarily—a fleeting urge—but the terrible needs of adolescent narcissism are much

---

[83] Henry Miller, *The Cosmological Eye* (New York: New Directions, 1939), p. 120.

[84] Miller's respect for the work of Anaïs Nin appears to be the single exception to the rule, perhaps in itself a reason for his enthusiasm over her productions.

[85] *The World of Sex*, p. 16. This short essay veers between aspiring to be a "serious message" on the subject, and its more pressing need to sell the title.

[86] *Ibid.*, p. 44.

[87] *Ibid.*

greater, the cheap dream of endlessly fucking impersonal matter, mindless tissue endlessly compliant, is so much more compelling. And the thrills of egotism are always there: the high of the con game, the excitement of lying, wheedling, acting, cheating, deliberately degrading, then issuing orders and directing the gull in a performance whose "bestiality" only confirms his detached superiority. All these comforts make up for the disgust of the act itself.

Finally, there is the satisfaction of evacuation—a general release of tensions, hostilities, frustrations, even thoughts. "During intercourse they passed out of me, as though I were emptying refuse in a sewer."[88] Americans never underestimate the virtues of indoor plumbing. Miller looks on woman in a surrealist dream and sees "a knot with a mask between her legs" and knows "one crack is as good as another and over every sewer there's a grating."[89] "Cunt" may be lobotomized earthenware, but "behind every slit"[90] is danger, death, the unknown, the exhilarations of the chase, and in Miller's "genitourinary"[91] system, the sexual comfort-station is a pay toilet whose expense is great enough to constitute its own reward.

Miller has given voice to certain sentiments which masculine culture had long experienced but always rather carefully suppressed: the yearning to effect a complete depersonalization of woman into cunt, a game-sexuality of cheap exploitation, a childish fantasy of power untroubled by the reality of persons or the complexity of dealing with fellow human beings and, finally, a crude species of evacuation hardly better than anal in character.

While the release of such inhibited emotion, however poisonous, is beyond question advantageous, the very expression of such lavish contempt and disgust, as Miller has unleashed and made fashionable, can come to be an end in itself, eventually harmful, perhaps even malignant. To provide unlimited scope for masculine aggression, although it may finally bring the situation out into the open, will hardly solve the dilemma of our sexual politics. Miller does have something highly important to tell us; his virulent sexism is beyond question an honest contribution to social and psychological understanding which we can hardly afford to ignore. But to confuse this neurotic hostility, this frank abuse, with sanity, is pitiable. To confuse it with freedom were vicious, were it not so very sad.

[88] *Ibid.*, p. 51.
[89] *Black Spring*, p. 164.
[90] *Ibid.*
[91] Miller is fond of this term and uses it often.

SEVEN

$\mathcal{N}orman$ $\mathcal{M}ailer$

I

Mailer is paradoxical, full of ambivalence, divided conscience, and conflicting loyalties. There is probably no other writer who can describe the present and its "practical working-day American schizophrenia" so well.[1] For by now Mailer is as much a cultural phenomenon as a man of letters, fulfilling his enormous ambition to exert a direct effect on the consciousness of his time. What he offers for our edification is the spectacle of his dilemma, the plight of a man whose powerful intellectual comprehension of what is most dangerous in the masculine sensibility is exceeded only by his attachment to the malaise. No one has done so much to explain, yet justify violence. Mailer is enigmatic enough to be a militarist with quasi-pacifist books to his credit, a man compulsively given to casting himself into the role of the "general" leading "his troops" when invited to appear as a celebrity at anti-war demonstrations.[2]

A prisoner of the virility cult, Mailer is never incapable of analyzing it. He even furnishes persuasive argument as to how this psychological set demands our general concern. For it is here that sexual politics intersect with

[1] Norman Mailer, *The Armies of the Night* (New York: New American Library, 1968, Signet reprint), p. 125.
[2] See *Miami and The Siege of Chicago* (New York: World, 1968) and *The Armies of the Night*, passim.

realpolitik. Here the oppression of women as a group is invoked to provide an emotional model, even a style, for patriarchal warfare. When pushed very far, an oppressive system tends to become vicious. In Mailer's work the sexual animus behind reactionary attitude erupts into open hostility. It is hardly surprising that a man whose most formative adult experience took place in the men's-house culture of the army might tend to see sexual belligerence in the terms of actual warfare.

When a novelist is obsessed with certain traits of behavior, his characters tend to repeat themselves from one book to the next. There is a character in Mailer's fiction who continues to appear under different guises, and according to the author's ambivalent response, may be villain or hero, or more likely villain as hero. The first such figure is Sergeant Croft of *The Naked and The Dead*, where the portrait seems to be as unfriendly as it is incisive. Like D.J., the prodigy ("there's blood on my dick") of *Why Are We in Vietnam?*,[3] Croft began as a hunter. Like Sergius O'Shaugnessy of *The Deer Park*, Croft has "the cruelty to be a man."[4]

The larger part of Croft's existence is passed in homicidal rage. His first murder, the cold-blooded execution of a striker whom he dismisses as a "dog," left him with a memorable "excitement."[5] It is an exhilaration he spends the rest of his life recapturing, both in sexuality ("You're all a bunch of fuggin whores . . . all a bunch of dogs . . . You're all deer to track"),[6] and in the organized slaughter of warfare: ("I hate the bastards . . . I'm gonna really get me a Jap").[7] *The Naked and The Dead* describes the American campaign on "Anopopei" in the Philippines. Since the Japanese who hold the island are without supplies and close to starvation, the invasion ends as a "Jap hunt," a Croftian holiday. Preparing to shoot a prisoner, Croft anticipates "the quick lurching spasms of the body when the bullets would crash into it,"[8] and the *frisson* which awaits him is the exact counterpart to what he knows of sexual experience.

Mailer regards Croft as the megalomaniac ambition of the frontier with no further room to exercise itself. "His ancestors pushed and labored and strained, drove their oxen, sweated their women, and moved a thousand miles." But in Croft this force has turned into an exclusively destructive energy:[9] "He pushed and labored inside himself and smoldered with an endless hatred," his "main cast of mind" a "superior contempt."[10] "He hated

[3] Norman Mailer, *Why Are We in Vietnam?* (New York: Putnam, 1967), p. 7.

[4] Norman Mailer, *The Deer Park* (novel) (New York: Putnam, 1955), Berkeley reprint, p. 198.

[5] Norman Mailer, *The Naked and The Dead* (New York: Holt, Rinehart and Winston, 1948), Signet reprint, p. 127.

[6] *Ibid.*, p. 130.

[7] *Ibid.*, p. 123.

[8] *Ibid.*, p. 153.

[9] *Ibid.*, p. 130.

[10] *Ibid.*, p. 124.

weakness and loved practically nothing."[11] Croft's most withering insult is to castigate his subordinates as "a pack of goddam women."[12] While a youth learning to track his first game (game whom he conceives to be female, because prey), he cursed himself with the same fury when his gun wavered before firing—"Jus' a little old woman."[13]

Another factor has contributed to Croft's maniacal anger—his wife's adultery: "It ended with him going to town alone, and taking a whore when he was drunk, beating her sometimes with a wordless choler."[14] Mailer suggests that it is the impetus of this sexual rage which has brought Croft to the Army and halfway round the world to vent his spleen on strangers.

If Croft stands for run of the mill fascism in the novel, General Cummings, the refined sadist at the pinnacle of the class structure which Army hierarchy represents so saliently, is the higher totalitarianism. He too considers killing sexual, and sexuality murderous. First a sample of Cummings the lover:

> He must subdue her, absorb her, rip her apart and consume her . . . [thinking] "I'll take you apart, I'll eat you, oh, I'll make you mine, you bitch."[15]

Next the general:

> the deep dark urges of man, the sacrifice on the hilltop, the churning lusts of night and sleep, weren't all of them contained in the shattering, screaming burst of a shell . . . the phallus-shell that rides through a shining vagina of steel . . . the curve of sexual excitement and discharge, which is after all the physical core of life.[16]

As sex is war, war is sexual. Can one deny "the physical core of life"? The connection between sex and violence appears not only as metaphor, but seems to express a conviction about the nature of both phenomena.

A superficial reading might convince one that Mailer's brilliant anatomy of these two cancerous personalities is rendered without any traces of admiring or positive identification. But in the last chapters of the book a subtle shift takes place in the treatment of Croft; a curious effort is made to persuade the reader that he is not mad but heroic. The novel goes GI and spoils itself in cheap patriotism.[17] Years later Mailer not only admitted that his ideas about violence had "changed 180 degrees" since his first work, but even con-

---

11 *Ibid.*
12 *Ibid.*, p. 405.
13 *Ibid.*, p. 125.
14 *Ibid.*, p. 129.
15 *Ibid.*, pp. 325–26.
16 *Ibid.*, pp. 440–43.
17 It is heartbreaking the way Mailer throws the book away on the last page by failing to stop at the proper moment, e.g., when the last Japanese is butchered. Instead he adds a final page of cute dugout humor which reduces the novel to a movie script.

fided that "beneath the ideology of *The Naked and The Dead* was an obsession with violence. The characters for whom I had the most secret admiration, like Croft," he remarks nonchalantly "were violent people."[18]

The ambiguity intrudes again in *Barbary Shore*, the quasi-political novel that followed, in which an undercurrent hostility continues to connect, even equate combat and cruelty with sexuality. In a book whose overt message is a shocked protest against the extermination camps of Nazi and Soviet, the brutality of our century, the hero and the novel's moral arbiter recalls with gratification how, as a soldier in enemy territory, he "made love from the hip:"

> I never saw the girl. Above my head in magnification of myself the barrel of the machine gun pointed toward the trees . . . I went back to the hay and stretched out in a nervous half-sleep which consisted of love with artillery shells and sex of polished steel.[19]

Mailer's chief quarrel with Nazi genocide turns upon a point of style; he disapproves of the technological nature of the gas chambers. Having promised Germany "the primitive secrets of her barbaric age,"[20] having offered the thrill of a chance to "*stomp* on things and scream and shout and rip things up and *kill*,"[21] Hitler paid off with nothing but the scientific tedium of gas.

During the Hipster period of "The White Negro" and *Advertisements for Myself* Mailer seems to have thrown all hesitation aside, and while still harboring reservations about the virtues of violence on a collective scale, appears to have fallen in love with it as a personal and sexual style. A rapist is a rapist only to the "square": to the superior perceptions of Hip, rape is "part of life," and should be assessed by a subtle critical method based on whether the act possesses "artistry" or "real desire."[22] Confusing the simply antisocial with the revolutionary, Mailer develops an aesthetic of Hip whose chief temperamental characteristic is a malign *machismo*, still dear to those in the New Left who have fallen under Mailer's spell in adolescence or continue to confuse Che Guevara with the brassy cliché of the Westerns. As the rampant individualism (domesticated Nietzsche) of Hip proliferates, it is interesting to observe the character Marion Faye change from the "homosexual villain" of *The Deer Park* into a banal movie satan in "Advertisements for Myself On the Way Out," achieving a final apotheosis in the theatrical production of *The Deer Park* in which Mailer travestied his novel. Faye is at first only a

18 Norman Mailer, *The Presidential Papers* (New York: Putnam, 1963), p. 136.

19 Norman Mailer, *Barbary Shore* (New York: Holt, Rinehart and Winston, 1951), Signet reprint, pp. 114–15.

20 *The Presidential Papers*, p. 182.

21 *Ibid.*, p. 134.

22 Norman Mailer, *Advertisements for Myself* (New York: Putnam, 1959), Berkeley reprint, p. 292.

sadistic pimp who goes about procuring "the kind of girl you could wipe your hands on."[23] But as the author's own admiring preoccupation with Faye's mastery of sex as manipulative power continues to grow, he invests this latter-day demon with an ambitious theological rigamarole, outfitting him with the glittery attributes of a cinema Faust and urban cowboy—Croft gone slick.

The Deer Park began as a sympathetic and middling-good study of how a corrupt commercial artist, the director Charles Francis Eitel, picks up, exploits, then breaks and discards a woman who his snobbery fancies is his inferior. The structure, the moral logic and the aesthetic unity of the novel properly require that it end in Elena Esposito's suicide, the final achievement of Faye's sadistic powers of suggestion working upon the promising material of her own self-destructive descent into prostitution. The anticlimactic resolution Mailer chose to give the novel instead in the defeat of her empty marriage to Eitel has its own pathos. But the drastically different denouement imposed upon the stage version, with Eitel's sad, self-regarding death, devalues the work even more outrageously as Faye is transformed from a sleazy hood with demented notions of Sin, to a sexual Faust of Hip, and Eitel is promoted from a plausible Hollywood heel to a hero of love.[24]

In *The Naked and The Dead* Mailer had presented Croft with a foil named Lieutenant Hearne. A weak liberal, a university man, Hearne is engaged in a forlorn struggle against both the insidious enticements of the Cummings' way of life among the rich and powerful, whose heir apparent his class origins destine him to be, and the brutality of Croft whose officer and fighting equal he is finally so anxious to become—the last a folly which permits Croft to have him shot. But in Steven Rojack, hero of *An American Dream*, the intellectual Hearne does at last manage to become a Croft of civilian life whose most precious memory is the night his platoon cheered their young lieutenant's histrionic victory over a nest of German soldiers. Rojack has ever since been possessed of a rage which only murder can quell, and he manages to bring about the deaths of two white women and a black man all in the novel's thirty-two hours. Mrs. Rojack is snuffed out by a blow for male supremacy, Cherry by her lover's sentimentality, and Shago Martin so that the white man may keep a corner on "his woman" in the face of black encroachment. The novelist assures us meanwhile that "murder offers the promise of vast relief. It is never unsexual."[25] In the sex war Mailer conducts throughout *An American Dream*, divorce is a "retreat," separation a species of cold war, sexual intercourse a "bang," or more explosively, a "bangeroo," male comrades are fellow "swords" and victory is announced in a froth-at-the-mouth Croftism:

I felt a mean rage in my feet. It was as if in killing her, the act had been too

[23] *The Deer Park* (novel), p. 159.
[24] Norman Mailer, *The Deer Park, A Play* (New York: Dial, 1967).
[25] Norman Mailer, *An American Dream* (New York: Dial, 1965), p. 8.

gentle, I had not plumbed the hatred . . . I had an impulse to go up to her and kick her ribs, grind my heel on her nose, drive the point of my shoe into her temple and kill her again, kill her good this time, kill her right. I stood there shuddering from the power of this desire . . .[26]

"Desire" is a happy verbal choice, for in the fantasy of virility which Mailer is so adept both at analyzing and at the same time identifying with in such a curious fashion, sexuality and violence are so inextricably mixed that the "desire to kill" is a phrase truly aphrodisiac. Nor is it very surprising that Rojack's victims should be women and blacks, or, with the exception of Rojack's service, the victims of Mailer's soldiers for three wars, Orientals: such are the white male's subjects, the objects of his dominant wrath.

Mailer's latest study of the Wasp male psychosis, *Why Are We in Vietnam?*, is perhaps his most interesting. It is carried out through the imagination of an eighteen-year-old pondering the implications of his recent rite of passage into the murderous order of his peers. Hollingsworth, the evil genius of *Barbary Shore,* had first introduced the notion of sexuality as butchery:

. . . he named various parts of her body and described what he would do to them, how he would tear this and squeeze that, eat here and spit there, butcher rough and slice fine, slash, macerate, pillage, all in an unrecognizable voice which must have issued between clenched teeth, until his appetite satisfied, I could see him squatting beside the carcass, his mouth wiped carefully with the back of his hand. With that, he sighed, as much as to say, "A good piece of ass, by God."[27]

Now the beguiling youth D. J. Jethroe, is introduced to tell us of the Alaskan bear hunt which has introduced him to "animal murder . . . and murder of the soldierest sort,"[28] describing his initiation into the company of men in a Hip-Pop diction whose metaphor is sexual-military: "Now remember!" he instructs the reader before the killing begins, "Think of cunt and ass—so it's all clear."[29] To convince us that sex and violence are inextricable in the culture into which he is being welcomed as an adult, D.J. offers us the evidence of his senses: "ever notice how blood smells like cunt and ass all mix in one?"[30] Already perfectly at ease among the "sexual peculiarities of red-blooded men," at home with the hero "who can't come unless he's squinting down a gunsight," D.J. renders the intercourse of his parents in terms of an explosion. Using a "dynamite stick for a phallus," Big Daddy himself ("he don't come, he explodes, he's a geyser of love, hot piss, shit . . . he's Texas

[26] *Ibid.,* p. 50.
[27] *Barbary Shore,* p. 146.
[28] *Why Are We in Vietnam?,* p. 7.
[29] *Ibid.,* p. 9.
[30] *Ibid.*

willpower") mother Alice is scattered over the southern states, "they found her vagina in North Carolina and part of her gashole in hometown."[31] Just as D.J. fancies his penis a gun to "those Dallas debutantes and just plain common fucks who are lucky to get drilled by him,"[32] he first gives in to the fever of the hunt when he catches sight of a great wounded bear splattering her death's blood into the forest. The transition from hunting and sex to war itself is Mailer's interest in the novel. Corrupt as that "High Grade Asshole," his plastic executive father, whose propulsion to kill is a means of "getting it up,"[33] D.J. now yearns after slaughter, inspired by an "itchy-dick memory of electric red."[34]

So the case may be with Wasps and Texans. Mailer is neither of these. There is a man in *The Naked and The Dead* whose name is Goldstein. He is not much of a soldier, he probably never killed anyone, but he does have the courage of fortitude and proves himself in an ordeal while carrying a friend's body through intolerable jungle miles of heat, thirst, and exhaustion. Oddly enough, this character never reappears in Mailer's fiction,[35] as hero after hero embody and then romanticize the Wasp viciousness of Croft or a mindless brutality presented as Irish, while Mailer grows more and more like a pillar of the American Legion, rhapsodizing in bellicose euphoria over the "sport," the "sensuousness of combat," the "soft lift and awe and pleasure"[36] of it; dilating upon the "sweetness" of war.[37] "Trust the authority of your senses," he admonishes with a veteran's nostalgia, conjuring by Hemingway through a busy career of aping the master's stolid martial airs—"If it made you feel good, it was good."[38] Perhaps, as an antidote to this enthusiasm, we may be permitted to quote another source:

You
Who have no channels for tears when you weep
No lips through which words can issue when you howl
No skin for your fingers to grip with when you writhe in torment
You

Your squirming limbs all smeared with blood and shining sweat and lymph
Between your closed lids the glaring eyeballs show only a thread of white . . .

In scorched and raw Hiroshima
Out of dark shuddering flames

[31] *Ibid.*, pp. 12–13.
[32] *Ibid.*, p. 42.
[33] *Ibid.*, p. 106.
[34] *Ibid.*, p. 122.
[35] Sam Slovoda, the central character in Mailer's short story "The Man Who Studied Yoga" (*Advertisements for Myself*) might possibly be the single exception.
[36] Norman Mailer, *Cannibals and Christians* (New York: Dial, 1966), p. 112.
[37] *The Armies of the Night*, p. 107.
[38] *Ibid.*

You no longer the human creatures you had been
Scrambled and crawled one after the other
Dragged yourselves along as far as this open ground
To bury in the dusts of agony
Your shriveled hair on scalps bald as the brows of Buddhist saints[39]

Mailer is at pains to convince us that the violence endemic in his novels and essays is in fact endemic in humanity, or at least that portion of it which merits his attention, since children, queers, and women fail to qualify and pacifists are "unmanly."[40] It follows that by definition the male is violent and for those blessed with this higher condition, "the message in the labyrinth of the genes would insist that violence was locked with creativity";[41] since it is "ineradicable," one stifles it "at one's peril" for it gives the holder "sufficient stature to claim he is a man."[42]

Moreover, the world of nature which D.J. and his still more manic pal Tex encounter in Alaska, the very "force of the North," with its sage "don't bullshit" air of reality, the essential environment of life itself, is one long lesson in violence where great prey upon small, male upon female.[43] Renouncing all technology in a parody of Faulkner's *Bear*, Tex and D.J. wander in the wilds and see all creatures speed toward death as a great male bear feeds upon a caribou doe, a fox upon mice, while the female herd is ruled by bulls designated as Fuck 1 and 2.[44] Under the burlesque of D.J.'s prose the ceremony is conducted with considerable seriousness. The outdated and ill-observed "Darwinism" of Mailer's glacier is presented to us as the true primitive mystery. In agreement with Lawrence, Mailer is anxious lest civilization "bury the primitive," believing that "what is at stake in the twentieth century" is "the peril that they will extinguish the animal in us."[45] Not only is D.J.'s puberty ritual an inevitability by this standard, it is somehow to take on the glamour of the splendid and the dangerous because Mailer conducts it as classical pastiche, palming it off as immemorial wisdom. Even with a smirk on his face, D.J. fulfills the requirements of his test, joining the ranks of the Hemingway cult. Most important of all, he has avoided the traps of homosexuality, compassion, and effeminacy, and emerges from the cold white summit with the very "power"[46] of the mountain Croft

[39] Sankichi Toge, "At a First-Aid Post," from *The Hiroshima Poems* translated from the Japanese by James Kirkup and Fumiko Miura. Mailer can't abide poets who write about peace, they make him want to flee the room. Toge is already dead of leukemia.
[40] *The Presidential Papers*, p. 128.
[41] *Ibid.*, p. 40.
[42] *Ibid.*, pp. 21, 22, 23.
[43] *Why Are We in Vietnam?*, p. 57.
[44] *Ibid.*, p. 191.
[45] *The Presidential Papers*, p. 200.
[46] *Why Are We in Vietnam?*, p. 157.

was unworthy to climb. Like much pop art, the novel is so ambiguous, so uncertain of itself, that it tends to endorse what it appears at first to parody.

Then too, the young murderer's charm and wit, his self-proclaimed talent—"a finger into the cunt of genius"[47]—make him a character too brilliantly conscious, too delightful a combination of Tom Sawyer and Holden Caulfield to alienate a reader. For all his elaborate cynicism, and pompous "alienation," D.J., like Rojack, is a caricature who ends by vindicating American virility. Yet because Mailer has insisted so often that the violence which masculinity presupposes, even requires, cannot be denied, we must conclude that the reason "why we are in Vietnam" is only because "we" must be.[48] Such is the nature of things. Sitting at their farewell dinner, Tex and D.J. happily anticipate going off to see "the wizard in Vietnam."[49] A considerable practitioner of psychoanalysis himself, Mailer protests he is against the trade because it would kill the mystery and spontaneity of human motivation, but one is reminded here of the popular Freudian formula: observe, codify, sanction, and prescribe. "Vietnam, hot damn."[50]

II

Under the influence of Wilhelm Reich,[51] the young Mailer once put himself forward as a hero of the sexual revolution, and true to form, saw it in terms of a stirring combat. But by his own account, Mailer's political position is that of a "Left Conservative,"[52] a confusing hybrid whose stress falls with increasingly apoplectic emphasis upon the latter term. And so the grand "war for greater sexual liberty"[53] amounted to nothing more than a crusade for an increased explicitness in the description of sexual activity, capped with the privilege of printing the taboo diction of four-letter words. This is all right as far as it goes. But, by a nice historical irony, the sexual libertarianism of the sixties had, in only a few years, managed to exceed anything Mailer desired, and in the course of time his attitudes have hardened so they might do credit to a parish priest. He is lyric about "chastity,"[54] ferocious about abortion, and wildly opposed to all birth control—"I hate contraception . . .

[47] *Ibid.*, p. 81.
[48] Mailer saw the years of the cold war as years of national disease, intimating any number of times that "an insipid sickness demands a violent far-reaching purgative." (*The Presidential Papers*, p. 134.) For some ten years he was literally crying out for war —the question is—which one?
[49] *Why Are We in Vietnam?*, p. 208.
[50] *Ibid.*
[51] See Wilhelm Reich, *The Sexual Revolution* (New York: Noonday, 1945). Mailer appears to have been influenced more by the books of Reich's decline, when the orgasm became a panacea to him. Mailer later endorsed a host of attitudes Reich had always deplored.
[52] *The Armies of the Night*, p. 143.
[53] *The Presidential Papers*, p. 139.
[54] *Ibid.*, p. 142.

it's an abomination. I'd rather have those fucking communists over here."[55]
Forbidding sexuality to the young by counseling abstinence, he condemns
onanism in the enlightened˙manner of a Victorian physician: "Masturbation is bad," it "cripples people" and ends in "insanity."[56] Finally outstrip-
ping both the Victorians and the Church, Mailer's line would sit well on a
Nazi propagandist: "The fact of the matter is that the prime responsibility
of a woman probably is to be on earth long enough to find the best mate
possible for herself, and conceive children who will improve the species."[57]

As the real implications of a sexual revolution became clear to him, Mailer
preferred to turn from such frightening possibilities to a new campaign.
Diverting his efforts to a war between the sexes in defense of male supremacy, he blossomed into an archconservative. "Sexual liberty" might, after
all, apply to women as well, might even threaten the double standard and
the subtle way in which "shame" is manipulated to control women. So Elena
preaches from the stage of *The Deer Park* that women "weren't born to be
free, they were born to have babies."[58] The dissipation of perverse guilt, the
Reichian hope of a "sex-positive attitude"[59] proved incompatible with his own
male-chauvinist propensity to give guilt a coercive function in sexual politics. He seems to cherish even the notion of guilt in men, a generalized guilt
associated with sexual activity itself, giving it the piquancy relished best by
a puritan sensibility.[60] While Mailer found he could appreciate the "mythology" of Lady Chatterley, the manner in which it encouraged the notion that
"sex could have beauty," he found it sadly ignorant of "the violence which is
part of sex," and later came to prefer the more amenable context of filth
which he so enjoys in Miller, arguing that actually, "most people don't find
sex that pure, that deep, that organic."[61] Instead, they find it "sort of partial
and hot and ugly."[62] Best to keep it this way, for sex is really "better off
dirty, damned, even slavish! than clean and without guilt."[63] Guilt, he would

[55] *Ibid.*, p. 131.

[56] Reich frequently denounced such attitudes. *The Sexual Revolution* has a long
chapter quoting this sort of opinion in scientific authorities and condemning them for
error and inhumanity. As Steven Marcus points out in *The Other Victorians* such convictions were also common among the medical profession in the last century.

[57] *The Presidential Papers*, p. 130.

[58] *The Deer Park, a Play*, p. 165.

[59] Reich had traced a great many social and psychological ills to the very negative
attitude our culture holds toward sexuality.

[60] Conditioned guilt produces fear of sexuality in women so that it may be imposed
upon rather than chosen by them, or it becomes a sign of their degradation. In men guilt
tends to take on an aphrodisiac quality. The severe dualism in all Mailer's thinking depends on an essentially negative attitude toward sexuality.

[61] *Cannibals and Christians*, pp. 197–98.

[62] *Ibid.*

[63] *The Armies of the Night*, p. 36.

persuade us, constitutes "the existential edge of sex," without which the act is "meaningless."[64]

Lawrence was content to manipulate, Miller to cover with contempt, but Mailer must wrestle. One does not exorcise the specter of an insurgent female spirit by epithet alone, so Mailer escalated to a more intensive sexual hostility. The short story "The Time of Her Time"[65] is his most notable exercise in this regard. Here dramatic conflict is stripped to essentials as the favor of first orgasm is conferred upon a Jewish college girl by that professional "cocksman," Mailer's own Sergius O'Shaugnessy, a "Village stickman" able to "muster enough of the divine It on the head of his will"[66] (Mailerese for penis) to effect some vague miracle upon Time which the author recognizes as "existential." This lofty purpose is secondary to the expression of sexual hatred, Sergius' real talent. Acting upon the principle that a female "laid" is a female subjugated, the hero strikes with his magic weapon, a penis, that his comic-strip bravado impels him to refer to as "the avenger."[67] The attack begins when Sergius overhears his victim venture a remark on Eliot. Such pretension to intelligence appalls his sense of propriety and he is on the instant "inflamed," the avenger urging him "to prong her then and there, right on the floor of the party"; so he brings her home afire for the moment he may "grind it into her," "lay waste to her little independence" and set all right.[68]

Things go wrong from the start. Back at the loft where Sergius operates a thoroughly improbable indoor school of bullfighting, the girl fails to succumb to that passivity which Mailer myth ordains is the only feminine route to the promised land of orgasm. The narrator deplores the error in grave literary tones: "she had fled the dominion which was liberty for her."[69] Nature rebukes the upstart by withholding sexual satisfaction; Sergius underlines the lesson by striking her across the face. When her dignity fails to collapse entirely and she answers his arrogance with a stubborn spirit of her own, Sergius is piqued by the challenge and willing to overlook the considerable drain on his business-like sexual economy (customarily loath to "score" twice on the same mark) and is willing to try another bout.

At their final match he suffers a momentary defeat through premature ejaculation, a blow to his careerist's reputation which requires the inflationary services of fellatio, thereby reducing him to what he regards as an inferior (passive, dependent) position. But recovering his resiliency with commendable haste, he imposes anal intercourse upon his opponent, slowly savoring "as the avenger rode down to his hilt" the outrage of pain and humiliation he has

[64] Ibid.
[65] See Advertisements for Myself, pp. 440 ff.
[66] Ibid., p. 458.
[67] Ibid., p. 450 et passim.
[68] Ibid., pp. 450–51.
[69] Ibid., p. 452.

inflicted, and grimacing at the reader "she thrashed beneath me like a trapped little animal," "caught," "forced," "wounded," and so forth.[70] Since Mailer's logic here demands the mortification of the woman as imperative (through a Freudian paradox)[71] both to the victory of the male and to her own bliss, it requires only the additional stimulation of Sergius' rasping racist whisper, "You dirty little Jew," and a quick switch to "love's first hole" to bring her over the brink of masochistic womanhood and into the fictive reaches of vaginal orgasm.[72] Were it not for the dead-eye perception of her parting shot, "Your whole life is a lie, and you do nothing but run away from the homosexual that is you,"[73] Sergius could claim total victory. But the match may be said to end in a draw.

"The Time of Her Time" is ethnic sexual politics. It is interesting to compare Mailer with Roth in this respect.[74] Portnoy's long *kvetch* is hilarious demonstration of how elaborate cultural penis-worship may produce, in a man of intelligence or sensitivity, a monumental infantilism whose only satisfactions are a contradictory blend of onanistic self-deprecation and the cheap glory of settling old minority scores in the sexual exploitation of women.[75] But Sergius the blond beast can scarcely be charged with sensitivity, and Mailer's sympathy appears to pander without unembarrassment before such *goyish* virility, a Mick brutality glamorized into Hip. And so Denise Gondelman is laid low, masculine pride so desperate a cause it can welcome alliance with anti-Semitism. "If Harry Golden is the gentile's Jew, can I become the Golden Goy"[76] Mailer wonders in a wistful verse, brooding over his romance with Aryan manliness, one of the most puzzling and ubiquitous of his paradoxical qualities. Since Mailer himself is inordinately fond of playing the would-be-Irish-buffoon,[77] it is pertinent to remember that O'Shaugnessy is an adopted name and Sergius an orphan, presumed to be Slavic by birth. As the anomaly himself acknowledges, gracefully disingenuous, "There's nothing in the world like being a fake Irishman."[78]

While his heroes are invariably studies in sexual vanity, Mailer's attitude toward their posturing tends to vacillate between mild irony and gratified

[70] *Ibid.*, pp. 462–63.

[71] Freudian theory stipulates that pain is satisfaction for woman, as she is, by her true nature, masochistic.

[72] *Ibid.*, p. 464.

[73] *Ibid.*, p. 465.

[74] Philip Roth, *Portnoy's Complaint* (New York: Random House, 1967, 1968, 1969).

[75] This callow method of shifting racial to sexual grudge and repaying injustice upon the oppressor's "woman" is the inspiration for Eldridge Cleaver's career as a rapist. By the most depressing racist logic, Cleaver first served an apprenticeship by assaulting women of his own race, content to mimic that staggering contempt white patriarchy habitually reserves for the black female. See Eldridge Cleaver, *Soul on Ice* (New York: McGraw-Hill, 1968).

[76] Norman Mailer, *Deaths For the Ladies and Other Disasters* (New York: Putnam, 1964), no pagination in the volume.

[77] See both *Miami and the Siege of Chicago* and *The Armies of the Night*.

[78] *The Deer Park* (novel), p. 22.

participation. His considerable insights into the practice of sexuality as a power game never seem to affect his vivid personal enthusiasm for the fight, nor his sturdy conviction (curiously reminiscent of, among other things, two decades of arms race policy) that it's kill or be killed.[79] At times he is gallant enough to render homage to the enemy as a worthy opponent, a good swinging bitch, but like any soldier hardened by his own side's agitprop, he can also fall into the jingoism of the sexual patriot: "Most men who understand women at all feel hostility toward them. At their worst, women are low sloppy beasts."[80]

Mailer's verses are bits of Avenger propaganda, whimsical pubic narcissism, always offered to the reader as "short hairs." One titled "Ode to a Lady" consists of a playful dialogue between male and female. The "lady" speaks with a becoming humility, conscious of her dependence and inferiority: "Create me/ dear singing loin of some manly harp/ create me for I stifle where I stand." Of course the poet is far too canny to be taken in by this sort of stuff, and he replies in stern recognition of feminine evil—"snake and foulest bitch, swine of a hundred feet." His suspicions are splendidly vindicated in her reply, "sweet lord you're kind/ Yes come to me honeybee/ and I will kill you."[81]

Love, when possible, under Mailer's sexual politic becomes a thoroughly ambivalent emotion. Or, as D.J. would put it, "love is dialectic, man, back and forth, hate and sweet."[82] Mailer is nothing if not sporting, and his combative urges, his eagerness after a sparring partner, causes the much lamented "bitchery" of the American woman to become a species of erotic currency. The desirable woman is more likely to be the tough fighting spirit of the heroine of "The Time of Her Time," or the greedy if vacuous Guinevere of *Barbary Shore*, than Elena Esposito, the beaten loser of *The Deer Park*, in the novel "a cocker-spaniel sinking inch by inch into quick-bog,"[83] but revamped into a feistier breed by the pert vulgarity she is given in the play.

In arming his opponent, Mailer has of course no intention of losing the war. He just likes a fight and is concerned with keeping up its interest and assuring the paying seats that the male struggle to retain hegemony will have the spice of adventure about it. Lest the contestants require ideology, he has exercised some ingenuity in concocting an existentialist-flavored home brew seasoned for genital man and hereafter referred to as "sexistentialism." The cult owes little to the French, a great deal to the Yank Army and the street.

Mailer insists on life after death, if only, as D.J. puckishly reports, that

---

[79] See *An American Dream*, "all women were killers," "women must murder unless we possess them altogether," etc., pp. 82, 100.
[80] *The Presidential Papers*, p. 131.
[81] *Cannibals and Christians*, "Ode To a Lady," pp. 142–44.
[82] *Why Are We in Vietnam?*, p. 126.
[83] The comparison refers to Marilyn Monroe, but fits Elena far better.

the "beeps" of orgasm, here taken as both the Grail quest[84] and a record of personal achievement, may be recorded and rewarded somewhere beyond. Sexistentialism is therefore religious rather than philosophic. As practiced by women, it is merely a hunt for fertilization, a minimal affair. As practiced by men, however, it is a thrilling test of self, played according to a demanding performance ethic which steers the athletic "hunter-fighter-fucker"[85] past the land mines of homosexuality, onanism, impotence, and capitulation to women. Through the perils of sexual traffic with women the courageous may "lay questions to rest" and "build upon a few answers" having "tested himself" and "fought the good fight or the evil fight" he is hereafter "able to live a tougher, more heroic life," his maleness certified, fortified.[86] Little wonder that Mailer's sexual journalism reads like the sporting news grafted onto a series of war dispatches. As the formula of "fucking as conquest" holds true, the conquest is not only over the female, but over the male's own fears for his masculinity, his courage, his dominance, the test of erection. To fail at any enterprise is to become female, defeated by the lurking treachery of Freudian bisexuality, the feminine in a man giving out like a trick knee at a track meet.[87] Since all this is so arduous, men are, Mailer believes, self-evidently entitled to victory, their "existential assertion." Reminding his teammates that "nobody was born a man" Mailer lays down the regulations—"you earned your manhood, provided you were good enough, bold enough."[88]

It would be difficult not to experience a certain amused compassion for such grandiose effort, were it not so remarkably smug, so sure of its monopoly on the human condition. Presumably arguing from the ardors of the sheets, Mailer's sexual politics reasons that men have more privileges, "more rights, and more powers" because life takes more out of them, leaves them "used more."[89] Women are supine during the only significant moments of their lives, but the male is forced to exert himself. And sexual effort seems to be much too taxing. Mailer's heroes conduct themselves as if there were just so much semen in the barrel of life, and sex an indulgence the prudent were best to shun: the resemblance to Victorian caution over the "spending" of semen is astonishing.[90] "You literally can fuck your head off," "loose your

---

[84] Part of the elite quality of the Hipster in "The White Negro" is his superior orgasm, orgasm being equated with existential *virtu*. Needless to say, Mailer subscribes to the most romantic theories of black sexuality which both Baldwin and Hansberry have pointed out are a new paternalism. "The White Negro" is in many ways an attempt to "cash in" on black alienation.

[85] *Why Are We in Vietnam?*, p. 157.

[86] *The Presidential Papers*, p. 141.

[87] These ideas are elaborated at length in "The White Negro" where the feminine is constantly equated with weakness and failure, masculinity with strength and success.

[88] *The Armies of the Night*, p. 36.

[89] *The Presidential Papers*, p. 144.

[90] See Marcus, *The Other Victorians* and the remarks in Chapter 6.

brains," "wreck your body," "eternally" Mailer warns Paul Krassner in an essay-interview.[91] His prose, both didactic and biographical, is full of terrified endorsements of Freud's prescription that sexuality is inimical to cultural achievement with harrowed accounts of sapped energy, wasted time. To Krassner's objection that sexuality is pleasurable and undertaken just on that account, Mailer responds like a grim semen bank on the verge of collapse, Jesuitically fierce over Procreation, nearly frantic that a seed be spilled in vain: "As you get older, you begin to grow more and more obsessed with procreation. You begin to feel used up. Another part of oneself is fast diminishing. There isn't that much of oneself left."[92] Erik Erikson is pained when ova go unfertilized. Mailer is preoccupied with worry over precious seed wasted upon prophylactic, the bedclothes, the onanist's hanky, the homosexual's rectum.

The Mailerite warrior-hunter is never too fastidious to obey the old maxim of "eat what you kill." His strategy of "fucking to win" converts intercourse to a procedure of absorbing the other's numa as the victorious sits down "to digest the new spirit which has entered the flesh."[93] This justifies the expense of effort and makes sexuality "nourishing,"[94] a diet of flesh which Mailer the ideologue recommends in the didacticism of his essays quite as much as in the overstated feasts of his fictive heroes. In fact, the most fascinating problem in dealing with his writing is to establish the connection between his fiction and his other prose writings, for ideas one is convinced are being satirized in the former are sure to appear with straightforward personal endorsement in the latter. Sergius expects to benefit from contact with Jewish intelligence by his bouts with Denise. Rojack goes even further. Contemplating his wife's corpse he imagines a cannibal dinner: "Ruta and I would sit down to eat. The two of us would sup on Deborah's flesh, we would eat for days: the deepest poisons in us would be released from our cells, I would digest my wife's curse before it could form. And this idea was thrilling to me."[95] Then he has a better idea—why not kill Ruta too and devour both of them? Appetite stops short of act, but having slaughtered his spouse Rojack immediately understands he has ingested her power. And it works. Applying the lessons of Mailer the pedagogue, Rojack explains his success with the cops and the Mafia is assured by the power he has acquired through consuming women: Ruta contributes cunning, Deborah meanness, and after she is beaten to death, Cherry, the golden-hearted whore, pays off like a good-luck charm in Vegas.

The same cannibalistic logic appears to operate in Mailer's essay accounts of how a writer "keeps in shape," wisdom imparted through the parable of

[91] *The Presidential Papers*, p. 144.
[92] *Ibid.*, pp. 143–44.
[93] *Ibid.*, p. 141.
[94] *Ibid.*
[95] *An American Dream*, p. 50.

a prizefighter who prepared to meet masculine hostility in the ring by absorbing the rage of "two prostitutes, not one, taking the two of them into the same bed,"[96] battening upon what might be taken either as their "evil" or their oppressed fury, their "meanness." Just, Mailer lectures, as "masculinity" is fed by "feminine" foods such as milk and chicken, which can be "dominated completely" because "compliant, tender, passive to our seizure,"[97] it is even further enhanced by the macho Eucharist, "bulls' balls," which he recommends with manic earnestness not only as a "delicacy" but as "equal to virility."[98] And that of course is the equivalent of grace in Mailer's system, "more than the stamina of a stud . . . power, strength, the ability to command, the desire to alter life."[99] A moral absolute, goodness is male.

Not only does Mailer conform to that curious pattern in American media which, as Diana Trilling once pointed out,[100] insists on portraying hostile society as a female intent upon destroying courage, honesty and adventure, he has gone so far as to conceive of masculinity as a precarious spiritual capital in endless need of replenishment and threatened on every side. True to the conflict between his perception and his allegiance, Mailer has frequently parodied masculine vanity: in the naïveté of the soldiers of *The Naked and the Dead* (Minetta, for instance, with his record fourteen "lays" —not bad for a fella my age, he hugs himself), or in D.J.'s wry allusion to the "grab for your dick competition snit."[101] Even with Sergius there are moments when one is certain the author knows O'Shaugnessy is a bully and a fool. But the comprehension of folly is so little a guarantee of its renunciation in Mailer, that his critical and political prose is based on a set of values so blatantly and comically chauvinist, as to constitute a new aesthetic. In a witty essay Mary Ellmann has described it as "phallic criticism."[102] It measures intelligence as "masculinity of mind,"[103] condemns mediocre authors for "dead-stick prose," praises good writers for setting "virile example" and notes that since "style is root" (penis), the best writing naturally requires "huge loins."[104] Really negative judgments are reserved for all that is or can be deprecated as feminine (here Mailer indulges himself unstint-

---

[96] *Cannibals and Christians*, p. 127.

[97] *The Presidential Papers*, p. 298.

[98] *Ibid.*, p. 297.

[99] *Ibid.*

[100] Diana Trilling, "The Image of Woman in Contemporary Literature" in *The Woman in America*, edited by Jay Lifton (Boston: Beacon, 1964); Leslie Fiedler's *Love and Death in the American Novel* (New York: Stein and Day, 1960) first formulated this thesis.

[101] *Why Are We in Vietnam?*, p. 176.

[102] Mary Ellmann, *Thinking About Women* (New York: Harcourt Brace, 1968). Ellmann is the first literary critic I know of to comment extensively on recent masculine reaction.

[103] *The Deer Park* (novel), p. 31.

[104] *Cannibals and Christians*, pp. 57, 128, 194, 250.

ingly), or like Jean Genet, can be baited as "unconscionably faggot."[105] As he settles into patriarchal middle age, Mailer's obsession with machismo brings to mind a certain curio sold in Coney Island and called a Peter Meter; a quaint bit of folk art, stamped out in the shape of a ruler with printed inches and appropriate epithets to equate excellence with size. Mailer operates on this scale on an abstract or metaphoric plane. His characters male and female, labor under simpler delusions. Guinevere is indefatigable on the subject of her lover's "whangs"; D.J. is paralyzed with the usual fear that someone else has a bigger one.

III

Mailer has a fine nose for sociological fashion and his hand-wringing over the "Womanization of America" at which "men have collaborated," positing a state of affairs where "women are becoming more selfish, more greedy, less romantic, less warm, more lusty and filled with hate" has a *Reader's Digest* character: "This country is entering into the most desperate, nightmarish time in its history. Unless everyone in America gets a great deal braver, everything is going to get worse—including the womanization of America."[106] It is vaguely depressing to see a literary man vending the same trash as those hundreds of psychologues and quacks whose jeremiads confound the public with such titles as "The Feminization of the American Male," "The Disappearing Sexes," and "The Flight From Woman,"[107] zealous tracts which thrash away at the cliché of overbearing modern woman, deplore the rising threat of homosexuality, and glamorize the blunter male supremacist style which the middle class is fond of patronizing as proletarian, or good-old-days. This order of "thinker," taking his own definition of "masculine" and "feminine" as both nature and nurture, innate and acquired virtue, announces any deviation from his norms as representing the most deplorable decay in moral standards, a weakening of the social fiber of the nation, which permits intolerable female gains and opens the way to a "flood tide of homosexuality," a "creeping virus of neuterization" which takes on the bogey aspect communism has for a true believer on the Right.

But Mailer is fully aware that the American male is sufficiently vicious, virile and violent. Surely there is as much proof of it today in *Why Are We in Vietnam?*, just as there was in the "Jap hunt" of *The Naked and the Dead*. Yet Mailer consistently pursuing his own convoluted and probably self-indulgent "strategy of self-consciousness" can only dramatize and illustrate the character of masculinist sensibility while remaining totally incapable of reasonable criticism of it. For against the logic of virility, it is pointless to reason,

---

[105] *The Presidential Papers*, p. 206.

[106] *Cannibals and Christians*, pp. 199, 201.

[107] See Patricia Sexton, *The Feminized Male* (New York: Random House, 1969); Robert P. Oldenwald, M.D., *The Disappearing Sexes* (New York: Random House, 1965); Karl Stern, *The Flight From Woman* (New York: Noonday, 1965).

pointless to raise any serious objections to "masculine aggression," since to do so is to frustrate nature itself, and, paradoxically, to demoralize culture as well. The military men's house must find wars and feed its cells upon victims, lest its values degenerate into the pacifism Mailer denigrates as "unmanly," or slip to the level of effeminacy and succumb to homosexuality. To renounce virility is tantamount to renouncing masculinity, hence, identity, even self.

> I think there may be more homosexuals today than there were fifty years ago. If so, the basic reason might have to do with a general loss of faith in the country, faith in the meaning of one's work, faith in the notion of one's self as a man. When a man can't find dignity in his work, he loses virility. Masculinity is not something given to you, something you're born with, but something you gain. And you gain it by winning small battles with honor. Because there is very little honor left in American life.[108]

With this ominous thunder Mailer acknowledges that maleness and masculinity are not equivalent states; the latter is earned, like Scout badges or plenary indulgences, acquired slowly through unremitting effort, which if slackened for a moment, plunges the subject into the slough of sexual heresy fuzzily described as lack of self-esteem or faith in the American Way of Life.

The real abyss which portentous phrases such as "existential dread" were invented to mask is the fear of nonexistence. That, or the secret terror of homosexuality; a mixture of sin, fascination, and fear which drives Mailer to his heterosexual posturing. To be faggot, damned, leprous—to cease to be virile were either to cease to be—or to become the most grotesque form of feminine inferiority—queer.

Believing that violence is an innate psychological trait in the male, Mailer insists that repression can only lead to greater dangers. In the strange personal mishmash of hypochondria and pseudo-medicine to which he subscribes, Mailer finds the genesis of cancer in throttled violence. Therapy lies only in expression, in "acting out." In a versified confidence upon certain trying personal experiences Mailer diagnoses how "The first unmanageable cell/ of the cancer which was to/ stifle his existence" made its appearance in the subject "on a morning when by/ an extreme act of the will/ he chose not to strike his/ mother." Since this was some "thirty-six hours after he had stabbed his wife," one is assured that hygiene is served by violence perpetrated, undermined by that restrained. Only when one's feelings are denied is there medical danger, or as Mailer elucidates, "his/ renunciation of violence/ was civilized too civilized/ for his cells which proceeded/ to revolt."[109]

Yet any attentive reader of Mailer's fiction is constantly made aware of how

[108] *Cannibals and Christians*, pp. 200–1.
[109] *Deaths for the Ladies*, "A Wandering in Prose for Hemingway, November 1960," no pagination.

explicitly he demonstrates the violence of his characters as springing directly from their stifled homosexuality. The anal rapes Rojack and Sergius perform are simply transferences (accompanied by sadism) of homosexual urges their elaborate masculinity seeks to disguise. In *The Naked and the Dead* it is made very clear that each homosexual indiscretion with which General Cummings chooses to embarrass young Lieutenant Hearne is followed by a gesture of cruelty. If his scarcely latent desire compels him to search out Hearne and call him to his tent while every officer in the company looks on, Cummings will visit his humiliating dependence on the younger man by throwing a cigarette butt on the floor and commanding Hearne to pick it up. Croft's violence also arises from a throttled homosexual impulse. All the beauty Tex and D.J. experience on the day they flee from their tainted elders to rove defenseless in the wilds is turned to cruelty when their adolescent affection sours into hatred before the taboo of homosexuality. In an essay on football, Mailer explains that it is the suppressed sexuality in the players' habitual gesture of bottom slapping (which he traces ingeniously to its origin in homosexual flirtation), plus the act of centering the ball "in the classic pose of sodomy" which "liberates testosterone" and enables the player, by the "prongsmanship and buggery at the seat" of his "root" to carry on and hit hard in the "happy broil."[110]

The constant interpretation urged upon the reader in Mailer's work seems to be that cruelty and violence spring out of the repressed homosexuality of men's-house culture, both emotions inevitable and beneficial because they constitute the only defense against homosexuality which Mailer's own sanctimonious sexual dogmatism regards as a greater evil than murder. This is nowhere made more graphic than in an account of the notorious Paret-Griffith prizefight in *The Presidential Papers*. "Now at the weigh-in that morning, Paret had insulted Griffith irrevocably, touching him on the buttocks, while making a few more remarks about his manhood. They almost had their fight on the scales."[111] The fight that did take place was an instance of murder acting as surrogate for sexuality. Ignoring both the bell and the referee, Griffith caught Paret in the ropes and struck him some eighteen times in three seconds, "making a pent-up whimpering sound all the while he attacked, the right hand whipping like a piston rod."[112] Sitting at ringside, Mailer reports he was "hypnotized" since he had "never seen one man hit another so hard and so many times."[113] "Off on an orgy," Griffith was uncontrollable: "If he had been able to break loose from his handlers and the referee, he would have jumped Paret to the floor and whaled on him there."[114] The expression "whaled on" is synonymous here both with

[110] *Advertisements for Myself,* "The T Formation," pp. 394–95.
[111] *The Presidential Papers,* p. 243.
[112] *Ibid.,* p. 243.
[113] *Ibid.,* p. 244.
[114] *Ibid.*

sodomize and kill. Paret died in a coma three days later, and the nasty incident gave boxing a bad name. Mailer's analysis of the event has a brilliant, unerring clarity. His defense of it is another matter. First, he informs us that "violence may be an indispensable element of life" then that fight managers are simply unheralded defenders of "an unstated view of life which was religious," and finally, he rationalizes all by declaring that the killer "sickens the air about him if he does not find some half-human way to kill a little in order not deaden all."[115] The fear of "deadening all" is clearly fear of falling into the plague of nonviolence, or the lethal defamation of homosexuality:

> The accusation of homosexuality arouses a major passion in many men; they spend their lives resisting it with a biological force. There is a kind of man who spends every night of his life getting drunk in a bar, he rants, he brawls, he ends in a small rumble on the street; women say "For God's sake, he's homosexual, Why doesn't he just turn queer and get his suffering over with." Yet men protect him. It is because he's choosing not to become homosexual. It was put best by Sartre, who said that a homosexual is a man who practices homosexuality. A man who does not is not homosexual—he is entitled to the dignity of his choice. He is entitled to the fact that he chooses not to become homosexual, and is paying presumably his price.[116]

One hardly wishes to argue against the right of sexual self-determination— but who paid? Paret is dead. Is the violence this choice appears to involve really worth it for anyone, even for frightened men? Or is its justification only some tortuous and deceptive fanaticism of Mailer's and those he speaks for, dependent on the fallacy that homosexual acts make one "a Homosexual," some odd and inferior being below the dignity of manhood? In a climate of sexual counterrevolution, homosexuality constitutes the mortal offense against heterosexual orthodoxy, the unforgivable sin that sends one off irreparably in the vast gray fields of virility's damned.[117] And this equation of homosexuality and non-violence as effeminacy is, of course, Mailer's own, or that of one time and place (America in the last two decades). Genet's hoods are as brutal (e.g. by Mailer's standards, virile) in their sexual as in their other habits. But Mailer's definition of masculinity does depend both on a rabid sort of heterosexual activism and the violence he imagines to be inherent in male nature. Should he slack in either, he ceases to exist.

Caste and class theology are curious affairs. In Dickens' work there is an equation of gentility with grace that accounts for the nightmare which Oliver Twist, to name but one example, experiences until his origins are

[115] *Ibid.*, pp. 245–47.
[116] *Ibid.*, p. 243.
[117] This despite the more recent trend to improve the "virility image" of homosexuality through the sadism of "leather bars," etc.

certified as bourgeois and he receives the class surety that represents salva-tion. In Faulkner's *Light in August,* in Sinclair Lewis' *Kingsblood Royal,* and other examinations of our native racism, the fear of a drop of Negro blood so unsettles a supposed white as to leave him suspended over Pascal's abyss. Mailer has constructed a theology on sexual grounds which operates in similar fashion. Despite the half-hearted apology of "The Homosexual Villain,"[118] its liberal patronization astonished at the idea that perhaps "homosexuals were people, too"[119] Mailer has never actually ceased to believe "that there was an intrinsic relation between homosexuality and evil."[120] So the devil is an anal force indeed—and the Mailer ethic teeters on its Manichean tightrope between good and evil, exhilarated at tempta-tion.

Not only do homosexuals constitute a pariah group, they do so because the pederast's act is thought to imply a descent into the foreign and inferior nature of the female. D.J.'s self-confessed anal compulsion, which leaves him a "shit-oriented late adolescent," "marooned on the balmy tropical isle of Anal Referent Metaphor,"[121] is matched by Mailer's own which dotes on scatol-ogy and drags on for pages about defecation.[122] But while buggery confers an extra honor on the "male" partner conquering a potential equal, "cause asshole is harder to enter than cunt and so reserved for the special tool,"[123] to be buggered is to be hopelessly humiliated. Since sexuality is inescapably a case of victimization in Mailer's mind, where the winner "prongs" or "brands" the loser, and having defeated the other, consumes the other's power, it is only natural that D.J. should hedge, poised uncertainly between the fear that Tex might "brand him up his ass" and the urge to "steal the iron from Texas' ass and put it in his own."[124] Sergius and Rojack just brand the female, easier to bully, a reasonable compromise, and safely within the ethos of sexual politics, for unlike Lawrence, Mailer is afraid that masculine cou-pling might undermine patriarchal hierarchy. In a sex war, faggots are de-serters. The presence of homosexuality or effeminacy negates the regenerative effect of the sacramental bull's balls: "What's the use of commanding women he could not command before, if he does not know how to fight off other men, and is not ready to learn?" Mailer asks, adding that "what freezes the homosexual in his homosexuality is not the fear of women so much as the fear of the masculine world with which he must war if he wishes to keep

---

[118] "The Homosexual Villain" in *Advertisements for Myself.*
[119] *Ibid.,* p. 209.
[120] *Ibid.,* p. 207.
[121] *Why Are We in Vietnam?,* p. 50.
[122] See *The Presidential Papers* on Waste and in *Cannibals and Christians,* "The Metaphysics of the Belly."
[123] *Why Are We in Vietnam?,* p. 203.
[124] *Ibid.,* pp. 202–3.

the woman."[125] Or conversely, the would-be homosexual's fear of the male he must conquer or "feminize."

Faced with the stalemate of desire and the hazards of the pecking order, D.J. and Tex conclude a blood pact whereby "they are twins, never to be near as lovers again, but killer brothers."[126] For they have comprehended that "it was there, murder between them under all friendship. For God was a beast, not a man, and God said 'Go out and kill—fulfill my will, go and kill.'"[127] Driven by its values and convictions, its dualist opposition between God and the Devil, male and female, virility and effeminacy, confronted by the twin perils of waning masculine dominion and the dangerous fascination of homosexuality, Mailer's "better to murder than to burn" has brought the counterrevolutionary sensibility to a breaking point of belligerent anxiety (and perhaps we experience it in other areas too as the practice of virility grows more and more at odds with life on the planet). *Machismo* stands at bay, cornered by the threat of a second sexual revolution, which, in obliterating the fear of homosexuality, could challenge the entire temperamental catagories (masculine and feminine) of patriarchal culture—this is where Genet is relevant.

[125] *The Presidential Papers,* p. 278. Note the discussion on virility and bull's balls is from the Presidential Paper on Waste.

[126] *Why Are We in Vietnam?,* p. 204.

[127] *Ibid.,* p. 203.

EIGHT

Jean Genet

I

It would appear that love is dead. Or very likely in a bad way. As to those practitioners of romantic love who linger on, the two most solicitous, Genet and Nabokov, are of suspicious orthodoxy. *Lolita* is as much a matter of kidnap, rape, and coercion as the terrible passion of a lost enamored soul who has followed his culture's blandishment of a child-wife to its literal conclusion. For the rest, hostility between the sexes has handily outdistanced romance in interest, a development due less to the inherent faults of the romantic myth (a sentimental idealism and traditionally, a rather inhibited sexuality) than it is to the animus toward women which their gains in this century have provoked from jealous patriarchal sentiment. The mistress or beloved is dethroned, even defamed; she has become a villain, a nuisance, or a deserving victim. As we all know, it has been open season even on mothers for some two decades. Those who continue to display a romantic enthusiasm for the amorous, tend like Humbert Humbert or Genet, to be members of the "sexual minorities."

There is a sense in which the homosexual is our current "nigger" of love, his[1] sexual life a bigger social risk and surrounded by a more hostile en-

---

[1] Following custom, the term "homosexual" refers to male homosexual here. "Lesbianism" would appear to be so little a threat at the moment that it is hardly ever mentioned. Once a target for liberal sympathies (Havelock Ellis' introduction to *The Well of Loneli-*

vironment, at any moment liable to pounce in ridicule or condemnation, than ever threatened Mailer's bullying "White Negro." In a great many places homosexual acts are still crimes under law, whereas Mailer's heroes, eager to offend society, must push on all the way to murder. In nearly any bar Divine could stand at bay and hear "herself" judged:

> She smiled all around, and each one answered only by turning away, but that was a way of answering. The whole cafe thought that the smile of (for the colonel: the invert; for the shopkeepers: the fairy; for the banker and the waiters: the fag; for the gigolos: *that* one; etc.) was despicable. Divine did not press the point. From a tiny black satin purse she took a few coins which she laid noiselessly on the marble table. The cafe disappeared, and Divine was metamorphosed into one of those monsters that are painted on walls—chimeras or griffins—for a customer, in spite of himself, murmured a magic word as he thought of her: "Homoseckshual."[2]

In pariah state there is some magic still, and the myth of romantic love has always prospered on the social hostility directed at star-crossed lovers, adulterers, or those who transgress the boundaries of caste and class. Its clandestine and forbidden character alone tends to grant homosexual love the glamour waning in literary accounts of heterosexuality, lost together with their guarded inhibitions and, regrettably, their tenderness.

Notwithstanding its romance trappings of sighs and roses, the love ethic of Genet's novels is even more atavistic than the romantic variety. Courtly in fact, it observes the traditional virtues of loyalty, secrecy, humility, and idolatry. From the perspective of sexual politics, it is possible to regard European courtly love as either a cruel joke—or the first entering wedge in patriarchal consistency. For by an anomaly social history is helpless to explain, the courtly lover, though *de facto* master, chose to play the role of servant to his lady. Genet has, with considerable political realism, turned this situation back upon its feet, and in the feudalistic hierarchy of his prisons, converted French abbeys founded by the nobility of the *ancien régime* and haunted still by the perfume of medievalism, it is the male partner who receives homage.

---

ness, T. S. Eliot's to *Nightwood*), or a screen for male homosexuality (Proust's Albertine) the woman as homosexual is today as decidedly a sexual object as other women. The two excited females in the bathtub on Forty-second Street screens pander actually to male fantasy which intervenes heroically between them, taking on the pair at once. Hollywood's *The Fox* and other productions of popular cinema are also likely to be directed at masculine audiences, while underground or art films ignore lesbians for the more explosive (because more realistically conceived) topic of male homosexuality. Whatever its potentiality in sexual politics, female homosexuality is currently so dead an issue that while male homosexuality gains a grudging tolerance, in women the event is observed in scorn or in silence.

2 Jean Genet, *Our Lady of the Flowers*, translated from the French by Bernard Frechtman (New York: Grove, 1963), Bantam reprint, p. 73.

The heroes of his romances are king-sized hoodlums, the courtly lovers at their knees not masculine, but feminine, whores and queens.

Although he is, as Sartre points out, a "passéiste,"[3] or one who lives in another age, Genet's feudal system is simply more honest than that of our other authors in its open recognition of power, its clear parallel to masculine cultures such as those of the Near East and the Orient, where older warrior was served by page, priest by acolyte, tyrant by the objects of either sex who suited his whim. In *Deathwatch*, Genet's first play and the one nearest to the closed milieu of his fiction, Green Eyes, the convicted murderer and therefore the most male or noble, sounds off before his vassals like a baronial paterfamilias: "Here in the cell, I'm the one who bears the brunt . . . I know I need a strong back. Like Snowball. He bears the same weight. But for the whole prison. Maybe there's someone else, a Number One Big Shot who bears it for the whole world!"[4] By such a structure does the patriarch face existence and live *for* his dependents, the nameless Misses, his offspring, his subjects, his chattels—minors all. At Genet's children's prison, Mettray, the inmates lived in "families" governed by a "head of the family" and his chief retainer, and "elder brother," a bully put in charge of the younger and weaker who are his concubines or "chickens." Genet's prison hierarchy is constructed in terms of sex: the pure virility of the killer at the top, on the next tier lesser Big Shots, macs or pimps,[5] then crashers (thieves who operate with a jimmy, breaking and entering) and on a lower plane, the queens and chickens who serve them. Chickens are subject to sale, "discipline" and even murder. Lowest of all are the jerks, pure scum, never selected for concubinage, but subject to rape. A jerk's life is hell.

Since all is precedence and rank, reciprocity is quite impossible and requited love as rare in Genet as it is fleeting. Homosexual love is a life of continual rejection. There is always a better-looking queen for the lord to expropriate; there is always one more commandingly masculine for the "chicken" to run to. Yet the obligation to loyalty rests heavily and exclusively upon the feminine partner for the male is permitted, even expected, to be promiscuous. Due to the regulations and the punishments of guards, intrigue is required, and in a world where homosexuality, like love, is both irrepressible

---

[3] Jean Paul Sartre, *Saint Genet, Actor and Martyr,* translated from the French by Bernard Frechtman (New York: George Braziller, 1963), Mentor reprint, p. 9.

[4] Jean Genet, *Deathwatch,* translated from the French by Bernard Frechtman (New York: Grove, 1954, 1961), pp. 147–48.

[5] Note the ranks of *mac* and *casseur* (pimps and crashers). "*Mac*" is generally translated as "pimp" and in fact it does mean this, but primarily it implies toughness, and an open contempt for women. As Philip Thody points out, the distinction the mac enjoys over the casseur depends chiefly on this last trait. Philip Thody, *Jean Genet* (London: Hamish Hamilton, 1968), p. 94. That "pimp" is an attribute connected with but occasionally separable from an occupation is attested to by the fact that in Mettray adolescent boys who have never known women are called mac, to which the English translation of "pimp" scarcely does justice. I shall use the two terms alternately.

and condemned, secrecy is a necessity against the scorn of all and sundry. Idolatry is also a feminine function. The mac is "daungerous" or hard to get, his most magnanimous gesture a momentary display of possessiveness. Tenderness or affection are beneath him: for a male to love would be to lose status. Every equality is forbidden. Proposing himself to another youth, Genet is rebuked with a dismayed "Huh? We're the same age. It wouldn't be any fun."[6]

In his account of Genet, Sartre constructs a theory, sturdily Marxist in bias, that it was the lifelong feeling of guilt branded on him as a child by his foster parents when they caught him stealing and sent him to spend the next fifteen years in the "children's hell" of Mettray that led Genet to homosexuality. The hypothesis is at odds with Genet's own assertion that homosexuality preceded his crimes against property.[7] And indeed, the dizzying shame, followed by a stubbornly resistant contumacy, which is Genet's stand toward the world, originates with sex, even with the "original sin" of his birth, a bastard and abandoned child. Weighted down with guilt, already an "unnatural" phenomenon in a society based on family and property, it is somehow logical that he should complete his fate by advancing to the "unnatural" life style of homosexuality, where he can further outrage "nature" by becoming a feminine or passive partner, furnishing a last touch by accepting the most ignominious role, laying claim to "the gravest insult"—cocksucker.[8]

Just as he resolved to be the thief they had made him by naming him one, Genet, once arrived at prison, insisted on living out the sexual guilt imposed on him both by his rape and the gentleness which provoked it. Discovering that the other boys were "stronger and more vicious" which in this school as unfortunately in most, is taken to mean more masculine, Genet insisted on living out the sexual or feminine shame they heaped on him—determined he would become "the fairy they saw in me."[9] The attitude implies a perverse

[6] Jean Genet, *The Thief's Journal*, translated from the French (New York: Grove, 1964), p. 140.

[7] Sartre, *op. cit.* Sartre acknowledges Genet's version only to discard it. See page 91.

[8] Jean Genet, *The Miracle of the Rose*, translated from the French by Bernard Frechtman (New York: Grove, 1966), p. 76. Genet informs us that "among toughs, it (the epithet, cocksucker) is very often punishable by death." *Ibid.* The degree to which eroticism and shame are inseparable in Genet is a nice illustration of how deeply guilt pervades our apprehension of the sexual, an unpleasant fact of sexual politics and hardly less true of heterosexual society than it is of Genet's: "I know by some indefinable, imperceptible change, that it is a shudder of love—it is both poignant and delightful, perhaps because of the memory of the word shame that accompanied it in the beginning." Such a sentiment is probably universal. *Ibid.*

[9] Genet, *The Thief's Journal*, p. 175. Frechtman has "malicious," but "vicious" is closer to the French "méchant." It is necessary we realize that "Genet" in this essay must stand only for that character around whom "the legend of Genet" has been constructed in autobiographical novels signed Jean Genet. Of Jean Genet's own life we know nothing, or next to nothing.

submission which is both fideistic and heretical, an implicit agreement with the prevailing social tenet that homosexuality and thievery constitute essences, rather than acts, and are immutable states of being. Because "thief" or "fairy" are words used to discourage one from being them, Genet's total acceptance of them is not only fatalistic, but covertly mutinous.

The grotesquerie of sexual role was, at Mettray, as it is elsewhere, acknowledged to be fated, even predestined. For a brief period Genet tried to evade his "wild nature," his femininity, by becoming a crasher and serving time at Fontevrault for breaking and entering, in the impossible hope of acquiring "the clear simplicity of manliness" through adopting the "steel penis" of a jimmy, an instrument from which he tells us "emanated an authority that made me a man," and would promote him above faggotry's "humble ways."[10] But even when a jimmy intercedes, the preordained is not to be cheated. Bulkaen, whom he courts to be his chicken, deserts him for the more impressibly virile Botchako and Genet ends where he began, mistress to the Big Shot Divers, still the queen he was at sixteen on his "bridal day" at Mettray. He is still nobody, still hardly better than a jerk.

Since for Genet, it is a case of rank by individual fate, sex role is established once and for all at two polarities of inferior and superior: the apparent deviations, young toughs like Our Lady and Bulkaen, are simply tadpoles, creatures in transition to a better destiny. It would be hard to find a more brutal or unsavory definition of masculine and feminine than Genet's, since it is simply an exaggeration of that in current use. Masculine is superior strength, feminine is inferior weakness. There is one exception however: Genet has jealously reserved intelligence and moral courage for his queens; for himself. The toughness of the toughs relies on their status, their largely decorative masculature (they disdain labor) and their meanness. Like Botchako they express their sexual mastery in choice phrases: "You bitch, you swallow it by the mouthful"; "I'll shoot it up your hole, you punk!"[11] Since their status is derived from their subjects, females or males feminized into submission, a pimp like Darling speaking out of the conviction that a mere woman would contribute less to his prestige, can boast when buggering Divine, "a male who fucks a male is a double male."[12]

Just as Genet's anti-morality is but an inversion of peasant folk-Catholicism —its sense of property, its literal apprehension of theological abstractions (grace, sin, etc.)—so his notions of sex role and rank are the most flat-footed ones available in his culture, quite without Lawrence's subtlety, archaic in their direct presentation of power and subordination: a vicious and omnipotent supervirility contrasted to a fluttering helplessness and abjection. In his world of prostitution and crime the woman or queen is ruled by force,

---

[10] Genet, *The Miracle of the Rose*, p. 27.

[11] *Ibid.*, p. 21.

[12] Genet, *Our Lady of the Flowers*, p. 253. (Here the page number refers to the hardcover, rather than, as elsewhere, to the Bantam reprint.)

by violence, and by ostentatious masculine disdain. Her femininity is pure servility, graphically enlarged beyond that bare abstract, almost discreet outline codified and prescribed by Freudianism: "masochism" is simply open self-hatred, "narcissism" a realistic sense of the self as object (vanity is a male prerogative), and "passivity" frankly fear, despair, and resignation. Since the pervasive effect of Genet's habitual ironic exaggeration is to unmask our common social hypocrisy, the fainter aspersion attached to the feminine by our other authors is enlarged to a candid repugnance everywhere in his work. There is scarcely need to fret over how Genet, a jailbird, may have come in touch with popular Freudianism (itself but a redaction of widespread and durable patriarchal assumptions) when far more remote literary references abound in his work, among them the most sophisticated allusions to the French poets. Dickens is also clearly an influence; the great trial scene in *Our Lady of the Flowers* is deliberately modeled on Fagin's sentencing in *Oliver Twist*.

In a sex ethic founded so solidly upon sexual guilt and inferiority, which, womanlike, Genet carries within him, sexuality itself must logically operate both as punishment and a confirmation of his status, the very moment of its enaction a fevered and mortifying accusation, a terrible reproach. As Sartre characterizes sodomy in the novels: "The sex act is the festival of submission, also the ritual renewal of the feudal contract whereby the vassal becomes the lord's liegeman."[13] And like Marie Bonaparte's properly masochistic female, Genet as queen is impaled, tortured, pierced, and subjugated by the male whose penis is a "sharp instrument with the cruel and sudden sharpness of a steeple puncturing a cloud."[14] Phallic heroism is presented variously in terms of a cannon, a dagger, a pile driver, an iron bar. The mac's very body is an erection, and even in infancy, toughs like Querelle can survey buildings in a landscape with naïve satisfaction, proud "at knowing so high a tower is the symbol of his virility."[15] As with many of the married couples whom Rainwater studied, sexuality is directed toward the male organ, thought to be the real actor and the purpose of coitus.[16] Since the male has so little interest in her pleasure, the queen, like traditional woman, rarely enjoys orgasm. Macs hardly ever condescend to jerk off a queen, and Divine is forced to finish in the toilet, place of excrement and shame. But like a theatrical whore or a dutiful wife, the queen groans and faints to convert her suffering to the appearance of joy.

Although "straight" society may be affronted at the thought, homosexual art is by no means without insights into heterosexual life, out of whose milieu it grows and whose notions it must, perforce, imitate and repeat, even parody.

---

13 Quoted in Sartre, *op. cit.*, p. 123.

14 *Ibid.*, p. 121.

15 Jean Genet, *Querelle de Brest* (*Oeuvres Complètes*, Tome III, Paris, Gallimard, 1953), p. 197.

16 Lee Rainwater, *And the Poor Get Children* (Chicago: Quadrangle, 1960).

Humanly judged, one is as perverse as the other; their pasts nearly identical, their politics eminently reasonable facsimiles. As Benjamin De Mott has pointed out,[17] Williams and Albee can say as much, and often speak more frankly than others about the horrors of family life, the tedium of marriage, the lover's exploitation of personality, the slow erosion of character in promiscuity.

The hostility which the swish provokes from a crowd of college boys and toughs, their taunts, their desire to strike down, their mindless rage, is as one critic observes,[18] the uneasy response of insecure virility erupting into violence to cover its own terror of a possible "false self," which according to the Freudian theory of bisexuality, is its hateful and sternly throttled femininity. Yet is not this very "assertion of masculinity" patently an expression, not only of the vandal's zealous heterosexual orthodoxy, his perfervid jingoist commitment to "normal" sexual behavior—but just as much a statement of contempt for the feminine itself?

For Genet's pimps and macs, the queen acts as a scapegoat for their own homosexual impulses, but also serves as the thing they hurt in retaliation for the horrified presentiment that their own natures might be tainted with what they palpably know is inferior, grostesque, female. The mayhem of the repressed homosexual is nicely demonstrated in Botchako's taunting a jerk in the prison yard: "I expected to see him strike the poor bastard, who didn't dare to make a movement, not even of fear. He instinctively assumed the sudden, shifty, prudent immobility of a frightened animal. Had Botchako made a single move to strike, he might have killed him, for he would not have been able to check his fury."[19] Botchako is only a crasher. The response of his superior, the pimp Lou Daybreak, is an amused "Go on, marry him! You're in love with him. Anyone can see it!"[20] The hero of *Querelle of Brest*, at the outset a militant heterosexual, is propositioned by a fairy, goes to his room and strangles him:

Finally, if a queer was like this, a creature so light, so fragile, so airy, so transparent, so delicate, so broken, so clear, so garrulous, so musical, so tender—one could kill it. Since it was made to be killed; like Venetian glass it waited only the big tough fist which could smash it without even being cut (save possibly for an insidious sliver, sharp, hypocritical, slitting and remaining under the skin). If this was a queer, it wasn't a man. For the queer had no weight. He was a little cat, a bullfinch, a fawn, a blind-worm, a dragonfly, whose very

[17] Benjamin De Mott, 'But He's a Homosexual . . .'" *The New American Review,* Number 1 (New York: New American Library, September 1967).

[18] George Dennison, "The Moral Effect of the Legend of Genet," *ibid.*

[19] Genet, *The Miracle of the Rose,* p. 20. Genet explains that Botchako's forehead was "too narrow to contain enough reason to stop his anger once it got going." *Ibid.*

[20] *Ibid.,* p. 22.

fragility is provocative and, in the end, it is precisely this exaggeration which inevitably invites its death.[21]

What Querelle is annihilating is an abstraction of the weak and the contemptible, the feminine. In punishment for this murder, indeed, as atonement, Genet causes Querelle to become the catamite of a brothel boss.

But as she minces along a street in the Village, the storm of outrage an insouciant queen in drag may call down is due to the fact that she is both masculine and feminine at once—or male, but feminine. She has made gender identity more than frighteningly easy to lose, she has questioned its reality at a time when it has attained the status of a moral absolute and a social imperative. She has defied it and actually suggested its negation. She has dared obloquy, and in doing so has challenged more than the taboo on homosexuality, she has uncovered what the source of this contempt implies—the fact that sex role is sex rank.

In *The Thief's Journal,* Genet lived as a satellite to Stilitano, a dim but virile one-armed bandit whose life's ambition is to be "the conquering hero of the comic books."[22] Serving the master by assuming the burden of dangerous trips across national borders with packets of opium, Genet reports that he acted "out of obedience, out of submission to a sovereign Power."[23] "It's perfectly natural," I said to myself. "He's a prick and I'm a cunt."[24] An operating pimp, Stilitano also runs a woman, the prostitute Sylvia, and so has two "cunts" in his service, Genet being the second. When a biological male is described as a "cunt," one gets a better notion of the meaning of the word. By revealing its primarily status or power definition, Genet has demonstrated the utterly arbitrary and invidious nature of sex role. Divorced from their usual justification in an assumed biological congruity masculine and feminine stand out as terms of praise and blame, authority and servitude, high and low, master and slave.

II

And of course there is something infinitely ironic in Genet's use of the terms, for as both his groups are male, role now appears more than simply arbitrary, it is revealed as the category, even the function of a nakedly oppressive social system. Particulars of status are observed with such excess of zeal, such tribal rigidity, that the final impression is humorous. Genet's own attitude fluctuates between obsequious acceptance and tongue-in-cheek mockery so that the total effect is satiric, and increasingly so as the oblique parody one finds in his prose fiction develops into direct statement in the plays,

21 Jean Genet, *Querelle de Brest.* Since the Grove edition is not yet issued, and the British Streathem translation virtually unobtainable, I have supplied my own translation from the 1947 Paris edition.

22 Genet, *The Thief's Journal,* p. 125.

23 *Ibid.,* p. 127.

24 *Ibid.,* p. 128.

where a feminine or oppressed mentality is extended to the other political contexts of race, class, and colony.

In the novels, Genet is forever arranging things so that his own feminine last shall be first, shall triumph somehow, even if it be the victory of despair and martyrdom. His queens embrace their lowliness with such fervor they convert it to grandeur, like those "Daughters of Shame" the Carolinas, a transvestite horde who march abroad in the streets of Barcelona, their "extravagant gestures" but a method to "pierce the shell of the world's contempt."[25] Through the miracle of Genet's prose ("my victory is verbal")[26] the masochism consonant with their role as slaves is converted to the aura of sainthood. How else does the good woman traditionally excel except through suffering? The church has, in fact, supplied Genet with an extremist solution to the lunatic pecking order of his world:

> The sacred surrounds and enslaves us . . . The Church is sacred. Its slow rites, weighted down with gold like Spanish galleons, ancient in meaning, remote from spirituality, gave it an empire as earthly as that of beauty and that of nobility. Culafroy . . . unable to escape this potency, abandoned himself to it voluptuously, as he would have done to Art had he known it![27]

Genet has art at his command and can effect through it the very transformation to nobility which Culafroy desires. Metamorphosed into Divine by the uncanny changes of faggotry, the miraculous is no longer beyond Louis' reach. Nor is art. Betrayed by her lovers, baited by hooligans, Divine invents a miniature painting on her fingernails; a tragic actress, she defies insult and forestalls criticism through bravura, calling herself a whorish old whore,[28] knowing there is no worse that can be said of her. An aged and fallen queen, the butt mocked even in fag hangouts, her pearl coronal broken and strewn upon the floor, Divine rallies the absurd courage to proclaim, "Dammit ladies, I'll be queen anyhow!"[29] ingeniously replacing the paste with her dental bridge, her crown of thorns. "Hewn of tears,"[30] the grim farce of her life has become her defense against the derision of the world. The most splendid character in all his novels, Genet has provided a place for her "among the Elect."

The martyred saint attracts Genet particularly, for unlike the scientist, the general, the industrialist, this is a hero who may be a heroine, and to the Gallic imagination this has perhaps a special likelihood, its own patron and national hero a woman "in drag" burned for a witch. In Genet's "eternal

25 *Ibid.*, p. 65.
26 *Ibid.*, p. 59.
27 Genet, *Our Lady of the Flowers*, p. 194.
28 *Ibid.*, see p. 116.
29 *Ibid.*, p. 193.
30 *Ibid.*, p. 194.

couple of the criminal and the saint,"[31] mac and queen, saint naturally takes the feminine form, "la sainte." For the mac provides only a body, the queen is the soul. Genet's feminine conquest is a matter of overcoming rank with the miracle of spirit. Here he is merely following the paradoxical logic of folk Christianity, as, in the eyes of God, a withered hag shines brighter than a king. Describing his place of sorrows, the Barrio Chino, Spain's most odious slum, Genet explains how

> . . . my life as a beggar familiarized me with the stateliness of abjection, for it took a great deal of pride (that is, of love) to embellish those filthy despised creatures. It took a great deal of talent . . . Never did I try to make of it something other than it was, I did not try to adorn it, to mask it, but on the contrary, I wanted to affirm it in its exact sordidness, and the most sordid signs became for me signs of grandeur.[32]

When he is arrested for vagrancy, the Vaseline found in his possession is but another sign of utter degradation because it only makes him more pansy, more vile in the view of the police and the secular world whose judgment they represent. It is for this reason more precious to him, stigmata both banal and triumphant. Associating it with his mother, also a prostitute, and overcome with the shame and tenderness both evoke, Genet claims "I would indeed rather have shed blood rather than repudiate the silly object," "its mere presence would be able to exasperate all the police in the world."[33] Christianity, the religion of the inferiority complex (humility) carried to the lengths of the Untouchable, transmutes this to beatitude. Casually jettisoning the ballast of its ethic, Genet has pirated its myth, content to prove that saintliness only means "turning pain to good account."[34]

But Genet's faith is incomplete, flawed by ironic analysis. Receiving the Eucharist, he experiences "nausea," tasting also "the magnificent structure of the laws in which I am caught,"[35] his fine and jaundiced eye remarking the icons of the Virgin in police stations. Completely removed from the bourgeois world, he can observe its totalist character, aware of how crime and the law are but each other's shadow. "Excluded by . . . birth and tastes from the social order," Genet went on to dare to "touch" it by "insulting those who composed it."[36] Louis Culafroy, child of a French village as Genet himself was, experiments with the sacred only to find it empty. Mounting the altar

---

[31] Jean Genet, *The Maids*, translated from the French by Bernard Frechtman (New York: Grove, 1954, 1961), p. 63.
[32] Genet, *The Thief's Journal*, p. 19.
[33] *Ibid.*, p. 22.
[34] *Ibid.*, p. 205.
[35] *Ibid.*, p. 173.
[36] *Ibid.*, p. 182.

of a deserted church and desecrating the host, he waits for the supernatural
to assert itself by a sign:

> And the miracle happened. There was no miracle. God had been debunked.
> God was hollow. Just a hole with any old thing around it. A pretty shape like
> the plaster head of Marie Antoinette and the little soldiers, which were holes
> with a bit of thin lead around them.[37]

Replacing this discredited god with crime and virility, Genet must also
find it hollow. The faces of his eminent killers, the heroes of the guillotine,
are really "vacant-eyed," "like the windows of buildings under construction,
through which you can see the sky."[38] Godlike in his world of fiction and
fantasy, Genet has contrived it that the pimp is a creature preternaturally
stupid, for with a revenge truly feminine he has undermined his masters by
turning upon them with the one insult woman has traditionally resorted to
in calling her lord a fool. Divine is often a burlesque of femininity,
celebrating July 14 in a way all her own, marking the day when the country is decked in the red, white, and blue of the tricolor, by tricking herself
out in "all the other colors, out of consideration for them because they are
disdained." But the cruel males whom she serves and Genet hymns are only
window-dressing dummies, fetishes of masculinity, rather than men.[39]

Genet's pseudo- or antireligion of homosexuality and crime has a third element in its trinity—betrayal. Although his role calls for perfect loyalty, he
delights in the perfidious,[40] a subversive even in his own realm, so full of
feminine guile that he corrupts and feminizes everything within reach, associating convicts with flowers, transforming the killer Harcamone's heraldic
chains and handcuffs into a network of roses, unmanning superman. Darling
was sadly mistaken in his expectation of becoming a "double male." After
a few years with Divine, the mighty pimp is as effeminate as his mistress.
Adrien Baillon, a promising young tough, is so infected by a brief cohabitation with Divine that he comes to be "Our Lady of the Flowers," consents to
attend a party in drag, and becomes a girl queen the same night.

Under Divine's influence even Seck Gorgui, her hulking he-man lover, is
softened. In the magnificent set piece where the three (Seck, Our Lady,
Divine) return bedraggled from their revels through the early morning streets,
Seck succumbs to an infatuation with Our Lady. The eternally rejected
woman, Divine has already lost her man by the time they catch a cab. Genet,
underlining a rare event, first advises us to "bear in mind that a pimp never

---

[37] Genet, *Our Lady of the Flowers*, p. 174.

[38] *Ibid.*, pp. 52–53.

[39] *Ibid.*, p. 105. Thody also comments on the "fetish" quality of Genet's males.

[40] See *Funeral Rites* (soon to be released in translation by Grove). Genet's delight
in betraying France calls to mind a common feminine response in wartime—*vide* the geisha
in Japan, the women of occupied Berlin and Paris. But the sort of betrayal Genet indulges in here is rather hard to forgive, and the novel disappointingly puerile.

effaces himself before a woman, still less before a faggot," and then describes how Seck, who, according to pecking order, should enter the taxi first, permits Our Lady to precede him.[41] This unique instance of chivalry is but effeminacy in Seck; a sign of regard for his new favorite utterly out of character in one of his station.

Our Lady of the Flowers was composed in prison while Genet was awaiting trial. The book is one long wish-fulfillment. It would seem that malice alone prompted him to invent the fantasy-figure called Marchetti—merely that he might be revenged on this handsome male by condemning him to a life sentence. "The charm that subjugates, the iron hand in the velvet glove," the absolute "Beauty" which inspires him to gush, "I am touched at the thought of it and could we weep with tenderness over his handsome muscles" is first paraded before us only that Genet may, with stunning acrimony, exterminate it:

> Marchetti will remain between four white walls to the end of ends . . . It will be the death of Hope . . . I am very glad of it. Let this arrogant and handsome pimp in turn know the torments reserved for the weakly.[42]

Gloating over the fate he has bestowed upon "the pimp, the lady-killer, the hangman of hearts," Genet addresses his creature with exquisite venom. "Your turn Marchetti . . . enjoy it as you can, deep in your cell. For I hate you lovingly."[43]

A spitefulness lurks within femininity, here defined not as the property of "a female in a skirt," but as a matter of "submission to the imperious male."[44] Genet's malevolence is a stubborn heresy cherished despite his self-proclaimed system of adulation, a lurking intractability. Slavelike, it shows itself in petty acts of betrayal and bitchiness. Refusing to accept the honor of a puff from the cigarette Botchako offers him, Genet, a mere fairy putting down a manly crasher, experiences a "triumphal moment."[45] The fag laughs at the mac behind his back. Just as he first rebelled from the social judgment of thief by embracing crime and converting it by "certain laws of a fictional aesthetic"[46] into his own version of evil as good, Genet has chosen to rebel from the ignominy of "cunt" status by creating *tantes* who transcend and outdistance their overbearing males.

Inscribing a copy of a book for a friend "Jean Genet, the weakest of all and the strongest"[47] he reveals he has always been a clerk among barons, a

[41] Genet, *Our Lady of the Flowers*, p. 224.
[42] *Ibid.*, pp. 184–85.
[43] *Ibid.*, p. 186.
[44] *Ibid.*, p. 235.
[45] Genet, *The Miracle of the Rose*, p. 220.
[46] Genet, *The Thief's Journal.*
[47] Sartre, *op. cit.*, reports to have seen this inscription in a copy of *Pompes Funèbres* (*Funeral Rites*).

part of him forever supercilious, aloof, and superior to the heroes he turns into poetry, donating gratis "those virtues they themselves *never* possess,"[48] knowing full well they are but overgrown bullies, clods, moronic adolescents. Their lawlessness, celebrated to appall the bourgeoisie whom Genet hates with a hatred more bitter and unrelenting than that of other contemporary French intellectuals (and with greater cause), is finally only the mugs' own bungled defeat before the fatalities of their class and education. But the Big Shots are cruel, and their masculine harshness, a stylized elaboration of the prevailing brutality of the world, makes them his enemies as well as his allies, his oppressors as well as his lovers.

The queen is continuously trying to absorb and become these lovers, to assume their superiority as Mimosa II swallows a photograph of Our Lady "like a host." Genet reveals the comic error in penis envy: to say he is infected is a gross understatement—possessing a penis, he has power envy. The very fellatio which is the queen's role and insignia of servitude is converted to a kind of castration rite wherein the pimp's hardness ("with Gorgui all is hard") is overcome by softness ("Divine is she-who-is-soft").[49]

An insight into the strangely subjective character of sexual power is contained in this brief description:

> From the way he talks, the way he lights and smokes his cigarette, Divine gathered that Darling is a pimp. At first she had certain fears: of being beaten up, robbed, insulted. Then she felt the proud satisfaction of *having made a pimp come*.[50]

In a conversion typical of slave psychology, Divine perceives the situation as one in her control, quite as the male imagines it is in his. Darling believes he had made Divine suck him off: Divine persists in the belief she had made Darling come. Caught in a power trap, each believes he/she is in command. The slave's manipulation of his master may distort, abridge—but never cancel —the distinction between them. Nor does it abolish slavery as an institution.

The final victory of Genet's subversive femininity is to cheat a spark of human affection out of the stony cliffs of virility. "What's eating you? Are you nuts or something?"[51] Armand grunts when Genet attempts to kiss his hairy arm. The mac is threatened, for he knows that fondness is feminine and can even make one vulnerable. By slow degrees he will be tricked into permitting egalitarian reciprocity, then need, and finally dependence. With insidious insubordination, Divine persists in telling Darling he is "pretty," un-

---

[48] Genet, *The Thief's Journal*, p. 23. Italics mine.

[49] Genet, *Our Lady of the Flowers*, p. 180.

[50] *Ibid.*, p. 79. Italics mine. I am gratefully indebted to Professor Richard Gustafson, not only for pointing out the ambiguity of this passage for me (my remark is but a paraphrase of his), but for a number of insights which I obtained from our conversations on Miller, Mailer, and Genet.

[51] Genet, *The Thief's Journal*, p. 134.

til the pimp is so unnerved he takes on her gestures and even goes to work. Caught shoplifting, his freedom evaporates in his victimization by the law. He is feminine now, beaten.

Genet's femininity is, as Sartre phrases it, a "hostile eroticism,"[52] delighted to ridicule and betray the very myth of virility it pretends to serve. By exposing virility's cowardice, its oppressive resemblance to the official adult world, the unfriendly society it mimics, his art is revenge springing out of "a humiliated adolescent's amorous hatred of the handsome big shots at Mettray" who first stigmatized him as feminine.[53] Like most of those restless in servitude, resentful of opprobrium, Genet has the little person's retaliation of derision and clever calumny.

But to be a rebel is not to be a revolutionary. It is more often but a way of spinning one's wheels deeper in the sand. Genet's hero criminals who achieve their martyr's crown at the guillotine murder inoffensive persons only that they may themselves be judged and murdered in return, leaving the system not only intact but actually stronger, for the lumpen proletariat has had its moment of symbolic self-expression through a vicarious participation in a pointless antisocial act, has enjoyed the execution also, maybe even more, and is now ready to become docile once again. And Divine's saintliness, her martyrdom, is only the destructive impulse, the masochism of her role carried to its fulfillment in self-immolation. Hers is the moral victory of true faith, but it is not freedom.

III

Because it did not cover Genet's last three plays, Sartre's biography leaves its subject still a rebel, failing to report his final metamorphosis into revolutionary. With *The Balcony*, *The Blacks*, and *The Screens*, we have a new Genet evolved beyond the imperfect subversive Sartre saw in the novels, *Deathwatch*, and *The Maids*. Genet's originally subjective antisocialism has gradually taken an objective form in the theater, aiming toward what he states in a recent essay to be his final ambition—namely, to disappear behind his work.[54] While irony increases, romantic myth drops away, and with it, that dichotomy between the two one finds in his earlier works, particularly the wonderfully urbane and self-conscious *Thief's Journal*. It is a feature of *The Miracle of the Rose* as well, which alternates between exaggerated celebrations of the prison world and jaded expressions of how "disillusioned" and bored with it Genet is becoming. Perhaps the very pitch of ironic attitude is reached in *L'Enfant Criminel*, a radio talk where, in the manner of a modest proposer, Genet urges greater inhumanity in reformatories, that youthful

---

[52] Sartre, *op. cit.*, p. 153.

[53] *Ibid.*, p. 149.

[54] Jean Genet, "The Funambulists," translated from the French by Bernard Frechtman, *Evergreen Review*, No. 32, April–May 1964, pp. 45–49.

offenders may "keep in touch with the revolt that makes them so beautiful."[55]

To advance past rebellion Genet is forced to discard the remnants of his ironic and paradoxical faith, for the step from rebellion to revolution is a step beyond nostalgia (for what one has known and hated and enjoyed defacing) toward the creation of new alternate values. Rebels can be "contained"—especially if they are sentimental ones.

The idea of "femininity" as presented in the novels: abject abdicating martyrdom, broken by an undercurrent of sedition, takes a new course in the late works for the theater, becoming an attitude of rebellious intransigence, which with Genet's expanding sympathy and humanity, his increasing interest in politics, grows into an identification with oppressed groups of both sexes: maids, blacks, Algerians, proles, all those who are in the feminine or subordinate role toward capital, racism, or empire.[56] The negative aspect of femininity as a slave mentality is now one which its victims struggle against with increasing fury, at first with futile self-destructiveness in *The Maids,* then with growing understanding and success in each succeeding play.

Oppression creates a psychology in the oppressed. Marxism, though adroit at analyzing the economic and political situation of such persons, has often neglected, perhaps out of nervous dismay, to notice how thoroughly the oppressed are corrupted by their situation, how deeply they envy and admire their masters, how utterly they are polluted by their ideas and values, how even their attitude toward themselves is dictated by those who own them. Genet has been a servant. When he states that servants are the "seamy side of their masters," their "unwholesome exhalations,"[57] and his maids, deep in self-disdain, refer to themselves as each other's "bad smell,"[58] he is describing a very real social and psychological phenomenon. His mature plays are studies in what one might call the colonial or feminine mentality of interiorized oppression which must conquer itself before it can be free.

The maids fail. Weighted down with self-hatred, their favorite game is really not to play at murdering their mistress, but to play at being her. The second game is so much more exciting that they never get around to the first. In the end, Claire, the more gentle and Divine-like of the two, drinks poison

[55] The talk was never given as the liberal prison reformers who were the other guests refused to show up. I am using Thody's translation of the phrase. The talk has been printed together with Genet's ballet, *Adame Miroir.* Jean Genet, *L'Enfant Criminel* (Paris: Paul Morihien, 1949).

[56] To argue as Richard Coe has done in *The Vision of Jean Genet* that Genet was undergoing a process which Coe calls "virilization" and identifies with freedom, self-realization, art, and every other good thing, is nonsense. Were such the case, Genet's plays should have sided with the powers that be, which all his life he had seen as masculine. By analogy, the transition from "niggerization" to black military is hardly a process of becoming white. Coe's terms explain his assumptions. See Richard N. Coe, *The Vision of Jean Genet* (New York: Grove, 1968).

[57] Genet, *The Miracle of the Rose,* p. 106.

[58] Genet, *The Maids,* p. 61.

so that the more craven and "masculine" maid, Solange, may pretend to a murder, enjoy the guillotine, and relish a tabloid notoriety. The play's raw material was the case of the Papin sisters, Lea and Christine, who killed their mistress and her daughter at Le Mans in 1933, capturing the popular imagination in their gory wake. Genet has made extensive changes in his treatment of the events, underlining the futility of the insurrection by leaving the employers untouched, and eliminating the daughter to add Monsieur, Madame's lover, the Man at the pinnacle of the hierarchy, who never appears, although he is referred to continuously, and exerts enormous authority over all three women from off stage. Madame claims to be his slave, and when the maids try to get him arrested by writing letters to the police, Madame rejoices in the melodramatic prospect of following him to Siberia.

The Maids is a study of female jealousy and resentment at servile status. "Filth does not love filth"[59] Solange proposes, explaining why it is impossible for the maids to rebel or take concerted action together. "When slaves love one another, it's not love,"[60] despising themselves, they despise each other, and there can be no solidarity between them, for like any well-trained women, they do not identify with each other but with males or with the rich like Madame. This is why Genet puts stress on the maids as proletarian as well as feminine, their immediate enemy their bourgeois mistress. Not until *The Screens* does Genet's identification with purely feminine circumstances clearly and decisively emerge.

Madame herself is kind, with the kindness of the comfortable middle class who can afford good manners. (To a lady who congratulated herself on giving her maid her discarded dresses, Genet quietly replied, "How nice, and does she give you hers?")[61] But the maids, playing at being mistress to each other, are not nice. Outcasts in an emotional complicity with the ruling order, they invent insults ("Servants ooze." "They are not of the human race")[62] exposing the poisonous effect their declared inferiority (agreed upon by others and agreed to by themselves) has had upon them. So much do they believe in their superiors' edition of their lives, they cannot escape servitude save in self-laceration, and their revolt is only the criminal's folly which inevitably rebounds back upon itself. But here, in contrast to the novels, it is presented for the first time with explicitness devoid of romantic sentimentality. The maids' suffering is exquisite, but their oppression is too effective; out of their predicament as selves defined by another, there is as yet no exit.

The Balcony, which concentrates on the political connotations of sex role as power, is another case of failed rebellion, but a great advance over the maids' claustral dilemma in that an actual revolution might have occurred

[59] *Ibid.*, p. 52.
[60] *Ibid.*, p. 61.
[61] Sartre, *op. cit.*, reports the anecdote on page 18.
[62] Genet, *The Maids*, p. 86.

if it had any alternate values to set up in place of the *ancien régime* it has temporarily destroyed. Armand names the problem: "I personally don't believe in their masquerade, not one bit. But is there any stronger force to replace them?"[63] A history of belief and co-operation paralyzes one. In Carmen the prostitute, participation in masculine fantasy has created such identification with the role that it becomes her reality; excused from the charade, she craves those heady moments when she was The Immaculate Conception of Lourdes to a bank clerk. In the same way, the participation of a whole populace in the ancient myths of the church, the law, and the army, bring about instantaneous capitulation when imposters standing in for these members of the "Nomenclature" are paraded through the city in state. Humanity is a bit infantilized, like the masochist in studio four who wishes only to be tied and spanked, so schooled in the old rites it loves them.

The revolution degenerates to counterrevolution because, lacking a creative alternative, the new order can only ape the old: "If we behave like those of the other side, then we *are* the other side," Roger, the most dedicated and intelligent of the rebels predicts, knowing that "instead of changing the world, all we'll achieve is a reflection of the one we want to destroy."[64] And so the popular upsurge, unaccompanied by any change of consciousness, can be merely a *coup d'état*, ending, as *coups* do, in a fascist junta. Illustrating the basic conventionality of the rebels, Genet again chooses to do it in terms of sexual role, through the conjunction of Chantal and Georgette. Though one is a fighter and the other a revolutionary intellectual, both are restricted to the stereotypic role of nursing the wounded. "That's a woman's job,"[65] a casualty recites smugly. Chantal's only alternative is to be a singer or a whore; to entertain or arouse the male. When the cadre raffle her off like cattle auctioneers (twenty ordinary women for Chantal) she performs the role allowed her and in the process helps corrupt the revolution. La Passionara is a figure full of romance, but one woman does not make a revolution, and one of the better tests of an actual revolution (as opposed to rebellion, riot, civil war, nationalist war, etc.) is the degree to which the female population participates.

Confusing sex with power in the same manner as their predecessors, the male rebels cease to think, and the uprising turns into an orgy of "shoot and screw," "one hand on the trigger, the other on the fly."[66] Of course they fail—"a carnival that goes to the limit is suicide."[67] Having nothing new to say, the insurrectionists fall into traditional follies regarding sex and power, sex and violence. Females are goddesses or packhorses as of old; nurses, bitches

[63] Jean Genet, *The Balcony,* translated from the French by Bernard Frechtman (New York: Grove, 1958), p. 67.

[64] *Ibid.,* p. 56.

[65] *Ibid.,* p. 60.

[66] *Ibid.,* p. 59.

[67] *Ibid.*

or whores, and males the familiar pack of mindless slaughterers, inspired not by freedom but by sexual delusion. A right-wing master politico who survives every rumble, the Envoy puts it neatly: "At first people were fighting against illustrious and illusory tyrants, then for freedom. Tomorrow they'll be ready to die for Chantal alone."[68] When the whistle blows, guilt and confusion find them at their stations, bowing before the customary notions of law and order represented by three dolls in lace and braid, the establishment's Justice, Piety, and Valor. Devoid of transforming ideas, they have earned their failure, and the police state closes in upon them, inexorable before Roger's suicidal gesture of literally castrating himself, a naïve bit of imitative magic, masochist as the maid's poisoned teacup, since it leaves the Chief of Police intact, sexually impotent as ever, but probably capable of ruling from his tomb with the truly powerful mythic phallus of fear. Caught in the toils of the sexual power game, rebel hope is "screwed" again.

In stipulating that the roles in *The Maids* be played by young men, Genet was not primarily indulging in a gay joke, but only, as Sartre observes, presenting "femininity without women,"[69] an abstraction, a state of mind. Since "nigger," like "cunt" is a status word to him, Genet employed a similar device with regard to black and white in *The Blacks*,[70] where he chose to have black actors ("behind the mask of a corner white is a poor trembling Negro")[71] represent the White Court who judge the ritual murder of whiteness as performed by another group of blacks, the Players. Since their situation in white culture makes them relative beings or mirrors of white ideas, the blacks seek to "entertain" their projected audience in the White Court, as well as an actual paying audience of Caucasians[72] with the one black act of greatest interest to the white, the brutal rape and murder of "his woman." This farce, whose function is to release black animosity, edify whites with a caricature of their bogeys, and affront them by a parody of their power establishment (the White Court) is, in fact, only a diversion from the real action, the beginning of an organized black revolution, inaugurated by the purge of Uncle Tom.[73] The probable traitor, Reverend

[68] *Ibid.*, p. 77.

[69] Sartre, *op. cit.*, p. 656.

[70] Jean Genet, *The Blacks*, translated from the French by Bernard Frechtman (New York: Grove, 1960). The French title *Les Nègres* is closer to "nigger" than to "black."

[71] *Ibid.*, p. 58.

[72] "This play, written, I repeat, by a white man, is intended for a white audience, but if, which is unlikely, it is ever performed before a black audience, then a white person, male or female, should be invited every evening. The organizer of the show should welcome him formally, dress him in ceremonial costume and lead him to his seat, preferably in the front row of the orchestra. The actors will play for him." Prefatory note to *The Blacks*.

[73] The play succeeded here splendidly. The only French or English critic who ever saw the real plot in early productions was Guy Leclerc of *L'Humanité* (Paris: November 1959).

Samba Graham Diouf is a compromiser undermined by the "kindness of the whites" into a "guilty meekness"[74] and full of hopeful proposals for a gray or gingerbread Eucharist. The blacks' own humorous solution is to make him the ritual victim of their rite and dispatch him to the "nigger heaven" of whiteness. Perched up on a tier there with the White Court, he can look down from his new eminence and report that "either they lie or they're mistaken"—whites are in fact "pink or yellowish."[75]

The Blacks will not perish through the same error as *The Balcony*'s rebels, for they have invented alternative values. Against the absolute value of white in Western culture, which has appropriated everything from God to cleanliness, they assert the power of black. In a prefatory note Genet asks "what exactly is a black? First of all, what's his color?"—a conundrum which implies both that color is irrelevant to common humanity, and secondly, that blackness is the route to revolution in a white supremacy. There is no insuperable contradiction here, for revolution would scarcely be a necessity to blacks as blacks, without the politicization white has effected upon black by basing its oppression on racial pigmentation—on blackness. In order to escape the identity their masters have given them, the blacks must first objectify it. They accomplish this by ridicule and exaggeration, the "niggerishness"[76] of their boot-blacking make-up, two-toned shoes, and flashy dresses. Next they must develop the identity of their own choice, for Genet is correct in assuming that the emergence of a positive collective identity precedes revolutionary awareness and marks the difference between it and pointless uprisings which only spin back into further reaction.

The Blacks is a turning point in Genet's exegesis of the politics and psychology of oppression, marking a move away from defeated self-hate to dignity and self-definition. And, finally, to rage. Blacks, colonials, women, all prisoners of definitions imposed on them by others, must, if they are not to become the victims of their own self-loathing (like the maids) or of their traditional illusions (like the people of *The Balcony*) find freedom by an angry assertion of selfhood and solidarity. Exploring the vexed and complicated problem of sexual and racial politics, Genet suggests that whites have divided blacks, as the *colons* did the Algerians, by introducing or capitalizing upon a variety of sexual hostility which provides a particular set of advantages for white ends. Among the blacks this has been effected by the proposition that the white master's aesthetic is embodied in "his woman," a bit of property he advertises so that it might be coveted, coveted so that the act

[74] Genet, *The Blacks,* p. 33.

[75] *Ibid.,* p. 89.

[76] In this context perhaps a better word than negritude. I heard it explained by Richard Richard, a black painter who based an aesthetic on it and described it in terms of Harlem interiors, pink chenille bedspreads, fancy table lamps and enthusiastically striped slip covers. All through his work Genet too has made an aesthetic out of "bad taste," e.g., the accoutrements of the poor.

may be punished. Meanwhile the black woman is imprisoned as her master's whore—"Every brothel has its negress,"[77] "I make my troops tear off a piece every Saturday,"[78] the White Governor chuckles.

For the white distorts love and sexuality in his subjects, forcing the black male to accept both the white woman's beauty, and scorn of the black woman. "I hate you," Village confesses to Virtue. "I began to hate you when every thing about you would have kindled love and when love would have made men's contempt unbearable."[79] Unable to "bear the weight of the world's condemnation," he has shared its disdain. Exorcising the myth which has bewitched them, the black lovers must first repudiate the white fallacy that the female is an aesthetic object and that beauty itself is white. Until this lie goes, Village cannot love Virtue, Charley's despised prostitute, who, of all the blacks, is "the only one who experiences shame to the bitter end."[80] The signal of the play's victory is his final acceptance of her.

Sounding the very depths of the colonial attitude, Genet demonstrates how the inability to accept the black woman is tantamount to a kind of self-hatred infecting the whole race. "Stately mother of my race . . . you are Africa, oh monumental night, and I hate you,"[81] Village bursts out. Felicity, the Black Queen, and the spirit of Africa, the matriarch who challenges and defeats the figurehead of the White Queen, is in fact the mother of this race: its future depends on its ability to come to terms with its origin, to identify with its negritude, the alternative value which will save it from the destructive standards of whiteness. In Felicity's magnificent evocations of Africa, the force and magic of an entire continent is gathered:

Dahomey! Dahomey! Negroes from all corners of the earth, to the rescue! Come! Enter into me . . . Swell me with your tumult! . . . Penetrate where you will, my mouth, my ears—or my nostril . . . Giantess with head thrown back, I await you all. Enter into me, ye multitudes, and be, for this evening only, my force and reason . . .

Tribes covered with gold and mud, rise up from my body, emerge! Tribes of the Rain and Wind, forward! Princes of the Upper Empires, Princes of the bare feet and wooden stirrups, on your caparisoned horses, enter! . . . Are you there, Africa with the bulging chest and oblong thigh? Sulking Africa, wrought of iron, in the fire, Africa of the millions of royal slaves, deported Africa, drifting continent, are you there? Slowly you vanish, you withdraw into the past, into the tales of castaways, colonial museums, the works of scholars, but I call you back this evening to attend a secret revel.[82]

[77] Genet, *The Blacks*, p. 38.
[78] *Ibid.*, p. 78.
[79] *Ibid.*, p. 36.
[80] *Ibid.*, p. 38.
[81] *Ibid.*, pp. 36–37.
[82] *Ibid.*, pp. 46 and 76.

Having made the world in the image of whiteness, white rule proposed its own narcissism as an absolute against which blackness, unable to conform, can only be defined as deviate, inferior. Against this myth, the anger of the black women is fiercest of all: "We, the negro women, we had only our wrath and rage,"[83] they seethe. Most oppressed of all, dismissed as a "tame captive"[84] even by men of her own kind, men whom they must ever suspect of desire for the whites' own ideal decorative feminine nonentity, the fury of women like Bobo or Snow is scarcely under control. "From far off, from Ubangi or Tanganyika, a tremendous love came here to die licking white ankles,"[85] Snow accuses Village, her distrust and resentment puncturing the ritual surface of the black mass with psychodrama. The real force of hate, the rock-bottom determination of the blacks lies with the women, who are not tempted like Diouf to sell out for the public office of "spokesman," or like Village, for the moonshine of white romance. At the bottom of the racial-sexual totem there is only one place to go. Archibald, the master of ceremonies, exhorts his players: "Negroes, if they change toward us let it be not out of indulgence, but terror," but he has no need to incite the women, only to restrain them. They are constantly transcending the ritual denunciation their role demands and breaking out into actual fierceness. Snow tears and bites the flowers which bedeck the catafalque, an act not called for in the rite and one rebuked as "needless cruelty."[86] Here, just as in *The Screens*, Genet has placed the most fearful revolutionary passion in the women.

Alone of our contemporary writers, Genet has taken thought of women as an oppressed group and revolutionary force, and chosen to identify with them. His own peculiar history, his analysis of expropriated peoples, inevitably lead Genet to empathize with what is scorned, relative, and subjugated. Each of his last plays incorporates the sexual into political situations: in *The Balcony* it is power and sex, in *The Blacks*, race and sex, in *The Screens*, sexual rank and the colonial mentality. Lawrence, Miller, and Mailer, identify woman as a annoying minority force to be put down and are concerned with a social order in which the female would be perfectly controlled. Genet, however, has integrated her into a vision of drastic social upheaval where her ancient subordination can produce explosive force. And, in fact, in *The Screens*, it is the women who are the revolution.

As the play opens the Arabs are immersed in a system of hierarchal situations; the European *colon* lords it over the Arab male, who vents his frustrations on his woman, who, if she is lucky, takes it out on her daughter-in-law. As the *colon* guards his fields with a mechanical glove suspended

83 *Ibid.*, p. 17.
84 *Ibid.*, p. 69.
85 *Ibid.*, p. 49.
86 *Ibid.*, p. 52.

in the air like a Blue Meaney, the Arab husband, during the hours of his absence, governs his females by means of his empty trousers.[87]

In the first scene Said, *The Screens'* anti-hero, is on his way to marry the "ugliest woman in the next town and all the towns around,"[88] fuming that he is stuck with her: In the scale of capital and marriage values, his own poverty is presumed to match her ugliness. It's hard to tell if her face is a real or imagined catastrophe, since Leila the bride wears a black bag throughout the entire performance, stark evidence of her nonentity, enslavement, and exclusion from human experience. Said's mother, a traditional Arab woman, tags behind him carrying a valise of gewgaw wedding presents. A devout male supremacist, she is persuaded her son would "be less of a man"[89] if he were to condescend to come to her aid in public. Leila is Said's salvation as well as his fate; her very odium epitomizes the Arab's colonial situation. Scorning her with a ferocious ardor, Said becomes a dangerously disgruntled colonial. More an allegory than a character, Leila the loathed woman, is a symptom of the general degradation of the Arab world. If Said the Arab hates her, he hates himself, for no people are capable of self-respect, if, like Genet's Muslims, they so fervently despise half their own population.

The folk humor of the ugly wife with which the play begins contains its central situation. Said's dissatisfaction brings him first to the brothel where the pariah prostitutes, creatures of a chiefly decorative function, assuage his native disaffection with mock-Western manners and ornate display. But even the house of illusions is not enough, and its essentially colonial character is explicit for both sexes:

> *Mustapha:* The French were pretty annoyed about our fucking their whores.
> *Warda:* Did they let you do anything else? They didn't. So? Here what do you fuck? Us.[90]

It is Said's very hatred of his own situation, not so much exacerbated, as summed up in his wife (who is his unrelenting *malheur*, his unique misfortune, the contemptible odor that follows him like a shadow from trouble to jail to a life of total alienation) which becomes the fuse of the revolution. Said's strange discontent is potential political dynamite.

But if Said becomes somewhat miraculously (in view of his determined apolitical nature) not only the model, but the "flag" of the revolution, its spirit and activity comes from a group of old village hags still more lowly than he. This is appropriate in Genet's scheme, a revolutionary politics whereby bottom dog should bark loudest. To the Arab male groaning under

[87] This actually happens. See scenes 3 and 4. Jean Genet, *The Screens* (New York: Grove, 1962).

[88] *Ibid.,* p. 12.

[89] *Ibid.,* p. 13.

[90] *Ibid.,* p. 20.

foreign occupation, the women present a longer and more complete history of colonial resentment:

> *Ommu:* For a thousand years we women have put up with being your dish rags . . . but for a hundred years, *you've* been dish rags: thanks to you the boots of those gentlemen have been a hundred thousand shining suns . . .[91]

It is old Kadidja who screams out the first words of insurrection at a sedate Moslem civil gathering from which she is officially excluded:

> *The Dignitary* (wearing a fez and a blue, western-style suit with many decorations. Into the wings): Remain quiet. Everyone must be dignified. No children here. Nor women.

> *Kadidja:* Without women what would you be? A spot on your father's pants that three flies would have drunk up.

> *The Dignitary:* Go away, Kadidja. This isn't the day.

> *Kadidja* (furiously): It is! They accuse us and threaten us, and you want us to be prudent. And docile. And humble. And submissive. And ladylike. And honey-tongued. And sweet as pie. And silk veil. And fine cigarette. And nice kiss and soft spoken. And gentle dust on their red pumps! . . . I won't! (She stamps her heel.)
> This is *my* town here. My bed is here. I was fucked fourteen times here and gave birth to fourteen Arabs. I won't go.[92]

And against the bumptious inanity of the landowner Sir Harold, it is Kadidja who cries out her people's first challenge—"I say that your force is powerless against our hatred."[93] In retaliation Kadidja is calmly shot down by the whites, whereupon (since *The Screens* is a surrealist dream play, its characters popping in and out of life in the most disconcerting way) her ghost begins the revolution.

It is little wonder *The Screens* incited a storm both in France and in Algeria. Presented in government-subsidized theatre in a superb production by Jean-Louis Barrault's company, *The Screens*, as Philip Thody has remarked, satirizes the French army as a body of "incompetent and attitudinizing [latent] homosexuals, and the one hundred and thirty years of French presence in Algeria as a totally ludicrous experience."[94] Broad, and often vulgar farce from start to finish, the play erupted into a riot when Genet's legionnaires patriotically farted "French air" in sober tribute over their lieutenant's corpse. In Algeria, *The Screens* is equally unpopular, for it accuses the

---

[91] *Ibid.,* p. 134.
[92] *Ibid.,* pp. 90–91.
[93] *Ibid.,* p. 96.
[94] Thody, *op. cit.,* p. 206.

revolution of becoming the very pattern of its colonial predecessor, leaving the masses, Said and the women, as wretched as before. The last scenes are a duel between a group of prophetic matriarchs, grand in their poetic rage and their visions of an ongoing revolution, and the pale and automated males of the new order, carbon copies of their French enemy, bursting with narcissism and military discipline, *la gloire,* and the organized slaughter called valor.

Obviously under Fanon's influence (probably via Sartre),[95] Genet is remarkably indulgent toward the violence the insurgents, both men and women, perpetrate in the terrorist stages of the uprising. One of the most impressive and frightening scenes in the play is the depiction, through drawings after drawing upon the screens, of the atrocities the guerrillas commit. As screen after screen fills with blood and fire, Kadidja, the first martyr and presiding figure of the insurrection, pronounces her unrelenting hatred and satisfaction at the human sacrifice. Genet's justification would doubtless be that oppression rightly seeks revenge, a stupid argument however fashionable. Violence of itself accomplishes nothing that revolutions are created to accomplish: in fact, it is likely to be the leading counterrevolutionary symptom, as Genet himself demonstrated in *The Balcony.* As means to the end of social justice, revolutionary crime is self defeating since it merely replaces older oppression and inequity with new.

But Genet's contempt for military murder is quite a different affair. In the lieutenant of the French legionnaires, he has created a splendid caricature career officer, an idiotic martial narcissist ("Let every man be a mirror to every other man")[96] a Maileresque case of repressed homosexuality finding its only outlet in cruelly eroticized violence, where love is hate, death is life, and war is sex. Here is the "brick and mortar," spit and polish maniac giving orders to his troops:

> I want the army to send your families wristwatches and medals caked with blood and even with jissom . . . Preston! . . . . my revolver. . . . Warfare, screwing . . . I want pictures of naked babies and holy virgins sewn into your linings . . . on your hair brilliantine, ribbons in the hair on your ass . . . And your eyes like the bayonet. And screwing. Get me: war's a rip-roaring orgy. Triumphal awakening! My boots more brilliant Preston! I want war and screwing in the sun! And guts oozing in the sun! Get it?
> *The Sergeant:* Got it.[97]

---

[95] This is not to say that Fanon and Genet are always in agreement. The patronizing and male-chauvinist attitude which characterizes Fanon's chapter on Muslim women in *Notes on a Dying Colonialism,* a portent of how Algerian nationalism exploited and co-opted this oppressed group, could not be more far removed from Genet's own radicalism in supporting their liberation.

[96] Genet, *The Screens,* p. 118.

[97] *Ibid.,* pp. 78–80.

The brothel is a sort of barometer of revolutionary and counterrevolutionary progress. During the stupor of colonial despair, it was the refuge of dreams and hope, where Si Slimane, the first martyr-agitator, was honored. When the insurrection actually occurs, the whores lose their leper status, are united with the village women and become one with the national cause. For a while they dispense free service. Later they even consider closing shop. But as the revolt is co-opted by efficient native patriarchal authority ("We want to be the stronger"[98] the new soldiers preach to the village) the prostitutes fall back to their traditional outcast standing. One is murdered by the village wives and the rest settle back into the normalcy of divided female camps, inflationary prices, and an ill-disguised hostility for the men who use them.

Kadidja and Ommu were the personifications of the popular rage. The new Arab army, like the French Legion, are but the old oppressive virility cult subsidized by the state, another set of bullies, in power through a new establishment. And as officials, they are infinitely more noxious than individualist criminals or the Big Shots of Mettray. Of the triad of matriarchs who proclaim the spirit of the revolution, Kadidja and Said's Mother (who grew so unconventional she lifted her hand to a man and strangled a French soldier) have been ghosts long enough to be beyond politics. Only Ommu is left. And her only course lies in "bottling" Said, the symptom of that crushing ignominy which, through the example of its ulcerous spiritual condition, first excited the tumult. Said is the product of the colonial system, a way of life, which, since it produced the revolution, must never be forgotten. If the shame of the past were to be obliterated, the Algerians would also be left without purpose. So Said must be preserved in art, or as Ommu puts it, he must "become song."

Turning upon a soldier of the new militia, Ommu taunts them as a new set of bosses: "You lousy little stinker, you snot nose . . . go join the other side where there's stately beauty . . . maybe you've already done it, you're joining them and copying them excites you. To be their reflection is already to be one of them."[99] For the "expected" has come about, and Ommu sees her own sons have "reached the stage of uniforms, discipline, jaunty marches and bare arms . . . parade and heroic death."[100] Not to mention "martial beauty" which as she points out, equates lovemaking with murder quite as the Legion had done.[101]

While the soldiers of the new dictatorship prattle of "the efficacy of com-

[98] *Ibid.*, p. 137.
[99] *Ibid.*, p. 135.
[100] *Ibid.*
[101] The historical accuracy of Genet's version of the Algerian Revolution has been attested to. Thody sums it up very well: "The dissension between the women, representing the criminally undisciplined upsurge of revolt, and the triumphant revolutionary army, with its cult of discipline and clean living, also reflects what happened in Algeria itself, and entitles the play to be considered as historical drama. Thody, *op. cit.*, p. 209.

bat," Ommu's ancient wisdom counters—"the aesthetics of decease."[102] Already anxious there will be none honest enough to succeed her in agitation, she lectures a priggish young bit of militarism: "Soldier of ours, young prickhead, there are truths that must never be applied, that must be made to thrive through the song they've become. Go die facing the enemy. Your death is no truer than my raving. You and your pals are proof that we need a Said."[103] What Ommu seeks in Said is proof that there is a humanity grander than drilled heroism.

Said, independent maverick to the end, refuses to belong to either camp: "To the old gal, to the soldiers, to all of you, I say shit."[104] Like Leila, he never arrives at Genet's heaven of paper screens at the top of the stage, but passes into the national atmosphere, the completely unreconstructed man. Impervious even to firing squads when the military government cuts him down, he persists as a compost of humiliation and the sordid past—"save the little heap of garbage since that's what inspires us," Ommu had advised.[105]

While Said and Leila become legend and memory, Ommu or some other prophetess will go on agitating, preserving the meaning of recalcitrance. Curmudgeon folk figure, one counts on her not to "kick off" as she'd like to, but to carry on "burying this one, screaming at that one: I'll live to be a hundred."[106] Emblem of woman, she has lived to see mulish arrogance once again stifle her freedom and suborn her humanity. Having been a "dish rag" for a thousand years, she has time, patience and experience. Since she is deathless resistance and a new spirit in the world, there is hope yet. And the revolution which liberates Said and Ommu will not only be the last, but the first.

102 Genet, *The Screens*, p. 195.
103 *Ibid.*
104 *Ibid.*, p. 197.
105 *Ibid.*, p. 185. The correspondence to Genet's own way of thinking about himself is noteworthy.
106 *Ibid.*, p. 200.

POSTSCRIPT

Genet's homosexual analysis of sexual politics was chosen, not only for the insights it affords into the arbitrary status content of sexual role, but because it was against the taboo of homosexuality that Mailer's counterrevolutionary ardor has hurled its last force. Yet there is evidence in the last few years that the reactionary sexual ethic we have traced, beginning with Lawrence's cunning sabotage of the feminist argument and Miller's flamboyant contempt for it, has nearly spent itself.

Other progressive forces have recently asserted themselves, notably the revolt of youth against the masculine tradition of war and virility. Of course the most pertinent recent development is the emergence of a new feminist movement. Here again, it is difficult to explain just why such a development occurred when it did.[107] The enormous social change involved in a sexual revolution is basically a matter of altered consciousness, the exposure and elimination of social and psychological realities underlying political and cultural structures. We are speaking, then, of a cultural revolution, which, while, it must necessarily involve the political and economic reorganization traditionally implied by the term revolution, must go far beyond this as well. And here it would seem that the most profound changes implied are ones

---

[107] Civil Rights was undoubtedly a force, for second-generation feminists were, like their predecessors, inspired by the example of black protest. The disenchantment of women in the New Left with the sexist character of that movement provided considerable impetus as well.

accomplished by human growth and true re-education, rather than those arrived at through the theatrics of armed struggle—even should the latter become inevitable. There is much reason to believe that the possession of numbers, dedication, and creative intelligence could even render unnecessary the usual self-destructive resort to violent tactics. Yet no lengthy evolutionary process need be implied here, rather the deliberate speed fostered by modern communication, in an age when groups such as students, for example, can become organized in a great number of countries in a matter of some two years.

When one surveys the spontaneous mass movements taking place all over the world, one is led to hope that human understanding itself has grown ripe for change. In America one may expect the new women's movement to ally itself on an equal basis with blacks and students in a growing radical coalition. It is also possible that women now represent a very crucial element capable of swinging the national mood, poised at this moment between the alternatives of progress or political repression, toward meaningful change. As the largest alienated element in our society, and because of their numbers, passion, and length of oppression, its largest revolutionary base, women might come to play a leadership part in social revolution, quite unknown before in history. The changes in fundamental values such a coalition of expropriated groups—blacks, youth, women, the poor—would seek are especially pertinent to realizing not only sexual revolution but a gathering impetus toward freedom from rank or prescriptive role, sexual or otherwise. For to actually change the quality of life is to transform personality, and this cannot be done without freeing humanity from the tyranny of sexual-social category and conformity to sexual stereotype—as well as abolishing racial caste and economic class.

It may be that a second wave of the sexual revolution might at last accomplish its aim of freeing half the race from its immemorial subordination —and in the process bring us all a great deal closer to humanity. It may be that we shall even be able to retire sex from the harsh realities of politics, but not until we have created a world we can bear out of the desert we inhabit.

BIBLIOGRAPHY

Works Consulted in Anthropology

BACHOFEN, J. J.: *Myth Religion and Mother Right,* a translation of *Mutterrecht und Urreligion,* a selection of the writings of J. J. Bachofen, edited by Rudolf Marx, 1926; translated from the German by Ralph Mannheim (Princeton, Bollingen Series, 1967).

BETTELHEIM, BRUNO: *Symbolic Wounds: Puberty Rites and the Envious Male* (New York, Collier, 1962).

BRIFFAULT, ROBERT: *The Mothers: A Study of the Origins of Sentiments and Institutions,* translated from the French, three volumes (New York, Macmillan, 1927).

BRIFFAULT, ROBERT: *The Mothers* (1927), abridged by Gordon Battray Taylor (London, George Allen & Unwin, 1959).

CRAWLEY, ERNEST: *The Mystic Rose, A Study of Primitive Marriage and of Primitive Thought on Its Bearing on Marriage,* revised edition, two volumes, prepared by Theodore Besterman (London, Methuen, 1927).

DURKHEIM, EMILE: *The Elementary Forms of Religious Life* (1915), translated from the French by Joseph Ward Swain (New York, Free Press, 1965).

FORD, CLELLAN S., and BEACH, FRANK A.: *Patterns of Sexual Behavior* (New York, Harper, 1951).

FRIED, MORTON H.: *The Evolution of Political Society, An Essay in Political Anthropology* (New York, Random House, 1967).

HARRIS, MARVIN: *The Origins of Anthropological Theory* (New York, Columbia University, 1969).

HARRISON, JANE: *Prolegomena to the Study of Greek Religion* (1903). Cambridge, England, Cambridge University Press, 1922, 2nd Edition.

HAYS, H. R.: *The Dangerous Sex, The Myth of Feminine Evil* (New York, Putnam, 1964).

LÉVI-STRAUSS, CLAUDE: *Structural Anthropology*, translated from the French by Claire Jacobson and Brooke Grundfest Schoepf (New York, Basic Books, 1963).

LÉVI-STRAUSS, CLAUDE: *The Savage Mind*, translated from the French (Chicago, University of Chicago, 1966).

LÉVI-STRAUSS, CLAUDE: *Totemism*, translated from the French by Rodney Needham (Boston, Beacon, 1963).

MAINE, SIR HENRY: *Ancient Law* (London, Murray, 1861).

MAINE, SIR HENRY: *The Early History of Institutions* (London, 1875).

MALINOWSKI, BRONISLAW: *Sex and Repression in Savage Society* (New York, Humanities Press, 1927).

MALINOWSKI, BRONISLAW: *Sex, Culture and Myth* (New York, Harcourt, Brace, 1962).

McLENNON, JOHN: *The Patriarchal Theory* (London, Macmillan, 1885).

MEAD, MARGARET: *Sex and Temperament* (New York, Morrow, 1935).

MEAD, MARGARET: *Male and Female* (New York, Morrow, 1949).

MORGAN, LEWIS HENRY: *Ancient Society* (1877) (New York, World, 1963).

MURDOCK, GEORGE PETER: *Social Structure* (New York, Macmillan, 1949).

SCHURTZ, HEINRICH: *Alterklassen und Männerbünde* (Berlin, Georg Reimer, 1902).

TIGER, LIONEL: *Men in Groups* (New York, Random House, 1969).

VAERTUNG, MATHIAS and MATILDE: *The Dominant Sex, A Study in the Sociology of Sex Differentiation* (London, George Allen & Unwin, 1932).

WESTERMARCK, EDWARD: *A Short History of Marriage* (New York, Macmillan, 1926).

WESTERMARCK, EDWARD: *The History of Human Marriage*, fifth edition, three volumes (London, Macmillan, 1922).

WESTERMARCK, EDWARD: *The Future of Marriage in Western Civilization* (London, Macmillan, 1936).

Works Consulted in Biological Sciences

BRECHER, RUTH and EDWARD: *An Analysis of Human Sexual Response* (New York, New American Library, 1966).

GLASS, DAVID C. (Editor), *Biology and Behavior* (New York, Rockefeller University and the Russell Sage Foundation, 1967).

KINSEY, ALFRED C.: *Sexual Behavior in the Human Male: In the Human Female* (Philadelphia, Saunders, 1949, 1953).

MASTERS, W. H., and JOHNSON, V. E.: *Human Sexual Response* (Boston, Little, Brown, 1966).

MONEY, JOHN, editor, *Sex Research, New Developments* (New York, Holt, 1965).

SHERFEY, MARY JANE: "The Evolution and Nature of Female Sexuality in Relation to Psychoanalytic Theory," *Journal of the American Psychoanalytic Association*, Volume 14, January 1966, No. 1 (New York, International Universities Press, 1966).

STOLLER, ROBERT J.: *Sex and Gender* (New York, Science House, 1968).

Works Consulted on the History and Status of Women

General Bibliographies

McGREGOR, O.: "The Social Position of Women in England 1850–1914; A Bibliography," *British Journal of Sociology,* March 1955.

BANKS, J. A. and OLIVE: "List of Relevant Books and Pamphlets to the Woman Question Published in Britain in the Period 1792–1880." An Appendix to *Feminism and Family Planning* (New York, Schocken, 1964).

CISLER, LUCINDA: *Women: a Bibliography.* New York: Lucinda Cisler, 1968, 1969, 1970. 6th edition (1970). $2.50 plus s.a.s.e. from Lucinda Cisler, 165 W. 91 St., N.Y., NY 10024.

There are helpful bibliographies in Sinclair, Klein, and Neff.

Books

ADAMS, MILDRED: *The Right to Be People* (New York, Lippincott, 1967).

BANKS, J. A. and OLIVE: *Feminism and Family Planning in Victorian England* (New York, Schocken, 1964).

BARDÈCHE, MAURICE: *Histoire des Femmes,* in two volumes (Paris, Stock, 1968).

BEBEL, AUGUST: *Woman and Socialism* (1885), translated from the German (New York, Socialist Literature Company, 1910).

BIRD, CAROLINE: *Born Female* (New York, McKay, 1968).

CHERNYSHEVSKY, N. G.: *What Is to Be Done?* (Russia, 1863).

DANGERFIELD, GEORGE: *The Strange Death of Liberal England, 1910–1914* (New York, Capricorn, 1935, 1961).

DE BEAUVOIR, SIMONE: *The Second Sex* (1949), translated from the French by H. M. Parshley (New York, Knopf, 1953).

DE RHAM, EDITH: *The Love Fraud* (New York, Clarkson Potter, 1965).

DITZION, SIDNEY: *Marriage, Morals and Sex in America—A History of Ideas* (New York, Bookman Associates, 1953).

ELLMANN, MARY: *Thinking About Women* (New York, Harcourt, Brace, 1968).

ENGELS, FRIEDRICH: *The Origins of the Family, Private Property and the State* (1884), translated from the German by Ernest Untermann (Chicago, Charles Kerr, 1902).

FARBER, SEYMOUR, and WILSON, ROGER H. L., editors: *The Potential of Woman* (New York, McGraw-Hill, 1963).

FAWCETT, MILLICENT GARRETT: *Woman's Suffrage* (London, The People's Books, 1912).

FLEXNER, ELEANOR: *Century of Struggle: The Woman's Rights Movement in the United States* (Cambridge, Massachusetts, Belknap Press, Harvard University, 1966).

FRIEDAN, BETTY: *The Feminine Mystique* (New York, Norton, 1963).

FULFORD, ROGER: *Votes for Women* (London, Faber and Faber, 1957).

FURNESS, C. F.: *The Genteel Female, An Anthology* (New York, Knopf, 1931).

GILMAN, CHARLOTTE PERKINS: *The Man-Made World: Our Androcentric Culture* (New York, Charlton, 1914).

GILMAN, CHARLOTTE: *Women and Economics* (New York, Charlton, 1898).

GRAHAM, ABBIE: *Ladies in Revolt* (New York, The Woman's Press, 1934).

GRIMES, ALAN P.: *The Puritan Ethic and Woman Suffrage* (New York, Oxford, 1967).

HERSCHBERGER, RUTH: *Adam's Rib* (New York, Pellegrini and Cudahy, 1948).

History of Women's Suffrage in six volumes, edited by Susan B. Anthony, Elizabeth Cady Stanton, Matilda Joclyn Gage, and Ida Husted Harper, Rochester, New York, 1881, 1886, 1902, 1922.

KANOWITZ, LEO: *Women and the Law, The Unfinished Revolution* (Albuquerque, University of New Mexico, 1969).

KLEIN, VIOLA: *The Feminine Character, History of an Ideology* (London, Kegan Paul, 1946).

KRADITOR, AILEEN: *The Ideas of the Woman Suffrage Movement* (New York, Columbia University, 1965).

KRADITOR, AILEEN: *Up from the Pedestal, Landmark Writings in the American Woman's Struggle for Equality* (Chicago, Quadrangle, 1968).

LIFTON, ROBERT JAY, editor: *The Woman in America* (Boston, Beacon, 1964).

MILL, JOHN STUART: *The Subjection of Women* (1869) (London, Oxford, 1966).

NEFF, WANDA FRAIKEN: *Victorian Working Women* (New York, Columbia University, 1929).

NEWCOMER, MABEL: *A Century of Higher Education for American Women* (New York, 1959).

O'NEILL, WILLIAM L.: *Everyone Was Brave. The Rise and Fall of Feminism in America* (Chicago, Quadrangle, 1969).

O'NEILL, WILLIAM L.: "Feminism as a Radical Ideology," in *Dissent: Explorations in The History of American Radicalism,* edited by Alfred E. Young, Northern Illinois University Press, 1968.

PANKHURST, EMMELINE: *My Own Story* (London, Everleigh Nash, 1914).

PANKHURST, SYLVIA: *The Suffragette Movement* (New York, Longmans Green, 1931).

PATAI, RAPHAEL, editor: *Women in the Modern World* (New York, Free Press, 1967).

ROGERS, KATHERINE M.: *The Troublesome Helpmate, A History of Misogyny in Literature* (Seattle, University of Washington, 1966).

RUBIN, THEODORE ISAAC: *In The Life* (New York, Macmillan, 1961).

RUSKIN, JOHN: *Sesame and Lilies,* "Of Queen's Gardens" (1865) (Chicago, Homewood, 1902).

SINCLAIR, ANDREW: *The Emancipation of the American Woman* (New York, Harper, 1965).

STRACHEY, RAY, editor: *Our Freedom and Its Results* (London, Hogarth, 1936).

STRACHEY, RAY: *The Cause: A Short History of the Woman's Movement In Great Britain* (London, G. Bell, 1928).

THOMAS, W. I.: *The Unadjusted Girl* (1923) (New York, Harper, 1967).

THOMPSON, WILLIAM: *Appeal of One Half of the Human Race, Women, Against the Pretensions of the Other Half, Men, to Retain them in Political and Thence in Civil and Domestic Slavery; in Reply to a Paragraph of Mr. (James) Mill's Celebrated "Article on Government"* (London, 1825).

WALSH, CORREA MOYLAN: *Feminism* (New York, Sturgis and Watton, 1917).

WHITE, LYNN: *Educating Our Daughters* (New York, Harper, 1950).

WOLLSTONECRAFT, MARY: *A Vindication of the Rights of Woman* (1791) (London, Dent, Everyman Edition).

WOOLF, VIRGINIA: *A Room of One's Own* (New York, Harcourt, Brace, 1929).

WOOLF, VIRGINIA: *Three Guineas* (New York, Harcourt, Brace, 1938).

Periodicals and Pamphlets

Handbook on Women Workers, United States Department of Labor, Women's Division and other of the many pamphlets published by the Women's Bureau on the condition of female labor in the United States.

Report of the President's Commission on the Status of Women—American Women, and other reports of the President's Commission, dealing with education, employment and so forth. U. S. Government Printing Office, Washington, D.C.

Sweden Today: The Status of Women in Sweden Report to the United Nations (Stockholm, The Swedish Institute, 1968).

"The Sexual Renaissance in America," special issue of the *Journal of Social Issues* XXII: 2 (April 1966).

"Sex and the Contemporary American Scene," special issue of the *Annals of the American Academy of Political and Social Science,* Volume 376, March 1968.

Works Consulted on the History and Status of Women with Special Reference to:

Nazi Germany

ABRAHAMSON, DAVID: *Men, Mind and Power* (New York, Columbia University, 1945).

BRADY, ROBERT A.: *The Spirit and Structure of German Fascism* (New York, Viking, 1937).

HITLER, ADOLF: *Mein Kampf,* translated from the German and edited by Chamberlain, et al. (New York, Reynal and Hitchcock, 1940).

HITLER, ADOLF: *My New Order, A Selection of the Speeches of Hitler,* edited by Raoul de Roussy de Sales (New York, Reynal and Hitchcock, 1941).

KIRKPATRICK, CLIFFORD: *Nazi Germany, Its Women and Family Life* (Indianapolis, Bobbs-Merrill, 1938).

LAQUER, WALTER: *Young Germany* (London, Routledge, Kegan Paul, 1962).

LOWRIE, ROBERT H.: *Toward Understanding Germany* (Chicago, University of Chicago, 1954).

REICH, WILHELM: *The Mass Psychology of Fascism,* translated by Theodore P. Wolfe (New York, Orgone Institute, 1946).

REICH, WILHELM: *The Sexual Revolution* (New York, Farrar, Straus, 1945).

SEYDEWITZ, MAX: *Civil Life in Wartime Germany* (New York, Viking, 1945).

THOMAS, CATHERINE: *Women in Nazi Germany* (London, Gollancz, 1943).

The Soviet Union

BROWN, DONALD R., editor: *Women in the Soviet Union* (New York, Teachers College, 1968).

FISCHER, LOUIS: *Soviet Journey* (New York, Harrison Smith and Robert Haas, 1935).

GEIGER, H. KENT: *The Family in Soviet Russia* (Cambridge, Massachusetts, Harvard, 1968).

HALLE, FANINA: *Women in Soviet Russia* (London, Routledge, 1933).

KINGSBURY, SUSAN M., and FAIRCHILD, MILDRED: *Factory, Family and Women in the Soviet Union* (New York, Putnam, 1935).

MACE, DAVID and VERA: *The Soviet Family* (New York, Doubleday, 1963).

MAKARENKO, A. S.: *The Collective Family* (1937), translated from the Russian by Robert Daglish (New York, Doubleday, 1967).

SCHLESINGER, RUDOLF: *The Family in the U.S.S.R.* (Documents and Readings) (London, Routledge, 1949).

TROTSKY, LEON: *The Revolution Betrayed*, translation by Max Eastman (New York, Doubleday, 1937).

Works Consulted in Psychology

ABRAHAM, KARL: "Manifestations of the Female Castration Complex," *International Journal of Psychoanalysis*, Vol. 3, March 1922.

BONAPARTE, MARIE: *Female Sexuality* (1953) (New York, Grove, 1965).

BROWN, NORMAN O.: *Life Against Death* (New York, Random House, 1959).

DEUTSCH, HELENE: *The Psychology of Women, A Psychoanalytic Interpretation* (New York, Grune and Stratton, 1945) Two Volumes.

ERIKSON, ERIK: *Childhood and Society* (New York, Norton, 1950).

ERIKSON, ERIK: "Identity and the Life Cycle, Selected Papers," published by *Psychological Issues*, Vol. I, No. 1, 1959 (New York, International Universities, 1959).

ERIKSON, ERIK: *Insight and Responsibility* (New York, Norton, 1964).

ERIKSON, ERIK: *Identity, Youth and Crisis* (New York, Norton, 1968).

FREUD, SIGMUND:

The Standard Edition of the Complete Psychological Works of Sigmund Freud in thirty volumes, edited by James Strachey (London, Hogarth Press and the Institute of Psychoanalysis, 1953).

Collected Papers, edited by Joan Riviere, in five volumes (New York, Basic Books, 1959).

Dora, An Analysis of a Case of Hysteria (1905, 1908, 1909) (New York, Collier, 1963).

Three Contributions to the Theory of Sex, translated from the German by A. A. Brill (New York, Dutton, 1962).

Totem and Taboo, translated from the German by James Strachey (New York, Norton, 1950).

Civilization and Its Discontents (1930), translated from the German by James Strachey (New York, Norton, 1961).

New Introductory Lectures on Psychoanalysis (1933) translated from the German by James Strachey (New York, Norton, 1964).

Letters of Sigmund Freud, edited by Ernst L. Freud (New York, Basic Books, 1960).

Letters, The Origins of Psychoanalysis, edited by Marie Bonaparte, Anna Freud, and Ernst Kris, translated from the German by Eric Mosbacher and James Strachey (New York, Basic Books, 1954).

Works Concerning Sigmund Freud:

JONES, ERNEST: *The Life and Work of Sigmund Freud* in two volumes (New York, Basic Books, 1953).

FROMM, ERICH: *Sigmund Freud's Mission* (New York, Grove, 1959).

LA PIERE, RICHARD: *The Freudian Ethic* (New York, 1959).

RIEFF, PHILIP: *Freud: The Mind of the Moralist* (New York, Doubleday, 1961).

KAGIN, JEROME: "The Acquisition and Significance of Sex-Typing," in *Review of Child Development Research,* edited by M. Hoffman (New York, Russell Sage, 1964).

KRICH, ARON, editor: *The Sexual Revolution, Pioneer Writing on Sex* in two volumes (New York, Dell, 1963, 1965).

LUNDBERG, FERDINAND, and FARNHAM, MARYNIA: *Modern Woman: The Lost Sex* (New York, Grosset and Dunlap, 1947).

MONEY, JOHN: *The Psychologic Study of Man* (Springfield, Illinois, Charles C. Thomas, 1957).

NEUMANN, ERICH: *The Origins and History of Consciousness* (New York, Harper, 1962).

REICH, WILHELM: *The Sexual Revolution, Toward a Self-Governing Character Structure,* translated from the German by Theodore P. Wolfe (New York, Farrar, Straus, 1945).

REIK, THEODOR: *Ritual: Psychoanalytic Studies; The Psychological Problems of Religion, No. I* (New York, Farrar, Straus, 1946).

REIK, THEODOR: *Of Love and Lust* (New York, Farrar, Straus, 1957).

REIK, THEODOR: *Myth and Guilt* (New York, George Braziller, 1957).

REIK, THEODOR: *The Creation of Woman* (New York, George Braziller, 1960).

REIK, THEODOR: *The Temptation* (New York, George Braziller, 1961).

ROBINSON, MARIE: *The Power of Sexual Surrender* (New York, Doubleday, 1959).

RÓHEIM, GÉZA: "Eden," *Psychoanalytic Review,* Vol. XXVII, New York, 1940.

RÓHEIM, GÉZA: "Psychoanalysis of Primitive Cultural Types," *International Journal of Psychoanalysis,* Vol. XVIII, London, 1932.

SAMPSON, RONALD V.: *The Psychology of Power* (New York, Random House, 1968).

SHERFEY, MARY JANE: "The Evolution and Nature of Female Sexuality in Relation to Psychoanalytic Theory," *Journal of the American Psychoanalytic Association,* Vol. 14, January 1966, No. 1 (New York, International Universities Press, 1966).

Works Consulted in Sociology

ADORNO, T. W.; FRENDEL-BRUNSWIK, ELSE; LEVINSON, DANIEL; and SANFORD, R. NEVITT: *The Authoritarian Personality* (New York, Norton, 1969).

BENDIX, TEINHARD, and LIPSET, SEYMOUR MARTIN: *Class, Status and Power: Social Stratification in Comparative Perspective* (New York, Free Press, 1966).

BERGER, PETER L., and LUCKMANN, THOMAS: *The Social Construction of Re-*

ality: A Treatise on the Sociology of Knowledge (New York, Doubleday, 1966).

BERNARD, JESSE: *The Sex Game* (Englewood Cliffs, New Jersey, Prentice-Hall, 1968).

CALVERTON, V. F., and SCHMALHAUSEN, S. D.: *Sex in Civilization* (New York, MacCauley, 1929).

DEUTSCH, KARL W.: *The Nerves of Government* (Glencoe, Illinois, Free Press, 1963).

HACKER, HELEN MAYER: "Women as a Minority Group," *Social Forces*, Vol. XXX, October 1951.

HERKHEIMER, MAX, editor: *Studien über Autoritat und Familie*, Forschungsberichte aus dem Institut für Sozialforschung (Paris, Librairie Felix Alcan, 1936).

HERNTON, CALVIN C.: *Sex and Racism in America* (New York, Grove, 1965).

HUGHES, EVERETT C.: "Social Change and Status Protest," *Pylon* (Vol. X, 1st Quarter, 1949).

KOMAROVSKY, MIRRA: "Functional Analysis of Sex Roles," *American Sociological Review* (Vol. XV, No. 4, August 1950).

MEAD, GEORGE H.: *Mind, Self and Society* (Chicago, University of Chicago, 1934).

MERTON, ROBERT K.: *Social Theory and Social Structure* (Glencoe, Illinois, Free Press, 1957).

MILLS, C. WRIGHT: *Power Politics and People: Collected Essays of C. Wright Mills* (London, Oxford, 1963).

MYRDAL, GUNNAR: *An American Dilemma* (New York, Harper, 1944, 1962).

PARSONS, TALCOTT: *Essays in Sociological Theory*, revised edition (New York, Free Press, 1954).

RAINWATER, LEE: *And the Poor Get Children: Sex, Contraception and Family Planning in the Working Class* (Chicago, Quadrangle, 1960).

SIMMEL, GEORG: *The Sociology of Georg Simmel*, translated from the German by Kurt Wolff (New York, Free Press, 1950).

SMELSER, NEIL J.: *Social Change in the Industrial Revolution* (Chicago, University of Chicago, 1959).

TAYLOR, GORDON RATTRAY: *Sex in History* (London, Thames and Hudson, 1953).

THOMAS, WILLIAM I.: *Sex and Society* (Boston, Richard G. Badger, 1907).

VEBLEN, THORSTEIN: *The Theory of the Leisure Class* (1899).

WATSON, GODWIN: *Social Psychology: Issues and Insights* (New York, Lippincott, 1966).

WEBER, MAX: *From Max Weber: Essays in Sociology*, translated from the German and edited by H. H. Garth and C. Wright Mills (New York, Oxford, 1964).

WEBER, MAX: *The Theory of Social and Economic Organization*, translated from the German and edited by H. M. Henderson and Talcott Parsons (New York, Free Press, 1964).

WEBER, MAX: *On Law in Economy and Society*, translated from the German and edited by Edward Shills and Max Rheinstein (New York, Simon and Schuster, 1967).

WIRTH, LOUIS, editor and LINTON, RALPH: *The Science of Man in the World Crisis* (New York, Appleton, 1945).

Core List of Works Consulted on the Sociology of the Family:

ARIES, PHILIPPE: *Centuries of Childhood, A Social History of Family Life,* translated from the French by Robert Balick (New York, Random House, 1962).

BELL, NORMAN W., and VOGEL, EZRA F.: *A Modern Introduction to the Family,* revised edition (New York, Free Press, 1968).

FOLSOM, JOSEPH K.: *The Family and Democratic Society* (New York, John Wiley, 1934, 1943).

GOODE, WILLIAM J.: *The Family* (Englewood Cliffs, New Jersey, Prentice-Hall, 1964).

PARSONS, TALCOTT, and BALES, ROBERT: *Family, Socialization and Interaction Process* (New York, Free Press, 1955).

SCHUR, EDWIN M., editor: *The Family and the Sexual Revolution* (Bloomington, University of Indiana, 1964).

WINCH, ROBERT F., McGINNIS, ROBERT, and BARRINGER, HERBERT R., editors: *Selected Studies in Marriage and the Family* (New York, Holt, 1962).

D. H. LAWRENCE

NOVELS:

The White Peacock (1911) (Carbondale, Southern Illinois University, 1966).
The Trespasser (1912) (London, Heineman, 1950).
Sons and Lovers (1913) (New York, Viking, 1966).
Sons and Lovers (1913) *A Critical Edition,* edited by Julian Moynahan (New York, Viking, 1968).
The Rainbow (1915) (New York, Viking, 1967).
Women in Love (1920) (New York, Viking, 1960).
The Lost Girl (1920) (New York, Viking, 1968).
Aaron's Rod (1922) (New York, Viking, 1961).
Kangaroo (1923) (New York, Viking, 1960).
The Plumed Serpent (1926) (New York, Random House, 1951).
Lady Chatterley's Lover (1928) (New York, Grove, 1957).

POETRY, SHORT STORIES AND SELECTIONS:

Selected Poems (1916) (New York, Viking, 1959).
Pansies (Poems) (1929) (London, Martin Secker, 1929).
St Mawr (1925) and *The Man Who Died* (1929) (New York, Random House, 1953).
Four Short Novels of D. H. Lawrence (1923) (New York, Viking, 1965).
The Complete Short Stories of D. H. Lawrence, in three volumes (New York, Viking, 1961).
The Woman Who Rode Away and Other Stories (New York, Berkeley Medallion Reprint, 1962).
The Late D. H. Lawrence, 1925–30, edited by William York Tindall (New York, Knopf, 1952).

The Portable D. H. Lawrence, edited by Diana Trilling (New York, Viking, 1946).

Phoenix, The Posthumous Papers of D. H. Lawrence, edited by Edward McDonald (London, William Heinemann, 1936).

Sex, Literature and Censorship, edited by Harry T. Moore (New York, Viking, 1959).

Selected Literary Criticism, edited by Anthony Beal (New York, Viking, 1966).

ESSAYS:

Twilight in Italy (1916).

Sea and Sardinia (1921) (reprinted together; New York, Doubleday, 1954).

Psychoanalysis and the Unconscious (1921).

Fantasia of the Unconscious (1922) (reprinted together; New York, Viking, 1960).

Studies in Classic American Literature (1923) (New York, Doubleday, 1953).

Reflections on the Death of a Porcupine (1925) (Bloomington, Indiana University, 1963).

Apocalypse (1931) (New York, Viking, 1966).

Etruscan Places (1932) (New York, Viking, 1957).

BIOGRAPHICAL MATERIAL:

Letters of D. H. Lawrence, edited by Aldous Huxley (New York, Viking, 1932).

Lawrence, Frieda, *The Memoirs and Correspondence,* edited by E. W. Tedlock, Jr. (New York, Knopf, 1964).

Chambers, Jesse: *D. H. Lawrence: A Personal Record* by "E.T." Revised Edition (New York, Barnes and Noble, 1965).

Moore, Harry T.: *The Intelligent Heart, The Story of D. H. Lawrence* (New York, Farrar, Straus, 1954).

WORKS OF LITERARY CRITICISM CONCERNING D. H. LAWRENCE:

Bentley, Eric: *A Century of Hero Worship* (Philadelphia, Lippincott, 1944).

Clark, L. D.: *Dark Night of the Body* (Austin, University of Texas, 1964).

Freeman, Mary: *D. H. Lawrence, A Basic Study of His Ideas* (New York, Grosset and Dunlap, 1955).

Gregory, Horace: *D. H. Lawrence, Pilgrim of the Apocalypse, A Critical Study* (New York, Viking, 1933).

Hoffman, Frederick J.: *Freudianism and the Literary Mind* (Louisiana State University, 1945).

Hough, Graham: *Dark Sun, A Study of D. H. Lawrence* (New York, Putnam, 1956).

Leavis, F. R.: *D. H. Lawrence, Novelist* (Knopf, 1956).

Spilka, Mark: *The Love Ethic of D. H. Lawrence* (Bloomington, Indiana University, 1955).

Spilka, Mark, Editor: *D. H. Lawrence, A Collection of Critical Essays* (Englewood Cliffs, New Jersey, Prentice-Hall, 1963).

HENRY MILLER

AUTOBIOGRAPHICAL NOVELS:

Tropic of Cancer (1934) (New York, Grove, 1961).
Black Spring (1936, 1938, 1939) (New York, Grove, 1963).
Tropic of Capricorn (1939) (New York, Grove, 1961).
The Rosy Crucifixion, Book One, Sexus (1949) (New York, Grove, 1965).
The Rosy Crucifixion, Book Two, Plexus (1953) (New York, Grove, 1965).
The Rosy Crucifixion, Book Three, Nexus (1960) (New York, Grove, 1965).

ESSAYS:

The Cosmological Eye (1939) (New York, New Directions, 1939).
The World of Sex (1940, 1959) (revised edition; New York, Grove, 1965).
The Wisdom of the Heart (1941) (New York, New Directions, 1941).
The Colossus of Maroussi (1941) (Harmondsworth, England, Penguin, 1950).
Sunday After the War (1944) (New York, New Directions, 1944).
The Air-conditioned Nightmare (1945) (New York, New Directions, 1945).
Remember to Remember (1947) (New York, New Directions, 1947).
The Books in My Life (1952) (New York, New Directions, 1952).
The Smile at the Foot of the Ladder (1955) (San Francisco, California, Greenwood Press, 1955).
The Time of the Assassins, A Study of Rimbaud (New York, New Directions, 1956).
A Devil in Paradise (1956) (New York, New American Library, 1956).
Big Sur and the Oranges of Hieronymus Bosch (1957) (New York, New Directions, 1957).
Stand Still Like a Hummingbird (1962) (New York, New Directions, 1962).

COLLECTIONS:

Henry Miller on Writing, edited by Thomas H. Moore (New York, New Directions, 1964).
The Intimate Henry Miller, edited by Lawrence Clark Powell (New York, New American Library, 1959).

LETTERS:

Letters to Anaïs Nin, edited by Gunther Stuhlmann (New York, Putnam, 1965).
Lawrence Durrell and Henry Miller, A Private Correspondence, edited by George Wickes (New York, Dutton, 1964).

WORKS OF LITERARY CRITICISM CONCERNING HENRY MILLER:

Baxter, Annette Kar: *Henry Miller, Expatriate* (Pittsburgh, University of Pittsburgh, 1961).
Hassan, Ihab: *The Literature of Silence: Henry Miller and Samuel Beckett* (New York, Knopf, 1967).

Orwell, George: *Collected Essays*, including "Inside the Whale" (London, Martin Secker, 1961).

Porter, Bern: *The Happy Rock, A Book About Henry Miller* (Berkeley, California, Packard Press, 1945).

Wickes, George: *Henry Miller* (pamphlet, University of Minnesota Pamphlets on American Writers) (Minneapolis, University of Minnesota, 1966).

Wickes, George: *Henry Miller and The Critics* (Carbondale, Southern Illinois, University Press, 1963).

Widmer, Kingsley: *Henry Miller* (New York, Twayne, 1963).

Wilson, Edmund: *The Shores of Light* (New York, 1952).

NORMAN MAILER

NOVELS:

The Naked and The Dead (New York, Rinehart, 1948).
Barbary Shore (New York, Rinehart, 1951).
The Deer Park (New York, Putnam, 1955).
An American Dream (New York, Dial, 1965).
Why Are We in Vietnam? (New York, Putnam, 1967).

SHORT STORIES, VERSE, AND OTHER:

Advertisements for Myself (New York, Putnam, 1959).
The Short Fiction of Norman Mailer (New York, Dell, 1967).
The Deer Park, A Play (New York, Dial, 1967).
Deaths for the Ladies and Other Disasters (New York, Putnam, 1962).

ESSAYS AND REPORTAGE:

The Presidential Papers (New York, Putnam, 1963).
Cannibals and Christians (New York, Dial, 1966).
Miami and the Siege of Chicago (New York, World, 1968).
The Armies of the Night (New York, New American Library, 1968).

JEAN GENET

PROSE FICTION:

Our Lady of The Flowers (*Notre-Dame des Fleurs*) (1943 limited edition, 1951, trade edition). Translated from the French by Bernard Frechtman (New York, Grove, 1963).

Querelle of Brest (*Querelle de Brest*) (1947), translated from the French by Roger Senhouse (New York, Grove, 1967).

The Thief's Journal (*Journal du Voleur*) (1949), translated from the French by Bernard Frechtman (New York, Grove, 1949).

Miracle of the Rose (*Miracle de la Rose*) (1951), translated from the French by Bernard Frechtman (New York, Grove, 1966).

Pompes Funèbres, Le Pecheur du Suquet, Querelle de Brest. Tome III Oeuvres Completes (Paris, Gallimard, 1953).

PLAYS:

Les Bonnes (*1948*) *et Comment Jouer les Bonnes* (revised edition, 1963) (Décines Isère, France, L'Arbalète, Marc Barbezat, 1963).
The Maids and Deathwatch, translated from the French by Bernard Frechtman (New York, Grove, 1954; revised edition, 1962).
Le Balcon (1956) (Décines Isère, L'Arbalète, Marc Barbezat, 1956).
The Balcony, translated from the French by Bernard Frechtman (New York, Grove, 1958, revised edition, 1966).
Les Nègres, Clownerie (1958) *Pour Jouer les Nègres* (Décines, Isère, L'Arbalète, Marc Barbezat, 1963).
The Blacks: A Clown Show, translated from the French by Bernard Frechtman (New York, Grove, 1960).
Les Paravents (Décines, Isère, L'Arbalète, Marc Barbezat, 1961).
The Screens, translated from the French by Bernard Frechtman (New York, Grove, 1962).

POETRY:

Chants Secrets (Limited Edition) (Lyons, Marc Barbezat, 1945).
Poèmes (Décines, Isère, L'Arbalète, Marc Barbezat, 1962).

ESSAYS:

L'Atelier d'Alberto Giacometti (including *Les Bonnes, L'Enfant Criminel, La Funambule*) (Décines, Isère, L'Arbalète, Marc Barbezat, 1958).
Lettres à Roger Blin (Paris, Gallimard, 1966).
Letters to Roger Blin, Reflections on the Theatre, translated from the French by Richard Seaver (New York, Grove, 1969).
"The Funambulists," translated from the French by Bernard Frechtman, *Evergreen Review*, No. 32, April–May 1964).

WORKS OF LITERARY CRITICISM CONCERNING OR RELEVANT TO JEAN GENET:

Artaud, Antonin: *The Theatre and Its Double*, translated from the French by Mary Caroline Richards (New York, Grove, 1958).
Coe, Richard N.: *The Vision of Jean Genet* (New York, Grove, 1968).
De Mott, Benjamin: "But He's a Homosexual . . ." *The New American Review*, No. 7, 1967 (New York, New American Library, 1967).
Dennison, George: "The Moral Effect of the Legend of Genet," *The New American Review*, No. 7, 1967 (New York, New American Library, 1967).
Driver, Tom: *Jean Genet* (Pamphlet, Columbia Essays on Modern Writers Series) (New York, Columbia University, 1966).
Esslin, Martin: *The Theatre of the Absurd* (New York, Doubleday, 1961).
Guicharnaud, Jacques: *Modern French Theatre From Giraudoux to Beckett* (New Haven, Yale University, 1961).
McMahon, Joseph H.: *The Imagination of Jean Genet* (New Haven, Yale University, 1963).
Sartre, Jean-Paul: *Saint Genet, Actor and Martyr*, translated from the French by Bernard Frechtman (New York, George Braziller, 1964).

Pronko, Leon Cabell: *Avant-Garde, The Experimental Theatre in France* (Berkeley, University of California, 1964).

Thody, Phillip: *Jean Genet, A Study of His Novels* (London, Hamish Hamilton, 1968).

MISCELLANEOUS

Burn, W. L.: *The Age of Equipoise* (New York, Norton, 1965).

De Rougemont, Denis: *Love in the Western World* translated from the French by Montgomery Belgion, Revised and Augmented Edition (New York, Pantheon, 1956).

Houghton, Walter: *The Victorian Frame of Mind* (New Haven, Yale University, 1957).

La Fourcade, George: *Swinburne* (London, Bell, 1923).

La Fourcade, George: *La Jeunesse de Swinburne* (Paris, Les Belles Lettres, 1928).

Legman, G.: *The Rationale of the Dirty Joke: An Analysis of Sexual Humor,* First Series (New York, Grove, 1968).

Marcus, Steven: *The Other Victorians: A Study of Sexuality and Pornography in Mid-Nineteenth-Century England* (New York, Basic Books, 1966).

Packe, Michael St. John: *The Life of John Stuart Mill* (New York, Macmillan, 1954).

Praz, Mario: *The Romantic Agony* (Oxford, 1933).

Ratchford, Fanny: *The Brontës' Web of Childhood* (New York, Columbia University, 1941).

Wilson, Edmund: "Swinburne of Caheaton and Eton," Introduction to the *Novels of A. C. Swinburne* (New York, Noonday; Farrar, Straus, 1963).

Wilson, Edmund: "Dickens: The Two Scrooges," in *The Wound and The Bow* (New York, Oxford, 1965, Corrected Edition).

Young, Wayland: *Eros Denied* (New York, Grove, 1964).

ACKNOWLEDGMENTS

SIGMUND FREUD

Excerpts from *Civilization and Its Discontents* by Sigmund Freud, 1930. Translated from the German and edited by James Strachey. Copyright © 1961 by James Strachey. Reprinted by permission of W. W. Norton & Co., Inc., publisher. Also found in a revised translation in the *Standard Edition of the Complete Psychological Works of Sigmund Freud*, Vol. 21, revised and edited by James Strachey; The Hogarth Press, Ltd., Sigmund Freud Copyrights, Ltd., and The Institute of Psycho-Analysis.

Excerpts from "Femininity" from *New Introductory Lectures on Psycho-Analysis* by Sigmund Freud. Copyright © 1933 by Sigmund Freud. Copyright renewed 1961 by W. J. H. Sprott, Copyright © 1964, 1965 by James Strachey. Translated from the German and edited by James Strachey. Reprinted by permission of W. W. Norton & Co., Inc. Also found in the *standard Edition of the Complete Works of Sigmund Freud*, Vol. 22, revised and edited by James Strachey. Reprinted by permission of The Hogarth Press, Ltd., Sigmund Freud Copyrights, Ltd., and The Institute of Psycho-Analysis.

Excerpt from "The Economic Problems of Masochism" by Sigmund Freud, 1924. Translated under the supervision of Joan Riviere for *The Collected Papers of Sigmund Freud*, Vol. II, edited by Ernest Jones, M.D., published by Basic Books, Inc. 1959. Reprinted by permission of Basic Books, Inc.

Also found in a revised translation in the *Standard Edition of the Complete Psychological Works of Sigmund Freud,* Vol. 19, revised and edited by James Strachey; The Hogarth Press, Ltd., Sigmund Freud Copyrights, Ltd., and The Institute of Psycho-Analysis.

Excerpts from "Some Character Types Met With in Psycho-Analysis Work" by Sigmund Freud, 1915. Translated under the supervision of Joan Riviere for *The Collected Papers of Sigmund Freud,* Vol. IV, edited by Ernest Jones, M.D., published by Basic Books, Inc., 1959. Reprinted by permission of Basic Books, Inc. Also found in a revised translation in the *Standard Edition of the Complete Psychological Works of Sigmund Freud,* Vol. 14, revised and edited by James Strachey; The Hogarth Press, Ltd., Sigmund Freud Copyrights, Ltd., and The Institute of Psycho-Analysis.

Excerpt from "The Taboo of Virginity" by Sigmund Freud, 1918. Translated under the supervision of Joan Riviere for *The Collected Papers of Sigmund Freud,* Vol. IV, edited by Ernest Jones, M.D., published in 1959 by Basic Books, Inc. Reprinted by permission of Basic Books, Inc. Also found in a revised translation in the *Standard Edition of the Complete Psychological Works of Sigmund Freud,* Vol. 11, revised and edited by James Strachey; The Hogarth Press, Ltd., Sigmund Freud Copyrights, Ltd., and The Institute of Psycho-Analysis.

Excerpt from "On Narcissism, An Introduction" by Sigmund Freud, 1914. Translated under the supervision of Joan Riviere for *The Collected Papers of Sigmund Freud,* Vol. IV, edited by Ernest Jones, M.D., published 1959 by Basic Books, Inc. Reprinted by permission of Basic Books, Inc. Also found in a revised translation in the *Standard Edition of the Complete Psychological Works of Sigmund Freud,* Vol. 14, revised and edited by James Strachey; The Hogarth Press, Ltd., Sigmund Freud Copyrights, Ltd., and the Institute of Psycho-Analysis.

Excerpts from "Some Psychological Consequences of the Anatomical Distinctions Between the Sexes" by Sigmund Freud. Edited by James Strachey for *The Collected Papers of Sigmund Freud,* Vol. V, edited by Ernest Jones, M.D., published 1959 by Basic Books, Inc. Reprinted by permission of Basic Books, Inc. Also found in a revised translation in the *Standard Edition of the Complete Psychological Works of Sigmund Freud,* Vol. 19, revised and edited by James Strachey; The Hogarth Press, Ltd., Sigmund Freud Copyrights, Ltd., and the Institute of Psycho-Analysis.

Excerpts from "The Psychology of Women" by Sigmund Freud, 1933. Translated by W. J. H. Sprott and edited by James Strachey for *The Collected Papers of Sigmund Freud,* Vol. V, edited by Ernest Jones, M.D., published by Basic Books, Inc., 1959. Reprinted by permission of Basic Books, Inc. Also found in a revised translation in the *Standard Edition of the Com-*

ORVILLE G. BRIM, JR.

JEAN-PAUL SARTRE

JEAN GENET

HENRY MILLER

Index

SITA

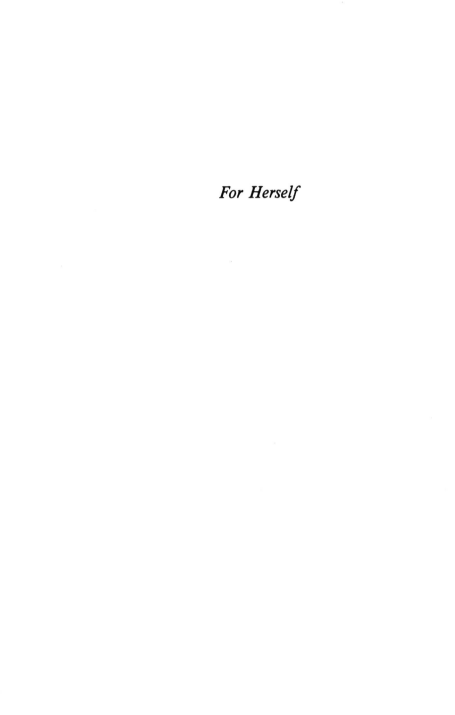

For Herself

Preface to the Illinois Paperback

Here is a new edition of *Sita,* together with the first of the prose elegies to Sita. Space and costs prevented us from printing the poems and drawings of the *Elegy* as well as the other three prose elegies, but we are able to bring part of "the end of the story," for *Sita* has a sequel beyond the book first published in 1977 by Farrar, Straus and Giroux. There was another book, the *Elegy for Sita,* published by William Targ in a limited edition of 350 signed and numbered copies, printed on lovely deckle-edged paper and bound in linen, an "inner circle" book published in 1979. Sita's death still recent, my own sense of loss, that of her children and of women throughout the country who had looked to her leadership. For the last twenty years I have longed for a popular edition of the *Elegy,* and if this portion of it pleases, I look forward to providing the whole of the matter.

For it did not end with the phone call that concluded the original *Sita.* I made a book of the notebooks and presented them to Sita herself, and we were reconciled. We would never live together, but we would continue as lovers in something more adventurous, "always an affair," a long, lifelong liaison that suited us better than cohabitation. This worked until her sudden and still inexplicable death, the mystery at the center of the *Elegy.*

As for the perils of cohabitation, rereading *Sita* itself at this distance, I undergo the "disease" of love with much the same chagrin as before, although tempered a bit with humor and the perspective that must come with time—and the mellowed satisfaction of knowing that we did, for a while, carry off our ambitions. Only to lose them before the great and real fact of death. And even then . . .

But here in *Sita* is all the fever of love, the obsession, the mania, the despair of a love affair on the slide. Grabbed after in panic, examined with the microscopic attention of the rejected, recovered only to become problematic again, ambivalent again. The tug of war between distant cities and across a continent and two incompatible ways of life, personality, and destiny. New York is a character in the book. So is California. So is the loft studio. And Sita's university post and her admirers.

The text moves with the speed of living, or the mind itself, consciousness hopping from observed detail, even domestic detail, to peripheral and then to central persons, and back to the arrangement of a room through the eye of the new arrival from an alien place returning to paradise only to find everything transformed for the worse and intent on remembering better days, the memory of past happiness a torment. We seem to have lived in a great hurry then, full of political hope and intensity and social experiment: everything was possible if one just kept the faith. And the end of love seems like catastrophe, counterrevolution. Watching love diminish is to be diminished, perhaps to disappear, a kind of dying of the self as well as the future. This is always so of course, is timeless, but the tissue of our theories and politics added dimension and energy.

The story of the end of love, the death of a love affair, studied and noted day after day, is the very stuff of the Western romantic tradition. The French insisted on calling Sita a "roman," not quite negating it as autobiography but recognizing it as a familiar form even if the protagonists were both women. In America it was given less permission: there was a great deal of disappointment that Sita did not give love between women a "better image." I was scolded for "masochism," for failing to enact success, for having presented such a poor advertisement for lesbianism.

My heart was with the French, *Sita* is my "European" book; I prayed to Proust every night I wrote it because I wanted his music, his understanding of nuance and discretion, that daring of his that would insist on the essential and often unwelcome truth even if he had to use disguises, his reliance on the melody of memory, the power of nostalgia to evoke and even persuade. And Violette le Duc, my only model all the way back through the dark to Sappho. There had been no language for this love, no examples.

That is why I am particularly pleased that this edition is more complete in lesbian matter, however early and primitively outlined, that it has not only celebration and complaint, ode and apostrophe, narrative and dialogue, erotic adventure, interior and social life, but even elegy and dirge, the entire round of an experience beginning to announce itself as a new phenomenon in letters as well as in life.

—Kate Millett
New York, 2000

Sita

I fall back on the bed. The nightmare change of it all. "You haven't seen the house since the gypsies took over," she'd said in Sausalito. All that, of course. Hit me in the first few minutes: the bits of fabric on the walls where Sherman's drawings had been, the bedspread draped over what was once the breakfast nook, now little Emily's bedroom, the rumpled rugs, the hodgepodge of bureaus and tables in hallways. Each like a slap against what had once been our house, the house the two of us had taken together, furnished, loved.

"But you've rented a loft in New York; you've been away for months. Remember we had Paul and Valerie move in for the summer when we went to Europe? Well, when you stopped off in New York and I came back here, I just let them stay on." My bedspread in her son Paul's room, the front room he shares with his girlfriend Valerie, my towels on everyone's rack in the bathroom. "Then Pia moved in. I was down with bronchitis and she took care of me. She and Dan had gone on the methadone program and they needed to be here." Of course it was good, good that she have her children with her, the commune she used to dream about. When she called me and said that Pia had moved in and I needn't worry about the rent for a few months, it seemed a good solution. She didn't mention Dan, she didn't mention Emily. It was all temporary, till the kids got on their feet. I love Sita's two grown children, but I don't want to live with them. "Listen, Kate, I will not throw them out," she shouted when she came to New York at Christmas. And she nearly didn't come. Days of evasions on the phone, lies at the office and at home, Pia telling me she was out, fibbing outrageously when I telephoned time after time. And then she did come. Sita in the great white light of the loft, Sita for Christmas. Four days of lovemaking and wine and quarrels over the house. But it was good, all the old power. If our thing had gone shaky, those four days brought it all together again. I would come back for sure, stay the winter as we'd planned, teach a course at the university. I would live half the year in each place. Since the loft was cheap, I could still have the excitement of New York and the stability of my life with her. Both. All. Everything. Even hold on to New York, my old town, my old life. All as we'd planned.

But there was so much I'd never guessed at, so many changes. She had made a new life without me, a life from which I was eliminated. I might have done that in New York, too. But I kept the old schedule, the old plans. Had returned to them now. Had come back to Berkeley and our house in the hills. To find it gone. Vanished into another existence, into a commune, a crowd. Well, adjust then, be flexible. Of course it was good she should have them with her, we have been over that a hundred times. When she came to New York at Christmas, it began to dawn on me that she had given our house over to her children, that I had been dispossessed. But I hadn't *seen* it yet.

Memories of the old life, the few things left, the bedspreads, in Paul's room and the one here in this room too, the drawings on the wall behind me, the three nudes I'd done of her that hang over my head. Evenings in a hotel room in Mexico City, her brown and lovely body, the quiet luxury of drawing her while we sipped tequila, while the traffic in the Zócalo grew still outside the windows. Mexico, the night before we left. I had just got well enough to come home. Knew the very shrimp that poisoned me, knew it as I put it in my mouth, could see it hadn't been cleaned, wonderful night we had dinner on the roof of the hotel, looking out over the cathedral and the square, the black line of poison sliding down my throat. Then the hell of it, even crapping on the rug, impossible to

4

get to the toilet, shitting and throwing up all at once. The intravenous feeding, the diplomatic English-speaking doctor, miraculous recovery. But that night it hit her, leaving me to run like a maniac to check us out, pay the bills, tip and bully porters into getting medicine at four in the morning, inventing Spanish. Cajoling the doctor's office by phone, struggling with the nurse who couldn't find her vein, haranguing her in gibberish and English while Sita, who is our Spanish, lies gray, eyes closed, her veins collapsing. And this ox jabbing her without pity. Until I bellow enough to bring another nurse, one with wiser hands. Wondering while I wait how I can get hold of a thousand dollars, pay for a hospital, my mind screaming at the thought of a funeral. Urging the next nurse with sheer force of will to find that vein, begin the intravenous feeding, save her. My Sita so nearly gone, the whole journey, which had started in such luxury, ending in a bad dream. Even the luxury of the first afternoon, making love in a cheap room that reminded both of us of all the existential wonder we had known in third-class hotels when we were students. Then moving to the grand place on the Zócalo, the sheer arrogance of it, our dinners on the roof, our sumptuous room, the whimsy of changing from one double bed to another, the long afternoons turning to evening while I drew her naked in the evening calm. That same body dying on the bed unless I can make this creature find a vein. Sita an ashen thing that can hardly cry out now when they stab her. But somehow I saved her life.

And last spring, living here together after we got the house, the two of us. How it hurts even to summon that time, how it stings the eyes. Now the place full of other people, their things, their paraphernalia. Sherman's big yellow painting should be on the wall before me, but it's gone. In its place a Mucha poster advertising Monte Carlo, probably something of Pia's. She stares at it too. "You won't believe me, maybe"—her voice hesitant, then definite —"but I like that better. Yes, a lot better. I guess I'm a gypsy too." She has taken sides, taken a stand. I lie back on the bed and close

5

my eyes. My things are foreign here now, unwanted. My paintings and drawings and photographs are taken down. The room, once our bedroom, simple and stark and lovely, the yellow canvas, the Greek bedspread, the white walls—now crowded with random furniture and posters and lamps. Funky—the kid's taste. And it's her thing too; it was all along.

Well, this is endurable somehow. Mustn't get hung up on aesthetics, objects, possessions. Why not share, have a commune? In New York it had sounded vaguely romantic, a relief from the loneliness of trying to write there, the terrible solitude I'd grown to hate and be afraid of after she'd been with me at Christmas. All these changes, well, really to be expected, so many people living here. But what murders me is the sight of another room just glimpsed while climbing the stairs. Crowded and unfamiliar now. Stuffed with others, stuffed. "Pia's room," that's what it's called now. That was where I worked. My "study," she'd called it. The room where I wrote, my big lovely table before the two windows and the bay. All of San Francisco and the Golden Gate at my disposal. The hills of Berkeley at a glance, and then the water, the city, and beyond it to the west the great orange bridge. I look again. Pia's big bed, table, bureaus, Dan's armchair. "It's a house full of love," she keeps saying. I lie back and close my eyes. "There's nowhere for me to work, my room's gone, nowhere to put a table." "Maybe you can rent a little studio some place. Pia has a friend who's just moving out of one."

"Just set up your table in a corner of the bedroom," she'd said in New York. As if it were a trivial problem about furniture. "I can't sleep and work cooped up in the same little room all day and night," I protested, looking up and down the magnificent space of the loft. Why should I leave this for California? Why indeed. And she'd never urged it. Was punctilious about that, keeps reminding me how she never insisted I come. But I came anyway. Unable to forget or be away from her after those four high days at Christmas, the loft suddenly turning sour after she left, lonely. Life in New

6

York, the new independence of it all, living alone after the wreck of a ten-year marriage, the man gone, even the studio where we lived torn down by the city. And starting out on my own again in the town, my own studio, but it had somehow lost its effervescence after she left. New York, my New York; all those mellow bohemian years grown cold as an empty plate. After Christmas, after the joy of her, the rest was solitude. And Christmas had been bed and champagne and fighting. Holding her that first afternoon, listening to *Bohème,* the album I'd given her as a present, routinely listened to—I did not realize it would affect me. We had heard it once together at the farm, but it only reminded me of Zoe and our early days on the Bowery. Sita had tried to translate it and to sing it for me, but I was angry and impossible and berated her for not being an artist, for not being Zoe. Regretting that time so as I listened then, both of us going back to that crazy little rehearsal we'd watched in the square at San Gimignano when we'd first come together over that music. Holding her that first afternoon in New York, sitting on the sofa in the winter dark, all the poignant grasp of her, listening, the two of us sitting on the sofa, and suddenly it is here, the great wrenching lyric speaking as direct as the knowledge of death, the flesh of her arm in my hand, the months, the years of loving her. And came to her now in January, knowing that I was helpless—couldn't get away.

Following that dream back to California. But already it was wrong. Even before we got to the house. The weekend. Coming down the ramp I saw her, coming to meet my plane. Sita standing patiently behind the barrier. The shock, as it is always a shock, to realize I am in love with a middle-aged woman. A plain, rather intimidating face, off-putting behind her hard shell-like glasses. Her armor. Only when she takes them off do you realize she is beautiful. It is only when you know her. And the manner too, the stance, an attitude that warns away the Anglo world, America, vulnerable as her touch of lameness, withdrawn, slightly arrogant. The foreigner's defensiveness, hauteur. It always takes a moment.

7

Then sliding again into her beauty, her spell. Her wit, her tenderness. The perfume of her exoticism.

We would have the weekend in Sausalito and then go back to the house in Berkeley. There would be some little transition before the new reality. But the weekend was a downer. Disparate, fragmented. Making love was not what it had been in New York, the great shuddering need to come together, weeping in her arms as after a terrible absence. There had been no great swell or volume. We had even been afraid to start. Both of us were. Rushed out and bought a bottle of champagne, postponing it. Her passion for champagne. As if that would begin things, make it possible, that talisman. She must have been just as conscious as I how the need did not transcend the shyness, the awkwardness, the uncertainty. Both of us seeing it: how we could wait, how we didn't have to have each other. I reminded myself there was time now, less pressure; this time it would be no mere four days. But I saw it like a crack in a bowl. We who had once been such lovers, so hot, so intemperate.

And the thing perfunctory almost when it happened. I had wanted to make love all afternoon; that had been my fantasy, one whole long slow afternoon, every variation and possibility explored, savored, every sensation lingered over. Yet the room seemed defenseless; noises in the hall and next door. And the room so small, without even a bathroom, one we'd never had before in all our visits; this old hotel our rendezvous how many times. Sausalito, the great nights of our love ago, the fire burning in the big room, our bodies spread out before it on a rug, nights once, or afternoons, long late mornings of being every experiment in the great mahogany bed. General Grant's own hand-carved bed in the plushest room of all. A room I remember, can conjure by. Every moment in it precious, irretrievable, the hurt of its very pastness as certain as burial. Even how she wept and shivered before the fire that one night, lovely in the naked brown skin of her body, crying because she had an interview in Los Angeles the next day and was

8

afraid of the job, afraid they'd hire her, afraid they wouldn't. Wanting Berkeley more, but the other paid better. And was she old? Would they sniff at her credentials? And could she go on standing on her own after a lifetime of marriages, and was it worth it, these jobs you killed yourself to get and then hated? And would they see all that right there at the interview and humiliate her? Her body shaking in my arms. Another Sita out of my thousand Sitas. I had never seen her scared, only the serene competence of the absolute campus politician, the administrator, the fighter for civil rights, the feminist, the subtle and magnificent bringer of change, my Machiavel. Her womanliness, her intelligence, her courage. Latin diplomacy, finesse, the loveliest manner, the charm of her age and her breeding saying the same things as the radical toughs, but saying them smoothly, reasonably, concisely; better yet, getting it done. For an hour this lost and terrified woman rocking naked before a fire. I comforted her, I listened, I reassured. The look and the feel of her in that room that night, a room just down at the end of the hall but a million years ago. I remember its bow windows, her wicker traveling case, the scent of her perfume in a scarf as she stood before the windows in the morning. It echoes in the mind like the feel of silk. Like the soft flesh of her name, Sita. Formally Innocenza, stately, nearly pompous; the humor and irony of it—*Innocenza di che*? In Italy and in Brazil, where she grew up, other children playfully softened the name, reshaped it to Sensita and then, to make it handy, cut it down to Sita, the most private of names, the dearest and most secret. Pronouncing it is like a kiss, the sound in the mouth like the lips grazing over soft flesh.

Now this disappointing little room. The hurry of it, the confinement. There was a dismaying absence of romance this weekend. Like the fear you have of sex sometimes, looking forward to it but afraid you will not be able, not be open, not reach orgasm. Lying in bed watching her prepare to dress on Sunday morning, realizing she is already wanting to dress, to leave. While I had been waiting for her to finish her coffee, come back to bed, begin some delicious

9

or leisurely exploration of one kind or another in the two fine hours before noon and check-out time. She stands before the mirror brushing her hair. The silver of the mirror, its strange empty light. The mercury gray of her hair. The feeling she gives off is impatience, irritation. Yet how beautiful she is, poised before the watery space of the mirror—the dark skin of her face, her lovely hair, the brush. A loveliness at odds with her exasperated, "Why did you wait till now to suggest it? I've long since lost interest. I'm ready to go." Seeing her pack, the neat efficient little gestures, a sinking feeling. It's all over. Suddenly all over. Almost as if it were already Monday. The weekend collapses into the prosaic sidewalks and concrete of a weekday. A workday.

It was wrong even when we went to visit Sherman. A visit lifeless, almost ceremonial. After visits made so many times, visits hilarious or tragic or inebriated. But this one almost silent, formal. Sherman, this old painter recluse, my friend for twenty years, strange dyke saint of art, in a new studio, cramped, broke, her canvases spread in new rooms now, smaller, shrunken. Yet somehow the old flair there still, her gift for turning any ordinary room into a work of art, a place of rest. But even then something was off somehow, anticlimactic. Though Sherman is my friend, it was Sita who talked to her. I said nothing. Had nothing to say, astonished to discover I had nothing to say, feeling estranged, distracted, removed from myself and the two of them. Sherman's face turned toward Sita. I am observing their friendship, moved by the sight of it, feeling an affection for it. Yet the displacement remains; it is as if I am not there, have evaporated, vanished. Listening to Sita's news: "Danny's leaving. He's moving out of the house. Such a relief. Now maybe Pia can get it together and do her own thing, she'll be free of his influence. Dan holds her back." Sherman nods. Behind it is Pia's long addiction to heroin, discovered again after five years when we thought she was clean, the five years since she had kicked the first time, alone with Sita in the old house in Sacramento. And then last year it turned out she had been using

all along. Came to light only when she began the methadone program with Dan. The two of them would be cured together. Then
maybe they could do something in music, in life. They are through
it now and have come out whole and triumphant. But Dan just
drives his truck. He will never go back to his drums. Years and
years in a basement, he'd told me, living only at night. No life at
all, he said. So he drives a truck in the produce market. "I want
to devote myself entirely to my family now," he says solemnly.

I search for something to say, anything, anything, any sign I am
alive, feel, exist. Nothing comes. I had looked forward to this, yet
I feel nothing but emptiness, unease. They go on talking. What am
I doing here? It is all a rerun of the past, California last time, the
time before. But with all the sensation gone. Weekends in Sausalito
with a stop at Sherman's on the way home—how magical they used
to be, how euphoric those early weekends, how every moment with
Sita glistened, whatever we did: driving or shopping or lunching.
Long wineglasses and fruit and the lights of the bay through mellow dinners at the Trident. At dinner there last night there was not
enough conversation to fill the hour. Our silence embarrassed me,
made us conspicuous. And now at Sherman's, watching the two of
them gossip. Sita has plenty to say, and I look on and relish her
vitality. But it is not for me. With me she is silent. Sherman's
weathered face and denims, such a contrast to Sita's beringed
fingers, her supple and elegant leather boots, her gloves and her
bag. Sita goes on about her job, how her provost is an ass, a
pompous fool, how they pay her one salary to do two jobs, how
they thwart her at every turn, how overworked she is, how there
is not one weekend free till April. I watch the two of them, everything closing in, becoming trivial. Are we old?

Finally Sherman questions me perfunctorily about New York.
Fumio. How is he? The muscles of my stomach tighten and then
turn liquid. How long will people go on torturing me with this
question? How long will I go on with my pat answers—that he is
busy working for his next show, that we see each other often, that

we are great friends, that he sends his regards. "How about your place?" Another nerve. The house I lived in fifteen years, grew up in, the dear old Bowery house where I lived with Fumio ten of those years, crazy wonderful 1806 Dutch masterpiece of zigzags and leaking roofs, condemned now and torn down by the city. Everything ends at once. Fumio, the house. Our eviction the signal for his escape. "So what are you going to do?" "I got another loft. My friend Ruth badgered the city until they came through with relocation." "You're lucky." "Yeah. Yeah."

"How long will you be out here?" Awkwardness. "Maybe two weeks, maybe the semester. I might be teaching a writing course for Sita's program." "You don't know yet?" A pause, Sita laughs to cover this and looks away. "Well, we'll kind of see how it goes." I still have no idea. Two weeks or four months—there's a difference. And I simply didn't know when I left, Ruth promising to forward the mail, water the plants. It would depend on how things went, it would depend in fact on the commune. And Sita. Everything depends.

They go on talking together. I go on being apart. What am I doing out here? What a fool I must look, not even knowing my own plans. A beautiful studio in New York and I'm hungering around out here where I have a table in the corner of a bedroom in a menagerie of hippies and children. I dread seeing the house again, I dread the weekend being over, cheerless thing that it was. I dread the visit with Sherman coming to an end, terrified of my own silence, my vacuity. Surely they must notice it. Sita, who decides everything, decides we must leave. A spiritless ride back to Berkeley, the sight of San Francisco, the great bridge, the bay—all curiously without effect. The Queen City, I always called it in my mind, used to worship the sight of it coming into view as you cross the bay; now only distant, unlovely, pointless. Even beloved landmarks like the Hills Brothers Coffee sign, an old friend now regarded with indifference. A mistake, the whole thing a mistake. Shouldn't have come.

I fall back on the bed. Thank God, they're not all here, the bunch of them looking on at my dismay. It will be just between the two of us. Or just within myself. I knew what I was getting into, or should have. This many people in the place, of course it has to change. She stirs beside me. "Shall I drive you to the airport?" I look at her, a long terrified look, realizing that if I were to say yes, she would simply do it. Calmly and easily do it. She will not budge an inch. Now even more than at Christmas, when she shouted she would not kick them out. "Who says kick them out?" I had argued. "Surely they know I'm coming back, they're there just temporarily, you say Paul's moving over to Marin soon anyway. Wouldn't this be a good time for them to find their own place?" It had seemed so reasonable then. They were taking my place in the house, sub-stituting, but now I was home. They were taking advantage of my absence, but now I would be coming back. The rent was my obliga-tion and I paid my half through the summer and part of the fall until Sita told me, *fait accompli,* that Pia had moved in. Paul and Valerie pay no rent, never have. But Pia and Dan would pay my half for a few months and this would solve the problem through the fall. And now I was back, only to discover it was no longer my house at all but theirs, hers, and in some mysterious way, her brood's. Sita melting into them as she did, the group of them merged and standing away and at odds with me, the outsider, the stranger. They are her family, I am merely her lover. A family, and I the interloper. It has taken me so long to understand.

When Hatsie came back from California in November, she'd warned me about this, but I was in no mood to listen. "Sita's really into this motherhood thing now. She says she hasn't had all her children together with her for years." "But they're grown up, they're not even children any more." Pia's twenty-six, Paul's finished high school now and has lived away from home for years. "Don't ask me, but she says being together with her whole family this Christmas will be the most beautiful thing in the world. "No, she's coming *here* for Christmas, to New York." "Oh, really?"

And then of course she almost didn't come. Crisis with her job, she said. Canceled and then let me persuade her to make the trip for just four days. The four days that brought me back. Because when she canceled her trip at Christmas I was ready to give up. There had been the months apart, the telephone tricks, the terrible memory of the summer in Italy, the great five-thousand-dollar catastrophe I had treated her to. "Two glorious months in Italy and Ireland," but we never got to Ireland, spent the summer in her brother Paolo's villa under family guard and in separate beds, a summer when she was with me not at all, hardly bothered to speak to me, a summer during which she openly despised me. Then the parting in September, she to California, I to build my loft in New York.

But the four days at Christmas when it all came back, came together again, all the months and years, the two, nearly three years of this impossibly lovely and exasperating affair reasserting itself, the old passion, the old sweep of it. And I'm here again, here in the house where we set up housekeeping together last spring, my marriage over, a breakdown and the suicide months that followed. Over, everything of the past over. New York behind me—or almost, and I came to the house here where we began our pseudomarriage last spring, the two of us. Until I got another loft in New York. And then it was to be half and half, here and there six months each year. Back again now to find the house as I knew it gone. And the life we had there utterly erased. Throw in the towel and give up entirely? Go home to New York and the bare empty loft, tough it out? Wanting her, even as we lie here, even in this anger and despair, wanting her.

The sound of the front door. An odd sound. Never before while we lived here did anyone ever turn a key in that door while we listened. But now there are so many, so many keys, so many footsteps on the stairs. And now Pia's voice—"Hi, you guys." Pia on the stairs. And Dan. I am as surprised to see him as Sita is. But it is Dan who hugs me hello in the hall, Dan who is warm and friendly. The other loner, interloper, outsider. Pia is her usual breezy delight. But not after a moment or so. Sita is cold to her, annoyed that Dan is still with her, still in the house. Suddenly Pia is furious and shouting, "Mom, where *are* you, I look at you and I don't see you, where'd you go, what's with you?"

We follow them down to the kitchen where Pia has started cooking chicken. We had planned to go out for dinner; a little more privacy, more time of our own. Pia is obviously cooking for us too, demanding we stay. I am not committed to this chicken and don't want to be, but there is no time to confer. Pia before the stove, brutally angry. "Dan's my old man, and he's staying if he wants to stay. He's my man and he can be here if he feels like it. He's my person, he's my friend, he's my lover. I can have him here." I lean against the cupboard, embarrassed. Envious. How I wish Sita would say this of me, stick up for me. Because I am under attack too. "You said this was our house, Mom. Didn't you, didn't you promise us that? Didn't you say it was *ours?*" And I am not one of ours. Odd that if Pia is entitled to her husband in my house, my own standing should be so precarious. Or rather, putting it the new way, if Pia is entitled to a husband in her mother's house (since everyone sees it as Sita's house now), why should I as her mother's lover find it so hard to justify my existence while leaning against a counter? Noncombatively. Because I answer Pia's assault with silence, terrified of her shouts. It will all be over in ten minutes. The children will drive me out. Paul and Valerie have arrived by now, Paul not even shaking my hand. How I used to love these kids, their chatter and pot, their parties and music and good times, but especially their music. Now they are strangers. Paul, who used to hug me against the bare chest of his gawky, six foot four, affectionate late adolescence. And now nothing. His Valerie beautiful and distant. But then I hardly know her, met her only once. They go off to their room together in the casual alienated way life seems to take here. Dan has also disappeared. I remain in the kitchen with Pia. With Sita, who is also silent. Waiting out the yelling. The

15

chicken goes on sizzling through Pia's recriminations. "This was *our* house." I listen, fighting my tears and humiliation. "And by God, it's *staying* that way." If only I had her fight, if only I could fight for my place. Is this some pecking-order savage society? If only Sita would speak out for me, settle it, say anything at all. Pia's voice is terrible. The commune is hell, a jungle. And it could have been fun. I never meant to quarrel with these people. We used to be friends till we had to live together. Pia wheels around from her chicken and toward me. "What's the matter with you?" "I have no place to work." "Tough shit." "Do you know what it means to me? Do you have any idea?" "Too fucking bad. Look, Mom—you promised, you fucking promised. And we're staying. This is *our* place." "No one questions that, Pia." "We belong here, see?" "Sure." "And Dan can be here till it suits him. Yes, he's going. We are splitting up. But it's going to take him some time to get his stuff together, to get himself together, and he can have just as long as he wants. See?" Sita never answers, but her very silence is a humbling acquiescence. The chicken sputters contentedly, its aroma a mocking invitation to dinner, celebration, conviviality.

Pia slams together the contents of a salad, Valerie assists. They refuse my help, Valerie's movements stiff and angry. I watch them, two very beautiful young women. Pia's fragility, Valerie's blond virago type. I am outclassed. They are younger, prettier, tougher. I hear Sita in conference with the two men. Then the sound of my table being carried up from the garage and installed in our bedroom. The chicken purrs on: we are stuck with it, the joyless family dinner. My fantasies of communal delight wither at the crowded table. The awkwardness of people feeding an unwelcome guest, the silences and broken jokes. Only little Emily is glad to see me. At eight she can ignore the opinions of the others. My old friend of dress-up games, my solemn fellow artist who shows me each new drawing. Pia's Emily, this strange grown-up child who has survived her mother's odyssey into drugs, hip, the music world, the white high of heroin. Sita's treasure, this granddaughter, the only one to remind her of Italy. Pia and Paul are fair and repeat their American fathers. But Emily has the darkness in her eyes.

"Whatsa matter with all you guys?" Emily's face examines us one by one. No one answers her. Dinner marches on. I do not even look at Sita any more; appeal is futile, the numbers between us cancel our relationship. You are on your own here. The others are couples, but we are not a couple. Sita is the matriarch, it is her house, she is the center, the authority, the power. Pia and Dan, Valerie and Paul, the pairs, each guarding the other, backing them up in the fierce battle for space and prerogative. Emily and I the extras, but Emily has the privilege of childhood, is owned by and appended to Pia. I have none of these claims of mate or kin. As the bizarre meal progresses like a mechanical farce, a movie parody —the communal act, tedious, empty, hostile, surreal—an amazement comes over me, trying to remember that I used to live here. As if it were a lie.

She is already asleep, and I next to her, smoking one last cigarette—the first day is over. Survived it. Go on surviving? This is not life. This is masochism. Get out of here. The suitcases still unpacked, shapes in the dark of the room. Leave? Leave her? Call it quits, the whole thing? Behind me in the dark those drawings, and beyond the room where I used to work, and Paul's room, which used to be our library, so rich we were in space; the dining room downstairs, scene of our candlelit steaks and artichokes, the yard where we would read or lie in the sun, the garden and the gardener, only a matter of bills to pay now. The life that was. And isn't any more. Your own fault for leaving, for wanting New York too, for needing a loft and a sculpture studio, for the extravagance of that independence, for feeling confined by last spring's "marriage." Last spring, when the place was your hospital after you lost the studio in New York, after you lost Fumio, after you lost your mind for the last and final time, the suicide trip. And then, well and recovered a bit, first thing you do is get another place in New York,

17

set up shop, and do a couple hundred drawings and try to write . . . And nothing comes, and the manuscript you drag around with you now will never be finished. Bits in notebooks, pages here and there out of the chaos of a life wrecked: your madness, your separation, your attempts to die. How would you ever put that together? Nerve endings, blood, hunks of flesh. Tomorrow you have to pull the pages, file, put in order, begin to type. The room spins at the hopelessness of it.

Write? Here? Are you crazy? The table in the corner, huge, obstructing the room. Write in a goddamn bedroom? 'Cause that's all they've left you—when you have that great big loft in New York? Or pack? Give up one more time, one more person, love, hope, chance—run one more time? Leave here and there is nothing left. Nothing but the loft. Empty, still unfinished. Loneliness. Distilled loneliness. The solitude of years. Being an old woman eating alone. No one to call. Friends too busy. You need an appointment a week ahead, can't just call up and say, Let's eat together. If it were not for the eating. Sleeping alone is almost easy. But the nights after she left. Wanting her every night. Holding back, trying not to, despising it; masturbation, second-rate, still somewhere ashamed, ashamed that it is such a substitute, saying her name, almost weeping it, saying her name, talking to her, the sweet obscenities, touch me fuck me take me from behind yes baby yes cries weeping to remember the taste of her cunt in my mouth as I came, all illusion more bitter afterward than the fact.

Lying next to her now, bitter too. Bitter even the touch of her hand on that part of me which waits for her in such heat and need. Always that I want her. And she does not always want me. That, just that, that inequality; the lever, that fulcrum of power and loss and defeat even before battle; conquest operable in any area of life from money to ideas. That dependency, that humiliation of need and desire. Because it has occurred to her, perhaps in compensation, compassion, pity, who knows the mind of the ruler—it has occurred to her to take me now. Here in this bed surrounded by others, here where one cannot make a noise. I had been afraid we would never make love, since the presence of her children had always made it impossible before—after a visit to them in San Rafael, she was always frigid when we returned to be alone in our hotel or at the house.

But it is her making love to me. She will not have me, I may not touch her. Even this, even this I take, accept, taking all I can get, beggarly, without pride, taking the heat of her hand on me, in me, taking the slim affection it betrays, the sense, if nothing else, of power. Of remembrance. Remembering, always remembering the power of her fingers inside my body, their absolute strength. I had never been fucked. I realized it the first time with her. I had never been fucked by a woman, hard, thorough, entire as by a man. Never by a woman, never before. And I discovered it the first time, coming upon the knowledge like a hallway mysteriously entered, taking me to where I imagined I could not bear the pain and then beyond to where there was no pain at all. But always the breathless force of her blows, how they caught in my throat like an elevator falling, the near terror of this new place, this new force. And to realize afterward in her gentleness that it was passion, that she could fuck that hard, be that ferocious, because of tenderness.

Sacramento—in her bedroom there with the great tree painted over the ceiling and along the windows of the morning. I had come to teach out there; she was the "welcoming committee." We will never stop being amused at having stumbled into love in this banal way, fulfilling our friends' cynical expectations, astonishing ourselves. When I saw her in the airport I saw a homely woman in a raincoat and glasses, a being not very interesting, a little scary, "Third World," taller, politically tougher. And as for the "Third World" business—more like a Puerto Rican who's made it, I grinned to myself: establishment, administration rather than faculty, an official person, a bureaucrat to my bohemian and artist. And then her tacky little house full of madras bedspreads across the windows, like a hippie pad. Over a good steak I discovered her sense of humor and began to call her Chiquita Banana to tease her about her recent flight from expensive suburbia and the way she'd embraced this funky place.

Over dinner she told me her tribulations in the land of the Anglos: demeaning jobs, and how the D.A.R. had handed out soap to the immigrants at her naturalization ceremony and she was given a paper to sign that demanded foreigners give up their foreign titles. I looked at her over my wineglass, high; growing to like her, challenging the whole thing, an outrageous joke. "And did you tell them you were the Pope?" "In Italy I am a countess. With that and fifteen cents you can buy yourself a cup of coffee." Chiquita Banana indeed, I thought, astounded, a little ashamed; suddenly I wanted to apologize for America, for the snobbery of every lesser soul (the D.A.R. ladies stopped handing out soap and began to curtsy), for all her poverty and humiliations, raising two children alone in a stony country. Because I am growing fascinated with this woman, her courage and her sufferings, her wit and now her beauty. Which is coming to life as a paper flower opens in water. She does not wear it in the street. There it's the trenchcoat and the opaque steel glasses.

The first night I wanted her. And could not understand why. And feared it. Was I merely adventuring? Consider her age, she is older than you. Is it honest to seduce her (assuming you could, she has two children and is probably straight, though she mentioned an affair with another woman)—but still, seduce her and then just trip off to your professorship and your new apartment and meet the other prospects here and that be the end of it? No. Lighting cigarette after cigarette. Wishing that she would turn on the light in the living room, invite me to have another joint, any excuse to make contact, at least see her. But I do see her, from my room at the end of the hall I see her going back and forth to the bathroom. Naked. Her habit to go around the house nude, she had said. Disturbing habit.

And the next day I met the others and they made no impression on me at all. I only wanted her. I knew it now, had tested it, waited, decided. Wanted her seriously and not merely to trifle. Loving her, sliding deeper and deeper into loving her, the improbable choice, her age, her looks new to me and at first unattractive, her life, her history so different, a life of marriages, wifehood, being rich, being broke too, but utterly unlike my life, my friends' lives, the art world downtown. And when the others had left, we sat on the couch and smoked a joint and talked the movement and understood each other in a mere sentence on this or that personality or issue. I mentioned rape, and she told me, in mere phrases, of being raped, how she had run out of gas one night in the desert. A car stopped and six men got out. "And all I could think of was how happy I was to see them." The help that turned into nightmare and mutilation. How they had had to sew her up, the clitoris nearly torn clean off and replaced imperfectly. I remembered this at odd times all through the next day, mixed in surreal apposition to the sheer delight I felt in my nipples that she had touched them, that they were like new flowers, changed, changed utterly for the rest of my life. Then my anger would return, this new and overwhelming rage that anyone could have harmed her, a livid desire to kill them. A pacifist and I wanted to kill. Avenge this. I had never heard anything before that had made me hate men. This fury coming back like an electric shock at stoplights, and then the memory, the equally improbable memory of her hands on my body. I had loved her for her suffering. And now for her passion. The whole day drunk on these bits of recollection, lost at stop signs, how her fingers felt inside me fucking me, fucking me into a whole new apprehension of fucking—exploring Sacramento, giggling as I noticed a sign in a seedy part of this little town proclaiming FIFTH AVENUE, getting lost, finding my way to my new apartment, to campus, buying furniture, remembering this new miracle. At first I thought I could not endure it, completely unused to that force, imagined it was pain, would leave me ragged and torn. I did not understand that a woman could even be that strong. That fierce, that passionate. But she was, and her long, slender, her most beautiful hands. After that I was hooked. After that there was no going back. There is none now.

Remembering now as she enters me, remembering everything, two years of the thing between us, a thousand occasions. Remembering, in her hasty and perhaps even indifferent touch, other times, times like hallucination, times when all time stopped as she held me, her fingers at the core and the center of consciousness, places within me I knew not, bends, wrinkles, plateaus, mountains and hillsides, and sunrises, caves and secret recesses, time hanging still above us as I asked her to be perfectly still within me, not to move at all while the silence held like a species of meditation. And all so that when she moved, were it the slightest tremor, it would be felt the more, a tremor would be like an earthquake. And then the whirlwind of her sudden and strongest gesture, her hardest fucking. Dizzy and hardly able to bear it, seized, forced to cry out, to gasp, to wonder if I would faint or die with pleasure. The lovely terror of it.

How she knows me, rules me, masters me, plays me, pleasures me. How I am always there for her; ready, open, writhing with desire. Knowing all this and against her new indifference, hating it, hating her power, the lever of control, the abuses of domination I am subject to. All love becomes vulnerability, the doorway to cruelty, the stairway to contempt. The very passion and adoration is now our undoing, the means of our evil, I in despising myself for loving, she in despising the one she had loved. Love turning back on itself, becoming its opposite.

All that had made us lovers now unmakes us. We are the end of the cycle, the bottom of the lie. The process draws to its conclusion as her hand finds me in the despairing dark. Still the fire, still the desire building. To stay or to go? The suitcases' shadows in the corner of the bedroom like crouching dogs. And her hand finding me, stroking a thigh, like the heat of music or death on the matted hair at the pubis, the soft flesh beyond calling her. Liquid like sparks or snow, the touch of her fingertips on the wet smooth flesh. Wet to receive her. And then a blow a storm a convulsion, she enters me. Hard and at once, fierceness and power like some creature beyond the mere human who trembles to receive her. Energy and indifference of the divine. Churned over and over in the force of her thrusts to fall spent on the shore of bliss, saying in the last place of the mind, I will stay. I will stay. I will stay. I will endure it, outlast everything that stands between us, not only will I stay, I would never leave you. And in the lonely moment before sleep, now without any certainty whatsoever, whispering to myself in secret: Not only will I stay, I'll beat this.

I watch her dress. She is at home in her body. Her perfect and lovely body. Marvelous that a woman nearly fifty should possess such a body. The luscious curve of her breast, the great brown Indio nipples, the place where she is neither Italian nor aristocrat but Brazilian aborigine. Nothing about her is so poignant, so moving, so "of herself" and individual as those nipples. Wonderful brown aureoles, I would know them beyond death. The line of her flanks as she moves, tracing it with my morning eyes. The ripples of her spine as she bends over to pull on her stockings. The flesh supple, delectable; I lust for it, watching.

"Lady," we always call each other, partly a joke, partly in earnest, using still the old word, in its full flavor a kind of exorcism against "saleslady," "old lady," "ladylike." Relishing the anachronism, even the formality a type of aphrodisiac, a contrast to our delight in the horny, the vulgar, the vernacular which we cultivate just as ardently. Lady, because the distant courtliness of the term, her idea after all, has a necessary charm, is maybe the last memory of her beginnings. She fastens her belt and pulls on a sweater. Gestures definite, complete. The mother of a son and daughter, the

23

grandmother of a granddaughter. That most of all I loved. How can I resist a grandmother? I used to laugh to myself, falling in love against all expectation.

Let me celebrate this, this perfection in age, this ripeness and fullness. The fig-like fall of her breast, the mellow coffee of the flesh on her long legs and slender buttocks, the easy slimness of her waist. Even her little hint of lameness, an injury from a fall years ago that occasionally gives her movements a childlike vulnerability, and which, like her accent, makes a special appeal to my tenderness and to the world's kindness and forbearance, now even this seems absent as she moves about. It is seven in the morning, she is dressing for work, moving quietly, smoothly, intending not to wake me. Knowing what she does, who she is, how she will spend her day. I remember my manuscript and wish I hadn't. It yawns in wait for me like the mouth of suicide. Today I was supposed to put it in order, begin. She zips up her beautiful leather boots. Fitted and glovelike and perfect. How I envy her everything.

At home in her body, its supple strength, the spring of her step. Once I was youth and thought she fed upon me as I fed upon her, love making me still younger, forever young. Far otherwise now. Watching her, I am old. Yet I am younger, Sita is nearly ten years older than I. But this ten years I am her junior is nothing, only my own emptiness. She is a being made for living, I am not. She goes to rule, administer, put in order. I stay only to fight confusion and lose. It is easier, being her. Not only easier than being an artist, it is being art, which is better. Beyond that, she lives in the real world, with adult cares, mature responsibilities; things I partly despise and partly revere. There, she is at home, capable, majestic. Even in a job she frequently loathes, where she is consistently underpaid and overworked and threatened with layoff. A job that begins at the ungodly hour of eight in the morning. And yet she is ready, eager, I feel her eagerness. I even resent it. Envy it. Wish it were eagerness toward me, for whom she now has so little eagerness, so little enthusiasm. I who was once such a paragon in her eyes. She never

24

tired of telling me I was pretty when she first knew me, my long, brown hair soft under her caresses, my long, brown hair endlessly laundered for her enjoyment. Once when she came to visit me at my farm during my breakdown and I was busy being crazy and had neglected to wash my hair, she hit upon that as the most visible proof of my madness. Wrote a nasty letter to all my friends and family bringing my deplorable condition to their notice on this account. I was already a damaged product. But not at the outset. At the outset I was a catch. I was a sculptor who had written a book which made me a minor heroine for a few months, a momentary genius. And I was pretty, she thought, quietly purring under it as a cat sits carefully when being stroked. Small and dark and almost demure I was, and so pleased with this taller and older woman's flattery. "Pretty," how rarely she says this to me now. And how enormous my sense of physical inferiority as I lie watching her. At home in her body, both plant and machine, this tool of flesh for the consummation of her will. Content inside it, the mellow light brown of her flesh, creamy yellow, smooth, graceful, the corporeal extension of her intelligence.

Who is she finally, this brisk and efficient woman; slim, elegant, off to administer her university programs in the gray January morning? Yet sensual, always, even at this hour in the morning, always there is this perfume of sensuality about her, in the brown of her skin, in the glow of her face and hair, in the sinuous movements of her long legs, in her delicate and lovely breasts, in her hands as she ties a scarf. And her history, how it fascinates me, how I retell it to myself. Born in Milan, daughter of a literary Italian count and a Brazilian opera singer, raised in convents, older sister to an adored little brother, the heir. A childhood severed in the middle as her mother's affinity for artists, for Jews, and for smuggling them to Brazil began to come to light. Sita's father was arrested by the Fascists, her mother fled back to Brazil with the two children. Being poor there, not nobility any more, poor relations to her mother's rich and indifferent tribe. To improve their fortunes it was decided Sita should marry, should be sold to a rich American. She was just out of school, he was fifty-five. After a child was born she escaped, divorced. Set out on her own with Pia in this new country. Until she fell into another marriage, even worse. Paul was born. Another divorce, another marriage; better, but still unsatisfactory. And then freedom. Now, near the end of her life, its ripe maturity to be her own, her own woman.

One night she showed me a box of old photographs of herself, the years of her young womanhood: Sita with babies, Sita with husbands, with Ben, who loved to take pictures, Sita the wife of his bungalow and his madonna with a dainty Pia, and pudgy Paul, her face a set smile, so strained it belied her good looks. Even her hair rigid in its forties and fifties hairdos, artificial, bent on pleasing and conforming, answering other demands. And that frozen wistful grimace in picture after picture, the look of someone completely ill at ease with life itself, with captivity within her own body.

But there was one picture, grand and glamorous and large, that denied all the others. Professional and on fine matte paper in contrast to all the little glossies of the candid home product. It was Sita one summer day before her second marriage. John Ford had come to the little Southern town and called for movie extras. She applied with her roommate and they got the parts. They'd be in the movies, they'd earn a hundred dollars a day for one bewitching week and wear long, old-fashioned dresses and big hats and walk across the lawn of illusion. A photographer had captured her doing this. And she was grand. And she was beautiful. Tall and stately, lady and aristocrat, her head fine under the great hat, her long neck, her benign carriage. Ebullient and quickening as she walks toward you. The mouth entirely sensual in its smile, perhaps even a little cruel. But confident, regal, utterly sure of itself. It was the only picture where she was alive, of herself. The only moment where she could be what she could be. This illusion was more real than her real life had ever been.

26

I am ten years younger, but I am not my own self. May never be. Am lost still nearly two years after a breakdown and a separation, lost in my work and my writing and my self. I have none of her assurance, can only envy it. And hate it—where it pushes me away. Coming here, I have lost myself utterly, relinquished the little world constructed with such effort in New York. The new beginning, shored up from the ruins of the ten years I lived there married. Fumio. All the agony of that severance fresh as a dismembered limb. Going back to New York, alone, the last time, and in those few months I was away from her, putting together a new studio, fixing up a loft. But in this time she had started over alone. Instead I kept to our plan, leaning toward her, always living three thousand miles away in part of my mind. And in returning to her now I lose my work and my studio and my self; ego and identity. Nowhere to paint or sculpt, nowhere even to write. Coming back only for love then. And the love is gone.

Artists who hazard their work for love commit a terrible sin. And for me she hazards nothing, would hazard nothing at all. She has never even considered living in New York. Her job is here, her life is here. New York is loathsome, she says, California the only place to live. She risks nothing, wouldn't think of it. Indeed, she scarcely considers inconveniencing herself on my behalf. The children, for example, are here to stay, they must not be disturbed, their welfare and happiness come before mine. If I mention that I have come far to be with her, been to time or expense, gambled my plans or work, ambitions or intentions—she only says that it was my own decision, she cannot take any responsibility. And I must not remind her; she will have no "guilt" imposed upon her. "You must come to California for yourself, not for me. Not on my account." Since nothing in the world would drag me to California except her, this leaves me nothing to say. So the proof of my affection is only another count against me. Time after time trying to explain to her that I am uprooted here, bereft of my friends, my work, my whole system of support and familiarity. Trying to make

27

her understand. And she will not. Finding, even as I explain, that it becomes a fault. Why don't I have friends in Berkeley and San Francisco? Why do I cling and have no plans of my own, no calendar, no busy schedule to fill all the days and nights she will find it necessary to be gone from me, "busy," otherwise committed, and so forth. Because she is very busy now. This will be a crowded semester. She is even booked on weekends, every weekend until April she'd said at Sherman's. So ominous it sounded. Why did I come? I will be marginal in her time and her life, just as I am marginal in the house, an extra body tucked away in a bedroom typing, a fringe person without a room or space of her own. In a house where I was once mistress the whole day through.

I must speak to her. I must communicate, connect where we have ceased to be connected. My eyes find her like hunger. And are turned away. There is no chance to speak at breakfast, so thoroughly does the presence of others murder privacy, stifle, prevent intimacy. Her car is being fixed today, I can drive her to the garage and then to work. Sitting through the grim boiled egg, Valerie's impatient gestures. "Valerie's one of those people who don't speak in the morning for fear of an explosion," Sita warns me. I try to pour Valerie's coffee when I pour ours. I use a cup and saucer. Without speaking Valerie forbids my hand and presents a mug, taking the pot and pouring it herself. The coffee I had poured her grows cold as an insult. I can't do anything to please, it seems. The hell with it. Yet I'm sorry, too, the commune fantasy still tugging at me, my admiration for Valerie's remarkable beauty, the terrible vitality of her youth. Sita and I are silent through breakfast.

In the car, still silence. Searching frantically for an entrance, a way to begin. Finally, just for anything to say, anything at all, Berkeley going by, the road down from the hills and Indian Rock, the Marin Circle, Shattuck. Each bit remembered with a greater sense of loss. Last year. When this was all ours and there was no one else but the two of us. How she protected me then, how carefully she would give instructions so that I would not lose my way in the town, how endlessly kind and considerate, how careful of my time, how she watched over me, treasured me. Once. And now I am merely a convenience, or rather an inconvenience who can occasionally be put to some use. Of course she didn't urge me this morning; Pia could drive her if I didn't want to. But I grabbed for it—a chance to be alone with her. The poverty of this situation, the cheap irony—that I would scramble up at seven in the morning just to have ten minutes alone with her. A woman I used to live with, share a house and life with. And having the chance—the last one I would have for twelve hours or so, until we are in our room after dinner tonight—and having the chance, the precious privacy —I have nothing to say at all, am in too much pain and confusion to talk. Too blank and desolate to have any topic to embark on, even any words.

Coming upon a piece of notepaper engraved with her matron's name and address, Mrs. Martin Richter: one of her former lives. When she was married to Martin and lived in the suburbs, the sprawling successful businessman's house he built for her. She used to have a picture of it in the hall, together with those strange and magical photos of the house in which she grew up in Italy. Palace rather than a house, its walls painted like Fragonards, its stiff ornate chairs, its monumental sideboards and lacy sofas. Photographs of rooms empty of people. All but one. Sita, in one touching picture, sitting primly on a silken chair. Staring out at the world from immense unhappy eyes, prisoner of this place she always describes as a penitentiary of unease. And yet she keeps the pictures. They have hung in the entranceway of every place we've lived. All the houses of her past as well, these last talismans of who she was born. The old Milanese house was destroyed in the war, I saw only its shadow down an empty alleyway last summer. It exists now only in these photographs, only in the unhappy eyes of its child.

And this piece of notepaper, before me, fit only for grocery lists. Echo of still another life. All the former lives, so many of them, her many selves. It was for this perhaps that I fell in love with her, captivated by her multiple personae, the sinuous change from one woman to another. In Sacramento once she went to lunch with me wearing a wig. Great silly blond thing of curls and peroxide. I did not know her. Excusing myself in confusion, I went into the bathroom and leaned against a wall, appalled to realize I was already involved, hell, in love, with someone who could look so grotesque, so different from my world and its values, aesthetics, its snobbery of scholar and artist. And came out, risking it, only to be overcome by a woman in a pants suit with vast bell-bottom trousers and that outrageous abominable wig, a woman of a kind and appearance I had probably never spoken to before in my life. And found her enchanting.

It was a "test," she told me. A test to see how much of who she was or had been I could absorb. And all that she has been, it bewilders me still, after three years. There was a certain photograph on the wall near the phone in my place in Sacramento just to remind myself of what constitutes efficacy: Sita with the determination of Il Duce on her face and a huge improbable Louis XIV hairdo, steel platinum mounted over a flowered dress, receiving an award for being the most enterprising woman in her housing development. "Woman of the Year." Sita in her suburban self, woman of the year. Before her independence, before her amicable divorce from Martin, before her present political and administrative eminence.

In three marriages you are many women. First a rich officer's wife, then the victim of a drunk, then finally sheltered by Martin's stability and kindness, which could pay for Pia's polio and the operations on her back and save Sita from the line of menial office jobs, the tired battle to raise two children, one of them dangerously ill. Martin saved them and then Martin became too small, his world too confining. Then Hank beckoned, a hippie painter from the commune Pia had taken off to live in. Only a few years older than her daughter—hairy mountain of a man, rough and crude as an early settler—yet he must have been like sunlight to her, his youth, his shaggy virility. Hank was the way out, but after a year or two she struck off on her own, beginning again alone after forty. Brave, new, both courageous and afraid. It was that that I loved, both the determination and the vacillation. Because I knew she would always come through it, because I sensed that this sort of woman was something new in the world.

All my Sitas: countess, courtesan, matron, flirt, mother, wife, lover, gossip playing with blouses or jewelry, administrator, coquette. Years of her, of her moods and troubles and gaieties and ardor. And now only this dead sensation, this hostile screen about her and between us, forbidding me even to speak. For my silence comes from her as well as from my own bafflement.

Her face. Watching her face as the desperate need to recover her comes on again, wanting to grab after her, the realization that I've lost her, that she is relinquishing me, putting me aside as she might slip off a sweater or a glove. The face I have loved so long. The fine aristocratic profile. Watching her so often in profile, preferring it even, because the front view is less perfect, too rounded perhaps —surprising myself that I should prefer even the distance of profile, its objectivity, its near indifference—all for the marvelous pure line running from brow to chin and throat, a line I covet, would draw, would capture, would possess. And the treasured dent just at the throat, how soft the skin there, how delicious to kiss, holding her very life in my lips. The gray of her hair, the brown of it going to gray. But that still doesn't satisfy her—my God, the very contrariness of tinting one's hair gray, confronting age and pushing it along, is characteristic of her. She insists on it despite my remonstrance. I was aghast when she did it first—to make yourself old, how perverse it seemed, but she laughed and refused to listen.

The gray lines of her hair about her face. Like silverpoint in an old engraving. The gray of her hair against the fine soft brown of her skin, how tender and inescapably sensuous, warm with that earthly warmth she has always, gives off continually like kindness. How that face shone on me once, adored and worshipped and cherished me like a living miracle. Even now, when I see its indifference or hostility, the old glow blocks my perception for a moment and delays me in registering the change, even crueler when the recognition comes. It had seemed a permanent state, her love. Absolute and entire, a great passion clung to with the patient tenacity of Latin womanhood. The way she forgave me for missing the plane that first time into Sacramento. I had been organizing a women's prison strike in Iowa, living in continual excitement and what even appeared to be some danger—and just as we were winning I remembered a flight landing in Sacramento. I had just plain missed it. Called and apologized desperately, her terrible inconvenience, she would never forgive me. But she only laughed. "You don't know anything about Latin women," she said. And forgave me. As she forgave the madness and the breakdown. But she forgave it less. And she never did forgive me for taking a loft in New York after we had rented the house here and begun to live that curious little marriage she now so bitterly despises. Now that she's her own single self again, matriarch of a commune, administrator in a university, a woman available to men. And there are some about, strangers at the edges of her life. She told me about one at Christmas. Chuckling, confiding, women chattering, half-deprecatory. Lovers too, snuggled in our pillows sipping wine.

He was young, she said, she'd met him at a conference in Virginia City. Everyone went off to a meeting and they stayed in the bar and had a few drinks. She told him women were better lovers than men. He was challenged. She took him up on it. An adventure. Told after the story of another adventure, her deplorable behavior at Emily's birthday party. Got utterly sloshed and took on some handsome fellow and even another lady. "I never called him back, but the lady was a bit more interesting." "You're terrible." I laughed. "We were worse than that. Imagine the garden party and the eight-year-olds and there we were getting it on in the upstairs bedroom. Even Pia and Paul didn't know how to deal with it all." "And you a grandmother." We are helpless with laughter while she invents and embroiders, they were "hanging moons" from the upstairs window. "You're making it up. You got it from Chaucer." "Or Boccaccio. But what are you going to do if you're two stories up and you need more wine or marijuana or want to tell someone down in the yard they have a telephone call?" "Shameless. Blessing you didn't get arrested." "It was the back window." I kiss her, laughing. Not knowing what to think. Not even quite believing. Like the stories she used to tell of how she celebrated her divorce from Martin by screwing some total stranger at the end of a party on her hands and knees under the dining-room table, the rug burns on her shins a joke between us for years. That there is somewhere a wilder self within her—promiscuous, a hussy—is only a probability, never a certainty. And piquant, teasing my own lust for her. Somewhere it is also terrifying, a hidden and dreadful threat. Amused as I am, admiring even, when I hear these stories I am also, at the very back of my stomach and near the spine, in panic, poised over a trapdoor that could open.

But the danger now is the very shut quality, the closed and decided set of her face lately. An expression I had never known before. Or seen only as something she gave to others, all the others she excluded from her beauty and herself. Whereas for me she was always open, my mystery, my good fortune and treasure—what for the whole world she would somehow shut like a shopkeeper's metal front rolled down. The reason other people often had no inkling of how beautiful she was, no notion of her stunning good looks. The face that opened and shone for me like the sun, warm, reassuring, protective. Permanently and definitely loving. How fatuous I was to believe, to imagine that. Nothing of love is permanent, ever. Yet I believed it; so passionate she was, so ardent, so entire in her promises, so Indian in her patience, so Latin in her attentions, so tender, so elaborately considerate. The package of cigarettes she kept in her purse. In case I should run out. She who doesn't smoke but was never without fresh Marlboros. When I landed I remember her mentioning that she had matches in case I needed them. I smiled a wry smile inside, registering the difference.

I am a spy in the house of love. A figure on staircases thrust into the role of eavesdropper. In what was once my own house. Populated now with hundreds. Emily is finally off to school. Valerie has stormed her way out the door and into the old black truck she and Paul own but still haven't paid for. As usual it will not start. This requires running it down a steep hill and hoping. Paul gets up to help her. The truck has a broom attached to the back of the cab, erect as a tin soldier; it would do well in a musical or a nostalgia film about the fifties. It has all the goofy charm of youth, just as they do, the childlike helplessness, the day-saving final ingenuity, the sense of adventure, the fantasy, that their life is grim and difficult. I find myself trampled and annihilated by their beauty, their youth, their carefree indifference. Pia rouses herself from bed, eats breakfast, and settles down with a book. She is supposed to be looking for a job, but there will be no pretense of that today. She glides around in a nightshirt, tall, slim, delicately and remarkably beautiful. Coming on the fragile and childlike perfection of her face, its utter innocence, you would never believe she was a junkie. Years in hip-pad filth, a filth imposed on Emily in neglect and abuse, the child's hair hopelessly matted, Sita said, when they showed up in Sacramento for cold turkey. Years of Janis and her crowd at the Trident in Sausalito, years singing and not going anywhere with it, not really working very hard, "laid back" and easy with dope and wine and the white song in the veins. "The greatest high in the world," she always described it to Sita. And now it's over. But the methadone is depleting. Pia and Dan slept most of the day for the first two months of withdrawal. Now that it's over, Dan's back at work driving his truck. Pia is free to do whatever she wishes: get a job, sing, study music, go to school, leave Dan, strike out on her own, join a band, make the contacts with musicians that her friend Michael is providing, wait for the mood or the moment to strike. Beginning life all over again.

We sit at the table drinking coffee, making small talk. Very small, because we are uncomfortable together and have nothing to say. I am uneasy with her. I would love to help, encourage, exert some benign influence. Sita always says I have influence with Pia, that she respects me and looks up to me. The teacher takes over and yearns as toward an undergraduate, a younger artist. If I could bring her along, sustain. And part of Pia lingers at the table for this. But part is distant with a new distance. Closed toward me as her mother is, taking her cue. She doesn't want me here. And she doesn't want what I offer. Or wants it only a little. I feel her teeter on the brink between an old life and a new. I must be very careful not to push, diplomatically pursuing her with questions about bands, this or that contact in San Francisco, the new women's groups. She has leads, but they are all vague, and you can never put your hand around what she says. It seems she has to get to know a few more people. There's a real tough lady in the city who could put her on to some good things. She'll be getting around to meeting her pretty soon. Nothing's hurried. Is she practicing, rehearsing? Well, a little bit with Paul. But it seems you really have to have a band, know what kind of material they do, there's the right stuff and the wrong stuff, and a lot of that rock 'n' roll shit she "just can't get into." Everything is pushed away, ideas and events and activities seem swept off to arm's length, floated away from the dining-room table and out to the living room. I see reality dismissed in the wave of her hand toward the living-room sofa. I must be very careful not to push.

Paul comes home and disappears into his room. Sleeping. It is terrible that there is no connection between us any more. There had been such a fondness. The parties and visits in San Rafael when the kids lived there together and Sita and I visited them on weekends.

35

But they were always parties, visits, special occasions, celebrations. And Sita there to mediate our shyness, transmit her great affection for me then, show me off, even. For they had been impressed at the beginning. The nervous breakdown settled that. I was scarcely impressive after that. After that I was an embarrassment, a broken instrument, an uncertainty. I had caused their mother pain, and that was unforgivable. Their loyalty to her, how I had loved and admired it even then, their fierce devotion. How they would stand against anyone who hurt her. Pia in her loyalty lying to me over the telephone last fall, probably hating what she did as she did it, and her own friendliness for me making her hate it still more. But she did it for her mother. They are blood together. And always I am not. My fortunes rising or falling on precisely whatever quotient of interest or disinterest Sita signals. They have no real relationship to me at all. Valerie passes me on the stairs, brusque, almost bullying in her size and her haste. Only Emily holds out. But even Emily picks it up. This morning when I bundled her off to school she was cross and tyrannical, dying to get away, to go off fifteen minutes earlier than she needed to and superior about what coat to choose, disdainful of my notion of red tights to set off her dark blue dress, and suspicious I wouldn't really be in touch with the correct time.

I am letting myself grow paranoid. It is hard to be one in a household of seven. I must buy Emily a little present, I must connect again. I must buy the rest of us some feasts, a carload of groceries. There is endless talk of poverty. Paul's job as a dishwasher hardly runs his pickup truck. Valerie teaches a class or two, but that only pays her tuition. Paul doesn't want college, talks vaguely of repairing guitars, and does a little inlay work in the basement, bits of ivory fitted into the top of a jewelry box, the neck of a guitar, the handle of a knife. His mother is proud: her son the artist. As if Paul were still so much a child his hobbies could pass for a profession. It used to be her son the rock 'n' roll star. And at seventeen it seemed that Paul might make music his life; he had his little band, his little gigs at pizza parlors. But since Valerie he has grown shadowy and stands behind her radiant energy in some contented nonentity that may satisfy him a long time. Valerie is determined; she will survive beautifully. She studies now to be a schoolteacher. Later she may take over the world. But I worry about Paul.

Paul will be fine, Sita says, Valerie will see to that. In being a male, he is already complete in her eyes, she has named him after her brother, Paolo, she has even given him her father's ring, the signet of the count, which Paolo had gallantly given to her. After a moment's annoyance had passed when I heard this, I realized I had wanted Sita still to wear it. Or Emily. Or Pia. But one doesn't hope for Pia; Sita has passed her by utterly. Yet oddly, for all the approval she showers on Paul, all the calm and assured affection, the easy and obvious favoritism, it is with the woman-child Pia that she has the stronger, more passionate relationship, even in its disappointment, its long, probably lifelong disapproval, even in this it is fuller and more fierce and more wonderful. To watch them together, to feel all the waves of energy and emotion, whether they are playing at lady friends comparing jewelry or whispering about men, or whether squaring off for battle, for chilly refusals or grief-filled embraces—it is always a matter of equals. Paul is a raw young page sitting on the rug at his lady mother's feet: but Pia is a queen and rival, they sit side by side.

Misplaced, I think, I am simply misplaced in life, incompetent, unable to cope, as lately I have been unable to speak, to make conversation, chitchat, jokes, any sound at all. As if tongue-tied, becoming a moron, a cretin, an idiot. Does the withdrawal of love produce all these symptoms of degeneracy? Remove every vestige of confidence, ability, intelligence?

Upstairs each object menaces. Remnants. I have so many clothes here, having meant to return, to stay, to arrive each year, to have my life here. So many books, feeling ashamed of the extravagance that bought them, a whole library of politics, thinking I would write and study. Shoved now, all of them, into the hall closet. We used to have them lining the floor in what is Paul's room, and I was going to build bookshelves when I got around to it. Now they tumble out of the closet at me. They have been displaced, as have all my other things that I come upon in corners, closets, the garage.

How would I ever bring it all home, assuming New York were home, all that's left? Boxes, clothes, files of papers, dressers, rugs, Sherman's paintings. Even a car. The car most problematic of all. Too much stuff to pile everything in and drive cross-country—an old car, might not even make it. And the long, lonely trip. I clench my jaws thinking of it. Giving up. Admitting it didn't work, is over, Sita a part of the past like other lovers gone. Leaving a car here was a guarantee always. Taking it away marks the end. Absurd, of course. Mere material objects, how they structure life. But having a car in a place, even a used and leaky Dodge convertible, is some sign and assurance you actually live there.

And I came back to find it gone, the place vanished, invaded, transformed by others. Sita, just one now among a horde of persons, and herself changed, preoccupied with them, absent from me, chilly when I recall her, her resolute new expression of face and shoulders, hostile under the surface politeness, waiting finally to snap, call it off, tell me to go. Impossible therefore even to complain or confront—it would only bring about disaster. I cannot afford confrontation.

The sounds of the commune go on relentlessly—Emily comes home from school and sits before her idol the television, Paul's dog pads up and down the stairs. The day is almost over, concentrate. Try to get a few letters written, anyway. Remember New York details, the mail, the bills, the plants. Ruth watering the plants. Her very expensive favors. Meant to ask Linda, who lives downstairs, to look after them, but Ruth offered, insisted she would enjoy it.

A mistake to become lovers again with Ruth. The night they tore down the old house, or rather that dawning—fifteen years of my life and a marriage, a good so good existence made there, loved it

38

as I loved him, not loved, adored—all down under a wrecking ball. The night before, late so late, did I intuit it?—that it would be that very dawn when I would wake and the old studio would be gone —only a hole in the street. Fifteen years. Rubble. Bricks. Friends I kept running into for months confided after the usual condolences, while I grimaced or kept my face like starch, that walking by they'd picked up a brick and saved it. Relics. Even of their own good times, the high fine drinking talk those rooms had known, my sculptures, Fumio's mobiles floating against the ceilings. Did I intuit it all by calling up Ruth—Come on over here. It's four in the morning. And I'm asking her to come over and fuck me. Must have even said that. Dead drunk I was. Dinner with Hatsie and for some inconceivable reason got blasted. Outrageous, raucous, even made a fool of myself at a club where Esther Phillips was singing, almost got us thrown out. And came home blind and called Ruth. Did I know it would happen, that they'd blow the house that bleak top of the morning? Months of the props and beams against the old walls and wrecking crews who wouldn't even let me in to say it goodbye. To gather the few last tidbits, the shutters from the front windows, the other ones in my studio, the ones with paper windows that I'd made by hand. Big gruff men who wouldn't bend. Not even the foreman. Sure to collapse, look at that crack in the wall, are you crazy, lady? And crazy and drunk and alone on a foam mattress on the floor of the new place, not even a bed yet, and called Ruth, pleading with her to fuck me. And she came. Unspeakably kind, patient, generous.

Bad faith, it was all bad faith. Never should have started. Bad faith when she's in love and you're not. Sexual friendship sort of nonsense doesn't work, not against her adoring obsession. She said it would, of course, sex not important to her really, only another dimension of friendship. Our real bond being sculpture. And so forth. Came and was kind. Healed something broken that night. Hatsie, her report on visiting California. The news that Sita's children snickered and ridiculed me, criticized my housework, said that I was selfish, I ought to have a maid, and so on. And Sita was cold. That came across. That she might not bother to come at Christmas. That there would "be a lot of changes," that if I came back it would "certainly never be like last time." All mysterious and hesitant. Hatsie dense as smoke, all hints, portents. Dreading even to hear the report, sounded so ominous when she first came back to town and telephoned. Was it disloyal of me even to listen? Put her off for two days. And then I had to know. Spent the dinner getting lush, proclaiming how I loved Sita, her charm her fascination her beauty her passion. Hatsie benign, gossipy, full of intrigue —pumping me: "Really shouldn't ask, but I'm so curious, how did Sita afford that trip to Europe with you last summer; did you pay for it?" Point-blank like that, I admitted it, hating myself for admitting the truth. Off my guard, swept away with my romantic rant.

Building all evening, Hatsie's little gestures, crab-like movements toward letting me know the truth. That I was in trouble, that I couldn't trust either Sita or the kids, that they'd changed. Nothing there to count on. And if I'd sinned in counting on Sita too much in the past, it was all over now, the group of them, only sand shifting. Blowing another way. No. It can't be, just can't be. It's got to be Hatsie. Merely Hatsie, Hatsie the trifler, the meddler, she's famous for it. And she landed on them, an unwelcome house guest, of course they'd all thoroughly disliked one another. Dismiss it. Keep believing. No, you can't dismiss it, the bug of unease, the germ of doubt is set now. To grow.

Slamming down on the mattress, I called Ruth. The call of an orphan, a sick call. And she came. New York. Ruth. Fumio and Ruth. And Dobie. Dobie the casual buddy. Fumio the rigid force that shuts me out. Ruth. Don't want to go back to Ruth. I want it to be over. Again and again, against her infatuation, insisting it isn't fair, can't return it, merely be friends. A much better thing. When I go back I'll break off, no more sex—remembering a lover saying that to me once—punitive, it seemed, perverse. To separate

40

sex from love from life from the rest of a friendship. But with Ruth I can't keep it up, the pretense of romance. A sexual friendship, as the phrase used to go. Ruth. Enormous sensuality. The great lush body I've drawn thousands and thousands of times. Fine. But not the obscene presence of her worship, that almost religious dependence on the magic object. For that's what I am. From that first speech at Columbia probably. And all my efforts to prod her along in art, make her believe in herself as a sculptor, all never fill the maw of her fixation. A thing she's done all her life. Crush on Greta Garbo when she was eight. Every day after school roaming the Upper West Side just to bump into her. And she did. Same terrible awesome child-radar still. Does it to me, can locate me anywhere on the Lower East Side within thirty minutes.

I can't be responsible for this. And being with Sita now only confirms it. And I can't respond either. The body makes its own decisions. All the ripe sensuality in the world, all the languorous drawing sessions when Ruth poses for me, all our naughty afternoons when the paintbrushes end up in bed, all nothing to the terrible tenderness that first time when Sita came at Christmas, choking almost, the absolute necessity of tears.

Stupid to choose. Sensuality's a fine thing too. But the choice falls elsewhere. In that Ruth's in love and I'm not. And won't be. Gratification is not the same. But Sita's not in love and I am. She was once. Once, once is the past. You don't get it back. Even sitting here and hoping. Even hanging on. Quit and go home. Even if you go home to nothing.

I sit next to her on the rocks. She is tired. When she came home I rubbed her shoulders. When she came home, the sound of the front door I had waited to hear for hours. And then she was upstairs at the door of our room. "Her room," in the commune. Though it seems ours again these first moments. Sita spreads out upon the bed, exhausted. Lady, I will take off your boots. Managing the first, its long, blue body of glove leather, its elegant shape, its sinuous zipper. Pia comes up the stairs. We will be seen. I will be caught in the strange erotic posture of taking off a boot. Sita feels it too and springs up to sit, doing the second boot herself. Then lies down again on the bed. I lie next to her. More noises in the hall. I shut the door, making the gesture, shutting the door, shutting out the world and the commune. But the moment is past.

And the sun is setting. Heroic across the bay, the city beyond. It pulls me as it always does here, the one spectacular moment for which the whole day is prelude, the drama building already at four o'clock, that special golden light beginning to filter into consciousness. And from there you are always aware the rest is coming, preparing yourself for it, wondering if you will be in the right spot when the moment comes, if your work will be finished, if you'll be in sight of the water. Because the moment is coming, the climax is approaching with one light and then another and then all. Memory, the memory of these sunsets last year. How well we are placed to see them; my old study had a superb view, so does this bedroom. But a better place is outside on the rocks at the crest of the hill. "Shall we go out and watch it from the rocks?" I ask. Neutral, not an invitation to the Marina and drinks at Grundy's, the best place of all, heeding the warnings that she would be too tired for this worldliness, effort, expense.

And she is companionable on the rocks. We perch next to each other, I knead her shoulders, trying to take away the day's tiredness, the frustrations of the job. "I had my secretary send out letters to your students today, canceling your class." I'm thunderstruck. Last night, having dinner at Grundy's, she had asked me what I wanted to do about the class. I still didn't know, but was doubtful if we could order the books in time. And she had simply canceled it. "I thought that's what you wanted, I thought you wanted to write while you were here." I hardly know what to say, embarrassed by my own malingering over the class, my inability to decide whether to do it or not, even my fear of the project, the responsibility, the way it would tie and compel me to stay here for ten weeks. When part of me wants so desperately to run. The class would commit me by contract to stay. But if she's canceled it, perhaps the inference is that I should go. I sit confused and humiliated next to her. "If I don't do the class, may I stay on anyway?" "Of course, you should do whatever you like. I just didn't want you to be under any pressure." Not to be under any pressure, not to be doing the class as a favor to her, not to be under any obligation to go to California—this has been her line since Christmas. I am as confused as ever about my fate. The future is impossible but also mandatory: the course required me to decide. And now she has decided for me. I am both relieved and disappointed. Had dreaded the class but also looked forward to it; in my unproductive time it would be work, something to do, the pretense and perhaps even the actuality of activity, meaningful activity, any activity at all. And now it is gone. I watch the sky, thinking of the class, thinking of her, thinking of the past. All the things lost. I don't speak because I don't dare. There is so much to tell her, but if I told her she would withdraw, grow angry, distant. And I would lose what little I have, this pretense of intimacy, two persons sitting high on a rock formation watching the sun set over a bay. The air growing chilly, the extinction of light and color a prefiguration of death.

In a little while we will have to go back and join the others. A few hours and then the few moments before sleep. All there is in a day. Last night at Grundy's we reminisced over the way we first became lovers that long wakeful night in Sacramento when I lit cigarette after cigarette and she made innumerable trips to the bathroom, both of us appalled at our own desire. It was not hospitality, it was not correct, laughing at ourselves, but the laughter a bit automatic perhaps, a bit too polite, perfunctory. I felt more like tears than laughter, the remembrance of our good times only makes the present more hateful, and to watch her playing at being a lover is more humiliating than outright rejection. Yet I am such a coward, I prefer it, would have even that, am greedy for whatever

43

moment, whatever absentminded smile. Even the stolid companionship of her body here upon this stone looking to sea, the little lights of Berkeley's houses coming into the darkness, the sweep of San Francisco's skyline, the melancholy shadow of the bridges as the air grows blue and cold. Once I thought I would grow old with this woman, our love going on for years. I have been here three days. How many days have I left?

I read the paper. The *San Francisco Chronicle,* delivered each morning to the house. My solace, my sedative, my shame. Idleness and the terror of idleness. I have no work here, why am I staying? The class is canceled. She has canceled it. And my own work only a void; dry, sterile, hopeless. She works of course. Was off before eight in the morning. And I merely read the paper, my fear of death in every murder, in every high-placed heart attack, my worry worries at the layoffs, the depression. Every item finds my soft gray spot of vulnerability, locates my dread, I suffer with all the losers in obscure places, cringe with corrupt officials exposed and indicted, experience a vast amorphous despair over a planeload of Japanese tourists poisoned by their scrambled eggs. Two days later the official in charge commits the inevitable suicide of responsibility. I've tried that too, but it didn't work.

As soon as she leaves in the morning, I am seized with anxiety, heart-pounding, throat-closing panic, pacing the floor. For what? I ask myself. Because my life means nothing, is essentially over, is useless, inactive, unemployed. That I age and grow ugly and reach the end of love. That I love her and am not loved, love and am no longer loved. But if I were, would I stay here? Hungering for New York, yearning back after it, the little beginnings I had made there, my own loft, the scraggly little circle of old friends. Who were never enough. Knowing I was bored there too. And what is boredom? Perhaps the inability to find meaning, to complete a perception, to arrive at an understanding: partly grasped, but forever just

44

out of reach. It is not lack of interest, but interest frustrated, cut off, imperfectly held. So says the *Chronicle* today. But for me it is the fear of emptiness.

I see her life and realize that my own is shallow, improvised, empty of the things she is rich in—family, children, grandchild— the young; and even the respectable: position, employment, col- leagues, community. Would I ever have noticed if I hadn't come here, or gone on imagining my fringe bohemia was an existence without comparison? Asking myself now, Do I envy this here? Yes. Do I want it myself? No. Then why the flurry, the terrible grief this house inspires? The past haunting me, last spring when it was only the two of us and the house a kind of music. Yet I didn't want to stay, limit myself entirely, so I went off to outfit a loft in the city. Meaning of course to live both lives, one here, one there, half a year in turn.

You can't live in two places, of course it's impossible. No one is so vain, so full of hubris, so full of illusion to imagine such a thing. It isn't done. The world isn't constructed that way. You live in one place or another, but not two; one world or another, but not both. You stick with town, the Big Apple, where it all happens, the artists and the dealers and the publishers and the machine that rules the earth—or you follow a will-of-the-wisp and decide on sunny California, lie back and settle for nature and landscape and an easier way of life. You don't say to a confirmed and unswerving Californian, Look, I have personal and professional reasons to need New York: it's my home these fifteen years, my friends and my known world are there. She is not an artist, the art world and the necessity for its dubious oxygen mean nothing to her. And without her I began to be stifled there. So here I am.

Reading the paper. Saving the funnies for last. Dreading the moment when they run out, when I get to Herb Caen, the second section with its two frivolous columnists, then Caen fronting the obituaries and the want ads, the three of them "witty" in that sophomoric manner of daily journalism, even that spark rebuking my lassitude. Surely this morbid sloth is only self-pity: reasonless and gigantic terror of life, hollow, vacuous, and inexcusable angst. But it comes down to this: that I don't know what to do today. Have nothing to do. Now or ever. Write, work, but I cannot work, loathe the aging dried manuscript upstairs. The first day after I arrived I was determined, forced myself, tore out all the old hand-written entries from their notebooks and filed them in order. A week of blood, the sight of that old stuff, the time and memories it evokes, nearly nauseating. Time of the separation, the break-down, the suicide trips. The idea was to type it up, fill in the holes, mold it into a book. But I doubt now it can be a book. And I can't work here in this madhouse, this uncertainty, this emotional whirl-pool. If I went home, back to New York . . . remembering how it paled after her visit, how the well-made little plan, the fresh growth of the new life wilted, how I longed to leave and then just started packing, keeping the appointed time. "I'm not trying to talk you into coming back, things are very different now," she'd said. How different I never guessed. "Come only of your own free will. Don't come unless you really want to."

To be this age and have so little direction in one's life. The emptiness of my freedom. She cannot go to this coast or the other, there is always her job. So it is for most people. Never having choices, they don't bump up against the strange gray limits. Or do I trot out these vague generalities only to try to obscure my disap-pointment in her, the knowledge of love dying, another place of safety closing? No, it's my own dissatisfaction with myself. My disappearing self, which had lived in my work and is now homeless. Other people live without work, would love to be unemployed, can think of nothing better. But the artist, staring and impotent, unable to work, deprived of the saving and sustaining art. Hideous that experience, that knowledge of failure.

And so I drug myself with Cypriot warfare, pop stars, the price of crude oil, new ideas in home decoration, the machinations of the C.I.A., shake-ups in the prison hierarchy. And the comics. So delicious, over so soon. If life resembles the newspaper, so huge, so various, so dull, it is love which resembles the comics, so charming and so brief. When the comics are over, you have, wherever you may have begun, even if you began with the comics, you have finished the *San Francisco Chronicle*. The only dependable part of my day.

Hating myself for the triviality of this crutch, because when the paper is over I have to face working, trying to work, deciding to leave, deciding to stay. And how smug and alone with themselves the others are—Sita, her competence, her matriarchal and managing power throughout the house; Valerie in her long red skirt and her Cossack boots off to school in her definiteness; Paul lying lazily in bed; Pia slopping around looking lovely in the most bedraggled nightgown, chatting on the phone or prone across her bed reading a book. They are certain, they know who they are. I know nothing, only this crippling fear. In a week I have lost all my bearings, utterly at sea among these people, strangers. Lost in life. And in a few moments I will have run out of train wrecks, the heroics of firemen, the arrests of extortionists, the opinions of editors. It is all merely how to spend the day while she is gone—all of it's just time waiting for her.

Our commune is invaded by new faces. Friends of Pia. Yesterday there were Jeff and Tina who were supposed to be arriving with good music. The music never happened, but they stayed two days. Today it is Hedy and her little boy, Jon-Jon, and an Englishman of indeterminate status named Pete. They sleep in the living room, and when you come down for breakfast you inevitably wake them all. Pete yawns and approaches the dining-room table with his shirt off. Jon-Jon cries and will not be comforted. Hedy and Pia discuss long-lost friends from Beech Street, their first commune ten years ago. We are polite and uncomfortable. The arrival of Hedy, Jon-Jon, and Pete brings our total to ten persons, plus Limbo the dog. Presently in heat. No one can open a door without the danger of Limbo's escape. This is her first heat. She is Paul and Valerie's dog,

47

but we are all responsible twenty-four hours a day to prevent her impregnation. There are bells attached to the handle of the front door and I must leave my work and run downstairs and stand guard over Limbo each time they sound. Pia can't be depended upon, the solemn duty rests largely on me. Life becomes more and more unbearable. The presence of the visitors limits me to the bedroom without respite for the entire day, since I cannot walk through the downstairs without disturbing them. Writing, the solitary art, grows more and more impossible. Sita takes no notice at all, she is only here in the evening and by then they have usually gone out. And perhaps she relishes the intrusions of young persons who treat her with elaborate respect; how "groovy" this grandmother must appear to them, how fond she is of their awed deference which understands that this is ultimately her house, no one else's. And perhaps she welcomes anything that will drive me away, convince me finally to leave, to surrender my hopes of reclaiming the place. And herself. Sita, who is now so distant and disagreeable to me, who forbids any complaint whatever. This is the way the place is, if you don't like it you can leave. She keeps suggesting I look at Michael's studio apartment. He's moving out this weekend. "I didn't come three thousand miles to live in Michael's apartment." She regards this remark as unreasonable. She is not responsible for me, she will not be made to feel guilty.

Pete talks of nothing but his passport, the need to get his visa extended, his troubles with the officials. Hedy dreams aloud about a trip to New Orleans they have planned. Got to get the car in shape first. Long disquisitions on the car and its condition. They have no money, everything seems dangerously vague. Hedy calls it being on the road. She transports two curious little sculptures with her. Pia and I admire them on the living-room rug. Pia asks if I will show them photographs of my sculptures. I would like to, but in the confusion of my effects I cannot locate the albums. No one notices. I spend two hours searching and give up. Hedy and Pia are still chattering on the rug. I am worried that I cannot find these valuable pictures, unique copies most of them, annoyed at the waste of time, the presence of strangers. Finding myself irate and hostile toward these gentle and innocent people, good souls wandering around the country meaning no harm. Hating myself for meandering through the day without purpose, for joining in the aimless drift of all those around me, their lunches, their snacks, their telephone calls. Endlessly conveying messages for Pia from employment agencies, suitors, creditors, gentlemen who might need a typist, the insurance company against which Paul and Valerie have laid a claim for a dent in their truck. The insurance money is their El Dorado, it might even pay for the truck. If not that, then the utility bills. They have spent the money a hundred times over, like lovable children. The company is slow and unwilling. Innumerable calls are necessary. Paul's earnest young voice playing man over the phone, nearly crumbling into tears when the check arrives with a stipulation that it cannot be cashed for a month. Who will cover it, meanwhile? They want to spend it right now, and they do not have enough in the bank to cover it themselves. Sita is uninterested in advancing two hundred dollars, so am I. I have made bad loans to the kids in the past and the job of making them solvent would never end. I listen to the mounting hysteria from the bedroom, sticking to my desk. First Pia negotiates with the bureaucrats, then Paul. A call to Valerie in Marin. The inevitable calls to Sita for advice. Further calls to lawyer friends of Pia's. Explanations of the delay. Paul again on the line to the company, brother and sister between calls furious and bellicose, but admirably patient when dealing with official stupidity. A call to the bank. How well I know that outrage, that sense of insult before pointless obstacle. I listen with painful empathy below my amusement, but they have used up three hours of my time with their emergency. The phonograph blares. Emily is home from school and has turned on the television. It's already four o'clock. Sita will be home in an hour. Hedy has decided to stay another day.

49

When we come in, the usual funky furniture from some improbable long-ago living room, the pictures rotting in junk stores twenty years. Camp. Kind of stuff Pia loves. The eternal dress-up of old satin, ankle straps, moldy ballads. Lampshades with fringes, pink overstuffed chairs, ponderous frieze sofas. Oleg's has expanded, taken over the adjoining storefronts, leaked its funk over two more rooms. Acres of depressing memorabilia in which to wait for lunch. Arrogant young man playing maître d'. He will call our table when he gets around to it. Signed us up as "Sita." Refused to bother with a last name. She permitted him. Will we drink? She won't. I will. A Bloody Mary at noon, despite the manuscript, the typing. Celebrate life, enjoy the time—a voice I locate as sanity. Death, the emptiness of time ahead. Fight it off, think of something to say. Since I am silence. This most of all, that I have nothing to say, am hollow—this most of all will drive her away.

"Did you take a look at Michael's place?" It is long and hard even to get out the word—yes. "Well, what do you think of it?" "It's a nice place." Hovering, holding fire. We look at each other through the silence. Palpable, almost visible. Visible surely in the slight annoyance on her face, the eyes blinking, the chin line hardening in impatience. I sympathize, I agree it's tedious. But what is there to say? Nothing or too much. Start out bravely, the truth—or some of it. "I think I'd be too alone there." I stop and then risk it: "I'm afraid I'd spend all my time waiting." She shifts at the end of her sofa, flicks back her hair. Gesture I love, seeing it now in fear. The wave of hair that falls across her forehead, always the same piece, always the same way. Throwing it off her face, perfect dip of the wrist, pat of the long competent fingers. My fingers.

She had expected a more satisfactory report, is still waiting for one. But how can I tell her that I took one look at the place and foresaw the most desperate future? One room, a nice-enough room, view of a nice little garden behind, fashionable neighborhood. Perfect bachelor apartment for someone like Michael, a young lawyer-about-town. Behind me at that moment, nuzzling Pia, with whom it is transparent he's having a thing that totally engages them both, leaving me, ostensibly the purpose of the visit, an awkward intruder. Pleasant little place, we all agree. They expect me to love it and take it on the spot. I look around the room and imagine life here; table by the window, fireplace, kitchen, shower—a life of waiting. Waiting all day until she finishes work. Waiting each evening until she tears herself away from the commune on the evenings she comes. And the evenings she doesn't come? Telephoning the house. Being told she's out. Being told she's at a meeting. But no, I'm only supposed to work here daytimes, stay at the house otherwise. How do I pay both rents? And I know already that if I took it I would be exiled here finally; it would come to be regarded as considerate or convenient. And here I would lead no other life but waiting. The life of Victor Hugo's mistress comes to mind. Here in this little room with its partial view I would learn all there was to know of waiting, exasperation, hope deferred, sad patience, the doglike expectation of a sound in the driveway, a step on the path. No, damn it, no. It would be hell to live it, hell to live like that. The most slavish conditions, the most insufferable circumstances. Accepting the last defeat, becoming her occasional visit, the creature she has stored away in a room in the hills, visited only when the mood strikes her. Marginal before, I would now be completely expendable.

Meanwhile, she goes on persuading me from the sofa at my side. The place needn't be seen as a penitentiary or a punishment, after all. It might be a great convenience to both of us; I would have a place to work and we would both have a place to be together, to be alone together. "A love nest?" I challenge her. "Sure, why not?" she agrees, seeing that's a good line to follow. And I follow it, despite the irony of our paying three hundred fifty dollars' rent to have a house together which she has so filled with people that I should now be expected to pay another hundred seventy-five so that we can have a little privacy. In addition to paying rent in New York. Perhaps I should. Maybe I'm being cheap, maybe I should just go ahead even if I can't afford it, go for broke. Love doesn't go by money, after all. A love nest, how charming; a place of assignation, a rendezvous. Delightful. Then I see the room and remember its true scent: waiting, merely waiting. Hours at the whim of her caprice, a life on tenterhooks. The terrible loneliness the place gave off predicted, even warned me, of itself. She expects me to have agreed by now. I haven't. Her name is called and we go in to lunch.

Oleg's garden is all under Plexiglas, the light generous and easy, the sensation of air and sky and plants is carefree and Californian and beguiling. I had forgotten there's nothing I like on the menu. There is no time to study it anyway, because she is lecturing me. I am pressing too close, take up too much of her time and energy. She wants and needs and insists upon a greater independence. I look on, helpless to argue or interrupt, not really understanding what she is talking about. She is talking about her own individual life, which had flowered and developed in my absence and which she is now in no mood to relinquish. "I don't want you to relinquish anything," I sputter, forgetting even to consider how much I relinquish. There is no way to parry her when she attacks. It seems there are a great many friends she has not seen since my arrival. "I've only been here a few days," I say weakly. There are a number of people dear to her, she goes on, her voice getting hard, building to its crisis, and she has no intention, absolutely none, of giving them up. "Who would ask you to?" I say innocently. "Men friends." "Really?" "People very dear to me." "I see," "Neal." "Who's Neal?" "I told you about Neal at Christmas." Neal, whom she seduced by telling him women were better lovers than men; Neal, who seems to owe his success to her particularly cruel use of me as a challenge. Neal. "He was a very good lover," she'd said. "Gentle, really very good." I'd winced for a second at the recommendation, but it was frivolous talk, giggling in bed. "Men don't really count, after all." She'd chuckled. And I'd weakened and told her about my friend Dobie. Whatever Neal was, Dobie is really only a friend, impossible to mistake our two abortive efforts at sex as being lovers. "What's Dobie like?" "He's black and was an actor a long time with the Living Theatre. He wants to practice their anarchist philosophy, so now he's running a bunch of food co-ops in Harlem, he's decided to devote two years to it. Very nice guy, he's helped me a lot with my loft, lives in the neighborhood. He's a buddy, we eat together a lot." "Men don't really count"—it seemed an awfully smug thing to say, however reassuring, and now I find that Neal does count, a great deal. Over and over she reiterates that Neal is part of her life, being free to see him is indispensable. "I'll be here only a short time, couldn't he be sort of—in abeyance?" It would never occur to me to impose Ruth or Dobie upon her. The time I am with her I am only with her. No, she doesn't see it that way at all. "Of course when we're apart it's understood we might have other lovers, but when we're together . . ." "Look, I live here all year round. I have to make a life for myself here. Just here. Nowhere else. And there are people in that life who matter to me." "I see." "You don't see. I insist upon having complete independence." "But you *have* it, whereas I don't. You have remarkable independence and I have none at all."

Now you want more: complete, total, totalitarian—all things I might say but don't. Can't, don't dare. Instead, I sit before her playing with my food, growing a little sick, my forehead hot with shame. No one hears us, the waiter approaches and withdraws at her commands, and yet I have an enormous feeling of shame, as if everyone there were party to my humiliation. Which proceeds. She taunts me: Wasn't I the great advocate of sexual liberation, where was all my nonsense jargon of "multiple relationships" and so forth now? I don't know. I know only that I feel the most craven fear, insecurity, even jealousy at the prospect of sharing her with Neal. She will go on seeing Neal, that is for sure, that's settled, she tells me. "Why should you possibly object?" "Of course not, how could I? I had only thought the thing could wait until I left." The inference seems to be that Neal has no interest in waiting. At Christmas she had mentioned telling him about me—"Neal understands, knows how much I love you"—but at Christmas Neal seemed a one-shot affair, nearly a joke, no rival at all. And now he is someone who makes demands, takes precedence, will be fought for. For the worst thing of all is that she makes this a fight, her fight for independence against my brutal and possessive ways. And her rhetoric is precisely the rhetoric of the woman's movement. I have somehow become "the enemy." This on the day I inspected a place where I was supposed to take up residence as the little woman, spending eons of lonely afternoons and evenings waiting for her to arrive like a masterful seigneur. The whole thing is too confusing. And I don't want to fight, lose even in peacetime, have fallen already, here in the sun and the hanging fuchsias and potted greenery, have fallen into a nightmare. The thought of going back to New York occurs only like further mortification. Lunch is over.

When I reach my car, I have to search for the keys. Have I lost them? Frantic for a second till they swim into view at the bottom of my purse. When I hold them in my hand I realize this is really all I have in California.

Lunch today. The No Name. They would not let us sit in the garden. "It's winter." When will winter stop? I wondered. "Too chilly to serve you out there." The garden shining beyond the window in the sun. We used to have such lovely afternoons there.

Squeezed into a disappointing little booth, and she touched my knee. It is what I remember afterward. My trophy. With the long wait ahead I examine it and weigh it against my losses. The winning and losing of love, the balance of points, the quick little slide into failure.

"I found that whatever the relationship, I kept turning it into marriage," Sita announces. The poet nods. She is taking a woman poet to lunch and has invited me along. "Man or woman, that was all I knew, that tight little . . ." Sita cups her hands illustrating her point. The poet nods again. I munch, agreeing and nodding, my compliance at odds with the knowledge inside me—she is talking about me. Last spring she had "married" me. Now she is all vehemence against it. My leaving for the city again, my needing it, wanting it still, taking the loft there, that was defection and betrayal.

Now Sita has seen her errors, she finds them contemptible. Marriage in any form (and it's a chameleon) is the enemy. She goes on attacking it, how it keeps cropping up. The poet nods. They agree perfectly. The poet's divorce. Her book of poems which chronicle it staring at me from the tabletop. "My daughter's going through a divorce right now." Dan, the lonely figure in cut-off dungarees I ran into in the kitchen last night, his lovely body defeated in its flesh, the naked legs, the bare vulnerable chest—Dan a divorce Pia is going through. His long, yellow hair haggard on either side of a face trying to be brave, keeping his dignity. Before me even. Dan pouring a glass of milk, his voice gently saying hello in the middle of the night. And this morning he was gone.

Only last night Dan was expelled. Martin was brought in to deliver the final blow of dislodgment, the whole execution taking place with disarming subtlety and discretion backstage in kitchen and dining room while Sita's inane committee babbled on in the living room. And when Dan balked, upstairs in the bedroom he shared with Pia, and seemed unwilling to leave, Martin, a domestic Kissinger, was forced to shuttle from whispered conference with

Pia at the dining-room table, where she was being promised school-ing and a secondhand car, up to Dan's den, where he suffered unknown humiliations as Martin came with kindly reasonableness to tell him he really must pack. And the whole thing going on side by side with a committee meeting, Sita's committee on male and female relationships. The committee busily eating a spaghetti din-ner while planning their coming weekend in the mountains. They went on earnestly about opening a new dialogue between the sexes, bringing a new respect to interpersonal relationships across sex lines. Bizarre, dreadful evening, the conjunction of their abstract jargon with the actual manipulations going on elsewhere in the house.

But even the committee had one reality: Percy. When I came into the kitchen to give a hand and make the salad, I met Percy. Black. Magnificent. Beautiful and arrogant and spoiled. The whole evening passed in an alarm of danger at the way he appropriated Sita, appropriated even the space of kitchen she stood in. And then at the Chinese table in the living room, each and every member of the committee deferring clownishly to his self-importance, to the cruel humor of his story of how he forced two young girls hitchhik-ing to get out of his car and walk the road again when he found one of them insufficiently docile. Pia watched him fascinated, later compared notes with Sita. "I've always been afraid we might flash on the same dude . . ."

"Pia will be a little blue." Sita guiding, directing, supervising at breakfast. Not all that blue either. Michael was leaving the house as I came home from the dentist midmorning. The employment agency called four times while Pia was in the shower. The radio plays. The phonograph. Pia, her long, luxurious teenage mornings. I try to type the mess I have sorted, hating it, waiting for lunch. For her body at the corner of the parking lot, the arm waving. The body I dream of seeing all day long, her body at the corner before an office, in the parking lot, or leaving her car at the curb and approaching the house in the evening. Waving now as I find a parking spot. Catching sight of this poet she has brought along to lunch. Her book of poems with photographs to match. Published it herself, a story I encourage her to tell as I consume my meal. Her friend Nancy who did the layout. Her best friend. Sita touches my knee. Her hand along the outside of my thigh. Sweet confusion. I do not move. Dare not even reciprocate by an inch. The poet breaks off with a commercial publisher, chooses her paper, takes bids from printers. Sita's hand is lovely where it is. I must make some slight move, some infinitely subtle gesture of gratitude. The hand deserts me, hesitates, returns. "What sort of paper?" "It's called Patina." I nod. "Picking out a paper could take forever, couldn't it?" "We ended up using this kind called Patina. It has to be sixty- or seventy-pound stock or the photographs come through to the other side." Knowledgeable nod. The hand on my knee as warm as a bank account. "And Nancy did all the layouts." "How did you set the type?" "We had a typesetter right here in Berkeley." Sita has decided we will have all three kinds of pie. Having coaxed me into the chocolate fudge. "Well, just to help you out," I tease. Her smile warming me like a hand.

Then in the street. Suddenly. Announcing, casually as if it were to both of us, that she is going to Davis overnight. The provost, his television film, his ego, her schedule. It's a bore but the provost is her boss. She'll stay at her friend Maud's. Just a few of them are going up from the office and the men will stay at a hotel. Neal? The poet says the street looks like New York. This is Shattuck Avenue and it has never looked like New York. Can it be Neal? Yesterday's announcement, ultimatum. Oleg's. Can she be lying to me? Would she do that, telling herself it's kinder? Accepting the ease of it, that it brings no confrontation. For I was bold, protested yesterday. The poet gurgling about this street and New York. Sita breezy about Davis, the provost, his folly. I can hardly see to walk. This street and New York, she goes on. Never in a million years, I mumble. The provost and his television film, the provost's magnificent goitered ego, chuckling in Sita's voice. They need it for a conference, preparations laid days ago, the better deal she got for them in San Francisco, the packaged crew, the provost's complete inability to judge time in media, the way he intended to drone on for thirty minutes all alone, this ham performer.

I had thought she might perhaps be late tonight, some meeting or other, was hoping for dinner out together at eight. Now instead this all-night vacancy. Immediately I try to improvise: I'll read, later go to a film. The sun on the pavement is hard and grim. "This friend of mine took me all over New York, I even rode the subway." The voice irrelevant at my side. Her cover. The reason why Sita invited her. The whole crashing news done so casually, three ladies striding along Shattuck Avenue and one happens to say, "I'll be out of town overnight and I'll go straight to work in the morning." Not even the sad ten minutes in the early dark, snuggling, the poached egg, the newspaper fragments, Emily's nightie bouncing at its place at the table, Valerie's definitive tread, Pia's wavering coffee cup. The silent ride to her office, driving her in order to have those few fruitless moments alone. None of these. Till lunch then tomorrow. Twenty-four hours. And will she even take lunch tomorrow? So hard to believe she will not be home at five this evening. The hour I wait for. This evening there will be a five o'clock and it will bring nothing at all. To endure dinner with the kids. Escaping to the movies. Reading magazines on the bed in our room upstairs, the only place I have title to.

Other times force themselves back: making love in Sacramento, my perfect little garden apartment there, the fuchsias hanging from the eaves so you could see them from the bed, even her old house on Fordham Way. This morning a woman telephoning for a lecture bureau said that she had sent me a wire at Fordham Way, the name almost buried, stinging as it bounced back from under those years. Those days, those first nights and days, the sight of our two coffee cups in the morning, the two of us standing together before a table naked, her nakedness and mine, her brown as syrup, beautiful large brown nipples, the smoothness of her skin was sense itself.

58

The other times here, even here in Berkeley last spring. Indian Rock, our house here on Indian Rock, her fortress made to treasure me against the world. Gone, invaded.

No, I am merely inflexible. Foolish, Possessive. Every vice I used to castigate in others. She's gone overnight on business, so what? Why the panic, the suspicion, the unreasoning terror? This is just a simple matter, friendship understands, takes it in stride. Can't be helped anyway, these are her responsibilities. You knew she was a very busy person. Even if you are here only a short time and get to see her rarely and under the most absurd and crowded circumstances, take it philosophically. You're in California only on a visit, it seems. A friendly visit. Enjoy it, the better climate. Pretend you're a jet-setter avoiding the New York winter or something. Take advantage of the landscape, the sunset from the Indian rocks, that sort of thing. And understand that this trip of hers is just part of her job; obligatory, boring. She is staying with Maud to avoid having to spend the night in a hotel in Sacramento. Where the men are staying. She used the plural. What men? The provost, yes. The other one? Neal? Were I to call, would Maud cover? Is she instructed? But I would never call. Not my sort of thing, despicable. Time stretches ahead.

I sit outside and write on the picnic table. Beginning this notebook. Or rather, acknowledging that I begin it. Begin? Begin what? "Begin" is inappropriate. All I'm doing is hanging on to the edge during a dizzy spell. Like that ride at Coney Island I went on a few Saturdays before I came out here. Innocent-looking thing. "Crack the Whip" or something. Round disks with cars mounted, a bench inside for two or three. And the whole car would spin about as it advanced along the larger circle, the motion itself making the light car whirl on its platform. So you'd be propelled by two forces, and the thing, which seemed matter-of-fact enough from the ground, actually built up a formidable momentum. You were whirled until your neck cracked and your stomach protested in nausea and terror. I had been insanely afraid, which delighted and amused my friends. Shut my eyes and prayed for life: just to get out of this alive.

Moments out here have the same panic. To come and find the house full of strangers and hostility and indifference. To find her changed past knowing, hardened past caring. I am lost here. Go back to New York or stay and go on suffering, experiencing whatever is to be experienced here? Maybe that's it, maybe the lure of the experience itself, painful as it might be, the experience in its learning and its sensations. If I leave I will not have had it. If I stay I can study it, even record, possess it. I hold on to the notebook and the ballpoint. As I held on to the bar in the carnival car. I am doing this, setting down words, just to survive, to fight off panic.

And the picnic table is warm. If I scribble something, I am writing rather than falling apart. Though it comes to nothing, is wasted time, doesn't even qualify as exercise or practice, it is still activity, some rag of work or doing to satisfy self-respect. Not merely pretense. "I'll be outside at the picnic table," I say as I go down the basement stairs and out into the yard, a face or two seeing me through the window, respectfully imagining that I work. When I only fiddle. Fiddle a forbidden tune: what would they think if they knew I recorded today's lunch, this morning's breakfast, this very four o'clock on a wooden picnic table, the little daisies in the grass, the rose tree still blighted with winter, or what passes for winter here? What would they think? Like a spy in the house of love, the house she claims is so full of love. Pia appears, opening a window to air a room, for a second as powerful as the appearance of a ghost. I saw her at the window of my study. Then it became her bedroom again. Not until the window is open do I realize it is another room, catching sight of her plants and her bed. There was no bed, there was my table once.

The thing was a surprise. I love carnival rides. Never been on the roller coaster, but I had negotiated almost every other offering.

And had not felt this horror since I was a child, when it was pleasurable and one courted it. So when this bit of silliness, experiment, bravado with friends turned into a nightmare, I was astonished. I felt old. It is how I feel all the time now. I turned forty last summer and it scared me. Since being here I am obsessed with death. Not the imminent death of my suicidal time, not a death you steel yourself to impose, but the "natural" and inevitable death that begins when the sense of age begins. If I was forty I was no longer young; when you are no longer young you are old. Old age is only the tedious and debilitating prelude to death, being dead while still being minimally alive. It is odd that I should feel so much older than Sita—ten years older than I, but she seems youthful and vital and alive. While I seem pale and gray and old. Losing her makes me old. It was the last love, the last conquest and romance, and losing it is losing the last chance. Having lost so much already, a marriage and a man and a home and a way of life. And now losing her, the last lover, the last resort or hope, and the time to come stretching away, so many empty years to kill before death.

I am aware that this is morbid. Desperation comes easy here. Like the old saying about running out of continent when you get to California; it's the edge, you fall off into the sea. Under the greenery and the complacency there is a lot of desperation. Everywhere people doing nothing with their lives. Pia gives off the scent of it below her studied cool, her beauty, her idleness, her outrageous camp clothes, the stockings with individual toes, each one a different color, the ridiculous six-inch wedgies she totters around on, the old silk gowns turned into afternoon dresses, the feather boas. I give it off in an old shirt and corduroys spotted with paint, pants I used to paint in at the loft, each spot a rebuke against the life I lead now. The manuscript abandoned upstairs whjle I fritter down here with a notebook. Scribbling because the compulsion is so great, because it might ease the pain, because like a primitive and magical gesture it might lance a wound, give me some control over what happens to me, upon me, beyond my control. If I could close my hand over this experience, capture it like a caterpillar or a grasshopper in a bottle, preserve it in its reality; useless to change it, one does not aspire to govern life, only to convey it accurately —accurately, but that's the problem, I will get nothing accurate, the picture blurred, lifeless. How to garner up events and persons and atmosphere I do not myself understand, am overpowered by?

And then I see her in the window. She has come back. She has come home. Finally she has returned after Davis, the night away. Her face shining on me, her arm waving. But she is not alone, some hairy hulk of a man in a denim jacket and Levi's, a beard, disheveled hair. Like another edition of Hank. But it's Mark.

"You mustn't be afraid of Mark. He's an old friend I've loved for years. Like one of my kids." "Yes, of course." I have heard all the descriptions of Mark, how they worked on the paper together when he was a journalism student and she was a housewife moving back into the job market. Then Mark's absorption into a commune of religious fanatics and LSD for the last three years, his efforts to recover his mind and his profession. "We were rookies together. You see, we're both hack journalists, it's our great bond. That we can yak away about our ratty prose. Something you'd never understand." A dig that stung more than all the endearments heaped up whenever he's mentioned.

Mark was the seventh and final personality laid on me when she came at Christmas. Not only that there were Pia and Dan and Emily, Valerie and Paul and Limbo the dog—but even someone I'd never heard of, all living in the house. This Mark Thorne person. All of them living at the house. Is he permanent or temporary? Permanent he seemed then. But he was gone when I arrived. Temporary then? All the arrangements of her life so fluid, so elusive, so provisional. And now he's back. Permanent or temporary? No one bothers to tell me.

And how he makes himself at home here. How free and easy he is, his great weight complacently settled in the fragile rocker. "I'll be taking the Toyota up to Sacramento tomorrow," he says with a coolness that appalls me. Telling her, not asking her, that he is borrowing her car. Dan destroyed her Mercedes, totaled it, but not until after Hank had damaged it to the extent of a thousand dollars' worth of repairs. When will she ever learn about lending her car to young men? Fortunately, her new little sports car is in the shop, Mark can't have it. Pia passes us on her way to an audition, a real band, a real job. She needs twenty dollars, she announces. No one moves. Sita hasn't been to the bank. Mark has no money. "Give her the twenty dollars," Sita orders me.

Later Sita handed me a letter. "This is not going to set you up quite like your mother's letter did." We sit politely in the living room opening the day's mail. Mark rocks in the rocking chair. Mother's letter with its dear, almost inexplicable last sentence—how happy she was to have Sita as a member of the family. Inconceivable once, and now finally, at this late date, approval, acceptance. The mother's gratitude reserved for someone who truly loves her daughter. Coming now when that love is running out. I unfold the letter Sita has handed me. Jaycee, under a neat letterhead and a new address, complaining in a letter which Sita has now casually passed along, Jaycee complaining that her new Karen has "turned out to be like your Kate, a nine-year-old tyrant." I catch my breath. Why did she bother to show me this? Why did Jaycee say it? Where would she get this attitude but from Sita herself? Is this what I am to Sita, this caricature reflected back through an old lover who should have known better, whose docile young follower I was once for four years. How persuasive Sita must have been. I swallow and say nothing. Mark in his rocker, witness to all of this. "Mark showed up at my office today so I came home early." Would she have done that for me? "We're going to walk down the hill to pick up some photographs. Do you want to come?" This long I have waited. To be invited along for a walk with Mark. Time with her so impossibly precious, so rare in this house. He will want her time as much as I do. She will want him along. The invitation mere courtesy and to be treated as such. With stoicism I decline.

63

When she comes back, she's buoyant. I have waited in the bedroom. Her smiles, her glances, her voice planning dinner, dispensing gaiety, relief, well-being. Should I mention Jaycee's phrase, confront her, annoy her, spoil her mood? I wait, savoring all the kindness, the charm, gobbling up the rare good humor, the warm moments. She moves to go downstairs. "I was very hurt by that phrase in Jaycee's letter." "Were you?" "Where would she get such a notion but from you?" "I can assure you, she arrived at it by herself." "I never did anything to deserve that description." "People remember things differently. But I promise you, I am not going to feel guilty for Jaycee's remarks." I know she is lying, yet I have to pretend to believe her. Either that or fight. Sita, her energy like a wall before me. She always attacks now, never stoops to defend. And this formula "not going to feel guilty," how frequent and emphatic she is with it. In New York she resorted to it whenever the summer in Italy came up. Cheerfully admitting she spent two months treating me like dirt, but it was just something she was not going to feel "guilty" over. Either something is past and we should simply forget about it, or else it is something she does not intend to feel guilty about—these two approaches: it is over or I don't care, or, better yet, I don't care and anyway it's over. She does not intend to "feel guilty." How popular this phrase, how often you hear it from friends, the moral back scratching of pop psychology. And Sita uses it like a gun. Her universal justification. Or rather, a negation of responsibility altogether, a refusal to discuss it. Yet what strict lines of conduct I am held to. For what offense am I a nine-year-old tyrant? What does one do to undo such a reputation?

After she leaves I try to imagine this view of myself. Is it true? Am I wrong at every juncture, and the two of them right? Or rather Sita's view of me as passed on to Jaycee, who wouldn't have thought of it herself but is delighted to apply it to her own friend when the affair begins to give way under her. Because Jaycee wants to come West and Karen, upon whom she has pinned all her hopes, is backing out. To be malicious, she compares her to me. To me, as Sita sees me and describes me to her friends? Maybe this is who I really am. I don't know myself any more, have no self to know, am only someone with two suitcases ready to pack who seems not to know when she's unwelcome.

And Mark making himself very at home downstairs. I don't think I can face that just now. Take a little walk up to the rocks and watch the sun go down. Meeting little Emily on the stairs. "Do you want to go with me?" "No, I want to watch television." Just as well, I prefer to be alone. I can't cope any more, don't understand, have lost my way and sense of direction. In every contest between us she wins. Since she has nothing to lose, is in no way anxious to keep me, has all the power base in herself, in the others, her own children, her own guests. It is impossible to quarrel. Impossible also to disagree.

I will be quiet then. Well-mannered. Faultless. Live down my past. I have put on the long dress she admired the other night. As I pass the kitchen, the sound of an ice tray being opened in the sink. For Mark's drink. I will be self-sufficient, entertain myself, walking to the rocks in a long dress, this absurd marginal figure staying on inexplicably in a house full of people with whom I have nothing in common, in distant California, asking myself as I go along what on earth I am doing here. Trying to remember I used to live here. Or trying instead to pretend this is a vacation, a short visit with a friend, part of an ongoing connection, a love affair that mellows for years on into middle age. Or—see it one day at a time, the alcoholic's slogan.

It's not that I like sunsets, I assure myself. The banal, tomato-paste sentiment of them. Only that the end of the day, its death in the sea, the explosion of color—is something against which I have no resistance. Even on days when it's forbidden by pressing activities, the disinclination of companions, the lack of a view, even on those days I can feel it coming, sense it in the light each moment through the afternoon, know its arrival, the gold of its imminence, the rose of the act like a vulva, the red aftermath. I watch on, stolid through the chill. The usual crew of rock-climbing enthusiasts. The six-year-olds, the lovers. I in my solitude, my outlandish dress.

And walking back I am astounded to see her coming toward me on the opposite sidewalk. If I had only waited, she might have joined me. I have committed another blunder. "I have made you a martini." "You did? How wonderful." And it is wonderful. That she has done this for me. Like a thousand-year plenary indulgence, Sita hating martinis and making one; martinis, the vice of a New Yorker, a drink I had no idea she even knew how to compose. "When you came downstairs I looked around and couldn't find you." "I'm sorry." How sorry—if I had only known, for in my treachery I had imagined that it was Mark's ice I heard in the kitchen. What folly, it was mine. My martini. "Let's hope it's still all right. I summoned all my bartending skills and you know what they are." Her laugh, her arm comfortably tucked in mine. The warmth of her body coming blissfully through my dress.

At breakfast Pia laughs and tells me she blew it. "You'll never believe what happened. You know I left here early. So first I went by to visit a few friends. Nobody home. So I went to this favorite bar of mine. Bartender says, This is your big night, honey. Buys me a corsage. Then this guy comes in that I really like. We start to split a bottle of mescal. Mescal . . . whee." She is lost, remembering it in the cigarette smoke she exhales in revery. I sit off to her side, she doesn't see me. "Never tasted mescal before. First thing I know, I'm throwing up in the john. Never got to the audition at all. Called up the band, drunk as a louse, gave them some fool excuse. Blew the whole damn thing. Can you believe it?" Now she turns toward me, she'll give it to me in the face. I mustn't wince. "Blew the whole damn thing. Can you believe it?"

I can. All too easily. Even the smell of mescal. The toilet and the air in the toilet and Pia's special fragile beauty humiliated there.

The other night it was just the two of us at dinner, and Emily. Dan was gone, Sita in Davis. Pia her most delightful self, pleasing, pretty, all the talk of Janis, Pia having been one of her set, how she lived, how she died. Billie Holiday records. The biography of Bessie Smith Pia loaned me to take to bed. Making dinner together, talking, enjoying her imitations of Billie, her love of the blues. I could read all the jazz-singer signs, the hypnotic fascination with danger, the blaze, and then the sinking out of sight. Booze. Drugs. Assorted suicides. The tradition solid enough now to demand self-immolation. And the thing expected somehow by all those who stand near, manipulating, participating, making it ready. "Those people around Janis, they needed her, needed her to give 'em dope. They needed everything she did, who she was. They thought *they* were Janis—yeah, that's what it came to, they were what she was. But she's the one who crashed. They didn't. They got out. Even that chick Sunshine, and I'll tell you, she's one strung-out chick."

After dinner she got out her high-school yearbooks and showed them to Emily. "This is what your mommy looked like." Pia in teased hair, bobby socks, cheerleader, American-girl pretty. The child fascinated, entranced by the myth of her mother as I have seen Pia entranced by Sita's baby book issued by Queen Elena, royal arms commemorating the beginnings of a new crop of nobles, pictures of an Italian childhood, summers at Lake Como, the count her father looking distinguished and appropriate, her mother florid and diva-like, Sita dark and homely yet somehow haunting, compelling, posing in absurd ballet postures, tutus, the long legs, the anguished face of self-conscious childhood imposed upon in some grotesque way by the world, yet half believing, more than half believing the fantasy of her silk roses, her magical shoes, her voile skirts, believing so earnestly perhaps that the betrayal on her face is not that they make her do it but that she cannot live there always. How different the stolid American face of Pia, grinning from out of a cluster of her classmates' smug Southern Californian crew cuts. "To a swell gal," "To a dreamy date," "To a girl with a great

67

future," "To a gal with real talent." "Is this you, Mommy, is this really you?" "I sure look different, don't I?" "Is this you, Mommy?" "Yes, Emily, I just told you so." The child loving the mystery of it, that the almost plump, almost woman, almost child blur of the photograph is her own slender beautiful wonderful mother.

The mysteries of mothers and daughters. Hard to believe that Pia is Sita's daughter, so fair she is, so Anglo. "They are both Wasps," she always says; "only Emily is like me." Emily with her dark eyes. Strange deep child eyes searching the glossy pages of meaning as she searches everything and everyone. Already orphaned. It is part of Pia's new regime of "doing her thing" to send Emily away to her father's mother, "the other grandmother," as she's called. Emily's father, Pia's first husband, was a musician on drugs, long since disappeared. "I never put him down in front of Emily, and Margaret's a good woman." Pia calling long distance, asking permission, making the arrangements. "You're gonna go on a trip, Emily, up to Gramma Margaret's, aren't you excited?" The child uncertain, already afraid, half in love with the adventure, half terrified of leaving her mother, Dan whom she calls Daddy, Sita, her world here. "Who'd ever believe that Joe and Louise would ever break up?" Pia crows, "Just goes to show." Margaret has told her that her other son and daughter-in-law are getting a divorce and she has both their children with her too. Seems like a lot for an older woman to handle, Pia speculates, but nothing will discourage or deter her now; it will give Emily two playmates and Oregon's a healthy place—"They have snow there now, Emily."

Hedy comes for breakfast. Pia repeats her story, a joke almost, a triumph. "Pia just plain bombed out last night. She just never got there," talking of herself in the third person. "Pia's your all-time fuck-up. Missing in action." Hedy has to laugh, so do I. The sporting and total admission, the absolute vulnerability, the summary judgment. We are left with nothing to say, she disarms criticism. And the whole performance, even its reenactment, is so classic, so steeped in tradition. I urge her to call back. She says they'll let her try again. Call them, I say, get another chance at it, you'll do fine. She says she'll call them, but she doesn't move. Pete comes in. Jon-Jon wakes up on the living-room floor. I escape upstairs. What am I doing here?

I put down one bag of groceries and go back for the rest. Valerie springs to help me. "My God, what did you spend?" I grin and she hugs me. I have shopped up a storm, feeling proud and a little silly as she marvels over the steaks, the Chateaubriands, the roasts, the chickens, the vegetables, the fruit. "I'm so glad to have you here," she says, "and not just for the food. It's good you're with us, I'm glad you came." It's not the first time she's said it. The other day, up in our bedroom, I came upon her chatting with Sita on our bed, mother- and daughter-in-law, or since Paul and Valerie aren't married, Sita invented the term "daughter-in-love." I remember a second's jealousy, seeing Sita sprawled on the bed talking with this beautiful blond young amazon. I went to the closet to search for something, perhaps to undress before bed. Sita got up to answer the phone. And Valerie lay on the bed and talked to me, saying it was so good I was there, how glad of it she was. I was astonished, overcome with gratitude, humbled before her goodness and generosity. So as her healthy size and big child's vitality shrieks and marvels at this vast windfall of groceries, I believe her. Somehow Valerie has accepted me. And Emily. I will keep trying, I will win them all.

The numbers rise and fall. Hedy, Pete, Jon-Jon, et al. have finally departed. But the next day another of Pia's friends, Pigtail, arrives. Days and nights of giggles and stories and reminiscences, the first mythical commune on Beech Street, the perfection of its chaos, the fate of each of its members. Pia ignores the employment agencies, they call to no effect, she is busy. And besides, she did go to one interview and the guy made her spend several hours typing his briefs "to try her out" and then never paid her. She has figured out that the salary he was offering was only three dollars more than unemployment. "Throw in the carfare and it's just the same thing." She gestures, droll, pathetic, vulnerable. "The whole thing's a rip-off. Life's a rip-off." Pigtail chuckles and they go back to entertaining each other, waiting for Michael, discussing last night's party, admiring a new pair of shoes. From time to time Pia wanders in to interrupt me and smoke a cigarette. "Art's very tough. You just gotta do it," she sighs. I encourage, buoy, prop up her confidence, remind her to call the band. She's going to, she'll get around to it soon. I must be subtle, patient.

Paul is removed. Stumbling in the round of his sleep and his toil and his inlay puttering and guitar tinkering. But he practices very little now, seems shadowy, a figure forever leaving for or being retrieved from work. He and Valerie spend most of their time going to and from Marin County, where his job is, where she goes to school. His conversation consists of jokes about his coming promotion to busboy, an elevation he takes very seriously. And fond, phony male-chauvinist jokes at Valerie's expense. There is no reaching Paul, this big gawky boy in long hair and glasses. But with all the others I will keep on trying, the trying an effort to bring back Sita herself. Through all those that she has put between us. I must survive in her. And if I win I have her again.

She snuggles my leg under hers. Solomon Grundy's with its great windows onto the sea. The old feeling. The old place. Like the night last week we had dinner here, talked about the first time in Sacramento, becoming lovers. That long night, lighting one cigarette after another. She was awake too. Her trips to the bathroom. Seeing her body in and out of the corridor, looking down the dark hall afraid to stir, to turn on the light. Hoping she'd ask me back into the living room, roll another joint, make it possible to come together. The barest sheen of her back floating away into the gloom, returning to her bedroom. What was I, crazy? Arrive here in the afternoon and already full of designs on my hostess. She laughed, remembering it. "Hospitality, you know, can't seduce the visiting faculty member on the first night." So we waited for the second. Waiting to be sure that I wanted her, was not acting out of some mere impulse toward a stranger, some perverse pity for her age, that she was older, waiting till I knew certainly it was just her age that I wanted, that this stranger was the very ripe and intriguing experience I chose. Sober, awake, with the whole day to think about it, to be sure. That I did not wrong her with philandering, curiosity. So we waited till the second night. And then it happened as if by accident, each of us ready on her side, happened in the middle of a sentence, sitting on the sofa talking politics a mile a minute. Suddenly our mouths kissing. I remember her voice telling me to come to bed. Like fate. Sent, knowing it was a finality like some sort of seal. Went anyway, wanting it. Then the astonishment of her lovemaking, the force of it. Nearly begging off, sure I couldn't bear it. But then I could, could just barely hold on through the terrible force of her hands, the power inside me nearly pain, at the brink of fainting, coming far ahead of will or realization, catching my breath only to drown again. Utterly commanded. Overwhelmed. The mastery of those hands—and yet her tenderness, the woman's passion of her. Falling asleep bewildered. No woman had ever fucked me before. The force of a man. I was hooked.

A sailboat goes by through the big windows of night. Ghostly gray in the black. I have never seen one in the dark. Daytime's serene shape, the white sails that flock around Grundy's in the sun are phantoms now. Her leg nestles next to mine, our knees warm and knowledgeable with each other. A mood perfect at the end of day, a day described, discussed, even the office settled. Even Pia's audition. Sita is disappointed, disgusted; all the times Pia has let her down. Even a pretense of hardness—she'll wash her hands of it. I break my rule of absolute detachment (it is none of my business and very dangerous to intervene) and make one suggestion—that the emphasis stay right on the issue, the audition, that Pia make another try and carry through. The point is not to hassle her but to get her started with a band. The knee squeezes me, I am content. Beloved as I used to be, cherished even. Because she is so anxious that I like the little Japanese restaurant she has picked for us tonight. "Finish your drink, I'm so excited to see what you think of the place." As I turn around to get my sweater, I see the sailboat again. Like a ghost in the pitch. Grim somehow, some strange and unexpected warning.

Pia slouches into breakfast. Emily fidgets over her food. Valerie storms in on us as she always does, the swirl of her red skirt, the definite strokes of the Cossack boots. Emily grumbles. Valerie scolds. "Keep out of this, Valerie," Pia shouts. "The kid is spoiled, she's got to learn," Valerie says and goes on scolding. Suddenly something is flying through the air. Valerie ducks, the cream pitcher hits the door frame and falls to the floor. We are all astonished. I cannot recognize Pia, know only her vagueness, her prettiness, her "cool," her vulnerability, her teen aura and idleness, her slippery promises. But never her temper. Raging now and still shouting at Valerie to leave the child alone, it's her child, don't you dare interfere. "Peace, peace," I say, trying to laugh, trying to make it a joke. Paul begins shouting on Valerie's side. Sita goes off to work.

That day I drove to Sacramento to see one of the prisoners in Folsom. There was still quarreling when I left. And when I came back home, there was no one. Until the phone rang—Pia from a bar explaining in her circular way that Paul and Valerie had left. There had been another fight in the afternoon. Pia hit Valerie, slugged her. "And I'm not sorry either." Though she sounds sorry and more than a little worried. "Don't tell Mom, or tell her just a little bit, make it easy for her." "Sure." The familiar "don't tell," when she borrows money from me, when she's late, when things go wrong and Pia can't "get it together," as she puts it. "Where are you?" "Emily and I are in a bar. Mom had to make a quick trip to L.A. and she wants you to pick her up at Oakland Airport at seven instead of eight. Do you know the way?" "She wrote down the instructions. Pia, what happened?" "So she kept going on about Emily and I couldn't take it, so I let her have it. Then Paul gets into it, my own brother, and he starts hitting me. And then they left. It was just crazy." "Where did they go?" "To Marin, Valerie's brother's got a place out there. I guess that's where they'll stay till they get a place of their own."

Paul and Valerie's closed bedroom door. Once another room, once a library. One of Emily's innumerable paintings decorates it. "I love Paul and Valerie," herself portrayed as a princess of the sun, bestowing blessings. Now there is war. Driving Sita home, I mention the thing offhandedly, gently, as if it were trivia. Just a spat between the kids. And fail to get the point across, though I break the fall. Pia does it, sitting disconsolately on the sofa as we come in. Crying. Weeping her daughter's tears while Sita strokes and comforts. I am in the way. I make a drink and sit in the kitchen alone, giving them time and place. An hour later they are still rapt in their own sorrow, Sita not even remonstrating, Pia contrite, remorseful, the sadness of years in them. I will cook them a good chicken dinner, roasting and basting the bird while reading in the kitchen on a little stool. They protest they are not hungry. I am chagrined, but go on, since I have started. And at dinner they are hungry and revived and Pia stops weeping to eat. I am useful, my patience is rewarded.

The rest is confusion. Our commune is over, ended suddenly in one afternoon. Confusing how I regret Paul and Valerie's leaving, much as I had wanted them gone, much as I had never wanted to live in a commune at all. Yet there's a little sorrow in its passing. Sita's sorrow not least of all. It had meant so much to her, living with her children. Yet it seemed to mean so little to them. And the irony of it all vanishing the one afternoon I was not there to

73

intervene, perhaps to save it. Though I had wanted them gone—
no wish of mine, no preference or claim had ever had any effect on
them—yet what a relief that I had nothing to do with it.

The commune is over. Foolishly, I remember all the food. All
the food I bought that we will never eat, all the dinners, the guitars,
the music. Little Emily goes north soon. Dan is long gone. I feel
Sita's grief as she gets ready for bed, her exhaustion, her tears.
"Maybe they will come back." Though I want them away, I would
have them come back for her. She looks old, beaten. I feel an
enormous pity, and enormous tenderness. And am helpless to help.
Tomorrow I go to Texas for a speech. "I'll call Martin," she says.
As she always does, Martin still somehow the husband and father
even after four years of divorce. Martin, lately her financial agent,
who writes her checks since she has decided she will give up trying
to handle money at all. My beloved administrator cannot balance
her checkbook and is heavily in debt. Martin will bank her checks,
pay all the bills, get her out of debt, and begin to force her to save.
She will pay me back for the trip to Europe, the three hundred
dollars she borrowed after Christmas until that magazine in L.A.
paid her for her article on Latin women. I listen, not really expecting her ever to pay me, but touched that she thinks of it, glad she
will begin saving, glad there is Martin to protect her. My arms
around her tired and trying to absorb her tiredness, her grief.
Wishing there were love in her shoulders, feeling only the solid and
alienated flesh.

I have been away to Texas for a day, and landing, I remember what
she will look like. Standing in so many airport lines to meet me.
Two years now. Even that first time in Sacramento when I came
down the escalator and saw her, a stranger in a raincoat waiting
at the bottom. With a little bouquet of flowers, which surprised and
embarrassed me a bit. How she used to tell everyone about that
escalator, that she expected me to arrive with picket signs, fierce,

74

formidable. And instead I was small and gentle and wore a long dress under a peacoat. The peacoat, the dress, almost objects of veneration as she named them, telling people over and over how she loved me, how from that moment . . . Remembering now, landing from Texas after a speech and away overnight, remembering everything. San Francisco below me in a glory. Remembering another landing here two years ago, back from a trip to England and so fatuously in love with her, the first separation of any length, circling over San Francisco imagining Dante: that I would be a poet and this my home, exiled to a city fairer than Florence. And she would be waiting, the euphoria of that day. Then the breakdown that summer, an autumn away from each other and estranged, the break with Fumio in the winter, coming to her that spring to live together. Shards of the past, each so bitter because then is so much better than now. Remembering the Sita of now only as a dull ache, the new distance impossible to overcome. Remembering that she will be homely. That I will wonder all over again why I love her. Only after falling into that face again, making it beautiful, necessary, only after moments, the first almost-embarrassed greeting, the hug before the eyes of others. She will stand there looking old, that raincoat, those shieldlike alienating glasses, tense, awkward. Sita, my person to be singled out from the other persons. My person, at first strange, uninviting. I am not proud of her, can hardly remember her. And then she is upon me. And in a moment beautiful, the center of my world, and I am a satellite or a child tagging along to the luggage place. Already devoured in her face, my eyes turned up, hungry, utterly persuaded.

But not yet. Still separate in my seat. Why am I out here, the West, San Francisco coming into sight? Why the West? When I am a New York artist. Why pursuing this thing already over? Knowing that. Having just had a day and a night in Texas to think it over. That the time of love is past, the span of it that was creative, renewing. As if it were a line on a graph, a strip of fabric in a pattern, limited, mere inches long. And now what? The aftereffect, dependency, habit, the fear of endings. All endings. Time staring, my fortieth year looking toward death.

Last night I fell asleep in a motel room with the television still on. Hours then and this morning before bureaus and mirror facing my failure, my wasting life. Hours before mirrors and in showers deciding I'm getting fat, I'm not getting any work done, my life has no direction, I'm spending too much money. If only there were a job, activity, any usefulness. Motel drapes, motel bedspread, motel view of granite Dallas. The trip and the distance were no ease, only a better vantage to discover and assess, admit finally that I am lost. I have lost faith. Give up and go back to teaching? Could you even get a job? Watching the woman who has a job that afternoon, polite little luncheon at a graduate student's apartment, the professor on her sofa, describing her career, her rise, her years in service. Earlier, sitting in her grand office, watching kids troop to classes, familiar files of figures crossing lawns, the sounds of them in hallways, their faces looking up eagerly in classrooms. Electricity of people, exchange, youth. That teaching could now appear a life of action! You have to write and live alone to believe this, envy it, hunger for those student bodies on the lawn.

Sita surprises me by wearing her mink. A dress and high heels. I am always bewildered by how many women she is. Intrigued by it, captivated by this. In fact, she is all the women I never was; matron, mother, socialite, administrator, glamorous, the femininity my mere female never encompasses. Someone who can wear a mink and has lived in the suburbs and had a Mercedes and called it her ransom money after twelve years of marriage. "Prerevolutionary," I tease her about the mink. She has come directly from a luncheon in the city, Chicana bureaucrats with reactionary opinions who needed to be impressed by the mink. "How are things at the house?" "Martin came down yesterday and we had a conference. Paul and Valerie came over from Marin and made peace with Pia." I hold my breath, watching the road, feeling her expert speed.

76

"Are they coming back?" "Oh no, they're gone. But at least we all talked it over." How easily she accepts it, how serenely and philosophically. Her favorite project, her greatest hope. Having all her children at home. I was nothing compared to that. And now Dan exiled. Paul and Valerie defected. Emily sent to Oregon tomorrow. How suddenly it emptied.

She analyzes the combatants: Pia's stubbornness, which will not even apologize, Valerie's immaturity; the struggle between them for Paul. "Martin just said it right out loud, I was very impressed by him, Martin just told Pia right to her face that when a man takes a mate, that comes before his family." I am amused by the heroic biblical ring. How it impresses her. How she never sees the irony in our case or notices how firmly she put her family before me; not a mate in Martin's time-honored tradition, merely an awkward eunuch before the sacred straight conventions, a lover somehow invalidated, invisible. I cannot tell her this, cannot comment on Pia or Valerie or anyone. None of my business. The miles speed by, the bridge, Berkeley's lights. Just as before I left, the same problem returns—having nothing to say. Or too much to say, so much of it unsayable. The rare jewel-like moments we are alone, having no use for them.

And inside the house, the same dismal incompetent silence. I lie back on the pillows. Pillows we ordered for the apartment back on Derby Street, the first months in Berkeley when I played her decorator, her "New York faggot," we called me, loving the joke, the excitement of doing a place for her. No more of Chiquita's gypsy caravan, the countess would emerge into her own, a polar-bear rug to make love on in front of the fireplace, the works. Another time. It is painful even to drive near Derby Street now when I go through Berkeley. Now she sits in the rocking chair with the antimacassar, one of the gypsy things acquired since. Pia sprawls on the davenport watching Emily making the early-bird Valentines which are her last hold on this place and must be given out at school tomorrow since that will be her last day. Talk is

77

desultory, fragmented by Pia's phone calls. Should she go to that party tonight? Or make arrangements for Emily's trip, calls to Martin for the plane fare, Sita's report on today's conference? I am bored. Nearly to headache. I look in my martini. Why did I come back? Sita goes to heat up some clam chowder. In a while I go in to sit by her at the dining-room table.

"Campbell's. Tastes like nothing at all." I reach over and taste it, my arm resting on the edge of the table. I look down and see my gold watch face up on my wrist. Surprised a second later to feel her fingers caressing my forearm. The strange excitement of it, the power of this little statement. The day after tomorrow we go to Mendocino for a long weekend. Driving from the airport, she said it would definitely be her last free weekend till April. Classes start on Monday and she is teaching one herself in San Francisco on Monday nights. And on every weekend till April there is a conference, a special session, something. It is still January. I listen, furious. The satisfied, almost smug manner of her announcement, almost sadistic.

Driving up to Mendocino. The rain persistent, right somehow that it should be in the rain. Certain landmarks, the packing plant with its block-letter assertion FORMULA-FED BEEF, and the big, unreasoning steer's head painted along the rooftop as you leave Berkeley. The industrial detritus of Richmond, and then the hills begin. We are silent, always and awkwardly. But in the hills and as the redwoods began, she asked me a frightening question, "Where are you now in your life?" I could not answer, hated to add it all up —the series of defeats, breakdown, separation, and now this. She went on, answering the question for herself. Now Martin was in charge of her affairs. How he would get her out of debt and begin her savings. "I've always been improvident, have it and spend it. But I begin to realize I will get old." I see her old, and worry. I see myself old, and despair. Age, death, the subjects of my continuous anxiety now; different from the suicide trip, when death was something actual, something you could choose and impose on yourself if you had the courage. Now it only stalks, taking forever to get here, but certain, finally certain. I went through forty years of life convinced I would live forever. And at forty discovered I would die, and have been waiting for it since. This is stupid, unreal, I keep reminding myself. But there is nothing else to look forward to, nothing else to expect. My art defeats me and escapes, love and the comfort of another in time and through age have eluded me twice, first with Fumio and now with her. There is no certainty, only solitude waits for me. Art is not enough in life and my art

79

deserts me. Eating alone in a loft on the Bowery, evening on that mean street. Where will I go when I am old? She goes on talking at my side, planning her life, in charge of it, resolute. "Maybe Martin will buy that piece of land in Napa he's always talking about. And we'll all end up there, even his new lady, Laura." I cringe at climbing into the fold, imagining a pastoral forcibly shared with the kids and who knows what new lovers.

Though she has asked me to talk to her, to be full and open, it is impossible. The muteness has taken me. And the fear—if she had any notion of my desperation she would never ask. The sight of it would sicken her. The thing is obscene. Not only have I lodged unfair hopes in her, made her my reason for living—which is unforgivable—but the paucity of my other resources, my bankrupt personhood. Artists without work are naked, hungry, frantic. We do not live merely to live as she does—and how I envy her this—but for some other purpose beyond us. Merely instruments of our purpose, we are like corpses when it fails us, might as well be dead. Even feel we deserve to die. My yearning for suicide was always just the imposition of that sentence.

I do not even know how I will live in the time to come. I have money for only three years, and when it is gone there is no more to come. And then what? Teaching? Risky, I am too old for the tenure requirements, too subversive, have slipped their harness too long. There are no jobs now, and though I love teaching, I hate it too, the collar around the neck, the separation from one's own work. To grow old teaching? When I had had such high hopes? Books, sculptures, drawings. The redwoods going by, and I would like to scream that I am barren, ended. Something is wrong when you feel such despair amid such beauty. There is an inch of snow on the road as we climb a pass. She talks of turning back, and I tease her, desperate under my banter to challenge her into going on. The road dips down again into the huge mysterious trees. We are safe, we will get there.

And our host, a gnome named Quigley, has prepared all and built a fire for us in our cabin. Large windows onto a long lawn and a strip of highway and then the terrible sea and the rocks. The rain, always the rain, but never mind, we could not do better, here is our nest, our palace, our happiness. We have champagne and cheese and nuts, a table of hors d'oeuvres. It will be wonderful, it will be magical, one of the great weekends of our lives. Mendocino —the name already tearing at me, knowing I will remember this place forever, whether happy or wretched, to remember happiness years and years into death. These two brief days she will give me, this place, the mountains and rocks and ocean, the little sea town, part artist part tourist, even this silly but superbly appointed motel. Each cashew on the table, each sip of champagne, each glance of her eyes, now finally looking and seeing me, lost in their brown and their power when she opens them to me.

We look away to the lawn and are astounded. Three deer. Sudden. Already their last movement comes to conclusion as we see them. Now motionless. Each in its place. Still with the stillness of silence. Unmoving. Looking toward us. Three. And she and I. There are the five of us in the world. And the sea. The three strange beasts on the grass, stolid and magical, their heads up, listening in the coming gloom of evening. We watch them until we can barely see them. Cars go by on the road, but the deer do not turn and flee, their heads down occasionally grazing, first one and then another lost in the coming dark, then found again. These three creatures, our omen, our supernatural occurrence, our miracle given to us. And we know them for this, both of us, aware that their appearance marks a moment, blesses it, holds it aloft and still.

Then it is dark. And then we make love. Long and slow, and quick and hot and hard, taking her gently as she takes me fiercely, the moment waited for arriving at last and perfect. We are entire and made whole, one in the unique separateness of us, each for a moment beyond self into a further place beyond reason and finally even beyond consciousness into a distant and momentary peace. Her flesh so warm and delicate, so fragile and aromatic, smooth and golden and brown, so unutterably dear to me, consumed in it, seen as vividly with my eyes closed as open, touched as unerringly with my mind as with my hands, putting all the concentration of passion into the tips of my fingers, entering her knowing she wants me and has made room, made the way smooth and liquid, hungers for my tongue as it thirsts to drink her, devour and never finish, that very blossom once blasted, damaged, the rapists, the desert—"they had to sew my clitoris back on," she told me savagely that first time, "you'll find me a little beat up," warning me gallantly —but how precious and even dearer to me for its terrible wound, moved with what particular care and compassion, the most reverential gentleness, itself the most determined passion, for I would overwhelm it with tenderness, make up for, compensate, heal and erase the scars, the hurts, all the hurts of your life, lady, dearest and loveliest and most wronged of women, mine now, this moment entirely mine, coming as she comes, with the sheer force of adoring her.

And then she sleeps. I am quiet, a guard over her rest, her protector. I read, write, fiddle. The hours go by and still she does not wake. Time for dinner. The room gets cold. The fire has gone out. I work at restarting it. It is dismal in the dark and I dare not turn on the light. The fire cannot be rekindled; the rain falls. Euphoria passes into comfort and finally into boredom. She has left me, escaping into sleep, as distant now as long before I had her. This is a dull way to spend a vacation—sitting alone in a cold dark room. I could wake her, but it seems unkind. I try again to read and cannot concentrate, find the book tedious after ten pages. Disappointment sets in, the briefness of it, happiness but a moment within hours of waiting. The rain incessant, the room prepared for a feast that does not take place, or took place in an instant and is now over, though the trappings remain, and I, the solitary guest, still expect a party.

I did not want to buy a Mendocino poster. Attractive as it was, haunting as its blurred old-time photograph of seascape and summer clapboard, recalling Provincetown at the other side of the world. Knowing already when I saw the thing that I would hang it in my loft, after carting it absurdly across a continent, hang it there, near a door, or in the kitchen, somewhere where I'd see it all the time, where it would confront me every moment the rest of a lifetime, reminding me, mercilessly, endlessly reminding me—of this time, this slow-falling rain, this near-happiness, this near-despair, this semblance of lovers, of secret lovers appearing to be friends, inspecting the town, the little art shops, the galleries, affecting an interest, desperately bored, desperately interested, cheerfully going on in the mud to the next event, the town workshop, the gallery up at the fork of the road, inspecting the kilns or the painting room or the junk jewelry. I am disguising my snobbery, my contempt for most of the art. She is disguising whatever—her contempt, ennui, the thousand secret places of her soul that hide from me. And in a shop at the end of the lane I saw the poster again, and it was harder to renounce the impulse, ignoring it only with an effort. Curing myself with the man's collection of trivia and old phonograph records, just as I pretended to be absorbed by the old lady's clock collection on the main street, the china and saucers and matching fabric, Sita holding my arm and admiring them as if we were two old maids who doted on complete sets. The part of her that does. The part of her that would settle in the house in Berkeley and continues to remind me to buy her Minton when I go to England. A minor character. Not the adventurer, not even the patient and long-suffering woman who stifles her yawn in antique shops today. Standing now in this bearded fellow's shop, counter crowded with knickknacks, camp revivals, trying not to look at the poster, the picture haunting me from the back of my head. No, no reminders. It will be over and gone and I will not be tortured with a picture. And if it does not end I will not need the

83

picture to remind me. And because it will end, if not now, then someday, it would be a suicidal act to buy that damn photograph. She has no idea what goes on in my mind. I appear to be interested in a poster and then grow ambivalent, indecisive, full of pauses and hesitations over something that costs only two dollars and could never be important in any case. But if I bought it, every summer of my life it would remember me, destroy me. And winters? Don't even think of winters. If I hung it in my studio on the third floor? Make it impossible to paint, fill me with regret and despair and self-loathing every time I saw it. No, damn it, not that bloody poster. So, saying nothing and showing only my quiet, futile, ineffectual self, we leave.

Meals. Meals are a problem. Last night, when she finally woke, we ate seafood at a little joint we found in the pouring rain, the car hardly able to swim on when the neon appeared miraculously by the side of the highway, authentic roadhouse, fresh fish and sawdust floors, echoing of Provincetown and summers. But the meal made gloomy by our silence, her torpor, our pretended romance, our counterfeit holiday excitement. And at breakfast this morning, taken at the most colorful local pub—the place full of beards and mackintoshes and the deliberate wintry cool of the city types, flowers sewn on their jeans, all alarmingly young and hip—at breakfast we read the papers and I cringed at the display of our silence, our conspicuous pall. Warming up finally, she reads me bits from the Mendocino paper: the Wilsons' boy is back from Vietnam, the Gregorys' brother and sister-in-law are visiting from Oklahoma, Mrs. Franklin ran into Mr. Franklin while backing the car out of the garage, fracturing his shoulder and six ribs. Then come stories of her life on the little paper in Folsom when she started back to work again, emerging from her suburban era: one of a battle she won against the mayor. She is alternately tough and pathetic, whimsical and vindictive as she tells it. "I'd love to live out here and work for a little paper like this," growing lyric, sentimental, rural, pastoral, adventurous—when a moment ago she was herself in her mink of ten years ago, taking on a man rich enough to own a private plane and crash in it. She goes on considering life here, fantasizing: sneakers, jeans, and a shack, all you really need. I find myself falling into it. "Wouldn't you miss the city, San Francisco?" "You can go there any time you need, it's not far." "Four hours." "Nothing, you wouldn't even miss it." I look around the room at the creatures in their rural uniforms of commune hip, the newspapers spread on every table. No. Shacks at the end of dirt roads, broken-down cars, leaky roofs. No. Yet listening to her I'm almost hypnotized, her voice rhapsodizing about the sea. I would have her alone here. No, I'd go crazy.

Meals. Now the great meal, Saturday night, the planned and deliberate and dressed-for meal. Finding too late we've taken the wrong advice. Quigley should be strangled for recommending this vulgarity. Heavy Germanic pretension, compliments of the owner, but the rest is the most awful American falsity. Even plastic ferns, we grimace at each other. But it is already too late, the waiter has us in hand. Even then I want to protest, develop an emergency, decide we've left the car lights on, anything to get out of here. If she'd back me up. But she is philosophic, content. The meal is not the ceremony for her that it is for me, the crisis, the sacrament. Only something to get through. Dull, spiritless, each trying to rally. I waver between tears of disappointment, suppressed, and game attempts at humor, the best wine. There is even a residue of anger under the despair, resentment, hatred even for the waste of it. Meals used to be such feasts.

But then she disarms me, picking up some liniment at the store on the way home, she will rub my sore shoulder, she will massage my back. First a melancholy little drink in the hotel basement, where a nervous boy plays very difficult blues guitar almost well. "He was out of his mind on speed, couldn't you tell?" she announces as we climb the stairs. And again I am dumbfounded by her blasé, almost cynical worldliness. Then the great maternal comfort of her massage, her repeated tenderness, saying over and over how it pleases her to take care of me, nurse me, touch me, make me well. "Even this is a kind of making love," she says, her voice smooth and liquid as a caress, as the flesh of her body, as the flesh of her hands kneading my hurt muscles.

I realize as she falls asleep that it was a substitute for making love, a way of avoiding it, begging off without ever quite having to refuse, ruse and techniques I know as well as any woman, a tactic we are all familiar with, find useful with men. The startled humiliation of knowing that she has just used it on me.

I watch her sleep. Thinking of all the women she is, knowing all of them, loving them and long past judging the survivor, floozy, countess, liar and woman of honor, cornered animal and proud beauty. Speaking of her past, it is always of lovers she has left—reluctantly but necessarily—rather than further endure their wrongs. This pattern is held forth as a covert warning for the future. "My beautiful exits," she always says. "I make great exits," head held high, part parody, part melodrama. As if her whole life were a matter of walking out only because she had to, to save face, because pride was the most important thing, after all, the final thing, the only thing. Despite the occasional nearly vulgar little jokes on "class" and "classy," her rare, oblique, satiric references to her birth, this fanatic pride is the only proof that she still believes in it. And even the "we" in her "beyond everything we are proud" is indistinct: at times Latin, at times the downtrodden immigrant. Or it could be the royal "we" of the noble, Sita, drawn to her height, the head and shoulders swanlike and regal as she floats away from some mere American mortal. And I had thought each of them was a cad, knew they were unworthy, and smiled with relief that with me finally and at last she was appreciated, deserved, the connection passionate and permanent, just and immutable. Wincing at my folly now, a naked woman in a motel room, banal, ordinary, discarded.

The past like a lost glory assailing me, bitter even to remember.

Sacramento and then Berkeley and Derby Street, the bedroom I had made for her like a lavender powder puff, its great white fur rug, its endless aromatic bed like a white breast, a room perfumed with sensuality. Breakfasts she brought me in bed, her delight in serving me, a service I tried as joyfully to repay by washing dishes and cleaning the house while she was at work, afternoons I'd stay there to read for classes. Long, lovely afternoons staring at the bay between paragraphs, afternoons too perfect even to recall. The day she came home for lunch and a "quickie"—her mischievous ironical recourse to smut. It amused us, we could afford to play at it, parody it, our passion so sure it could run the gamut of lesser emotions. And such terms excited me, as it excited me early on, one day when almost apropos of nothing, while driving her car, she remarked, "I hope you'll understand, I really like the four-letter words in bed." I turned and saw her, this very elegant woman behind the wheel of a Mercedes, the world's last candidate to appear a lesbian, this woman who had so recently and tumultuously become my lover, making this dashing statement in the middle of Sacramento traffic. And on Derby Street, as calmly as a business executive sporting with a Fifty-seventh Street playgirl through a leisurely lunch hour, calling it a "quickie." I imagined myself her tart and adored it. As I adored the sight of her long, slim, brown body in and out of the bed to the shower, to the dressing room in the hallway, a room gone now but piercingly remembered: its beads, its treasure of silk and scents, seeing her here in the dark, then there framed in that doorway, making one last witty remark, blowing one last kiss, her lovely shoulders, the long line of her back, still seeing them duck around a doorway.

Like a litany, the places we've been together: Sacramento, her place there and mine, Derby Street, Indian Rock. Derby Street and how I used to perch on the kitchen stool while she made dinner. The low table in the living room where we ate. Wine. Pillows. Then she lived there with Hank in the months we were estranged after my breakdown. Until finally she decided her detestation of the landlady was too great to be borne any longer. Developed the first scheme of a commune with the kids and rented a huge old house in San Francisco. The night before they were to move in, Pia and Dan withdrew from the scheme, Hank split. And I was called for. Rang me up at the farm in the East, said she was desperate and all alone. Could she come to me for Christmas? Fumio was leaving me. If I didn't kill myself, I might join her in California and start over. She rented the house on Indian Rock and kept calling me away from suicide, calling me to share the house she readied for us. And so I went. Last spring and the little idyll. Holding her now in the motel night and seeing Derby Street again and Sita rising from the bed, about to go down the hall to the dressing room. How beautifully she moves in her nakedness, sliding past the door frame, the fruits of her breasts, their brown, dark-brown nipples, most precious of all. All lost. The tears coming at last. Gone even as she lies in my arms.

In the morning a growing sense of doom. Her shower running as I lie still in bed, still in the hold of sex, wanting and not daring to ask. Her movements of preparation, the folding of clothes, the opening of bags, the rounding up of stray objects. I remember the weekend in Sausalito, but things are worse now, darker, more malign. I woke in terror, feeling the loss of the class I was to have taught as a mother mourns a child. It is something I will never have, an experience, a job, a stretch of work and action torn away from me, irreplaceable in a future otherwise so empty. I am still afraid of the class, yet now I lust for it, hunger and starve for those thirty women. They would buoy me up, give me confidence again, an excuse to be alive. People I will never know now, widowed of them without ever having met them. Since the class was canceled, calls come, letters arrive, their regret, their consternation. At first they merely scolded me, underlined the guilt for my irresponsible, irrational behavior; contrary, ridiculous, indecisive—to schedule a class and then cancel it. And now reschedule? Absurd, a thousand times more ridiculous, impossible. But is it impossible? Lying awake, waiting impatiently for her to wake up so I can ask her, pretending it's all hypothetical and so forth, just wondered if the university would even consider, permit, and so forth. "Of course, it's very unusual, but possible. But this time you will have to mean it, otherwise I'll lose all credibility with the provost and the department." Ironical, painfully so, that the job I could once tell myself I was doing as a favor to her—the salary so trivial, the course itself so minor and negligible an effort—I have now messed up so grandly that she is doing me a favor in permitting me to regain it.

Never mind, teaching it would give me ten weeks to be with her, to be doing something definite. What are you working on now? people ask and I will finally have an answer. Accounted for, planned, the future projected, plotted. But could I stand ten weeks of this? There is no backing out, it's a state contract. They could sue me if I cut and run. Get her in trouble. But it means staying, committing myself to staying, to the women I teach. So why not, you're dying of having nothing, being uncommitted, joined to nothing, floating in the vacuum of writing that doesn't come, manuscripts that stay in the same place and do not move an inch or a paragraph. Okay, I'll give up working on the old manuscript, just teach, and work on the fool notebook I carry around with me and hardly ever write in. I'll stay with it, with what I'm doing now. I'll make it an experiment, see if I can record life as we live it, the moments ticking away in the house at Indian Rock. This love affair dying. Slowly, slowly like a diseased plant.

I will try it, crazy and useless as it probably is, a risk but also a promise. Better this, this last maybe desperate chance than going turn-tail back to New York and the emptiness, the loneliness, the dilemma of Ruth and Dobie, loving neither of them, burdened by both. Other people you call up and they're busy, the night comes on and you start drinking. I'll stay, I'll teach the course, shaking with fear and the continuous indecision that stays on like an ague in the mind. She is content. Hardly enthusiastic, but she says she is glad I have decided to stay, there will be just the two of us in the house now and Pia, three women, we will have a good time, it will be very satisfactory. It will be Pia and the two of us, she says again, the idea pleasing her, Pia will stay on.

We sat in bed an hour, talking it over. It was tense still from the decision, frightened, in panic till it was resolved, the plans for letters to be sent out to all the students, the day of the first class established, the die cast. And then I asked her. The humiliation of asking. I think I had hardly ever done it before, hardly ever had to. There being so many other ways to ask. But I asked now because all other approaches failed. And she said no, she did not feel like making love or being made love to, but she would make love to me if that was what I wanted. And it jarred so, stung. The kindly patience, the favor of it, the gentle condescension. No. Not to lie there while she dutifully went through with it. No. With what awful sadness, saying thank you, lighting a cigarette, trying to save face, think of any trivial thing to say. Waiting till the shower runs to let my face be its naked grief. Lying there hearing the shower and seeing for the last time each piercing item. Things, the things of our time here, the objects that have been our companions these two days: the Swedish fireplace gaily painted orange, Quigley's fancy kindling wood that never worked, the big wooden table before the window covered with books, the table of our snacks and champagne, and the appearance of the deer, a few magazines on the floor near the fire, even they full of portent, melancholy. The shower stops. And the packing begins, my nervous hurry, her resolute march, her stately efficiency. The brisk transpositions into the wicker basket she travels with. Relentless. Over and over as I watch us leaving, walking through the door, like a loop of film projected again and again, I see myself turning just at the door, looking again at the bed. I would know this bed all my life, see it beyond death; this bed and this room. This bed disappearing behind a closed door, while my body obediently follows her to the car and gets in, but my mind, the traitorous mind, stays behind, alone, isolated, eyes watching this bed which remains, which remains.

Even as I stop and get out of the car and pay Quigley his inflated price, Sita mentioning only then that she brought no money, her new habit of expecting me to pay, since she really can't afford it and if she goes places with me now it will have to be at my expense. Quigley surrounded by his tiresome ledgers and memos and scenic calendars, sprightly as ever, I'm even propitiating the little man, begging a card from him, "in case I should ever come back," recommend it to my friends and so forth. Needing, needing some proof of the place, even the printed evidence of its foolish and impossible name, Oceanspray Lodge, taking the card like a relic and preserving it in my wallet, even its embarrassing design and color precious now, what remains. We pass by the lawn where once the deer stood and are gone. Stopping again just before the road, because we'd brought a camera along and have never used it. So she obliges me for a few moments and I pretend to learn her camera, a Rolleiflex with a lens I am unused to and soon hate. I had been borrowing Ruth's Nikon in New York and was getting rather good with it and I have wanted for a long time to photograph Sita. Close-ups, intimate studies of her face after making love, knowing I could capture her, reveal her, the depth of her beauty, her sorrow, her intelligence, her humor. I have drawn her body over and over for years and still hardly approach it. Failure, caricature, awkward approximations, except now and then—but a photograph, I thought, if I photographed her, seriously, making it art, the concentration and the passion of art, brought that to it, and knowing her as I do, with what fullness and obsessive care, reverence, tenderness for her great and so often hidden beauty. Then I would have her. Then I would possess her in a certain and perfect way. She would be there when she was absent, she would remain the same when she had changed, she would be something I had discovered, unearthed, polished, breathed upon, adored, and brought to a timeless perfection.

But she is instead only a bored and impatient woman standing by a post while I am an inept idiot complaining that I cannot focus the damn machine. "It's the simplest thing in the world," she says. All the great pictures I would make of you, lady, but instead I am revealed as someone too stupid to handle your camera. The rain drizzles on. She is a wooden object, awkward in a heavy coat. This is not the pose I wanted or the place or the mood or the image. I take one more dull snapshot and we leave.

The redwoods wind ahead. She tells me the story of her second marriage, a long long story that lasts nearly until we are home. I listen, trying to memorize each detail, learn her, commit her to heart. Ben, the navy flier, the one I know least, remembering how she told the story that first time, during dinner at an old hotel up in the gold country, remembering how I gasped as she told it, the lives she had led, the woman she was, the woman I would never be. All that she had known: poverty and money and babies and husbands, life as a clerk in jerkwater offices and as a service wife in dry back-country towns. Remembering as she tells me now, the same story, but there is more of it, more detail, complexity, ambiguity. How he appeared as a blond god alighting from a Buick convertible, resplendent in uniform, a "knock-out," as she puts it, a flicker of rueful irony shadowing ahead to the slob he became. But that is not yet, still it's drinks at the officers' club, dinner and dances set against the small Southern town, its hot nights, the cheap apartment and the roommate, a waitress from Alabama who helped pay the rent, the tawdry detested job in the credit department of the water company, Pia to raise, groceries to haul, nights too tired to go out to the movies. But the roommate went to the officers' club to see what she could find. Sita, homebound, well-bred, demure, uncertain still about the country, persuaded once to go along. And there he was: superb, shining. And bought her a drink. And had another woman, whom he dropped. But still never a wolf, always the gentleman courting with flowers and that car and the officers' dance bands, gardenias converting the dusty streets to something glamorous, and men, men are the way out, the romantic strangers who descend to the rescue. "Pia went off to camp and he stayed over and proposed. But we still never made love. If I'd known then—but how could I guess he was usually impotent? The early days of that marriage I used to ache, actually ache from wanting him. I had never wanted Gil, my sexuality was only now coming alive, and I wanted Ben like a fever." The redwoods thin out, we lose them. "And the drinking. I didn't even realize how much he drank, or that he drank more than anyone else, I simply never noticed. He never seemed drunk. But after I married him, I discovered he opened a can of beer as soon as he got out of bed in the morning. I tried with that marriage, I really tried. I loved him that much. It was the second time and I didn't want to fail again. And by then we'd had a baby, Paul." Ben's slow decline, in her eyes, in the world. "They transferred him to a flight school, which he hated. He had to teach flying in one of those little tandem two-seaters, terrible things, you can't even see the student pilot. Of course it was very dangerous, and a few of his friends cracked up. Ben got so that he was terrified to go up. Headaches, migraine headaches. They put him in an office job then, which he really hated, because flying was his life. It was dull and pointless and he drank even more." And then the troubles began, creditors, brawls, misconduct, warnings and more warnings. They gave him one chance after another and finally he was cashiered. "It was like a death sentence for him. Outside that uniform he disintegrated. It was his whole manhood, his whole identity; the service was who he was. So he just sat around the house all day and drank and went to pieces. Of course he was driving me crazy too, as you can imagine." The redwoods are gone, we are past them now. They are gone forever. Mendocino is over. "Finally the only solution was for him to join the regular army, but as an enlisted man, not an officer. And then he got a chance for officer's training if he'd go to Califor-

93

nia. It was the last hope. We went. But things were no better here and I decided to leave him. It took months. I had two kids and no way to earn a living. Ben was being transferred to Germany. I let him go and rented a little dump for myself and the kids. It was all over." But the story goes on, on to the next man, on to Martin. After a time in the wilderness, after a still more grating and humiliating job as a "hostess" in a pretentious restaurant where the managers regarded her as some not very presentable half-breed, too dark to qualify as part of the upper staff, but not so unappealing that they could desist from whispered requests for blow jobs upstairs. Her dignity and survivorship living through this until the rape. And then she was broken.

Pregnant too, though the father might even have been Ben. "One last time, Ben asked me to go to Florida before he left the country, one last try at reconciliation. I took the bus all that long way. It was hopeless. He'd told me he had a vasectomy because I had such a hard time with Paul and was afraid ever to be pregnant again. Years later his mother told me he'd remarried and had a little girl. So he'd lied about the vasectomy." I see her with a suitcase in the heat of summer, her lameness, the bus and the exhaustion of the bus all the way back to California. And then it happened, the week after she got back, on her own now, driving in the desert one night, running out of gas, the panic, the glare of headlights, their laughter, their savagery. Her pride, how that must have undone her. "All I thought was how glad I was that someone had stopped." Because after her courtesy and her helplessness, her absurd predicament of being out of gas in the wilderness—did they ever get to the gas? —did they ever even listen to her, drunk as they were and she a lady, unmistakably giving off that sense of privilege and distinction, all that they in their drink and their brutality and demoralization, all that they despised and resented? Did she cry out or beg their mercy? I would never ask, yet I suspect not. Even when they left her torn and bleeding, she knew the futility of hope.

After the rape there was nothing. She was pregnant and she

wanted to die. It would be better for the children; Pia's father would take over her upbringing, he had a fortune and could easily pay for the operations on Pia's spine to correct the curvature caused by polio. And Ben's mother could take care of Paul. They would both be better off. She wouldn't have to bear another child, wouldn't have to struggle to go on. She took sleeping pills after seeing the children off for a weekend. A neighbor who also worked at the same restaurant came around on Saturday and found her. When she explained her predicament at the hospital, they didn't bother to keep her for psychiatric observation. The only problem now was time. And a method. Then Martin entered the picture. A decent guy who took her out to dinner once or twice. And he had a .22 caliber pistol in his glove compartment. When he discovered she'd stolen it, he came to visit and they had a long talk. The upshot was that he offered to marry her, to help, to take care of her, an abortion, Pia's doctors and the years of surgery, Paul. Martin was a practical solution, which is how she has always described him to me, a protector, which is what he still continues to be four years after separation.

We are almost home, the familiar blight of Richmond, the doldrums of the oil tanks, the ominous formula-fed beef marking the turn to Berkeley. Her life is folded up like a sample of fabric, her life which I love to gaze at, telling myself its stories over and over, its hardships, which made me love her, even its frivolities, which made me wonder or admire. In midtown Manhattan once we walked by Elizabeth Arden's and she laughed and told me how she used to get "done" there during her first marriage when she lived a whole winter at the Biltmore. It is always the life I never lived, neither its glamours and embassies nor its banalities of housewifery and office work. Everything about her fascinates me. Watching the lovely line of her throat as it descends into the fabric of her blouse as she drives, I imagine and possess that delicate flesh in its youth, in its extremes of passion or maternity, under the sun of summer or wet by the sea, speaking or laughing or in tears, sleeping, swallowing, speaking. And the long fingers on the wheel, the ring with the ankh to match the one she gave me, wearing her own on her first finger almost rakishly. I have worn mine religiously, superstitiously, even in the hell of the mental hospitals, bins she had helped put me in, and yet I wore it there as an amulet, a talisman that I would ever get out, all those dark claustrophobic days that terrible summer. And if not my salvation, then a memento that at least I had lived, at least I had known her before I went down into the pit, at least I had lived that high euphoric love, the existence of the ring proved it.

Jails she had helped to put me in. But like every sufferer in these places, I continued to love and depend on those who sold me into them. And she was one of them. Together with my husband, jealous of our affair, and my older sister, scandalized by it. And my own manic hysteria before the problem of saving a political prisoner's life from the hanging he had been condemned to in Trinidad. Assigned to this case by a consortium of other civil libertarians and artists. It broke me, shattered me. The responsibility sent me over the brink. I'd never had a life to save before. Lots of political prisoners, but never a lynching to stop. Somehow it unhinged me. I talked incessantly and didn't sleep, spent days making tapes for use in speeches, half the time with the machine not running. Fumio was on a visit to California. Neither he nor Sita could cope. My older sister was called out and ordered me to the loony. Which they achieved by trickery, I was led into a trap. Went along with them credulously, a visit to a doctor's office, only to discover the place was locked. I had agreed to see a psychiatrist, who remarked sadistically that my first mistake was in believing the people who brought me there. Who else was I to believe? Each of them dear to me as life. Yet they watched while two bullies in white coats, ambulance drivers with the mentality and legal authority of cops and weighing over two hundred pounds apiece, beat me to the ground in a parking lot and tied me face down on an ambulance pallet. Even then, even after this betrayal, I played Dante to Sita's

Beatrice in the elevator going to the locked sixth floor, she would be my guide to paradise after this hell. "Vergil did not get to see it, remember," I warned her, forgiving already. And each time they used her as bait when they moved me from place to place, so that the seventy-two-hour imprisonment the state permits in each of its ratholes would go on. And even then I forgave, even then I wore the ring, conjuring by it the empty days and the futile nights. I had trusted them. Gone to see their doctor, and was led into a snare, only to discover the place was locked. They had taken me by force. Only by cunning then, the cunning that pretends to agree but learns the law and waits the time, could I get out, only by patient cunning. And only through them, since the people who lock you up are also the people who can get you out, betrayers and saviors both. Not only did I need them, I loved them, learning only in my captivity the magnitude of that love. Which could forgive anything, understand even how misguided they were, and forgive that. Dependent upon their visits, the hour of coming like the last judgment each day. And that ring like the promise of salvation. That, and the amazonite in its silver band that Fumio had made for me. Sita, Fumio, my older sister—my three white horses, I used to call them, conferring symbolisms, ransacking Buddhist parable or Persian miniature or Yeats in my delirium, forgiving always after each fury at how they violated my trust and gave me into the hands of the healers, the culture police, the state and its locks and bars, loving and hating them as they must have loved and hated me.

These times lie between us always, though rarely spoken of. It was while trying to help a prisoner that I came to learn just what it is to be one. Learned what it was to have nothing, no rights and no recourse, not even a dime to call for help on the telephone. For ten cents you can start a call to anywhere in the world, and I didn't have that. Or my address book. Or the key to the door, a car to travel in, the freedom of airports or the price of a hamburger. Even a night in solitary carelessly heaped on my serious and lifelong claustrophobia: deliberately hallucinating brush drawings on the

97

walls, drawn with my naked eyes as if, by sheer force of will or imagination, to cast a spell against the dangers of sensory deprivation—for that night they had even taken my rings from me—but I did not kill myself, did not make my head a broken melon charging against the huge oak door. That was California. And then the second time I was captured that summer, St. Paul this time, compliments of my mother's gullibility before a local pundit who persuaded her to commit me so he could experiment with a wonder drug. And again with Sita's complicity. There was a trial with the best local civil-rights lawyers on my side, and I won. A sanity trial, the modern counterpart of an inquisition against a witch. Sanity is probably impossible to prove, but they couldn't prove insanity either. We won: I would not be committed for life. Free for a long, angry summer upstate at the farm. Sita coming for my birthday in September, and inevitably we fought and she left. Free again through the bleak autumn and Fumio's desertion. The studio condemned, eviction, Fumio despaired of. And the winter and depression and the drift toward suicide. One attempt after another and the thing longed for, lusted after, craved. To die, only to die. Finally the help of medicine, the depression lifting, the will to live coming back, the grief over Fumio and the studio receding. Sita and I repaired our quarrel, her own plans fell through, she came East to the farm at Christmas; she waited while I suffered through a lawsuit and the last hankering after death, she took the house on Indian Rock and waited there. And then that spring we lived together through my last convalescence. Then a loft came up in New York and I took it. Then the trip to Europe together last summer, the months alone in New York last fall while I fixed up the loft, drifting a little apart, then her visit at Christmas putting it together again.

And now living here again with her, just as by plan, but all strange and distant, painfully different. Different the silence—for the silence has come on us again—the stranger's figure next to me on the seat, different from the loving and passionate woman mistaken as she was in those hospitals, nearly breaking down herself and making the excuse always that the time in Italy was her breakdown, her delayed reaction; different from the protective woman of last spring, her kindness, her solicitude. Different now, I can already sense the difference as we park the car, as we explore the house for Pia, who doesn't seem to have been home for days, as we bring in bags and check the mail, as I hear her changing her clothes, starting the shower. A sinister difference. "I have to go out tonight, I promised some friends." My stomach clutches, she had not mentioned this before. There is something spur-of-the-moment even as she goes on explaining that it's a nuisance but she made the appointment a long time ago. Suddenly our weekend is truncated. I am unreasonably afraid. But there is a disastrous quality to her preparations, it is not only my own desperation, it is something in her manner too. And the oddness of her packing her wicker basket. As if she were bringing extra clothes. The irritation in her voice, the speech about her independence again, about having friends of her own, people she's fond of seeing. Who could they be? She doesn't bother to say or describe. I ask, trying to appear casual and am as casually told I don't know them. The inference is a couple who've invited her for dinner. Yet everything about her manner speaks more, speaks something dangerous, speaks dishonesty, the squirm of deceit. Mendocino, the weekend is violated. Relegated the moment we return. It had stood for a coming together, for a commitment, my own to stay and teach the course, and hers to live with me and Pia. We had re-formed, regrouped, made a new household. And she is already out the door. Only barely do I hear the line with which she leaves: "I'll call you tomorrow from the office."

Thunderstruck. Tomorrow. The office. For a second or two still not quite comprehending it. Then a rush, then a sudden rush of the heart to the door, to call out, to beg, to scream and wail, to denounce, to entreat, to grab her by the very throat I love and stop her. Waited till she was halfway out the door to say it. The bitch,

99

the damn incredible fucking bitch. This morning she was too ill to make love, a touch of stomach trouble, she'd said, grinning at me, not up to it, not feeling well. But she's well enough for him . . . Who? Neal? Another. I'll go mad. I am seized with the greatest fear, a physical fear even. As if the house were under siege and terrorists or police surrounded it.

Each room is darkening, closing in like disease. Every object in the house derides me, every line and shadow and banister depresses me—the banister, the cheap rug in the hall, the beautiful Grecian spread on our bed. Our bed. Of course, that was why she carried the wicker basket. Liar. "I'll call you from the office in the morning." Coward. The office, yet. Bureaucratic whore. To wait until I couldn't answer back, might not even hear her. We'd never treated each other that way before. Even in the beginning when we were both sleeping with other people. But not while we were together, living in the same house. Never just "took off" this way. There were Hank and Brian, but she had them at her house. And that one time I slept with Sarah at Meg's place in San Francisco, Sita in another room, she was rightfully angry; angry even when Sarah came back to Sacramento and stayed a few days at my own apartment. And furious when Bea slept there during the music festival, Sita having to stay in a motel.

But that was a long time ago. Living together last spring, we were faithful, as if there were no other way to live. During our separations there were other people for both of us, but that was understood; we were apart, after all. But to live together, to be living with her and hear her casually announce that she'd be sleeping with someone else, that she'd be with a lover tonight—I had no idea how it would stun me. No idea of the fury I would feel, the terrified insecurity, this helpless fear. Because I am afraid, horribly afraid. To be so at the mercy of another, to be so unprepared and face such amorphous and uneasy danger. As if my life were in jeopardy.

The house filling up with the evening. I can't stay here. For nothing in the world could I stay home tonight. Bitch, I whisper, bitch. I am tricked. Said I would teach that damn course, said I would stay. And you do this to me the first night afterward, bitch. Bitch, I say, but what I feel is the breaking of the heart; anger is nothing to my sorrow. The grief of knowing. The despair in realizing I am actually helpless. Because I love her still. Because I must suffer this, put up with it, have not walked out. And cannot.

The first thing I knew, even as she left, was that I couldn't stay in, spend the evening alone in this house. Which without her is the most foreign place in the world. When we lived here together last spring, one rare night when she was out, I spent an uneasy evening alone here. It was not a home at all I discovered that night. Without her, it was an utterly meaningless place I would never have chosen, an empty, rather heavy bourgeois house overlooking a strange bay; the lights outside were the lights of a foreign place, not my town. A voice spoke inside me, What are you doing here? As if I had wakened from a dream to find myself in some inexplicable landscape. The discovery that only her presence brought me here, kept me here, came like bad news long evaded. The house ominously still, unfriendly, like a dog whose master has left it in your care until, inexplicably, it bites you. It was her house, not mine. And the world outside, the lights, the landscape, and the city—all hers and suddenly unrelated, alien.

If I could drive the bridge tonight, if I could feel the speed and the air on my face, I could breathe. But if I stay here I'll strangle. The panic mounting in my chest. Sherman. Call Sherman. Thank God, there's one person. One person who is not her person. Because to go now to any acquaintance who would be, since they all are, her friends, not mine, would be betrayal. And I cannot betray her. Or us. The collective myth of our relationship. But Sherman is an old friend, my friend originally and still. I can tell her. Talk to her. The ease of it, having someone to confide in. Someone to eat with. But what if she's busy, not in, feeling unsociable? Then emptiness. There's only one person, only one person in this whole damn place. I have only one friend in California. Insane, insane I should live in a place where there is only one friend. Get out of here. Go home, back to New York. Knowing beforehand that is what I will say to Sherman. That I have to go home. But what if she's not there? Hurry.

"Look, I've got to see you. Can I come over?" "Sure." The salvation of it—my hands shaking on the wheel, fumbling with the ignition key—that there is this place to go in need. Sherman's talk, the understanding of old friends, dinner, the sight of their domestic bliss, even that, Marguerite making dinner, the kitchen, the warm light, the paintings, the bowls of flowers, the pots hanging on the walls, the old-fashioned stove Sherman brought along from the last studio. The ease of it. That they are a couple, that they are together, that some are, that some last, that it works. Even bringing this gaping wound, my humiliation, there where it will be all right, they will not laugh, despise me, no dishonor, no loss of face.

"She planned to leave you last fall, came over and told me you were wiped out, over." "Odd she never told me." "Really?" Sherman looks in her wineglass, a large glass cup, mottled, veinous, beautiful. "You mean she never mentioned any of this to you?" "Not at all. When we said goodbye after Europe and I stayed on in New York while she came back out here, the plan was for me to finish the first big work on the loft and come out around the end of the year. Then she said she'd come to New York for Christmas. She was on and off with that, but finally she came. We got it together again, 'cause she'd become very distant by November, it was hard to get her on the phone, I had started to worry about how things were. But at Christmas we patched it up, so I came out in January. To see how it would go. But I'd no idea she had ditched the whole thing when she got back last fall." "Well, she came over expressly to tell me it was all over between the two of you. That's why I was so surprised to see you the other day. That you were out here again. And to see the two of you together. Great, I thought, they're back together." I laugh, a discouraged, mortified laugh intended to be cynical.

The light falls in Sherman's living room. Marguerite is still at work. The chicken is defrosting, only enough for two people, but I have accepted an invitation to dinner anyway, desperate beyond good manners. "She loves you a great deal. She said that last September." I am accustomed to Sita's protestations of love, protestations made to my friends, often with tears; she adores me, I am the great love of her life, but impossible. Just before Christmas my friend Barbara was out in California and had lunch with Sita. Barbara was the first to bring me the news Sita was not planning to come. They had lunch in San Francisco. Sita wept. "She's so much in love with you, she loves you so much," Barbara reported. I smiled, pleased, self-conscious. "She's coming for Christmas." "I don't think she will be," Barbara said, her voice suddenly uncertain, embarrassed. "Sure she is, we've been planning it for months." "She told me she was planning to stay out there with her family." But I ignored Barbara, what would she know? Then Hatsie too, saying that Sita had told her that having Christmas with all her children about her was the most precious thing in the world. And indeed she had had it, flying East to me only the day after Christmas, but she'd said it was her job that prevented her coming sooner, they made her work on the day of Christmas Eve. And then it was her job that made the visit so short, a mere four days, they had demanded she be back right away. In coming she risked being fired. And I believed, just as I believe the reports of her passion, the tears, all of it. In her drama she loves me grievously, weeps for herself in renouncing me, believes in her grief as she renounces, is passionately convinced by her passion as she recites it. Then she goes off, works, administers, flourishes, takes on new lovers, shops for men. But on meeting someone who knows me, on reflecting, she will weep and declare her love. And whether she announces its end or gives intimations of its survival, the listener is profoundly impressed by her tenderness, her intoxication, her nostalgia, her grief.

103

"How much she loves you," they say to me, awed, admiring. As I have admired, as I have been in awe of this woman's genius at love, at the expression of love, the avowal, the declaration, the very sensuality of her voice. The soft Italian accent, the trembling vibrato of it, her beautiful eyes. Nearly three years I have been the captive of this performance, real and unreal, persuasive, compelling. My stomach melts at the sound of that voice speaking its love, I am moved past speaking or reason. Is it her love for me that I love, this melancholy and infinitely tender emotion figured forth, expressed with such perfect inflection and tone, fullness of eye? This extravagant love for me. That someone, a beautiful woman even, had loved me so plangently. This love for me now withdrawn, now bitterly withheld, hidden and eclipsed.

And of course it's been gone a long time, far longer than I knew. Sherman knew, other friends knew. But I didn't. The dusk coming into the room sad as the end of day, the paintings in their places. We are left always with things like paintings, the cold objects with which we console ourselves. It comes down to that. I walk around Sherman's studio, the little room next door: brushes, tubes of paint, pens, paper, stretchers, rolls of canvas, the messiness of a palette. I miss drawing. There is no place to do it out here; the basement, the only possible place, is still full of Paul's carving junk. And somehow that house never seems a place in which to draw. If I went home . . . suddenly wanting home, the loft, wanting to draw again, to work, to live on my own. Enough of this hanging around. Dependent sick shit. Having raved to Sherman, I already know I will stay, keep trying, hang on a little longer. I have even taken on the course. The thing we decided this morning. "It's important to you," Sherman said, assuming innocently that the course was a proper course and I a proper teacher, having no idea that the course is a pretext to stay, that I have put this love ahead of any adult considerations of work or profession, that I am simply diseased.

"Of course you can't stand it. I wouldn't put up with it for a moment," she said when I explained Sita's departure tonight. "But you see, I don't agree with you. I don't believe in monogamy, possessing people, the rightness or inevitability of jealousy. She has the right to go with anyone she likes. I'm on her side. It's just that it hurts me, it hurts terribly—I hadn't expected that; it even hurts that it hurts. It shouldn't hurt, I shouldn't feel jealous, I'm ashamed of the feeling." "Crap. Anyone do that to me, it's out the door with them." "Maybe it's the way she did it. This I'll-call-you-from-the-office business. I'm being lied to. I think I could take it if she just told me, if she were honest." "Pamela, for example, Pamela started not coming home and that was the end of it, damn it." "You see, if she explained how she felt, if she said, Look, I really want to do this; if she said, Look, here is someone I want, though I want you too. If I had the confidence I used to have in her love for me, don't you see?" "Bullshit. Nobody can put up with that stuff. It's not human." "I don't agree. There were times in the past she was with someone else, and really, I was *not* jealous. I was loved, I was convinced of that." "You and your half-assed theories."

At first I don't even know where I am. Then I see Donleavy's *Ginger Man* on the pillow next to me. Reading it in my booze. Went to sleep yelling my rage into the empty house and the glass of gin and a book. With the light still on. I realize she is gone. "I'll call you from the office." How the phrase sounded as she closed the door, the words barely audible, a flicker just before the noise of the door, then the sound of her motor, the sight of her car disappearing just as I began to understand what it was she had told me. "I'll call you from the office." Her exit line. The insult of it, the sheer contempt of leaving like that, the smug bureaucratese of the words, the dismissive arrogance of it. But more than anger, the humiliation, the crippling mortification that thwarts anger, when fury could be helpful. The result instead is despair. It is I who am worthless. The whole dizzy circle of despair, conflict, ambivalence.

Go or stay? When you so clearly ought to go. Stay, win her back; the whisper of insanity. Remembering when she did love me, remembering how real it seemed, how utterly convincing, how beyond doubt or change.

A hangover. Breakfast. The paper. Postponing thought, the dilemma of staying or going. Because I could not tell her at lunch —since she has indeed called me from the office and invited me to have lunch—so I could tell her at lunch, just tell her, Look, I'm going home, there won't be any course. Or is it too late, has she already set the machine in motion, told the provost, sent letters to the students? Today would be the first meeting. Two o'clock this afternoon. Is there time to avert it all? Is there even time to save it? Because in the slime at the back of my mind I know already that I want to stay and search now only for means.

The method, absurd as it is. To offer a course. Then cancel. Then reinstate. A course I don't even want, am actually afraid of. Am sure to be trapped by—and yet I want it, passionately. Because it excuses my presence. The folly of staying on here. The obscene need of her. Even her cruelty. Craven without either shame or pride. Wanting to stay. To keep trying. Hope. Getting her back. Having her again, to have that love intact again, mine, warm as my arm around her back, the long, lovely muscles of her back, the delicate carvings of the bones in her spine, the perfume of her shoulders, her delectable, infinitely tender flesh.

I am distraught again, walking the rooms of the house like a madwoman. Will I go crazy again, fail, fall, live every moment in panic? The lure of suicide again, the absolute loss of direction in life. Life being over. Life being Fumio and Sita, both gone. There is no living past their love, with its death I die, living on like a zombie now, a walking dead without hope or purpose. Swallow, the heart beats as in danger, the stomach in its cramp of fear. I am no one any more. I have no work. My art is finished, failed, over. Escaped me. The sight of the newspaper folded on the table. The rug. Whether to stay or go. Wine stain on the rug. Bought it together at Macy's, split the cost. The other one, the big polar bear under the pile of cushions, that was a present to her. When she first set up an apartment in Berkeley, and I was her fancy uptown decorator. Derby Street. To go, to go home finally, give up, throw in the towel. Not to fight for her any more? Should one fight? Why should one fight? It is only fighting her; she loves me or she doesn't, one can't change that. I would want her to love me of her own accord, not through persuasion or coercion. But remember her hostility lately, the meanness of her temper. You can't change the mind of someone like that. Through patience? Playing the saint of love? Bullshit masochism. Oh, it is all masochism, don't even bother bringing that up. The word has no meaning. I would advise any friend, even an enemy, against living this way. But for me, being inside it, this is—becomes reality, the only reality. Leaving is flight, surrender, the end of hoping.

Then unexpectedly I remember the deer, the three deer at Mendocino. The burning of tears as I make, actually make a note in my notebook, put down a phrase: three deer. Sudden. Already their last movement comes to conclusion as we see them. Each in its place. Still with the stillness of silence. Unmoving. Looking toward us. These three. She and I. There are only the five of us in the world. And the sea. Three strange beasts before us. Stolid and magical. And then break off. Simply the pain of it overtaking thought or effort. Do I stay because three deer showed up on a lawn once in a resort town? Do I stay because I am a writer and this is something to write about? Because I want to have this experience, simply that? However painful, silly, demeaning. To have this experience rather than walking out on it, not having it. To have it and to record it. Even if that is in some way immoral or wrong or sick, one makes choices and I choose this suffering because at least it is feeling, at least in the vast anomie of my life now lost, vacant, at least I am driven to put down thirty or forty words in consecutive order and this is the last grasp on sanity or usefulness, hope or the notion of a future.

Or is it for the future of life? Not writing at all, but living, life itself, the conviction I have had for three years that we would be lovers all our lives, that this was a permanent relationship, a marriage even, if you will, that a bond was made and soldered, and vows and understandings given. And I am just too stupid or too stubborn to give up and go home. Even when it's so plainly all over, past, done for, blown. Even when she has filled the house with others whom she would never ask or even permit to leave and who left against her will, even when she has hemmed me out, built walls against me, taken up new lovers, given preference to some muscular young man, anonymous Neal preferred over me, preferred with such thunderous rudeness, such disciplinary force. To tell me to get lost. And I won't. No. Bitch, I'm staying. Hurry, put something on, it's time for lunch; hurry, don't lose your course, your passport.

She is on me before I know it. A puff of hair, a kiss hello. Coming up from behind at the corner of the parking lot. "I didn't see you," I say weakly. The first thing I was to say this fatal interview and it sounded so puny. "I've just come from lunch with a woman running for office. She should do very well. All the right ideas, employment programs, the works." The brisk efficiency of executive women. Where are my batteries? my protest? walking humbly alongside her. Neal. Last night. I'll wait. Say nothing till we sit down. The gravity dissipating, becoming ridiculous. Only to be with her again. Do the course, just to go on having that. To be sitting across from her like this. Her face.

And then simply her eyes. Her very long look. Her eyes. Swallowed in them, floating in them. I hold my breath. Her beauty. Has she ever been this beautiful? The eyes open and take me. The absolute tenderness of it. I used to see this making love. And have forgotten. Her eyes. So brown. Their brown power over me. Opening as if by some voluntary exercise of power, opening to their full vibrancy, the pupils expanding, taking me in like a sexual act, the terrible eroticism of that look. She can do this if she pleases, I think, she can, simply, by an act of will, by a whim, look at me this way and I am naked, open, utterly disarmed.

She smiles. Impish, naughty, flirtatious, a female who's been out all night. An essence transported from him, whoever he was, to me. She is intact, humorous, roguish. The convent, Italy, serenity. I smile without meaning to. Unable to restrain, to refuse; to refuse would be like refusing to answer, refusing to dance, refusing to kiss. She says nothing at all. She only smiles, saying everything. Last night is discussed and settled in that smile. In making me smile, she makes me accept, become her accomplice. The moment takes on light, flickers, goes out slowly. The waitress appears. Sita exquisitely pointing out a wet spot on the tabletop. Her long finger pointing out the offending spot, though the whole table was freshly scrubbed, proof it had just been prepared for use, proof that this section is open, proof that we are fortunate and in privacy. Tea. Because she has already had lunch. And I will have tea too. To add to the coffee, the cigarettes, the diarrhea. Smiling again, just to be smiling at each other, to be two women smiling over sex, a peccadillo. Smiling as friends smile, sisters smile. The smile itself denominating the subject, nudging it to the center of the tabletop between us. And we sit in a tearoom, candy factory, soda shop. Female territory. And we smile in this debonair way, urbane, worldly. How beautifully worldly she is, this woman I love, my lady, how humorous and knowing. How she always makes being female a mystery, a joke, the romance of gloves and scarves, perfume and jewelry. How she has always made me love being a woman, and being a woman with her, its smiles and secrets, its fascination with fabric and texture, its nuance of leather or silk or the love of the flesh. The dressing room at Derby Street, how it represented her with its thousands of dresses and silk blouses, jerseys, belts, handbags, hundreds of shoes, photographs of children and ancestors, bureaus full of gloves and scarves, treasures of rings and bracelets. All gone as the place is gone, as the time is gone and who we were then, lovers tireless in bed in shower in repairing there to dress, to perfume ourselves, skin fresh as the lavender of her sheets, the fur rug before the fire, the tomato juice and coffee on sunny mornings, the cherry blossoms in a china teapot, the volume of Dante by the window, the long, sweet sex of our nights, insatiable and in all positions and places, the long line of her back as I took her or she took me, the cries and whispers of our comings, our sighs and ecstasy, the light of the fire or the dawn, the roses by the bed, the moon on her flesh, the tired tenderness of her exhaustion, for I would never have enough of her, now gone entirely and forever gone. Then, gone in now.

"Lady, I don't know where I am." "Just where you were yesterday when I left you." I look at her, bleeding astonishment, the cool of it. "I love you. I will always love you. You have a very special place in my life as you must know by now." Among how many? I wonder. Children, lovers, friends. But the eyes still underlying each nuance as I hear her, caressing with old caresses, forgotten, dead, I had even thought. Afternoons in my old place in Sacramento, the wonderful rooms full of sun and plants, fuchsias piled on the balconies, camellias everywhere. The flowers she always arranged for me on my desk. Mornings waking before class, waking early to make love while the coffee perked. The evening she played truant to her own party, a farewell party for Brian, to surprise me with candles and rosé, soap and towels for the new apartment, a big black dish for flowers (I saw it only yesterday, full of junk, unanswered mail, paper clips), and Sita aglow with the wineglasses and corkscrew, my "survival kit," she called it. I was new then. Brian was a lover too, but she had slipped away from his party, come to me. It did not even occur to me to worry about him, I was new then, I was the favorite. The period of my glory, this lovely woman courting me.

"Listen, there was that time in San Francisco at Meg's apartment and you carried on with Sarah. I was there. I even stayed through it." "No, you wanted to take the bus back," I remind her, ashamed still to remember what I put her through that night and apologizing again. "It doesn't matter, I stayed finally. And when Fumio was here . . ." "But we weren't living together then, there was always somewhere else to go. Some outlet, some out." "That hardly makes a difference." "Of course it does. Look, I also remember Brian and Hank and going back home to my apartment if I saw Brian's car in front of your house. His last night in town and of course I'd understand. And of course I did. Even Hank." Dimly remembering that I'd called her one morning when she must have been in bed with him. Blasé we were in those days. Gay, insouciant, and so forth. Hundreds of years ago. And the plant that would arrive from the florist midmorning on such mornings. Almost embarrassing, the richesse, the delivery man and the message. "Good morning, dear lady," the voice purring at me, caressing me. The call to follow it up. Almost embarrassing receiving the package at the door, the grin of self-conscious pleasure, the novel and vaguely ridiculous feeling of being courted, treasured, swept up with gestures. No one had ever courted me. Fumio's language of love was to sew a button on my coat; quiet things, lovely in their considerate ingenuity, their subtle thoughtfulness. Coming home to find that he had invented a book rest that kept the pages from turning when you wanted them to stay flat, that he had remembered to buy Coke, that he had found just the right brandy glasses. But not flowers, not Latin indulgence, not notes and telephone calls that began "Dear lady" and went on to become graphic about delightful sensations, sticky substances, flashes of heat.

"I want to be free. You know I have to have that. You taught it to me yourself." I am horrified, hearing her, my own undoing, my own stupid theories on life, even my own actions, my insistence on New York. "Last year I would have been your wife or made you mine. Now I know that's not the right thing." I would protest, but protest is futile, her tone forbids it. I wonder what it is that we are. Friends, sisters, lovers, she'd said. "I want to share the house with you and Pia, I want you to stay." I watch her, saying nothing, unable, hypnotized. She is making her terms, she is in charge.

III

"Remember at Christmas in your loft how you said you really enjoyed living alone. Well, I want to, too. Or rather, not alone"—flicker of eyes, correcting herself—"but with that freedom. You know about Neal. I told you at Christmas. And if I want to go out with him and spend the night once in a blue moon, I've every right to. I can't go around feeling guilty or being made to feel guilty." The defensive tone again, the defiance. I smile, helpless. Avert it some way. "Next year I may not even remember his name." I blink to escape the ramifications of this. "You know I love you and how deeply I love you." "But that's just it—I don't think you do love me any more, I think you're through, exhausted." Is it my exhaustion, I wonder, my own disillusionment with this affair, do I merely project my own anomie upon her?

Her eyes smiling at me, intimate, sensual. Is it my fatigue or her mood today that brings back the high tide of love, when it was there, when every moment was charged, when just passing her a cup of coffee, or meeting each other by accident on campus, realizing fifteen feet away as she bore down on me, her coat flying around her shoulders, her hand picking a branch of camellias, how she ravished me, how she shouted our liaison to the world. How proud she was once. Around us jaws work sandwiches, women spoon ice-cream sundaes, office workers hurry hamburgers. My eyes focus on the cashier and the windows and then back to her across the table, hair swept back handsome from her face. The same beads as yesterday. The same sweater. "Free, yes of course. I can hardly argue with you. Of course it's your right. But the way you did it . . ." "How else could I?" "That ratty little line about calling me from your office." "What else?" "Efficient bitchery. Why not just tell me? Be honest. Surely the truth is better than lies or one-line exits like that. There was something cheap about it." She flinches. I've hit the mark of her honor, we are both proud here, have been rivaling each other in magnificence and probity for years. And because she is struck she takes off. And fires. "I had to shock you into understanding. I didn't want to hurt you, I don't ever want to hurt you. But I had to make you realize. So I had to do something to shock, to dramatize." "I'd rather you tell me the truth." Knowing of course she was afraid to. Had to resort to that line and then run. Had to? No, preferred it. Just as she preferred making love with Neal.

"Look, we'd just come back from Mendocino, we'd just decided I'd stay and take the class, we'd just rearranged the house—you, Pia, and I. And suddenly you mumble something about 'seeing friends' tonight and go off announcing you'll call me in the morning. Naturally I didn't know where I was all over again, whether it was crazy to promise to teach that class, whether I could even stand it, staying that long." "Oh, that class, I wish we'd never started on the thing. Here's your letter."

She delivers the letter, my letter rescheduling the class, over to my side of the table. I had meant to use it as a lever, my bargaining point. And know far better than before that I dare not, that I couldn't possibly. She would urge me to cancel in a moment, is already repeating all her phrases about not wanting to put any pressure on me. Can I even rescue it from her? Helpless and afraid, knowing that I want to stay, must. And need the course as an excuse, a term of time, a stated interval. And the class, I think, something my own, mine. Touching the paper. Grasping at the students. Mimeographed names. The absurdity of it, to schedule the thing, cancel, reschedule. How like an indecisive fool. My face goes hot, thinking of it, the shame of all this.

And it may already be too late to recapture the students. Sita picking up the check. Back to her office, the telephone, we must hurry. Our meeting, our famous showdown took less than the full hour. And ended by her *indulging* me, *permitting* me to teach one three-credit course for peanuts. Walking up the stairs, I remember again that the first meeting is scheduled for two this very afternoon. We have twenty minutes. Sita on the phone through a labyrinth of bureaus checking to see if the sign canceling the class is up on the church door as ordered. "My God, a church?" "The First Baptist, no less. The university's very miserly with classrooms, we make do with what we can dig up. My secretary saw to the sign and then went home." Calls to the registrar to see how many students have transferred to other classes, collected their money. I pace, fume, sweat it out. "Hadn't I better go round there and change the sign?" Ten minutes before two. "The registrar will call back." The thin green slips of registrants in her hands. The class permits thirty-five; seventy had applied. The fragile papers on her palm, cradled by her long fingers. Five before two. "I'll go over there." "There's no point, the church is locked." More telephones, people, the green papers, tissue-thin. A sign somewhere on a door saying canceled. "I'm going even though I don't know where this place is. I'll find it. I can change the 'canceled' to 'postponed.' " "There's really no point in it." "Hell, I can't help myself."

Finding it almost at once, miraculously. Great stupid Romanesque and pompous. First Baptist. And the little sign, yellow paper and a Magic Marker, CANCELED. One lone girl turning down the stairs. Scruffy, looks the type. Gone by the time I park. Ten after two. Feeling foolish scribbling out the "canceled," trying to substitute "postponed" with a ballpoint that won't write at a vertical angle. "Do you want to borrow this?" The girl. And her purple felt pen. I add the telephone number for the office. Humiliated, ridiculous, while she looks on. Has no idea she's addressing the instructor. Saving grace. "So they're going to have it after all?" "Just call this number, they'll tell you all about it." Magically preserving my identity. Returning the pen. Foolishly back to my car.

Am I crazy? Buying a present. Passing a store and feeling the impulse. This morning I would have throttled her, struck, even struck her dear tender face. And now, buying a present. Just lost my last argument with her and I want to buy her a present. Sitting across from her at the teashop today, I knew for sure she would never live as I am living, in someone else's town, someone else's house, with the pretext of a silly marginal course paying only a token salary while I wheeled and dealed in my world, slept with other people while she waited up nights. Unthinkable. It is this that humbles me, this knowledge that she would not endure my circumstances one single week. And perceiving this, I worried most that she would despise me, because I gave in, took every insult. I cannot ask for gratitude, yet I so fear her contempt.

And having passed the afternoon with "other people," the other people she advises me to cultivate, having sat through coffee and a young filmmaker's epic about trains—miles of footage lavished on the Metroliner because the young woman who did it declares it's actually the "feminine spirit," the passion of her life, and so forth—I am hanging about in front of a record store hankering to go in and buy a present. The audience was so savage during the question period that I came to the filmmaker's defense, complimented the photography, the technique, the ghostlike effect in the old photographs she used. "There are always ghosts in a love affair, other people on stage," Susan Griffin whispered to me while we waited for the film to begin. "And ghosts of all the old moments of the love itself, the lovers as they were a month, a year ago, the love of then. Which is not the love of now," I said. Susan's a playwright, we were being literary. When they invited me for dinner after the film, I begged off, half regretting it later. For it had felt good being with other people, almost like New York. A life of appointments and friends and conversation. Not to be buried in that house. Morose, solitary, lugubrious place with night coming on. And yet I wanted to be alone again. To expect her again. To go home and wait. Knowing she'll be late. And passing a store, wanted to go in and buy her a present. Noticing the records, feeling the impulse.

Lovers and presents. How we used to buy them, hardly a day without them. Mostly hers. Flowers, records, a book or something to eat, trivia even. Flowers, heaps of them. Spending way beyond her means. The whole kitchen of plants she gave me when I moved in at Sacramento. Begonias, the two moccasin plants I used to literally run to water after our weekends in San Francisco. Furious they would be at me, crying out over neglect at the end of two days. Sita courting me those days. Something I hardly understood then. I had never known gifts in such profusion.

Now it's I who buy the presents. Passing the record store and then going back. Not knowing what to buy till I remember the Alice Stuart that Sherman has. Alice Stuart, recalling the name just when I need it, tossing it to the clerk. "Central aisle." Steward, no, Stuart, no, next to it, finding it just when I'd given up. The one with the motorcycle on the cover. And another one too that I haven't heard yet. Clerk wrinkles her nose at the other. Maybe she does me a favor. "It's early and not very good." "All right, just this one then."

Waiting for her downstairs, the record on the couch where I will not forget it. The rain in torrents. Will she stay at school? Put up with a friend? Go to Neal's? The time passes. Nine-thirty, when I expected her. Then ten. And past ten. And still the rain. Huge impersonal flood. How will she ever survive it? Then a taillight reflected through the glass of the front door. Seeing it like some sort of miracle, unforeseen, beyond desert. I call to her from the open door. Her voice answering me, her brown coat around my arms.

Settled on the sofa, we sit where she sat that night with Pia, comforting her after the quarrel with Valerie, and I hovered in the kitchen, cooking a chicken to comfort them. But tonight I sat where Pia sat, tonight it is I, the center of her attention, her delight. She crows over the record and plays it, listening in my arms. For the first time in weeks I feel she is actually present when she is with me. Her body speaks to me. "Makes you want to dance," she whispers. I remember dancing as from some former life. "Friday let's go dancing at Peg's," she says, bouncing nearly, having thought of it. Excited by her nearness, her kisses, the pressure returned against my body. But afraid to press further.

In bed she seems ready for me. Permitting me brief access, one bittersweet opportunity to enter and be her lover. Does she remember him and compare, measure me against him, Neal of only last night. If I went down on her, would I find him there, his odor still about her after a shower? Forget it, take what you have, what is given in her new sweetness, her willingness. The aftereffect of the other perhaps, the rebate, but still mine. Yet so short this turn of mine before she finishes, expels me, ceases to respond. My own inability or her lack of interest?

Then leaning over me, taking me, always what she prefers. Her face looking down on the joy given, registered unashamedly, uncontrollably. Her satisfaction. Her godlike powers. In and out of me each time stronger more certain more inevitable until she has found a new touch, slowly ever so slowly, touching the whole outer flesh, each stroke separate resonant astounding. I dare not speak, even encourage her with words as I love to do, sly lechery of language to excite us both, forgone now, I can only cry out softly with each stroke as she guides, controls, masters, nurtures, and completes. I the creature given over, straining, accepting, accepting all I am given. Stroke after stroke, curious the high of it, the cool

117

of it, and the plateau of it surprising and a little frightening. Wave after wave of heat. Stillness and motion, then the sudden shuddering. Have you ever done this to me before, I ask, bewildered, ever quite like this? That miracle, the finding, the discovery of new sensation where all was familiar, all had been known.

I am lifted, I am hidden, I am in danger and suspended in air and fall and rise again and dizzy, then battered, then exalted. I am her cunt and against my will I tell her so, slavish, owned, devoted, open, a thing to be used. At the mercy of her force and her strength and her fingers, her caprice or her tenderness or her majesty over me. Her eyes open to me, giving pleasure, knowing her certainty to make me rich or afraid or victorious with each caress. Giving because it pleases her to give now, this moment. As it pleased her to give another last night. And I can only admire, prisoner of the touch of her hand on the quick of me, the slow mysterious move of her fingertips around the lips of my mouth gaping to be filled with her, pleading for her fullness and her force in me, the blow of her arrival at the cervix, itself another mouth, another door opening to her touch. Have me, have me, I'm yours, altogether yours, my mind saying what I refuse to say aloud or say only to repent it, the complete abnegation submission surrender, the long fingers of her assaulting me breathless or sly shoved high and now and now this instant. Crying out in the little cries she gives me, crooning to me as I come to her, my creator, comforter. A coming strange and strangely disappointing.

Pia's home. It's been days now. The last note, the one found on Sunday when we came down from Mendocino, specified "a few days to think and get it together." Yet she never tells me where she's been. She stands at my doorway and I invite her in for a cigarette. She sprawls on the bed: long beautiful limbs, perfect and delicate girl's beauty, the face almost of a child. Like Emily's, but finer. "Emily's just great, loves it up there. The only thing she misses is her big Donald Duck." "Well, if that's the only thing on her mind, she must be taking to the change very well." "Sure, she's getting along just swell. That part's all okay . . ." We lapse into a silence. "Staying here while you guys were gone last weekend really got to me. Over in my room it's full of Dan's clothes and stuff. And when I go downstairs I see Emily's bed. Like the whole place was too full of echoes. So I just had to take off for a while, don't you know?"

I do, and then of course I don't. Have no idea where she's been. And the "being alone just to get into my own head" seems fairly unlikely. In San Francisco or even in Berkeley she would have had to stay with someone. Michael is out of the question; his wife has come back to him. I cannot ask her where she's been. And she clearly doesn't mean to tell me. Further silence. The phone rings. "If that's my mom, I don't want her to know I'm back yet." It isn't. We try a few topics: the income tax, the used car Martin has given her, the band. "Jack was supposed to call me back but he never did. Guess old Jack was just stringing me along, wanted to show me the sights, that number." I am disappointed. "They didn't play the right kind of music, anyway. Stevie Wonder. I can't get off on that stuff. It's all atonal and that big band honking away behind me. I need a melodic line, don't you see?" She fiddles with a bracelet. Wonders where she's left a glove. The cigarette is nearly finished. Is she back with Dan? Is she still clean? Wanting to ask. Unable. Awkwardness filling the room. "Gotta get these big old shoes fixed," displaying the outrageous pair of wedgies that made her fall down the steps into the front hall the last time she wore them. It worries me to see her wear them when she drives. "These are my only job interview trotters. Had 'em tacked together with a Band-Aid here but that didn't hold up so good." Smiles. Adjusts a bracelet. Leaves.

Back in a moment with "a few things." Nightgown, dresses. "I'm off again." My affection falters, wishing she would talk to me, stay. "I left this note for Mom." My eyes, scanning the thing pinned to the frame of the door, usual stuff about "needing time and space to think everything out." Sad little exchange about the note. "Do you think this is the best place for her to find it?"—the note tacked rather foolishly to the naked frame of the door. "I'll tell her it's here." "Well . . . off I go . . . oh no, did I forget those gloves again?" Long, elaborate search for the gloves.

It hardly seems an hour later when she calls. "The most terrible thing has happened. I hit somebody. Not in my own car, but I hit this guy." "Tell me what happened. Take your time." Her voice pinched, terrified, she keeps going over it until it's clear. "I was driving Dan's car, see . . ." I don't see, when she has one of her own, when Martin has just bothered to buy her a car of her own, part of the plan for her independence and rehabilitation. "And this guy on Van Ness, wouldn't you know he has to jump out and yell whiplash." "Start over." "Well, I was getting along fine in San Francisco and the hills and all, pumping the brakes. You know, Dan's car doesn't have any brakes." I close my eyes, knowing, remembering he was "going to get them fixed" at least two weeks ago. No use asking why anyone drives a car without brakes in San Francisco. "Well, I got to the stop sign at Van Ness and suddenly all the cars bunched up at once and I couldn't stop fast enough, couldn't pump 'em up quick enough and I rammed into this guy in front of me. Wouldn't you know, he disappears under the seat. And then comes roaring out with this whiplash thing." "Did you hit him very hard?" "Just my luck in this whole city to get the biggest creep!" I would laugh if I had the energy. Were not afraid for her. "So he starts yelling that it's a hit-and-run and the scene of the crime and all that stuff, just 'cause I can't stand there forever, 'cause I had to bring Dan's car back to him and get my own." Why? I wonder. "This guy has a Datsun or something and I haven't hurt his car too much, but Dan's front end is a mess. You know how those little Volkswagens just fold up." Bewildered, I am left with the knowledge of how Volkswagens crumple, this general truth, this commonplace. She bounds on. "So I took Dan's car back and picked up mine and I'm going back there now, scene of the crime, he calls it, just to show him I keep my word. But he's got this phone number and my address, so I just wanted you to know, in case he calls up." "Sure." "I'm terrified, I'm just terrified. He could go after me for every cent he could get." "Try not to worry right now, try to calm down. Relax a little." "What can he do to me? Attach my welfare check? I'm broke, man." "If he calls I'll talk to him." "I just wanted you to know ahead of time. Tell Mom not to worry."

Thinking that I have now, my stated interval, my term of time. Thinking it as I watch her at breakfast. My stretch of days, my allotment of proximity, days, weeks, months. Then nothing. Go back to New York and it will be over. But for now there is this, guaranteed. Thinking it as I watch her over breakfast. Warm, secure in her presence, momentarily secure, watching her eat. Her poise, her assurance, her movement taking a piece of toast and buttering it, both dainty and bold somehow, and curiously admirable to me, smooth and fluid like the smoothness of her skin. Admiring the shape of her breasts in their green sweater, her long legs as she stands and goes into the kitchen. Her movements as she cleaned the ice box last night, the stride, the efficiency. Even her confidence before a mess of spoiled vegetables, some recalcitrant stain. I would have made a project of this, dreaded it all day, stretched it to hours if I'd gotten to it at all. She does it in four whirling minutes. Even the arcane fittings of the plastic shelves, those troublesome boxes at the bottom, all deceitfully easy under her command, trays sliding neatly back into place.

Then her committee arrived for a meeting she'd assured me would last only three minutes. I went upstairs to read and be out of the way. Discovered I had left the glass of wine I was drinking downstairs. Too late. The book I'm reading inescapably dull, the print too fine, my neck begins to ache from reading prone on the bed. Try again, sitting up. Worse still. They have been down there an hour already. I begin to hate and resent them. It's dinnertime, why don't they go home? Percy, his boasting noise coming up through the floor. Then a white man's voice, nasal, irritating, going on about his asinine "five-point scale" for making decisions. "We must ask ourselves, will this experience benefit my intellectual and emotional growth?" I close my eyes, this sort of language always gives me the creeps. California hokum, therapeutic weekends, how can she bear these people? But this project, this "dialogue between male and female: toward a new communion and understanding," is at the moment the darling of her heart. It has already consumed two of our evenings and will devour a three-day weekend in February. It is about to overcook tonight's own chicken as well. The male voice goes on: "Does it take me to restful places likely to nourish and stimulate that growth?" Charming, well-modulated moron. Go home, the chicken will be overdone. This is my dinner you are drying out. I have a headache from hunger, from being cooped in a room like a domestic animal.

And when they finally left two hours later, she rescued me. Hearing her step on the stairs, I had already forgiven everything. The dear soft voice of her apology. How charming the Italian in its accent, which fluctuates according to the occasion but is always stronger when she is confused or sorry or ill at ease. Or perhaps it is the Portuguese, for it is the Indian in her that apologizes or waits, once waited two whole days for me when I missed a plane. Light-years ago. Never mind, she is laughing, hugging me, laughing at them, laughing with delight that they are finally gone, laughing at the chicken. And I am laughing too, warm in her embrace, the scent of her lovely sweater, the silk around her neck, the fine gold of the bracelet at her wrist. I forget everything in her presence: the absurdity of my position here, the unfairness. They are dismissed in an instant by her complicity, her romantic transformation of all life into an assignation. She'd once spoken, smiling, of "the proper conduct of a love affair." I had never realized that love affairs were conducted, I thought they merely happened. I had much to learn.

Now at breakfast she is planning Paul's birthday party. This or that couple from the office. One pair can't come because it's their fifth wedding anniversary and they have other plans. I do not look forward to it. It sounds very dull and heterosexual. "What usually happens is that Pia and Paul's friends end up upstairs playing music and smoking dope—I'll get beer and crackers for them—and the rest of us have a good time downstairs. George McFarland is coming. You remember George. And Neal. And I think I'll invite . . ." But I hear only Neal. I would have thought she could do without this, without making me meet him. Perhaps it's better. Perhaps if she has her own way in everything, is unopposed. Completely free. Is that freedom?

Last night when she woke in the middle of the night, because the back door was open and had been banging, I was positively surly. She laughs, repeating my growl. " 'Sita, what the hell are you doing?' is what you said, as a matter of fact." "I'm so sorry, darling." Wishing now I had held, had kissed her, enjoyed her, the soft of her flesh. "I've known worse. People who wake up in the middle of the night and talk. Talk, mind you. Hank used to walk around in his sleep." I see Hank, ghostlike, another past, his great naked body dwarfing his cock. When you are secure, they never bother you, never challenge, these pictures. You can flick them away. In the old days I triumphed so over Hank, over all of them, Sita so outrageously in love with me then that they simply never mattered.

Last night I did not offer lovemaking. Afraid now as always lately. Afraid of her rejection, even more afraid of her having to reject, finding a way to say it kindly. Or annoyed and forced to show annoyance. No, not forced, merely unable to hide it or disguise her antipathy. But this too puts a burden on her. And I am loath to put her to that trouble, that ill nature, that guilt. And I

123

am afraid, too, to know how bad it is, how small my chances are. And so it is always her decision now, a decision rather than what it used to be, a coming together and igniting and who knows which ignored, for it was that close, the spark in the loins that mutual, the fever coming into the forehead and finding relief in the mouth. Wishing as I held her in my arms before sleep, wishing as I have wished a thousand times to descend her body and eat, feast in the damp between her legs, drink as at a fountain. Suckle there and play and sate myself, hours of it, the greed of it, the concentration as I hear her cries, breathing in the scent of her, the dear lovely taste of her always so fresh. Time to do this, the afternoons we used to have, evenings devoted to lust. And joy. The joy of those times. Now there is neither time nor inclination.

But there is this stretch of weeks. There is this, there is still this. Over inevitably, as inevitably she will put down her coffee and go to her office. And leave me here to wait her return nine long hours later. But I will have this time, savor it, experience it as completely as I can, drain it. It is the end of love, the dregs. The last crumbling and embarrassed moments of its collapse. All that I am given.

Knowing it is limited. Not like before, when riches poured down, occasions came unsought, surprising me as she descended on me in a morning I did not expect her, casually, beautifully undressing, an act she always did with the most consummate grace and ease. Or Sita met by chance on campus, flattering me when she would burst into my office at the end of a day. A bunch of daffodils in her hand. Or found at the door of my classroom, Sita claiming she had just discovered a new place we should drive to for dinner. Once even with Hank, we drove up to the gold country, the three of us riding in the front seat of my convertible with the top down in the fine serene evening. If she likes, I could even take on Hank. Remembering a wistful comment she'd made that a woman lover she'd had once hadn't liked him, was unreasonably jealous, and that she had always wanted to have a weekend in the country, up at the ranch where Hank lived, the three of them, just to be in nature, to swim naked there and lie in the sun. Wondering if I could do that. Liking Hank. When we got to Sutter Creek and began to explore the ruins, he teased me, the three of us standing together, both of them so much taller than I, "shrimp," he called me, and I suddenly found I resented him, discovering I was not a woman to him but a boy, or he would try to convert me to a boy, someone smaller, and I was not the desirable stranger but a rival. At dinner he drank badly and was morose, jealous, irritating. But he insisted he drive my car down the mountain because I drove the pitch-black road so slowly. He had just wrecked Sita's car. But she did not back me up, said she was too tipsy to drive herself, and seemed to think it a fine idea he should. I refused to let him drive and he called me a cunt—"Just like any cunt in a bar, all cunts, whoever the fuck they think they are"—a remark she has always professed she never heard, even though he shouted it. I drove, but for the first time my confidence as a driver was broken. Her confidence in me too. When we go anywhere now, she drives. Even in my car. It is part of my subjection to her.

Mad, the whole thing is mad. Mad to be here, mad to linger in a relationship where you don't even drive your own car, where you are hanging on in somebody else's house and town and life without a purpose and your own sense of adequacy, ability, competence utterly shattered, so that you no longer really work or believe in your work. Thinking of suicide again. And congratulate yourself on having ten weeks of this guaranteed to you? Glad of it.

There is this space ahead, this time. Last night after dinner, merely watching the television. She sat beside me on the floor, then stretched out on the couch while I sat below her, an arm around her knees, giggling together at the pretensions of Bronowski or Alistair Cooke's narrations, the gravity of televised "culture," groaning at the superb generalities of their capsulized history but admiring their footage on Greece. Then lying back on the pillows in the bay window, no longer even watching the set and its dull pop-singer hero, only inhaling the fragrance of her flesh, the security, the eternal because so momentary safety of her arms. This time.

The sound of Hare Krishna people along Telegraph Avenue. Dark of a coffeehouse. Loneliness of the afternoon. A rainy day in Berkeley. Why am I wasting myself here, far from home, pursuing what has already fled? Why, when death is so soon? Around me beards and coffee cups, madras bedspreads on the wall, other people's conversations. The impenetrable lives of strangers. On the street a young woman carrying an infant covered with a blanket against the light rain. She looks utterly lost but has more purpose in life than I do. Young men in their ponchos and hats and padded jackets, their big boots and watch caps. All the paraphernalia of youth. I become old, watching. A youngster crowing over his professor: "This guy used to teach at Harvard." Waiters on their listless feet. "So I went into his office this morning and he told me two or three things that are gonna be on the midterm. With the answers, man. Be no problem there." The busboy picks up a dirty cup. "This guy writes so smooth, you know, it just flows." Pull of the espresso machine. A girl in the corner behind huge dark glasses drinks coffee soulfully. The espresso machine pulls again, suction and whistle.

She will be home late again tonight. Only an hour, an hour and a half together before she sleeps. A couple come in and discuss God. Are they madder than I? "They can still be saved," the woman's voice labors on, didactic, anxious. Ineffably tedious. He rattles her with questions, objections. "No, no, when you are praying, ask the Lord to help you with the things you can't accept. Having been a Christian for twenty years, I can understand a lot more than someone who's been in the movement for just a few months." He quibbles over her age, closer to nineteen really. Idiot reactionary fanaticism and this child calls it a "movement." How

126

self-important they all are, what a collection of phonies, of mediocre minds. Berkeley. The waiter finally brings my coffee.

I must not dig in too hard, hold on, anchor myself in her, I
thought to myself last night at the Riviera, watching her arm,
enjoying the rose flesh of it, my eyes touching it like fingers. Watching her during an Italian film; the woman director was present,
answering questions afterward. And Sita, her mouth half open in
delight, following the play of dialogue in both languages. The look
of joy on her face as she heard her own Italian spoken. And later,
outside the café, coming upon an Italian professor: *"E Mario."*
"Come va." *"Va bene."* How her voice dances over the words, rises
and falls and sings them. Her English so much more restrained,
restraining. But seeing her again speaking Italian, how she lights
up, how she relishes each word in her mouth. Her laughter, her
gaiety. I go on a few steps to wait for her apart, enjoying her from
afar, happy for her happiness. She calls me back to introduce me.
"You do not speak Italian?" the professor asks. I admit my ignorance, feeling irredeemably stupid before his surprise. It would take
too long to explain my lust for the language last summer, my
eagerness to learn it, and then the wall she lowered between me and
her country. "I could have picked up a lot, just didn't seem to have
the knack"—but no one hears me; they are reminiscing about
friends in Sacramento. After he leaves she tells a long and naughty
story about the professor's wife, the mood of the evening still with
her as she drinks cappuccino, her voice still floating into laughter,
into that particular lilt and vivacity it takes from contact with the
Italian. As if English were a kind of prison and America too a
duller place, heavy and plodding like its language, somewhere you
might go to escape a war or a depression, but tepid and ugly finally,
a cold exile from the Tuscan hills she loves so deeply. That summer, especially the last time she saw them, en route back to Germany and the charter flight, tears in her eyes so that she could
barely drive, she hated so to leave them. And I, looking at them

127

that last time, had actually come to hate them. And Italy. All that I had loved so in my Oxford days, the great trip to Italy alone after my examinations. Years ago, and had loved the place, the people, the profusion of art and excitement and good nature. And by the end of a summer there with her had come to hate it, the heat and the tiled roofs, even her good and always impeccably polite family. A hate that was love utterly disappointed. How easy it would have been to learn the language, how easy to love her family—how easy if she had not been there. Preventing. In some mysterious way preventing me from speaking or from becoming friends.

Her brother was invariably, even punctiliously kind. So it is hard to explain, but perhaps it was that little incident even before we got down to the villa and the shore and the countryside, the second day actually, just a few hours after we left Milan. I needed cigarettes. Paolo was not very eager to stop the car. And it was hot that day, not yet lunchtime, but the traffic was heavy already. I had to plead a little to get him to stop. Then I jumped right out and into the store, thinking to hurry. Hardly noticing his command that I wait until he was at my back in the shop, shouting at me. I had already used my new and experimental Italian on the shopkeeper, and made my request, was rather pleased with myself, when I turned to see Paolo furious. "Who do you think you are?" I'm astonished, merely stare at him. He countermands my order for cigarettes. I stand there discredited, ridiculous. He buys another package, pays, and orders me to leave. "What on earth is the matter, Paolo?" "Who do you think you are, going around like you know everyone?" He slams the door on his side of the car. I look back to Sita for guidance. She hasn't any. Like Paolo, she merely assumes that I stay in the car while a male deals with the world, keep silent in a country where I do not know the language. And be served. But paid for too? How many times has it been made clear to me that Paolo finds it hard to pay for the life he leads. I had meant only to save my host the trouble. And I had also taken it for granted that one helps oneself, is independent, and the American woman in me had no desire to be served, still less to put up with the bullying that comes out if you show any signs of independence. I found Paolo harder to like after that, though I did like him anyway. Or rather I admired his character in maintaining an exemplary courtesy to me through a whole summer in his house, when I knew he neither liked nor approved of me. I'm not certain what he imagined my relationship with his sister to be.

On several occasions he referred to Hank as Sita's lover of the moment, a fiction I did not know whether to contradict or not. During the first week of our stay he read a book I'd written, *Flying*, that was expressly lesbian in certain passages. Bravo, I thought, he has taken this extremely well. The next day our beds were changed from a double to two singles. The reason given was that Sita had a cold. She may well have asked for the change herself, though of course she denied it. On the rare occasions when we spoke. For she was consumed now, reabsorbed into the bosom of the family, the language, the ways, the countryside, the long afternoons at the beach, the conversation of her sister-in-law, her walks with Paolo, her hours of badinage with the children. She was lost to me, lost in the crowds of friends and relations, a couple from Milan, the grandmother, the maid, the thirteen who sat at dinner. And I was a shadow reading books in our room, grinning foolishly when addressed in English, puzzled and idiotic when addressed in Italian. In as much as she could arrange it, I was simply not there. I had been the means of transport, a convenience in bringing her to Italy, but now dispensable. In as much as I could arrange it, I would rather neither of us were there, but she would not leave, and our two-week visit slowly and hideously became two months. I begged and was occasionally conceded a weekend in San Gimignano, a night in Siena, and finally, by myself, fleeing really, a week in Florence.

That an entire summer in Europe could be so wasted, so boring, so friendless, seems hard to believe now. All the expectations I had had, the adventure of it, being with her in Italy, her Italy, so loved, so long talked about, imagined, planned, anticipated. And of course there was much in what we had that could have been enchanting, even glamorous. The great stone-floored villa in the fields, a farmer's house from the eighteenth century, huge, full of rooms and guests and long lunches, banquets at night, the party they gave for me the night I left alone for Florence, the champagne and cakes, the table spread outside in the mists of the evening, romantic it was, magnificent. Somehow only a mockery. Even our crazy dancing that night, the one occasion of hilarity, license, the whole lot of us, children and all in a frenzy of cha-chas and twists, tarantellas and rock 'n' roll. There will always be something lonely about remembering this, I'd thought at the time, thinking it was because I was leaving them all, leaving her here with them. But it was more than that, there was a strange betrayal even in the feast. An empty ceremony.

Remembering it now in a Berkeley coffeehouse on a rainy afternoon, I find it unspeakably bitter. To remember Italy at all is unpleasant, remembering it as I am losing her is unbearable. But why didn't I see it then? Not really believing her odd little explanations for her behavior—that she was suffering depression, that she was having a little nervous breakdown in return for my bigger one, and that I, if anyone would, should understand and sympathize. On other days she would say it was her health—glandular deficiencies, hormones, nerves, her doctor would look into all of it further when she got home. Poor lady, she was simply bored to death with me and had not yet found the way to relieve herself of the affliction. Coming home in September, she could serenely tell Sherman the affair was over and rearrange her house and life and associates accordingly. She had simply neglected to tell me. Till being here becomes finding out. And letting me come was a weakness she permitted herself after the visit at Christmas. There was still a spark. She wouldn't quite give it a chance, but perhaps she could not quite bring herself to extinguish it completely. She'd wait and see. So do I. I wait and see.

And I drink bad coffee in cafés on rainy days in Berkeley, and prowl bookstores, and have nothing to do for whole afternoons. Because I am waiting. Knowing already that if ever I were to win, I would be just as confused. I have done her the disservice of making her my need. I have used her to find purpose in my life. You can't do that to someone. My own terror lies like a mat under a rug; makes me tremble browsing through a bit of Henry Miller, his *Insomnia*, the obsession of an old man with a young and indifferent girl, but my story too. Yet whatever fool he was in the middle of the night, he was still a writer. And I have lost who I am. A follower following nothing, my hands empty along the way. Do I cling and pursue this love because I have really nothing else to do—or am I unable to write because my slavery to this infatuation makes work impossible? The former. No, the latter. The former because you have not finished a book in three years. The latter, because that is the period of time you have known her. Never blame problems with your work on other people; you have simply had no book to write for three years. Probably never again. Done for. And done for with her too. Both at the same moment. Nice timing. That curly-haired boy waiting on table knows who he is. The religious fanatic knows who she is. Even the wavering and uncertain figures passing the windows in the rain, even they understand who they are, each in his lazy California manner, "mellowed out," "laid back," whatever occult fizz passes for wisdom in their confused minds, they all know what they are doing. But I am only waiting for nightfall.

I spread her out on the couch. Laughing at me. "Kate! Why are you getting me to take off my clothes now? We're going out soon. You were going to call your sister before we left." "Later, later. This now." "But she'll be out here in ten days, we should confirm with her . . ." "I'll write her a note." "People can see us. If someone came up to the front door . . ." still laughing, unsure perhaps as

I am unsure. How she would have adored this once, the madness, the risk, the spontaneity. Now I am very far from sure if she will even give in, permit me. But sitting near her on the floor as she sat on the sofa, it came to me, like a wildness, like a hope—the notion of spreading her legs and taking suck. Suddenly how I wanted that —how charming and offhand, how silly and willful and easy it seemed. I had only to coax off her trousers, spread her legs, and the warm dark loveliness would be there at my mouth. If I can persuade her, cajole, tease. Appearing to be utterly sure of myself, without qualm or question. If I can make it be then, that time and its willingness, its lust and hurry and ease. We never refused each other anything those days, could often hardly wait until we got home. When I landed from Seattle once, we took a room in Sausalito simply because it was a closer bed than Berkeley. Rented a room because we could not wait or drive any farther. Deciding the thing in the airport parking lot, amused, feeling wicked and a little silly but very pleased with ourselves, with our savoir faire and nonchalance, our imagination and ingenuity—or rather hers, for it was her idea, I was far too provincial and stingy to think of renting a hotel room to satisfy an urge. But how charming the idea was when she suggested it, how worldly and blasé. Scarcely able to wait till we got there, falling upon each other, each as if by some mute intuition taking each other in the anus as well. We laughed—can this be the reward of a Catholic girlhood? Just as I'd laughed when she came to me finally at my farm that September after the break-down and the loony bins, the moment arrived at last when in touching her flesh again I would know all those nights in hell were over and had been worth it, had been lived through only that I might feel her in my arms again, her embrace, her skin under the fingers of my hand, and when she took me and entered me, I wept and said, the joke only a pretense for its utter earnestness—Ave Innocenza, do you realize you're my religion? But she had no idea what I meant. Maybe that was the beginning of the end, for we quarreled the whole time and she left three days later.

132

The anger of the bin was in me, my fury at what they had done in order to lock me up, to dope me and hold me and make me despair of freedom. I tried but I could not forgive her. And she would permit me no anger, imagined I was still mad. And I suppose I was, a little. And she drove me madder. The last awful business upriver at some college where she was to speak and was traveling as a big shot to confer with other big shots. I was supposed to perform as well, but hadn't accepted the invitation in time and had been replaced. So I traveled along as companion, baggage handler, nonentity, and then shamed her horribly by heckling from the audience. Stuffed-shirt chapel atmosphere and I put a bit of the old bomb-throwing radical into it, discomforting the little Wasp children in the audience and mortifying Sita. After that it was over. No amount of begging or pleading could get her to stay. A long tearful delirious night and she left on the 6 a.m. plane. It was over, all over again. Then, in the late fall, her plans for a commune with the kids fell through and Hank left because the rent was too high for him. She began calling me. Answered my first tentative gift. It seemed she couldn't forget me. Or perhaps I was handy, other options failing her. And mine were failing too. Fumio announced his desertion. I began the long spiral downward into suicide. Six tries, two of them in earnest. When the depression had run its course, she was there for me, she had taken the house in Indian Rock. We would live together, it would be our home. Refuge and asylum and all settled. Until I failed her, or it seems I did, by taking a new loft in New York for a few months of the year. Having no idea it meant so much to her, having no idea it would bring about the disaffection that came out in Italy, the slow, but perhaps not slow, perhaps sudden erosion of trust or even interest that must have taken place in her while I was in New York these past months fixing the loft. And so we come to here, what I find when I return, the house on Indian Rock alienated, Sita absent, hostile. The process I stay here fighting, the death of love, its breakup, its wilting, its decay.

133

Hoping by an act of fantasy now to revive it, hoping by such reckless gestures as spreading her upon a couch to reach some spring of Eros never touched and still new, still fresh. I know, even as I perform the miracle of undressing her, I know the futility of what I do. And do anyway, doggedly, stubbornly, with the faith of desperation. Because it is desperate: to imagine it would matter at all if she gave into my whim, submitted to my obsession—this once. What is once? What would it possibly matter in the sure and relentless loss of yardage, the inevitable sliding down the bank grabbing at saplings and weeds, what would it matter if once, a mere once, she indulged me? But that is what I want. As if this once were all time in one moment. Without consequence. As time is for lovers.

Further laughing and persuasion, yes, darling, just a little whim, it occurred to me we had a good ten minutes, just right for something instant, how pretty you are, your long brown legs, your soft brown hair here. She protests again about the door, about her shower, about her long day at the office and no shower, it cannot be pleasant, she would prefer to shower, she would prefer to go upstairs. And out of my clutches. And the shower too is a canard, she is as fragrant as she always is, tasting her as she laughs in resignation and places her hand on my head, crooning as I wish now I could croon and speak, speak the words of my love and lust, the words that would excite her further, stoke her, fire her to cries and madness. For she is interested, she is finally intrigued and then warmed and then willing. But not as I would have her willing. The very act of getting my way, of succeeding, is my failure, the realization of how alone I am. I had wanted her to love me back, to love me as I love her, as much, as compulsively, as passionately as we once both loved each other. But this is then and then is not now. Now is merely my diseased persistence, seeing again the beloved skin of her thighs, the soft brown hairs over her cunt. Her cunt that is almost a being to me, so long have I loved it, known it, kissed it, wept for its wounds, its small twisted clitoris. After the rape in the desert, the six drunks who stopped when her car broke down —the joy that help had arrived—the nightmare that followed the surgery. Why, after such outrage, why, when penetration must be so physically as well as psychologically painful to her, why would she permit, even seek Neal's probably large and certainly painful prick? Why, when she is loath even to let me go down on her with infinite gentleness and relish? Surely he cannot know and love her as I do. The old rancor, that she would fuck a man, permit him to enter, gross and rude and large after the crime of the six drunken rapists has left her so, why of her own free will accept another one? And why in preference? There is no knowing, only the moment with the sweet salt taste of her in my mouth, trying, trying to give her joy or bliss or something to come back for, accept me again because of some particular pleasure, some satisfaction for love or skill or even adulation. Because this is surely the act of homage. Saying to her once as we walked by the sea, saying what had been so hard to say, and saying it with a bitterness that surprised me— "Why is it always I who goes down, never you? Is that some of your damn European aristocrat business?" And she of course protested. But it was true, even in the early days, when all I saw was her great and enormous desire to make love to me, to give me such pleasures as I had never known; even then, she did not often perform that act. Yet now, it is still she who is the lover, her endless and wonderful ability to make love to me, all that is left of our sensual relationship. Whereas once she assured me no one had ever really given her pleasure before—and how easy I found it to believe that tribute, why not, there had been the rape, a succession of clumsy or inattentive husbands—now there is really nothing left but her making love to me. An exercise of power perhaps, a favor, charity, guilt. But to satisfy herself she has found men again, the one last time, others. Labor, even as I labor, listening for her cries and her hands stroking my cheeks, lighting around my head, I have no real hope. At bottom my heart already accepts defeat, expects the little sounds of her pleasure and then the sigh of her satisfaction—and knows it for fraud, if not the fraud of faked orgasm, the fraud of shallow and mere physical pleasure. I have lost my hold on her; even as I take her in my mouth, I understand how I have lost my hold. Were she to have refused me, I would not know with this same disappointed certainty. Having wanted and having gotten, now I know. Really know I have gotten nothing. Hardly even the heart to look at her as she speeds past me to her shower.

This is not love. This is sickness. Only some utterly negative aspect of what once was love. Like meat gone rotten. The failure of the illusion, the winding down, the acknowledgment of death. Debility, weakness, loss. All the hateful, the despicable traits. Dependence most of all, a paralyzing, humiliating dependence. The aftermath of love. Like its corpse. Long after the body ceases to live, the blood to run. But the vitality it gave off once, how it made me feel young, alive, intelligent, capable. Now this blue-gray thing of evening. Remembering her professions of love, an experience so deep it will go on to the day she dies, never leave her. She had never loved anyone this way before. Now I experience it ending. What she must have meant is that she will always remember having wanted me, not that she will always go on wanting me. But I had hoped we were exceptional, long-lived lovers. Not an affair of a year or two and then erased. And do I mourn her love's death or my own? Because I too cease to love as I knew it. What's left is not love, only despondency, fear, the little hopes, the great clinging.

But to think of a time without her. New York without her. Of course. But for how long? The day I can no longer be with her, the day I cannot come back. Finally it is her absence in the future that I fear. The line to the theater shifts, moves forward three feet. I am "entertaining myself" because she is gone tonight, won't be home for dinner, is staying at the office late because of registration. It is the third night in a row. It is possible that she is simply having dinner with someone else. Neal? Who? If you begin that route, you are sure to go crazy. Forget it. The line crawls on with film-archives tedium. She pins up the notices of the "cultural events" on campus in the kitchen. I pick almost at random, desperate for a way to fill an afternoon or an evening or the hours from five to seven.

I leave the line for a moment to make a note in my notebook. It has become my friend, solace, obsession. I will live in it, in the ability to record experience which makes me more than its victim. Putting feeling into words, and the words onto paper. Magical transformation of pain into substance, meaning, something of my own. The notebook then, like a shield against all that happens, each turn of events, the suffering of each evening. I am recording a process, keeping track of an event, noting with almost clinical observation and accuracy the death of something organic. But back in the line I am merely a nondescript waiting patiently to see a movie that fails to interest me at all. And even as I finish my scribbling, I am seized with the cold knowledge of New York, the loft alone. A future without her. Gray years stretching to death. The notebook assumes its real aspect, an untidy scribble without meaning or body or direction. The cheapest illusion. What will happen is what I have written and the cold understanding in it: finally, it is her absence in the future I fear.

I am home a little later than she is, her car is already parked in front of the house. As I mount the stairs I see her coming toward me in the hall, the familiar purple wool caftan (over her brown skin how many times) and that absurd flannel nightgown underneath. Watching television by herself. I sit down at a little distance, drinking a glass of wine. "Shall I bring a glass for you?" "No." Then I drink it alone, sitting alone, giving her space, sensing that she would like that just now. Or she may even move over toward me. A Japanese film tonight, long miserable business of hara-kiri. Just when I am settled into it, absorbed, I am startled to see her rise and leave the room. Probably just to the bathroom. Surprised to see her return with the ubiquitous curlers. "I'm exhausted, I'm going to bed. You stay up and watch it."

I am afraid, afraid of a middle-aged woman in hair curlers abandoning me to the little screen of shadows. Go with her? She doesn't want me. Nothing could be clearer. And I would now like to watch the film. Then be sensible, stay here. Letting a few moments pass before I must rise, go up the stairs, the room already pitch dark. "I wanted to say good night." Her kiss perfunctory, meant to repel, send me back downstairs. Well, I have tried. Watching the film again, the slow terrible agonies of the feudal code, its courtesies, rituals, obligations. Then the light is on upstairs. Without even saying it to myself, I know. She is choosing another bed. Pia's in one room or Valerie and Paul's in the other. Knowing already that the move is a command not to follow. I go to the bottom of the stairs. She is before me on the landing, taller, so much taller, the length of her nightgown.

"I am in one of my wanting-to-be-alone moods right now." I feel the tension in my shoulders, discovering they are raised three inches higher around my neck, my arms rigid. I look at her. "Have I done anything wrong?" "No, of course not." I feel the tension in my shoulders ease a bit, aware I am lowering them. Does she see me? "Are you angry?" "It has nothing to do with you. I've told you before, I need space sometimes, you'll just have to try to understand." The voice querulous, annoyed. She turns to mount the stairs.

The fear is greater now, a certain thing. I watch the film in a trance of dread, deadening myself with it, drugging my mounting terror with its patterns and images, faces and figures. The frame, the shot, the rhythm of architectural line, of black and white. You do not call back love. If one lover takes it away, withdraws bearing the missing half, then the unfortunate, the loser, the fool still willing, cannot furnish it alone. Her refusal is absolute, without appeal. And I do not appeal it, only wait for grace: a change of mood, the swing of the pendulum, the inevitable (no, perhaps not inevitable) rebate. After her night with Neal she was a greater sweetness to me. But this diminishes. May diminish to a smaller and smaller mite each time. Whether to play the lover as saint— "love must never beg or entreat or demand"—or whether to be modern, practical—insist on the rights of a peer? Vacillating between the two, successful at neither. Insufficiently committed to either course. Meanwhile, the shadows of an old world before me, the figures in the drama go about their predestined ways to death. Slow, graceful. The samurai condemned to seppuku with a bamboo dagger. Terrible their poverty and honor and courage. Extreme, remote, and perfect.

Alone in this living room thousands of miles from my home. And she, obdurate in her room upstairs, whichever room, whichever bed. She goes from me by steps, each expected but then surprising, each foreknown and then a shock as it occurs, something I could never have predicted. There is no way to forestall, as there is no way to recall, to bid back, to restore. That she does not want, that she does not wish—is everything, an enormous power. And wanting, I am powerless. Her serenity, her solid ego and identity—is it that she knows herself so sublimely, commands her time and place and destiny so thoroughly? How do you become so strong? Through denial only? I see her marriages anew, not as the inflictions she has described, but as the exercise of her will over Martin, over Ben, even over Gil. She could have made their lives hell. No, not your place to judge these things, you know nothing really anyway, watch the screen, the samurai preparing to die, the square tatami of his suffering. She is a presence above me in a room.

My eyes uncovering the empty bed. No need for the light. Or the stealth I had promised, were she here, stealth to undress without waking her. Banging the closet door against a hanging plant irritatingly hung at just the wrong juncture. Taking my nightgown from its hanger. Just yesterday she had praised its color. Out the windows, the desired view where I can never move my desk, the lights of San Francisco gleaming across the bay, magical, alluring, the old dream of living there. Teaching the course again next year, having a future for us here. Now in the dark seeing her pillow gone.

Of course I can't stay here. This will be recurrent. And Neal on Sunday at the party, and wondering all day if she will go home with him afterward. Monday my first class. Still time to cancel again. Before the students kick in their money. Go and explain graciously, urgent research, publishers' deadlines, family illness all require I return posthaste to New York. And merely stay through February. I can't stand much beyond February. My eyes traversing the rug as I get into bed on my side. The mere sight of the rug telling me in an instant of my boredom here, my dislike of the place. But what if she were to do as she did last year, make it a fortress, a castle of her protective adoration? I would strangle. What if she wanted me to stay, stay on through the year? Never leave California. No, I would die without New York, suffocate. So why not leave now? Why be here at all? No, these months, these few months, this last experience.

Lying in bed. Knowing she is lying in bed in another room. Pia's room behind the closed door. This night harder even than the other when she didn't come home, since then I could go out to Sherman's. The rain falls. Sounds of the house, this house of old sounds. Rain on the roof sounding as if it were falling directly through the ceiling and into the hall. Just a few feet away, the steady tap like a leaky faucet. The other night I could drink and rave, read *The Ginger Man* till I passed out in fantasy. But tonight her hostile presence just yards away.

I light a cigarette, unable to sleep. The lights of San Francisco if you raise your head from the pillow. Such a beautiful room for a bedroom, we thought when we got it, the great yellow painting on the wall, the black-and-white-flowered sheets, the Greek bedspread. Simple, perfect. And now this disorder of objects persists even after she has eliminated some, weeded the place out after we came home from Mendocino. And I had hoped so that I would be given Paul's room to write in. From the beginning, when we talked of shifting things around, using Paul's room, I was afraid, afraid it would be a matter of her moving herself out, away from me, rather than making a place for me to write as I hoped. My forlorn manuscript still all over the desk right at my elbow. I didn't get the room.

And now sleeping apart. It will go on. The damn class keeping me here, months of this torture, this bullshit. Monday is the first class. Over the weekend I must talk to her, ask her gently if she's sure she wants me to stay, or can foresee that it might be too great a strain, that much time. And then if we cancel it? Further looking foolish in public, but at least not bound by the law to stick it out. There's a contract. And state law. Have they got me already? Fear like a net over the bed. In what strange place have I fallen captive all by my own undoing? I had a life, New York pulling at me all day—get out of here. Losing myself in staying, losing her if I go.

In the morning I saw that she had slept in Paul's room. A peach-colored blanket, and under it a yellow one over the spread. There were no sheets. I had noticed before that when Paul and Valerie left, they took their sheets with them. I smiled and thought of them as children, indigent children in love. And she chose this. Chose to sleep without sheets under two light blankets. Preferred it. It was what she preferred.

Sitting on the couch Friday afternoon, the week over. A glass of wine. She is gay, relaxed, out of time, full of reminiscences. I enjoy her, simply and openly delight in her. "And what sort of people did you know in Japan?" She lies along the sofa, her body young, elastic, glamorous. "The Brazilian ambassador, who had grown up with my mother, and the French chargé d'affaires. His wife was a great friend of mine, she had a little girl the same age as Pia. Only a few Americans. But one couple, the O'Neils. Both over six feet tall, and she had black hair and blue eyes. Everywhere they went they were smashing. Then one night Tim O'Neil was coming home drunk and ran over a Japanese civilian. An old man with a white oxen and honey buckets and the oxen loomed up around a corner, but Tim just never saw the old man. It was a terrible thing: inquest, court-martial, the whole works. He deserved it." "Were the Americans bullies?" "For sure. Luckily I was not an American, so there were all sorts of places I could go that Gil couldn't. And this way I got to know a lot of Japanese, visited their houses, became friends." I see her in those days, young under great wide hats. Spoiled, beautiful. "Gil loved to buy me hats." The Sita of then, another Sita, the young Italian dragged out to Japan to join her American husband, forced to leave Italy because of an affair with a student there, her parents insisting she was causing scandal, her place was with her husband. And rejoining him, loath but obedient, for the distractions of diplomatic life, parties, cocktail dresses, the liquor ration that had to be consumed by the end of the month. Gloves and shoes and jewelry. A chauffeur. On the chauffeur's day off a mad ride in a jeep with Ginny O'Neil, the two ladies on their way to a garden party, the naval sentries unable to stop them and bound to salute the commander's vehicle. Gaiety, a swirl of people, dances, uniforms, gifts, invitations, clothes. A summer house in Karasawa. And Sita married to a man thirty-five years her senior, a man her mother had forced her to marry when they fled Italy for Brazil and poverty, the rich American who was to be everyone's means of escape. A good man and he must have loved her, but she grew to hate him. "When we were sent back to San Francisco, he wanted to buy me everything in Magnin's and the City of Paris and Gump's. He wanted to buy me San Francisco. It was the first time I'd ever seen California and I loved it. Then he was ordered to Detroit. I didn't want to go to Detroit, and my father had just died. That closed the door. I didn't have to be married any more. It was over."

It is almost time to go, to relinquish our cushions and comforts, to proceed with our evening. We have scotched a reception in the city and will just go straight to Matthew's for drinks, have dinner, and then dance at Peg's. Paul calls. Plans for his birthday. I move aside in a special euphoria, from the wine, the talk, hearing her relive an earlier life, learning her again in greater detail, further nuance. Then startled, as if a great hook has torn the flesh of my stomach, by what she is saying into the phone: "I've moved into the front bedroom, so you'll find all my stuff in your room when you come over." A laugh. "Yes, and I've been warming your bed." More bright laughter, then the expected closing, "See you Sunday." I sit stunned while she goes to change her clothes. Has she really moved into that room? Was last night the beginning of a permanent arrangement? I had heard her talk only about some posters, moving in her desk and the file cabinets, and her clothes, because the room has a big empty closet. And is this where she will sleep now? The whole structure falling again, the fragile little edifice of my peace, my sanity. Do I have to stay here ten weeks in separate bedrooms? Never. Cancel the class, I must cancel the class, get out of here. Now finally I must leave.

Thinking as we drive along, It's the last night. As we cross the long arm of land toward the bridge and the city. The dilemma burning inside me like a stomach ulcer. I will have to tell her this weekend. Tell her the course is off and I'm going back to New York. But tonight, bury it, bury all the agitation and grievance, live only in the moment, the moment of our last night on the town. Each segment still untouched, drinks at Matthew's place, dinner by ourselves, the dancing at Peg's. FORMULA-FED BEEF speeds by and the debris sculpture on the beach, those strange concoctions of old boards and driftwood continually made and destroyed and remade by invisible strangers—how they remind me of my own ephemeral life—and the great bridge spiring off into the distance, beyond it the enchantment of the lights and towers. Making our approach, we agree, surprising and lovely concurrence, that it is better to live in sight of the city, at a distance, where you can see and savor and have the thrill of entering this way, than merely to live in it, where you see little at all and never the skyline. I help her search for a parking place, I find the spot, I succeed for us in the little challenge. And her umbrella protects me like her arm. We

143

are one, warm, musical our rapport. I do not ask her about Paul's room. I will not spoil it.

The last night, each moment resonant and separate as a Christmas-tree ornament. Past the chic polyurethane panel Matthew has hung across his glass door, some ultra packaging device converted ingeniously to decor. And the red carpeted stairs. I remember them. And the plants, hundreds of plants. Most of all the brown rooms, that he had painted all the rooms a deep and elegant brown. A showplace, the kind of place that's good to visit because after you've admired it, it reminds you how much you like your own house—as she has said. But I compliment Matthew, am impressed, in awe of his house, one part of me just as delighted to be free of it as she is, but enjoying the creation of it, the peculiar achievement of it, that it exists with a greater authority than we do.

I meet Richard, Matthew's new lover, younger, very handsome. Richard talks all the time. From the moment we sit down we are his prisoners. He insists we drink a new concoction (contents unspecified—we must taste it first) that he calls a "Gold Dick." Sita laughs. "Haven't had one of those in a long time." A bit too cool, I think, growing uneasy. A not-so-veiled reference to her old flame Brian Oyama, a Nisei. But surely it was meant only to amuse. Richard goes on, insisting we hear all about each and every apartment he ever had in New York. Crowding us, suffocating us with his talk, his endless one-man avalanche. I am a New Yorker and he pulls New York away from me as a greedy child pulls away a map. An apartment he shared with his sister and three black stewardesses. We obligingly ask the right questions about privacy. "Oh, we got to know each other intimately, intimately. But what I couldn't stand was coming home to find Harlem in my living room. All those spooky dudes they went out with! So I moved over to the East Side, Upper East Side, East Seventies. I did much better there. Just couldn't handle that West Side funk, just couldn't handle it at all." "You were right not to persevere," I say, catching a wry, ironic grin on Matthew's face. Knowing his boy. Infatuated, but still knowing.

Richard goes on, indefatigable. I tune him out and save what is left to me, the sight of Sita kneeling to fix me a piece of farmer's cheese on a cracker, the comfort of our two leather chairs side by side, facing the men, the mere knowledge of her presence, Matthew's friendly being across from her, the beauty of the room. The drink draws to its close. This portion of the evening, this fresh and precious ration. Like seeing a fortune diminish.

And we still have not accomplished our mission. "What are we going to do about Sherman?" Sita asks. "Get her a show," Matthew says. "I can't do anything for her in the freelance way now, market's too tough. But let's see what we can do to get her a show." Richard's just full of ideas: rent a gallery on Saturday night and invite the dealers. Hire a band too, I groan to myself. Richard elaborates, flies off into public-relations fantasy, hoopla. I concentrate on Matthew, addressing him seriously, talking for the first time this evening, trying to fight through the silliness of Richard's hard sell to insist on Sherman's undiscovered greatness. She belongs squarely to the New York School, a peer of Gorky or Kline's, but always overlooked because a woman, not only that but a lesbian, not only that but a dyke who has worn it on jeans and men's shirts for years like a cross. Though her work is beautiful and original, she is a recluse painting in obscurity, suffering years of poverty and neglect, but always painting, painting in whatever neglect or despair or on booze or broke, painting still the great strong pictures of her own style structure and line. "She is yet to be discovered, but I don't want it to happen after she is dead," I tell him. A bit self-conscious after my speech. They murmur agreement, I've had my effect. They promise to see Sherman on Sunday. Matthew is an art director with many contacts in the city. We all have hopes.

On the last night even the smallest moments have an urgency:

the lifting of a piece of French bread at dinner, the passing of the butter, the choosing of the wine, even the choice of the place itself, a small fashionable restaurant on Castro Street, the awkward, overpublic wait for a table, the two of us poised right before a swinging door. My heart cries out to be settled down, at ease and in comfort over the meal, the ceremonial meal. And when it is begun, I already fear and anticipate its conclusion, the moment when it ends, the segment of the evening ending with it. This, the last night.

And at Peg's in the roar of music, the wonderful near-sinister rhythm of butch and disco and hard bartender, the great tall black beauties of women, the rabid finesse of the dancers, the whirling colored lights reaching from the ceiling toward every fantasy small-town prom and big band and nightclub and acid, but effective only if you will plunge yourself entirely, spinning until you stagger in your dizziness. And this is hard for us. Removed so far from this world, tourists once or twice a year, the first moments uneasy in the place. Because it is tough and gay and at the edge. Everything we admire in it, but still another world. Being here at all is some sort of commitment or declaration. I watch her to see its effect. Will her retreat from me show in this place, will the absurdity of the whirling lights, the jejune music, the frantic gyrations of the dance, the public act of dancing with another woman, will it all merely throw our futility into high relief? But with that smoothness of manner, that charming democracy, that tact and poise in any situation which I both love and hate in her, she smiles and is agreeable, exchanging a word or two with some woman whose drink sits next to ours on a railing (there are no tables, it's big Friday night), even accepts an offer to dance with a huge peroxided blonde I am forced to envy though thankful for the opportunity to watch, merely watch her dance. This is different from dancing with her, a thing I never do very well, Sita unable to match my American rhythms or I that odd little South American beat she never relinquishes. And yet tonight we are closer to being in tune than

146

in all the years I've known her, closer to having that euphoric sensation of being perfectly in step, communicating with the body, the face, the mind—all one integrated little pageant that has the special cachet of being performed in public, before spectators. Whether they watch or not, one is stating and proclaiming a relationship before the world, showing off an emotional attachment never otherwise permitted such display.

Perhaps it was for this reason I so resented the man. A nondescript creep, the sort who frequents this kind of bar, with hang-ups of his own, yet unlike the voyeur leaning up against the wall, or the two sailors who have come for kicks and to dare each other into getting one of these broads to dance. This one is different. Determined. Fearless. He asks woman after woman to dance with him. And succeeds. He has even split up a couple, engaging one of the women in something like a necking match, only to drop her the moment of his conquest, the moment she stops her embarrassed protestations, the moment she seems to have adjusted herself to his step and his insolent gnawing upon her neck. I watch, feeling a special humiliation. I am no bigot and would probably argue that such places were best open to the public, loathing rules and exclusiveness and bouncers at the door, but I hate this man. A sudden irrational anger, as if he were the center of all malice, as if his predatory way, his hunt and his stealth were the very image of all that threatens me, every danger in my life now. It is almost over, my mind keeps reminding me, this last night, this last occasion. I mention the man to her, pointing him out. She has noticed him too, agrees with me—yes, it's terrible how they come here, yes, it is annoying. Someone asks her to dance. She is gone from me again. The night is almost over. Bar calls for the last drink. Still watching the alien male closing in on a new partner. She is back with me now, holding me, taller than I am as we dance. Feeling at one with her and then separate as the lights explode, the final drink is bought, the voice booms at us over the microphone. They are having a ball game, a picnic, are a community with Sunday suppers

147

and birthdays and anniversaries. We do not really belong, there is her university across the bay, her neat administrative post, her necklaces and Italian leather boots, her children and grandchild, her party of straight couples tomorrow. The little tawdry world collapses as they turn on the lights, waitresses begin clearing the tables. It is over. Even the malign specter of the man has disappeared. Ahead of us only the bare late-night street, finding the car, the drive home.

All I remember of the party is Neal. But of course it took hours before that happened. The early afternoon and Paul's gang to be entertained, their tedious jokes about Allen's red car, about Paul's haircut, about Tom's skiing trips, about his girlfriends, about their busboy ambitions, the new restaurant in Sausalito. I watched the afternoon sun and tried to help entertain them but found it difficult. Pia relieved us a bit, Pia the prodigal returning home after the mysterious absence of a week, Pia seeing Valerie for the first time since their fight. Her entrance was remarkably dramatic, with effusive whoops, lots of jewelry sweeping into the room, trailing jokes and kisses. High. Very up. Seeing the unnatural energy, I wondered if she was on drugs again. But perhaps this is only strategy to cover an awkward situation. She kisses Paul and notices his haircut—the general subject of conversation for the last two hours. She does not kiss Valerie. I am shocked by her stubbornness, impressed by her bravura and defiance. It would have been so easy to be gracious—yet she wouldn't stoop. And yet she triumphs, gives us all a sense of life as we sit languishing in boredom. After Pia, the family party lapses into the general, hordes of people crowd the rooms. But for me nothing changed.

I think I have never hated a party so much. I have always loved parties, can even summon the nerve to speak to strangers at them. But I spoke to no one. Not even the few people I knew, like Marsha Crabtree, who once shot an unfinished film with me and now sits next to me, loyally and kindly urging me to go ahead and edit it.

"We've got some really good footage there," I dimly hear her say at my elbow. I nod, smile wanly. How can I explain I'm going back to New York, maybe tomorrow? The city yelling all day in my head, urgent as a suitcase to be packed. All day while cleaning the rugs and arranging potato chips I have packed and repacked my hopes—it remains only to tell Sita. Sita a figure in the distance, greeting her guests, performing hostess at her party; charming, beautiful, witty, and full of laughter and serenity. In charge, completely in charge. And I a tongue-tied figure in a corner, unable to say a word, peculiar, downright embarrassing, certainly noticeable. Nothing unfreezes my silent idiocy except the one anxiety. Neal. Imagining him in every man who enters the room. When a very handsome, gray-haired man walks across the dining room with her, tall as she is tall, it must be Neal. I am undone by how well they look together, how superb each of them separately, how they match and complement each other as a pair. One cannot argue with this perfection, I must of course defer. But she introduces him to someone as Walter. Of course, Neal is thirty-five, he could not have Walter's beautiful gray hair even over such a youthful face. Wait, watch again for Neal. He is coming. You have only to wait in a gut of nerves, moving often to cover the fact that you never speak, occasionally useful with chips and sandwiches, but essentially mute, useless. Only to wait until he comes, like a sentence to be executed.

And then I see him. A florid young man with huge mutton-chop whiskers. A bit plump despite her stories of his athleticism. Through some mysterious, baleful intuition I recognized his hunting jacket on a kitchen chair even before I saw his face over the dining-room table. He follows her into the living room, general introductions. He smiles a special smile at me. I cringe. He sits at her feet as she sits across the room from me by the fireplace, a little above him on the chair, and Neal, like the others sitting on the floor, a face in a sea of faces as she presides, queenly, regal, the prow of a ship around which they constitute the waves. Her manner of introduction somehow proclaimed him, his manner of sitting at her feet as well. I feel a subtle, nervous twinge go through the guests—they have sensed it, sensed Neal and myself and some displacement, some way in which his arrival has displaced me. There is the little extra burden of bearing up under ridicule. Or at least trying not to appear ridiculous.

But perhaps my inertness, my silence, is protection, the way I blend into the cushions or the wall. But of course that too is ridiculous. And ridiculous too when I find myself seated next to Neal, who has lumbered over and now squats on his haunches to talk to me. I can think of absolutely nothing to say. A crisis of inarticulateness. "I hear you're going to be doing some teaching for us." His voice is paternal, grand, as if his post entitles him to speak in avuncular fashion for the entire university. I look at him, this puffy, slightly shy young man, embarrassed perhaps as I am, but being decent for God's sake, trying, you've got to admit that. Almost liking him. My answer, which could have been witty— given the number of times I've made a botch of that course, there are ample opportunities for making my answer a joke on my own scandalous vacillation—my answer just a weak little smile and some drivel about looking forward to it. Neal then treats me to a gunner's report on courses that fail for lack of students, courses that must be canceled, courses where the instructor is sent home empty-handed "because the whole thing has to be run like a business, you know." That settles it—squatting back on his heels, he is a football player or a Vietnam veteran or a hunter beside his kill, but he is not the shy and likable young man I had conjured up a moment ago. He speaks *de haut en bas,* an administrator to a mere faculty member, a male to a female, and out of a wealth of masculine assurance and assumption that takes my breath away. How can she endure this pompous young man, how can she endure his heavy limbs and his quietly overbearing manner!

I look up to see her smiling at the two of us. Pleased to see us together. For her sake then, continuing to listen to Neal administer

151

the university, pay its debts, arrange its priorities, and watching him later as he sits across the room, a bit spoiled-looking, a bit put out that he should have to come to this party at all, see her with other people. I understand him, even sympathize. I am also on his side as he looks with annoyance at the proper young couple on the sofa, boring everyone with academic shop talk and subservient reference to the provost. I stay apart with Crabtree and her man and their hashish, hoping a bit of it will carry me out of myself, make it possible to talk, to enjoy the party. No luck. Neal prepares to leave. Will she go with him? Or will she simply install him in Paul's bedroom and subject me to having him in the house all night? She has a cold, she says. Is that a clue, a signal for her departure? Neal disappears. And soon she tells her guests her cold is driving her off to bed, but they must stay and enjoy themselves as long as they like.

It's an impressive performance, walking out on your own party. I cannot help but admire the sangfroid with which she manages it. But now I am left to conduct this foul event—it's not my party, these are not my friends; indeed the experience has convinced me that Sita and I don't live in the same world, could never really live together at all. I do not find these people interesting, even dislike them and consider their presence intrusive. And yet on another day she could invite fifty entirely different people. So various she is, so capricious. And tonight she quietly withdrew the moment she felt like it.

The guests linger. Pia and I see to the stragglers and sit up late with a neighbor who arrived at the last moment, one of the few interesting and likable people. But it is now past one, and even this real personality, with her talk of actual life, palls and flags. We see her out and I go upstairs to find "our" bedroom empty. She has gone out with Neal. Knew it, suspected it, feared it. If I knock on the door to Paul's room, will she be there at all? Will she be there alone? Will he be there as well? Her voice calls to me, feeble,

devastatingly ill, "Come in." She is by herself, very sick with a cold.
I am overcome with tenderness for her, remorse.

The class files in. I have done it, have gotten this far. After a whole
morning of intending to tell her I would cancel. But she was so ill
it seemed impossible to proceed, and my one oblique little attempt
—"What would happen if I didn't do the class after all?"—elicited
a very straightforward "Then I'd lose all credibility with the provost and my department." I could go no further, though the impulse to run was on me all morning, a morning spent in hectic trips
to the bank and then to the co-op for her medicines, lies to the
druggist that I am she, even the lie of signing her name to some
fool slip exempting them from responsibility when I innocently
asked to take the medicine in ordinary containers rather than those
with the elaborate and apparently standard "child-proof" tops.
There is a further hassle about whether she has a co-op number.
Pretending to be Sita, since I am afraid the co-op will not fill the
prescription otherwise, I feel particularly silly having to telephone
her for the membership number. Turns out you don't need one, but
I now realize I do not have enough money for all the medicine,
which costs more than the twenty-five dollars I just took out of the
bank. I cannot write them a check using my own name, so must
go again to the bank. All the while my inner voice is screaming,
Get out of here, for God's sake, go home, leave their lousy sunshine
and vegetation and prissy regulations and get back to reality
Downtown.

Back from the bank, the precious medicines in hand at last, I
leave her for my class, Mark having arrived to sit with her. The
class files in. We have been waiting a long time in the corridor for
the room to empty. I look around at their faces. Grown women—
how on earth am I to be their guru? If they only knew. And the
awkwardness of standing about, packed together, waiting for a

room in a stuffy YWCA building. Tacky, and off-campus, the Y scarcely seems an improvement over the First Baptist. We are packed into its depressing little foyer, staring in embarrassment at each other.

Maybe this will be only another error. I start out, trying to give off energy, to swell my voice, which sounds small and ineffective, my lecture notes squirreling around on the page before me. I make some distinctions for them, playing with the notion of a feminist sensibility versus a feminine sensibility in writing, the effect of history upon artists and then of artists themselves in turn upon their society and culture and those who come after. Their attention hangs on me, they expect too much. I go on, finding there is more to say than I had imagined. A few are bored. Afraid, seeing their faces withdraw, realizing they are too far away, crowded into the back of the room. No, still alive, very much alive, all of them, by this time speaking up, challenging. I am astonished at their information, how widely they have read, how many of them write. Will I be good enough for them? And an odd little hope that they can help me, that I can learn from them, benefit from the mutual support that one of them has just mentioned.

The period draws to a close, and I am almost sorry. I have been better than this with other classes, more vital, humorous, subtle, erudite—but that I could do it at all, pull it off at this time, there's a relief in that. Even a little triumph. Afterward I go for coffee with two of the students, Janice, a young college instructor, and Virginia, a poet. We sit in a little café near the parking lot while Janice describes Anaïs Nin to us. She has met her, says she is dying now in Los Angeles. "How does one come to know such a woman?" I ask, curious about the great and the extent of their accessibility. She tells me that Nin spends her evenings answering letters from her readers. I admire, I more than admire, yet the idea appalls me. The poet has with her some leaflets advertising readings in the city, a world beyond these confines, the claustrophobic world of Indian Rock. I have now met two people who know me rather than Sita.

I am lighthearted when we part, eager to buy another notebook, to write, to work, to study.

Crossing the street on this errand and suddenly believing I could teach again, make that a life. But where to find a job, the market being what it is now? Imagining myself teaching in New York, a life busy, active. No more of the loneliness of the loft and the struggle to write. A life full of people, students, colleagues, old friends fitted into a circle. Feeling confident and competent. No more of this dependency, uncertainty, homelessness. I find a few more errands, extending the time. Knowing I will miss her since she goes over to San Francisco for her own class tonight. I will get home after she's left. I even look forward to having the house to myself.

I am still floating when I drive up and see her car in front of the house, realize she is too sick to go to the city, has of course stayed home. And Mark is still in attendance. Upstairs to her room, seeing her enthroned on pillows and Mark like a son waiting on her, I wonder if I, too, return to her as to a mother. But also an enchantress, our goddess whom we serve with wine and toast and chicken soup.

Mark sits on the big corduroy couch with his shaggy hair, jeans, stocking feet. I sit on a little stool near the phonograph. A record of ballads, the mood for a drink. I bring us all wine. Mark borrows a pack of cigarettes. We smoke together. Our lady upon her pillows. Mark is silent, even more silent than I. As Sita and I chat over the day, Mark says nothing. He is a heavy presence in the room. Such a presence as I have been lately. How strange the dynamic of persons, their emanations, the effects of their mere movements or expressions. How more powerful and definitive finally than words. Mark interrupting something I am saying by slowly, awkwardly standing, going over to the bed, looking at something. He has destroyed what I said, smashed her attention, even my own concentration. Does he do this knowingly or instinctively, and what is the difference?

They have spent the day going over old papers of her—speeches, manuscripts, stories. She has made use of him to move the file cabinet out of Pia's closet and over here into "her room." The room that had been Paul's. The room she has been referring to so much lately. "The front room is mine," she tells people. I remember hearing her say it at the party, sensing Neal hear her say it. And her kids know of course, everyone around her does. Mark too now can observe the separate-bedroom principle.

I go down to warm her soup. Mark follows to heat up macaroni for himself. The food begins to burn in the pan as he forgets it. Almost unwillingly, I take it off the burner, stir it to save it for him. I am relieved to see him leaving, after one last attempt of several to borrow her car. He is pulling on his boots, ready to hitchhike. At last to be rid of him, to have him out of the way. Then I am inconsistent and regretful almost as he kisses me goodbye. How stupid of me to be so possessive. Yet his going leaves us a warm and lighted room, cozy, the intimacy of the sickroom. I have already appropriated the corduroy sofa, having envied Mark as my back ached sitting on the stool. Merely to sit with her, to read, to be together in the quiet evening.

I begin reading one of her manuscripts. It is not all that good, but that is not my interest. An introduction about a journalist "in search of a new angle," a series on the love affairs of older women with much younger men—a transparent device to tell her own story over and over again. It is Sita and Hank, Sita after she left Martin. And each of the three women is a side of herself: the plastic, high-powered, Los Angeles woman executive; the aristocratic woman moving in foreign diplomatic circles; and the one most like her in externals, a suburban housewife who follows her daughter to a commune where she meets a painter. Leaves her husband, a businessman, for the bearded artist and the countryside. The young man in each case an idealized, beautiful, erotic object, highly charged but utterly devoted. And the husband, a nonentity, a jailer. They'd had separate bedrooms for years.

Reading, I see her fantasy self, the drift of her emotions, her attitudes, her hopes and patterns, real or imagined. The pattern of husband as ogre, then rescue by a young man. She has imposed it again on this house and even on me. Separate bedrooms. Making me the husband, Neal the young savior. I tell her this and she laughs. "Neal couldn't rescue anyone from anything. He's young, he's very young. Impossibly young." "But don't you see?" "Not at all, don't be silly." I go on reading. What had hurt me so savagely when I first realized it, this parallel with a jailer husband—this blast against my womanhood, my love for her, this slander—now also seems tedious, simpleminded.

Very well, teach the course and leave. Till then live on your own, I tell myself. Picking up another manuscript, this one rather better, one she is working on now, a grim little parable of the war in Italy. She had protested, "No, don't read it now, some other time." "Would you rather talk," I asked, "or are you only being polite and would really like me to read it?" "I'm being polite." She is couched on her pillow, watching me. But when I leave off reading for a moment, I discover my eyes examine other parts of the room now, they do not run for hers like little fishes seeking food. I feel contained.

I feel free of her. The class and reading her story, with its naked and simple illusions, have freed me, left me a space for indifference, for neutrality, disengagement, even for self. I go willingly to my bedroom, suggesting my own withdrawal. "You must be tired now." She is standing, on her way back from the bathroom, and she hugs me. Inside her hug and feeling it merely as pleasant, as warmth without necessity. Lovely new indifference. "Perhaps if I'm better tomorrow I can come sleep with you. Get out of this hospital." She calls this after me as I close the door. "If I let you," I wanted to say. Wanting so much to say it even minutes after the time has passed.

But if I withdraw, it may be only another blind alley, another defeat. Remembering what she used to say of Martin, that he left her alone all the time, was married to his job, to mere money. By answering her departure of spirit with one of his own, he only contracted another fault, something else to be reported as a reason that he was impossible to live with, sterile, without feeling. "If I let you," I had wanted to say, even by teasing to imply that I too had choice, assumed it. But would I? Would I merely heat and want her, helpless in wanting, crippled by the fact of loving, handicapped by that, certain to lose. And how I loathe making a game of it, oneupmanship, maneuvering, outsmarting. How that cheapens it all.

Going away is better, cleaner, it does not profane the love. But I cannot go away now, am staying, committed to staying. By the class. Yet the class makes a turning point. Reading a bit before I sleep, I realize that tonight, strangely, for the first time, I am at peace. Remembering how just last night I read a few pages on Magritte without registering a word and was utterly miserable, a misery hard now even to recall.

The feeling holds. When I wake and cross the hall to the bathroom, past her bedroom, opening its door first to wake her gently, I can still feel it. That the class has made me alive and almost indifferent to her. I look at her sleeping face as at a friend's, but not as a creature looks upon its god. Its slave master. Very well, that's the point. We are all moderns and slavery is not progressive. I look at her face again. No, it is something new, if not indifference, then it's the cool thrill of liberty I feel.

And I feel well. As after an illness. I am someone again, if only the someone that conducts that class—at least a mind, some personality, a certain modicum of effective intelligence, purpose. I was swallowed by her and now I am coughed up; swallowed by her world, her friends, her family, her job. Not their fault, of course, but they simply drowned me. Brushing my teeth, I remember someone in New York, my friend Alita. I imagine conversations with Alita when I return, long afternoons in her studio, the cats on the rug, teacups, talking as equals. Delighted by that feeling, able to remember it again. Friendship, one's peers. The class has done this for me, restored me to the world I'd forgotten.

As I wash my face, the cold water restores to me my dreams of last night. Hectic, wonderful things. Alita telling me she had balled with Ken and another lady, Ken balling them both, and she loved it. I said I would never do that with Fumio, I would surely be too jealous. But then in the next sequence of the dream joyously balling with Rip and another woman. And then woke to realize that all this has never happened and that Rip is a rich SoHo art dealer now, not the gamboling blond athlete I used to know. But the dream had its sap, its pagan ease, its out-of-time, out-of-space pleasures, like a carnival and the people spread out in caves beyond the city, lecherous but languid, flesh shining in the misty evening light.

On waking I wondered vaguely if a man would want me or am I too old? Forty. Sita nearly fifty and has her men, all too many of them. Realizing that I think her the better woman: body, dress, manner. Beginning to take account of my subjection, this vast and monstrous sea of inferiority in which I have washed about for three weeks now. Emerging, I sit on my bed in the room that is mine now, rather liking that. Sherman's oil again, my own drawings, my desk, my big red Mexican sweater hung on the door, the beautiful blue and white bedspread from Greece. Even the carpet no longer haunts me. Perhaps what I had been so in terror of was living here alone with her, having nothing else but that enslavement to her. Now it is not that alone. There is the class. There is even some of myself returned again, coming back.

The piggy-back plant hangs high over my desk. The early-morning sky, gray clouds with the sun lighting them underneath. It is the first time I have been up before her in the morning, had the house and the day to myself.

Today is like yesterday. She was still sick then too, the two of us home all day together, yet curiously apart, estranged, remote.

She in her room and I in mine, the hours going by. I work, she sleeps or lies awake by herself, not needing me, not wanting me. She does not call out to me for things. I must suggest the soup, the tea, the apples. She looks tired and very old. She does not call me, she calls others, thinking aloud to herself that her friend Edith might be good at massage, or that Mary Jane could bring her papers from the office. When I go near her room, I feel a need to knock, to stand in the doorway and seek permission. We are in a curious place, we who used to be lovers, so headlong in it once, rapt, intoxicated. Earlier selves I can hardly recall or believe in now, and remember with wonder and astonishment.

Now neither of us speaks. The effort of repressing so much leaves us nothing to say. All talk is dangerous. I rebel against this continuously, go near her room, meaning to say something, anything— meaning to connect. And seeing her I cannot, something is forbidding in her tired face. Of course she is ill. The tedium of illness. Stopping off at the market yesterday, buying two steaks in the hope that she would be well enough to relish them. She wasn't. Only more soup. I ate yoghurt and waited for another night. But even entering the market I could feel that special foreboding you feel with illness in the house, foreknowledge that meals will not be celebrations, that the evening will go by unmarked by that coming together. When you can't even look forward to dinner, life loses most of its color, we used to say on the Bowery, an adage out of our bohemian days, our art world, bon vivant life. How far away it all seems now. It took so long for me to understand that her hedonism was not the same as ours. Not until I had learned much from her, a new way of life dedicated to pleasure, to the sun and California weather and the life apart from the job. But I don't have a job, my work is my life. There is always this difference between us, growing larger over time.

How gloomy the day is through the windows. I've finally gotten my table before the windows. Not the old ones of course, the ones in what is now Pia's room, though she hasn't slept there in weeks, but here in "my room"—what had once been our bedroom. Here with the same rains coming every day, the same lowering clouds, trees and bushes blowing, the city across the bay only a morose and steely blue. The rainy season. Last night when I came home from the market she seemed inaccessible. No wine, no music as when Mark was here, no recognition of the evening and its customary warmth, leisure. I took myself away, couldn't stand sitting on the little stool at her side, holding her prisoner with a presence she didn't want. "If you need anything, or even if you just want to talk, call." Almost calm, indifferent. An independence I achieved by watching the evening news downstairs. And then she astonished me, coming into the living room in flannel jacket and bathrobe, establishing herself on the couch, joining me of her own volition.

Pia and Paul are to play for an art opening in Berkeley tonight. Pia seems to have blown it already by not showing up for rehearsal, failing to get the guitar she was to borrow since she had never fixed the broken string on her own, and finally by leaving Paul stuck out in Marin County without a ride. I am happy with Sita, warm, at home, snuggled into a domestic moment watching a documentary on the Second World War, but I must go out, attend the opening, hear them play, be their audience—if they have even gotten there.

And the opening is a sorry sight. Six people when I arrive, soon reduced to four. Pitifully, there are no less than three homemade cakes for the guests who never arrive. I feel sorry for the artist and spend a long time looking at her pictures. Even sorry for the kids, who did come after all, and are even playing, though carelessly and without much effort. How their music fails to interest me at all now and yet how bewitched I was by it once. In the beginning. Disenchantment. How it all "went" with her when I first knew her, these beautiful children making music, the fragile and haunted daughter who sang, the funny and talented son who played guitar. And this lovely woman who was their mother, my lover. Sat at their feet and begged them to play, and she beamed, proud of them. Loving her was loving them, inheriting them as a gift. In all of her life there was but one thing I envied then, telling her once, If I envy you at all, feel poorer in any way, it is that I envy you your children. "You will share them," she had said.

But they were not to be shared, their allegiance was to her and her only, tough as the rind of a fruit. And I lost my sheen after the breakdown and grew discredited in their eyes as she passed through the stages of abandoning me. Last fall when she came home from Europe and told Sherman it was over, she must have told the kids as well; I was never expected to show up again. And they must know this is merely an aftereffect, like the last ripple in a pond long after the stone has fallen. Paul knows his bed is warmed, she's taken care to let him know that, and it must have registered. Yet Pia must still have some feeling for me, greeting me with a full performance of Brenda Starr: the neat new job she may get, the super bosses she may have, the big commissions, the hot salary—"Unless this chick who knows Dictaphone beats me to it. They were all so taken with my magnetic personality they just clean forgot to ask if I knew Dictaphone." I smile and try to be encouraging. She is so lovable, so vulnerable, doing her "routine" for us, acting it out, the bosses and the dewy-eyed new secretary, and a moment later, dancing the Charleston while singing a raunchy song. Lovable and yet so tragic, with such predestined sorrow. The job won't happen, the heroin may come again in this life she's now taken up with Dan at the Mission Hotel. Pia, her lovely face, the long, elegantly slender body, her ridiculous fashionable shoes. That face, so perfect in its Saxon beauty—how proud of that Sita is, that miracle of blond and blue to have come from her own darkness, her Indio blood.

When I first knew them all, having lunch in the city with Pia, high up in the sun at Ghirardelli Square, looking out over the water, Pia telling me her mother had pushed the Anglo look in her, worshipped it as all she could never be here, the fair ideal of this foreign place. And Pia had the singing lessons, dancing lessons, acting lessons, was a cheerleader, went the route, even modeled in

New York. Then rebelled with Leary's band of outlaws, Janis's crowd. Pia blaming her mother, then not blaming her, understanding the needs she was meant to satisfy vicariously. The sun shone on us. We were full of compassion and the most profound understanding that day. We were frivolous.

Which is the greater truth, that day of golden possibility or this evening of preordained failure? I know the first time was joy in living, Sita's love converting every moment, sight, incident into radiance. And now this life extended after death, the sight of the empty living room as I open the door. Back to her bed.

She thanks me profusely for having gone, knowing I didn't want to. I am touched, feeling sad little after-lights of love as she puts an arm around my shoulder, apologizing for being sick. Reassuring her, comforting, offering to rub her back with lotion.

And the sight of her back, naked and beautiful, surprises me with love. I thought I had stifled it, but there was the ache of it, the pull of it again. A flowering of lovely freckles, the firm delicious flesh, feeling it under my fingers, my eyes loving the wonderful lines of it, especially as it disappears under the covers into her white buttocks, the slenderness of waist and then their hidden fullness. I would lift the covers and see their round white flesh, the supreme moment when they part and come together, that so sensual ridge, declivity of flesh. The strange little mound of flesh she has just at the base of her spine—I would know her body in the dark by that sign. Stroking the small of her back, lusting to go below it, catching a glimpse of my desire by pulling off the covers for a moment. Satisfied and unsatisfied. Wanting her past speaking and into tears and then refraining.

Then back to her shoulders, the back of her neck, doing the work of a friend as well as a lover. I feel the tension in the shoulders ease, hear her sighs of gratification. Strange way to make love.

Bidding her good night. She promised again to be well enough to sleep with me tomorrow. "If I invite you," I said, softly smiling

163

at her. Very likely she did not hear me. And I wonder if my daring has paid off at all. Today she is more distant than ever. So where have we got to now? Stasis. The rains. The city in mist. Rain against the window glass, its strange irregular patterns, the suburban roofs of Berkeley. I have lost my opportunity to leave of my own will, lost it permanently. When April closes I will leave anyway, of course. But the chance to flee, to walk out on a bad job—that's over. The class keeps me here until something like the original expected period of time is over. When I parked my car in the driveway, I sat behind the wheel a long time, dazed, wondering what I should do with it when I leave. Because I will not be coming back. Nervous a little, even saying that, speaking the words. Teaching here every winter into spring, the old original plan, that's over. Over with the emotion that might have made it possible.

Rain striking the tin roof. The tulips she bought for me upright on my desk. And in the great shallow black dish, a group of camellias that she picked and arranged for me last Sunday morning. Like the tulips, rare deviations into the past, its old ceremonies. They rebuke me now. Ingrate. I hear her in the bathroom, the splash of her shower behind me, the rain before, this afternoon too has passed without speaking. A few words over the errands I have run—the bank, shopping. Giving her a telephone message just as she steps out of the shower, I come upon her nakedness, her legs below her sex and its poignant little patch of hair, how slender her thighs, almost piteous the way they part below the hair, how they hollow out a space, seem so fragile outlining the small void below the pubis. Has she gotten thinner through her illness, I wonder, or was there always this defenseless little space between her legs? Loving it just as I am surprised by it, almost a voyeur, catching sight of the forbidden, something never revealed before in all this time. She stands with the towel in her hands, drying her face, the absurd puff of a shower cap on her head, overtaken in her nakedness, her vulnerability. Bothered in her illness, with business, with

164

telephone messages. I feel a great protective tenderness, then I feel nothing.

Her face by candlelight. Sita peeling an orange and making fun of Henry Kissinger. "You missed the news. The fat little man's off again for Egypt and his big wife's bought herself a pith helmet. A huge inexplicable veil all over it like mosquito netting. Like a giraffe in disguise." After her shower she put on a long skirt and went downstairs. Instant action in the kitchen, beef stew begun and the whole house put in order in minutes. She is well again, or almost well. She comes back to me, talks, laughs, gives off energy. The silence, the despair evaporate. We have a full-fledged, comfortable dinner, with all her graces. Wine and candles and steak and good talk. It was probably how she talked at dinner that first made me love her; a love affair is all those evenings and the light of candles and the talk and the wine and her eyes suddenly at the end of a sentence. I can think of things to say again. By candlelight I can adore her, the classic loveliness of her face in profile, and her wicked, humorous talk.

Afterward she rests her head on my knees while I read, this delightful arrangement her own idea. But first she invites me to sit next to her on the couch. For days I have sat at a distance, the distance of her cold and her coldness. So close to her body now and our hands in each other's.

"Hang on to me, lady." I look at her, pleased by her saying that, but still not sure. "What do you mean?" "Probably that I want to hang on to you." "So?" "So." And then the subject changes, interrupted by a movement or some household banality impulsively remembered. Earlier she had spread herself along the sofa and, looking up at me, said suddenly, "I love you," transfixing me where I stood. "Thank you" was all I could say, not knowing, as I am forever not knowing now, how to respond, how much. Even whether I should at all. Or whether to go on withdrawing as a tactic. Absurd, hateful pretenses of love—you love or you don't—so why the game and the chess moves and the sleights? Or whether to withdraw in earnest, to go on extricating myself from love, attachment, dependence—seeing this becoming possible perhaps now. My indifference, friendly, even serene, as I go to bed alone this night just as the last. And the nights before it.

The lights of San Francisco across the bay, and above them a strange supernatural light, an aureole in the mist. The rain has cleared for a moment, and above the city and its million jeweled buildings, this peculiar halo of mysterious light, not a reflection of the diamonds in the windows of skyline, the sumptuous buildings crackling across the water, not that. Something other, some other prescient force lighting up the sky above them like a halo in an old picture.

But then I wake, caught, as by something unpleasant suddenly remembered, to realize that she may come back, may sleep with me tomorrow night. Would I have the courage to refuse her? Never. Could I, however sweetly, ask her not to come? Thwart her? No, I know already that would be beyond me. And if she offered lovemaking, then what? Looking back, I realize that I never have refused her. A few times in the past, yes, from being tired, but this was not seen as refusal by either of us, merely lack of response. Until this stay here, we had neither of us ever put it on the line, come to an open difference over it, a flat denial. "Learn to say no," she taunted me last week, the phrase still like a slap. And if I did, would she cease to ask? That is what I fear, just that. So little faith in my own powers to be coy, to attract, even to distract. I who have been on hand (grimacing to myself at the pun) or on tap anyway, every moment. There for her when Neal isn't, or the children, or committees, or Mark, or the job or the countless friends and well-wishers. I who have stood by, hangdog or carefully neutral, her shadow, her nuisance.

I sympathize with her impatience. Placed as she is, cooped up with a lovelorn soul she does not exactly love. Yes, of course, I can understand. Taken all around, she has been kind, remarkably for-bearing. For someone who does not love, to be immured with one who does is torture. But do I love? Or love enough for it to be so described? Though this is far too simple. Not only in that perhaps she does *indeed* love—to some extent, surely—but also in that *I* do not—or not entirely. I cannot leave my own ambivalence out of account, my longing for New York and my own life, my utter horror of staying here permanently or for any length of time. "Married" to her or to this house. For someone who does not love, to be immured with one who does is torture—was that last spring? Would it be this one too if she were still infatuated with me? Isn't it simply that she is the first to know the end of love, or maybe only the first to be honest and admit it? Don't I know it's over too, over within me—and am merely unwilling to let it end? Not wanting it to die, I proclaim its continued life by prolonging it as mere misery.

Mere vaporizing. This was supposed to be a life together. Maybe what drives me to frenzy is my failure before my own absolutes. Should I have loved her entirely and forsaken New York and, cutting all ties, come here to live—as she once wanted? But does no longer. Good enough then. She would never consider making such sacrifices for me—there had been one reckless offer to come East to live with me when I was so depressed and near suicide at the farm one Christmas, safe I'd never take her up on it, make her lose her job—no, it was obviously I who had to leave everything behind and come to her. Good thing I didn't. Or did she cease to want that only when I failed to give it, the turning point last spring when I took the loft? Did she just despair, give up, and not care any more? And will I do likewise, tiring finally, worn down finally, acceding finally to the separate bedrooms, the careful partition of lives like the cellophane and cardboard in the packaging of espe-cially perishable goods?

I'm not going to Los Angeles. She flies there tomorrow for a conference, had asked me along, and almost without thinking or knowing what the exact date was, I had said yes. Because it would be a chance to be with her, share one of those many weekends away. But a few nights ago, when she reminded me it was this weekend, I did a remarkable thing. Said I'd rather not. Would prefer to spend the Saturday preparing for my class. The trip is expensive, she would be busy all day, and faculty clubs are not good love nests. No, I'd prefer to spend Saturday working. Astonishing myself. The forbearance. Astonishing myself still further by acting to please myself—I really would prefer to stay home, work, see a film in the evening. Or maybe see Sherman. Suddenly there are so many things to do. A week ago it was hard to get through the day. Now I have resources, am beginning to stand alone. Still I have doubts, a moment looking around the kitchen, how desolate it always seems when she's gone. I wonder if I should have said yes.

When she returns from San Francisco after a long meeting, she asks about my day. Splendid, I tell her. "I finished that article on Sherman and had dinner with Susan Griffin." In fact, it was a wonderful day, sunny at last after the maddening stretch of rain, the joy of writing again, finishing something, typing it up, getting it ready to send off. The cure of work, its health. And the delight of another writer's company, a drink at the Marina in the full glory of the sea, sashimi at a little Japanese restaurant. Home to do a bit more work, even write some letters. Feeling cured, myself again.

When she came home she sat on my bed, reading my new piece and scratching her flea bites, Limbo's fleas, which eat us now that the dog has followed Paul out of the house. Next she stands in the door, talking to me. Then sits on a little wooden stool in the hallway, just beyond the door, as if there were an invisible line she is forbidden to cross. I laugh at her, the sight of her scratching away at the flea bites, laughing with delight, laughing a long time. "What in hell are you doing, are you forbidden to cross the threshold?" "Well, it's your room and I respect your privacy." Have we come to this with her separate-bedroom nonsense? Requests to knock and enter, etiquette. Suddenly the whole thing seems so viciously silly, tiresome. Too tedious to hurt any more.

Because I have mentioned a crick in my neck from typing, she offers to rub my back. I smile at the transparency of it all, pleased as well as amused. All evening I have thought she might deign to sleep with me. But she has to get up at six, still has a bit of a cold. When she recedes into her own room I am content. I did not have to face the decision, should she have asked, and did not ask her myself. Content then when she is off in her bed, her room and my room, content in my room to read late, to look out the windows at San Francisco's lights and water, to get up and write a note reminding myself to buy raw fish for Saturday, the night she will be away.

I had brought her daffodils, poking about the little wooden cart in front of the flower shop on Solano, wondering what I could get for the cash I had with me, realizing only gradually that it was Valentine's Day. Sentimental crap of course. Feeling a bit silly as I carried them up to the front door, then completely disarmed by the delight in her face. "How yellow they are, Kate, how much like spring!" The spirit of the day takes over, asserts itself against all better judgment, all hanging back. "I have something for you too, dear lady," she sings at me, brandishing a champagne bottle. Silver paper, great pink ribbon, she has been to Barber and Stewart, had it gift-wrapped. All for me. She has remembered. What if I hadn't absentmindedly bought those daffodils? She would have beaten me at what I had thought was my game.

But it is hers tonight as well. She has become the benevolent dictator, the fairy godmother. We'll have dinner at the Marina, she says, celebrate. The lilt of her at times like this, the call in her eyes, in the movement of her head. First we'll have a drink, wait till the sunset is just ripe before we watch it across the water. "The champagne now?" "No, let's save it for later; when we come back we'll build a fire, drink it before we go to bed." Something's up. Suddenly she is all romance, witchery, good fortune. Mellow the talk, the mood, the fine evening; like the past come back. She is restored to me in stages, in a glance, in a smile, in the full warm brown of her eyes. I do not want to believe but I feel myself sliding, persuaded. At dinner she is flirtatious, saying again that she does not want to lose me, her eyes full on me, the power of them open and compelling. I am being called, beckoned, even pleaded with. She is courting me from across the table, with a look or a smile or a joke, with teasing and reminiscing, with the flattering recall of a detail, an occasion, a friend.

The lilt of her at times like this, the call in her eyes, in the movement of her head. The pleading nearly in those fine brown eyes, the pathos of this aging and beautiful woman asking me not to leave her. "It's that I never felt or, rather, never felt before that you had any respect for me." "Sita, don't be absurd." "It's true. You never gave me the feeling that I was worth anything in your eyes." Maneuvers, I think, of course she must know how I admire her in everything, I have told her so a thousand times. And she has even used it against me. "I had to make you respect me." "You have only made me miserable." "Until this time, until you came out here this time, I've never been anything more than a shadow in your life, tagging along, someone in the background." "That's ridiculous." "It's how I feel. It's how I've always felt." I look at the great beauty in her eyes, the utter sincerity, the unimpeachable conviction. All completely of the moment, all true, all false. She has persuaded herself of this during the past five minutes and believes it completely. Five minutes ago or hence, she will be imperious again, mouthing speeches about her freedom, or full of sentiment, persuading me that what we suffer now is merely a moment in our long relationship, a mere segment in the band of time that unites us, will unite us always, each passage like a pattern in a bolt of cloth, now one color, now another, now a leaf, now an arabesque,

170

now a flower or a hill. "We have come to a very wonderful place in our relationship," she goes on. "We have come to a point of struggle where all the initial conflicts had to explode, be resolved. We will be more equal now, we've reached a point of separateness, independence. We've grown up in a sense." "I have no more expectations," I tell her, afraid even to say this, controlling the bitterness and the soreness of what I say. But she does not hear me, telling me again how deeply she loves me, the one great passionate love of her life.

There is no resisting her eyes, the softness of her voice, its little thrill of an accent speaking a word, softening it, making it intimate, nearly as intimate as the Italian words she used to say making love to me—"*tesoro bello,*" "*ti voglio bene,*" the most intimate sounds I had ever heard. I even forget that she no longer says them. Listening to her now, the gesture of her throat courting me, the liquid of her eyes pleading or snapping into the flirtation of wit, the coaxing of her humor, her mischievousness. Even her infidelities are proofs of her love; ploys, sleights, gestures to strengthen the fiber of this wonderful creation that lies between us.

We are at our old place on the Marina, Solomon Grundy's, with the sea and the city spread out beyond the glass walls, the gulls sweeping, the last sailboats hurrying home, their great wings brushing by our windows. Beauty of sky, sea, the lights of the bridges, and the city. This is our place, we are at home, each great moment of our affair played out somehow, echoed against this scene which is as much Sita as it is itself. She who is always California for me. If I should lose it . . . a tear stinging the thought. But before me now her whole self dedicated to the idea of retrieving me. Yes, I have expectations. "There's a Persian proverb I'll tell you when we're comfortably installed in front of the fire," she says.

Just as I light the fire, New York interrupts us with a quarrel and a petition, long, convoluted prose recited over three thousand miles of telephone wire and demanding immediate attention: prisoners and denunciations, informers and accusations, arrests, positions of principle. I want very much to say, "Look, I just happen to be busy making love now and cannot quite enter your mood." But I don't say it; no one ever does.

After this, the peace of the fire and the room and our quietude. We have hours to make love. Leisure. I will wait and let her seduce me, sitting back from the flames on a low stool next to the red Chinese table, watching the fire, sipping champagne as, gradually, by the slowest and most insidious of motions, her hand winds its way up the full sleeve of my gown. It is so deliberate, so agreed upon, so assured. The entire evening is prelude only to this moment, pledged to it, all preparation and diplomacy toward this consummation. Our talk is only a summons to this actualization.

Remembering how she took me sitting down, sitting on a low stool, her hand reaching under my long skirt, entering me as I sit. Legs apart, perched forward but still sitting. The little straw stool, drumlike, made of string and bamboo, curiously and elaborately fashioned over a straw frame. Pakistani, fruit of one of our enchanted shopping sprees at the import houses of San Francisco, on fine mornings two years ago when I first furnished my apartment in Sacramento, the great luxurious weekend visits of our first love, rapt hours of lovemaking at the Sausalito Hotel. Now the fire and her figure crouched on the floor next to me, her hand searching, reaming, digging within me. Somehow it is particularly exciting that I sit, that I am sitting just above her as she reclines on the rug, her arm extending up inside me. Sitting. The frisson of perversity in it. Forcing myself almost to go on sitting, which is difficult. So excited I am, so much I long to sprawl on the floor under her so she may hover above me, nearly mount me, and my legs flung wide and open. But sitting still, or if not still, yet maintaining myself on the little stool through the pure ecstasy of her explorations, her little touches, her experiments, her caresses, her attacks. Those long, strong fingers plunging into me, then withdrawn to hang about the lips of love, the small bud of clitoris erect, swollen, full almost to crying out. And still upon this little stool, this curious sedate little chair, gasping into her mouth, take me, take me, our tongues crowding into each other, divine intercourse each its penis and protrusion, or turn about, womb and cave-like the mouth arches and waits the other's tongue, pleading and prodding to fill, overwhelm.

Still perched upon the little stool. And finally can bear no more confinement but must have the floor, the great red Persian under me and the fire before me as I groan under her full thrusts, having quietly slid the stool away, slowly surrendering the strange gratification it gave, its limits and discipline. Now for the full open force of her, the full stretch of my legs, buttocks tense and taut as they raise me against her terrible entry, its power and fire. Hot you have made me, so hot, I whisper. Her tongue in my ear for answer, coquetry. Knowing so well her mastery, her authority. I would give her everything, blood, self, life. Open for her, whispering into her ear as she takes the higher inner ridge of flesh in me, wrings it and makes it come like rain, juices weep upon her hand, telling her as she brings one cloudburst after another from this strange hidden height, telling her I am hers, her creature her thing her woman her cunt her own to have, do unto, surrendering with each gush of that pink and hidden place she has only to press and it flows, surrendering self as well as body.

And now I will have her. Wanting to open her upon the floor, take her on the rug. There, then. Thirsting for her, already imagining how she will taste and feel, how it will be entering her, the joy of it, the great tenderness I bring to her body, subtle against her nipples, moved beyond myself, kissing her throat, wanting her now. "Wait till we get upstairs, I'm the staid type, I like beds." But when we got there she stops to open Emily's note. The child's block letters on the page. She hands it to me, turning away: "Dear Grandma I just wanted to say thank you very very much for the Little Lulu valentine card. Well I'm running out of things to say. Love Emily." Impossible not to smile. But she is weeping. Lost to me now. The sight of little Emily being loaded onto the plane, the sordid hamburger joint near the BART station where we tried to cheer her up, the odor of the coffee urns, aura of small-town bus stations and proletarian sorrow. Emily in her winter coat waving goodbye as Pia hurried her along and away. Grief has removed Sita miles from the woman of a moment ago. Grief and other people, dear, close, and with better claims. They have all left her now. A month ago she was a matriarch presiding over a home bursting with family, now there is only me against her loneliness. I share her sadness; loving her, I feel a strange little pain over all partings and separations, like the knowledge of death, but I want her back, my lover again. Not possible. She is gone.

Waking, I fight the sadness of every waking here, the moments before I beat down panic, assure myself I am safe, that the sun is shining and I am recovering myself, learning to survive. But she is gone, the bed is already empty. "Phony," the word coming up out of my subconscious, I hardly recognize it for a moment. "Phony, she's phony." Come on, have you no gratitude for last night, for all she gave? But that is the point. I was seduced, won over again, coaxed back into the cage only to be abandoned there again. Nonsense, she's just gone for one day, she'll be back from L.A. tomorrow. A pleasant day by myself, study, some first-rate Hawaiian tuna, if I can find it, eat it raw for dinner, a film. And she's restored to me tomorrow morning. We are going to the museum in the afternoon and to see Susan's play in the evening. Sita has already seen it but is going again for my sake.

The note is waiting for me on the ice-box door. I don't even read it right away, imagining at first it's the usual "Beautiful Lady, etc.," the charming and inevitable little message admonishing me to enjoy the day and meet her plane at such and such an hour. And then incredulously reading: "After consulting my schedule I find that I will have to stay over an extra day in Los Angeles and so won't be back until Monday morning." "Consulting her schedule," "discovering" she'll have to stay another day. Lies. So Neal will

174

join her there? So there will be no Sunday together at all. "Due to flight schedules" she cannot be home until Monday. The whole weekend without her, the whole weekend alone. How can she do this after last night? Didn't it exist for her, was she only adventuring? Neal will be just as interesting an adventure on Sunday.

I remember when I suggested the Beat Show at the museum and wanting to see the play, I remember saying then—in my own room, out of sight, even with a grin—"We could go somewhere else, or maybe you might want to see Neal that night since you've already been to the play?" Hearing her miraculously drawl back that no, she'd be pleased to go with me. Lies. And when did she change her mind? When did she call him? Had she arranged it with him before last night and our feast, our lovemaking? Neal. Or someone else? Someone there in Los Angeles. Why not tell me, why not give me the truth, at least that? Because this is "kindness"? Then this hateful little note blasting the weekend and all its hopes, hopes built since yesterday. Built on lovemaking, built on new tendernesses, dependencies, the ties of the flesh, the feel of her in my hands, the quick of me hot under her fingertips. Only a new trap, a new deficiency. God, why did I whisper those bits of folly, that I was hers, her woman, in friction and heat vowing that it was hers, this place in me, entered and held, her "house," she'd laughed in my ear, taking me. What a fool to give myself. She'd made no such commitments, simply enjoyed it.

And what can I do? Passing the Mixmaster on the way to the bathroom, its aluminum bowl registering irrelevantly out of the corner of my eye. Prisoner all weekend of this empty kitchen, these meaningless objects. Why didn't I go with her down there? What a mistake that was, that little notion of independence. Nothing, I can do nothing. Am helpless, impotent, the initiative is always taken from me. She acts and I react. This is subjection. And how clever of her to have been the one to bring up the idea of "respect" last night, insisting that I did not respect her. Even mentioned the word "subjection," that we had never been equals before, that she used to feel everything revolved too much around me. She has certainly changed all that if it were ever so in the first place. But how clever to steal a march, appropriate these very complaints to herself, put me in the position of assuring her of the depth of my respect. Monstrous and feudal respect. Virtual despotism. I am her inferior in everything now.

And then the note stymies me again, staggers me with its duplicity, its smug hit-and-run language. Like the routine of telling me she'll call me from the office. How do I get through this weekend, rebuild enough self-sufficiency to last through it, enough films, enough reasons to visit the city? And all the usual bland talk last night that we will be lovers always, for years and years, permanently, whether together or apart, this long and splendid relationship. No, we will not be lovers after I leave, nine weeks from now it is over. And yet she can't give me her free time even now. Next weekend is her committee's workshop in the mountains. Friday, Saturday, and Sunday, all three days. And who will it be then? Neal, Walter, who is going to attend? "Such good friends for so many years—probably because we've never slept together." She may elect to change that. There's also Percy. You'll go nuts thinking these thoughts. Stop.

Remembering how she took me sitting on the little straw stool. How good it was, knowing she would make love to me, knowing I would get that, have that again, that it was certain, the luxury of time. Folderol. Bullshit.

Look out the window, it's magnificent weather. The city glistens across the water, beckoning. You're in California, even if it's empty and without purpose. The sun of spring. There's good work to do, places to go, a glorious weekend. Absurd to mope around and be tied to her. How much better to be free, to be myself, whole, new. Very possible, this new independence, very possible, this new self every day closer within my reach. An end to being haunted, to neuroticism. Love is ridiculous, Sherman and I agree over the phone. She is leaving Marguerite. Soon I will be leaving Sita, though it is hardly the same thing.

Chewing it over in my mind. And on paper. The blue notebook, the one out of sequence, the one I can ramble through, the one for problem solving and obsessions. And the things most difficult to say. Sex, for example, my continuous sense of exasperation and defeat there. Is this what we fight over? Over sex? How undignified. She resists me, will not let me make love to her. Will not let my passion inspire her, holds out against my love and defeats me. Even these terms, how demeaning, how distant from love itself, how redolent of war and struggle and hostility. That it can come to this, this plague and vexation and undercurrent of animosity. When what I began with, the emotion, the reaching out, the desire and the urge to touch, was so different, so flushed with tenderness. And then it is turned back, snubbed, thwarted, mortified, and defeated. I will never get her back. I will never have her completely, entirely open to me, laid bare and open, a road panting and waiting and wanting me as I am, completely hers. Instead, I am the one saying it, even against my will and principles, theories and scruples, all the rest mere nonsense when she enters me, saying aloud or crying it in my mind—I'm yours. Your cunt your clitoris your heaving thigh and belly, your cheek of ass, your anus, your vulva, its soft thick flesh turned to clinging velvet turned to soft butter, waiting like a survivor alone on an island waving at a ship, waiting for the rescue of the stroke of your hand.

But she does not want me the same way. Only the brief permission of entry, the few moments of my skill, artless and without direction, the soft sigh of her finishing. I want to spread her limbs and eat her, devour her for hours, savor the sweetness of her odor and her taste. But she has no such ambitions. Always in my unsatisfied mind, always in my thirsty hurt unconscious, only there shall I open her legs and the little dark mouth and sup and dine

177

and drink, the brown legs open only in my mind, the terrible sweetness of her soft mouse-colored mound, the tender hair. Only the mind can have her heave and struggle with passion, cry out for more and more and all: entry, tongue and fingers burrowing, opening further, taking her anus as well as the cleft below the thatch of hair, tongue laving all. Even the forbidden, turning her over, caressing the beautiful globes of her buttocks, smooth perfect shapes, stroking them over and over again and taking her, entering slow and moist and gentle.

But it is just this I cannot do. Just this abandonment I cannot bring about. Her ardor is for me, or for her own magnificent powers as a lover, her mastery, her control, the perfection of force and intimacy in her fingers, their speaking power over me. But not as the beloved, not as the one given to passion, surrendered to emotion and desire, helpless for it, lusting and craving and needing. No, she does not need. She gives. And when it pleases her. Otherwise not. So I do not initiate, I wait. And the waiting is my resentment, my continuous frustration, my grief. I rage and grumble: this is unequal, this is unilateral, this is without reciprocity.

In sex one wants or one does not want. And the grief, the sorrow of life is that one cannot make or coerce or persuade the wanting, cannot command it, cannot request it by mail order or finagle it through bureaucratic channels. And I live with her knowing she does not finally want me. And have the humility or cowardice or weakness or despair to go on living with her in the hope that it will change.

I examine the past, searching for clues. Was it different during the days in Sacramento, the first wild wonderful days? Those first two nights probably I never noticed, so overcome by the way she made love to me, the power in her fingers. Their articulate voice came later. At first it was merely their force. No one had ever used such force within me, surely no woman. I was stunned, almost afraid. It would destroy me, cripple me. And yet I could bear it. Just bear it. And then it became easier and easier. For I learned to listen to her hands, apprehend what the fingers said, talking to me, each thrust, each minute or subtle move a whole essay of love, a sentence of passion, fierce, naïve, romantic, manly or womanly, intimate, sisterlike, the lust of a stranger or a mate. Sometimes I would still the heave of lust and lie very quietly with her inside me barely moving, charting my interior, which I had never so under-stood before, discovering new crevices, hearing her fingers' blood beating against the cervix, her fingertips discovering a shield near the rear of the lower portion of the canal which when touched caused automatic spasm. This is the place of the orgasm, we thought, marking it in our minds. And I marked it too in her body. But how open was she then? Wasn't the emphasis then too upon her making love to me? And upon her scars and bruises, the disfigured clitoris that I loved with a fiercer love because it had suffered every crime and indignity and I would avenge them all, heal with the fine euphoria of my adoration. What arrogance. I could not heal it. Now I can scarcely rouse it. She who will let Neal's great penis, or some other's, enter here, an object of a size and force that must surely hurt, will not or will only rarely let my mere finger enter, my soft and adoring tongue genuflect and wor-ship. Having to live with that.

Every morning when I wake I search for the sign. Waking is terrible. Out of dreams so dark, so irrational, waiting for the clue of today. Imagining it will come in a word, in a thing recalled or formulated, in some line or direction taken. And then there is only the good clear sky, and the bewildered fear subsides; it is a fine day, it is Sunday. I am still alive, well, sane, have little to fear, much to look forward to. The city, the museum, a visit with Sherman in the afternoon, the theater in the evening. It's all planned, pro-grammed.

Making breakfast alone, I grow philosophic. I've simply been a victim of jealousy; ignoble, the most ignoble of emotions, the most reactionary. Why shouldn't she have other lovers, enjoy her freedom? Love is not to be constrained. We have one of your modern relationships, self-conscious, slightly hypocritical, built on a good large dose of ideology. It's supposed to be an "open" relationship with room for other lovers during the months we're apart. All you have to do is extend that to the months when we're together, which is what she's pressing for now, and provided there's a good foundation of trust and affection, the rivals aren't rivals and they don't threaten what lies between us. The trouble is that they do. If I felt her love, if I had the sureness of its presence, I really would be able to bear the existence of other lovers and bear it very well, much as I used to. But her love simply isn't there any more now, is not persuasive.

So give up. I leave in a few weeks. It is only a matter of time. What was it that I wanted, anyway? Simulated domesticity strangled me. The sight of her graying hair, nightie, slippers, hair curlers, all in some permanent state of guard over me would make me cut and run faster than this, this strange prolonged waiting for the end. The fact is, she interests me now. Hardly her purpose probably in pursuing her own way, but surely its effect. Sita in her long, green-trousered legs, her slender waist, her green sweater over the lovely shoulders and breasts, her gold necklaces, her hair swept back from her face, pursuing her way. Lively and radiant somewhere. Somewhere in L.A. or Berkeley or San Francisco. Gladdening Neal's day or someone else's. Maybe even attending her conference, flirting with the world, scattering her vivacious Italian charm, or the darker, nearly Indian tranquillity of her Brazilian side. Beaming at the people around her, many of them younger, duller Sitas, beaming them her humor, her grace in age, the miracle of her subtle erotic self.

Wherever she is I bless her, admire her, salute her. What if I were to renounce the last remnants of vanity, gradually burned away by my humiliations here, and embrace a really selfless love? Not merely the foxy taking what I can get, what bones of affection and attention are thrown to me, but to lay off my hands altogether, bring them away palm upward and back to my sides, clean, asking nothing at all? Bid her to be, simply to be, since her being is such a triumph over life, her own past, her age, her own disappointed hopes, the lives she wept for never having had last Saturday when I came upon her listening to *Bohème*—it was knowing, she said, knowing she would not, would never be the writer or the conqueror she'd dreamed of being once in some earlier self, the adolescent ballerina with her huge haunted eyes. Now a woman facing fifty.

"Really feeling her oats, isn't she?" Sherman had rumbled over the phone when I mentioned Sita was gone this weekend. And why not, why shouldn't she have that, that last glorious burst of energy, not merely erotic but total, giving her whole body zest, her walk, her voice, her face. Why shouldn't she have it? Maybe I have never loved her enough, or well enough. To love is simply to allow another to be, live, grow, expand, become. An appreciation that demands and expects nothing in return. The end of love—or its beginning.

She surprised me by coming back as early as ten on Monday morning. It's a school holiday, Neal has the day off too. I'm taken aback, had never expected her so soon. The dishes from my long bachelor weekend aren't even washed. I am ashamed, a little confused. Suddenly she is with me again after the long absence. Yet I feel nothing at first, only a neutral nothing when she hugs me hello, this stranger in her pink wool blouse and sweater, her face a little aged in the morning light. Strange, neutral feeling, my main concern the unwashed dishes. "I didn't fly all the way from L.A. to worry you about the dishes." She laughs, sitting herself down at the table where I'm reading for my class, nervous because I'm not yet through the assignment, while she describes her conference. "I saw your old friend Ivy yesterday." I wonder, did she really spend the whole time in Los Angeles? Was I wrong, was she really telling me the truth? She goes on describing a comic band that entertained them Sunday afternoon. "One hilarious lady with a pompon and a headband—like this. And these, what do you call them, gloves without fingers and big wide open sleeves. And there was one like you, delicious, voluptuous little thing shaped like a turtle dove and poured into this brown dress with a pelisse, and a bustle, you know, that she'd bump and grind in time to the music." A turtle dove? I wonder. Was she really there, did it really happen, or did it just happen on Saturday instead?

"Some damn-fool guru and his disciples were on campus too and held us up for hours Sunday, we couldn't get into our meeting room, so we convened very late Sunday evening, but we got a lot done, made a real start for women in California. Maude Tracy was elected our part-time advocate for the whole state. We have almost enough in the treasury to cover a salary." I listen, confused, my mind partly on the dishes, partly on the book I must finish reading in the next few hours. She goes on, spinning, weaving, embroidering, creating a whole weekend, event after event, meetings and people and the college where they stayed, the faculty club, the participants. Even the band and the musicians, their outrageous clothes, their spirit. I no longer know what to think, am numb with trying not to care.

Then as I wash the dishes, she reads the paper, sitting on the couch. When I have finished, counting the hours and minutes left before class, I decide to risk joining her for a little while to test this bewildered indifference. I sit down next to her, discovering there is not enough room, awkwardly obliging her to move over, feeling silly. She puts her arm around me, says she is glad to be back. I see her and feel her, not really seeing or feeling. Why do I feel so little? What does she feel? The same neutral emptiness probably. But she is kind. It is a sort of happiness just to feel her warmth, the rose-colored wool of her shirt sleeve around my shoulder. I no longer know any more. Except that it hurts less. Even that is a loss; to arrive at mere indifference after such a love. Refusing even to remember the reunions of the past, their ecstasies, their gifts and surprises, their surges and throbs of voluptuous pleasure. We would surely never have restrained ourselves, would surely have made love. Couch, floor, kitchen, dining room, nothing would have stopped us. And now I go dutifully upstairs to read my book.

Wondering, as I sit sequestered here, off in "my own room" with the door shut, hearing her busy showering, the sound of her rearranging the room Paul and Valerie have stripped over the weekend, even their bed gone, leaving only a little sponge-rubber pallet on the floor ("her bed" in "her room"?), wondering if she will miss me, feel any want or emptiness now that I am out of reach for the whole morning and early afternoon until the class. Then a knock, polite, discreet. Would I like anything to eat? Some tea, an apple? Bringing a whole tray replete with teapot and a small camellia blossom, the lovely flower smiling at me against the brown wood of my desk; elegant, precious, framed upon its snapping dark-green leaves, having ridden serenely upstairs upon a pretty blue napkin. Such touches as I fell in love with.

After my class, after her meeting, we are to have drinks on the water at Solomon Grundy's. I arrive home first, having turned down coffee with my students. No, I tell them, I'm going to have a drink at the Marina, want to hurry not to miss the sundown, sure of myself, young, excited, the evening ahead of me, the happiness of a Friday night or a holiday, the night glamorous and full of promise, the bay misty before me down through the hills as I drive. She is not home yet. I debate what to do—leave a note asking her to meet me there? or wait for her here? The sun is setting, the special moment hurrying on. She'll probably go straight to the Marina from the city. Go. Hurry. Leave her a note. Hasty thing composed by two faltering ballpoints, the first giving out halfway. But plain enough. And with a foolish little flower scrawled on the bottom.

And then I begin down the hill, going a new way, faster, one of her methods. But missing the exit, imagining there's a special one for the Marina just beyond the University Avenue exit. No such thing. On my way to Oakland or some such fate. Off again at the nearest ramp. I will miss her. Long, desperate search for an entrance back, going the other way, returning to Berkeley. A sign tells me I'm headed for Sacramento, seventy-eight miles. I curse a New Yorker's curse on California, freeways, the modern world. And look up to see the University Avenue exit. Saved. Now a little sign pointing to the Marina. I follow. A long frontage road going nowhere. She will have come home, seen my note, gone to the Marina, seen I wasn't there, gone home again. Turn around, go back to University Avenue. Give it another try. Through long streets of warehouses and railroad tracks back to the main thoroughfare, the only one I understand. I will miss her, I will be late. She will have left. The signs, the correct turns. Wondering if I should turn back, go home. Surely it was a mistake to leave the note calling her down here. But it was agreed we'd go. No, she will think it peremptory. She may get home and decide she doesn't want to go out again. Just what I was hoping to prevent with the note, to assure that she'd come. And now the sun has gone while I have been lost on freeways, the moment over and past that we had come to see. That note, the whole device was an error. I had thought it independence, fire, temperament. An act on my part, going ahead, taking the initiative.

The conduct of a love affair, I say to myself, seeing the parking lot finally through the car window—arrived, safe—the conduct of a love affair requires the right moves, adroitness. And this is misconduct, error, mismanagement, bungling. Walking up to the place, loving just the sight of it. Solomon Grundy's is built like a Japanese castle on the sea, with great wooden beams, a bridgeway across a chasm of water, the waves rolling under it echoing to the towering beams and the delicate wooden fishbone of the canopy overhead. All the sides that face the sea are nothing but pure glass, section on section of sky and water sealed in view as from a gigantic observation platform. I look along the side of the building to the

184

windows of the bar, way back near the sea where they begin. All the hundred occasions of our love have met here.

Surprised and glad to find a table, lucky really, even though the sunset has long passed. Of course she is not here. Or not yet. Beginning to grow afraid. Will she make me wait here for nothing? It's inconceivable. But she may come home and just decide not to bother. Telling me later that she was tired, that she didn't want to drive so far. How long should I wait? Till eight? Past eight? Call her? That gives her a chance to refuse, and by now I need her here. The waitress comes by for my order. I say I am waiting for a friend.

Sitting before the pitch-black sea beyond the cold windows, I feel utterly helpless. Nothing I can do to change anything, affect her in any way, draw her back. No tactic, no device. When it becomes a question of wills, the one who has made it so holds all the cards and the one who goes on loving is powerless. When it becomes a game, there is already no winning. To hurt back, to take revenge is both impossible and unwanted. It is she who makes every decision, every demand, every stipulation, who conditions every peripheral aspect of our lives. We are eating at home tonight rather than here because she is tired of restaurant food after a weekend in hotels. Just as we get up in the morning at the hour we do because of her job, just as I wait for five for it to release her to me.

But it is not in these material, inevitable things that she controls me. It is in her silences or bursts of affection, her willed absences, her hundred methods of withdrawing, evading, leaving me nothing but sisterly good nights, a friendly good morning. "Have a nice class," she said as I left, as she got into her own car and headed for the city. Yet I was hungering for her; for luck almost, I climbed out of my car again to see her face as she drove down the hill, feeling blessed that she had thrown me a kiss.

Her greetings, now so measured, objective. And her "I love you"s, her "It's nice to see you again"s, how perfunctory, polite, without meaning. The black water through the windows; she did

185

not bother to come. The terrible sadness of the end of love, its loneliness. The illusion no longer shared. I look out at the waves and at the lights of San Francisco, the wharf and the bridges. The two small stars, the planets Venus and Jupiter that my students had mentioned—how airy and delightful it was with them today—hang isolated and poignant in the sky. Just as promised. Hum of the people around me, reflection of the bright fireplace in the windows, this intimate and cozy place impossibly lonely. She hasn't come, isn't going to. I realize finally that it is perfectly possible for her to yawn at my note on the door, find her keys in her bag, and simply decide not to bother—"She'll come back when she gets tired of waiting."

I turn around and see her, coming almost shyly toward me in her tired camel's-hair coat.

To be two women living in this house. I look off to the sea and away to the city. To be two women living in this house, to what profit, to what purpose? How narrow the margins grow, the limitations close in. She made love to me last night. After permitting me the same, or rather, not really the same, a short, almost futile attempt. Men interest her more now, at this period of her life—that was how she put it to me as we lay in bed afterward. And I am no Neal, no great stretch of flesh within her. I watched her face, both as I struggled to give her pleasure and as she turned to me next, looming over me. It was the face of someone I loved, a wealth of tenderness for its wide cheeks and beautiful dark eyes, loving its line of chin and lips and nose, its brows and lashes, the mole just above her lip. I looked straight into her eyes as she entered me. Looking straight into her eyes and seeing nothing. Her Indian eyes. Under her beautiful mask of the loving and sensual woman, under and beyond that, the inscrutable Indian self buried and obdurate.

I had never thought she would come to me last night. Had seen her sitting naked on Pia's bed. Is this to be "her bed" in "her room," now that Paul's bedstead is gone? I wondered, despairing at how she outwits me, eludes me at every turn. Now that Paul's bed is gone, the sponge-rubber pallet may not be to her taste, I had thought. She'll come back now to "my bed," which was our bed. But then the sight of her in Pia's room, calmly sitting naked on the bed, waiting for me to finish with the bathroom, that was too much. I would have wept if I had the energy, if I did not feel such despair.

187

Sitting in bed, waiting for the good nights to be over, waiting to read myself to sleep. And then she appeared in the door. "Are you open to receiving guests and other wayfarers?"

How she disposes, how all is at her disposition, how I am acted upon, passive, hedged about. And how willing, having her in my arms, how willing to be hedged and warmed and heated and alive to her leg between mine and my hand to find her. "I have wanted to make love to you all day," she says, "all evening." And how was I to guess, how even to believe? Believing.

We'd gone out to the movies, a little rustle of festivity since we so rarely go out at night, coming home late. And the day had been good, going swimming with Susan at her club, seeing the trees and the hills rise like a bowl all around the water, looking up at the apartments perched steep above us. And the concentration of twenty laps, the sting of chlorine, the hot shower after, and the sauna. Gratitude of the flesh for motion and water and warmth, the comfort of its exertion. Never mind, I had thought, I will live here, in my body; perfect it, isolate it; I will become essentially solitary, an independent existence, send down a root from my backbone into the place where I stand.

And she slept with me that night. Usual folderol of wonderment, her arbitrary preparations in Pia's room, the expectation she would come, the certainty she wouldn't, renewed expectation. The drama of her nightly arrangements. How I tire of it, am humiliated and sated, able to bear no further misery. Yet go on bearing. Pompous she is, absurd, but all-powerful. How many people go through this business of separate rooms, visits, beds declared vacant or closed or independent, nightly hopes, fears, disappointments. Everywhere in the world it must go on and I never thought much about it, believed everyone slept in double beds without a qualm or a flurry. Never suspected the possible stratagems, moves, advances and retreats of pieces and pawns, the thousand possibilities of inflicting torture, withering little shoots of hope annihilated in the soft closure of a door. I'll read, I decide, smoke, enjoy my solitude, keep later hours—still listening to the sounds in the hall, the precise stage directions of the bathroom, the toothbrush, the faucets.

And then her figure in the door. A woman in a wrinkled flannel nightgown. I have set my heart and life upon this apparition. Though tonight, unlike last night, it turns to sleep in a moment, tonight she is separate, off on her side of the bed, the warmth of her body my only reward.

And yet the very next day there is a new deprivation. She will be very late tonight. Her friend Maud, her great conspicuous friendship with Maud—"Maud, my best friend," she always says, the statement never failing to hurt and irritate me. Or Neal, I wonder, is this just a cover for having dinner with him? And then an overnight I will only discover when the time comes. Yet when I come home from hanging out with my students in a coffeehouse, she is already in bed. Pia's room. Asleep already, but she has left me a note, says she tried to call me in the afternoon, has to get up very early tomorrow morning. Doesn't want to "disturb" me. "You are loved," the note says. Just like the other one, the night of the party. And for a crazy moment I wonder if the note is a ruse, if she's even in the house.

I undress quietly without waking her, but around eleven-thirty the telephone rings. A man's voice. Neal's? But there are others: Mark, Walter, how many others? She wakes as I am answering it and I hand her the receiver. "I'm sound asleep," she keeps telling him. "Yes, yes, I'm glad your speech went well." Neal, precipitate fool, at this hour waking her with news of his vain little speech. Hairy-armed Rotarian. She disappears swiftly back into her room, an irritated specter. I lie in bed alone, having come three thousand miles to the cold comfort of separate bedrooms, knowing everything, knowing it all to its dregs, all the folly of it. And still here. There are eight weeks left.

Unexpectedly, I remembered what it was like. Realizing only through the contrast. In the coffeehouse last night, one of my students reading a poem describing some lovers. It was all there again, the frankness, the joy, the ease and intimacy of bed. Sitting up and chatting, laughing, getting up for coffee, diving back into the flesh again. As the poet read I could feel the sliding fabric of sheets, mornings of lovemaking, coffee cups, whole afternoons of sex, sunlight that is luxury and time without hurry, without goals, only the goal of living in that high moment which is forever, both past and future, that second which expands to fill the world, blotting out childhood and old age, transforming each segment of life into the refracted light of now, the moment to which all others led and can only follow.

And I thought of our taut and nervous bodies now, like two long, gray metal bars laid parallel in bed. Suddenly it seemed curious that we can sleep at all, our flesh now so without ease or spontaneity. So out of touch and harmony. But it did happen once. And that's what I remember now, having almost forgotten it. How we sat up in bed and chattered, drank wine, smoked. Sacramento those first dawns, making love before classes or as soon as the world released us into evening. The speed and grace with which she removed her clothes, how it always astonished me. Quite wonderfully, without shame or hesitation. Her arms removing a blouse on entering the room. And suddenly she would be there in her brown skin and flanks, the great brown circles of her nipples. And we had all that, that ease, the freedom of feeling, quick and alive, young in our joy, our frank knowing of each other in flesh and spirit and talk. Such a feast of talk, endless talk. Our naked bodies moving between bed and bath and kitchen, downstairs to the coffee or the plants, the talk continuous, witty and relaxed, intimate but objective, or gossiping or partisan, lofty or flippant, talking of a book or a meeting or a personality. How it all flowed.

The little bedroom there, its shadowy light of candles the nights she visited, its pearl-gray mornings after I had stayed up all night reading for a class, having to cram because we had spent the evening in lovemaking. And then she would sleep while I kept vigil, doing the two hundred necessary pages before a nine o'clock. I cross the hall from my study, sensing the strange pale light, knowing that now I must wake her. Hesitating, hating to do it. But after a moment, there is no sorrow at all—we were never tired. Sita waking to love again and a shower and coffee. Mornings when her presence, her great happiness was like a song through the house, through the coffee, through the clean early sunlight. How different we are these mornings. Strained little moments at the dining-room table, each reading the paper. Or if she does not read, I also forbear in courtesy. And the hope of a moment's attention. But I lust for the paper, the opiate of it, the cover to our emptiness, our so obvious emptiness.

It is the distance of our bodies. That more than anything, that is the index, that our bodies no longer know each other in the same way as once, are no longer friends. It is the distance in our bodies. And our minds and our souls. But you see it in the bodies. If you can even remember, of course. But I remembered it in the poet's phrase, a certain piquant image of lovers and their bodies, the good friendliness of their bodies in bed, their good will, their excited, almost childlike escape from all self-consciousness, their special camaraderie. Only then did I feel the loss, the difference, and understand the terrible change. As lovers how our movements now are curtailed. It is difficult for us to be ample, attend to the whole body, be generous with care and attention; I cannot throw back the covers and find her thighs with my mouth. Our lovemaking is cut-rate now, short of fabric, skimpy. Like girls in boarding school fearful of waking a house mistress, campers sly not to arouse the counselors—no, they all enjoy themselves—like prisoners then. Like prisoners, stealthy and adroit, minimal. Sly we are, secretive. As if we were ashamed.

Once how far otherwise, free with our flesh, our bodies nude from room to room, unconcerned about our cries through the thin little apartment walls. And now, merely this hasty little act below the covers, this mockery. Hidden, out of sight. Is it always so, the end of love? Always that abbreviation of the former drama, its play and invention and embroidery, its long, serene caresses snipped, eliminated, pruned, divested of their ritual, leaving only a quick push for orgasm—the goal, the finish, the having it over?

It was not a remarkable poem, only that it conveyed the magnetism between bodies; together with their innocence, their friendliness even. And that made me understand, with one blow, measure the distance and be appalled. What do you do then, when you realize you have fallen so far, when you can calculate and must admit it, like an account finally investigated by a bank auditor, the evidence confounding you? What do you do? Admit it's gone? Leave? Or relapse into vacancy, into not knowing, into hope, into expecting change? Do you confer? But conferences are already admissions of failure, and our failure is too ominous to withstand a conference. If I take a hard line, if I say it is over, she will agree. If I do not, she will go on about the years ahead, how I "will always be a part of her life," how we are in a "stage," a particular "moment of growth." And say that she loves me, with that diluted, almost sisterly affection she now considers love. But we are not lovers, our flesh has lost its knowledge of each other. Not only that glorious electrical affinity that kept us up all night, but even its relaxation, its contentment, its friendship. And you cannot define something so nebulous as the trust between bodies. Or restore it merely by taking note of its absence.

If I had not listened to this poem. If I had not remembered. If I had not realized. If I did not know.

A life of waiting. Waiting till she gets home at night, till her day is finished, till she gets back from Sacramento, where she has a meeting today. Days consumed in waiting, days empty except for the prospect of her return. Existence relative, dependent, vacant. I might be a wife, a child, or some marginal and parasitic creature. My own work is little comfort and does not sustain. Hardly her fault; my failure is my own. But her absences, her withdrawals, psychic as well as physical, leave me drained, impotent, unable to concentrate. Yet once when she left each day I was filled, replete, eager to work, believing. Why should my belief be contingent upon her love, hers or anyone else's? If you are an artist, you work, simply that; the belief has to come from within.

Now I no longer believe, only wait. Waiting, finally and eventually, for the time when I leave. Eight weeks. So little time. And then it's over? Finally and eventually over. Harder than waiting for evening, this prospect. When a thing saps you, corrodes, dissipates your energy . . . I say to myself, being sensible. Rational. Thinking of self-preservations, smelling disease.

But life beyond and without her? Not freedom, only greater poverty. Life closing down. Fewer and fewer remain. Ruth and a few friends in New York, the man I used to be married to—lately a strange, nervous friendship, new in places but underneath the same tragic fiber and fabric. And Sherman. So few people, so little left. Age closes in. She and I were to share it together somehow, an idea she still professes to believe in, talking about Martin's retreat in Napa. I see myself there in age and solitude, coming there afraid of the cold, reduced, glad even to share the sun with Neal or whatever other Neals show up.

When you can live neither with nor without her . . . Absurd, but it comes to that. Is it only need, loneliness that ties me to her? Memory? Memory of the past, the love then, its food and health and quality. Or some strange mixture of the two, the second, failing, becomes transformed into the first. And dignity disappears. For the defeated lover such things are luxuries hardly remembered. But how one gets to hate this creature inside oneself, this rag without selfhood or pride, unable, quite unable to afford such things. The other, older self, the self who was loved and cherished, seeing love disappear, bridles, pulls up sharply. Pampered, it cannot imagine itself despised, makes as to leave, simply to exit from such an untenable circumstance. And falls just before the door, its leg tied in some explicable way to memory. Inconceivable that this could be taking place, this thing of being no longer loved, when memory knows such a different world. There, in memory, in the past, staring right at you from the same face that now rejects you, a face hardly changed, slight changes compared to years and the distance of a continent, only this faint shift of expression between boredom and infatuation. And then you are addicted to that inch. If you could move it, erase it, slide—imperceptibly at first but by subtle degrees—slide it away and restore the past. Or wake up to have it suddenly intact again one morning.

I wait for her now to come home from Sacramento. Lately she has taken up a yoga class on Tuesday evenings, one more little escape from me, one further evasion. I heard her describe it as you might listen to someone explaining how they'd wrecked one side of your car. Such a theft it seemed of the little time I am given. The hour grown later and later. We will miss Susan Sontag's talk at the university. Dishes washed, salad made. I am of two minds whether to season the meat yet. Going to the door or the window, looking out. Pulled, yearning, like a wife in an old fable. The table set, the candles ready for lighting. A car pulls up. I hurry to finish my preparation, sure it is she, not needing to run and look out. But I do, only to see the car pull away. Maybe she just changed her mind, decided it would be more amusing to look up Neal, got home and just didn't feel like coming in. Or maybe she wanted to turn the car around, drive up to the top of the hill and come down and park on the other side. Waiting for the headlights again. They don't come back.

Later and later. We will almost surely miss the lecture. To keep from going mad, to prevent hysteria, I will read. Half a page before the phone rings. She is at the bottom of the hill. Will be home in a minute. Like grace.

Curious the operations of jealousy. And jealousy too simple a word. At dinner she mentioned, quietly and in passing, that she would not be home Friday night. I never blinked. Neal. Neal's night. And in bed she wanted me, her hand finding my breast surprised and willing. My mind measures and resists—tomorrow is Neal and so tonight, the night before him, and perhaps Saturday too, the night after him, there will be this rebate. The payoff. Is it her guilt or actual desire? No way to judge. My body doesn't judge at all, the loins wanting her, writhing for the touch of her hand, the bud of flame between the legs lit by her touch, her fingers sauntering, dallying, expert. Hot and cold as she circles, opening, preparing. "Talk to me," I whisper. "I have wanted you all day. You were everywhere around me in Sacramento, I remembered you in every street and building. I've waited for this." "You never say so, you never say these things." She chuckles, raising herself on her elbow as I lie under her, cloaked and covered and tremulous and waiting the moment when she plunges inside me, when one sensation gives way to another. I tell her we do not take time as we used to, time to enjoy our bodies fully, to explore and savor. Telling her in my lust the things I would do, my hands covering her buttocks, stroking and caressing the line of parting before the cleft I do not enter but only touch, each fingertip exciting me as her hand on my cunt faster and faster excites me now to frenzy. I do not even think any more, only thrash, her creature as she enters me.

Afterward I wept in her arms. "It will be all right," she says, holding me. But she would not give herself, let me make love to her. Immediately I think of Neal. I have lost, been outclassed by the competition. Wanting to make a joke of it, and not daring. I feel tricked now, cheated. What if I had resisted? But I wanted her. So often these days, during so many occasional moments, I ask myself—brushing my teeth or working or parking the car—what if you refused, went without? How would she react? Further withdrawal? Or perhaps she wouldn't care at all.

Surely this is wrong, foolish, reactionary. Surely she has a right to her pleasure and I none to my pain and misery. A love without possessiveness, restraint—surely we both believe in that. Or rather

I believed and proclaimed it and she was jealous, violently and painfully jealous, when on two occasions I took a lover. I will never forget the sight of her standing up naked on my bed one night in Sacramento, a diva in full tantrum because she had just been bitten by one of Bea's hairpins lurking treacherously in the sheets. I very nearly laughed. But whenever she felt jealousy it was sorrow, and her every sorrow grieved me. Sita never struggled with jealousy— it came upon her and it happened. She was a Latin, she was entitled to it. It was I who had notions, terms, theories, and Sita who was fiercely possessive, protective as a lioness, forbidding. There were times when it became unreasonable, even grotesque; she punished me for weeks over an affectionate indiscretion she came across in a letter, a letter to a prisoner, where it was merely academic if he would ever spend Christmas with me one day in the country, a thing I proposed to cheer him up. Having read the letter by accident, she wrote me a dramatic note to the effect that we were doomed. She used to date my defection from then, regarding the loft I took merely as confirmation of an essential infidelity. But now she has come round to my views, practicing them with a vengeance. And I am not proof against them.

This morbid curiosity, the sense of betrayal, the world upset by a word, by a segment of time missing, stolen away, by a night away. The emptiness stretching between now and tomorrow. Her voice on the phone this morning calling from her office: "So I'll see you tomorrow afternoon then." She will be away all night with someone. The thing accepted, taken for granted between us at breakfast and when we drive to the garage to pick up her car—see you tomorrow, hear from you tomorrow. Tomorrow, when she is taking me to the Chinese New Year parade and dinner in Chinatown —my reward for patience. As if I were some particularly well-behaved child. Or perhaps simply a child, a dependent being one buys with treats and favors. Why should it be such a humiliation, this bright sensible new way to live?

Just as I had perfected my gloom and self-pity, she called and asked me to lunch—she is thinking of firing her secretary. I am the secretary living in fear throughout lunch.

After a night with Sherman, drinking and complaining—Marguerite's illnesses, Sita's infidelities—like two old boozing pirates, boring ourselves and each other. In the restaurant at one point I thought I would scream with tedium, as Sherman expounded to her old friend Selma why New York is so exciting and San Francisco is so dull, a performance I have heard a thousand times. My left shoe hurts, my foot is going to sleep. Even with the shoe off the foot hurts terribly, the bones seem squeezed. Selma describes the filth of New York, the rudeness. "I was there just one weekend and it was two days too long for me—never again." I put my foot across my knee and massage it under the table. Selma and her child lover, a college girl, finally rising to leave.

Sherman's voice when they are gone, droning over my pain: "I needed to see you tonight. I've really had it. I can't paint in this mess, I can't even live. She's totally dependent on me, has no family in this country, no money,   place. Now the damn hospital, the hospital bills. Just what wiped me out last time. I can't even think any more." We are back at our first conversation, while drinking a few hours ago in a tough gay bar on San Francisco's Broadway. Sherman had called early this evening, looking for me, got Sita, just dressing to go out. "Sita was on her way to a seminar." "Bullshit. She's on her way to Neal." "Who's that?" "The guy she's fucking tonight." Appalled at my own voice, the crudeness and violence of the term. Almost an assault. An assault I would never have made but for the lie. And my fears that she may have persuaded Sherman, seduced her to her own views. "I'm really disappointed," Sherman says softly.

But I must find out more, what else was said. In fear now that I have lost my only ally. Sherman reverts to Marguerite, staying

197

with a friend tonight, right near the hospital. Her illness is very serious and may last months. The doctors are finding it hard even to diagnose. "I can't stand it, I can't stand living like this." "I feel the same way, endless distraction, up and down in her moods, her decisions, her nights in and out. It's a completely totalitarian relationship." "I can't go on this way, just fucking can't." "Neither can I, but I do. Loving her, not loving her." "She says you have lovely times in between." "Sure, great romantic fires, fireworks. Then she's off again." "She told me on the phone that she wanted an adult, independent relationship." "That means she fucks Neal when the mood strikes her. And I put up with it." "Never, I'd never be able to stand that." "For some reason, I can. Just barely. Look, I believe in her freedom." "Sure, she's seeing age and she wants to live—zoom." Sherman gestures in a line with her finger.

"I can appreciate that," I say, the feel of the bar stool under me, the clink of glasses, the faces along the bar facing the evening, drinking their Friday evening, the jukebox, a band setting up in the back of the room. "Look, Sherman, I can appreciate it all, even admire it aesthetically, if you like, Sita's a beautiful woman. And if she wants to grab life and wring it dry—why not, we all do. And I don't really even know what I want from her finally." "She keeps you interested, that's more than I can say. This being-sick trip is driving me up the wall." "Well, Marguerite doesn't want to be sick —you're acting like it's her fault." "Yes . . ." But Sherman turns to Moxie on the right, quips with Selma behind the bar, acknowledges a gaggle of young lesbians eyeing her from the end of the counter. How can I keep her to my subject, attacked again and again till I understand it, as if talking aloud might solve it, bring insight, undo the riddle? Selma finishes behind the bar and joins us. We will have one more, then go for dinner. Dinner alone, the two of us, with our two obsessions.

But it's Peter's birthday today. Wonderful, who's Peter? Bartender at the restaurant we're going to, a new one. Sherman says the Air Freight, our favorite haunt, has taken a nose dive. Or rather, since she prefers gestures to words, a habit particularly emphatic when she drinks, she does the nose dive with a gesture of her thumb descending like a crashing plane. So we must go to this new place, and Selma and her lover (young, silent, pretty) will go along with us just for one more drink and to wish Peter a happy birthday. I'm fond of Selma, an old crony of Sherman's, a retired union official, tough and gentle, but tonight I wish her away as I suffer through the monologues Sherman directs at her, waiting for my time, for my obsessions to reassert themselves. When the other two leave, the dialogue goes on, even repeated: Sherman's frustration before Marguerite's invalidism, psychic and physical—"Cortisone the rest of her life, can you imagine? Poor damn kid, but how can I go on with this, sick, all the time sick, day after day, it never stops." And my own complaints, each indication from Sita, what it portends, even as I talk feeling the bones of my foot aching in this odd inexplicable way, wanting to leave, to walk, to exercise, to stamp out the pain. And wanting to stay, to keep gouging the wound, exploring it.

"I don't know where it goes. I want both things, here and New York. But it can't work." "Beautiful if it did, to be able to have all that. But your cake and eat it too? Now really." "Overambitious"—feeling guilty before Sherman's monogamous judgment, her settled life in one town. "But otherwise it just means going home at the end of a few more weeks, giving up." "She won't let you go." "Sure she will, she'd drive me to the airport tomorrow." "You're wrong. She loves you." "I love her too. But I don't know what it means." More wine, more repetition, more spinning of the wheels, less understanding, further despair. More statements of impatience, more punching and kicking at circumstances, less hope for change. Sherman's bearish voice: "Let's quit, I'm sleepy."

Back home I see the living room transformed subtly as for company. Neal. He came here to pick her up. Since I was in the city at the doctor's, he was able to call for her here. Be entertained. Glasses in the kitchen? Don't bother looking. But a silent butler on the Chinese table, the cushions hunched up under the windows, the shape of his back implanted. And flowers, the chrysanthemum plant I bought her when she was sick, wilted in its pot lately. But she has clipped the flowers, put them in water, where they shine in a little majolica pitcher. What a genius she has for making a room special, festive with merely a touch, the slightest rearrangement. But something else is new, Sherman's other painting is on the wall above the console, replacing Pia's hideous Maxfield Parrish poster. For a second I am furious. Even before I can admire, rejoice that the painting is hung again, brought out from under the sheet where it had been banished when the kids moved in—even before I am glad, I am furious. My friend Sherman's picture was hung for Neal, Sherman's painting hung to impress him, to make the room "gracious" for his reception. No, forget it, mount the stairs. Read a little. Sleep. She is not coming home tonight.

The first note is on a little rocker before my bedroom door. Yes, of course, there'll be notes, the usual nervous little assertions that I am "loved." And the expected instructions on how to get to the hotel in San Francisco where we meet tomorrow—the exits, times, locations. She has even changed the time. Not four now, but five. Merest wince of disappointment. Well, I will read myself to sleep. Turning on the bedside lamp to find another note posted beside a huge pink-white hydrangea filling a Chinese bowl. *"Tesoro bello,* this exuberant blossom—with its delicate pale-pink petals and its simply luscious fullness—reminded me of your breasts. File this under H for horny thoughts. My love, Innocenza."* More than a genius—this flower, what we used to call a "snowball" when we were children—was, until she touched it, merely a large ugly thing on a stalk in the front yard. Now it is a miracle in a blue bowl, now it is a message. I am touched, persuaded, conquered. Somehow between dressing and transforming the house and doing the dishes, somehow in all her preparations, preparations for another lover, somehow she found time and thought to do this. In her strange, excited eroticism, which borrows from one to give to the other (and

I have known that feeling too, loved one lover more for loving the other, another), she has stretched the perfume of her sensuality across us both. I see the little note pinned to the lampshade and believe, am flattered with the old, almost shy embarrassment of riches her courting used to give me. Such courtesy, such charm. I am treasured and cherished and wrapped in the furs of her attention. Reading alone in bed on a night she has left me for another lover, I am loved, adored, protected, watched over as if by spirits.

And in the morning I notice another note set for me at the dining-room table, more chrysanthemums, the piece of paper leaning against them. "Good morning, my love"—though she wrote it last night—"Another outrageously beautiful sunset . . . and they will go on—longer than we will, and then we won't even miss them. But I missed sharing this with you now. Death is forever—and life is so short—love a beautiful sunset, always changing, always the same, always too brief. Beautiful Lady, I miss you. Share my sunsets—share my love—share my life." All this while she waits for Neal. Incredible, exasperating, beautiful woman. "Let's give each other joy. There's not enough of it in life and we have much of it to give each other. I love you. Innocenza."

In the kitchen an obituary is pinned to the bulletin board, a friend of ours who has died very young of cancer—and beside it Sita has written her own name, and "Alive, but for how long?" I pour my coffee and reread her note. To love or not to love? To live together or apart? Never mind. "Let's give each other joy. There's not enough of it in life." Yes, yes. Let's give each other joy then —how much I want that, to end the tussle of wills, the setting up of obstacles, the turning away of the face or the back or leaving the room, the withdrawals of self and affection. To give, to have that joy to give. Am I worthy, able? This heavy silent and depressed being of mine, how I must bore her, weighted down with my convictions of futility. To give each other joy. Longing already for the moment we'll meet in the streets of the city. The Chinese New Year, the festival. Firecrackers and dragons and parades.

This is the giddy time, her weekend. When the world turns on its heel and goes carnival. Monday to Friday are grim and efficient, early to rise and to bed, an immersion in mediocrity and hated detail. Then for two days each week life becomes romance. An artist has no weekends, any day might be a workday or a holiday, but you are never off work, never free of worry and the obligation of art. And yet any day might be romantic; there is no schedule or division, only a continuum. But never mind that difference now. Or any other difference. And all your tedious grief and whining. She waits for you, are you up to the challenge? Can I smile, laugh enough, be light? All right, I will try, I will meet her, try to set off this explosion, this ignition she calls for. Joy. How well I know what she means, that there is not enough joy in life. The very scarcity and paltriness. And there's the fact that we could, since it is there and possible, if we ceased opposing, we could produce this very jewel, this precious substance that makes life wonderful rather than merely bearable—by an act of will, turn our association with each other into the good and the creative. As it was before? In essence, but in everything else different, of the present rather than the past, new as today is new, this crystal morning. All right. Then dedicate this morning, this moment, to that hope.

All right, Lady, you've said it, what I might have wished to say, longed to tell you, to propose. To set forth as a plan of action. We are not finished, I think we are merely starting.

Arriving late. Her instructions were off. There is no hotel at Sixth and Market. Or rather no hotel likely to house a conference. Only an old transient thing called the Shaw. Hardly likely. I search frantically for another clue. Realize I hadn't bothered to write the exact name of the hotel, Hilton something, Sheraton something. Sixth and Market seemed clear enough. Now it isn't, now it's an enigma. What a fool I am. And she in her great goodness, her magnificent efficiency, had plotted this out for me so carefully, even leaving a copy of the schedule of the conference. I was appalled to see she had a workshop Friday night, last night, what I had taken to be Neal's night. What if she had dutifully gone to that workshop last night, the "seminar" Sherman mentioned, which I had casually defined as a fuck. And staying out all night? Well, maybe at the hotel, attending the thing wholeheartedly; parties were listed for after 10 p.m. No. Yes. Never mind, just find her.

The one clue, New Montgomery Street. The hotel's parking lot was on New Montgomery. Scratching through one-way streets and blockades and streetcars and the narrow lanes of Market Street and No Left Turns full of flea-bag transient hotels and filling-station attendants and parking-lot boys and motorcycle cops with inaccurate directions—cop said Post was next but it's not, it's Ellis, what will I do?—until finally and a precious thirty minutes late I find the Sheraton Palace. She is not in the lobby. Despair. Ask the desk. My eyes devouring each shabby sofa, each plush and stodgy armchair. And then way off to the left, so familiar, so unglamorous, so beloved. Her knitted patchwork vest, her camel's-hair coat, her long, lovely legs. To think that I have made her wait, when every moment was so precious with the new promise of her note, the bargain it had struck.

Her conference drones on inside. The ballroom, with its dais and tables and the foot-soldier fleet of folding chairs. She leads me inside. Like hell, like chaos, like tedium. The exhaustion of two days' talk on every face and body. "Shall we just go?" "That would be lovely." "There's a party as soon as this is over." "Well . . ." Uncertain what to say, willing to please her, to go to the party, to try to enter her mood. The conference is of the new journalists, there are some people I know here. "Let me just put my briefcase in the car." The few moments on the street already make us feel free. Forget the party, let's go on our own way, to Chinatown, the parade, our long-awaited dinner. She is feeling the freedom too, we decide to go off alone, ignore the party, the droves of people. A woman stops us in the street, an old acquaintance from Sacramento. It is an eternity until she releases us. Then finally, finally on our way. Fancy-free, two figures arm in arm, dwarfed by the buildings, almost skipping with the exuberance of having escaped, going off on our own, our adventure, our night on the town.

Everything is enchanting, delirious, infinitely pleasing. The drinks before the parade begins, the hundred foolish high-school drum-and-bugle corps, the majorettes, the clown. Even the fat sheriff in his limousine. She holds me, standing behind me, warming me in the cool night air, reassuring me. Even when my feet are tired from standing, even when her body leaning against my back makes it actually harder to stand, even then I am full of delight. As we drank she described the evening before, the sun setting when she was alone in the house. "It's the first evening I've been alone since you came." The solitude had made her melancholy, thoughtful. "I had a hundred Zen insights." She laughs, covering her face. I remember all my evenings alone there and say nothing. "Coming across Ann Scott's death in the papers, then watching the sunset. It went on and on. Where were you when the sun went down?" "On the freeway, coming back from the doctor's." "If you'd come back then, I would have canceled my engagement for the evening." Neal, I think, forgiving just as the snap of logic fits. "But it was a commitment and I had to honor it. Though by this time, nothing could have bored me more." I smile, feeling a little limp, confused. She turns the full force of her eyes on me. "It comes down to this, I don't want to lose you, lady. I don't want to lose you." "I'm so glad," hardly knowing what to say. Some voice in the back of my head saying, "You already have," and knowing it for the lie of mere revenge. I look at her, her beautiful eyes loving me, wanting me back. She has returned. For how long? Later, when I made a remark about my habitual inability to answer my letters, complaining that I'd really had trouble with the mail today, she misunderstood me, thought I had said "male" and meant Neal, she gratuitously swept him away, half in apology, half in dismissal. "Call it senility, call it a last fling." "I only meant the postal service,

204

darling"—laughing to cover her mistake. And during the parade she held me.

My hand stroking her cheek. Suddenly aware of tenderness, the awful nameless pull of love, its desire to possess, consume. Lying next to her and painfully aware of it as I had not been all day, even that evening, entertaining friends, when we had laughed, flirting with each other, lovers laughing into each other's face at a joke or some gossip repeated by one of the guests, making the joke our own, special, private, intimately shared. And then we tired of them, wished them away. Longing for our peace and our rest. She is especially tired, hungrily wants sleep now. I feel desire stroking my thighs but do not disturb her, say nothing. Wondering if she intuits it. We turn away to sleep.

But I cannot sleep. Surprised by my restlessness. I always sleep so easily with her. One moment ago warm in the warmth of her body, content as always in the mere nearness of her and ready for sleep. Then of a sudden seized by a stricture in my chest, like smothering. I cannot breathe. Pulling for air. The suffocation of claustrophobia. Absurd, lying here on the low open bed, four windows around me—two looking onto the expanse of the bay and the city. What could be the matter? A terrible fear. The strangling is about the fear of staying here. If I stayed on past the time, if I settled, I would suffocate. Wanting to cough. Gulping for air. Hardly daring to move, not wishing to wake her. The friends who came by tonight, old friends from New York. I was gay, slender, witty, young, laughed with my head back, realizing I have not laughed for over a month, the whole time here. Laughed and went on laughing, enjoying it like some novel sensation. And now holding my breath, then opening my mouth to breathe. I cannot get enough breath. Turning once, cautiously, my innards screaming with some fearsome incoherent premonition of their own, the body taking revenge.

She wakes. "Would you like me to sleep in the other room?" "No, no, I'm terribly sorry." Lying very still now. I never thought this would happen, yet I would like her gone. I would like to read. To smoke. To stake out the black-and-white-butterfly sheets for myself. My bed, my territory, my peace, my solitude, my own pursuits and space. I turn over on my back, stealthily. It will have to be better now, the breathing will have to improve. If I could just lie higher on the pillows. Memories of imagined asthma attacks at the university, damp spring nights dreading examinations. Nonsense. Years ago. Breathe easily and deeply. Get hold of yourself. If you don't beat this tonight, it might go on, become impossible to sleep together, surely you don't want that. Try, for God's sake.

Trying, lying on my back, feeling the lights of the city, which I cannot see, only feel. Their dim glow on the ceiling over the window hardly more than a vibration. Breathe. The breath constricted, painful in the chest. And beyond it mind and stomach in panic at the threat to life, the possible closure in the throat. If I could sit or stand. Ridiculous. This can't go on. I will go into the room across the hall, Pia's room, sleep in the cold, unfamiliar bed. Not force Sita to move. She lies beside me, asleep. Without waking her, clumsy but rising noiselessly, almost surprising myself for having surrendered the attempt, for doing what I so detest, banishing myself to the other alien bed. Not alien to her of course, her refuge. But to me utterly loathsome. Cold damp sheets, a musty room. Never mind, pick up the cigarettes by the bed, slip downstairs and get your book. And just as I am standing, she wakes. "I'll go over to Pia's room." "No, I'm already away, I'm up. You stay there, go back to sleep." But now she too is standing, ghostly in Pia's flimsy white nightgown. We are two ghosts on either side of the bed, a bit ridiculous, perplexed. But she has already outmaneuvered me. Her brief goodbye kiss. "I guess we're both restless. See you in the morning."

For a moment disappointed. Then relieved. Ensconced with lamp and cigarettes and book, reading Anaïs Nin to the last wonderful pages of the second volume, the death of her romantic life in Paris as a world war begins, the vitality of this bohemian world and the tragedy of its dissolution never more poignant and compelling than in those last throes, farewells, exiles. Conclusions.

At the faculty club. Lunching in the sun. Half satirizing, half appreciating the place. Its elaborately shabby elegance, the vast masculine comfort of armchair, the luxury of good wine at the end of a cafeteria line. Going to the lobby to buy cigarettes, I pass dazed old professors with their newspapers, jolly tables of young departmental hustlers. The world of academic bliss I might have had were it not for art—an old envy coming back, an old fear of the lonely future. So much drabber now, without her. Yet she is still there waiting at the table in the sun, its good warmth on her back. I feel it in my hair, glistening in the light, how pleasant as the sun filters into the scalp, down to the very vertebrae. We are leisurely and contented. She is reminding me of some annual dinner, Martin and his new woman friend are coming down to the city for it, will pick us up. I should be one of the party. Laura will want to meet me. "It will make her feel entirely in the family. She's already met the kids and Stanley and Neal." "Who is Stanley?" I ask automatically. I have never heard the name. "Haven't I ever told you about my friend Stanley?" "No. I've heard about Neal, but I didn't know there was anyone else." "Oh, I haven't seen Neal in a long time." I am bewildered.

"Stanley's a testament to the power of advertising." I look at her. "I put an ad in the paper. The kids said I was crazy. But I really wanted to try it, to see if there were actually any sensitive intelligent men left in existence interested in friendship and conversation, which was how I chose to phrase it." I watch her, feeling a curious pity but also admiration. Was she that lonely? Or this brave? I watch her, her mellow beauty, her ability to laugh at herself. "Box

207

number of course, no name. And then the replies started coming in. Pia and Valerie and I put them all in the middle of the bed and read them out loud and laughed and laughed. Of course they were mostly just nuts. Illiterates. Horny creeps. But at the bottom there was a good letter just signed 'S,' which is how I'd signed mine. From a lawyer with several children going through a painful divorce. It was on university stationery with his department on the letterhead. So of course I looked him up in the catalogue and in a few easy steps found out who he was. Naturally he had no idea who I was, just a box number and the initial 'S.' I decided I'd let him hang on the ropes a while, play with him, enjoy myself. So I called his office and left a message saying I was Serena—I swear at that moment it was the only other name beginning with 'S' I could think of. He called me back and I teased him—'I've got your number, I know just where you work and all about you.' So he started trying to find out who I was, went through the catalogue, played CIA. And couldn't come up with anything. No Serenas. Finally I gave in and agreed to have a drink with him. He picked me up at the house, and there it is, we've been seeing each other for months."

She smiles, the same half-bashful, half-willful, naughty smile she had over Neal. "He's just a nice middle-aged man, forty-five years old, who loves his children and sees them weekends. He's moved over here to the East Bay to a little apartment, and his kids think it's a great treat to bring their sleeping bags and camp out with him on the floor. He's shorter than I am and has a bald spot." The last, like the deprecations of Neal's youth, published to appease, to ease the hurt. Merely bewilderment still as she goes on to enumerate Stanley's virtues, the pleasure of his company, how delightful it was to introduce him to Martin, who happened to stop by once, how Stanley hopes he and his former wife can arrive someday at the pleasant friendship she and Martin enjoy.

Somehow the introduction of Stanley is tolerable, even interesting and sympathetic. There is more of the truth. Stanley is a new rival, another ghost of the nights of her disappearances. How vast, amorphous, yet overwhelming her mysteries, the pitfalls of her betrayals. It is terrible to add Stanley to what I fight against and am losing to, but at least the stranger is named, a real human being, an actuality. We fall to talking of the house, how the rent will be paid when I'm gone. Should we get a roomer? No resolution. And then to trivia. Suddenly she turned and smiled at me, and she asked how I liked it, did it make life more exciting, every day a new catastrophe around the corner? Teasing me. And then we fell into the quarrel. Her independence. Her right to her independence. Lovers of the past, her past, my past, whether they had interfered, whether it had been hard to bear—her material. Mine—that the time here so far had been very hard, the house full and alien, feeling her love so much diminished, the loneliness of these weeks and weekends, days and evenings, and for a clincher, that I was here for only a short time, a matter of weeks, and it mattered terribly to me how things went—it was only a short time, then it was over. Would I write her off so soon? she asked. I did not know how to answer. The sun beating down, the campus in green and blossom and springtime. The terrible contrast between us and nature, between us and the idyllic scene, the strolling professors, the carefree kids, the bicycles and dogs.

"After a few months you're going back to New York again. Then what have I left?" Of course. She lives here year round. She must have people around her, provide for herself. It is all sensible, reasonable. It's I who am unreasonable. "You yourself agree with me. You have all sorts of ideas about freedom." "I know. I don't believe in possessiveness. It's just that when you live with this it's so much harder than you think. I've never asked you to live with it like this, day after day." She looks away. "And maybe I just couldn't live up to my ideas," I confess, ashamed, looking down at the table as she gets up to leave.

We begin to cross the campus. "Do you suppose boredom is inevitable in relationships?" I ask, watching the professors and the kids, wondering if our differences are only temporary, common-place. "Of course, relationships go in cycles. They grow and go through phases," she lectures me. "At one time they're very sexual, then it may die down for a time, take another direction, and then it may come back, flare up, die down again." She goes on and on, playing sage, but now I feel she is talking down to me. We pass a grove and blossoms and a tower. "You've just got to be made to understand that I am free to do what I like." "I do understand. I've been made to understand." My gorge rising at her tone. "And I can't see any reason why it should bother you if I see other people. Both of us have done that in the past." "But it was at a distance. We weren't living together." "There was Sarah, there was Bea," she insists. "How do you suppose I felt having to stay in a motel that night because you were with Bea when she came up from L.A.?" It is not till hours later that I realize she didn't stay in a motel, she drove back, furious, to San Francisco. How contrary she is. Jealousy then was natural, at least if she felt it. And I was flattered, took it as a sign of caring. "The times you mention were only two nights in three years. And you had them too—Brian, Hank. But somehow it worked. We did not have them while we lived together; we had our own separate places then," I argue. She is hostile, determined. It is her manner that makes me despair, just as it was her lying to me about Neal; if she had come to me and said, "Look, I want this," I could have understood, but it was the if-you-don't-like-it-go-to-hell quality, the bullying. How to explain the difference to her? Her voice is hard against me, negative, con-temptuous. She is berating me for not seeing more people, having more friends. Suddenly I am very angry. The patronizing tone stings, hurts like malice. "I don't live here. I don't have friends here." "You don't even try." I keep silence, going along a fence and a sidewalk, the dirt hot and dry, the place ugly and without mean-ing, so angry I could strike her, nearly choking. "Look, I know exactly four people, only one of them is a friend, the other three are acquaintances. One of them I haven't reached yet, she's never home. The others I pursue all the time. Sherman I see whenever I possibly can. Susan too. Alta I just sat down with for the first time yesterday. Believe me, I try. I chase them." Feeling foolish saying it, but insisting she realize the truth, admit how alien I am here, that I am here for her, only because she is here. Something she has forbidden me to mention, since she's not interested in having any "guilt" about it.

But it is not the issue, trivial or continuous, that matters. It is her contempt, her ease in treating me like a child underfoot who should go out and play, find playmates. Or someone socially inept who has failed utterly to adjust. We walk along beside the football field. Still astonished at how easily she despises me, still hurting. Astonished by my own anger. We draw near her building. One hundred more yards and we will say goodbye. I fight in my mind for the thing to say, to do. Apologize? Say I was a poor sport, suffered a jealousy that I shouldn't have, stand before her contrite, conquered all over again? I say nothing and we part.

And the next night much the same thing. The suffocation, the rigid waiting. And something new: my fists double up, a convulsion all through the body. Anger. How could it be anger? I hardly dare investigate the idea. Once this was a bed for sleep, reading, conversation, lovemaking. I would sit up and read half the night if I chose, it never bothered her, she used to suggest it, encourage me to read, smoke, do what I liked. But now I cannot even move, am afraid, forbidden to stir. A prisoner here just as circumscribed as in every other aspect of my life. The hour we go to bed is chosen by her. I could stay downstairs, but really I cannot, too fervid not to miss the few moments of intimacy per day, moments when I lie close to her, feel her warmth, her body, moments when she might make love to me. Of course it is that, just that—that she might make love to me.

She has turned away, ready for sleep. Is it a frustration merely sexual? I ask myself. Just as last night I felt a moment's desire, then banished it as she turned away. I supply all the usual reasons; a week night, her job, tiredness. But tomorrow she is taking the day off, we go to Napa. Never mind. After the quarrel at lunch today, what could there be tonight? The quarrel. After I left her, a curious thing happened. I went home and answered all my mail, the stack of letters I never answer, my reservoir of guilt, of inferiority before her matchless efficiency. Attending to all my affairs. I will not be a victim. Doing something for myself. Then I went out and bought us a chicken. Dinner was passable despite the quarrel. Afterward we read. Out of the evening there must have been one good hour. Lighting the fire I teased her, that I am the better firebuilder. Leaning over, I laughed into her face and my lips brushed her breast. Then I remembered I had a pimple on my chin and lowered my head.

I turn on my back, hoping to breathe better. Moving in stealth, surrounded by prohibition. No use. After minutes trying to slide up the pillows, to have my throat and shoulders higher. More air. The room across the hall beckons. My own space. A book. Cigarettes. I lie waiting to escape, to glide out in the dark, mind already lighting up and opening a paperback. She turns and shifts in her sleep, noisily, without fear, unconscious. I lie on my back again, waiting for courage or the need or the maniacal fear of suffocating to become powerful enough. But tonight more courage than fear, tonight it is possible, more possible to leave her, to rise and go. I toy with staying, beating it, afraid of the nights to come. But it is too desirable, the room over there, my privacy, my ease, and my interest. I lust after it. All that against the grave I lie in, the stricture in my chest, the futility of staying.

Slowly, carefully finding the cigarettes and the book. Then, in an instant, fighting the creaky places in the floorboards, in an instant more crossing the hall rug, pulling to the door, using a silk scarf hung on the doorknob to ensure against the sound of the lock. I am safe. Free.

All the way to Napa heckled by the past. Starting out grim and silent driving through Richmond's oilfields in my closed convertible. Our dull and speechless holiday. The weather gray and uninteresting, without promise. Every detail mocks the great high junkets of our early times. Other trips, other selves who drove the road, top down, radio on full-tilt, going down to San Francisco eighty miles an hour with her hand on my thigh. Even in an open car I sat close to her, the sky around us shouting for joy—whatever the motorists thought, we were youth and intoxication, we were every summer in the world, we had finally discovered love, invented it. If ever I think of those early days, it is often a picture of us in the car on some back-country road near Napa. The hood just cresting a hill, trees, even a cow. We are laughing, holding hands, and singing pop songs; dreaming aloud, planning where to eat, telling our old loves and past lives, composing long, extempore paragraphs of pornography for a fantasy publishing house we have named Flaming Crotch. "We must remember to bring a tape recorder along sometime and get filthy rich." "All we need is a press, there's no point making a whole lot of work out of it, we'll just secrete it when we're horny. The world needs a new pornography." "And we'll just toss it off on the side, juicy tidbits when we can spare the time." She would squeeze my hand, and the word "juicy" would inspire us to flights, to smut and endearments and laughter and the risk of the lewd and the tender together.

Sita doing eighty on the highway, the magic road from Sacramento to San Francisco and our great golden weekends, the hills like green mossy breasts on each side of the road. Her California, the hills she taught me to love. Just as she taught me to live those times, taught me food and wine and the sun of our own Mediterranean—California and all it meant, promised. For once not the tawdry of Hollywood or the tourist's Frisco, but the real California, which was always her self, those soft green hills, her ripeness and beauty and wit and good nature and knowledge of the world, teaching me this as she gave it, as she taught me youth and how to be young, that it was a feeling you permitted yourself once the lock was broken by love, a rapture, a fine full air of spring.

And this other spring today. Three years later we are the gray pygmies of today. Speechless for miles with nothing to say. Forced comments on a house or a car or a billboard. I turn and look out the window and fight tears remembering the thundering sunlight of that other time. Our bodies are dead between us. I sit on my side of the seat as she drives now. It would be unthinkable to sit near her, it would never occur to her to lay her hand on my thigh as she used to, or even to put the top down. I hear the psychiatrist's phrase in my head: "inappropriate behavior."

Then and now. It is this that sickens me each time, this disparity between what we were and what we have become. The suffocation of that joy. Even—and this is a more dangerous thought—the disparity between what we are and what we might be now if we had love again. Because it is all possible. Objectively speaking, we have everything: a car and a trip to Napa, a good lunch and the wine country. The hills begin to be a lovely green and the mustard is beginning to bloom in the fields. But instead, this heavy silence, this discouragement. Boredom. How bored she must be, driving with her eyes on the road, completely removed from me. I feel it too, thoroughly bored. But it is worse, it is grief.

Sita had suggested that we make a side trip to Jack London's house in the mountains. And it was there, after the photographs and first editions, after the artifacts of a manly life of boats and extravagance, fine jerseys and sails and old letters and handmade chairs, it was there we had our fight. Or as close to a fight as we've ever gotten—twenty bitter minutes in the trees by the parking lot. It had been my idea to sit on a bench in the little glade and recover from the efforts of literary tourism, smoke a cigarette, enjoy the pale efforts of the sun and the view. Never guessing what would come. Though of course I'd had my little plan. Given the scene, we would talk, would communicate somehow, close up the gap before it widened, get in touch, come together again. Floundering about for words, for a way to say it all, the feeling so urgent but the words so inadequate, especially the appropriate everyday words, the spoken language. To find the permitted conversational words that are not slang or jargon but still have the purity of simplicity. Meaning my overture to be almost a bouquet, a hopeful gesture of courting, probably a halting and feeble rigmarole meaning at the end only I love you, but meaning it with a fresh force, some novelty, something to catch her heart again.

And she astounded me with venom, with fury, an outraged female reciting her grievances, movement rhetoric, a feminist tract. A parody of our situation, hypocritical, dishonest. "This is some watered-down version of *A Room of One's Own,*" I said. Hurt that she would see me as the enemy. "Exactly, that's exactly what I mean, that I need a room of my own." "Virginia Woolf didn't have lovers in mind but writers." She ignores me. "I want to be free of you. I need space. I had to show you that. I had to teach you that, whether you wanted to learn it or not." I look at her, amazed. Each word is a blow. "So you had to be taught. You just had to be made to learn. Even if it took something dramatic. And that's what Paul's room is about. That's what my staying out all night is about. I need my freedom. I insist on it." "Of course. No one in the world has the right to question that." I stand up, ready to go. I don't want a fight, I want peace. But there is no winning with her. And no talking, except to quarrel. She will have her freedom, well enough. She should have it, I am only sorry about how she defines it, that it increases as I decrease, that it needs to eliminate me in order to flourish. She walks ahead of me back to the car. I would like to shout at her—but there is no freedom for me. What about me? What do I get? You withdraw further and further, reserve a room for yourself, take lovers, and I get to wait for you, to see you in your odd moments, to come three thousand miles to be fitted in as a quickie before or after one of the real people, the men. Her back is angry, righteous, frightening. I follow it into the car.

We hadn't meant to have lunch at Juanita's, just a drink. It's out of the way if you're going to the vineyards, but some old impulse got us there to the big ramshackle house full of overstuffed chairs and roosters and mice urinating in cages, and Juanita herself like a great overstuffed sofa, fat, mean, cantankerous, as bizarre and full of antimacassars and old plantation decadence as the place itself. And wonderful, its very crudeness, the plaster saints, the run-down "antiques," the monkey that used to get drunk at dinner—how it all challenged and bewildered us that first time. After a look at the place, after the odor of the mice and the realization it was their urine soaking the newspaper in the big cage in the central hall that perfumed the whole rambling building, after one pass by the monkey, trying to climb my leg, we quietly took our bags and left. Fascinating place of course, but we just couldn't take it. This was no place to spend the weekend, even though Pia swore it was "pure camp" and I remembered Juanita from the years she had her houseboat in Sausalito, where Sherman took me on those first glorious trips to San Francisco to have hot cakes at all hours of the night with highway cops and pop stars and all the butter you wanted. No checks, just take what you want and declare what you ate at the door. But Juanita was a dim presence then, off in her corner trading obscenities with troopers and truckers. Now she was a huge presence right smack in the front door yelling, "Where are you going, girls?" We with the bags and all, caught dead in our tracks, escaping her. Even Sita's presence of mind slipped a bit at this, but we invented some innocent errand and drove hard to the next hotel. She'd stayed there once. A converted monastery, sounded just the right thing. But on inspection altogether too Protestant. Antiseptic, a Hollywood aqua chenille bedspread, a motel lamp. And that was it. The barest room I ever saw. We were ready to go back. Both of us as ashamed as we were amused by our cowardice. As if it were some special forgiveness we could afford, being so in love with each other, we could condone even this typical female shilly-shallying, this timidity before monkeys and mice and the bizarre in a house.

Back in our room, or rooms, for Juanita, conferring the favor of letting us stay all night, for which you needed connections, gave us a sitting room with a Victorian couch and a bedroom with a bed I imagined from a nineteenth-century house of prostitution, bed and bureau and washstand so redolent with sensuality, with Impressionist nudes washing in tubs, with Madame Bovary and the throes of romantic love in illicit places—back in our sitting room, safe from the mice and the rooster and the monkey, I could look out our windows into the flaccid and overgrown yard and realize that this room was every ruined plantation, the real dangers of sloth and heat and the past grown rank, probably beyond anything Tennessee Williams could bear. But how he would love it. It turned out that his friend came here often. It also turned out that the halls were full of tourists, and that after we had made love and she slept while I read for a class, they invaded the halls with their noise, their foolish trying of the door, their comments, their exclamations, the violations of their footsteps. So I put a sign on the door of the bedroom where she slept and spent the next three hours listening to them reading aloud in ringing tones, "Please be quiet, someone is sleeping." Listened like a dragon in its den, ready to spring, so fierce I was to protect her, my adored and sleeping lady, to protect her with the little power I had to protect, protection being always her prerogative to extend toward me. But here was my chance, this rare time when being younger I could be older, knowing less I could be wiser, the beloved I could be the lover.

That was the weekend of Sally Jean, our eponymous double, our mythic and joint alter ego. It began with the high-school yearbooks on the bedside table. Once between making love she read to me from these, her accent making the maudlin prose hilarious, the scrawled inscriptions, "To a great gal," entirely new and wonderful comedy. She had, through Pia, even mastered the idiom and could hold forth in it for hours. "Look, Sally Jean, you're just gonna have to keep putting it out for me, baby. You put out real swell, honey," her eyes beaming at me, her hand lascivious along my stomach. I had never seen or heard anything as amusing, as absurd as this impersonation. And called her Sally Jean too. We were both converted into peroxided American teens, gum-chewing, vulgar, horny, lazy, dumb. The perfect fantasy, the perfect charade and escape. Everything that we were not, a release into our antipathies, opposites, reversed identities. The mirror we plunged into for our most salacious games and roles and smut. Even the contempt in Sally Jean was flattery, the perfect assurance we were ourselves. Somehow the pretense in Sita-as-Sally-Jean patting my ass, her patronizing lewdness, "Sally Jean, just keep putting it out, baby," was the grandest compliment, the most intimate bond between us. Our secret selves. Selves no one would ever believe or understand. A code. Like the black and white sheets. Wonderful Beardsleyesque patterns splendidly drawn and printed; we both came to own a set and they were a talisman, fetish. "Remember me? I'm the one with the black and white sheets," she'd drawl. "If you ever get confused, just remember them black and white sheets, Sally Jean."

All so far away now when we enter the bar, the huge shabby bar where we used to drink before dinner, the great Rabelaisian dinners of Juanita, dinners of steak and roast beef together, dinners you could never finish and stopped eating somewhere in the middle, limp with exhaustion and defeated greed, dinners where a woman played the autoharp for us, coming specially to our table, spying us as lovers probably, suckers maybe, but came and sat before us and played us everything we liked. And Sita liked a song that asked, "Will you still love me tomorrow?" I saw in it her age, her fear that I would leave her, her surprise I did not gather the whole host of young women she imagined lurked or assembled everywhere for me to take them. There was a line in this song, "You gave your love so sweetly," that I felt always must be her feeling about me, about my coming to love her, about my docility and gentleness, a thing she had never expected of me, going by my reputation as a female Don Juan and bomb thrower, but a thing that completely

disarmed her, and that by degrees perhaps, but very soon, I surrendered myself to her, so the words had a specific sexual or
perhaps one should say amorous content, but against it was always
the threat of time and her own age—will you still love me tomorrow? And the woman must have caught this and, whatever her
notions of these things, been touched by it, for she sang the song
over and over. She was near Sita's age. And I thought how foolish
of them to worry. And I was right.

This irony, along with so many others today as we sit in the bar.
Catatonic with silence, dying to strike up any pleasantry with the
barmaid, the tourist couple to our right. I order a gin-and-tonic.
Sita orders a Campari. I am pleased that she will drink, pleased
that in our black mood she will do anything at all, speak to the
tourists, charming them, or to the barmaid, democratic. Even take
notice that lunch is in preparation. She suggests we stay. I had been
hoping for more neutral, less haunted ground, some new place. She
says she is hungry and the driving has made her tired. Well then,
of course.

We sit in a little booth off by ourselves, usual Juanita collection
of fifties frieze, the hideous made quaint through attention. Sita
eats the main course, roast lamb. I made a mistake in not ordering
it, choking down a gigantic tired assortment of breakfast things
instead. We eat. We do not speak. There is nothing more to say,
nothing to say at all. In time past we ate here and were happy,
rapturously happy. And now are miserable. Is this all it is, I scream
quietly inside myself, does it come to this? She eats her roast lamb
with poised, polite bites, she asks if I would like a glass of water.
In the midst of this insanity of decor and arrangement, of despair
and loss and disappointment, she is a lady.

The moments spent in that odd little booth composed of some
absurd tulle hanging for a canopy, some deathless pink armchairs
out of the houses one loathed visiting as a child, and the great
succulent dishes of food suddenly unappetizing, even nauseating,
so that I wonder as much if I will vomit as over the bereavement

of time, the terrible falling off—how do you have love and lose it? —how can it be there at one time and gone at another?—how if they loved you then, do they no longer love you now?—how does one stop loving? I never have. The moments like a funeral, a grim little mockery I imagine every hippie kitchen hand must see and find funny, Sita wondering aloud how Juanita can ever possibly make the profit she needs to buy the place if she feeds all these kids. The moments that are the worst of all. That little booth our coffin.

In front of Juanita's there is a round stone fountain. Sita took a picture of me sitting on the edge of it that first time we came up. I am wearing a black turtleneck sweater, rough wool that always seemed full of Paris and the art world—I used to call it my "existential" sweater—and a new pair of black trousers she thought particularly sexy. I am *tesoro bello,* I am the light of her eyes this day. I have taken off the smart straw hat I had been wearing and my long brown hair shines in the sun. I look very good. But to her I looked wonderful and she used to show people that picture with a frequency and fondness that made me nervous. "I took this picture of Kate when we were up at Juanita's one weekend, in Fetters Springs," she would say, showing the kids, showing the people in her office, showing friends. As if the little Kodachrome were some wonder.

As we go out we pass the fountain of course, the fountain where Juanita's police-like bellow stopped us, the fountain of the photograph. And beside it the raunchy little enclosure for the animals, donkeys and ponies and a few morose sheep, the usual untidy collection of roosters. Seeing the fountain, I steer us around to the animals and pretend an extraordinary interest in what mules eat. But finally passing the fountain on the way to the car, I see my ghost, a girl with shining brown hair in a black sweater gazing in ecstasy at the dead eye of the camera, out of faded paper eyes looking with blind miraculous delusion toward her certain tomorrow. I pass by as one passes a maniac or a corpse.

I had thought of it even before we went upstairs. Thought of it as you might contemplate the marvelous, a miracle, something you'd never be able to bring off or be able to do. Then doing it. Undressing in our room, growing sure I would do it, then panicking and heading for the bathroom as she undressed in Pia's room across the hall. But then coming to the door of "my" room, I watch her ensconce herself in what is at the moment "our" bed, and softly say to her, "Had a lot of trouble sleeping the last two nights. I think I'll go over there so as not to disturb you." Hearing her protest as I reach the other room, safe, strong, miraculously strong. "Well then, *I'll* change," her voice calls after me. "No, just stay there where you are."

Realizing that I forgot my book, have no cigarettes. Ducking back to get a paperback. The book, but still no cigarettes. Do I dare go downstairs for some or will she jump in and replace me, forestall me in Pia's bed, my gesture ruined, my effort turned to nothing? For it is not merely that I want to sleep alone; it is that I want to *choose* it, to have the power and initiative of choice, never mine till now. Finally not daring to go downstairs but planted firmly on the bed and in the room of my choosing. I will wait till she goes to sleep. Then I'll go down. With cigarettes and book and privacy and my victory. Meanwhile, just sitting on the empty bed.

Realizing what it means: sex. I'd said to myself, You will have to give up even wanting it. You will have to go that far. Her insult from weeks before when I'd told her that all initiative was hers, that she had created a situation where only she could initiate lovemaking. And that this was unilateral, unfair, unequal, without reciprocity. "You'll just have to learn to say no," she said, laughing. "Time has taught me that if nothing else." "You'll just have to learn to say no." Like a slap. All right then, I *will* learn.

A tap on the door. I'm amazed. When she took to other beds, I never dared to knock on her door. Why didn't I think of that? But of course it would never have worked. And I know already as she enters and sits beside me that it will work for her. "Please come back. You're beginning to make me feel like someone who uses the wrong deodorant or forgot to buy the right toothpaste." "You're not the first one to feel that." But she is certainly not the one to put up with it. Wheedling me now to come back. Her inconsistency —that will brook no rejection at all and yet impose it whenever she chooses. And makes it stick, terrible in her irritation, her authority.

Utterly unaware of her inconsistency. Like a child, having what she will. I can know all this and yet cannot resist her. "What can I do to bring you back? What can I say to make you happy? How can we start again?" When her voice says these things, I am helpless. Then she stops. She has already tired of wooing me. Just as I was about to rise and follow her. I look at her beside me. Her neck seems thick, she looks old. Her hair is in tight curlers because she is "going out" tomorrow night. He gets the curls, I get the curlers. I am tired. I would like to read. She is bored, it takes too long to court me. I wish I had a cigarette. "Come now, get your book and come back to bed." Why my book? She will not let me read in bed these days, or is this a new offering? I look at her, wondering if she plans to stay here and send me back across the hall. "Aren't you coming with me?" I say as I stand up. "Yes, if you want me to." Diabolic. She has arranged it so that I am asking her, inviting her to bed.

We settle in. The warmth of her snuggling against me. Then she turns away to sleep. I do not wait long for the stifling to begin or to escape it. Rising quietly, cigarettes, book, the short space across the room, across the hall carpet, and into my sanctum. Have I somehow kept faith with my resolution?

We meet on the stairs. Dark here even in daytime. Kissing, merely kissing hello. She smells of the sun, the glorious day outside, its light and urge in her hair her skin her lips. Our tongues slip into one another's mouth. I move in my jeans, surprised, not having meant to. Never expecting this. We break and meet again, mouths open, loins touching, warming moving heating.

And then it's over. She hands me the mail. We go upstairs. She has chosen the bed as the place to open and read the mail. I calculate my chances and look at the letters. A dull thing from New York about my loft, a boring letter to write in answer. The mail strewn around us as we sit on the bed. She begins to describe a demonstration at the governor's office. The reasons she would participate or refuse to, the inanity of driving up there without an appointment. I watch, only half listening, listening instead to my senses. Will she? Will she, when she finishes describing what she said to the demonstrators on the phone, will she revert to the scene in the hall? Was it a prelude, a promise? I have forgotten all my resolutions, I am only waiting to see. "Would you join me in some titillating . . ." giving me her lips. Probably the sentence was supposed to have ended in "lunch," but she does not end it. Our mouths continue their own dialogue, the soft warm thrust of tongues, sexual beyond sex or the sex of the genitals, an intercourse of its own, preamble, overture. Wanting to unbutton my shirt, her hand already finding its way inside my pants. Hot for her, giving, wet, hungering.

The sun of early afternoon on us, our bodies in the frank light of day. Waiting for her is waiting at my desk, noon passing and losing hope. She said she would be home at lunchtime, after some errands. At one o'clock I'd given up. Then a car stopped, her keys in the door, as now her fingers in me. Waiting a second, then meeting her on the stairs, the kiss igniting. As now she has me in sunlight, our old ease and extempore, the sense of surprise, the unplanned, the spontaneous. Remembering one lunchtime at Derby Street, our frantic and yet leisurely heat, a "quickie" she mischievously called it, or even "chicken soup." Her delightful vulgarity, its miraculous contrast to the serene and stately lady, even to the sensual woman bending over me, sure of her power.

223

Taking her breast in my mouth as I come. Then making love to her, the old disappointment. It was there that it went wrong. There where the current shut off. There as I stroke her legs and stomach and pubes. There as we take off her clothes, wanting to quicken the flesh, part the legs, breathe fire into her, drink her. But she will not have me. Only the gentle friction on her parts, only the moment's little spasm. Never even entering her. And then she will take me again. And again I am willing, but less so. Already the imbalance depresses me, penetrates my lust, still consummate upon the lovely flesh of her leg, its last crying wave, already despair enters my mind.

A minute after, the terrible disappointment. This really was a quickie. It does not stay on in euphoria, doesn't heal, comfort, or expand. The mind falls back at once to the sidewalk of reality, the smell of tar and asphalt, the ordinary. Letters on a desk. A letter from my prisoner telling me his appeal has failed again. "Shall we finish this off with some sandwiches and coffee?" She is already up, brisk, dressed, back in the world of offices and clocks. I follow her downstairs, disillusioned, remembering she had mentioned that she would be "busy" tonight, "an old friend from the South." At the time I thought that might merely mean dinner. Realizing now that she will be away all night, realizing it because the lovemaking preceded it. Precedes and follows all the nights out, the men. My rebate. Perhaps scheduled for last night. And last night I had denied her. And when I did come over to her bed it was too late or she was no longer in the mood. Or maybe she even felt that I wasn't—but we cannot so presume. So this noontime flight is the alternate schedule, the substitution, the fill-in. How tidy she is. How just, how rigorously fair. My mind accepts it all, understands; my heart and stomach despair at the understanding. I have been had. Against all resolution, used. How much wiser if I'd kept the resolution, went without this. Its prospect so fair and sunny as we began. But afterward, seeing the shame. I have lost. Lost that little bit of pride.

And now the dining table, formal behavior, politeness, small talk. Shaken inside and calmly eating lemon yoghurt. She is quick and alert, in a bit of a hurry to leave. I am leaving soon too, a doctor's appointment in San Francisco, cheerfully forgotten during her visit. Finding my bathing suit and a towel, planning to meet Susan at the pool afterward, I look for her wicker overnight case which I usually borrow, but cannot find it. She comes back into the house, has forgotten her purse. I give it to her, going out with her to her car. Wondering if the overnight case is on the seat, if she has already put it in her car. Hating myself for wanting to look. Stopping short on the pavement, not doing it. Preventing myself. "See you later" is all she says. No "I'll call you tomorrow." Perhaps she isn't going to be out overnight after all, maybe she's changed her mind. Last night she had said, "I know a few things I can do to make it easier for you, happier." Could she have meant that, could she have gone that far? But I would not have her cancel her freedom merely out of pity. If only she would give them up, no longer wanting them, wanting me instead. But not merely to please me or propitiate. Freedom is freely giving. She has every right to her freedom, I would never want to take it away. I sit in my car after she has left. What is it I want?

And what could I have, anyway? She will go with them. She will stay away nights. Well then, the rest of the time. I will have that. Content myself. Yes, but if she could only really *be* with me the rest of the time, really be there for me, actually be with me when she is with me—what would the other times matter? Why should they? Any more than if she were away at work or a conference. Absence is merely absence. But unfortunately it is not. It is time charged like air, poisoned. And when not absent, when present, she is the dead or hostile being of Napa. I myself dead much of the time, passive, a mere reactor to her moods, hot on a staircase, nervous eating yoghurt. All initiative is taken from me. I was so afraid even to put my hands on her shoulders today as she kissed me on the bed, terrified to presume, to begin, to brave misunderstanding or rebuttal. I can hardly respond, carry through, keep up my half of the dialogue.

A dilemma. Her polygamy, my monogamy; her activity, my passivity. This is not reciprocity, an equal relationship, her much-touted adult and independent business. By the very nature of the circumstances it cannot be. Were I to have other lovers, yes. But there are none. I know none out here. Beat the bushes to find one? I don't want to, don't want to be so pushed. And knowing no one I want, want no one. The circumstances of a masochist. Was she cunning enough to contrive a situation where my recurrent ennui, or even hers as well as mine with our bland "marriage" of last year, should become "inspired" by masochism to go on being "interesting" through pain?

And to go on with this lame thing, this suffering, to go on how long, wearing me out how many weeks until I leave? And in New York having only emptiness, the complete absence of her. To go on doing this, spring after spring. Year after year. Her plan. And the alternative? To break off entirely. My plan. Then to have nothing at all. There is no winning.

She called in the morning, having stayed out all night. It had been the movies alone and popcorn, then a Japanese film on television, reading in bed. Careful diversions, carefully timed. Then the telephone as I'm reading the newspaper, calculating the hours till I see her. Her cheerful good morning. Aggressively cheerful. I am subdued, polite, not cheerful, tempered, trying hard for just that moderation. She would like to have lunch with me but she has an appointment. However, she would like to get together after work, maybe drink down the sunset at the Marina or go over to the city. Fine, I say. When she hangs up, I am sorry. Contrite that I didn't try to be "bouncy," with "Good morning, Lady," and so forth. By sounding merely ordinary, unenthusiastic, have I perhaps given her guilt, the thing she cannot, will not, abide? Was it absolute joy she wanted in my voice, absolute love, utter forgiveness, a total welcome? Were she given this, would she return to me in delight? And not given it, will she be surly when she returns, will the time assigned me turn sour? I can think of nothing else now, am obsessed with my mistake. An hour later she calls to tell me the political-science students want me to visit their class. I am bouncy, glad, laugh with her. She is coming home an hour early from work.

The evening began well enough with drinks on the Marina. "Look at the people," she said, "the black men are so much more exciting than the white." Obediently I look and agree that I, too, have always found black men more attractive. But she doesn't hear me, has fixed her attention on a chic black woman with an arresting, elegant, thirties-style gown. Her attention shifts back to the men. "Look, they are all in costume, look at them, the one with the tiger's teeth around his neck, the one in the huge velvet trousers, even the ones with maroon polyester pants and white belts around their big waists." I watch, wanting her attention finally to come round to me but glad she is in a good mood, interested, lively. At least we converse and do not sit empty and inert. A black man stops at the table before us against the windows. "He looks like a shark," she says admiringly. He bumps against her chair and apologizes. She forgives him delightedly, flirtatiously. When I look up a moment later, I find him staring at me. I look down, confused, embarrassed. She listens to him talking at the table behind her and decides his accent is Jamaican. "A wonderful thing, a lilting sort of English," she says. I look out the window and find him staring at me again. He seems to be speaking to me, his mouth moves but I cannot hear his words. He stares on. I am covered with confusion. I look down, feel foolish, want to escape. Later she chides me: how could I resist smiling, whatever he had said? I do not know how to explain to her that he might have been a pleasant adventure were I alone. But that I am with her, and that I want to be. And that he therefore doesn't exist.

After dinner we are given fortune cookies. Mine reads, "You

have a particularly magnetic personality." Life's little ironies. I fold it and put it away. What does it say? she asks. I answer in the Irish manner, by asking her what hers says. She seems nearly as reluctant as I: "Lucky in love." The mockery is rather too much, and it hangs between us across the little restaurant table. Maybe that was the turning point. Or maybe just the way the weather had turned earlier. All day it had been gorgeous, warm, tempting. But I kept on working, writing letters, waiting for the magic hour when she got off from work. We would go to the Marina, watch the sunset, lovers in the thankful luxury of a Friday afternoon. We had started off so bravely in the sun, so gaily, with such anticipation. And then the weather changed. In the space of ten minutes as I stopped off at a supermarket to buy an apple so that I wouldn't be drinking on an empty stomach. When I came out of the store, the mist had already formed. By the time we reached the sea, it was nearly a storm. I was cold in my fancy Greek shirt, which an hour ago had seemed festive. Inside, it was already full. There were no window tables.

And she watched the men. Somehow that was bearable, "amusing," food for conversation. The dinner was excellent and we ate with zest. But somehow the "lucky in love" phrase was too much, too bitter. After last night, after all those other nights, Neal and Stanley and whoever the others are, even the men at the Marina, the shadows of men just at the periphery of our lives, strangers hulking and threatening from a hidden place in the wings, waiting till she approaches them, preferring them, stands and lies in secret with them, as she forays back and forth into my life. And you call that lucky in love? To sit there a fool and hear her say it. It was fortunate we were going, just leaving then for the movies. In another five minutes the darkness would cover me, my moods or mistakes or withdrawals, my exasperation or malaise. Fury, impotence, despair.

Coming home, I pleaded headache, told her I would read my

228

way out of it. She had to get up early, had already set the alarm, and so went off to Pia's room to sleep. How eager she is always that if one of us is to move, separate herself, it should be she. That the controlling power of action be in her hands. That the room-of-one's-own decision be hers alone. I lie in bed, the charm of reading stale now, lonely here, my resolution exhausted. If she were to knock on the partly closed door, if she were to come to me now, how sweet. Coming into "my" room tonight, I stood by the bedside table a second. The phrase "confused, merely confused" going through my mind. What is it I want? Her fidelity? No, I would not circumscribe what she calls her freedom. I can't, have no right to. Then what? Not her fidelity but her love. Her love, having as many lovers as she chooses, only loving me as well? Something like that. Yes, sometimes. But tonight it didn't work. The rebate didn't come through. The ardor with which she usually returns from these men, the spill off from them or toward me, I'll never know, but always there is some quickening. Gratitude that I endure it? Guilt turning to sentiment? No way to analyze. Yet it is there. And I'm thankful, hungry enough to drink it in without asking.

But perhaps now I inquire too much. Perhaps I am bored or jaded. Cynical or sated, past hoping or starting again or believing at all. Yet if she would only come through the door, I would forgive everything, forget every moment but this, begin all over. She does not come. I do not go to her. And now the bay is misted, air and water the same identical gray. And I think of the weeks ahead, fewer than the fingers of my hands.

Undressing tonight, we had talked of going swimming tomorrow when her conference is over. "Call me," I'd said, "and I'll see if it's okay to bring a guest. I'm still not a member of this club Susan takes me to, but call and I'll see if they'll accept my application on a Saturday." "I won't have time to call, I'll be too busy," her voice out of Pia's room, snappish, impatient. I went to the door of her room and gently explained it all over again. "There may not be any

229

phones." "But surely you'll break for lunch?" "I'm busy then too." I went back across the hall to my room, "our" room, partly closing the door, quietly exasperated.

As I read, the door rattled once, softly. I hadn't closed it firmly enough, the bolt wasn't in its groove. Thinking to myself, In a moment I will get up and shut it quietly without disturbing her. Then astounded to hear a rustle behind it, then a loud bang. It irritated her, and she had seen to it herself. But the vehemence, the violence. Like an insult. My face burns with a strange kind of shame. Sitting up with my book, feeling as if she had struck me. There was something cruel about the gesture, more cruel than anything she has done before.

When I look up at the door, I notice the balloon we bought at the parade. She had tied it to the outer doorknob when we came home that night, and with the slam of the door, it has ended up on my side. Wilted, shrunken, like a headhunter's trophy mocking me. Time goes on inside the room.

She is at one of her conferences. Another day drags by, another Saturday. She is bringing her friend Maud home to dinner and to stay the night. And they are late, hours late by now. The frustrations of waiting, of pacing the kitchen, checking the preparations for dinner, making myself ready. Because I am near tears and mustn't weep, determined to go through the evening with perfect stoicism. If Maud were to see anything amiss, since she's Sita's friend and her friend only, she would see it as a matter of my "being difficult," "giving Sita a hard time," "being a drag." They may well have discussed me in those terms already. Maud herself gives me only the slightest attention and, possibly for this reason, has bored me increasingly in the years I've known her. Because she is Sita's friend and not mine (as if it were not possible to be both), there is always a taut sort of politeness between us, always more brittle as her claims as Sita's friend begin to outweigh my own as her lover.

I will be perfect. I have already prepared a magnificent steak dinner and I will be charm itself, the good hostess, the good sport. Meanwhile, I will withdraw utterly inside the realm where it matters. I will murder caring. And so this paradox, the happy home, the good dinner, the lively conversation; but inside I will have abandoned them both, gone away clear out of reach.

Do I do this to save my face or Sita's? For it would never occur to me to make a scene before her friends and I am just as eager to put on a fine show as she is. Our devotion, our discretion, our graceful and courteous behavior toward each other before others have been my pride as well as hers, years of it now, the joint enterprise of our relationship, the product of our two personalities merging to create a third, the "us" of each combined with the other, this remarkable and passionate friendship, so permanent and immune to distance or separation or time or differences in age, this image of ourselves we had projected to be admired, admiring ourselves in the process, the narcissism of love, this public self, the hardest thing to give up, this externalization of love, the bitterest thing to relinquish when the private love is dead. And so I will be perfect. And I will murder caring. Both at the same time. For I have come to the end of something. And waiting for them, I feel it.

The dinner is splendid. Maud, who never eats, eats more than she perhaps should. I watch her finish her steak, feeling like the mother of the world to see her happy, forgetting that her lover is fatally ill, that her parents have spent three months visiting her, that she is in danger of getting fired again in her yearly crisis at the university, that she's maybe even had more to drink than she should. I also try to forget another dinner here last year, when she spent most of the evening in the toilet throwing up. But it is the Sita on that occasion that I want to forget. Sita with just that extra glass of wine, delightfully tipsy, cooking a roast chicken she continues to baptize in sherry, Sita in a silly and even rather ugly apron, huge, disfiguring, and yet in retrospect painfully lovable, Sita laughing and gesturing and being Italian and bending down her beautiful head to open the oven door one more time and baste that poor critter with wine, the rest of us too amused even to remonstrate after a while, merely enjoying her so innocent high.

Having eaten and drunk so richly, Maud grows sleepy and a bit disappointing after dinner. She sits on the couch and nods. I light a fire. In a few moments she is ready for bed. Sita and I stay up, deserted by our guest.

And I don't know just how it started. A chance remark I will probably never remember, but in a minute we are fighting again: the old fight, but for once I am fighting back. To my astonishment I hear my voice telling her that it's over, that I can't take any more. "I just can't stand it, that's all. I thought I could, but I can't." "Then what do we do?" "Call it quits." The still air in the room echoes the ominous words. I have gone this far without ever meaning to; without measuring the distance of the jump, I have said it. Part of me huddles its collar around its neck and waits in pure terror. Part, a part I never knew existed, keeps right on going. It is utterly silent in the room, the silence before disaster. "Would you do that?" "I have to. I can't bear living this way. You are not *with* me any more." "Well then . . ." She is accepting it, she is receiving my bloody little resignation and filing it away for the official stamp of my departure. It was that simple. She never objected at all. The air in the room so empty, so full of fear, as if a murder had taken place. I have done it. I have said the words I cannot retract. And it's over. Finally it's over. "I'm sorry, darling, I'm sorry I couldn't take it. I tried."

"Then I will give them up." At first I don't even know what she means. And then it comes to me—she will give up the men. "I don't want to lose you." Looking at me with all her power, sitting above me and at some distance on the sofa while I lie back in the pillows, looking alternately at her and at the fire. She has tears in her eyes, her beautiful eyes, weeping, love me. She will even give up others for me. At once I would have her take it back; merely the statement would be enough. And I hadn't even been thinking of them. But of course, if she gave them up, it would be a new start, the end of one set of fears. It is not that she loves others, but that she doesn't love me—a significant difference. But perhaps this is her way of loving me again. And surely a gift. Such an act of caring, of commitment on her part. "I don't know what they're good for anyway, really, maybe I was just convincing myself of something." Keep them, keep them, I want to say. Give up nothing for me. If young men make you feel young, if their attentions give you joy, have them.

While at the same time the serpent gloats, wants them gone. And beyond that the voice of victory flushed with pride that she would do this for me. "Don't do what you don't want to, it would only make you love me less," I urge, the serpent already winning. "I only want it to go on, for us to stay together." Her voice choked, moved, and I watch her amazed. For the first time she has capitulated to me—because I meant it, was serious, was gambling the whole stake? I watch her, humbled by her humility, realizing that she is vulnerable, finally vulnerable. "It's three years, that's too much to throw away," she says with this new weakness, tragic in its frail humanity, moving me to a rush of endearments for her, esteem, compassion, all the things that first brought her to me. Now like a miracle, rising, rising even in her tears, rising and coming toward me, toward the great white polar-bear rug I lie on, the luxurious pillows, the firelight sealing us as I fold her warmth into my arms, her sobs in mine. And making love is wonderful, a discovery, all harms past, a new pact. The tears and anger leavening the tenderness we feel, the renewal. We have come that close to nearly losing each other, nearly parting in consternation and bitterness, nearly calling it quits and meaning it. And now to have it back. We lay a long time by the fire, and when we came we wept.

At my desk, to my right, these magnificent roses. Orange, actually orange. Perhaps fuchsia. A touch of pink in them, but really they are orange, literally orange. The most wonderful roses I have ever seen. They light the room, already full of the cleanest morning sunshine. This moment is a touchstone, I think. Fragile as the roses themselves; already one stem is broken. Hold back time, do not take them. Or this moment. A touchstone, I called it, a peak. The very perfection of it a kind of pain. Glowing like these strange vital flowers against the lovely brown of the worktable, the dark Japanese blue and white of the vase. My writing table. Having it again. Having my room again. The view of the city and the sea and the bridge. All restored. My first morning in a room of my own.

The roses are astonishing, the power and intensity of their color is such that it's hard to keep my eye on the page, to read for my class. The very fact of being rushed in the reading and of not being able to write and do my own work today, even this does not mitigate my pleasure, only increases it and my anticipation of tomorrow. The sun pours in. No other moment here will be as perfect as this morning. The realization itself a sorrow. Just as these roses go, roses that she bought for me yesterday as we were going to dinner in the city, buying them on impulse. And the roses radiate her, her gift—it is all her gift—the sun and the sea and the table, clean, waked, fresh for a fresh start in a fresh room. She has given it all to me. Given it back, restored it. All I took for granted last spring, having my room to work in, my warm cocoon of her love. How little I knew then what it was like to lose it. Spoiled, coddled, complacent.

Looking back on the ragged weeks. It is all restored now, returned to me, each piece falling into its place. Sunday afternoon while she plotted a trip to Mexico with Maud this summer—a trip I'll miss, being already in the East by then—I scrubbed the floor in what had been Pia's room and is mine again, while Pia moved all her belongings out. She and Dan have found a house in the city. She has taken a waitress job at a truckers' place in the Mission and does imitations of the customers. She didn't mention Emily, and when I asked about her return, Pia was vague. The new apartment has wonderful light, she said, her plants will love it. And I loved scrubbing that floor, waxing it, putting down the rugs. My own floor again. Moving my worktable back in, hanging some drawings. It is all ready for me. Finally, after all these terrible weeks of patience.

I read for the class, happy, excited, lucky in the insights and perceptions one hopes for in doing this work, falling into its method of thought but looking up every now and then to be astonished again, to savor the roses, their outrageous color, their pure loveliness, their so sensuous form, petal upon petal folding, vulva-like, some paradisaical vulva repeating its liplike crevice avariciously a thousand times. Each time I withdraw from the book I'm reading, make a note or look about me, the sunlight and the roses overwhelm me again, pleasure so close to pain, joy so much a premonition of sorrow.

I will have to leave here. Suddenly it is neither rescue nor escape. Suddenly it is loss. For the first time, absolute and irremediable loss. Finally I understand her—"You will leave again in a few months for New York and I will be left alone, why should I risk it?" I had felt that too, coming here. That I would be gone and without her so soon. Why invest again? Of course, how unfair I am. Coming here and divesting her of all she had built between her and loneliness: children, lovers. The kids departed on their own, but the

235

lovers are made dormant by her promise for the few weeks I have left here. Or until she tires of what she promised.

Her goodness has restored me to my room, my view and my time and my roses. And her love, her attention, are slowly turning back my way. And just as my full resumption of place ripens, this moment of sun and these miraculous flowers. Just then, I know it's ending. Feel it coming, like fate, imminent as an amputation. I stayed and gambled and am this fine moment winning. Losing, I threw and took the risk, and now see another loss coming at me.

Only a few weeks and I return to New York. Just yesterday, leaving Sherman's studio, I remembered the roof of my loft, how pleasant it would be to put some chairs out there, watch the sunset, invite friends over. I'll buy geraniums, I thought, the thought almost like an infidelity as I followed Sita down the passageway, surprised when she turned and kissed me.

Walking to dinner in North Beach, we passed a flower shop and looked in the window. "Shall I buy you a posy?" "No, please don't bother, darling," worrying if she had enough money, anxious she not be extravagant, but delighted. "What do you like?" "Well . . ." following her into the shop. "Pretty flowers for a pretty lady." She laughs with the shopkeepers. Then I saw the roses, their utterly incandescent color. Six for a dollar. Why not? During dinner she put them in the water glass. With each step of the way they became more precious to me, more magical. The waiter admires them. Coming out of the shop I was only flattered, but during dinner I grew infatuated with them. She is tired, tired with that enormous fatigue of her Sundays now, one day to rest after a six-day week. I drive her home, protecting her.

The tiredness is possibly boredom. Perhaps she is already regretting what she promised. I would have her undo it. Perhaps she already feels unfree, tied. I long to undo what has been done, but am afraid to mention it, fear her annoyance at my inconsistency.

And the roses on my table, like a triumph. What if I never went home? Gave my loft to someone who needs a studio? Fumio has been looking for one for a couple of weeks. After the money spent and the months fixing it up, painting, plumbing, scraping floors? What if? I say it but cannot imagine it. The idea only a toy. The way people say, What if I were to get run over this afternoon? Because the loft is my self and my salvation, my only independence. But what if? And would she be imprisoned here with me then? It is what I felt last year and so did she, or she said so afterward. Yet while I was here she wanted me to stay forever, live together entirely, the "marriage" we refer to so bitterly now.

But do I owe it to her to stay? Having got it all back now, am I obligated somehow? Will I feel like a rat when I go? I had never had to worry about it till now—saw the time as the moment of release only, dreaded nothing but that it was a permanent break. And now I am by no means sure that it will be. I think of coming back next year. She thinks of it too, I am sure, though we hardly mention it yet.

To be happy now. To have joy. These flowers and this sunny morning. The class, which I'm truly enjoying now, and this evening dinner with my students, then to meet with Susan and Alta afterward. A full day. And the days ahead, days of work, swimming, the fine weather and the city. To be able, simply, to savor time as it comes. And yet these strange orange roses have already put the period on time, added the piquant note of finitude just at the moment they have signaled the top. I call her up to thank her, not really having the words, only the roses and my gratitude for being so happy this morning. As if the shock of their color, the bend of their graceful little stems, the crisp little green of their leaves were in itself her devotion, protection, tenderness. She does not quite understand but sounds pleased. How like a lover her voice can be, how like the very flesh of her body as it touches me.

Will there be another spring here? And if there were, what would it be like: January's coldness, new persons in the house, the unseen presence of lovers, the ghosts of men I never meet? Or meet only to suffer the more from. Or her lack of interest, the hostility breaking out so many times in quarrels and bitchery, her love's gradual diminution.

Who knows? You take your chances and so forth. I have thought once or twice of an entanglement of my own, if I were to meet some new person in the months away, some relationship that mattered, absorbed. But none do. And I am held here, Sita. By these roses, their small elegant pot, the lovely brown of the table, the sunlight over all and bouncing across the walls, the room mercifully transformed, emptied of Pia's hangings and plants and pictures and overstuffed chairs and beds. All gone. Mine again. My own room. And the great sweep of sea outside it, the span of the golden bridge. This moment having it all.

After my class is over, I'm in limbo with a few hours to waste. Was to have dinner with some of my students but there's been a mix-up: they thought it was next week, I thought it was today. Another student offers to eat with me if I'm "at loose ends." I keep face and mumble something about an appointment. Coming away from class high, excited, with the special enthusiasm that comes after a good class and then has nowhere to go. Neither have I. Or rather, that particular nowhere which is everywhere: home, the Mediterranean café, the Marina, the city. Home to my table and the roses on the desk, work a while before I go over to Susan's this evening. And then perhaps Sita may be home. Standing in the lovely campus evening, the rhododendrons in flower, the tulip trees, the scents of spring, trying to decide. I go to get my car. Rummaging for my keys, I realize I have forgotten to lock my classroom. Duty requires I hike back and do it. Coming out of the building again, still undecided between a café and home. The evening so fine, the promise of a spectacular sunset. But if she is home, if she stopped off there a moment on her way to her class in the city . . .

And she is home, her little gray car in front of the house like a present. I am thrilled to find her, carrying the whole burden of the roses and the morning, full of feeling. "I'm so glad to see you." "Well, I'm glad to see you too." She looks up from doing the taxes, putting her papers away, her mind in another place altogether. There is no echo to my mood, my clumsy ways to say it. She's spent her few moments busily, is now hanging out the wash. I struggle to help her, plodding downstairs and into the yard against the pieces of linen. Practicing phrases, hoping to come up with some-thing, some arresting series of words. The small grass underfoot, the billowing sheets. While I hang one, she has hung all the others. I look around for more to do but she has already gone into the house. She munches cold chicken in the dining room. I eat cottage cheese out of the carton, watching her. "Do you have time for a glass of wine?" I'd asked when I came in, relishing the idea of a sociable little drink. "No, I'm in a hurry." Eating, she still gives off the sense of hurry. My gratitude, my love cramped inside me as I watch her. Later maybe.

And later she thwarted me too. Coming back from Susan's early, tearing myself away as soon as I could. Because she'd be home by now. I am even late. She may be in bed already, asleep. Planning to be stoic, silent, to slip in beside her and not wake her, merely feel her warmth. The front light on. Maybe she is still awake, maybe we could talk a little. Coming up the stairs, I know it all in the sight of the closed door at the top, the door to Paul's room. Now that Pia's is my workroom again, there is only the foam mattress in Paul's old room for her to run to for asylum. And she has done that. Sensible, of course, she didn't want to be awakened when I came in. And turning the corner, I see the rest. The lamp beside our bed in "my" room, the covers folded back, a note on the pillow: "Lovely Lady, sleep well, sweet dreams. I'll wake you in the morning." A flower sketched whimsically at the bottom of the page. Fragrant maternal sweetness of these notes, how ironic, al-most treacherous. The room is lovely, inviting, empty.

This evening after she left I took the roses from the refrigerator (where I keep them in storage, covered like an icon, hoarding each precious moment of life), put them on my table, and sat a long time watching the sunset till it was dark. Even then I preferred the stars and the city lights reflected in the water to the room's bright overhead light, and so I lit a candle and went on sitting, merely sitting till I was hungry.

"When you're in a bad relationship . . ." someone had said tonight at Susan's, the phrase sticking in my mind. How easy, the time being past, to label it, to condemn it as hopeless, something you got into once, were well out of later. The pat little phrase comes back to haunt me. Susan and Alta both agreed. "When you're in one of those awful relationships, and believe me, I've been in plenty . . ." I nod my head; we are imitating women of the world.

And of course they're right. I said nothing of my own situation but I have read them a bit of my journal, since we are all reading aloud bits of our journals and they know very well where I am. They spied the wound and were kind about it. Probably would like to persuade me back to health. We are friends and fellow writers. A few generalizations about life and love and what is "good," what is "destructive," what is "hopeless."

But you don't understand, I want to protest, I love. It's because I love that I go on. Hoping. Trying. Delusions, romantic delusions, the phrase replies with its tidy view of life. But I want to live by my own standard, by love and the life of the senses. Or should one instead find refuge in a phrase—"a bad relationship" like that— and explain imponderables, explain passion this way? And the phrase sounded so convincing when Alta said it, so full of the conviction with which she had extracted herself, and would do so again if need be, tough, good woman that she is. You live by what goes far down, I could have argued, where you find energy, where you are convinced or can find belief, the faith of experience. But this is largely pain, they would have argued back, frustration, bafflement. True, or in this case true. But I have lived this. Deeply, all the way. I can remember it when I die—it is even a kind of dying in itself, or rather the losing of it is—because it was something from the beginning so sharply, so vividly and intensely lived, that the morality of "good" and "productive" and all that are irrelevant. But I tremble before their reasonable judgment and was afraid to read when it was my turn, hungering to communicate, to tell someone my plight, yet terrified to do so. And when they reply with good common sense, I insist upon my sickness, even arguing its value, turning it into a perversity, something clung to. Because it is mine, because it is my whole life now, my obsession. Sita.

Somewhere at the very bottom—the kernel, the heart—I suspect, of the problem is that love has failed us, failed us both. That we simply can't love any more as we used to, that it wore out, that it died somewhere, that fine aroma, that intoxication. And we will neither of us admit it. She chooses her mildly interesting affairs and a life of insecurity. I my angst and then my escapes to the East. And we are afraid to throw in, risk everything, and try making it whole again. Because we can't.

New York prevents me, anyway. Then it's I who broke the circle, taking a place in New York as long ago as last spring? Or was it she, deciding I had broken it by doing so? Was it she who broke it in Europe, those two terrible months during which she never even spoke to me? Tease the problem, find justice here or there—or blame or answers or riddles. It is not this, it is simple. Simple as the current between us, whether on or off; living together or apart; it can become in an instant alive or dead. If the current is there. But living side by side without it is nauseous, a moment-by-moment agony, something obscene when you compare it to the alive and living, the time of connection.

But isn't there something to be said for steadiness, continuity, security? If I had never left. If I had given up my town and my people, my studio and much of my art, the art world and its opportunities, my gallery. How much should you sacrifice? I sacrificed half. Foolish, probably not enough. Yet she doesn't consider these questions late at night.

But still it might have worked, this half-time life. If we had the current, if the lifeblood were there, it would have held us and the absences might have made it only the more exciting. Might. Might. Theoretical. Meandering. The real situation is her body inert in another room, and the closed self of this evening, the remote self of tomorrow's breakfast.

Her face in the light of two candles. I've done a London broil, striving for variety as meat chef. This one from a real butcher, not the usual Safeway thing. It's too rare for her, she says, "but it has a lovely taste." More wine and we edge toward what is usually a quarrel, but tonight we stay precariously balanced in a serious discussion. And then lapse into sentiment. She draws her chair closer. "And what am I to do when you leave? Does that ever enter your mind?" It had come up in the kitchen while we were cooking. "When do you take that trip to Puerto Rico?" I ask. "April twenty-sixth." "Then I guess I won't see you again; I have to speak in San Diego the twenty-fifth." And I'd been planning to go home to New York at the beginning of May. New York again without even saying goodbye? Suddenly the wall in front of me, the end. I look up at the cupboards, off to the stove. Her back is to me, preparing the salad. "How long will you be gone?" "Just four days." "Then maybe I could wait till you get back before I fly East." "You could spend the weekend in San Diego, it's beautiful down there. You might even want to go down a few days ahead." She goes on in her California tour-guide manner. I listen, incredulous. Can those last days together be so unimportant to her that she can cheerfully pack me off to look at scenery instead? As always it is so hard to understand the brisk managing side of her, the capriciousness.

Is it caprice now, her hand on my shoulder, asking about the future? "We have a lot to discuss here. Your belongings. The house. If you're coming back. All of it." One candle gutters. Her eyes by the light of the single candle, so very beautiful, so full of feeling, tenderness. Compelling. "Maybe if I had a connection that

could keep on supplying me with underground classes at substand-
ard wages?" I tease her, opening the way. Wondering, as I do it,
if I want to come back, so unsure myself. Yet part of me assumes
it now; I will come back, I will always come back. It will go on,
it will always go on. "You don't seem very eager," I say, nudging
her, sorry the very instant I do it, not having meant to, wanted to.
"I don't want to push you. Not until we both know what we want."
"And the fact is, we don't," I conclude. We smile. A wan, hopeless
smile.

"Now when I think of leaving, it makes me very sad. It hadn't
been this way when I first came. Things were so hard then that
leaving was rescue. Now that we've come closer together I dread
the time I go back." "It will be very lonely here without you." Her
eyes telling me this, canceling the others, the friends and lovers and
diversions. "It's very lonely in New York too, damn bleak in that
loft a lot of the time." "Maud used to tease me, that when I came
back from Europe last fall I almost systematically started surrounding myself with things and people and activities." Her hands
move, describing the things and people and activities, moving them
around the polished surface of the dining-room table like small
wooden counters. "Maud used to tease me that under it all I knew
just as well as she does that there's the house wine and there's
champagne. It's that simple. You're my champagne." Laughing.
"And you know my extravagant tastes." Her eyes, mischievous
and full of light, snapping in the warm glow around her face. "I'd
be able to forget for days in a row, and then when I'd be dressing
or walking to lunch, I'd suddenly remember. I have felt the greatest
tenderness for you, more than I've ever felt in my life for anyone."
She puts her lovely head on her arms, her white sweater gleaming
around her shoulders in the candlelight. Utterly beautiful to me.
I sit drinking wine, loving her, admiring, telling her my admiration, adoring her in words, words I am normally too shy to say.
Emboldened a little by the wine, by our closeness tonight, our final
ability to talk. Even to talk without argument or bitterness. We are

243

lost in our situation, hopeless as the distance between our worlds, a whole continent, three thousand miles, two radically different ways of life.

There is the art world and my need of it, which she saw when she came to explore it at Christmas; a small foreign child she was while I dragged her through slums, through the Village and SoHo, exclaiming softly, "Now I see, now I finally see where you live." We talked of it again tonight, the sense she has of being excluded there, her hatred of New York, her love of California. "But if I went to New York, if I arrived at your door, the door of your loft, you know you couldn't stand it." "I think it would be super," I say. "No, you don't. Four days maybe, but not much beyond that." Wondering if she's right, if I want New York to be alone in, free, my own place.

But wanting while she goes off to telephone Maud, wanting simply to admit how empty and alone New York really is. Wanting to say that Dobie, for example, is just a nice guy to build bookcases or go dancing with, but that's all. That only twice was I drunk or dumb enough to sleep with him and it wasn't any good. That even Dobie prefers a platonic friendship out of some dingbat romantic notions of his own. Wanting for some crazy reason to tell her all, to show her the utter barrenness of my days there, admit even that I'd been sleeping with Ruth and that it is nothing but guilt and disaster and that when I go back I won't do it again, that the whole thing with Ruth is a species of crime because she loves me and I do not, cannot love her, maybe—the terrible thought again—as I am Sita's crime because she cannot love me. The old analogy; as Ruth is to me, so am I to Sita. Wanting to tell her New York is solitude, that there is no one and nothing there for me. And yet not saying it. Shyness? Self-protection?

She comes back to the table to talk again and drink wine. It could work, she says, hard as it is to live our lives together only half the time. It could work. She wants me to come back next winter. We talk late and until we are very tired. As she was undressing in

Paul's room, where she keeps her clothes, I found her and my arms brought her to bed with me.

During the night she escaped, but I did not mind, waking to a bit of a hangover to see that it's barely dawn. Coming back from the toilet, I walk softly, crossing the treacherous floorboards before her open door.

"Come here." I stop like a thief in a pantomime. And then dive into the warmth next to her. "Snuggling"—surely the most pleasant thing in the world. Scrunching further and further into the mattress as we struggle closer and closer warmer and warmer nearer and nearer, our bodies like a letter fitting into an envelope, my legs over her legs, our hips sliding against each other, her arm tighter and tighter around my shoulders, my face nestled more and more firmly into her collarbone. It is bliss. The simplest and most primitive bliss. A childlike, sexual, friendly, animal bliss.

A garland of her notes. Notes left on the pillow wishing me sweet dreams, notes that Susan had called, or that she'd be an hour late, notes wishing me good morning or good night. Each with its caricature flower drawing, its old-fashioned and ironic salutation of "Lady." How many notes that start with "Lady" these three years, the word half courtly, half mocking, given what weight of tenderness by now, what smooth slopes of eroticism beneath the growth of familiarity. I have saved them, saved every scrap of paper she's ever given me. Letters. Notes. All the visible proofs of her love, even of her existence. It began when I first met her. I could never bring myself to throw away anything from her hand. Almost as if I knew from the beginning that one day she would be only a memory, a series of relics from some strange lost love, the beautiful older woman who had loved me once. Like a full rose that had bloomed once in my life. Even in those early days the sense of fatality, the telescope vision, seeing it already from the other end, from afterward. Why, when it is so present now? But now it's only a present suffering, the bitter ending of it, not the delight of then.

Now it is an hourly humiliation so unlike the past with its light quick moments of intoxication. Now in contrast to then—a disappointment so sharp it is a kind of mortification.

Yet her voice on the phone this morning was humorous and caressing. She thinks she has sold one of my drawings. Real money. We are both pleased. "I'll take my usual commission," she teases me. "I'll let you take it out in trade," I counter. An old joke, her joke, a joke from the old days. "Would you like me to apply in writing?" "That will be satisfactory. But I must inform you that carbons are now required, because of the demands on the property." "Would Xerox be an acceptable alternative?" "Well, since you're an old client . . ." "Old? The oldest! Would you like a statement from my doctor to that effect? Or certification that I'm free of contagious social diseases?" "You have fleas." "No, they've left." "Really? I got bitten twice last night. You see what happens when you abandon me?" "They couldn't resist your body. Succulent. It's that succulence. I'm beginning to feel it way over here." Hearing her voice, loving it. Mellow, capricious, sensual, teasing, its urbane shuttle between her office and its bureaucratic realities and our own private and forbidden pleasures.

The past like music flowing back. How the telephone would ring on my desk in Sacramento, a desk crowned with the flowers arranged for me in the big shallow black bowl. I would be reading for class. Those long, rich days of reading and thinking, getting up only to walk the floor and pull a few dead leaves off my plants, waiting for a thought to form, for a note to be made. Rooms full of flowers and the sun and quiet. And her call, her voice Italianate and full of trills, like bubbles running up a glass, a voice full of invitation, ideas for dinner or explorations into the countryside. Or late at night a voice Indian and full of longing and desire, sadness and distance. When I answer the phone in New York and she says her name, she always says it as if she expects me to have forgotten who it is. Cross-country calls these three years. Her voice hurt

246

often, lonely often, rarely reproachful. You fail love with distance too.

Or do you merely say "a bad relationship" and dismiss it? As a carriage is hurled across a typewriter and on to the next line. Are people like used cars that you trade in, the object being efficiency or health? Health, surely, that's the model for such phrases, the psychiatrist's "well-being" as measured and therefore imposed by the "objective" observer, authority. Or do you stand by the thing you have made, experienced, created with hours of friendship and lovemaking and talk and boredom and companionship and quarrels and enjoyment and the power to remember?

But I do not have the fixity to carry this off, to cleave, settle. The courage of matrimony, its complacency. I am more romantic, believe more in the nostalgic than the everyday, have more faith in the music of the past. To say, "Here it is, I stick by it," is impossible for me. I stick by nothing. Or rather only that which has the ring of music, experience which leaves a fragrance behind it. I can envy the honest stolid matrimonial everyday, its commitment to the banal in exchange for security. But I cannot live it.

Let it always be an affair then between us. The way she laughed at Christmas, watching me cook dinner, sitting in my only chair in my big Mexican sweater, throwing back her head when she said it: "Let's always be having an affair. Wherever we meet, however many times a year—let it always be an affair." And I was excited and flattered and a little challenged, perhaps even made a little nervous by the idea; yet it struck me as perfect. To go on year after year with no more safety than the hazard of that. Perfect.

Of last year here, last spring, our settled time, I remember almost nothing. Only that it was comfort. That she brought me out of suicide. Separation from the man I'd lived with so long, the studio I'd had so long, then an almost fatal depression. And then I came to her. The place was reassurance, here I took the first steps back to living. And then walked off to New York. Clear away. When I

247

joined her in Europe that summer, last summer, the balance had already shifted. I was no longer beloved, cherished, covered by her passion and nestled in her affection. Her passion of the early days, the great protective affection it ripened into. All gone. Only the steely resentment of a stranger, the nightmare of being in a foreign country with a woman who despised me and seldom spoke. And next the stranger when I came here this time. Now melting slowly back into the lover. How to trust it? How to take the steps, permit the folly of believing again?

I have never doubted the past, the Sita of then, a woman dead now. So full of love, of eagerness, of extravagant gestures to please, to surprise, to delight. Nothing was too much trouble, too far, too long, too expensive, too troublesome, too tedious, too obscene for intimacy, too silly for words. This garland comes from that time, the ghost who composes these notes knows the old music. Speaking to me on paper, she speaks to someone who was, and is no longer, but in the act of writing comes alive again for a moment, the one I was when she loved me.

I watch her face as she talks to me. Animated, entertaining me, talking for fun, for the recitation of it. A string of wooden beads around her throat, how I love the skin on her throat as I listen. A light flannel blouse, pearl-colored, handsome. Her hair curling around her face, its gray almost pearl-colored like her shirt, shimmering in the early-evening light. A story about a woman who arrived without an appointment and stayed all afternoon. Sita performs the bore who showed up in her office. "You won't believe it, but this woman is actually named Dr. Doctor. She's not a medical doctor, only a Ph.D. Might as well have been an idiot, took up two hours of my time and managed to say absolutely nothing. Silence. Dead silence. Just sits there. One of those moment-to-moment talkers, you know, the kind who may manage a whole sentence in an hour. But she'd come to see me because she wants me to give her a job teaching something she calls Assertiveness Training for Women."

248

She is laughing, waving her arms. Her beautiful features are lit with amused malice, with the delight of her impersonation of Dr. Doctor, varied with one of a dead body slumped in a chair, which alternates with her own vivacious account of the interview, her hands flying in Latin articulation, the rings on her fingers sparkling in the twilight. Her gold ring slaps the table for emphasis. "Dr. Doctor did manage to tell me a story. How she'd gone to a store, an art-supply store. And the man ahead of her had gotten a piece of cardboard from the clerk. When he offered to pay for it, the clerk said it was free. Dr. Doctor said it took her five full minutes to get up the courage to ask for a piece of the free cardboard too. And this woman wants to teach assertiveness!"

I know exactly how Doctor felt, have been Doctor all my life. I ought to take assertiveness training too. But instead I say, "Maybe she should give it a little whirl as a student before she starts teaching it, whatever it is." "That's just what I suggested—very tactfully of course." Sita beams. I merely enjoy her. Unable to judge, uninterested in judging; for all my sneaking sympathy with Doctor and the Doctors of the world, I am enchanted and beyond morality watching her. "Then at a quarter to five—she didn't leave and she didn't leave—I said I just had to get out my mail." Running into one of her silly puns, "You know, though Doctor didn't, that I keep a little male under my desk and at five I trot him out." Her smile lush on me, mischievous, sensual. "If you keep him on a leash coming home, he may even do his duty," I say, grinning at her, the word "duty" catching up with me as I say it, like some nightmare prediction.

"I think I'll put cinnamon in the coffee," she says, stretching. Should we go dress yet? I wonder, not wanting to yet, cherishing her mood, her company, bored by the political cocktail party at which we must appear soon. "Cinnamon. Do you like cinnamon?" she asks, being cinnamon as she asks it, aware as she says the word, repeating it over, smiling its syllables out, aware she is cinnamon itself, its very color and flavor. "Do you remember those little red cinnamon candies, red on the outside, cinnamon on the inside, do you remember them when you were little, how hot they were?" Her mouth imitating their shape, their supernatural hotness. "Hot, hot, hot." She laughs at me. I smile and appreciate. Just the way she says the words is sex, playfulness, eroticism, every form of coquetry, the word warm in her mouth. Is she this way with them, with men; was she this way with every lover, with the men of the past, the husbands and the lovers? A great flock of birds rises into flight. It is that time of day. The bay sparkles with the last light of all.

I put the coffee cup away and rinse egg off the dish. Morning. The time of facing your soul and starting to work. There is the old manuscript upstairs in its manila folders, the record of the year of the plague, the death book. Supposed to be working on it, but instead I indulge myself with this notebook business. This account of her and me. Really of her. If I could make an account of her. A tribute? An act of love. Fix her on paper. But it's complicated, sheer adulation is tedious, false, fictitious. If you are honest you have to tell things they later regard as unflattering. With lovers you don't merely love, you hate too, you disapprove, you recriminate. You're unfair because love is unfair. And this whole notebook's unfair probably. And inaccurate. Too close, too intimate. It should be described as an experiment in charting and recording a relationship. Day to day. No one's ever done that. Surely not of two women. Which is just what makes it risky. Risky especially for her. Risky for me too; on behalf of the great generalized hostility of the world, I have here perfected the instrument of its revenge. I have lodged its loathing in a ball inside my stomach.

Last night I had dinner with Christiane Rochefort, the French writer. Susan had introduced us. Christiane is middle-aged, and a writer of fiction in the great tradition. I liked her Parisian art world toughness, her gentle, aging woman's face, soft as her cashmere scarf. I liked her and she was kind to me. But we are of different generations. Under her prodding—"What are you doing now?"— I told her I was keeping a journal. "I kept a diary once," she said, making a face, "but it was not literature." I mentioned my two unfinished manuscripts. "Aborted manuscripts," she said. "One can never do anything with them." I don't believe she meant to be unkind; she was merely relating her own experience. I listened, hoping she might not be right.

If Sita were someone else, and if I were someone else, if we had the cover of fiction, would our experience be more worthwhile, less disreputable, even more "real" to readers? Or would we be only a "story"? Robbe-Grillet caught something of jealousy—the gut reaction, the sweating palms, the obsession. Yet in his novel there are scarcely any personalities at all—only counters for the exposition of that emotion. And I think that was what I was after at first too, with all my "process" propaganda. But personality could not be suppressed. Hers anyway. I am too fond of it, too involved, admire too much not to want to convey it, every detail of her life is sacred, fascinating to me, my only fear that I will not express it sufficiently, fail to do it justice. A person always so much more than you can get on paper.

Meanwhile, I am left with my doubts, my notebooks, my hopeless task, its obsessive desire to record, study, analyze, preserve.

Turn it to fiction then. Since you're so fond of thinking you are at last drifting that way—out of the suspect waters of the personal, the autobiographical, the experiential—and into the safe harbor of fiction. High art. Didn't you tell Susan the other day that you were at the edge of fiction because you were describing a phenomenon even more than persons, doing an event, the end of love, just that essence, that moment, that experience, that process, process for its own sake. Using the first person, but the narrator didn't matter at all, could be anybody—it was the process that mattered, that held the stage. Blah blah.

So in fiction then, thinking in fiction. I could turn myself into a painter. Repress my writer self. Even my sculptor self. Just say I paint, am someone who paints—not drawings, mind you, paintings in oil. But then I almost become Sherman in my mind, someone who paints in oils. Blue denim shirts, Grumbacher brushes, tubes of Winsor & Newton, that old six-dollar cadmium red, I remember it well—probably up to twenty bucks by now. Oil, the smell of oil paint, the time of painting, the slowness of oil, all the times you light a cigarette and stand back and look at the canvas, the time of day, the pauses in sunlight, the body time, the long daylight hours. A painter in oils. Someone else, not me. Like me, but not me. But less and less like me as she becomes someone else, a fantasy self. Sherman? Or someone else entirely. She keeps becoming Sherman. No, let her become someone else, someone you don't know. But then I don't know her and stop knowing about her. Characters take on lives of their own. Which is why they can have plots and murders and unexpected events, events unexpected even to their creators. Christiane Rochefort told me that one of her characters died apparently of his own volition in an automobile crash several minutes before Christiane could prevent it or even decide if she approved of the idea. But I am writing of something experienced, something known that particular way. Not imagined, not fantasized, but known in the gut way that you know a stomach cramp.

But try, try being a painter. It would be so convenient. Noticing once or twice I have almost written down "painting" for writing, canvas for manuscript, carefully guarding my writing table to be flexible enough for later revision into easel, studio for study, etc. Little points here and there where I protect my identity so it might still be switched. Little points of dishonesty or self-preservation or malleability. And I walk around the house thinking all the time of other names for her, different streets, towns, places. The disguise of fiction, the defense of it. The nuisance of my give-away geography, New York, California. But it is just these two points at the opposite ends of the continent which compose the situation, are its

252

very essence—how do you deal with them? Not wanting to. Wanting to just go on and on writing it as it happens, keeping a record of time and experience, perception—however imperfect.

And it is so imperfect. Holes everywhere. Whole passages unwritten, key events never set down. Laziness, inability to record accurately, well, completely. Like a shoulder badly drawn looks so awful, so awkward. And the vulnerability of intimacy, how do you rifle it, expose, betray to strangers? Even the solitary page?

The phone rings, 9:30 a.m. I wake to discover I am still dressed and stretched out on the sofa. Sherman's voice telling me she's called the restaurant. They have the notebook. She'll walk down and collect it later today. Gratitude for her goodness, shame and amusement and surprise at my present situation. How did I get here? Coming home from our bachelor dinner in town, Sita gone again, a quick trip to L.A. which will bring her back this morning, another mysterious trip to L.A.—when I questioned her she asked if I needed proof it was university business and offered to show me papers—of course I was ashamed. Ashamed again to wake up on the couch and remember I have lost my notebook. I had worked all day for the class, which left me only an hour to write before going out. Wanting to write. Not even wanting to go to town. But then, dressing, I had; had suddenly wanted the city, bars, restaurants, the night. Thinking all the time that I would go somewhere, some café, afterward, write—better yet, come home and write. And then in the street late at night in front of Gino and Carlo's, drunk, the bars nearly closed, standing in the street saying goodbye to Sherman, realizing I'd lost the notebook.

And last night I told Sherman I was writing it, that it was a process of something struggling for life or dying, that I was keeping track of a process. "Good," she said, "do it." I was surprised. Here was sanction. But Sherman's an old pirate of an artist, she'd understand. Does losing the notebook mean I must tell Sita? Picking it up this weekend, the errand of recovering it—does this involve me

253

in revelations? And would her knowing predict events, subject life to control? All the old questions. You should have gone into them before.

What am I doing on the couch? The down of remembering. Coming home already nicely lit—and playing records. Wanting to hear music. Alice Stuart, Roberta Flack, Nina Simone. Every song that had ever mattered between us, that replaced her absence. More wine, maudlin after finishing the open bottle of Riesling. Dancing even. All by myself dancing around the living room. Having wanted to dance at the bar, but Sherman was having none of that and there was no one else. Sherman's Wild West bar empty and sinister tonight because the bands are all downtown playing a concert. Atmosphere of a place where nothing's going on. Only our long-chinned talk of loneliness. I remember telling her how much I had loved Fumio, that I would go back to him even now. "She knows that, she'll never forgive you for that." Then switching and telling her the other side of it, how he used to ask me every morning at breakfast what I wanted for dinner. "Don't you see that could drive someone crazy?" She nods. "I not only didn't know what I wanted for dinner at that hour in the morning, I didn't even know if I wanted to be home for dinner. I just knew that I hadn't worked yet. Just that I wanted to work and then I'd think about it, when I was ready to play. But I felt trapped."

In the morning light remembering this crap. This sludge of sentiment, half-formed, two-faced, partial truths, bad faith. Bitter or in tears over this love or another, all gone down the wind of my own errors. And lost the damn notebook too. Has its humorous side, and a headache you can count on. Get up and go undress in the bedroom. Be ready when she comes, wait for her in bed.

Earlier than I'd expected. The key in the lock and her steps, then silence. Looking up to see her just as I feel her weight softly on the edge of the bed. "You came. You came back." "Of course." She takes me in her arms. "Forgive me, darling." "For what?" "For nothing at all." At once she launches into tales of the tedious dinner party last night, the hosts who wouldn't drive her to the airport. "Toddling about at six having to take a cab. And I had only that ten dollars I pinched from the food money. The cab comes to six dollars. The limousine to two-fifty. I was terrified I'd never get my car out of the airport parking lot. If the limousine had cost another dollar, you'd have had to drive to Oakland just to rescue me from a seventy-cent parking charge." Her arms enfolding me. We sleep again. The whole weekend is ours.

The whole weekend. Two long mellow days. On Saturday I draw her from the nude. She reads a book and does her hair while she models. An almost irritating cleverness at entertaining herself while the process goes on. I do drawing after drawing of her back, the pose most convenient to her other pursuits. Each time I fail. I imagine her sneering at my poor and inadequate efforts, for I cannot capture her today. I try other poses too, the lovely sinuous line of her side, the slender belly and loin and shoulder, the superb fruit of her breast, its brown berry in profile. "Do you despise what I'm doing?" I ask her finally, confronting her for a moment in the bathroom. "No, of course not, I love it that you draw me, no one has ever paid me such a compliment before." And then I believe her again. It is like that, the up and down, the on and off of faith.

This weekend which is to give so much. The only full weekend for a month. Next weekend she is off with her committee to their retreat. The following is my trip to New York. No, not the end, not going "home" (already it no longer seems home), but a short visit of a week, a book tour that my publisher has asked me to make. And when I am back in California, it will already be the end of March. Then there is only April till I leave. So this weekend is precious, promised to me all week ever since she first mentioned it last Sunday, taking just as she gave, by telling me the retreat followed it. I made a face but accepted and spent the week in expectation. We had even thought of going away, Sutter Creek, the gold country. But we didn't call ahead early enough, the inn was nearly full, there were only single beds. Sita put her hand over the

255

receiver and grinned, saying, "I'm not driving eighty miles for a single bed." You can have that at home, I'd wanted to say, but held my peace. And now the weekend, its weather uncertain, the bay gleaming one hour, beckoning us out and to the city; glowering an hour later. For a while I have her, then washing her hair claims her attention. Or a newspaper or the phone. Her mood is elusive, shifting, her attention so hard to capture.

I had promised to take her to dinner in the city, but as we drive along she decides instead on the Marina. Eating dinner at four-thirty in the afternoon, how odd it seems, even ridiculous. She is delighted, however; we'll get to the city with plenty of time to park before the concert tonight, we'll even have time for a walk on the pier. Solomon Grundy's big windows frame the sea, the mounds of Angel Island, Buena Vista, Treasure Island, the three great spans of bridge: Bay, Gate, Richmond. Our kingdom this, and the sailboats and the city sparkling way off; this is the panorama and the place she had stretched out for me from the beginning, this the sunlit world of California, this for the city-rat eyes of a downtown New Yorker.

Always she won me this way, over and over this glistening spread of water and seagulls and island and city and bridge and sky. Clear and immediate as the sailboat whose canvas nearly touches our window. Of course I loved her world, it being she, she being California itself. No poor American thing belonging to smug blond children but to the buoyant and vivacious northern Latin, the Mediterranean great lady who spread it out before me, nobly and affably displaying her jewels, pressing them into my hands. Half of her. And the other half, the South American Latin, dark, even Indio in her long patience, also discovered it for me. The "brown wren," this one calls herself, having believed most of her life that she was homely, slighted. Just as the other woman in her has always been beautiful and known that beauty, reveled in it, flirted with it, rolled it like a Sienese banner of silk unfurled and snapping in the wind.

256

Sita across the table from me now. And her world spread before us in the sun. We are very happy. I can feel the moment, even remember it ahead of time, the curse of foreknowing that, even as it is sweet now in the mouth, warm along the arm, it will be some cold New York nightfall bitter on the lips to remember. Some time after she is gone from me, some solitary hour closer to death. It is this, this foreknowing of mine that makes it impossible to live in the moment. And the dubiety, the lingering skepticism.

The man at the table behind us sermonizes his wife and his son and his daughter-in-law on gift taxes, inheritance taxes, the value of his house, his boat. We grimace at each other, hating him. "I'm going to ask Martin to put my boat on the lake this summer. I can stay at Maud's and use it on the weekends," she says. I tease her for having sold the boat to Martin though she goes right on using it herself. "I'll pay the dock fee," she says. We both smile. Suddenly I realize I will not be here this summer. The little pain of it, just as when I heard her discuss the trip to Mexico with Maud, or her drive cross-country. In a few weeks I go out of her life again. The bay spreading at our elbows. The man behind booming that he can give son and daughter-in-law thirty thousand each without any taxation. Sounds awfully high, wonder if he's right. "Now, the house is worth eighty thousand of course, get that without any trouble at all." Must be some house. "Course your mom and I gotta pay taxes on the eighty grand, you know that." I wish he'd stop shouting. I wish he'd shut up. The figures of his self-importance booming through my efforts to concentrate on Sita, the little time left in our lives. "Now, that's the gift tax, you can work it around real good if you know a good lawyer." Motherfucker, why don't you shut up, you're poisoning my lunch.

Lunch, I'd call it. Dinner, she'd call it. We rally each other over the word. I try again to tell her of my love, telling her over and over lately, because she keeps saying she never did feel loved by me. "I was a way station, a provincial outpost between one person or another in New York, because New York was all that ever mattered to you, all that was real." The sea stretching away at her hand and her beautiful face that has courted me so many times and does no longer. "This became real. The first time I came I was out here just for a while, remember, a temporary job. New York had been home, after all. Anyone would see that all this was beautiful, but you made it take hold." The old confusion between the two places. And soon I go back to New York. But already this scene, which was merely landscape at first (and New Yorkers are suspicious of landscape), now begins to replace the broken buildings of my slum, erase them.

The hurt I can feel even in my cunt—the fear of losing this place. Then the old questions. Can you have both? Love both? Can people live in two places? Students always live in two places, at college eight months of the year, at home during the summer. Can people really live in two places? Or is there an attrition of energy, some loss of attention? The artist in me is terrified of this, that my concentration will be dissipated, fewer works produced. And then there are practical matters, the opportunities of New York, publishers and art dealers and events, and the collective energy of other artists.

"Finish so we can walk on the pier." The man's voice is booming away behind us still, his investments, his taxes. I don't want to finish, I want to block him out and go on talking of love. The honey of its words, wanting her to tell me more, and again in greater detail. I want the sweetness of these moments to go on and on— the sea and the bridges, the islands and the city, our enchanted scene, familiar, beloved, paradisaical. "Why do you want to leave —just because of that boor behind us?" "No, I want to put my arm around you when we walk." Disappointment gives way to pleasure. And when I didn't understand how the sun dial on the pier worked, she laughed and showed me. Walking away with her arm around my shoulder, still laughing.

Sunday morning. Waking in terror. She is all I have against the world. Against failure. Death. The disappointment of my work. Manuscripts discarded, unfinished, useless. "What's the matter?" she asks. "I'm scared of life, scared of work, scared of death." And for once I can tell her that my life was always a surprise once, full of kinks and turns as a subway tunnel, not knowing the future, the where or the what in store. "And that was always good. But then last year it turned 180 degrees, and when I'd gone through the suicide trip and losing Fumio, it all seemed suddenly a straight, flat highway with just death at the end of it. Like the lights of some town, just how far away you couldn't tell yet, but it's flat as Kansas and death is the only thing ahead." She holds me, comforting. "Do you worry about us too?" she asks. "Of course." "What can I do to give you assurance?" I tease her: "What do men and women do? on these solemn occasions?" "What they do is jump out of bed and get married. Shall we get our crazy friend Frieda to marry us in that gay church of hers?" "Really!" "I'm serious. Would you feel better if we made some pledge to each other?" I close my eyes against her collarbone.

Pledges are just what I dread. It is just that certainty, like the flat black road surface to death. And yet, and yet the surety of there being someone in the future, in age? She goes on, her mouth above my head, repeating the line from Browning at the end of a play on television we saw the other night, "Grow old along with me! The best is yet to be," Laurence Olivier leading Katharine Hepburn off into senile romance. I had been strangely moved; she had gone upstairs to weep and I wished she had not left the room. How odd we are and at what cross purposes. How we fail to guess or communicate even over a television drama. A month ago, the pledge she speaks of—which terrifies me now and which I sedulously avoid replying to by keeping my head down and smiling and remaining silent—a month ago it would have released me from hell.

Sunny Sunday morning. We make love over and over. The weekend indolence I have coveted for weeks. But it did not begin this way. Finally bringing myself to say it out loud, the disappointment of yesterday, of the other days stretching back and back as I lie now in her arms, listening to her tell me she loves me. "We don't make love, we aren't lovers any more." "But of course we make love." "The last two times you've made love to me you haven't even bothered to finish. And you never let me make love to you." "I haven't felt comfortable." Thinking: Is it that you need a man, prefer that, require that, that six inches of flesh—feeling defeated.

"I haven't felt comfortable because there is no time, no energy. But now there is." Taking me and letting me take her. Over and over in the sun of the morning. Taking me and giving herself to me to be taken, hand or mouth, tongue or finger. Lapping the sweet juice fresh between her legs, the flesh like fruit in my mouth, the ineffable sweetness of her little mound or pouch of flesh, sweet as my hand reaches it, its swell, the soft hair under my fingertips, the nearly painful sweetness of it, this ridge at the base of her belly, this crevice between the thighs, its thrilling and terrible sweetness to the lips, its sweetness to the tongue and mouth. I am insatiable, still thirsty for her after she has finished, wanting to go on mouthing and licking and beginning again. Taking her over and over in my hand or mouth, my tongue teasing to enter her as she opens wider and wider, stroking the dear desired triangle even after she is done, stroking to another heat and spasm. And wanting more, still more. The delight of having her again, taking asking and getting, opening her thighs to kiss again this sacred spot, this mystery, my mouth on those lips, the source, the source of her. Forgetting the denials, the refusals, the rejections, the rebuffs, desire turned away, turned rancid and bitter. All forgotten now in the joy of having her again. It all comes together, contentment and triumph.

After breakfast she calls to me from the couch: "Come and join me in here, those dining-room chairs are so uncomfortable." I settle in with my newspapers. "I've been thinking about it and I get the impression those people in New York who handle your books aren't very good." It is rare and lovely for her to be interested and I'm flattered, though a little confused by her taking up my career. "I really think they're pretty good and they do save me having to do it myself." "But how do you know they're not just dragging their feet? I know more about public relations than any of them." New York, the world she hates, fears, and could not conquer and manage as she does here. Talk of New York brings her to Fumio and the woman he lives with and into the dark backwaters of the end of my marriage and the nervous breakdown that came before. "If it's any comfort to you, a lot of marriages founder after something like that. They snap under the strain."

Today we talk about the breakdown. We usually don't. She was with me, stood by me through much of it. I thank her now, realizing how rarely I have, how the whole memory is so bitter I habitually avoid it. Hoping to avoid a quarrel, since it is hard to remember what they—my elder sister, my husband, even Sita—did to me, hard to forgive their naïveté, stupidity, bad faith. Perhaps that's the wrong order, for it was naïveté more than malice. But the capture, giving me over to guards and jails when I was confused and afraid, having me beaten up in a parking lot, wrestled to the ground, tied, trestled, bound upside down into an ambulance. That they stood there and watched, when any of them, especially my sister and Fumio, who were kin and legally empowered, could at any moment tell the huge two-hundred-fifty-pound guards to let go, lay off her, not to hit her any more, to stand back and let her be: We'll talk to her, she's just scared. I looked up at each one, pleading, and they did not move.

"Don't you understand?" I ask her. "Anybody that scared freaks, but if you give them some room, talk to them . . ." "We didn't know what to do." "Yes. And you'd started machinery you couldn't control any more and you couldn't stop." "True, all through the thing. And whenever they wanted to move you from one place to another or get you to do anything, they sent me. They realized I was the only one you'd listen to, the only one you'd even hear." She stops. We look across the room, embarrassed, in pain, even to remember is painful. But she keeps on remembering, how this or that friend tried to make me see reason, how Frances, for example, a psychologist friend of ours, wanted me to go to the country for a week. It goes on and on, the old reproaches, the number of occasions when I was impossible, incoherent. "You were like someone on speed. Amphetamines. People who take amphetamines are like that." "And I still don't even know what happened, what caused it. Pressure? Michael X's case, trying to prevent his execution? Teaching? Filming the music festival?" "It started a month earlier when your other sister was here. Then it kept on escalating through June. You were a wreck when you got back from that trip to England." I want to tell her that I was fine in England, worked like a whirlwind for Michael and was probably effective. Just exhausted and overexcited when I got back. "No, it was when Fumio came out West, to visit, right after that. Having you and Fumio in the same place. It made some strange, terrible pressure. Some awful enormous incoherent guilt for loving both of you. I think I couldn't stand it. I think that's what made me jump the rails."

Silence. "But I'm sorry for what it cost you, for what you suffered too," I say, looking up at her. She is sitting on the arm of the couch above me. "We've been through so much." "Sometimes that makes it harder," I answer. "Or richer." There is tension and silence and then other words, the coming back together after exploring the terrible, the wounds and mysteries, the reaches avoided, proscribed. "And what do we have when you leave?" she asks. "What do I have, anyway? It will be lonely here." "New York is lonely. There is really no one there for me, eating alone, living alone, no job even to go to, no 'colleagues' and that sort of thing. I'm lonelier there than you are here, more isolated; I know fewer people." "What do we have when you leave? What commitment do you make? It's not fair . . ."

Odd, even crazy that she should talk commitment, she who had shed me permanently a month ago, replaced me, leaving no room even at the edge of her life. Then it was I who wanted to talk commitment, to hold her to the letter of some past agreement. Fair —the word makes me wince. Surely I didn't mean to be unfair. "Look, Sherman told me you'd decided you were done with me last fall." "I was finished. Yes, that's true." "Well, not having been informed, I arrived anyway, fell out of the sky in January to find there's no room in the commune. But I stuck around. The kids bicker and split, all on their own and with no help from either of us—you to make them stay or me to make them leave. But one day Valerie and Pia just start pulling each other's hair and it's all over. Then . . ." But the next thing is hard to say, the gray figures of men between us. "Then you're still a mile away and I can't reach you. You're wrapped up in other people and your conquests." Exchange of wry little smiles. "But somehow you decide to look me over again, somehow"—my voice changes—"you began to care for me again. How I don't know. Why I don't know either. Lady, you dragged me around Europe like an amputated limb. Then you dumped me. Now you've changed your mind. When will you change it again?"

I lie back and relax. The camellia and the note beside me on the pillow. Her infinite sweetness in writing this, finding an old envelope because she couldn't find a sheet of paper, wishing me good night with a flower. She is asleep in the other room. I feel no resentment at all for that any more. I am late tonight, having dined with my students and having had a wonderful time. One student got drunk and was very tedious, a layer of hostility under her compliments, but even that didn't faze me.

I could live here, I think. Getting to know enough people so it even seems possible to live here. That student who showed us slides today is really a brilliant photographer, such an air of strangeness about her pictures—"Fictions," she calls them, people in the most ordinary situations yet surrounded with an odd stagnant air, a vacuumlike atmosphere: a girl in a barren room, a floor lamp photographed all by itself, a man with his head deliberately cut off by the camera's framing, couples whose very postures speak volumes of anxiety. It would be nice to know her. And there are others. I tote them up. A few other writers out here whom I should try again to reach. Yes, it would be possible.

Everything is possible in this satisfaction—stretching out, lighting a cigarette, deciding not to read. I should finish off that manuscript on Japan I was working on out here last spring. It wasn't "interesting" enough, I'd decided, leaving off in what was probably the best passage, the time after Yoshiko died and Fumio and I first fell in love. Too painful to write so soon after breaking with him? Or was I merely interrupted by the return to New York, the trip to Europe? I could finish it. My life a mess of unfinished manuscripts. "Aborted manuscripts, there is nothing you can do with them."

And the other manuscript, the dead folders that sit on my desk. "My season in hell," I snarled tonight at the drunken student who was needling me to know what I was writing. That black murky junk still on the desk, the year of the plague, the job I'm ignoring completely in favor of this stuff, my "microscope," I called it tonight, refusing to tell the student what I'm really doing, though she has a whiff, I suspect, from Susan, who's also a friend of hers. "What did Susan tell you?" "Just that you'd read from something new and that she'd liked it." "Everyone in the world must be keeping a journal this spring," I'd said, dismissing it.

But it's true. My students. And their students. Janice, the student who got drunk, has a class of senior citizens and *they* keep journals. Virginia teaches black teenage boys from the ghetto, and they keep them. But mostly it's women, the new women, the new women writers, the new sensibility of women finding its way onto paper now. Fervid, secretive, then abandoning all secrets. But I find myself still caught up in secrecy. I have still not told Sita about this notebook. Close to it so many times, with oblique references, half disclosures. That day at the faculty club. Yesterday over dinner out in Sausalito when she told me what name she wanted to have if I ever wrote about her. Suddenly, apropos of nothing: "If you ever write about me, you should call me Sita. Of all my names, it's the right one."

The camellia she has left for me on the pillow. If I went to her, would she mind, be angry? Wanting her, wanting to lie next to her, to feel her warmth. Only that. Gratitude, a new kind of affection, friendlier than anything I could feel in the bad days, the weeks past. Liking—realizing that I like her now. And couldn't like her then, not when she gave pain. How to be sure even of this? Love in one or a dozen of the senses of that word: longing, desire, the need to possess, need of a hundred kinds. But this affection now, this liking is different, elusive, tantalizing. If I lie next to her, I will know what it is that I feel, I will satisfy something. Not afraid to go—which must perhaps be some signal it is out of good faith? Quietly, ever so quietly. Not to wake her. Treasonous floorboards, the rustle of covers. Moving slowly with the patience of a madman or a mother or a friend. Then the warm, waterlike ease of the foam-rubber mattress, the current of gently heated air, the assurance of flesh giving off heat, the full balance of her weight next to me. In her sleep her foot reaches out to touch mine. Like a kiss.

"Commitment," she'd said. The word was a stone around my neck when she said it. But doing the grocery list I add glasses, hardware, rings for the bedroom curtains, so they can be closed easily and the morning light will no longer hurt her eyes. I will fix the door Dan and Paul removed so cavalierly, losing the hinge pins in the process. The bookcase? She wants a bookcase for the front room, later Paul's room. And maybe it can again become what we used to call it, the library. All my books are still in the hall closet, where they were stored while the kids lived here. Gradually, step by step, the place is restored to me, to the two of us, to me and the

Sita who is with me, rather than the Sita who was with them. Should I build her that bookcase? Time, money, tools. Buy one? Commission a carpenter? Commitment is building a bookcase. When I came here I certainly had no such intentions, came and found the place gone, full, occupied, given away. I wanted to run. And decided to stand my ground, fighting for space, fighting the ghosts of men I never saw, or saw only once, sitting across the room from Neal. Stayed and am winning.

How contrary I am. It is just now that I'm scared and want to run. Commitment? Do I lose the future, its unknowns, its possible adventures? And otherwise? To be an aging woman living alone in New York, solitary meals, a body going toward death. Grow old along with me, she'd said. Hell, I don't want to grow old at all. I never want to die.

New York. Publications. Exhibitions. Will I lose as an artist, staying here? Even staying part time? My friends, others my age, running on ahead of me. And this age, this decade, one's forties, the time when the most work is done, the prime of maturity. But it's not merely that which would elude me. More. Love affairs, parties, encounters, a fistful of experiences never had. In loving her do I lose the world?

How contrary, how irresponsible I am. Wanted her when she was gone from me. She returns to me and I want to run. And stand still not out of integrity or faith but out of cowardice. I don't dare tell her I am afraid to be caught. She was right after all to withdraw. Her instincts were sound. "She goes away," Sherman said, "because she can't stand being the victim of her feelings for you." I stood by and waited till the children were gone, till she had given up the men. And now I leave? Now when her eyes turn toward me, all others being gone, departed, forsaken or forsworn. I stand in the kitchen ashamed of myself.

A trifler then? But I never meant to trifle. The thing catches me on every side like a machine out of control in a Chaplin movie. When she is cold it is my fault somehow, when she is fond it is my responsibility. I fear having her on my hands, and I am afraid and ashamed of that fear. If she knew? She would be furious, would never forgive. Her superb mad pride would take her off at one leap. But I can no more forgive than she can—and it's just that, the failure of faith, the wavering in loyalty, the shallowness of character in her that could have sworn love so persuasively in the past and then grew so fickle, so rude, so sullen. For all my patience, all my doormat masochism, there is a current of rage in me, a strand of malice that can never forgive the defection.

I am someone in a fairy tale transplanted to a beautiful kingdom every year. A place of springtime and sun and flowers. But one year I arrive to find my queen or fairy godmother or princess or whatever completely obdurate. She no longer loves me at all, no longer even remembers. Then slowly, by infinite degrees, I warm the ice which surrounds her. She comes to life. She smiles and loves me again. And then I say I cannot live here, prefer my winters and my darkness and my shanty at the bottom of the mountain, and tell her that the paradisaical kingdom is not enough, is not habitable.

This is ridiculous. So what is it I miss, then? My solitude? The very thing I fear. My independence? For with her I lean. And since she cares less she is always stronger. I depend, give way to her superior force and personality, her facility in decision, her efficiency, her certainties. I who have no certainties. So it is always an unequal relationship, even when it's happy.

What else do I fear? Coming back, coming back each year. The waiting, hers as well as my own through the intervening months. The attention always stretched to someone far away, not seeing those who are close, the things that are near, the day-to-day. Other relationships never really form or take hold. One is always coming from or going to the rendezvous.

She mentioned the loneliness ahead of her, the empty summer. I don't want to inflict that on her. It isn't fair, just as she said, it isn't fair. Not that she'd be as isolated as she says. The men would come back, or other men. She'd take lovers of course. But they would be temporary, marginal, tangential. As mine always are. Or else they would take hold and replace me. And then I couldn't come back. And I want to. Mostly I want to be able to—to have that door open. The way to the sun.

Each winter, to have that escapeway clear, each winter as the depressions of my winters settle in, the apathy, the longing for suicide. To have her older face waiting for me in the place of the sun, her serenity, her ease, her comfort. Making love once in the old days on Derby Street—the time I was mad or beginning to be mad—late late at night, having exhausted her, exasperated her, and now insisting on this act too, my face along her thigh, the soft hair of her pubis on my lips, I understood it. One of those impossible insights that I loved in madness and the others hated so. Comprehending at one bound the myth of Demeter and knowing that she was Demeter, that the fountain between her thighs was my own youth and I Persephone, who had come to her in spring and would come forever, for she was my youth, older than I and yet my youth, my ever-recurrent spring, and spring itself only a metaphor for the source, the waters, the hidden river, the tunnel of life between her thighs.

Lady, how I exasperated you. How I fail you still. Wanting. Not wanting. The moods and vacillations, the morbid speculations of a love as contingent as this, as voluntary and unsanctioned and insecure. She must feel the same, has felt the same. But doesn't speak it. Nor do I. Silent all those crucial moments on Sunday when she asked for a pledge. Sly I was, and pledged not. Afraid to lie outright. Yet as much as I can, I suppose I gave it. Yes, and I know that it is being leveled at me now.

St. Patrick's night she got drunk, a rare occurrence and even a little funny, though she herself wasn't funny, she was angry. Bounced up and down in bed and almost yelled at me, she who never yells. "How can I know you won't go back to Fumio? Can you promise? Can you promise that if he wanted you back you wouldn't just go back to him and live with him there in New

York?" "He has no intention of having me back. He's delighted to have me out of his hair." "That isn't what I asked you. I asked you if you could promise you wouldn't go back." "No point in it, it will simply just never come up." At this juncture she burped and I had to smile and didn't actually take her seriously. As I didn't earlier, about Molly. The day before Molly had come to the house to interview me. I liked her as well as the attention—that somebody was taking me seriously as a writer. Molly has a nice Irish humor, a dark and roving eye, a cap of curly black hair. Young, but I rather fancied her. Under the cover of her questions she asked if I were in love. I hedged a little, the question was too complicated and more than I felt like divulging. I was probably flirting with her too. Nothing important. Molly can play the fiddle, would be at the neighborhood bar on St. Patrick's and invited us to come and hear her. A rare thing a real fiddle, the jigs and the reels and so forth. So we went. And it was very lively, Sita got tipsy and jigged away. But there was one odd little moment. A young woman sidled up to us and asked, what would I like to know about Molly. "She's a good friend of mine and I can tell you anything you'd like to know." I'd nothing to say whatever, but Sita said, "Do you really think she's going to ask with me sitting right here beside her?" It was absurd. I was embarrassed, even humiliated by both of them. And yet sharply pleased that Sita could still be jealous. After all the broad hints that I should find my own "interests" now that she had a few going. Perhaps she was merely annoyed that it was said in front of her. Or annoyed because she's given up her men. But it was lovely still to see her jump and pounce again. Bullying and proprietory as her jealousy had always been; unlovely thing that jealousy always is, it was lovely somehow to have it back. As for Molly, I haven't given her a thought since then, except to make certain not to be home when she came by to pick up the copy of the interview she had sent me.

I go to dinner with Sherman the way other people go to their psychoanalysts. Perched on a bar stool at the Tivoli, gazing at the collection of old light fixtures lined up above the bar, odd Chicago art-deco stuff, always mysterious, hypnotic over me while we sit here talking, going on about art and how to live our lives. Always the brave pretense that art matters more, that we put it first. "So what if I just folded my wings and settled down to live in Berkeley, California? After all, it's not the art world finally that makes New York home." "Oh, that fucking art world." "No, you don't understand. If I folded my wings and settled here, how can I explain what it is I'm afraid of?" "New York has energy." "It's also lonely as hell sometimes. Look, what I'm afraid of is that there might be fewer books, that there might be some book I never wrote." "You said yourself you can write here. She's supportive of that, at least you're not sabotaged there like I've always been. They see me paint, they watch that day after day." Little gestures of painting, a big clownish grin. "And gradually, they come to figure out how much it means to me. And then—oh, unconsciously, mind you—they start hating it." She breaks off with the usual dismissive wave of her arm. "Hating it, man." Turns. "But that's not your problem." "No, I would write if I stayed. Maybe. But there might be some book lost, some book I'd never meet. Some adventure, I can't explain. And no sculpture. There's no place to sculpt. I have a show scheduled next December. The gallery's in New York. My studio's in New York. I hate sculpture, it terrifies me. But . . ."

"You need it, for some damn reason you need it. And you need this"—she slams her fist into her palm. "Yeah." "You need that, that goose in the ass, that stimulus. That's New York." "It's not that simple. I go nuts in that loft some nights."

We drink and Sherman accepts the homage of the regulars as they come in for a drink after work: like an old and acknowledged master in her big denim jacket, her beautiful head, the cropped androgynous hair, her ringed fingers holding a glass or gesturing, the majesty of her height and age and courage; everyone in the quarter knows her. I go on explaining to her wisdom, "It's that if I stayed and settled and didn't go on I'd never know what I'd lost, what book or sculpture or drawing—I'm not even drawing here and I used to draw two hours a day every day in New York. You know what I mean, all those discoveries of living alone, whatever adventure or love affair or growth or change. Instead, it would be settled. You can stay in one place and start seeing the end. I don't want to see the end. I don't want to know what's ahead." "So it's New York. Gotta be." "No, it's not that clear-cut. If I leave her, there's no one I'm close to in New York. And it means giving up that nice warm living-with-someone thing." We smile, acknowledging all this.

"I love living with someone, Sherman, I've done it most of my life. It's good. You work all day, then they come home, dinner, a fire, sleep together." "Yum yum." She snaps her ringed fingers, grinning. "Look, Sherm, that's life, just life. Just for the sheer living of it." "Like most people." "Yeah, the lucky bastards, none of this garbage about making art. Just enjoyment. Take it as it comes. When the sun shines they roll up their sleeves and they can feel it." "Bullshit. They're frantic. All they do is wander around having to score. They gotta score a car, some sex, a game of pool, a permanent, a job. They gotta worry about what's on TV or if the kids' school can teach 'em to read. They're driven. They're just as driven." "Maybe you're right; let's order another drink." "Of course I'm right." The laughter of comrades.

"I keep thinking of age, of living alone and being old. And not having kept this when I had it, of having thrown it away." "You're really morbid." "Hm. But you know what? It's better now. She's come back to me in some strange way." "Only to disappear for the whole weekend again." I defend, protect, explain, produce reasons, commitments. "I think she really didn't want to go this time. The committee bullied her into going at the last moment." "And how soon do you leave and go East?" "Beginning of May. But there's this little trip next week. Just a few days. Then I'll be back to stay all through April." "You can't be both places. You just can't. No way." Her arm wipes out the possibility in the air, one of her most definitive dismissive gestures. "I don't see why not. I don't see why I can't live here six months a year. She thinks it could work too." "It hasn't." "No, when I came back this time it was a nightmare. But it doesn't have to be that way." "When you're gone she entirely regroups." Neat gestures of her hands making boxes on the bar top. "Rearranges her whole life, substitutes. I don't blame her." "I don't either." "So when you come back, there's no room any more. Why should there be? You can't have it both ways." "So it would appear." "You don't believe that though, do you? You think you can." "It might be possible if we had some fine and special under-standing and really wanted to live that way, wanted it enough." "Crap."

Her body bringing me the phone. "Call Marguerite, she's in the hospital." Sita's body: elliptical, pear-shaped, Modigliani. The lovely lines of her hips and ass disappearing now in the frame of the door. How many times I have drawn these lines in my mind, with a brush, with the eyes opened or closed, remembering or imagining or recording on paper? Does consciousness of an experience change it? Writing is so much more problematic than drawing, full of moral pitfalls, ambiguity, public responsibility. If you record a day of your life, does the decision to do so change the shape of that day? One of Doris Lessing's days in *The Golden Notebook* is fifty-four pages long. It's complete; the rest are summaries—the "impression" of a day foisted artfully upon the reader by providing a few details. Fiction is made this way—as lineal perspective gives the illusion of three dimensions in drawing. But does the selection of a day—that you begin by knowing you must remember and observe—really affect it? Do you change the balance, distort the truth? The period itself, its choice and selection, does that not in itself constitute a kind of misconstruction, and the rest follow subconsciously?

What do you leave out, what do you falsify? What do you mar by the imposition of a pattern? Recently I was sure I was recording a natural pattern—decline and fall. But where am I now? I read de Beauvoir's *The Woman Destroyed* the other day and was transfixed—she had already done everything I had hoped or intended. Her story went straight as an arrow to the murder of a relationship and the woman dependent upon it. There, I thought, that's it exactly. And it wasn't. For days I felt a special anxiety because I was not following that pattern, the tragic tangent. What I thought was the pattern. I would have imposed it on the notebook, but I could not impose it on events. Instead she returned to me, turned and returned. Would I have preferred the expected, the reasonable shape and continuation of events? Preferred some trite and "logical" pattern I could impose on a notebook? Wanted a notebook more than a lover, preferred a bit of scribbling to life? Or did the pattern only seem inevitable and rescue from it arbitrary, temporary, artificial, more cruel in the end?

This notebook business. The keeping of records. Good for an occasional *cri de coeur* maybe; but when it becomes bigger than what it recalls, takes on a life of its own? When the time comes that it has to be owned up to? I stand accused. Trapped in my own device. I have even told her I was writing the notebook. It seemed only fair to do so finally, not knowing what to expect as I told her, perhaps even expecting her wrath. She was only amused, regarded the thing as a hobby horse, a waste of time, an evasion of real writing. She was witty, teased me about it charmingly.

When I came here and things weren't as I'd hoped, I could have just gone away quietly, someone with any pride might have. And no notebook. I realize now that I may have stayed to write it. To experience and then analyze that experience. I'm reminded of that morning in the dining room after she'd been out all night, the night we'd come back from Mendocino. I'd decided at Mendocino to stay in California, a decision that was almost immediately invalidated by her departure for the night with that exit line about calling from the office. I was pacing the floor in the dining room, just before I went to meet her the next morning, and the course had to be decided on finally, since that should have been the first day of class. Pacing the floor and remembering the damn deer at Mendocino, remembering them, just then and even in the state I was in, writing a sentence on those deer and saying to myself, I will stay, because if I leave it I will not have had the experience and I want to have had it.

On Valentine's night when we drank the Asti, I wanted to drink it in bed; my notion—frivolous, silly, vain—that it would be such fun to intersperse the Asti with sex, imagining taking a sip and then going down on her, alternating the tastes. A bauble of course, a fancy, some bit of ingenuous decadence. Harmless enough. But written out—what does it make? Lessing says that when Joyce wrote about Bloom crapping on his pot (I believe she says "defecating"—perhaps a different activity), the passage shocked, which was ironic. Because it was precisely the opposite of his intent. Joyce had meant to rob the words of their power, of course, talk us into accepting our own humanity in Bloom's outhouse. We don't get much closer.

I don't even defend what I do, though I should. As long as writing is perceived as magical, it will be so. And as long as it is magical, it will be given an aura of reverence—of which the charge

274

of exploitation is but the obverse, the analogue. And the defense that you wrote this to understand, merely to understand your own experience, even to select your own experience and then to study it as it occurred—nonsense too. Your methods are too imperfect yet to understand anything well enough to justify making an issue of it. And what after all is your own experience? How do you possibly separate it from that of others? And you stayed—remember—you chose to stay. In order to have this experience. And to have the record of it.

Or is that the most specious bit of silliness yet? Was the notebook just the last and most pathetic ploy of all—to stay. The course being a bit tottery just then and you needed a really ponderous reason so you could go on suffering in love—pretending it was work, telling yourself you were staying, not in the forlorn hope of recovering Sita, Sita dead or a stranger or disappeared on you, but you were hanging around here because really you were doing this "for yourself," and so forth? And anyway, are you ever even going to finish this notebook? You go to New York in a day or two and you haven't written in it for five days. You hate it now. You loathe working in it, put it off from hour to hour. You will never be able to fill in all the days you left out. Your opening is weak and would fail to prepare the reader—assuming there were one—to enter into the characters or the situation with enough information and impressions. The day-to-day business of course is unspeakably tedious, inherent defect of the journal as a form. But the fact is, you have really lost interest in the project. And the more she returns to you, the less you need it. The notebook was only useful in her absence, a poor substitute. But of course she comes and goes. And there is no assurance her return is permanent or even real. What if I let the notebook slide to find only at the end that she had eluded me too? And the time was past to recapture her even on paper.

What then if I have neither Sita nor the notebook of Sita? The shape of her thighs, the ellipse of her hips, the delicious handful of her ass, the hunting spring of her long legs, the almost solemn line of her spine and vertebrae, that little saddle of flesh at the small of her back. The line, the line of her hips. That outline. That ellipse.

A dark little counter overlooking the airstrip. L.A. The beginning of the trip. The writers' conference already behind me, with whatever fuel it provides—tidbits imbibed and already spent, devoured, and the plate empty. I'm scared of this trip. Scared of going home. Scared of the cities I must visit and the media, the public, being examined, making a fool of myself on the radio. A glass window into the night. Landing lights. A gin-and-tonic ordered and on its way. Thinking the thoughts of great blank glass windows, neon lights, the cocktail-lounge mumble droning behind me, thoughts of airports and strange towns and unsteady hotel nights. Thinking of where I am on the dirt road of my life: the self, rising high on each airplane's wings, looks down and sees its double bent over, hiking along, a dot on the artery of time. Spotted, pinpointed. Where am I now, the time running out?

She is always on my mind, hovering behind the forehead, an echo coloring all, even the conference moments, its applause and camaraderie, encouragement, late-night talk, laughter, all those other women engaged in the same strange process.

Waiting room. Kennedy in the morning after the all-night flight. A Hasidic Jew in a great long beard and round black hat. I am home. I will see Ruth. Have breakfast with Fumio. If I can reach him. The phones on the Lower East Side have been out of service for a month now. A fire at the telephone company. Strange. It is all strange. I will see Second Avenue again, climb the five flights of stairs to my Bowery loft.

The skyline at dawn. And at the end, at the bottom, the fear finally reached and discovered, I see the loft. White. Empty. Unfinished. The furniture I still haven't rewebbed, the wooden arms and legs of chairs and sofas still undone. The pillows I never ordered. The rugs I haven't bought. Can't afford. The green of the bedspread quilt. The plants piled up by the windows where Ruth faithfully waters them.

No, it isn't really the unfinished quality, the fact that there still isn't even a cabinet for dishes and groceries, or the great cavernous space of its white walls a hundred feet long, not that either, or its fine high white light. It's the emptiness; that it's empty. Alone, solitary. The life before the life with her. For a while the new life after the ten years with Fumio. The single life instead of the life with her. And this odd, unlooked-for, accidental, even unnatural return for a few hours. (I land at six and leave for Washington at 7 a.m. the next day—will sleep only one night in my bed and for a few hours this morning before going to find Fumio and Ruth.) Like some bizarre trial. A taste of the old life, the new life beyond the one in California. Life alone versus life with another.

I like them both. But living with another hinders, limits, impinges. And being alone has so many empty places, bald spots, with an uncertain and possibly terrible future.

On the wan Bowery pavement, the two big suitcases to carry up the five flights. Trembling to see it again. Anticipation. Anxiety. Passing the third-floor studio without even opening the door. The hundreds of drawings in there, like corpses laid out in a mortuary. One suitcase and then the next. But I must, I simply have to open the door to the fifth floor right away, can't go back down for the next bag, must rest, must see it again. Confront the specter. My home.

Looking both ways up and down its length. It didn't seem all that huge, only empty. You could fit the Berkeley house in here easily. And be civilized in the meanwhile. My heart hangs fire while I check for catastrophes. No broken windows. Only later do I discover the pane is missing over the heater vent, fallen aside. A day's work on a ladder, but I have no time or energy now. Bless Ruth; the plants are thriving, the mail is neatly piled.

The morning is coming, rose light into the east end of the loft illuminating the kitchen. I never see this light when I live here, am always asleep at this hour. Lovable, it becomes my studio again. Romantic as the day I found it. The new life it would represent. Now dubious. The place does have potential. But so unfinished, rudimentary, little more than a cave whose walls I've painted, floors I've done. The expensive mystery of plumbing installed in the bathroom and kitchen. And there a glass sits on the drainboard where I had left it three months ago. Time like a hammer falling, the old agony and terror of time. Life running out and what have you achieved, you with your fancy and extravagant studios? Some drawings. A manuscript you didn't finish. That good red lobster painting on the dining-room wall, the blue and green one in the bathroom. Using the toilet, then reaching for the brush to scrub away the months of rust in the bowl. No brush. There is one in Berkeley, there is one at the farm, there was one in Sacramento, even one at the old studio on the corner, now torn down, just a hole in the line of buildings like a vacant tooth, my studio for fifteen years and now destroyed. All the damn toilet brushes I have bought and here there is none. Maybe the third floor? Forget it.

Go back and see the rosy light of dawn filling the kitchen, illuminating the great still white walls. Brick, pure, freshly painted. Tomorrow the tour begins. There is only today in New York. Sleep a while, then see Fumio. Have dinner with Ruth. Don't go to bed with her. Keep your promise and don't give in. For her sake, don't start it again. No time for others, and anyway, there are so few others. Here there is Fumio, who is mine no more, fights me off, transcends me. And Ruth, whose adoration I cannot bear. Always I tell myself, There are so many in New York—old friends, art-world buddies, movement women, the nebulous circle of friends and acquaintances. But they vanish when I name or invoke them.

You don't call New Yorkers on the spur of the moment. So it will be just the two. Ruth is waiting. Fumio may be hard to find.

Coming in, I met Carey, the hippie kid on the first floor, and he said that seventeen thousand phones were put back in operation yesterday. But mine's still out. Fumio's probably is still out too—our slum is bound to be the last restored. Sleep then, and when you wake, find him. Terrified that I might not, might spend the day, the single precious day, hunting him down from studio to apartment. The apartment he shares with Bonnie. No, I can't call him there either. I had no way to tell him when I'd be coming, no definite date till the last minute, and then no way to call. No way to guess then how absolute the need would be when I arrived, how he would stand out against the little figures who are almost enough to get by on most days here. Enough for dinner or a drink. But when you come from far for a visit, it's only the people who have mattered long and hard who are enough.

Like Sita. Have I come all this way only to miss you, to measure the distance, to see my brave beginnings here, my solitary artist life grow gray and pale and pointless? What am I deciding now, knowing the stopover here was for deciding? And not just to hang up some clothes and beat out a few wrinkles before the media ordeal, closing my eyes in dread of the next four days. Lying down in my own house. Back to the real self, the self that knows its guilt by looking at its unanswered mail on the desk, the self below that one, which knows how few pages were written here. The restlessness of evenings, flights to the roof to see the sunset. The days were not so bad. But when you see the last sunlight go off the buildings. Then. Times I missed her most, will miss her; times you miss someone, the lover, the friend, the person to eat with as dark comes and hunger and the terrible loneliness of this city's nights, the nights of life going on to death.

Before I lie down, once up to the roof to see the morning come, no longer the great rose of dawn it was in the kitchen but an ordinary day. Already at seven, the sun well up. A good day for

New York, but after the first light, almost banal, each building in its place, the Empire State, the two silver sheaths of the World Trade Center like twin cigarette lighters. But with some new up-start blocking the base of one of them—did they build that piece of crap since I left? Pacing the roof. This summer I'll put down wooden skids, steal some of those loading platforms they use in the warehouse district. A deck made out of them. Trees. Geraniums. Outdoor furniture. Parties here. And paint the third floor. Build my worktables, get tools, make it ready for the sculpture show in December. The overpowering list of things to do. If I dare. If I can make it.

There's something unpleasant about talking to Hiro, even be-yond the fact that Fumio isn't there, that I've climbed all these stairs in cold fear and he isn't even there, so now I'll have to try phoning him at Bonnie's with the hateful possibility that she may answer the phone. Asking her permission to speak to him. Hiro's embarrassed—he remembers too. The time when we had moved the stuff out of the old studio and up to the country and at the end of the day Fumio sprained his back but still insisted on going back to Hiro's that night. He wouldn't stay with me. It was the first time or maybe the second that he refused to sleep in the same bed with me. We never have again. Ten years and then late one night, late, when he is hardly able to move out of the back seat of the van, the bastard insists on walking five blocks, though he is right next to his own house. Or what had been. The condemnation order still gave us another week. But he wouldn't come. I begged him. Because if he didn't come with me I knew I'd try to do it again that night. I had the night before—went to sleep with the two-inch pipe wide open, the gas so loud it almost kept me awake. But I meant it; woke up in the middle of the night, heard it still going, the huge danger-ous stink of it, and went back to sleep. This is your chance to change your mind, I thought. But I didn't want to back out. I knew just what I was doing, though the akvavit helped. And then I woke up at seven and it was moving day and I was still alive. Everything else was over, the marriage, the old house, the old life, my chances of sanity or work. And he stood there on the sidewalk, probably even aware of what I'd been up to. But he wouldn't come in. His face distorted with the pain in his back. And for that I was sorry. But it was also the first time I'd ever been able to see him suffering or even unhappy—this adored man—with a part of me merely standing and watching. Not caring. Not all that much. He'd stopped caring entirely.

The next morning I called Hiro's to see how he was. Hiro was clearly embarrassed. He should have been. A friend for ten years now lying to me. He "didn't know" where Fumio was. Of course he was at the apartment, Sakai's old place, which they used as a hangout. And probably with Bonnie. Hiro claimed not to know the number. I was stunned. Surely Fumio was a friend, surely I could check on his health, whomever he was with. Hiro's voice tentative, hideously self-conscious: "I don't think he wants you to know the number." I was humiliated. I was now a woman whose husband instructed his friends to keep his whereabouts secret from her. We had come to that.

Today Hiro's face and manner seem to recollect all this as he so very politely tells me Fumio hasn't arrived yet. The telephone at the apartment over in the Village is working. Do I know the number? All graciousness. Yes, I know the number, thank you very much. Hiro, whose paintings I used to baptize with six-packs and long arguments about art. Such a good friend once, such a stranger now.

I walk along Great Jones Street toward the Village, looking for a phone booth. How odd to be using a public phone, to be calling Fumio, calling him at another woman's house, making appointments with him. Fortunately it's Jack, his apprentice, who answers. And then Fumio's peculiar little frog-like voice, half adolescent, half old man. He agrees to breakfast, though he's already eaten it, is probably on his way to work at the studio, isn't relishing interruptions. And at Sandolino's he's distracted, bored. The perfect Sunday breakfast place, I'd thought, with fantasies of lazy mornings and the *Times*. But instead it's packed, impersonal, the management rude, dismissive. Fumio makes it plain he finds the place a drag.

We walk back and climb the stairs to his studio. Half the objects in the room are from the old place. That chair, the bureau, the maple table we ate at for ten years. I cannot look at these things without tears. When we broke up we were casual about the furniture, each picking what we liked, the other too depressed to care or even notice, let alone argue. In the few days the city gave us before the building was to be torn down, saving the sculpture was the main issue. Both of us lost many pieces. Furniture was unimportant. For over a year I hadn't even known where much of it was. Whether given or thrown away. Now I see one familiar object after another while he makes tea for me, being kind, patient, polite. That high stool we used to have in the workshop. That battered old pan we used to cook artichokes in. The little wicker stool. How nice to see it again. Then, unexpectedly, this thing, a shabby little stool I used to sit on when we had guests, because you could pop right up from it and into the kitchen. You almost squat rather than sit on it, but it was always my favorite perch. This little stool, this ragged funky thing suddenly a vise squeezing memory, every moment of those ten years contained in this humble object. The seat of it some unusual, unidentifiable kind of wicker, the legs simply four little black pegs. How many martinis consumed on this, my throne? How I argued here and held forth on this thing, how I dispensed drinks and coffee and opinions. Popping up to get someone more ice, loving to have guests about me. Fumio too, for he adored people and was a delightful host. The beautiful rhythm and balance we had in entertaining people together. All the hundreds of people who came to that studio those ten years. Gone.

Even when he shows me his new sculptures, my eyes keep examining the edges of the room and finding new reminders. He seems utterly oblivious, something I'm thankful for. If he noticed he might see how down I am, how helpless before him, how depressed in my very soul, how without hope as an artist. I do not want him to know that vulnerability.

And at the end he is very sweet, giving me a pair of wooden clogs he bought in Sweden. The six months in Sweden with Bonnie. Never mind, he has carted these unwearable shoes all the way home for me, remembered them in one or another shopping bag and several moves, and kept them on hand just for when I might visit. And a drawing too. A pair of lamb chops, a study he'd done for a wooden sculpture that he says never did work out. "But the drawing's not so bad." His old habits of understatement, criticism, rare praise. Looking at some others, I see a flower drawn just at the edge of the paper. And beg it from him, feeling no guilt whatsoever since we always swapped; last time he came to my place he picked out three things he liked, a series I'd called "Samurai." I said they were for him, meaning that I'd thought of him. "Thank you," he had said, quite pleased, and so of course I gave them to him. This little man sitting across from me, ten years older than I but looking still a boy. "What will you do when you begin to age, pass him off as your son?" my mother used to tease me. But it didn't last that long. I couldn't keep him. Strange self-contained little person in his tight shoulders, the dear flesh around his neck showing at the throat of his shirt. He wanted only to be rid of me. And now he is. Our leave-taking as polite and futile as the day has been. Does it come to this? I want to scream. But say nothing. And going down the stairs I swallow and refuse to cry.

Ruth had left me roses by the bed. She knew I'd be coming today, and when I call she says she'd be delighted to have dinner. We meet at a restaurant over on Barrow Street. But in person she's a changed and rather unfriendly presence. First, there's the hassle about the mail. "I find I resent doing this for you any more." "Sure, I've already notified the post office. They'll forward it from now on." "You owe me money for postage due." "I'll write you a check." "The plants are getting to be a nuisance." "I'm awfully sorry." Why remind her that it was her own idea? It would have been easy to ask the woman downstairs. "I've bought some automatic feeders for them so I don't have to bother coming over." "Fine." "They were expensive." "Just tell me how much and I'll include it in the check." "My analyst thinks I shouldn't see you so much." "That's nice." "She says I'm obsessed with you; it's destructive for me." "Probably right." "My mother doesn't think I should model for you any more." "Does she know what went on at our sessions?" Anything to tease her out of it, restore some semblance of friendliness. I will miss Ruth, whose great body I have drawn thousands of loving times, the cheerful sensuality of those long afternoons. "My mother thinks I should concentrate more on my own work." "A good idea." Ruth growing up as a sculptor, no longer the student, the kid I used to lecture and exhort and berate into taking herself seriously as an artist. "And I won't be able to work as your apprentice on your next show."

One blow after another. Ruth, who was too staunch, too convenient, too good. Ruth, who decided to fall in love with me one day up at Columbia when I was making a speech, Ruth star-struck and determined, hunting me down over three years' time. She begged to help me on the last exhibition, wouldn't take no for an answer. I said there was probably something undemocratic about having an apprentice, but she stayed anyway, worked like a demon, learned. But it has always been wrong. Her infatuation, her obsessiveness, her maniacal patience, her services, her dogged devotion. I had been "picked." But had no part in the picking. Ruth loved me, it was never my idea to love her. I was located and decided on. Her adoration always seemed unjust to me, imposed upon. At terrible cost—the guilt and recriminations that settle on me when I reject it. There is something selfish and predatory about Ruth's selflessness. But when she showed me two years' worth of writing, up at the farm, two years of writing with myself as its subject, I relented. Flattered. It was good writing. The summer I was mad and Ruth

285

seemed the only friend left. Ruth to play her guitar and her Israeli folksongs and model and take photographs. A nice idyll until Sita came back and Fumio decamped and things got serious. But Ruth saw me through the hard days too, the suicide times, the homeless months after I lost the studio. Just friends again rather than lovers. Until that night last October when I got drunk having dinner with Hatsie and I called her, roaring and sodden and said, Just come over and fuck me, and the good soul did. That morning they pulled down the old house, but I was too sick to get up and watch it go out the window.

And now I sit across from her, having wronged her, determined not to sleep with her tonight. Don't wrong her again. For you it's a good lay, friendly sex. For her it's different, she's in love. And angry. "My analyst has helped me get in touch with my anger." I hate this sort of talk and am at this moment trying not to get in touch with my own anger. It's getting to be a pretty tedious dinner. Come home to New York and you come home to nothing. "I think we should be friends." "So do I, splendid idea." "I take it things are better in California now?" "Quite a lot." I have even used Ruth as a confidante, called her once when I was very depressed and told her how badly it was going. Meanwhile, she's freed herself. I watch her unwrapping herself from me. Good. Good that she's getting her own studio, that her analyst has taught her how to balance her checkbook and stop taking money from her parents, that her stomach ailments are better, that she's finally finished that portrait of me and can go on to something more promising. Good that she's growing up.

But the process seems to require losing her even as a friend. Perhaps it was not my friend she wished to be. And yet she's been the deepest, staunchest friend at times. Now she's become this irascible alien. We order dessert. Rhoda, who worked on a film with me, is at the next table. She comes over, and then takes off, having hardly said hello. I nursed her through a crack-up last fall; but tonight she seemed hardly able to remember my name. Ruth is a hostile presence across the table. Suddenly I feel lonely the way New York makes you lonely. What's the point of it all? I wonder. People are like sharks here, no one ever does anyone a favor without a huge price tag on it, you think you have friends here but you have nothing, you go around hanging on to the memory of this place and your bloody art world and they are nothing but a pile of shit.

Ruth walks me home but pauses a good ten feet from the door. We say good night. As I climb the stairs I realize that her coming up with me was never an issue. I think of her walking up the Bowery alone, her back and shoulders in an old blue peacoat and wonder whether she feels as righteous and dejected as I do.

Now Sita again. Framed in the door. How small she looks. How dark. And how young her hair, nearly its own brown again. Lively as a gypsy, my old Chiquita, some adventurous caller from another world. It all goes away, the bad day in Boston, the good day in Chicago, the chill of New York—all disappear. We feel stealthy as she slips in the door of my hotel room. "This is the craziest place in the world." "I've got New York on the line, I'll be right with you." How it all goes wrong; first having to come out of the shower to deal with the maid who wants to get the room ready for the night. Why not, this night of nights, when Sita comes to me air freight from San Francisco on a university errand cleverly sched-uled so we can rendezvous in the midst of my tour, a stolen night of our own.

The Beverly Hills Hotel had been just a name to me; some dotty motel L.A. pink-stucco thing probably, the ubiquitous vinyl mon-ster beloved of travel bureaus. Not the marvel that greeted me, rumpled, out of a taxi before the haughty eyes of women in long skirts, still more haughty doorman. Hollywood, the real Holly-wood, with stars and starlets off to a premiere. On closer inspection just overdressed Los Angeles. Humbly past the desk, the labyrinth of corridors that lead to my seclusion, my luxury. I examine the room—excellent furniture, a balcony we've no time to use, alas, a swimming pool far off. And room service, an elaborate and compelling menu. Order up champagne or wait? What guilt attends it?

And now this gypsy at my door, more precious than ever, this co-conspirator of mine. But why does everything go wrong? The maid turned out to be undoing the bed, which to her surprise I bid her redo. The yellow silk of its coverlet is our tablecloth, our drawing room, our very house tonight. The maid sulks. I feel remorse. And then the blamed phone just as Sita knocks on the door. All should have been in readiness. At least I showered. And at last I am off the phone. At last she is in my arms, laughing at our naughtiness, our intrigue.

"I have no idea why I feel so wicked." "Neither have I. Let's order everything on the menu." She looks around the room. "I love it. I have a real affinity for the expensive." "Isn't the furniture good for a hotel room? That green chair, for example?" "How will we ever get that lovely armoire out of here and onto an airplane?" She sets down her wicker case and comes to join me on the bed. "Speaking of airplanes, I've got one at 8 a.m. Do they have limousines?" "My dear lady countess, limousines are a thing of the past. Let's see if they have taxis." Already she is going from me. The morning so soon.

"Should we make love?" I ask her uneasily. "This is making love," she says, sipping champagne and stretching out. "We will —slowly, gently." And till then we talk, a feast after nearly a week's hunger. Every detail of the house and the garden and friends and the tour, its prickly interviews only whimsical now, jokes to present her with, all that had been forbidding, humiliating. The good things too, like that woman reporter from the Chicago *Tribune*. "Hey, I met Mary Travers of Peter, Paul & Mary." "What's she like?" "A right-on lady, reminded me of Nell. So did Shirley MacLaine. Good tough women, troopers, actresses." The champagne excites us—we could talk forever, kissing, embracing, breaking away, showing off, amusing, reassuring, rejoicing, trumpeting our happiness.

"When I got here, you won't guess what was hanging from the doorknob of the room. A pair of women's underpants." "You're putting me on." "My first thought of course was that you'd arrived ahead of me and were leaving a calling card." "Where do you get these depraved ideas?" "I assumed it was some sophisticated little joke of yours. An invitation of a sort. Naturally I accepted. And besides, I didn't want the bellboy to see them. On checking, however, I discovered they weren't clean. And that the odor was not the correct one." "So?" "So I threw them in the wastebasket." "They call this a good hotel." "I think they belong to the couple next door, who seem to be out." "Unless they're in there listening to your every word."

But they aren't, we are safe in our joy, private in our delighted reunion in Nirvana, in a state of frivolity remote from any reality. It will evaporate. As soon as we check out in the morning, it will never have happened. We will only remember, have only the tintype of the mind. But solid now this moment, like that beautiful green silk chair across the room. I will carry it in my mind like an emerald of remembrance. Sacred, holy, to be invoked on high occasions or in the hardest need. Like a licking stone carried in a child's pocket.

We have already passed the dinner hour. Must settle for supper. "Pity, no chocolate soufflés with Grand Marnier." "We'll have to make do with Cabernet and filet mignon." We are obscene in luxury, rotten with decadence, resplendent with vice. And happy. Also exhausted. Falling asleep as we come finally into each other, our flesh all good-willed exhaustion, sated merely by the touch of her breast, the infinite sweetness of her downy hair, the soft triangle between her legs, the sharp hot joy of her finger finding me, parting the hair to reach the lips, enter and, entering, seal all; finish we never did.

And a few days later she meets me when I land in San Francisco. Home again. Drinking at Señor Pico's, looking out over the bay, how splendid our city is, how glad I am to be home. Juanita's has burned to the ground out in Fetters Springs—Sita has clipped the article from the paper for me. It is a piece of the past gone, snipped as with a scissors, excised from time and place. Even this one elegiac note doesn't matter as we watch the perfect sunlight on the bridges and the islands. For dinner we go down to Fisherman's Wharf, to a tourist trap with nasty waiters. Sita is exhausted, nearly falling asleep over her seafood. Only exhausted—or bored? I run into dread again.

She came to my class. Appearing magically in the hallway near the door, wearing my own gray jersey and the string of wooden beads. "I'd like to sit in, unless it cramps your style." Why didn't I say that it would? Because I never suspected that today would turn out to be the one day the students would just sit woodenly, refuse to answer, shy away from discussion. The book we've read is Violette Leduc's *La Bâtarde,* and of course they're afraid of its lesbian passion, of its immediacy, its personality. My comments on style and technique collapse around me. I start to sweat and can smell it. A circle of silent, embarrassed women. I panic. I have run out of notes, out of things to say. We're in a windowless basement room. Thirty women on hard plastic chairs. The bright fluorescent light. Linoleum tiles. The week of the tour gave me no time to prepare and the book is huge, enormous. But I've read it many times and have just spent six careful hours reviewing it today. Even if I were unready, alone I could wing it. Or face the first defeat in solitude without her face coming at me from the right side of the room, a seat set back just near the door. Seeing her face, the gray jersey, the beads, the gray of her hair and her glasses swimming into my terrified vision. Her face calm and kind, encouraging, never meaning to destroy.

It was disastrous. The class that is my hope, my joy, my consolation. My own thing against the heavy encroachment of love. Teaching, which I'm so proud of, so good at. My high dinners after class, with group after group of students vying to entertain me. Our buddy sessions around the coffee machine in the ten-minute break. Why are they letting me down so? These women whom I try to turn into writers, whom I urge into life, now sitting dumb and forlorn. And Sita watching. There is no energy at all in the room, none in the circle of our chairs, none whatsoever in my body. Where is Gretta today, with her psychopathic babble, talking until the others revolt? I could use her. A few others monopolize the little that gets said, but they are repetitious, haggle over trivia, harp stupidly and subjectively on the author's personality. The rest abide in stony silence. They give nothing, offer nothing.

My love looks on. This is my celebrated class. And I cannot take hold, give direction, and command. The little talk dies away into silence again. My eyes grab for the notes on the page. What else did I mean to call to their attention, dazzle them with—the passage on tearing up her father's photograph? No, skip it, not important enough in this vacuum. The use of the adjective, Leduc's superb qualifiers—the "charity" of a lover's shoulder blades. But it elicits no response. The technique of personification and apostrophe? No, I've mentioned that already. On a good day I could get some thirty minutes of mileage out of that. But not now. The clock drags.

Okay—face it: what do they think of the portrayal of lesbian experience, the erotic content of the book? Did it shock them? Laying the groundwork by mentioning a previous class, the class in Sacramento, how hard it had been for them to discuss this. Embarrassed silence. One admits she was shocked but can go no further. One found it "very erotic," "lovely" even. And falters. We switch gears to the great act of betrayal in the book, the incident in the room of mirrors, the brothel where Violette has brought Hermine to try her or to break her. I say I find this passage shocking, gratuitous. Evil. They don't. The one who has been glib with Proust for an hour finds more Proust. The rest don't find anything at all. I glance again at my notes—I have run out. There will be an eternal silence. Desperately I take another tack. Someone had just mentioned one of the passages from childhood, how Violette, while out walking with her adored grandmother, occasionally permitted her attention to stray away from her companion, a thing she describes as being "unfaithful." "I would pick up a stone or a pebble and then run after her and give her my free hand. When the stone or pebble was warm I let it fall on something soft: the grass or sand. Then I could breathe with the satisfaction of having had an existence of my own." I pounce upon it, how the word "unfaithful" here, so strange and extraneous to ordinary usage, is indicative, even typical, of Leduc's sense of sin and of the absolute in love. I see Sita gather up her jacket. In a rush I turn to the problems of registration, part of the reason she is here. People attend the class who are not registered. Others whose registration is somehow imperfect due to the process of canceling and then rescheduling the class, attend and even write essays, though their names do not yet appear on the roll. I labor through this, hating the police aspect of it, the bureaucracy. But solve it finally, even pleased with myself by the solution. I look up to find she is gone.

Walking toward the house, I accept my failure, knowing beforehand how it will be to live with that all week. Who can know the love of a teacher, its ups and downs between Monday and Monday, its symbiotic existence upon a group of strangers, its hungers and thirsts and deprivations? The tragedy of a bored or empty lecture, the victory of a set of essays or even of one clear and perfect illustration. I'll tell her that it was their off-day and mine too. A fluke. A pity we hit the wrong time. Say all this to her lovely brown eyes, with the windows of the living room open to the early-evening air flowing serenely past us as we huddle together on the couch, our arms warm, our heads comforting each other's shoulder. She is kind, kindness. "They didn't get the book; it scares them." "It wasn't so bad." All the usual flagellation of self-hatred dissolves. I forgive myself. And I realize I am divinely happy, a happiness saved from a thousand destructions. I will believe her, believe in

292

her. I will ask no more than this. To be in her arms, to feel the soft gray jersey on my cheek, the fine spring air from the open windows.

There is no purpose even in writing this notebook any more. I have decided only to live in this happiness. Lose a manuscript? My work? So what? Supposedly so precious, actually nothing but the bottom line of survival. Merely living is better, living in this enormous comfort and this breathtaking peace. I have arrived at rest. The air so clear gold going toward the rose of sunset. We cannot bear to part from each other. I will go with her to the city for the evening class.

It's over. I should throw the notebook away. It's to no purpose any more. Quit it. Junk the whole project. Whatever end it served no longer exists. Yet the pity of leaving off, dumping it. Another abandoned manuscript. This on top of the Japanese stuff, the death book that will never be a book. The wrench of giving it up. On the trip everything surged toward the newest book, the book about the murder of a child. I had been longing to write about things outside myself. And I was confident again.

If I stop this journal, is that a sign of coming to rest? Of committing myself to her, leaving no out, no outlet? Or would that be only another failure, another submission? Or is it peace? To stop examining, reporting, recording the bloody emotions. To stop prying. To have a life so fine, happy, somehow *holy,* that it will bear no scrutiny, would resent the third eye of an interloper. To live merely for living. And then what do you do with your life?

An hour ago she telephoned: "I'm looking at four daffodils and wishing I were seeing your face through them. Someone in my office just handed me these flowers and I wish you were here to complement them. I've missed you all morning." The singing of her voice, its amorous ingenuity. That, or the hard little scrabble with words? What do I care? What do I care, when living itself goes on so perfectly?

I will have a party for her in New York when she stops off on her way back from the conference in Puerto Rico. It will soften the separation, soften my going back East, because in a sense she will be going back with me. This will be her second visit to my loft, and it's now much further along than the rough space she saw last Christmas. It will be her second visit of many, for we will share our cities now. Each time she comes to New York she will admit, on my account, to hating it less, learning it all over again, like a new city. Downtown, an artist's city, not the dull rich lady's city of her old days, the world bordered by Bonwit's and Saks and the Biltmore. And each time I will make it magic for her, pore for days over the entertainment guide, take her to the shows in SoHo, the right streets in the Village, the restaurant she hasn't been to yet, out-of-the-way museums. Each time it will be that much closer to a balance.

So I will invite all my friends—or rather, the best ones, the ones that matter most, are dearest rather than "interesting" or "famous" or "impressive." They will meet her and know her. She's accused me of hiding her, has complained that I have never introduced her around. This will be in her honor then. All of them will be called to admire her, to appreciate her—all these tough New York types summoned to pay her homage, see her fineness, render their approval. I am pleased and excited by the idea, compose new invitations in my mind each day.

The idea of her coming to New York, her idea, how clever it is. Nearly erases my departure from California. We will merely part for three days, only to meet again in my town, my world. I would not have wanted it that way before, was even a little uneasy when she first suggested it. Once I had just wanted to leave. The gesture of leaving California and going home, the gesture I had been trying to make for months. The gesture of walking out. And part of me still held to that, I suppose, when she first mentioned it. Saying goodbye in New York seemed to cancel my gesture and its inference of independence. How insidious she is, I'd thought, listening to her outline the plan—that she could stop off in New York on her way home from the conference in Puerto Rico—how insidious to have taken even my leaving away from me. Because this way, of course, it is she who will be leaving me. After the magical week she outlines: "You know what a wonderful time we had last Christmas. Well, it'll be a whole week this time, not just four days. A whole week just to do nothing but make love and drink champagne and admire your pictures and your beautiful white walls and go to the theater and sleep and not worry once about this damn job . . . but after that you have to put me on an airplane and send me home." Always that moment at the end, that moment in Kennedy. Watching her leave the Christmas she came to my farm—wanting to scream and run after her, tear at the arm of her mink coat and at her smart cocked hat and never let her out of my sight. So close to death that Christmas. "All I can remember of your loft is that lovely green quilt on the bed and those huge white walls. And I think that's all I'll need," she goes on, outlining, arranging, selling me the idea. Of course, of course, to have her in my home again, to show her more of what I love—funky things like Second Avenue below St. Mark's, but would she ever understand it? Always like a child, nearly wanting to hold on to my hand when I lead her through my slum, her eyes huge and appalled, intrigued perhaps or astonished that anyone would actually live on the Bowery by choice. When one could live in San Francisco, in Berkeley, California? Walking very close to me, and I am always surprised and a little amused at how foreign and insane and squalid it must be to her, keeping so near to me, a countess on Second Street amid the wine bottles and the bums, the debris and the wild dogs at the corner where some old derelict is squatting, too poor to feed the mangy beasts. Sita climbing the five long flights to my loft on her lame leg; tenderly I wait and carry things for her, carefully I arrange life so there are only a few trips. Sita lighting my dingy corridors, my empty spaces, my dark unpainted studio on the third floor. I will sit her down like a patron, show her drawings, not just spread out the portfolios as I do sometimes for other artists, everyone just squatting on the floor or sitting for hours on their haunches. No, she will sit on a chair like a patron. She will become austere as she sometimes is, grave and judicial, a snob; her ancestors commissioned pictures for five hundred years and one of them was a Pope. The idea delights and intimidates me. Will she understand my pictures? More important, will she like them?

The idea of her coming to New York has hold of me now. Once I wouldn't have wanted that. But that was before, when I merely meant to leave. And it would be the end. Now it is no such thing. I will be back. We have arranged about the rent and she is looking for someone to share the house with, someone to rent Paul's room. If no one satisfactory turns up, I'll just go on paying my half until I come back. Extravagant, and it becomes more and more so as time goes by and my little pile of royalties runs out, but worth it: the house is mine now and will go on being mine. And I wouldn't want her to have to put up with someone she didn't like. We will go on. The future is all there now, each winter I will come here to her; each summer I will go back, but she will come to me. She has the month of August for vacation this year and she is now talking about driving cross-country to be with me, come to the farm, go up to the Cape. If she flies (and I will find her the money if she hasn't got it), then we will have more days to be together. And during the months we are apart until January, there will be trips, conferences, speeches—we'll manage this, the prospect amuses and delights us. The permanent "affair" she teased me about: "There'll be years and years of our rendezvous in different cities, all those hotel rooms, lady, we can make a career out of it." She had sat in my big Mexican sweater when she came to New York last Christmas and watched me make dinner and laughed, throwing her head back. "We should have a permanent affair, it should go on for years. Maybe it should always be an affair for us. We're better that way." But we even talk now of the time when I give up New York and settle in California. We look at houses out of the corner of our eye.

Once I wanted just to leave when May came. But now of course it's entirely different, because she is so different, so good to me now. Like the frog, for example. At breakfast the other morning my cigarette fell out of the ashtray and burned a hole in her favorite blue tablecloth. It seemed past repair, and I had nearly been afraid to confess. And then last night she came home with this absurd embroidered frog. Seems all you do is iron it onto the fabric and you have a delightful readymade patch. The frog touched me enormously, it seemed a symbol of all her goodness, her kindness to me, her patience and gentleness, a goodness beyond what we mean by friendship or even the maternal, something almost Buddhist in its endless warmth and care. That was Sita as she used to be, a Sita whose love was at first so expansive and generous I feared for it, terrified I should in some way exploit or abuse. "I saw a future of indulgence in her eyes," Leduc says somewhere about a woman who loved too abjectly. I remember quoting Sita the passage, dragging the book over to the phone once in Sacramento. "Look, there's something I want to read to you because I never want to take advantage of your goodness." And she was a bit amused and said yes, she would certainly watch out for that sort of thing. I was warning her, warning her of herself and of me. And yet I think I never loved her quite so purely as that moment. Protecting that infinite tenderness and sensitivity and kindness which were at the very heart of her love, the love that I loved— goodness I suppose it was actually. Even virtue. Or what virtue would mean if it were a word still permitted to have meaning.

And so to celebrate this frog and my starting the new book— the book about a child who was put to death, which I have talked about writing for so many years—we opened champagne and lolled on our cushions and drank toasts. The evening sun filled the room and I think we have never had it so good here. The time is itself now, doesn't need to be compared to other times, as it used to. In the future it will be a time to be compared to.

At dinner Sita was tipsy, and made a long, long speech about politics, about her responsibilities to Latina and Chicana women. Which seem to preclude her being a known lesbian. Because the Latin community is so conservative, prejudiced, Catholic, macho, reactionary. All of which together is too powerful to be ignored. I am silent and admiring and entertained by the La Pasionaria aspects of her performance, and so charmed by the refrain of "You are my life and my love, but still . . ." that I probably do not listen carefully enough to the rest. Was it her fears of the world that swayed her toward men when she drifted from me, the ease of being "straight," the convenience, the political convenience, the social approval? Listening, I drink in all her wonderful and extravagant professions of love and almost ignore the rest. "Who's requiring you to tell the Latinas you're gay?" I ask languidly, wondering after all what the fuss is about, assuming that she is really just enjoying the business of posing as the heroine of her people tonight, the proletarian Chiquita whom I adore, the Sita who harangues money from the city council for the *conferencía femenil,* the Sita who has spent years in civil-rights groups. Once we attended a drug workshop with Pia during which everyone made some statement about themselves. Sita announced to them that she was "Pia's mother and a lesbian." The last identification seemed so gratuitous I nearly laughed, for whatever "lesbian" meant to the wrecked young people in the room, it was scarcely a word that applied to the beautiful, early-middle-aged woman they saw or to the Sita whom I or anyone else knew. Somehow she has always seemed to be a woman who might love another woman, or had, or did even then, without being what the world imagines is a lesbian. And so I listen with only half an ear now, sure that she does not really have to face this issue in real life but that she is experimenting only for herself in saying it out loud—that she would not want it known, that it could cause her trouble, hurt her reputation. Or rather, that it would render her ineffective with the Latinas who are her special constituency, make it impossible for her to help them, render them services she is dedicated, and uniquely qualified, to give. All very strange since in the past I have been far more discreet than she, scrupulous largely on account of her job. And it was Sita then who would laugh and say, "But of course they all know we are lovers. How could anyone not know by now?" Proud of it, a bit proud of me, her "catch" once. And now I listen to her, gradually dumbfounded by what seems to be coming through her sweetly disheveled fulminations, her revolutionary posturing, and it seems to be fear. "So if I have to, I'll deny it." "Really?" "Don't you see, I can't afford to be open about it?" "No one's kicking you out of the closet," I tease, to reassure her. But it's disappointing, the coward's way. It's not like her.

In the morning she couldn't even remember what her speech had been about or how I got her to bed. "With smiles and the fondest patience," I say, kissing the back of her neck, the coffee-brown skin, the softness of it, the delicacy. The sun shines into the room. Again these days of happiness, the sun, swimming each day, great roaring dinners with a fire afterward, again these days perilous on the rim of love, of joy balanced over fate, days of happiness even when things go wrong or a student of mine is in trouble and arrested in a fight and Maud calls that she has finally lost her job, or a letter arrives from Italy reporting that Pia has borrowed two hundred dollars from Sita's brother there.

"In all those years I lived in shacks and worked for the damn water company and starved and brought up two kids, I never asked them over there for money." Sita bitter and scornful, her honor dashed, her heart broken by Pia's guilty malice when confronted, a child caught at wickedness turning spiteful, calling her names. Martin has come to dinner to report that Sita is still not living within her budget. She is still in debt for the kids' extravagances during the time of the commune. He is grave and pessimistic. She cannot afford to go with Maud to Mexico in July. But she will bring him around somehow; Martin enjoys playing curmudgeon and shaking his head, and the dinner is as mellow as old friends.

There is still peace, even happiness. For the first time I am sure I am able to comfort, that merely lying next to her at the end of the day I am strength for her. And the happiness winds around me like a cocoon. The rhythm of workdays—the swim in the afternoon, our drinks, our dinners. Our weekends. Our every precious day until it is over. And the new book growing, its pages growing from eight to eleven to fifteen. As I swim laps in the spring evening, I find an idea in one lap, a method in another, waiting for the time I must give up imagining and begin research on the events the book will be based upon. The evening sun glinting on the water, the pool on the top of a long hill, and far below the bay and the bridges and the towers of San Francisco, spread out like a faerie city, mystic in the curve of the shore, the twist of bridge floating to Treasure Island, poised for a second in invisible space, then floating again to the mainland and the crown of spires.

These are good days, these are the best, an oasis in the desert of the past, the past I less and less remember or even believe in, her voice angry and impatient when I do—"If you're going to start hassling me about that again," she'd said, when I made a face that we'd have guests this weekend and because there's a meeting on Sunday. And I learn to keep patient, to trust, to accept less than all. One odd moment listening to her shower, wondering if the banquet at Santa Barbara, a farewell for a university official, a man retiring but already condemned to death by cancer, the banquet which means staying overnight down there, wondering if it means a night with Neal too. And cease to wonder. Listening to the sound of the water, her sound, her lovely body glistening through the room a moment from now. There are only moments. Live in this one. The happiness of these days.

This notebook, the narrow-lined one, will contain the final entries. It's late April and the experiment will end May eighth in New York at the close of that last week there together. Even to write down those words makes me feel weak. The entire experiment was a failure. Abandoned any number of times and particularly lately, the last week or so when I find I only make lists of moments over a weekend. "Maud here. A meeting in San Francisco on Sunday, I looked out at the bay and wondered." Or hungered or yearned or some similar tedious and repetitious emotion, too vague, too diffuse, too challenging or insufficiently challenging to put into words.

Yesterday she cleaned her desk. Always admirably efficient, she completely rearranged and updated all her papers in an hour. Then she told me, as we sat close together on the couch, that she had saved every letter of mine, even valentines, along with six inarticulate poems I loathe and am in dread of ever seeing again. "No one had ever written me poems. My three husbands never even saw me. I was a body washing dishes and raising children. They never saw me. But you, you've written me poems, you've made drawings of my body. No one ever said it was beautiful before."

To hand her these pages. Some proof, some testimony of love. Inconclusive. It is as much a testimony of hate, uncertainty, ambivalence, indifference, boredom, resentment. And if it convinced for a while, it would pall soon. You can read and be pleased and then put aside. Easily, very easily. It would constitute no way to hold her. Even the fact of obsession, still more obsession exhibited—this would necessarily cause her to stiffen and reject. Nothing is so odious as unsolicited adoration.

Then say I did it for myself, since it is just whatever I wanted to bother putting down on paper. And of course it was here that it broke down altogether. Because I never *got* it, never got it at all. Not even such a simple thing as the air in the bathroom when I look at the walls and remember she wanted them painted after the fire they had here during the commune. Now there isn't time for either before I leave. Not getting something like the blue-and-white Greek bedspread in the bedroom, all it conveys of our cohabitation, our intimacy, afternoons when the sun falls on it and she is gone. And I think of afternoons the sun will fall on it when I am gone, when I no longer exist for her. Or the riskier and more difficult atmosphere of the front room, Paul's old room, the so-called library whose bookshelves are yet to be built; guest room, space for a future roomer, scene of her nights away from me—its foam mattress on the floor and a chintz quilt she has thrown over that, the pillows at all angles, her sunlamp aimed from a lamp onto the mattress where she bakes herself listening to country music on the radio.

Hundreds of things that will be gone soon, maybe forever. Surely forever from this notebook or my attempts to place them with any permanence. Things I scarcely understand myself but will miss like a cry of pain. The sight of the kitchen when there are dishes to wash and I would rather write, the sight of them somehow baffling me —as they would never baffle her—until I pull myself together and remind myself I do after all know how to wash dishes, even understand by now where they are supposed to go, where each thing is to be put away after all the changes of the commune. The commune gone now, buried like a lost civilization, and I have wangled my way back into her heart. Yes, and leaving now. How can she forgive me? How, for that matter, can I forgive myself? Doing it, leaving, I know not even why.

True, my sculpture show must be done in New York. But that's late, next fall. And I dread it and hate it anyway. Cancel? No, it's a necessary recovery of the self. Stick with the new book? You can write that anywhere and might do better writing it here, in a settled life. But I know I want to leave her. If only so that I can stop writing this damn record, a record begun as consolation for losing her love. Having regained it in some measure, writing about it has come between us, forcing me to escape for a while just so the notebook can come to an end.

And the end too, how feeble. Seven days together in New York. I do not even leave her. She leaves me. Gets on an airplane at Kennedy, disappears down a chute as I have seen her do how many times. She has arranged it thus. But what we have instead is amorphous, as amorphous and inconclusive as life. There are no solutions, resolutions. Only the repetitions of the rise and fall of the heart: rejection, then a little less rejection, then acceptance, then rejection again—subtler and more malicious. And on the other side, vacillation again. Followed by dread, the old dread but a little smaller; dread of life, either alone or together.

First we went to Grundy's for a drink. We were on our way elsewhere for dinner. Even as it happens, I know it is to be remembered, pressed in the book of the mind, uncovered in other places where remembering it will hurt, will tear in the New York evening, will haunt me in age if I lose her. But what was it like? We are two bodies in a car on a long coast road. I feel the line of the bay in my heart, my fingers tracing the water and the sand and the road itself. The bay in the pink of the sunset, the sun itself a fire falling, heaving down upon the hills, heaving itself to extinction each second faster and farther. The line of the bay, the sheen of the water nearly alive with the strange powerful light on it. Cars have stopped to watch. She pulls over. For a moment or two we stare at it mutely. "It will get harder and harder to live in New York." "Maybe you'll have enough of the Bowery someday, enough bums, enough cold, enough suffering." "Sixteen years might almost do it." I laugh because she is teasing, just as she did in the parking lot leaving Grundy's. We were going some place new, a restaurant on the water over in Oakland. The bridges and the sea before us like thunder. "Such a beautiful place to live," I said. "Well, of course it doesn't have all the advantages of the Bowery. Picasso succeeded without living in New York, Colette, de Beauvoir. Even Dante." "Turn off the engine, we've only got a dollar's worth of gas." "All part of the adventure." We are silent again, looking to the sea. Suddenly she starts the car. We pass other cars that have stopped, others willing to drop everything to gape at the moment. The sun plunging farther, nearly touching the hills. Great eternal force.

303

"Where are we going?" "I've got a great idea. A surprise."
"Where?" "Back. What we had is the best, why bother to explore?"
"You're right, you're exactly right."

And so we went back. I cannot explain how this little episode,
a bit of indecision and then inconsequential decisiveness over something as trivial as where to eat dinner, I cannot explain how it
mattered to me, how it portended. Or even what it portended. Yet
it seemed to put a seal on things, a curious kind of commitment,
a vote cast. And for more than our favorite restaurant. For the
notion of us perhaps. And yet I don't think she felt it so deeply as
I, was probably not aware of anything but the power of the scene.
And that power was probably something else. A landscape is something different to each person who sees it. And I expect she did not
see it as us, or feel it as a crisis. She did not even think of it as the
last time. I think not, no, not at all. When we were home I saw her
come out of the shower, her beautiful body almost old. Going down
on her, trying to make love to her. "My body lets me down," she
said, and then a long, uncertain discussion of the menopause, if it
can affect a woman who's had a hysterectomy years before. Then
she talks of the insecurity of the relationship. A few days ago she
said that if we were either of us to fall in love with someone else,
it would hardly matter if we were together or apart. "If it were
going to happen, it would happen anyway, wouldn't it?" I say New
York is my independence and that I'm swallowed here now, now
at any rate, and that I need the city, need to be away. She turns
away from me: "Maybe we never could have learned to live together, anyway." I stay awake, sipping wine, reading and rereading
the page of a book. A medium despair—not like the old one. But
the next day an ongoing anxiety.

Pictures of her. If I should lose her, against that time, to have
some copy. Sita in the doorway of my study, an apparition in an
orange bikini. Wonderful she is, brown, young, slender. "Have you
heard about the banana scandal?" Eating one as she asks, playing

herself, playing Chiquita Banana. "Very slippery case really." I begin to laugh, but forget what I have been typing, an essay about the Iranian political prisoners, my last sentence a description of death by torture, one of the cases documented by the London *Sunday Times*. "I'm serious," she says. "It's in all the papers. United Fruit's been giving out all this payola. It's been going on for years." "Your usual South American government, the expression 'banana republic,' for example?" I grin at her. "Under the skin," she intones mysteriously and tweaks the edge of her bikini. I forget the prisoner, forget my rage of a moment past, reading and transcribing horror in another place, and I sketch the words as she goes on, trying to catch them, to etch them on my brain, scribbling on the back of my draft of the essay. It is like trying to sketch her body, always she escapes me, evades me, slips past the fingers of my pen. Engraving her on my mind, on the backs of my eyelids, in the black spaces behind my eyes, so that if I close them someday afterward the brown body in the absurd shreds of orange cloth will be there, will always be there, even though she goes back to her sunlamp and I return to my prisoner.

It is an hour of the day when I am usually careful to absent myself, having lately chosen it as the time to swim, the hour or so just after she comes home from work. She had let me know that she would like more time to herself, a bit of time on her own after a day in an office full of people. And though I wait all day for the time of her return, a day entirely alone, it seemed only the simplest kindness to be away when she returns, one of the things I could do to please her, an opportunity even. There is so little time. The parting is so soon, only days now. She spends the time in the most mindless and lovable bliss under her sunlamp, listening to cowboy music. Perhaps it is the combination of all these mad details, the banana, the terrible suffering of the Iranian political prisoner as he dies, six months ago and several thousand miles away. According to the *Times* report of January 19, 1975: "He was placed on an electric oven and burned in his sacral areas. His wounds were not treated for a long time and the smell became unbearable to all. He was half paralysed and he was taken to court and shot soon afterwards in this state." Perhaps it is nothing but the reality of her lovely body in that doorway where it stays now, where it will always stay, her patter of wisecracks and her wholehearted adoption of American vulgarity. Perhaps it is all and nothing of that, but a step beyond toward the forging of an icon, her gesture of tweaking the edge of her G-string, that particular insouciance, which cannot cancel but maybe balances the agony of the prisoner, maybe assures one that both these phenomena exist in the world. This man called Asgar Badizadegan: "He was slowly burned by means of an electric fire while his hands and legs were tied to a bed. He was so badly burned in the lower lumbar area that it reached some of the vertebral bones and he fell into a coma . . . He was then transferred to prison hospital and underwent several operations. But he can no longer walk, only crawl on all fours." I have been enraged all afternoon by this and her appearance is a kind of sanity for me, reminding me that there is also sensuality and humor, bikinis and country music and the lazy early evening, the time when work is over and you have a drink and the light grows golden and ripe like a swollen belly pregnant with the bloody sunset within it.

But there is always the jarring note of where I am and where she is, where I was when she came in, my mind absorbed by horror and injustice, her saucy bikini mood so free it seems an impertinence. We quarreled later, perhaps this set it off, perhaps the thing festering for weeks already. Pajaro Dunes, a place where she has another one of her tiresome conferences this coming weekend, our last weekend. I am to come with her, smuggled along, as it were. But we are uncertain, afraid she might get in trouble for bringing me. When I bring up my doubts again, she says, too easily, "Why don't you just stay here, it makes no difference to me whatsoever." We descend into quarreling: I confront her with my greatest fear, that by now she feels contempt for me. She denies it in an openly contemptuous way. As I leave the room, she fires at me: "It has nothing to do with me at all. You are simply a person who doesn't like yourself very much." That last phrase burns my ears all night. Because it is true. True here, anyway. I have despised myself here day after day in a manner I often thought I couldn't bear. And yet I bore it. She is right, perfectly right. But what makes it so? Is this to be a permanent state, this forgetting of normal self-respect? What is it about this love that destroys the self? When it was reciprocal, mutual, joyous and fresh, I lived in a shocking state of self-esteem. Hubris even. And now, loving and unloved, I fold like a broken tent. No pride, no personhood. Get out. I've got to get out of here.

I close the door while she brings the car around. Pajaro Dunes. The deep-blue walls of this little room facing the sea, the weathered driftwood outside. How I have come to love the remarkable cobalt blue of the walls of this little cottage, our place for two days. Two days which she spent waiting on other people, the tedious conferees whom she served as cook and waitress. The enormous task of cooking for thirty persons here to elevate their minds with Gestalt psychology. The psychologists exceedingly important and knowing, the conferees enthusiastic suburbanites exalted by their status as clientele, and Sita and I the drudges who serve their dinners. I am small enough to feel resentful, but she is generous, gracious, the camp cook and matriarch. A countess who can wait on the noisy herd and never move a muscle of her disdain.

During the free moments we walked the beach and fell in love with the sandpipers and the terns, the tiny, quick-legged birds that keep hurrying mindlessly toward the water as if in pursuit of food or magic, something that never seems to be there. So they fly ten feet away and begin again, the very image of yearning patience, the persistence of these saints of hope. The scurry, the unbelievable speed of their little feet, their nearly invisible steps, the twiglike legs spinning as they rush. Over and over and again and again; a little movie of love. Impossible and imploring.

307

Some of that in myself. She was elsewhere much of the time, even when she was with me. Wanted to walk the beach alone, wanted the solitude of sunning herself, her body stretched on the porch, ripe and mellow but forbidden. Two of your general California underfed teenage specters sunning themselves next door, no more than five feet away. The gray of the weathered buildings, a resort compound composed of a thousand cubicles, the bleached wood and deckboards speaking of Provincetown and Eastern things I love. Then the mirage vanishes and you remember it is new and California. Which is why the little apartment is such a break. It's not really old, of course, but the furniture is antique, oak pieces from another time, a bottle of wine to greet us, and those wonderful blue walls.

I would like, in some inarticulate and puzzled way, to thank it. It was our last home, our last place. Soon it will all be over, all be gone. Only a few days now till she leaves for Puerto Rico and I for New York. So this was the final landfall. And then too something happened here, a strange minor miracle. I think I had her, finally. Not that it carries over. Making love to her Saturday night and she cried out as she hasn't in a long time, perhaps never, that way. The animal intensity of it, the glory of moving her so. Not, as I say, that it carries over. Indeed, the very distinction was that it happened and then ceased to happen, stood for a moment and then disappeared. The occurrence was the very proof of its never having occurred. Maybe it was just good sex, the pleasant fulfillment of lust, the orgasm you give yourself because you are merely taking and the other serves you and serves well. Or perhaps what I saw is the joy she has with another, with any other, with all the others. For I did not feel it was for me. "That is how it should be," she had said, almost as if she had forgotten and was reminding herself. Yes, of course, I thought, would that she wanted it so always, responded, pleasured herself this way every time. And yet I was not there with her, not really, did not ride the waves of it along with her, did not feel what she felt as she felt it, as once I did. So long

308

ago, Sacramento. Did not even have the rapport and connection I usually have when I make love to her, however stunted and remote that can be at times. No, she was somewhere else and I did not really feel I was her instrument, only a friend nearby, delighted at her luck.

It winds down. And now I must let go even this odd little holiday with its blue walls and its ocean, where the incomprehensible, perhaps even solitary act of our love was enacted. It was as if she shot past me. Even as I was supposed to be reaching the goal and giving her the pleasure that would bind her to me, cause her to be possessed by the particular gratitude of the flesh that cements a pair of lovers, bolting them together in memories so intimate and intense they can never quite forsake them—even then I felt her pass me. Not the usual passing beyond of profound orgasm, where for a moment all life and persons, even consciousness itself, is dimmed or goes out in something near fainting. No, not that, but the passing beyond of someone moving ahead and away, like the wind of a fast-moving car overtaking. And I never saw her go out of sight, she simply vanished.

And now in another world—how other—she is waiting, perhaps even annoyed by the delay, as I linger wanting to say goodbye even to the sink, to the glasses, to the table where we drank the wine and she told me of Rio, the lights at night, how many miles of them along the shore when she was a girl there, the animals hanging from the roofbeams dripping blood onto the dust of back yards, blood for the voodoo. "And do you still believe in it?" I asked. "Of course," she said—another Sita, another from the one crying out in the little bedroom, and another still from the testy, middle-aged woman waiting impatiently behind the wheel of the station wagon for me to drag seven bags of leftover groceries up the hill and into the dull tailgate of the mediocre university company car, so that we can sit and be silent all the way to San Francisco and the house on Indian Rock whose rugs I hated so particularly yesterday.

The magic disappears, evaporates, is left behind. Doors close on rooms with blue walls and the white of nearly New England windows, the sea is gray and waiting for the rain that will come today at five o'clock. And the room remains behind as the door closes and you see the warren of other cubicles up to the right and the walk off to the left, and beyond the communal garbage dump the car waiting, its totally pedestrian color. Paper bags of groceries. Ahead. Forget ahead a moment. And the time coming. A long time. More than you'll need. The deep blue of the walls, the clean white of the woodwork, the light in the little bedroom, such a yellow light, almost the light of vigil lights, the Catholicism of our childhoods, the yellow, strangely yellow, shrine-like quality of that light and then its darkness and then her cry. What did it say?

All the way to New York, seeing the continent crossing through the windows of the plane, seeing the time there in the sky as it passes, taking me away. A spring of instinct screaming, Fool—you have left it. Your happiness, what you had of it, by the end you had something. No, no, she comes to me there in New York, Sita in New York in three days, she has promised. Cheerfully ignoring the color movie and the headsets of canned music. Not reading or writing either. Outside the little window, Wyoming, then Kansas, Indiana, Ohio. The long way, the full distance, and that one terrible voice mocking me, You had it and you left. Other times—the Sita who put you on the plane for New York that first summer when you went home for Fumio's show. The fondness, the doting, the almost astonishing pain with which she saw you to the helicopter in Berkeley. "The way you looked going off in your straw hat," she said later, "I could hardly bear to let you out of my arms." And Sita seeing me to the helicopter the last time, when I went to New York for the book tour, Sita bored in the waiting room, fidgeting, wanting so badly to leave before the 'copter even arrived, but too sporting or conscientious, or aware she was being watched, dutifully lasting it out.

No, these things don't matter. The first trip back was after all the first; she may have worried I wouldn't return. And the last time she knew it was merely for a week. After all, people get used to each other. Her boredom is surely no news to me now; conquering it, that's the news, winning her back, courting her with my city, my friends, the party I plan for her, the theater, the restaurants, the right streets, just the right streets, certain parts of the West Village. Barrow Street and Morton, Grove, strolling there in the evening, the sense you get of the life in those places, the romance of other people's lives, strangers with books that go up to the ceiling, that is part of the charm of New York; the avocado trees that grow in the windows where painters live, I will show her how if an avocado grows it's sure to be an artist's studio. I will take her through the loft district and make my little speech about how in these few square miles, these twenty blocks or so, all the books and paintings are made for the whole country. And she will smile and squeeze my arm and call me a provincial. And what if she doesn't come?

Leaving the house at Indian Rock, I buried little notes like Easter eggs sown in secret places, notes she'll find in drawers, surprises. Notes beginning, "Lady, I love you, so I snuggled up against your bras and stockings, waiting for you to find me." And when she finds them, I will be already gone from her. Don't even think of it. Or the last days at the house. Sita already gone to Puerto Rico and her friend Walter installed in the house. That she would give the house to someone else, turn it over to a housesitter while I was still there—as if I were a piece of furniture—an arrangement she announced at dinner a night or two before she left. I had just told her how I liked the Bay area now, loved San Francisco. And she informed me that Walter would take over and that it was more convenient for him to move in on Friday rather than waiting until after I had left. Arranging it all without ever mentioning it to me beforehand. If it is not convenient for me to have Walter and his son underfoot while I pack, it doesn't matter. I heard her in a helpless kind of fury. Already I was displaced. After Walter leaves in July, there would be another roomer. Walter would be no threat whatsoever, she assured me. "Though of course I don't plan to be celibate; I'm not that kind."

I should never have left. Should have stayed and guarded what was mine, stood sentry over the house, my car, my papers, all that

I left there, had begun to make there, the students, the friends, it's madness to go back to New York. I had everything there, was a fool to leave, the claustrophobia seizing my throat; turn this thing around—I've made a mistake.

But no. No, she's there. She's East already. She's coming to New York. I go to join her, not leave her. I will see her in only two days. Just enough time to get the loft cleaned and ready.

That night, as I was washing out the refrigerator, I heard the doorbell. Odd, I thought, no one knows I'm back. A wayfarer, an artist buddy wandering by, needing company or a drink or having a nervous breakdown; all the reasons people don't call beforehand. Or a nut, a drunk from the street. I lean my head out the window into the quiet and comfortable rain—I am home, no one can harm me, I am making ready. "Western Union." And already I feared it—but you fear other things, your mother's death or something happening to a friend abroad, or just someone who's decided your telephone is broken. An honor or a catastrophe. My hands shaking with that particular fevered hurrying as I walk up the stairs trying to open the envelope, my legs tired already from the climbing, my forehead hot with dread. But even then it was almost entirely a surprise: NEW YORK TRIP CANCELED. SCHEDULE CHANGED. LETTER FOLLOWS. SITA.

An hour later I still cannot believe she has done it. The traitor, the bitch, the liar—and in that asinine telegramese. "New York trip canceled. Schedule changed"—what I had based my life on torn away in that smug business language. "I'll call you from the office." More of that. Who is she there with? What stud of the moment has caught her eye, who is she fucking, what anonymous male encountered on an airplane, in a dining room, at a meeting; whom does she ogle and then offer herself to? I can hear the come-on, "Perhaps you don't find older women attractive?" And of course he does, of course by now it's a point of honor that he does. As she unfolds, becomes her beauty her charm her wit her fascination, removes the formal self, the cold eyeglasses, the efficiency, becomes the Latin, the woman of passion and feeling and sensibility. Do you read them Neruda too? "Body of a woman . . ." "No, it sounds better in the Spanish," she always said, her mouth kissing the words, *"Cuerpo de mujer, blancas colinas, muslos blancos."*

Stop, you will go mad. Call Puerto Rico again. The operators are out on strike. Call them until they answer, call Bell Telephone. Screw their damn telephone strike, screw the Statler Hilton, get through, grab her by the hair with your voice, seize her, don't let her get away. Lies; if she lies, say nothing, get her back. Finally, at three in the morning, her voice: "I've just been writing you." I close my eyes and stop the tears by main force, just as I stop seeing that hotel room and whoever is with her. "Sita, what are you doing?" "But, darling, I've been weeping, I'm so bitterly disappointed. I'd wanted so to come." If she weeps you may not call her names, only a friendly little "Maybe you met someone there and would rather stay?" "No, no, nothing like that, they lost my provost's film at the airport, I've been three days tracking it down." Long, involved, expensive descriptions of her troubles, the nuisance of the provost's film, the odyssey of recovering it, the further nuisance that she is obliged to bring the film over to Florida to show it to a conference there. "Which is why I thought I couldn't come, but now I think I can manage a few days with you. It will only be from Sunday to Thursday, would you like that?" Of course I'll take anything, forgive anything. If only she comes. Then it is not over. Because it had seemed that the telegram killed everything. Walking away from the phone, saved now, I tell myself surely that was exaggerated, surely there will be January when I come back to live with her again in California. Surely this is an ongoing thing, don't jump to conclusions, don't foresee death and the void. Like last week, when I came home from shopping for dinner and she said Maud had called from Sacramento, was in a terrible state, her lover's illness, losing her job; she must go up and take care of her tonight, drive up after dinner and stay over. I made a face, I suppose, though I said, "Fine, that's probably necessary." And I remembered I needed something else at the store and went back to get it. When I came home she had disappeared. Simply vanished. No note, nothing. Then I remembered that going out I had slammed the door. This was my punishment then, that she had not stayed to eat the dinner I was making but had gone straightway to Maud's. But at first I did not even guess where she had gone, I only stood in the house with its engulfing, paralyzing emptiness. Like the first night she went off to Neal. The same desperation as now. But never mind, it's fine. She's coming.

And so she came. Coming from Florida on Sunday night. Everything is ready. I have bought furniture, scrubbed, laid in provisions, wines, champagnes, steaks, lobsters. Walking into the lower level at Eastern, I see the flight sign and at first don't understand it. Flight 42 from Puerto Rico. I look at the telegram again, the second telegram. FROM FLORIDA FLIGHT 42 9:40 P.M. It can't be. Did the airlines make a mistake? Does the flight originate in Puerto Rico and stop off in Florida? I check. No. Flight 42 is a direct flight from Puerto Rico. I sit down. I am a little dizzy with the idea that she has lied to me. That she has lied perhaps over and over. That her story on the telephone was also a lie. She never went to Florida at all, stayed in Puerto Rico the whole time and would have stayed there until it was time to return to California if I had not caught her in her hotel room and—what—shamed her into coming? And now she goes on lying, when she gets off the plane she will go on saying she has come from Florida. If I let her. She will lie and lie and go on lying, divesting herself of that fine integrity she wore like her pride of birth.

"Did you come from Florida?" "Yes." "The plane comes from Puerto Rico, the sign says so." "Then I came from Puerto Rico." "What did you really do?" "Stop bothering me and help me carry

315

this thing," the provost's film, a great stupid plastic can of it. I help, still asking, still wanting to know. But there is no knowing. "I was supposed to bring it to Florida but they lost it again. Just carry it, I'll explain some other time." And crossing the road—"Don't ask me questions, just let's enjoy the time together." And I realize there never will be any explanation. She will never admit that she lied, nor will I ever force her to. From now on I must accept what I get. She lies and will go on lying. And I will know it and have to keep silence. It changes things, changes them completely.

But there is still the time ahead, the four fabled days. When there is no more truth, when you no longer trust someone. And they know it too, know that you are someone to lie to, and are therefore despicable. Yet they forbid you to ask, forbid you to brave them and call them liars, demand instead that you acquiesce, pretend that the lie is not even there to be seen, or that answers given you are not even there to be heard, humiliated by. So pretend that you are deaf and dumb and merely carry baggage very carefully across the airport road. And when she seizes you and embraces you and says that we must have a lovely time and not quarrel, nod and turn before the tear on your cheek is discovered. Then get the car. And tell yourself a thousand times until you have memorized it and can really act on it . . . this didn't happen. All that matters is that she's here, that you have her these four days. Now, only now. Begin from now. Picking her up in the car in front of the terminal, loading the luggage, taking her hand at the stoplight. Now it begins.

And so she came. And we spent the four days, the week that had melted and shrunk, spent them at the theater, at a dull serious play uptown and an uproarious farce downtown, and I loved being with her. Even at *Equus,* which bored me so much I went to sleep. But merely being with her, sitting next to her in a theater uptown where I hadn't been since college, even that had a curious charm. And laughing at the wickedness of Off Broadway, the audience yelling and standing to cheer, all the boisterous homeliness of it, that too.

316

And the party, and giving her to my friends and the two of us dancing and showing off, the particular harmony and compatibility of that moment, even what she wore, a soft pale-rose wool shirt, and how I loved her breasts in that shirt, the lines of her torso and hips as she moved in the dance. How shy she seemed then, shy and somewhat reserved; yet the next day, walking uptown with her from the Modern along Fifth Avenue, she said, "How nice it is to walk with you uptown," and I laughed and said, "Here we are in full view of all the best places, not just Rizzoli but Tiffany and Cartier and right over there is Miss Elizabeth Arden, where you used to spend the whole day getting done." "In another life." She smiled back at me. And her arm was in mine.

Quickly the moment came again at Kennedy. She got out of the car very fast and gave her bags to the porter and waved me on. Was it because she did not want to say any more goodbyes, the way she did not want me to make love to her the last night and left me in despair, then making love to me after she had refused me herself, making love to me almost insultingly, just so much kindness. Or was it only because she loathes goodbyes? I rolled over on my stomach, wanting to cry, and she took me from behind. Just as now the porter removes her and the cop waves me on bitterly, vehemently. Over and gone.

Then two weeks later she called. Early in the morning. The phone reached me still half in sleep, trying to make a pot of coffee. Her voice pronouncing my name: never the crisp English syllable, but a sound all her own, plaintive, today even ominous. Already I'm scared. I had not recognized her at first; understandably it made her nervous and angry. But she goes on to the weather, almost as if she'd lost her nerve. Then: "I have something to tell you . . ." "Can you hold on a moment?" I lean over to turn off the coffee. Going to find a cigarette. I'm really scared now. When someone is three thousand miles away and reaches you on a machine, you are at their mercy. And my life is wonderful now, the

317

work goes well, I am happy living alone, my friends come round me, Fumio is kind again, I draw every day, the manuscript speeds along. What if she reaches out this long way and disturbs my precarious peace? And there is good news too—I will see her again in a few days. Unexpectedly, I had gotten a free ticket to the Coast to speak for the Iranian political prisoners at the University of Washington in Seattle, and after the speech I'm being flown to San Francisco for a press conference. "I didn't imagine I would be seeing you again so soon, lady, isn't it wonderful?" I'd crowed at her. "That's what I wanted to talk to you about," she said. That must be it. My stomach panics, she is going to say she will have to be gone the twenty-first, when I'm in town. That I can't see her. I'll go where she is then, I think, picking up the extension phone at the other end of the loft, sitting down on the rug, trying to light a cigarette.

"I have something to tell you. I'm in love." "In love?" "Yes." I am still thinking of the weekend, the twenty-first, I'll see her. She can't take that away. In love—it's so pretentious I would like to laugh. To scream. To tear the machine out of the wall. But I only shake, completely unable to light the cigarette, strike the match, hold on to the receiver. Which has just shot me dead with a word, a phrase. In love. "Well, I suppose I'm glad for you." Trying for the sublime in good will. Remembering we are friends; friends wish each other well. *Ti voglio bene.* Even trying for a chuckle. "It's a nice thing to be in love, you couldn't wish anyone better luck than that." Thinking, All right, let her be in love. I won't be back till January, I can be in love any number of times before then myself. Wishing to God she hadn't told me. I wouldn't mind not knowing just for once.

"I could have fallen in love last night at a party," I say, "but I wouldn't call you up to bother you with it." "No, this is serious." And it is, her voice makes it so. "It's very painful for me to tell you, but it seems only fair." I am too beaten for any recriminations; I remain silent. "This is really it for me." "I see." The little hope is gone, leaked out into the rug like my strength, like my will to fight, to go there and capture her, confront whoever this is, win her back, struggle, argue, plead. "Who is it? Do I know this person?" "Well, what is there to say? He's thirty-five years old. He's from L.A. . . ." The little touch, the first thing she says about him is his age, younger than I by five years, younger than she by fifteen. And his sex, revealed by a pronoun. If it were a woman, I think, I would try. But a man, no, you can't beat a man with her—no, her voice alone presents this as the ultimate triumph, the real achievement. A young man. The glory of it. L.A. All those trips to Los Angeles. All the boring people whose houses she had to stay at, the husbands of university officials who wouldn't drive her to the airport in the morning, leaving her and her insufficient funds to cope with cab drivers. It all comes together as it falls apart. I'm coming to the West Coast and so she has to tell me she won't be home this weekend, she'll be in Los Angeles with him. She can't spare even a day to see me, has given him all her future. But it's more than that. She is calling to say goodbye. She will be living with him. "No more room in your life for illicit affairs in distant places?" "No, I'm afraid not. He insists on monogamy."

It is all done in a telephone call. There is no need even to write, none whatever to see me in person. She discards me. The young man is named Erik. He used to teach at Sacramento. But then he was married. Now he's getting unmarried. They have been "seeing each other" since last November. On her visits to Los Angeles. On his visits to San Francisco. They have corresponded and talked on the telephone. In those afternoon hours after work when she liked to be alone? It was all going on while I was there. While I was intent upon Neal, there was Erik. What a fool, I never guessed. She goes on, telling the story of their love, their meetings, their plans. "I want to share my life with him," I hear amid the ruin. "I won't bother you now with arrangements about getting your things"— this small mercy, that I do not have to move my papers and books and clothes this very night. "And of course if you're in the Bay area this weekend, although I won't be here, you are welcome to use the house. Maud is here. And Walter. They're having a little thing." The trivia of Maud and Walter and their little thing is too much to bother with; I brush them aside without troubling to register. "No, I'll just cancel the trip to San Francisco. I've promised to speak in Seattle, but afterward I'll just come straight back home." "I'm sorry it worked out this way." "Sure, so am I."

The second is approaching when she will hang up, when it will all be permanently and entirely finished. Her voice winds toward that pause, picks up, but then changes: "You know, for what it's worth to you, whether you believe it or not, and without knowing just what it means now—I still love you." "Yes, I do too. Always." Wanting to say, And if . . . But not saying it. "Goodbye." "Goodbye." And then the line dead.

I do not know yet that I am free.

I go on then. Wanting to recapture her. Having lost her, wanting to recapture that time, and, against the future and its emptiness, to have some copy. Like the photographs we never took. Like the Sita in a long gown in the old movie still, the lawn and skirts of her afternoon, her broad straw brim, her wide-mouthed smile, young and a beauty and in a film. Sita in another life, one I never knew but was favored to catch a glimpse of. Because John Ford came to the little town where she was a waitress and she got to be an extra. Because the hand of time stopped for a moment, was suspended, in an act of art that would last forever, so far beyond its subject. Like the slides she found once at the farm, nude photographs of Ruth I'd taken one day at Provincetown when I got tired of drawing and out of whim and pique and foolery grabbed the camera and said, "This does it quicker and without mistakes." So we made a game of it, photographed each other, composing the frames, heaping a crimson coverlet around her great Olympian white skin. "Like Velázquez," I said, "very classical," the whole thing half in mockery, half in earnest. Naughtiness, experiment, good times. But how to explain these pictures to Sita, who was only jealous? And angry. I cursed myself for not having put them away where she would not come upon them.

All evidence of life. All the pictures, even these, the life we had out there, the house, its hours and light, its glasses of wine, its dinners and bedtimes. Its dullness, its interest, its anguish or mellowness. But away and beyond now and always, some Sita anywhere and everywhere: the way her back would move walking down a street in Rome, the lovely ellipsis of her hips, the way her leg might pause on a corner in New York, the lame one with the long cut on its knee, the sight of her walking out from the foam at Santa Cruz the weekend we were there two years ago and I was aghast watching her come out of the water in her orange bikini, brown and slender and belonging so to water and ocean. Marina —one of her so numerous middle names, and she was of the water, loved it in a way nearly ominous. Because it said California and the Coast and no other place. She would never live away from it now. Now that she was free of husbands and the desert where one husband or another had made her waste seven years. But coming out of that water she was her own woman, her head up, listening to her own echoes only. I was on the beach and her companion, but I had vanished, become invisible.

And if I could succeed, it would be in honor of that Sita, the one who doesn't even know me, the Sita who would go on walking in streets that are mysteries to me, to eat dinners in restaurants I'll never see, visit towns I've never heard of, sleep in beds with others I'll never meet, the pure essence of herself. All that she has gained or achieved or fought for in her struggle to be free, to come to independence out of all the obedience she was bred to, trained by circumstance or necessity, children or husbands or privation.

No, beyond that. Surely the essence is not even in this created self, deliberate and consciously formed, but in the unconscious grace of her movements and her character, the loveliness of her body and its gestures, the kindness and sympathy, the amazing ingenuity of her attentions, her delicate favors and remembrances, the very tenderness of her consideration. Almost as if a child very much in love permitted its imagination to work in the placing of a flower by a plate, a note scribbled where you would find it by surprise. Sita as lover, the eroticism of thoughtfulness or of wit or of mischief. Or worldliness. Sophistication, toughness, my slum queen Chiquita, my Sally Jean, my countess, that delight in all things sensual, the most inventive hedonism. Behind it the memory of suffering, war, rape, poverty, humiliation. The mixture of these together producing the woman, the lover, the companion. That she had suffered much and had learned how to live. And taught me some of that, honored me in knowing her. Sita.

Afterword

There are so many ways to remember her. Sita in the prime of life, the late afternoon sun filling my loft, spreading like soft gold over the heads of all the people who had come to celebrate the publication of her book: Sita in triumph, an aura around her head as she danced. "I can see why you loved her," my editor said. Those who knew her knew she was Sita, otherwise her real identity was protected with her privacy. The loft was crowded with friends and well-wishers, so many people, and that amazing light flooding through the big windows facing the west, floor to ceiling all across the front of the building—one saw a hundred heads in silhouette, glasses, the roar of talk.

All was restored. Two years before this party Sita had dismissed me with a phone call, long distance from California to my loft in New York. Time had stopped then. It was over, finished. So finally then there was nothing to do but copy out the notebooks into which I had bled my gradual loss of her that season in Berkeley, add to them and shape them and make a book, holding on through mere paper, maintaining my obsession, insisting on a solitary and foolish one-sided fidelity to something already past which I could make still present, even future.

I stayed in the loft, I did nothing else, I saw no one, I spent a summer without even going up to the farm. I concentrated. And when it was all done, when the last pages were written at Province-town in a borrowed empty room looking out to sea, I could take them back to the loft and rewrite them again for another winter.

Finally I could give them to my agent and we could wait for months to see if anyone would print them. When they would it became serious: Sita would have to read this, approve, give permission. She was off somewhere, had run away to sea on someone's yacht. Then one day she called: she would see me, she would read it.

We were both very nervous; it was a house I had never seen before, but when she took my suitcase and strode into her bedroom with it I had reason to hope. It was Valentine's Day and it rained hard; she read her book in twelve hours without stopping and then we both cried and laughed and were lovers again. I had written it to prove myself, it seemed. For by then I understood that the original defection was really mine; we separated because I got a loft in New York. Now, having patiently won her back after another defection to the East—to my home, my world, my art, my studio, my farm—a letter arrived while I was still in Berkeley with photographs of a new loft, a piece of the rock I could have. My old loft had been destroyed, confiscated and condemned by the city marshall, but here was another which a friend had found for me. For the taking. I took it without hesitation. And ended our life together. She had a job in California and couldn't move; I could but I wouldn't. She was an absolute Californian; I was a New York artist.

We would always be a continent apart. We knew that now but somehow it didn't matter anymore; the book was the needed evidence of my commitment, and I was taken back. Like my suitcase, carried with such assurance. She approved the book, permitted its publication; she would even come to New York for its birth and christening. For a week she forgot her hatred of the place, of its money and snobbery and power: her New York had been meetings in Peacock Alley at the Waldorf, mine was the Lower East Side. Hesitantly, as if almost afraid she would be tempted to stay, to defect—to show up one day on my doorstep no longer a university administrator but a gypsy, her mediterranean climate surrendered for my slum—she let me show her my downtown: cruddy cafes

324

and miles of derelict buildings, the beloved bizarre streets that we walked for days on end. Showing it to Sita made it an adventure again. And coming home one night from eating dinner at the Tin Palace and listening to jazz, walking past CBGB's, my neighbor Hilly's place, Hilly was standing out in front of the door; he waved and said that Patti Smith was inside and had just started her last set, we had to come in and hear her. Wonderful happenstance; I'd never heard her before and that night: as the Japanese say in praise of the real blues singers, she "gave blood." Everything was smooth and fragrant and magical, Sita in my loft and my town.

We were reconciled; we were together now in that fragile and wonderful liaison we had invented by the end. "Let it always be an affair," her way of putting it, because we both knew we could not live together by now. There were two coasts and there would be other lovers: romance, not marriage, suited us. We would meet many times a year in her California or my New York or even in between. Ingenious, frequently humorous arrangements, clever comings-together coat-tailing on a conference somewhere, or just driving down from San Diego into Mexico; a future with so many possibilities, islands, and airplanes. What we lacked in domesticity and marital fidelity, daily life and cohabitation, we could improve upon with a lifetime liaison, the friendship ripening out, perfected and serene: we would make up for settled couplehood with a superior longevity. Because we would maintain this passion all our lives. Variations on the Sartre–de Beauvoir ideal.

Those last visits to California presaged it all; we could merely sit together of an evening, have a drink and watch the light, hardly needing to talk—communion was there already, maturity, confidence. We could still fight, there were rivals, there were explosions of lust or rage or deception, but in this fragile truce we were coming at last to trust and believe; we had already endured so much for so long: other lovers, the pull of different work, different places. But now there stretched before us a new and tolerant confidence, a common spirit and sure continuity, a final complicity. So that when

325

we met we were completed. This would last. We had found the formula.

Two years later someone found me in the Colorado wilderness where I was boning up on Chaucer to teach a course. They had walked the mile down the mountain from where the road ended, not with groceries, but with the word that Sita was dead. Suicide. Robin Morgan had called from New York; Robin knew Sita, it was not a mistake. Sita was already dead. I could not go and tear the terrible pills from her hand, talk her out of it, I was too late. I had been a week out of reach by telephone, maybe for the first time in my life; would she have called me? Sita—who found me once when I was trying to sneak away after I lost my first studio, my marriage over and Fumio gone too, alone in a condemned building the night before the movers were to come, the place derelict and empty but the phone still on and she caught me, reached out all the hell from California to New York and caught me—I hadn't caught her.

Sita had made it to the other side, was brave enough, resolute, had the determination of a warrior, a noble. But why, why, why? You go mad trying to understand, you argue with the dead, remonstrate against this betrayal, you try to let go. Suicide is a riddle: there was the usual young man; there was being passed over for a vice-chancellorship; there was a doctor's verdict of liver cancer; all reasons, her reasons. But there was still a mystery and my own sense of betrayal to surrender. Letting go, I wrote poems in drawings alone at the farm, a little crazy on martinis and grief. In the months that followed I did four prose elegies, arguments with the dead. Over time I crafted them together into a beautiful book which a friend published in a limited edition of three hundred and sixty signed copies. It was a work of love: I chose the paper and the type, even did the specifications and reductions of the various large drawings to one consistent set of proportions. I had made Sita another book, one which I hope someday the readers of this book can read as well—so little is said of suicide and this may be the only elegy for a lesbian ever published. All the copies of this private printing are gone now, and a popular edition should be done so that one may know the end of the story.

For me Sita is not really dead nor even that absent. Though, of course, after having lost her once and got her back, I lost her again to what appeared to be the permanence of death. Writers would cheat death somehow, artists too: during that last visit she made to New York I had playfully, lazily, shot a roll of film one morning, shots of her head lying on its pillow. The eyes were open looking at me. Afterward—everything means so much. Finding this roll of film when she was dead, I learned how to print photographs for the first time—watching the image come up in the developer was like causing a soul to live again. The one miracle in the visual arts, the chemistry of the darkroom, gave her back to me. I did an exhibition of these pictures together with the elegy drawings, the printed sheets of the prose elegies.

I have her still in so many ways, far more important than things done on paper. Images of Sita from a thousand moments of her life: her hand raised to tuck in a stray hair from a perfect chignon one night in a restraurant, a lady and a countess, a hippie activist in jeans, Sita clothed for the world in good wool and her perfect Italian boots, or naked, or rising from the sea at Santa Cruz in a bikini—she can show up certain nights for conversation, and I forget even to notice what she wears now since she is immaterial, pure spirit.

At other times, the living and the dead merge into one beloved woman won and lost again, a ripeness and intelligence absorbed into myself as a pinch of ashes are consumed in Japan, as the communion wafer is consumed, bone of my bone into the very marrow of my being, cells now within my cortex, breath and blood and heartbeat empowering me, I become Sita, I take on her mana. Even as I become her, learning by memory, recollecting all she knew, absorbing her savvy, re-inventing her competence, reviewing all the lessons she gave me in doing and getting done—in another and richer way—I also still experience Sita as outside myself, a voice entering consciousness, a discussant, argument giving way to conversation, advice.

And then those rare times of visitation—awake or asleep or falling asleep. Then she is with me undiluted, not merely that surface self which I have absorbed—my mentor, the administrator and politican, the diplomat and fighter, the intense political being who is also a sensualist and romantic, frequently also sentimental and enthusiastic, a lover of comfort as well as the struggle—but the real Sita, her actual self, through all the layers of her soul, her selves both adult and child, the core. Death reveals the core of being, it is why death is important and powerful, bringing the whole of a life together and into focus. The sound of her voice, even that, "Tesoro bello," the Mozartean lilt of Sita, her flirtation and courtliness, the coffee and chat of *Così Fan Tutte,* the romp, the gossip, the humor and malice and naughtiness, tact and consideration, teasing or kindly, the thousand sides and faces of this being, her variety.

Past death there is now a grandeur, and Sita now a great protean presence, a protector, the guardian spirit of the Farm remembered at Obon Feast nights, in toasts and candleboats, in poems sent out to burn on a raft in the center of the pond, yet experienced all year long as well, communed with in every crisis and decision, the place displayed for her inspection—here's one of those women's organization things that actually works, that hasn't self-destructed—both of us painfully conscious of the early movement's burning fuselages, wrecked hopes, trashed friends. Sita's death itself was seen by some as a casualty in the battle, a life unrealized because, all the while it wore itself out in opposition, advancement and security never did come to its rescue. Here at the Farm it's in quotidian strategies that I feel her wisdom most: in letting things pass, in giving responsibility to the restless and headstrong, in remembering the purpose and the goal.

The other day my aged Irish mother began a sentence in the following way: "When I'm dead and you kids pray to me . . ." I was taken aback. "Do you have ambitions for canonization?" I teased. "Don't be silly—when someone very important to you dies and you talk to them later it's praying," she instructed me. And I guess it is. So I'm asking Sita to give us a hand with this place. Praying in the old sense of begging a favor, trying to use "influence" with "higher-ups."

Sita, you who loved the Farm and hated it, its emptiness and loneliness and cold, its remote isolation—before it was a colony and full of life—how fortunate if your political genius and intention might be prolonged and perpetuated here. Pioneer organizer, suave and perfect in your golden California, let yourself be transported with the ease of an idea and without a trace of physical discomfort even to New England. Preside here with us still, and always.

—June 10, 1991, The Women's Art Colony Farm,
Poughkeepsie, New York

Elegy for Sita

In 1977 *Sita* was published. Sita herself took her own life in June of 1978. This elegy, composed during the course of that summer at the farm and at Provincetown, completes the work with regret.

* * *

Again the long hours and the sea. Provincetown. You never got here. And now, because of four hundred little green pills—there were still a few in the shag rug of your bedroom when I sat chatting with your daughter Pia the morning after your funeral—you never will. Unless you are here already, curious presence I imagine with me now that you are no longer a continent away in California, but nowhere; everywhere the being is summoned, remembered, invited. You could have come here with me this year's end, this after Labor Day, the beach quiet and perfect, the best time, they always say up here. Or the farm this summer. If I'd known. If you'd spoken.

Because when Robin called it was too late. It would be forever too late. "I've got some terrible news for you; is there someone there with you?" Before she will even tell her news I must answer her. The question merely an annoyance, repeated like a fly buzzing around fruit, fruit already terrible and ugly through the terror in her voice, her tears crying already for what I don't yet know. Because it took so long for her to say it. Waiting, I inventory: my mother, Fumio, the farm. Which catastrophe? And why Robin? Why would Robin be the one to call? "Is there someone there with you?" "Yeah, Dakota Rosie's here." "Who?" "Dakota, you know, my friend Skippy."

And then she said Sita and it fit. Because Robin knew her too.

331

There must be something wrong with Sita, preparing for the blow: anger, sickness, disaffection. "Sita committed suicide last Wednesday." I only hear Wednesday, it is the first thing, the other phrase I cannot touch yet I only hear Wednesday and know this is Monday morning in an office where I've gone to use the phone, out of a camper's life in Colorado. Teaching Chaucer for fun in Allen Ginsberg's private English department at Naropa, a pseudo-Buddhist academy of hip poets in the mountains. And at one of their crowded busy little desks, these words are attacking me on the phone from New York amid late registrants, applicants for Tai Chi and meditation, triplicate forms, seven other calls on lighted buttons, everyone else's sensible conversations in the eight desks around me, the twenty-four phone lines to matriculation, course selection and public relations. And an old friend weeping into the earpiece is perfectly seriously saying these words. Words I would have her take back. Eat them. Swallow. Keep them down. And don't weep. It shows you believe it. I would have you scream. I am just choking my own scream back. Because panic is what it should be. Terror. The fear of all fears, death. When you are dead . . .

"O my God, I'll call you back." No changing, no reversing it. You are utterly helpless and it has already happened. Days ago. Where were you on Wednesday? I was even, damn my soul, in California, Los Angeles. Two hours away from the bedroom in San Diego. The bathroom. The little study, the new condominium that was still only an address. Jesus. I was staying with Skippy—"It's nice you have someone," Sita'd said. Finishing the fat lady sculptures, moving them in trucks, bargaining for storage, for shipment, for Shelley Winters to put one by her swimming pool. Wednesday night I may even have been drinking with the movie queen in the Hollywood Hills. And some old chorus-line chum of hers who'd read Sita on her own and liked it. "It ought to be a movie." Skippy high on the idea too, on the way home we stopped off and had one of Lucy El Adobe's margaritas on it. The piece was delivered, we even got to swim in the pool. And the old chum had praised the book, her husband was a director. "These folks got all kinds of money, they could do it, you know," Skippy's high and taking on her Dakota Rosie drinking personality and I'm laughing. An hour later the old chum, her eye on being Sita, shows up for dinner at Dan Tanna's dressed the part. A Lady. And with a brand new cultivated Mid-Atlantic accent. Not yours. And she not you. Not Sita. Never, I think, but I go on drinking, exploring Hollywood like a bumpkin in Disneyland. And maybe that night you died. At the moment old chum has us back at her house, booze and cocaine and then suddenly throws a fit because I said I had several lovers and she is on the instant bellowing I'm promiscuous, on into vulgarities and I'm amused, explaining my modern claptrap about "multiple relationships." "Just whoring," she's yelling. "You don't understand, I love these people, they're my family, I'll know them all my life, this is permanent, committed," dithering away, trying to convince her mounting outrage, more and more inappropriate and erroneous. Disconcertingly hostile. This pretender to Sita, thinking then, the way one remembers treasure, Sita, I am always most sure of this love. Sealed somehow by our last visit, the serenity of it, the resolution at last. After all the quarrels and renunciations and amnesties, that it was fastened, that I would always have this great fragrant love, always. The very irony of these contrasting circumstances maintaining my good humor.

Was it Wednesday? Or was it Thursday? And you already dead. The irony waiting to clobber me when the coroner gave way to the kids who called friends who would call me. When they could find me. And it took days. I who am so rarely out of reach. But it was to be part of the charm of the trip. After the hassles with sculpture and trucks, Colorado would be days in the wilderness re-reading Chaucer by a stream in the cabin at Duck Lake. No telephone, running water, heat, light, gas, electricity—nothing but peace, a chilly spring, fires in June, the Rockies to bring back adolescent summer jobs in a West never seen again for twenty years. Then a mad scheme with Skippy to buy a piece of land over Duck Lake, a little mining claim, a gold stake without gold but cheap in the purest wilderness.

And even, when we began playing house in Naropa's standard faculty apartment, how like my "townhouse" in Sacramento where we played house—now how painful to see it after the call. But it was still the first innocent day of class. "Call Robin Morgan," I'd been told—another message in addition to the pair of Amazon child dykes who mysteriously appeared at Duck Lake yesterday, strangers coming up and saying Robin Morgan was trying to find me, the message coming in to Big Moma Rag in Denver. And these two explorers knew by some telegraph that I had friends in the fastness of Duck Lake. Or maybe they only happened by. Having no notion of why Robin needed me. Or maybe they did know and were sparing my feelings, waiting for the older comrade to tell me, the friend of years and years. Probably they had no clue at all, just pass the word.

I hope they had none. Since my response was utterly trivial. "There's a phone down the road at Ward, at the Windmill, the bar, you can call her right now." Probably just another petition, I figured. Remember Sita, the last petition? We were making love when Robin called. She is still laughing over coming upon that in your book. This is my Sunday, I thought. We're already a half mile into the wilderness, why pack all the way back out now? Call when you leave in the evening for dinner, at Gold Hill, they'll have a phone. And forgot. The excitement of taking pictures all day, of finding the gold mine, plunging with Skippy into fantasy, buying it a hundred times over, designing a cabin to build in the woods by the lake, all our Middlewestern childhoods summoned, improved upon, inspired with candlelight and wine, sketches on the back of the restaurant check. I came across the thing yesterday, the brittle paper, the messy hopeful ballpoint, the log cabin that marched up story over story and even arched in a little bridge over the road, the dirt track bisecting the property, "studio" and "photog" and "writing" inscribed optimistically on half the nest of rooms.

Someone else bought the land. Though Skip went back another time to Boulder to try to save it, to haggle, to hang on. And the next morning you were dead. Having been dead already five days. It seemed more important than ever to get it then. Land seemed so sure, solid. To dare buy something with someone, to gamble. It was too late to ever buy anything with you. Would that have kept you alive?

334

For the reasons for your death come bearing in now. After I grab Dakota's arm and steer her away from earnest conversation with some harmless young man: macrobiotic food, Eastern mysticism, Tai Chi—whatever, it evaporates in the news I bear, myself now telling it, making it true, repeating the impossible all the way home in the car. She drives me, kindly, patiently; I am seething. There is no home anymore. What if I had heard this news at the farm? The Bowery? Would those rooms be haunted forever? Even the little townhouse Naropa gives us, its resemblance to that other, to ours in Sacramento, previously a relish, a recall of delight. Now a rebuke— it was in a place like this I first loved her. Stretched my independence from Fumio and New York and fell under the spell of Sita, the easy spontaneous living. Now mere nomadism. Without even a telephone; the urge, the necessity, the madness to have one. Robin again. Hear it. The why of your dying. At first so secondary, now so urgent. As if the reason could make sense of the event.

Ginsberg has a telephone. The only one. Our chairman, mentor, host finally; Dakota having fetched permission, coffee, cigarettes. Installed on Allen's balcony, a little cement veranda in the air above telephone lines, the mountains incongruous in the distance. My milk, my coffee, my cigarettes ridiculous beside the phone, itself ridiculous on this tiny shelf midair, Allen solemnly pursuing poetry with his private student behind the glass door as I sob eighteen and then thirty-eight dollars into Robin's ears, hearing what little there is to know, fighting the event still, and how a suicide scars all lives around it. The cheat, the fucking robbery of it. That I had no idea. The few who knew her depression not telling me, not seeing it themselves as fatal. "She was bitter in a letter I had in March," Robin says, "A little fatalistic even. They hadn't given her that promotion to Vice Chancellor, something about how they'd as much as told her a woman, a woman and a little bit brown too, wouldn't have a chance—but I'd had no idea."

"Listen, I called her before I went to Paris in April. She was okay. She was wonderful. She sent me off in triumph and I wrote her picture postcards of Notre Dame telling her how, the baby we called it,

335

the book—was taking the town. I'd called her because we had to tell her brother the book would be out in Italian and I think that worried her a little, the name, they called her Sita there; her brother, good bourgeoisie, you know, God fearing, Catholic devout, that sort of thing—so I wrote him a letter and read it to her—she thought it was perfect. Do you think my book?—it's too hideous to think of."

"Look, she went to New York to the book party to proclaim she was Sita, to bask in it, to be delighted and delightful. She was radiant that day. You're way off the track. Her friend Maude saw her the weekend before she did it and even she's puzzled. Sita was down, but none of the things seemed enough, everything was awful but none of it was important enough. There was her job and she had some cause to fear she'd lose it. There was some young man and he'd stood her up, told her he was going to marry some other lady. And she'd bought a condominium and she hated it. So Maude says sell it. Forget this idiot guy. And wait and see about the job. Or quit it. Write. Beachcomb. Do the things you're always talking about. And then she'd do that, pursue that line, decide to sell the house and take off and live. And then another crying jag. Maude was beside herself. Sick of it. Helpless. Sita went from mood to mood. Maude said she was fifty people that weekend. But mostly she was beaten."

Her age, the job, the young men, the last young man of all, was he the one I met last time? A fool. Jerk on a motorcycle, middle of the night. Weird, kept trying to give me artificial cocaine. A cretin. Did he dare to trifle with her? Where did she have to be to find a creep like that important, anyway?

"Maude said the same thing. She said Sita knew all this, told her she wasn't in love with him but that right now she needed him, like a bad habit."

Sita and her young men. The last one. Burned her out. This one was only the ashes in her mouth. After Eric left her, there was one part of her that never recovered. He was beautiful, had a motorcycle too, was even a Ph.D. But this one, this guy Warren. Was not beautiful. Was drugged probably most of the time, but sober would be below average intelligence, perhaps impaired. I was afraid for her, knowing such people. The buddy with him was coming off coke after blowing his nose his life his health: long semi-literate descriptions. They arrived in the middle of the night, slept on the couch. Sita and I sleeping together in her room. "He knows all about it, he knows you come first." The assurance of the lady of the world. I am on an obscenely short visit between planes and I rather wish he'd stay at the Hogg farm, or wherever he lives, so irrelevant he seems to me, so tangential, so obtrusive. And yet so minimal I entirely believed her. Not only that I maintained the curious distinction of being her only woman, but that her love for me was really a thing apart from whatever dumbbell reason Warren rode the highways and found shelter.

In fact he found rather a lot. Since February he'd come up to San Diego, taken a place nearby. Sita's son and his lady being at her own house, she spent a great deal of time at Warren's. Then he jilts her. Got another woman, fixing to marry her. Sita as opera queen. Sita as Tosca. Sita at fifty-three and stricken. "Over this moron?" I yell at Robin. "Well, it's the combination, it seems. The job, she couldn't have that kind of job and hang out with him. I mean the guy's not what they call presentable. Maude said so too. Got a record, no credit, can't own anything. She had to put his motorcycle in her name." "Jesus." The stupid ugly pockmarked face, belligerence practicing good humor on me. The idea of that beautiful woman committing suicide over this lout humiliates me. As a woman. As a human being. Does our predicament, our endless vulnerability, our relentless condition reduce us to this? Did Sappho jump her cliff over a boatman? Surely he was pretty, had grace, the light of a boy.

But this nondescript—putting it together from Robin, from Maude, from what Sita's daughter Pia has told them both. And then there's the doctor, the point that she was unwell, had been for months, the pills foisted on her. Maude saying how many, how various, how chemically tanked she had been under his care. An experiment in hormones, in chemical balance and imbalance. "Why don't you throw all that crap out and get another doctor?" Maude taking the bull by the horns. As I had wanted to once when I saw all the junk and didn't like it or this man who seemed to manipulate her life. Her loves too. Well, maybe she would, but then the next minute he'd be her oracle. I believe he decreed celibacy that last fortnight we went to Mexico and consequently were miserable and quarreled. Renouncing me once more she called him from the airport just to confirm instructions before putting me on the plane.

There was always so much I never understood. She is dead and gone to me, compliments of nameless university officials, coroners, and a nobody in a motorcycle jacket. Ranting still at Robin, "She didn't need to die, she could have lived at the farm, she didn't even need a job—she could manage the project, she could run that ladies' art colony or whatever we're gonna call it, she was the most beautiful administrator I've ever known, she could have run the women's movement if they'd let her, she ran it in Sacramento and they had forty-seven courses in women's studies alone, don't you see what a waste it is. For us. For all of us. But Jesus, for herself. She threw it all away. For what?"

"Yeah, yeah. Still, it's her prerogative and we don't know."

"Sure, it's all you got, all you really own. That one life. Sometimes the only right you got is to take it. And it's gutsy as hell. I know, I tried, I didn't make it."

"Well, you're not sorry either."

"But I'm sure sorry she did. Don't you see the mistake, the fucking mistake, the fucking waste. And it leaves me so poor. Robin, I've got two different tickets to the coast this fall. She won't be there. I'll go and look around and she won't be there. She's taken the very future away. I was going to know her all my life. I counted on that. We'd even finally . . . "

Robin's husband, Kenneth Pitchford, comes on. What am I teaching tomorrow? "Chaucer." "Yes, but what?" It comes back to me. "The Miller and the Reeve." We laugh maniacally. "It's probably all for the best, the Knight's Tale or the Franklin could lay you out. Troilus would be fatal."

"I remembered Troilus for Sita."

"I'm not surprised."

In a thrice it is Allen Ginsberg's balcony, the coffee cold, the milk soured in the sun, William Burroughs crossing the street below looking like an accountant in the St. Louis Grain Exchange. Allen droning benignly to his student.

"Old Girl Friend?" Ginsberg asks as I decompartmentalize myself by sliding the glass door away from my audible privacy. I wince, realizing that for all their charms and goodness, the men here on Olympus do not and probably never will read me. Allen says Buddhist things about death, all very wise, all utterly useless. I begin to live with it, going back to Dakota and a long day on other people's phones. And Chaucer, thank god for work, for the buns of Millers and Reeves and Hendy Nicholas the clerk and hanging moons—all things you would enjoy Sita.

As dead, you begin to live with me.

KATE MILLETT was born in 1934 in St. Paul, Minnesota. Perhaps best known as a feminist activist, she is author of *The Prostitution Papers* (1973), *Flying* (1974), *Sita* (1977), *The Loony Bin Trip* (1990), and *The Politics of Cruelty* (1994). Her groundbreaking work *Sexual Politics* (1970) helped usher in the so-called second wave of the women's rights movement and helped pave the way for the growth of women's studies in the United States.

Millett is also a sculptor, and is committed to her farm in Poughkeepsie, New York, which is an economically independent colony for women artists, writers, and musicians. She lives in New York City.